AF071874

Koren Talmud Bavli

THE NOÉ EDITION

BAVA METZIA

Steinsaltz Center

KOREN

תלמוד בבלי

KOREN TALMUD BAVLI

THE NOÉ EDITION

בבא מציעא

BAVA METZIA

Daf 103a through Daf 119a

COMMENTARY BY

Rabbi Adin Even-Israel
Steinsaltz

EDITOR-IN-CHIEF

Rabbi Dr Tzvi Hersh Weinreb

SENIOR CONTENT EDITOR

Rabbi Dr Shalom Z Berger

EXECUTIVE EDITOR

Rabbi Joshua Schreier

•

STEINSALTZ CENTER
KOREN PUBLISHERS JERUSALEM

Supported by the Matanel Foundation

Koren Talmud Bavli, The Noe Edition
Vol. 22f: Tractate Bava Metzia, Daf 103b through Daf 119a
Paperback, ISBN, 978-965-7766-07-1

First Hebrew/English paperback edition, 2021

Koren Publishers Jerusalem Ltd.
PO Box 4044, Jerusalem 91040, ISRAEL
PO Box 8531, New Milford, CT 06776, USA
www.korenpub.com

Steinsaltz Center

Steinsaltz Center is the parent organization of institutions established by Rabbi Adin Even-Israel Steinsaltz

PO Box 45187, Jerusalem 91450 ISRAEL
Telephone: +972 2 646 0900, Fax +972 2 624 9454
www.steinsaltz-center.org

הִנֵּה יָמִים בָּאִים, נְאֻם אֲדֹנָי יֱהֹוִה, וְהִשְׁלַחְתִּי רָעָב בָּאָרֶץ,
לֹא־רָעָב לַלֶּחֶם וְלֹא־צָמָא לַמַּיִם, כִּי אִם־לִשְׁמֹעַ אֵת דִּבְרֵי יהוה.

Behold, days are coming – says the Lord God – I will send a hunger to the land, not a hunger for bread nor a thirst for water, but to hear the words of the Lord. (AMOS 8:11)

The Noé edition of the Koren Talmud Bavli
with the commentary of Rabbi Adin Even-Israel Steinsaltz
is dedicated to all those who open its covers
to quench their thirst for Jewish Knowledge,
in our generation of Torah renaissance.

This beautiful edition is for the young, the aged,
the novice and the savant alike,
as it unites the depth of Torah knowledge
with the best of academic scholarship.

Within its exquisite and vibrant pages,
words become worlds.

It will claim its place in the library of classics,
in the bookcases of the Beit Midrash,
the classrooms of our schools,
and in the offices of professionals and business people
who carve out precious time to grapple with its timeless wisdom.

For the Student and the Scholar

DEDICATED BY LEO AND SUE NOÉ

Steinsaltz Center

Executive Director, Steinsaltz Center

Rabbi Meni Even-Israel

Managing Editor

Rabbi Jason Rappoport

Senior Content Editor

Rabbi Dr. Shalom Z. Berger

Editors

Rabbi Dr. Joshua Amaru, *Coordinating Editor*
Rabbi Avishai Magence, *Content Curator*
Amy Kaplan Benoff
Aryeh Bernstein
Menucha Chwat
Rabbi Yehoshua Duker
Betzalel Philip Edwards
Rabbi Dov Foxbrunner
Rabbi Yonatan Shai Freedman
Raphael Friedman
Rabbi Alan Haber
Noam Harris
Rabbi Raz Hartman
Rabbi Tzvi Chaim Kaye
Rabbi Yonatan Kohn
Liron Kranzler
Sholom Licht
Elisha Loewenstern
Rabbi Jonathan Mishkin
Rabbi Eli Ozarowski
Yosef Rosen
Rabbi David Sedley
Jay Shapiro
Rabbi Michael Siev
Ami Silver
Avi Steinhart
Rabbi Yitzchak Twersky
Ami Vick

Copy Editors

Aliza Israel, *Coordinator*
Bracha Hermon
Ita Olesker
Debbie Ismailoff
Shira Finson
Ilana Sobel
Deena Nataf
Eliana Kurlantzick Yorav
Erica Hirsch Edvi
Nava Wieder
Sara Henna Dahan

Language Consultants

Dr. Stephanie E. Binder, *Greek & Latin*
Rabbi Yaakov Hoffman, *Arabic*
Dr. Shai Secunda, *Persian*
Shira Shmidman, *Aramaic*

KOREN

Design & Typesetting

Dena Landowne Bailey, *Typesetting*
Tani Bayer, *Jacket Design*
Raphaël Freeman, *Design & Typography*

Images

Eliahu Misgav, *Illustration & Image Acquisition*
Daniel Gdalevich, *Illustration & Image Acquisition*

Introduction by the Publisher

The Talmud has sustained and inspired Jews for thousands of years. Throughout Jewish history, an elite cadre of scholars has absorbed its learning and passed it on to succeeding generations. The Talmud has been the fundamental text of our people.

Beginning in the 1960s, Rabbi Adin Even-Israel Steinsaltz שליט״א created a revolution in the history of Talmud study. His translation of the Talmud, first into modern Hebrew and then into other languages, as well the practical learning aids he added to the text, have enabled millions of people around the world to access and master the complexity and context of the world of Talmud.

It is thus a privilege to present the *Koren Talmud Bavli*, an English translation of the talmudic text with the brilliant elucidation of Rabbi Steinsaltz. The depth and breadth of his knowledge are unique in our time. His rootedness in the tradition and his reach into the world beyond it are inspirational.

Working with Rabbi Steinsaltz on this remarkable project has been not only an honor, but a great pleasure. Never shy to express an opinion, with wisdom and humor, Rabbi Steinsaltz sparkles in conversation, demonstrating his knowledge (both sacred and worldly), sharing his wide-ranging interests, and, above all, radiating his passion. I am grateful for the unique opportunity to work closely with him, and I wish him many more years of writing and teaching.

Our intentions in publishing this new edition of the Talmud are threefold. First, we seek to fully clarify the talmudic page to the reader – textually, intellectually, and graphically. Second, we seek to utilize today's most sophisticated technologies, both in print and electronic formats, to provide the reader with a comprehensive set of study tools. And third, we seek to help readers advance in their process of Talmud study.

To achieve these goals, the *Koren Talmud Bavli* is unique in a number of ways:

- The classic *tzurat hadaf* of Vilna, used by scholars since the 1800s, has been reset for great clarity, and opens from the Hebrew "front" of the book. Full *nikkud* has been added to both the talmudic text and Rashi's commentary, allowing for a more fluent reading with the correct pronunciation; the commentaries of *Tosafot* have been punctuated. Upon the advice of many English-speaking teachers of Talmud, we have separated these core pages from the translation, thereby enabling the advanced student to approach the text without the distraction of the translation. This also reduces the number of volumes in the set. At the bottom of each *daf*, there is a reference to the corresponding English pages. In addition, the Vilna edition was read against other manuscripts and older print editions, so that texts which had been removed by non-Jewish censors have been restored to their rightful place.

- The English translation, which starts on the English "front" of the book, reproduces the *menukad* Talmud text alongside the English translation (in bold) and commentary and explanation (in a lighter font). The Hebrew and Aramaic text is presented in logical paragraphs. This allows for a fluent reading of the text for the non-Hebrew or non-Aramaic reader. It also allows for the Hebrew reader to refer easily to the text alongside. Where the original text features dialogue or poetry, the English text is laid out in a manner appropriate to the genre. Each page refers to the relevant *daf*.

- Critical contextual tools surround the text and translation: personality notes, providing short biographies of the Sages; language notes, explaining foreign terms borrowed from Greek, Latin, Persian, or Arabic; and background notes, giving information essential to the understanding of the text, including history, geography, botany, archaeology, zoology, astronomy, and aspects of daily life in the talmudic era.
- Halakhic summaries provide references to the authoritative legal decisions made over the centuries by the rabbis. They explain the reasons behind each halakhic decision as well as the ruling's close connection to the Talmud and its various interpreters.
- Photographs, drawings, and other illustrations have been added throughout the text – in full color in the Standard and Electronic editions, and in black and white in the Daf Yomi edition – to visually elucidate the text.

This is not an exhaustive list of features of this edition, it merely presents an overview for the English-speaking reader who may not be familiar with the "total approach" to Talmud pioneered by Rabbi Steinsaltz.

Several professionals have helped bring this vast collaborative project to fruition. My many colleagues are noted on the Acknowledgments page, and the leadership of this project has been exceptional.

RABBI MENACHEM EVEN-ISRAEL, DIRECTOR OF THE STEINSALTZ CENTER, was the driving force behind this enterprise. With enthusiasm and energy, he formed the happy alliance with Koren and established close relationships among all involved in the work.

RABBI DR. TZVI HERSH WEINREB שליט״א, EDITOR-IN-CHIEF, brought to this project his profound knowledge of Torah, intellectual literacy of Talmud, and erudition of Western literature. It is to him that the text owes its very high standard, both in form and content, and the logical manner in which the beauty of the Talmud is presented.

RABBI JOSHUA SCHREIER, EXECUTIVE EDITOR, assembled an outstanding group of scholars, translators, editors, and proofreaders, whose standards and discipline enabled this project to proceed in a timely and highly professional manner.

RABBI MEIR HANEGBI, EDITOR OF THE HEBREW EDITION OF THE STEINSALTZ TALMUD, lent his invaluable assistance throughout the work process, supervising the reproduction of the Vilna pages.

RAPHAËL FREEMAN, EXECUTIVE EDITOR OF KOREN, created this Talmud's unique typographic design which, true to the Koren approach, is both elegant and user friendly.

It has been an enriching experience for all of us at Koren Publishers Jerusalem to work with the Steinsaltz Center to develop and produce the *Koren Talmud Bavli*. We pray that this publication will be a source of great learning and, ultimately, greater *avodat Hashem* for all Jews.

Matthew Miller, Publisher
Koren Publishers Jerusalem
Jerusalem 5772

Contents

For the vocalized Vilna Shas layout, please open as a Hebrew book.

Introduction to **Perek IX**

Do not oppress your neighbor and do not steal; the wages of a hired laborer shall not remain with you all night until the morning.

(Leviticus 19:13)

If you take as collateral your neighbor's garment, you shall restore it to him by when the sun goes down. For that is his only covering, it is his garment for his skin; where shall he sleep? And it shall come to pass, when he cries to Me that I will hear, for I am gracious.

(Exodus 22:25–26)

He shall not take the lower or upper millstone as collateral, for he takes a man's life as collateral.

(Deuteronomy 24:6)

When you lend your neighbor any manner of loan, you shall not go into his house to take his collateral. You shall stand outside, and the man to whom you lend shall bring forth the collateral to you outside. And if he is a poor man, you shall not sleep with his collateral. You shall restore to him the collateral when the sun goes down, so that he may sleep in his garment and he will bless you, and it shall be righteousness to you before the Lord your God. You shall not oppress a hired laborer that is poor and needy, whether he is from your brothers or from your stranger that is in your land within your gates. On the same day you shall give him his wages, and the sun shall not set upon him.

(Deuteronomy 24:10–15)

You shall not pervert justice due to the stranger or due to the fatherless, nor take a widow's garment as collateral.

(Deuteronomy 24:17)

This chapter consists of three sections. The first discusses the *halakhot* of sharecroppers and contractors leasing fields, the second focuses on delayed payment of wages, and the third discusses the *halakhot* of taking collateral.

An individual would often give a portion of his field to another to be worked. This person would work either as a sharecropper, who receives a certain percentage of the produce, or as a contractor, who gives a set amount of the produce to the owner. Generally speaking, individuals could contract business arrangements in any manner they chose, without the Sages intervening.

The majority of the halakhic discussion in the chapter revolves around specific cases of these agreements, especially with regard to issues that are not explicitly dealt with in the written agreement. Problems often arise with regard to determining which methods of working the land are acceptable and unacceptable. In addition, difficulties also arise in situations of natural disasters, such as droughts, flooding, or crop disease, which may prevent the cultivator from fulfilling his responsibilities as stipulated in the agreement, and also remove the possibility of the landowner's earning a profit. The bulk of the halakhic analysis of this chapter involves finding the proper, just manner in which to resolve these types of disputes between the cultivator and the landowner.

An important principle to keep in mind when discussing such matters is that even when the two sides enter an agreement concerning an issue where the *halakha* is not clearly defined, not everything is entirely arbitrary, and the sides must take care to uphold the principle, stated in the Torah: "And you shall do that which is right and good" (Deuteronomy 6:18).

The second section of the chapter discusses situations where the Torah itself sets the standards for the definitions of what is considered "right and good." It is possible to suggest that these *halakhot* themselves are considered beyond the letter of the law and are a demonstration of doing that which is "right and good."

The Torah obligates an employer to pay his workers for their labor immediately and without any delay. This raises numerous practical questions. First, does this apply to all workers or only certain types of workers? Second, when is payment due for a worker who is not a day laborer but who is hired out for a set period of time that may be shorter or longer than a day? After what point does one violate the prohibition of delaying payment of wages and who precisely is liable?

Concerning the appropriation of collateral, the Torah greatly limits its permissibility, both with regard to the method of taking the collateral, as well as with regard to retaining it at times when the debtor needs it. Similarly, a prohibition exists with regard to appropriating collateral from specific individuals as well as taking certain types of items. One of the fundamental issues here is identifying the nature of this collateral: Is it taken to ensure that the debtor pays back his debt, or does the collateral itself constitute the collection of the debt? In addition, what is the permitted method of appropriating items as collateral? Moreover, does the prohibition against taking collateral from a widow apply to any widow or only to a poor widow? Finally, what are the methods for determining which items may not be taken as collateral?

All of these and many related questions are the primary focus of this chapter.

Perek **IX**
Daf **103** Amud **a**

מתני׳ הַמְקַבֵּל שָׂדֶה מֵחֲבֵירוֹ, מָקוֹם שֶׁנָּהֲגוּ לִקְצוֹר – יִקְצוֹר, לַעֲקוֹר – יַעֲקוֹר, לַחֲרוֹשׁ אַחֲרָיו – יַחֲרוֹשׁ, הַכֹּל כְּמִנְהַג הַמְּדִינָה. כְּשֵׁם שֶׁחוֹלְקִין בַּתְּבוּאָה כָּךְ חוֹלְקִין בַּתֶּבֶן וּבַקַּשׁ, כְּשֵׁם שֶׁחוֹלְקִין בַּיַּיִן כָּךְ חוֹלְקִין

MISHNA With regard to **one who receives a field**[N] **from another** to cultivate, either as a tenant farmer, who, in exchange for the right to farm the land, gives a set amount of the produce to the owner, or as a sharecropper, who cultivates the land and receives a set proportion of the produce, the *halakha* is as follows: In **a location where** those cultivating the land **were accustomed to cut** the produce, this one **must cut** it as well. In a location where they were accustomed **to uproot** the produce, not to cut it with a sickle or a scythe, this one **must uproot** it as well. If they were accustomed **to plow**[H] the land **after** harvesting the produce, this one **must plow** as well. **All** farming of the land shall be conducted **in accordance with regional custom. Just as** the *halakha* is that the owner of the field and the one cultivating it **divide the produce,**[N] **so too** the *halakha* is that **they divide the stubble and the straw. Just as** the *halakha* is that the owner of the field and the one cultivating it **divide the wine,**[H] **so too** the *halakha* is that **they divide**

NOTES

One who receives [*hamekabel*] a field – הַמְקַבֵּל שָׂדֶה: Several different arrangements exist between a landowner and one who cultivates his field: A renter pays money to the owner, and has full control of the field for the duration of the rental period. A tenant farmer gives a certain amount of the produce to the owner and keeps the rest. A contractor gives a set proportion, such as one-quarter or one-third, of the yield to the owner, and he keeps the rest. A sharecropper is essentially an employee of the owner. The owner pays for expenses such as seeds, fertilizer, and other necessary equipment. The sharecropper cultivates the field and receives a certain proportion of the yield as remuneration. According to the Meiri, a sharecropper receives one-half of the yield, while a contractor receives more. The use of the word *hamekabel* in the *mishnayot* in this chapter in connection with cultivation of a field is not specific to one type of arrangement. Rather, it is a general term that can include anyone who receives a field to cultivate under any of these arrangements. Some of the *halakhot* discussed apply only to a contractor or a tenant farmer while others apply to anyone cultivating the field.

Just as they divide the produce – כְּשֵׁם שֶׁחוֹלְקִין בַּתְּבוּאָה: Some explain that this refers to a location where there is no established practice for cutting or uprooting what remains after the produce is harvested, as had the local practice been to cut it, what remains in the field would belong to the owner. In the absence of an accepted practice, if the one cultivating the field elects to cut the crop, he divides the remaining produce with the owner (*Torat Ḥayyim*).

HALAKHA

To cut…to uproot…to plow, etc. – לִקְצוֹר...לַעֲקוֹר...לַחֲרוֹשׁ וכו׳: In a location where the custom is to cut the crop, one may not uproot it whether he is a contractor, a tenant farmer, or a sharecropper. In a location where the custom is to uproot the crop, he may not cut it. In a location where the custom is to plow after the harvest, he must plow at that time. If either the cultivator or the owner wishes to depart from the accepted practice, the other party may object (Rambam *Sefer Mishpatim*, *Hilkhot Sekhirut* 8:6; *Shulḥan Arukh*, *Ḥoshen Mishpat* 320:4).

They divide the stubble and the straw…the wine – חוֹלְקִין בַּתֶּבֶן וּבַקַּשׁ...בַּיַּיִן: Just as the *halakha* is that the owner of the field and the one cultivating it divide the produce, so too the *halakha* is that they divide the straw and the stubble. Similarly, just as the *halakha* is that they divide the wine, so too the *halakha* is that they divide the vine branches (Rambam *Sefer Mishpatim*, *Hilkhot Sekhirut* 8:10; *Shulḥan Arukh*, *Ḥoshen Mishpat* 327:2).

Perek **IX**
Daf **103** Amud **b**

בַּזְּמוֹרוֹת וּבַקָּנִים, וּשְׁנֵיהֶם מְסַפְּקִין אֶת הַקָּנִים.

the branches pruned from the vines **and the poles. And the two of them,** i.e., the landowner and the one cultivating the field, both **supply the poles.**

גמ׳ תָּנָא: מָקוֹם שֶׁנָּהֲגוּ לִקְצוֹר – אֵינוֹ רַשַּׁאי לַעֲקוֹר, לַעֲקוֹר – אֵינוֹ רַשַּׁאי לִקְצוֹר, וּשְׁנֵיהֶם מְעַכְּבִין זֶה עַל זֶה.

GEMARA It was taught in a *baraita*: In **a location where** those cultivating the land **were accustomed to cut** the produce, the one cultivating this field **is not permitted to uproot** it, and in a location where they were accustomed **to uproot** the produce, **he is not permitted to cut** it. **And the two of them,** i.e., the owner and the one cultivating the field, can each **prevent the other** from deviating from the custom.

״לִקְצוֹר אֵינוֹ רַשַּׁאי לַעֲקוֹר״ – הַאי אָמַר: בָּעֵינָא דְּתִתְבַּן לִי אַרְעַאי, וְהַאי אָמַר: לָא מָצֵינָא. ״לַעֲקוֹר אֵינוֹ רַשַּׁאי לִקְצוֹר״ – הַאי אָמַר: בָּעֵינָא דְּתִינָּקֵר אַרְעַאי, וְהַאי אָמַר: בָּעֵינָא תִּיבְנָא.

The Gemara explains the *baraita*: In a location where those cultivating the land **were accustomed to cut** the produce, the one cultivating this field **is not permitted to uproot** the produce even if he wants to, because **this** one, i.e., the owner, who wants the produce cut, can **say: I want**[N] **my land to be fertilized with stubble,**[N] i.e., the remains of the plants. **And** if the owner wants him to uproot the produce, **that** one, i.e., the one cultivating the field, can **say: I cannot** uproot the produce, since that is too labor intensive. Similarly, if the custom is **to uproot** the produce, the one cultivating this field **is not permitted to cut** it even if he wants to, because **this** one, i.e., the owner, who wants the produce uprooted, can **say: I want my land to be cleared** of stubble. **And** if the owner wants him to cut the produce, **that** one, i.e., the one cultivating the field, can **say: I want** to uproot what remains so that I can use **the stubble.**

״וּשְׁנֵיהֶם מְעַכְּבִין זֶה עַל זֶה״. לָמָּה לִי? מַה טַּעַם קָאָמַר; מַה טַּעַם לִקְצוֹר אֵינוֹ רַשַּׁאי לַעֲקוֹר, לַעֲקוֹר אֵינוֹ רַשַּׁאי לִקְצוֹר? מִשּׁוּם דִּשְׁנֵיהֶם מְעַכְּבִין זֶה עַל זֶה.

The *baraita* teaches: **And the two of them,** i.e., the owner and the one cultivating the field, can each **prevent the other** from deviating from the custom. The Gemara asks: **Why do I** need this statement and what is its purpose? The Gemara answers that the *baraita* **is saying what** the **reason** is for its ruling: **What is the reason** that in a location where those cultivating the land were accustomed **to cut** the produce, the one cultivating this field **is not permitted to uproot** the produce, and in a location where they were accustomed **to uproot** the produce, **he is not permitted to cut** it? It is **because the two of them** can each **prevent the other** from deviating from the custom, as each has a justified reason for opposing the deviation desired by the other.

״לַחֲרוֹשׁ אַחֲרָיו יַחֲרוֹשׁ״. פְּשִׁיטָא! לָא צְרִיכָא, בְּאַתְרָא דְּלָא מְנַכְּשֵׁי, וַאֲזַל אִיהוּ וְנָכֵישׁ. מַהוּ דְּתֵימָא? אֲמַר לֵיהּ: הַאי דְּנָכֵישְׁנָא – אַדַּעְתָּא דְּלָא כָּרֵיבְנָא לָהּ. קָא מַשְׁמַע לָן דְּאִיבָּעֵי לֵיהּ לְפָרוֹשֵׁי לֵיהּ.

The mishna teaches: If they were accustomed **to plow** the land **after** harvesting[H] the produce, this cultivator **must plow** as well. The Gemara asks: Isn't it **obvious**[N] that he cannot deviate from the custom? The Gemara answers: **No,** it is **necessary for** the situation of **a place where** the custom is **not** to **weed** the fields, **and** the one cultivating this field **went and weeded** anyway. **Lest you say** that he could **say to** the landowner: When **I weeded** the field, I did so **with the intention of not plowing it** subsequently. Therefore, he should not be obligated to plow it. To counter this, the mishna **teaches us that** the renter **should have specified** this intention explicitly **to** the landowner beforehand in order to exempt him from the requirement to plow.

״הַכֹּל כְּמִנְהַג הַמְּדִינָה״. ״הַכֹּל״ לְאֵתוֹיֵי מַאי? לְאֵתוֹיֵי הָא דְּתָנוּ רַבָּנַן: מָקוֹם שֶׁנָּהֲגוּ לְהַשְׂכִּיר אִילָנוֹת עַל גַּבֵּי קַרְקַע – מַשְׂכִּירִין, מָקוֹם שֶׁאֵין נָהֲגוּ לְהַשְׂכִּיר – אֵין מַשְׂכִּירִין.

The mishna teaches: **All** farming of the land shall be conducted **in accordance with regional custom.** The Gemara asks: **What is added**[B] by the use of the term **all?** The Gemara answers: It serves **to add that which the Sages taught:** In **a location where** landowners **were accustomed to rent out the trees**[H] in a field **together with the land** so that the one cultivating the field receives a share of the fruits despite not needing to care for the trees, the trees are presumed to be **rented out.** In **a location where** landowners **were not accustomed to rent out** the trees in a field together with the land, and the one cultivating the field does not receive a share of the fruits, the trees are **not** presumed to be **rented out.**

״מָקוֹם שֶׁנָּהֲגוּ לְהַשְׂכִּיר מַשְׂכִּירִין״. פְּשִׁיטָא! לָא צְרִיכָא, דְּכוּלֵּי עָלְמָא יָהֲבִי בְּתִילְתָא וַאֲזַל אִיהוּ וִיהָבֵיהּ בְּרִיבְעָא. מַהוּ דְּתֵימָא? דְּאָמַר לֵיהּ: הַאי דְּבָצְרִי לָךְ – אַדַּעְתָּא דְּלָא יָהֵיבְנָא לָךְ בְּאִילָנוֹת. קָא מַשְׁמַע לָן דְּאִיבָּעֵי לֵיהּ לְפָרוֹשֵׁי לֵיהּ.

The *baraita* teaches: In **a location where** landowners **were accustomed to rent out the trees** in a field **together with the land** so that the one cultivating the field receives a share of the fruit despite not needing to care for the trees, the trees are presumed to be **rented out.** The Gemara asks: Isn't this **obvious?** The Gemara answers: **No,** it is **necessary** to state this ruling in order to include the case **where everyone** in that region **gives** land to sharecroppers to cultivate in return **for one-third** of the yield, **and he,** the landowner, **went and gave it for one-quarter. Lest you say that** the landowner can **say to him: This** concession on my part, **that I reduced** my portion of the yield **for you,** was done **with the intention that I would not give you** a share of the fruits **of the trees** in the field, the *baraita* **teaches us that** the landowner **should have specified** this **to him** in advance.

NOTES

This one can say, I want, etc. – הַאי אָמַר בָּעֵינָא וכו׳: Some commentaries question why it was necessary to offer these explanations, as it would seem sufficient to simply state that one must follow the regional custom without explaining the basis for each custom (*Nimmukei Yosef*). One explanation is that in general, even where a regional custom exists, if there is no significant difference between that method and another, one who insists on acting in accordance with the regional custom in a case where this causes unnecessary effort or difficulty to the other party in the process, is considered to be conducting himself with the attribute of Sodom, a biblical city known for the extreme cruelty of the residents in the domain of interpersonal relations. Therefore, the reasons for each custom are specified so that each party may insist on following the regional custom without fear that this will be construed as conduct characteristic of Sodom (*Tosefot Yom Tov*).

My land to be fertilized with stubble, etc. – דְּתִתְבַּן לִי אַרְעַאי וכו׳: Some commentaries explain that this applies not just to a contractor, who gives a set proportion of the yield, but also to a tenant farmer, who gives a set amount of produce. Although a tenant farmer gives a set amount of produce to the owner, and accordingly, one might think that it does not matter to the owner if the field is fertilized, nevertheless, the owner has an interest in improving the quality of the produce that he receives. Therefore, in a case where the custom was to cut the produce, the landowner might desire to have this done, since it fertilizes the soil and enhances the produce. Conversely, where the custom is to uproot the produce, he may prefer this method, since fertilization can lead to the undesired consequence of the produce ripening quickly and consequently rotting quickly (commentary attributed to the Ritva).

To plow after…isn't it obvious – לַחֲרוֹשׁ אַחֲרָיו...פְּשִׁיטָא: Although in the context of cutting and uprooting the Gemara explained the basis for each custom, this was necessary because there were differing customs, each with its own advantages. By contrast, it is obvious to all that plowing is beneficial to the soil. Therefore, it is understandable why the Gemara asks: Isn't it obvious, specifically in this case. This is also the reason for asking: Isn't it obvious, with regard to renting trees in the field (Rid).

HALAKHA

To plow after harvesting – לַחֲרוֹשׁ אַחֲרָיו: In a location where it is customary to plow after harvesting, the cultivator of the field is obligated to do so. In a location where this is not the universal custom, if he specified that he planned to do so, he may not renege on the obligation. But if at weeding time he stipulated that he was weeding on condition that he would not have to plow, and the owner was silent, the owner is considered to have agreed to the stipulation, in accordance with the Gemara (Rambam *Sefer Mishpatim, Hilkhot Sekhirut* 8:6; *Shulḥan Arukh, Ḥoshen Mishpat* 320:4).

In a location where landowners were accustomed to rent out the trees – מָקוֹם שֶׁנָּהֲגוּ לְהַשְׂכִּיר אִילָנוֹת: In a location where cultivators are accustomed to partake of the fruit of the trees in the field, a cultivator may do so if it was not specified otherwise, even if the landowner increased the cultivator's portion of the other yield of the land beyond what is customary. The landowner may not claim that he did so to preclude the collection of a portion of the fruit by the cultivator. But in a location where cultivators are not accustomed to partake of the fruit of the trees, then even if the cultivator contributed more to the landowner than was the custom, he still may not partake of the fruit (Rambam *Sefer Mishpatim, Hilkhot Sekhirut* 8:6; *Shulḥan Arukh, Ḥoshen Mishpat* 320:5).

BACKGROUND

What is added – לְאֵתוֹיֵי מַאי: The Gemara occasionally asks this question with regard to a seemingly superfluous word, phrase, or sentence, particularly when a mishna contains a list of items to which a certain *halakha* applies as well as a general statement that covers the items on the list. The question means: What case is included in the *halakha* based on this addition that would not otherwise have been included?

״מָקוֹם שֶׁנָּהֲגוּ שֶׁלֹּא לְהַשְׂכִּיר אֵין מַשְׂכִּירִין״. פְּשִׁיטָא! לָא צְרִיכָא, דְּכוּלֵּי עָלְמָא מְקַבְּלֵי בְּרִיבְעָא, וַאֲזַל אִיהוּ וְקִיבְּלָהּ בְּתִילְתָא. מַהוּ דְּתֵימָא? אֲמַר לֵיהּ: הַאי דְּטְפַאי לָךְ – אַדַּעֲתָא דִּיהַבְתְּ לִי בְּאִילָנוֹת. קָא מַשְׁמַע לָן דְּאִיבָּעֵי לֵיהּ לְפָרוֹשֵׁי לֵיהּ.

The *baraita* teaches: In **a location where** landowners **were not accustomed to rent out** the trees in a field together with the land, and the one cultivating the field does not receive a share of the fruits, the trees are **not** presumed to be **rented out.** The Gemara asks: Isn't this **obvious?** The Gemara answers: **No,** it is **necessary** to state this ruling in order to include the case **where all** the cultivators in that region **receive** land in return **for** giving **one-quarter** of the yield to the owner, **and** this cultivator **went and received** the land in return **for** giving **one-third** of the yield to the owner. **Lest you say** that the cultivator can **say to him: This** concession on my part, **that I added to your** portion, was done **with the intention that you** would also **give me** a share of the fruit **from the trees,** the *baraita* **teaches us that** the cultivator **should have specified** this **to him** in advance.

״כְּשֵׁם שֶׁחוֹלְקִין בַּתְּבוּאָה כָּךְ חוֹלְקִין בַּתֶּבֶן וּבַקַּשׁ״. אֲמַר רַב יוֹסֵף: בְּבָבֶל נְהִיגוּ דְּלָא יְהִיבֵי תִּיבְנָא לְאָרִיסָא. לְמַאי נָפְקָא מִינָּהּ? דְּאִי אִיכָּא אִינִישׁ דְּיָהֵיב – עַיִן יָפָה הוּא, וְלָא גָּמְרִינַן מִינֵּיהּ.

§ The mishna teaches: **Just as** the *halakha* is that the owner of the field and the one cultivating it **divide the produce, so** too the *halakha* is that **they divide the stubble and the straw. Rav Yosef said** with regard to this statement: **In Babylonia** those who enter into such arrangements **are accustomed not to give stubble**[N] **to the sharecropper.** The Gemara asks: **What is the** practical **difference** resulting from the assertion that this is the practice in Babylonia? The Gemara answers: The difference is **that if there is a person** in Babylonia **who gives** the sharecropper the stubble in addition to the produce, **it is** considered merely as though he has **a generous disposition, but we do not learn from his** actions that this is the general practice.

אָמַר רַב יוֹסֵף: בּוּכְרָא וְטַפְתָּא וְאַרְכַּבְתָּא וְקָנֵי דְּחִיזְרָא – דְּבַעַל הַבַּיִת, וְחִיזְרָא גּוּפֵיהּ דְּאָרִיסָא. כְּלָלָא דְּמִילְּתָא: כָּל עִיקַּר בַּלְמָא – דְּבַעַל הַבַּיִת, נְטִירוּתָא יְתֵירְתָּא – דְּאָרִיסָא. וְאָמַר רַב יוֹסֵף: מָרָא וּזְבִילָא וְדַוְולָא וְזַרְנוּקָא – דְּבַעַל הַבַּיִת; אָרִיסָא עָבֵיד בֵּי יְאוֹרֵי.

Rav Yosef says: The first, second, and third[NH] elements of the earthen barrier surrounding the field **and the poles** used **to** support **a thorn** fence are the responsibility **of the owner** of the land, **but the fashioning of the thorn** fence **itself** is the responsibility **of the sharecropper.** The Gemara explains: **The principle of the matter** is that the **main** part of **the boundary** of the field is the responsibility **of the owner** of the land, while any **additional protection** required is the responsibility **of the sharecropper. Rav Yosef says: The hoe and the shovel**[NL] **and the bucket and the irrigation device**[L] must be provided **by the owner** of the land, while **the sharecropper** must **make the irrigation channels.**

״כְּשֵׁם שֶׁחוֹלְקִין בַּיַּיִן כָּךְ חוֹלְקִין בִּזְמוֹרוֹת וּבַקָּנִים״. קָנִים מַאי עֲבִידְתַּיְיהוּ? אָמְרִי דְּבֵי רַבִּי יַנַּאי: קָנִים הַמּוּחְלָקִין, שֶׁבָּהֶן מַעֲמִידִין אֶת הַגְּפָנִים.

The mishna teaches: **Just as** the *halakha* is that the owner of the field and the one cultivating it **divide the wine, so** too the *halakha* is that **they divide the branches** pruned from the vines **and the poles.** The Gemara asks: **What is the purpose** of the **poles** used for the vines? **They said** in **the school of Rabbi Yannai:** This is referring to long **poles that were divided** in half, **with which they support the vines.**

NOTES

In Babylonia they are accustomed not to give stubble – בְּבָבֶל נְהִיגוּ דְּלָא יְהִיבֵי תִּיבְנָא: Early commentaries note that this statement indicates that when the mishna states that the cultivator and the landowner divide the stubble and straw, this division is also subject to the local custom, as this was not practiced in Babylonia. Why, then, does the mishna state this ruling in absolute terms, and not teach that it depends on the local custom? Some answer that the mishna is teaching that although the local custom is always followed, in a new community, where there is not yet a fixed custom in place, the custom described in the mishna should be followed (Rashba; Ran).

The first [*bukhera*], second [*tafta*], and third [*arkavta*] – בּוּכְרָא טַפְתָּא אַרְכַּבְתָּא: Some commentaries explain that the first layer was a furrow about six handbreadths deep, while the second was only three handbreadths deep. Others say that while the first layer was a ditch and the word *bukhera* is related to the term: Location of digging [*bei karya*], the second was a mound of earth rising from one of the banks of the furrow of the first layer (Ra'avad). With regard to the third layer [*arkavta*], some say that it was dirt brought from elsewhere to heighten the mound (Meiri). Others suggest that it refers to trees with holes through which the poles were passed (Rabbeinu Ḥananel). According to Rashi, the *bukhera*, *tafta*, and *arkavta* were three layers of earth that would be added successively to the mound as it was tamped down over time.

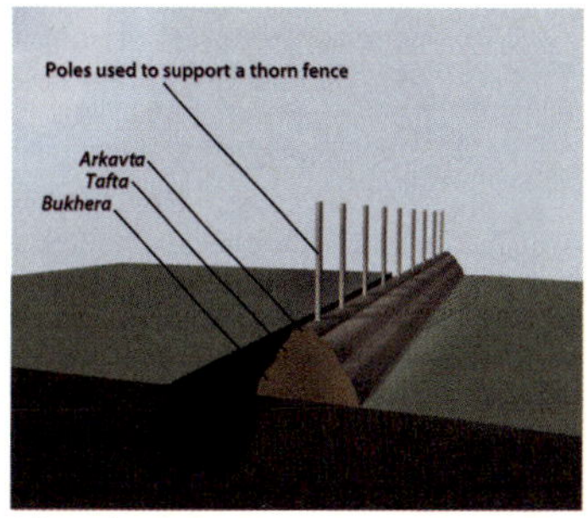

Bukhera, tafta, and *arkavta,* and poles for a thorn fence, according to opinion of Rashi

Shovel [*zevila*] – זְבִילָא: Some say that *zevila* was fertilizer, which was incumbent upon the owner to supply (Ra'avad).

HALAKHA

The first, second, and third, etc. – בּוּכְרָא וְטַפְתָּא וְאַרְכַּבְתָּא וכו׳: The owner is obligated to maintain any item that serves to mark the boundary of the field. Any item used for additional protection is the responsibility of the cultivator. The landowner must provide the equipment used to cultivate the field, while the cultivator is responsible to do the work. Some say that in the case of a tenant farmer, the landowner is not obligated to supply any equipment or boundary marker (Rambam *Sefer Mishpatim, Hilkhot Sekhirut* 8:2; *Shulḥan Arukh, Ḥoshen Mishpat* 320:3, and in the comment of Rema).

LANGUAGE

Shovel [*zevila*] – זְבִילָא: Apparently related to the word for manure [*zevel*], the word was then borrowed to refer to a tool used to move manure. According to the Talmud's description of the tool, it is similar to a spade.

Irrigation device [*zarnuka*] – זַרְנוּקָא: Possibly related to the Arabic word زرنوق, *zurnūq*, meaning a water pipe or channel. The Sages use the word to refer to a leather bottle used to transport water.

BACKGROUND

Irrigated field [*beit hashelaḥin*] – בֵּית הַשְּׁלָחִין: Opinions differ as to the precise meaning of *beit hashelaḥin*. Some explain that this term refers exclusively to a field of grain (Rif). Others maintain that it refers specifically to a vegetable garden (Rid; Riaz). Yet others say that it can refer to both a vegetable garden and a field of grain, but not to an orchard (commentary attributed to the Ritva; Meiri). Many early authorities maintain that it can refer to an orchard as well.

״וּשְׁנֵיהֶם מְסַפְּקִין אֶת הַקָּנִים״. לָמָּה לִי? מַה טַּעַם קָאָמַר; מַה טַּעַם שְׁנֵיהֶם חוֹלְקִין בַּקָּנִים? מִשּׁוּם דִּשְׁנֵיהֶם מְסַפְּקִין אֶת הַקָּנִים.

The mishna teaches: **And the two of them,** i.e., the landowner and the one cultivating the field, both **supply the poles.** The Gemara asks: **Why do I need** the mishna to state this? The Gemara answers that the mishna **is saying what** the **reason** is for its ruling: **What is the reason that the two of them divide the poles?** It is **because the two of them supply the poles.**

מתני׳ הַמְקַבֵּל שָׂדֶה מֵחֲבֵירוֹ וְהִיא בֵּית הַשְּׁלָחִין אוֹ בֵּית הָאִילָן, יָבַשׁ הַמַּעְיָן וְנִקְצַץ הָאִילָן – אֵינוֹ מְנַכֶּה לוֹ מִן חֲכוֹרוֹ. אִם אָמַר לוֹ חֲכוֹר לִי שָׂדֶה בֵּית הַשְּׁלָחִין זוֹ אוֹ שָׂדֶה בֵּית הָאִילָן זֶה יָבַשׁ הַמַּעְיָן וְנִקְצַץ הָאִילָן – מְנַכֶּה לוֹ מֵחֲכוֹרוֹ.

MISHNA In the case of **one who receives a field from another** to cultivate **and it is an irrigated field**[BN] **or a field with trees,** if **the spring** that irrigated the field **dried up or the trees were cut down,**[H] he does **not subtract from** the produce **he** owes the owner as part of **his tenancy,** despite the fact that he presumably considered these factors when agreeing to cultivate the field. But **if** the cultivator **said to** the landowner explicitly: **Lease me this irrigated field,**[H] **or** he said: Lease me **this field with trees, and the spring dried up or the trees were cut down,**[N] **he** may **subtract from** the produce **he** owes as part of **his tenancy.**

גמ׳ הֵיכִי דָּמֵי? אִילֵימָא דְּיָבֵשׁ נַהֲרָא רַבָּה – אַמַּאי אֵינוֹ מְנַכֶּה לוֹ מִן חֲכוֹרוֹ? נֵימָא לֵיהּ: מַכַּת מְדִינָה הִיא! אָמַר רַב פַּפָּא: דְּיָבֵשׁ נַהֲרָא זוּטָא, דְּאָמַר לֵיהּ:

GEMARA The Gemara asks: **What are the circumstances** of the ruling of the mishna? **If we say that the large river** from which all the channels originate **dried up, why** does he **not subtract from** the produce **he** owes as part of **his tenancy? Let** the cultivator **say** that it is the result of **a regional disaster.** Consequently, he should be able to subtract from the produce he owes. **Rav Pappa said:** The case in the mishna is **where a small river** that irrigates this field alone **dried up, as** the landowner can **say to him:**

NOTES

One who receives...irrigated field – הַמְקַבֵּל...בֵּית הַשְּׁלָחִין: According to the Rambam, who bases his opinion on the statement of the Gemara (104a) that equates tenant farmers and contractors with regard to the *halakhot* discussed in these two *mishnayot*, even a contractor may give a smaller portion of produce to the landowner in the case of a regional disaster, due to the additional effort expended on the field. Conversely, the Ramban and others hold that this *halakha* applies to tenant farmers, while a contractor is still obligated to contribute solely based on the yield at the time he received the field for cultivation.

The spring dried up or the trees were cut down – יָבַשׁ הַמַּעְיָן וְנִקְצַץ הָאִילָן: In the Jerusalem Talmud it is stated that if the spring did not dry up completely and water could be accessed through deepening the channel, or, alternatively, if only some of the trees had been cut down but there were still ten trees per *beit se'a*, the area required for sowing one *se'a* of seed, left standing, the tenant farmer may not subtract from the produce he owes as part of his tenancy. The reason for this in the case of the spring is that extracting the water is difficult but not impossible, and therefore it is incumbent on the tenant farmer to do so. With regard to the trees, the fact that there are now fewer trees in the field means that those left will produce more fruit if cared for properly, allowing the cultivator to earn a similar profit.

HALAKHA

The spring dried up or the trees were cut down – יָבַשׁ הַמַּעְיָן וְנִקְצַץ הָאִילָן: If a tenant farmer or contractor cultivates an irrigated field and the spring or channel from which it is irrigated dried up, but there is a larger river nearby from which water can be brought to irrigate the field, he may not subtract from the produce he owes as part of his tenancy. If a tenant farmer or contractor cultivates a field with trees and trees are cut down, the one cultivating the field may not subtract from the produce he owes. But if a regional disaster occurs, e.g., the main river dries up, then both a tenant farmer and a contractor may subtract from the produce owed (Rambam). The Rema holds, based on the Ramban, the *Maggid Mishne,* and the *Nimmukei Yosef*, that a contractor may not subtract from the produce he owes (Rambam *Sefer Mishpatim*, *Hilkhot Sekhirut* 8:4; *Shulḥan Arukh*, *Ḥoshen Mishpat* 321:1).

Lease me this irrigated field – חֲכוֹר לִי שָׂדֶה בֵּית הַשְּׁלָחִין זוֹ: If the landowner stands in his field and announces: I am leasing this irrigated field, or: I am leasing this field with a tree, if the spring subsequently dries up or the tree is cut down, the cultivator subtracts from the produce he owes per their arrangement. Some say that if some of the trees in the field are cut down but ten trees per *beit se'a* remained, or alternatively, if the spring did not dry up completely, he may not subtract from the produce he owes (Rema, citing *Tur*). If the owner did not stand in the field and announce: I am leasing this irrigated field, or: I am leasing this field with a tree, then even if the spring dries up or the tree is cut down, the cultivator may not subtract from the produce he owes. Some say that this is the *halakha* if the landowner makes the stipulation to the cultivator, but if the cultivator himself stipulated in this way, then even if he is not standing in the field he may subtract from the produce he owes per their arrangement (Rambam *Sefer Mishpatim*, *Hilkhot Sekhirut* 8:4, and see *Maggid Mishne* there; *Shulḥan Arukh*, *Ḥoshen Mishpat* 321:2, and in the comment of Rema).

אִיבָּעֵי לָךְ לְאַתּוּיֵי בְּדַוְולָא.

You should have brought water **in a bucket.**

אָמַר רַב פָּפָּא: הָנֵי תַּרְתֵּי מַתְנְיָיתָא קַמָּיְיתָא מַשְׁכַּחַת לָהּ בֵּין בַּחֲכִירוּתָא בֵּין בְּקַבְּלָנוּתָא. מִכָּאן וְאֵילָךְ, דְּאִיתָא בְּקַבְּלָנוּתָא – לֵיתָא בַּחֲכִירוּתָא, וּדְאִיתָא בַּחֲכִירוּתָא – לֵיתָא בְּקַבְּלָנוּתָא.

Rav Pappa said: With regard to **these first two** ***mishnayot*****, you find** that they are correct, **concerning both tenancy,** where the tenant farmer gives a certain amount of produce to the owner and keeps the rest, **as well as** the case of **a contractor,** who gives a set proportion, e.g., one-quarter or one-third, of the yield to the owner, and keeps the rest. **From this** point **forward,** i.e., from the third mishna of the chapter until its end, that **which is** relevant to the case **of a contractor is not** applicable **to tenancy, and** that **which is** relevant **to tenancy is not** applicable to the case of **a contractor.**

״אִם אָמַר לוֹ חֲכוֹר לִי שָׂדֶה בֵּית הַשְּׁלָחִין זֶה״ [וכו׳]. וְאַמַּאי? לֵימָא לֵיהּ: שְׁמָא בְּעָלְמָא אֲמַרִי לָךְ. מִי לָא תַּנְיָא: הָאוֹמֵר לַחֲבֵירוֹ בֵּית כּוֹר עָפָר אֲנִי מוֹכֵר לָךְ, אַף עַל פִּי שֶׁאֵין בּוֹ אֶלָּא לֶתֶךְ – הִגִּיעוֹ, שֶׁלֹּא מָכַר לוֹ אֶלָּא שְׁמָא, וְהוּא דְּמִתְקְרֵי בֵּית כּוֹר.

§ The mishna teaches: **If** the cultivator **said to** the landowner explicitly: **Lease me this irrigated field,** or he said: Lease me this field with trees, and the spring dried up or the trees were cut down, he may subtract from the produce he owes as part of his tenancy. The Gemara asks: **But why** is this so? **Let** the owner **say to him: I told you only the name,** i.e., the type, of the field, but this does not mean it would actually be irrigated during the time you are cultivating it. **Isn't it taught** in a *baraita*: In the case of **one who says to another: I am selling you a** ***beit kor***[B] field **of dirt,**[NH] **although** the field **contains only a half-*****kor*****,** once the buyer purchases the dirt **it has come to him,** i.e., he may not retract from the transaction, **as** the seller **sold him** the dirt **only** by **the name,** and he did not mean that its size was precisely a *beit kor*. The *baraita* adds: **And this is** the *halakha* only **where** that field **is called** by people **a** ***beit kor***.

כַּרְמָא אֲנִי מוֹכֵר לָךְ אַף עַל פִּי שֶׁאֵין בּוֹ גְּפָנִים – הִגִּיעוֹ, שֶׁלֹּא מָכַר לוֹ אֶלָּא שְׁמָא, וְהוּא דְּמִתְקְרֵי כַּרְמָא. פַּרְדֵּס אֲנִי מוֹכֵר לָךְ אַף עַל פִּי שֶׁאֵין בּוֹ רִמּוֹנִים – הִגִּיעוֹ, שֶׁלֹּא מָכַר לוֹ אֶלָּא שְׁמָא, וְהוּא דְּמִתְקְרֵי פַּרְדְּסָא. אַלְמָא אָמַר לֵיהּ: שְׁמָא בְּעָלְמָא אֲמַרִי לָךְ; הָכִי נַמִי נֵימָא לֵיהּ: שְׁמָא בְּעָלְמָא אֲמַרִי לָךְ!

The *baraita* continues: Similarly, if he said: **I am selling you a vineyard,** then **although it does not have vines,** once he purchases the land **it has come to him, as** the seller **sold him** the field **only** by **the name; and this** is the *halakha* only **where it is called a vineyard.** Likewise, if he said: **I am selling you an orchard,**[H] then **even though it does not have pomegranates,** once he purchases the land **it has come to him, as he sold him only** by **the name; and** again **this is** the case only **where it is called an orchard. Apparently,** the seller can **say to him: I told you only the name. So too** here, **let** the seller **say to him: I told you only the name.**

אָמַר שְׁמוּאֵל: לָא קַשְׁיָא; הָא דַּאֲמַר לֵיהּ מַחְכִּיר לְחוֹכֵר, הָא דַּאֲמַר לֵיהּ חוֹכֵר לְמַחְכִּיר. אֲמַר לֵיהּ מַחְכִּיר לְחוֹכֵר – שְׁמָא בְּעָלְמָא אֲמַר לֵיהּ. אֲמַר לֵיהּ חוֹכֵר לְמַחְכִּיר – קְפִידָא.

Shmuel said: It is **not difficult; this** *baraita* is comparable to a case **where the owner of the land said to the tenant farmer** what he was leasing him, while in **that** mishna **the tenant farmer said to the owner of the land** what he was leasing from him. The reason for the difference is that if **the owner of the land said** the terms **to the tenant farmer,** then he can claim that **he told him only the name,** and the tenant farmer cannot object. But if **the tenant farmer said** the terms **to the owner of the land,** then he was clearly **particular** to receive a field that would be irrigated when he cultivated it.

רָבִינָא אָמַר: אִידִי וְאִידִי דַּאֲמַר לֵיהּ מַחְכִּיר לְחוֹכֵר. מִדְּקָאָמַר זֶה – מִכְּלָל דְּקָאֵי בְּגַוֵּיהּ עָסְקִינַן. בֵּית הַשְּׁלָחִין לָמָּה לֵיהּ לְמֵימַר? דְּקָאָמַר לֵיהּ: בֵּית הַשְּׁלָחִין כִּדְקַיְּימָא הָשְׁתָּא.

Ravina said: Both **this** *baraita* **and that**[N] mishna are referring to a case **where the owner of the land told the tenant farmer** what he was leasing him, as implied by the mishna, but **since** the owner **said: This** irrigated field, **by inference we are dealing with** one **who is standing inside it. Why,** then, **does** the owner **need to state** the fact that it is **an irrigated field?** It is obvious simply from looking at it that it is irrigated. Rather, the owner must have **said to him** by way of emphasis that he is providing **an irrigated** field **as it currently stands.**

BACKGROUND

Beit kor **– בֵּית כּוֹר:** A *beit kor* is an area of land that can produce a *kor*, or thirty *se'a*, of grain. The amount of land required to produce a *se'a* of grain is fifty cubits by fifty cubits, or 2500 square cubits. A *beit kor* therefore contains an area of 75,000 square cubits, which is approximately 18,750 square meters.

NOTES

A ***beit kor*** **of dirt – בֵּית כּוֹר עָפָר:** The Ra'avad claims that the correct reading of the *baraita* is: This *beit kor*, and: This vineyard, and: This orchard. Although the buyer can claim he thought he would receive more land from elsewhere or that vines would be planted for him, since the seller mentioned this particular field and this plot is called by this name, the transaction is still complete. But if he did not mention specifically this field, the seller may not give the buyer less than the stated amount.

Ravina said, this and that – רָבִינָא אָמַר אִידִי וְאִידִי: The commentaries consider the relationship between Ravina's opinion and Shmuel's. Some explain that Ravina agrees with the distinction made by Shmuel and is adding an additional distinction. Others say that Ravina holds that his own distinction is the only relevant one (Rambam; Ran).

HALAKHA

A ***beit kor*** **of dirt – בֵּית כּוֹר עָפָר:** If one says to another: I am selling you a *beit kor* of dirt, then even if the field is smaller than a *beit kor*, the transaction is complete, as he meant only that the field was called a *beit kor*. This is the *halakha* provided that the seller can prove that the field is in fact known by this name (Rambam *Sefer Kinyan*, *Hilkhot Mekhira* 28:14; *Shulḥan Arukh*, *Ḥoshen Mishpat* 218:17).

A vineyard…an orchard – כַּרְמָא, פַּרְדֵּס: If one says to another: I am selling you my vineyard in such and such a place, or: I am selling you an orchard in such and such a place, then even if the land does not contain any vines or pomegranates it is a proper sale, provided the plot is called by that name (Rambam *Sefer Kinyan*, *Hilkhot Mekhira* 28:14; *Shulḥan Arukh*, *Ḥoshen Mishpat* 218:18).

HALAKHA

One who receives a field…and lets it lie fallow – הַמְקַבֵּל שָׂדֶה...וְהוֹבִירָה: If one receives a field in order to cultivate it, and he lets all or part of it remain fallow, the court appraises how much it should have produced, and the cultivator must pay the owner his share of this amount. Even if this condition did not appear in their contract, it is considered as though it were written, as maintained by the Rambam and *Tosafot* (Rambam *Sefer Mishpatim, Hilkhot Sekhirut* 8:13; *Shulḥan Arukh, Ḥoshen Mishpat* 328:2).

Expound common language – דּוֹרֵשׁ לְשׁוֹן הֶדְיוֹט: With regard to legal documents, the local custom is followed. Therefore, even if a certain practice was not a rabbinical ordinance but merely the common practice, it is treated as though it was written in the document, despite its omission. The same applies to communal ordinances or other city customs (*Shulḥan Arukh, Ḥoshen Mishpat* 42:15, and in the comment of Rema).

Brings the offering of the rich on behalf of his wife – מֵבִיא קׇרְבַּן עָשִׁיר עַל אִשְׁתּוֹ: A husband must pay for all offerings that his wife is obligated to bring. If he is poor, he brings the offering of a pauper, and if he is wealthy, he brings the offering of a rich man (Rambam *Sefer Korbanot, Hilkhot Shegagot* 10:6).

מתני׳ הַמְקַבֵּל שָׂדֶה מֵחֲבֵירוֹ וְהוֹבִירָה – שָׁמִין אוֹתָהּ כַּמָּה רְאוּיָה לַעֲשׂוֹת, וְנוֹתֵן לוֹ. שֶׁכָּךְ כּוֹתֵב לוֹ: אִם אוֹבִיר וְלָא אַעֲבִיד אֲשַׁלֵּם בְּמֵיטְבָא.

MISHNA With regard to **one who receives a field from another** as a contractor **and** then **lets it lie fallow**[H] and does not work the land at all, the court **appraises it** by evaluating **how much it was able to produce** if cultivated, **and he gives** his share of this amount **to** the owner. The reason is **that this** is what a cultivator **writes to** the owner[N] in a standard contract: **If I let** the field **lie fallow and do not cultivate** it, **I will pay with best**-quality produce.

גמ׳ רַבִּי מֵאִיר הָיָה דּוֹרֵשׁ לְשׁוֹן הֶדְיוֹט; דְּתַנְיָא, רַבִּי מֵאִיר אוֹמֵר: אִם אוֹבִיר וְלָא אַעֲבִיד אֲשַׁלֵּם בְּמֵיטְבָא.

GEMARA **Rabbi Meir would expound common language**[HN] used in legal documents written by ordinary Jews to deduce halakhic conclusions. Although these formulations were not prescribed by the Sages, one can nevertheless infer *halakhot* from them if they are used in legal documents. **As it is taught** in a *baraita* that presents a similar case to the mishna: **Rabbi Meir says** he is liable to pay, as the document states: **If I let** the field **lie fallow and do not cultivate** it, **I will pay with best**-quality produce.

רַבִּי יְהוּדָה הָיָה דּוֹרֵשׁ לְשׁוֹן הֶדְיוֹט; דְּתַנְיָא, רַבִּי יְהוּדָה אוֹמֵר: אָדָם מֵבִיא קׇרְבַּן עָשִׁיר עַל אִשְׁתּוֹ, וְכֵן כׇּל קׇרְבָּן וְקׇרְבָּן שֶׁהִיא חַיֶּיבֶת, שֶׁכָּךְ כּוֹתֵב לָהּ: אַחְרָיוּת דְּאִית לִיךְ עֲלַי מִן קַדְמַת דְּנָא.

Likewise, **Rabbi Yehuda would** also **expound common language, as it is taught** in a *baraita*: **Rabbi Yehuda says:** In a case where a woman who has given birth is commanded to bring the offering of a childbearing woman and her husband is sufficiently wealthy, **a person brings the offering of the rich**[N] **on behalf of his wife.**[H] This is so even if his wife does not possess money of her own and perhaps should have been considered poor. **Similarly,** he may bring **every offering that she is obligated** to bring, such as a sin offering or guilt offering. He pays for all these offerings **because this** is what **he writes to her** in her marriage contract: I accept **upon myself** to repay you for all **obligations that you have,** even those **from beforehand.** Consequently, he must fund all of her offerings.

NOTES

That this is what a cultivator writes to the owner – שֶׁכָּךְ כּוֹתֵב לוֹ: The early commentaries ask: If he wrote an explicit condition, he must certainly fulfill his word. What, then, is the novelty of this statement? Rabbeinu Ḥananel explains that this is a case where the condition was not properly drafted, as it is not formulated as a compound condition, stipulating both positive and negative outcomes. Furthermore, a stipulation of this kind can be viewed as a transaction with inconclusive consent [*asmakhta*], as he does not expect to have to fulfill it, and such a stipulation is not binding. Therefore, if it were not for the principle discussed in the Gemara that common language is expounded, the document would be rejected. Other early commentaries contend that these claims concerning the formulation of the stipulation and the *halakhot* of an *asmakhta* are not definitive (see Ramban and Rashba). The majority of early commentaries and authorities agree that even if this condition does not appear in the document, it is viewed as if it were written, as this was generally the local custom. Its omission is merely assumed to be the result of a scribal error, and the terms of the document must be fulfilled regardless. In the Jerusalem Talmud it is explained in this way as well (*Ge'onim*; *Tosafot*; Rambam).

Expound common language – דּוֹרֵשׁ לְשׁוֹן הֶדְיוֹט: Various interpretations of this expression have been suggested. According to some commentaries it means that the conditions discussed in the Gemara are treated as requirements established by rabbinic ordinances, and must consequently be followed even if they were not written in the document. They add that the word: Expound, indicates that Rabbi Meir regards the contract as if this clause were written even when it was omitted. Alternatively, the expression can be explained as does Rabbeinu Ḥananel, that even though one used common language without carefully formulating the details, the language in the document is accepted as binding. Other early commentaries, such as the Ramban and the commentary attributed to the Ritva, point out that these explanations do not fit well with the word: Expound.

Most early commentaries accept the interpretation of Rav Hai Gaon and Rabbi Yehuda of Barcelona that the word: Expound, has the same meaning here as elsewhere. According to this approach, although these common contractual phrases can be explained simply in a far more limited way, the Sages expounded and inferred halakhic principles from them as though they were written in the Torah. Consequently, they arrived at binding legal conclusions based on omissions from and imprecise formulations in actual contracts. In this particular case, although the document can be understood simply as hyperbole, an assurance on the part of the tenant farmer that he will work the field and pay the standard amount, the Sages inferred that he must in fact pay from the best of his possessions. Similarly, with regard to a marriage contract, one might have thought that writing: I accept upon myself to repay you for all obligations that you have, even those from beforehand, is merely a vivid way of saying that the groom accepts upon himself the duty to pay for the household expenses, similar to other flowery terms written in the marriage contract. Likewise, a straightforward reading of the marriage contract from Alexandria indicates only that after the wedding, the woman will no longer be betrothed but have will have the full-fledged status of wife, and the statement concerning the collateral merely attests that a deposit was taken. Nevertheless, in all these cases the Sages read the wording as carefully as if were written in the Torah itself, and expounded all its meanings (see Ramban and Rashba).

The offering of the rich – קׇרְבַּן עָשִׁיר: The reason the Gemara mentions the offering of a wealthy person, which is a reference to the sliding-scale offering, is because this category of offering applies to a woman following childbirth or a woman who is a *zava*, both of which affect the husband as well. Consequently, it might be thought that only in such cases is his financial status taken into account. Rabbi Yehuda therefore teaches us that the same principle applies even to offerings that are only for her personal atonement (Rid; *Tosafot* in *Nazir* 24a; see *Tosafot*).

הִלֵּל הַזָּקֵן הָיָה דּוֹרֵשׁ לְשׁוֹן הֶדְיוֹט; דְּתַנְיָא: אַנְשֵׁי אֲלֶכְּסַנְדְּרִיָּא הָיוּ מְקַדְּשִׁין אֶת נְשׁוֹתֵיהֶם, וּבִשְׁעַת כְּנִיסָתָן לַחוּפָּה בָּאִין אֲחֵרִים וְחוֹטְפִים אוֹתָם מֵהֶן, וּבִקְּשׁוּ חֲכָמִים לַעֲשׂוֹת בְּנֵיהֶם מַמְזֵרִים.

Similarly, **Hillel the Elder**[P] **would expound common language** as well, **as it is taught** in a *baraita*: **The inhabitants of Alexandria**[B] **would betroth their wives** a significant amount of time before the wedding, as was customary in those days, **and at the time of their entry to the wedding canopy, others** would **come and snatch** the women **from their** husbands. **The Sages** consequently **sought to establish the children** of these women as ***mamzerim.*** This is because with regard to sexual intercourse with other men, a betrothed woman has the status of a married woman. Consequently, if she is taken by another man, her children fathered by that man are *mamzerim*, just like children of a married woman who were fathered by a man other than her husband.

אָמַר לָהֶן הִלֵּל הַזָּקֵן: הָבִיאוּ לִי כְּתוּבַּת אִמְּכֶם. הֵבִיאוּ לוֹ כְּתוּבַּת אִמָּן, וּמָצָא שֶׁכָּתוּב בָּהֶן: לִכְשֶׁתִּכָּנְסִי לְחוּפָּה הֲוִי לִי לְאִינְתּוּ, וְלֹא עָשׂוּ בְּנֵיהֶם מַמְזֵרִים.

Hillel the Elder said to the children who came before him for a ruling on their status: **Bring me your mother's marriage contract** for examination. **They brought him their mother's marriage contract, and he found that** the following formulation **was written in it: When you will enter the wedding canopy,**[N] **be for me a wife.** This shows that the marriage would not take effect at the time of her betrothal, but only after she would enter the wedding canopy. Consequently, the marriage did not occur at all, as she never entered the wedding canopy, **and** therefore these women **did not cause their children** to be ***mamzerim*** by engaging in intercourse with the other man.

רַבִּי יְהוֹשֻׁעַ בֶּן קָרְחָה הָיָה דּוֹרֵשׁ לְשׁוֹן הֶדְיוֹט; דְּתַנְיָא, רַבִּי יְהוֹשֻׁעַ בֶּן קָרְחָה אוֹמֵר: הַמַּלְוֶה אֶת חֲבֵירוֹ לֹא יְמַשְׁכְּנֶנּוּ יוֹתֵר מֵחוֹבוֹ, שֶׁכָּךְ כּוֹתֵב לוֹ: תַּשְׁלוּמְתָּא דְּאִית לָךְ עֲלַי כָּל קֳבֵל דֵּיכִי.

The Gemara adds: **Rabbi Yehoshua ben Korḥa**[P] **would** also **expound common language. As it is taught** in a *baraita*: **Rabbi Yehoshua ben Korḥa says:** One **who lends** money to **another may not take more collateral from him than** the value of **his debt, as this** is what the debtor **writes to** the creditor if the creditor temporarily returns a deposit for the debtor's use: **The payment to which you have** a right, which it is **upon me**[N] to pay, **corresponds to the entire** value of **this** item, indicating that the item cannot be greater in value than the debt itself.

טַעְמָא – דִּכְתַב לֵיהּ הָכִי, הָא אִי לָא כְּתַב לֵיהּ הָכִי – לָא קָנֵי? וְהָא אָמַר רַבִּי יוֹחָנָן: מִשְׁכְּנוֹ וְהֵשִׁיב לוֹ הַמַּשְׁכּוֹן וּמֵת – שׁוֹמְטוֹ מֵעַל גַּבֵּי בָנָיו!

The Gemara infers: **The reason** the creditor acquires the collateral is **that he wrote this to him. But if** the creditor **did not write this to** the debtor, would the creditor **not acquire** the collateral? **But doesn't Rabbi Yoḥanan say:** If a creditor **took collateral** from the debtor **and returned the collateral to him and** then the debtor **died,** the creditor **removes** the collateral **from** the debtor's **children.**[H] The reason for this is that although movable property of orphans is not acquired by their father's creditor, the collateral is considered to belong to the creditor, and he can collect the debt from it.

BACKGROUND

Alexandria – אֲלֶכְּסַנְדְּרִיָּא: This port city, which lies west of the Nile delta, was founded by Alexander the Great in 332 BCE. In its glory days, during the Ptolemaic rule in Egypt and until the end of the mishnaic period, Alexandria was one of the largest cities and cultural centers in the world. Many of the greatest scientists, doctors and artisans of the time lived in Alexandria.

NOTES

When you will enter the wedding canopy – לִכְשֶׁתִּכָּנְסִי לְחוּפָּה: Rashi explains that this formulation was written in the marriage contract for their betrothal. This explanation is puzzling, as marriage contracts were not usually drafted at the stage of betrothal. The Rid therefore claims that it is more likely that this formula appeared in the marriage contract given to the woman at the wedding. Accordingly, Hillel the Elder was not saying that the clause written in the marriage contract in and of itself renders the betrothal a conditional one, but that from the presence of this clause in the marriage contract one can infer that the betrothal was a conditional one.

The payment to which you have a right, upon me – תַּשְׁלוּמְתָּא דְּאִית לָךְ עֲלַי: The main purpose of this formulation is to prove that the collateral should be considered as belonging to the creditor, so that if the debtor happens to sell it the creditor can claim it from the buyers (Rid). Alternatively, it means that if the deposit decreases in value, the creditor must bear the loss, and he cannot claim the amount of the deterioration (Ra'avad).

HALAKHA

He removes it from the debtor's children – שׁוֹמְטוֹ מֵעַל גַּבֵּי בָנָיו: If the debtor passed away after the creditor had temporarily returned his collateral, the creditor may take it from the debtor's sons and does not have to return it to them (Rambam *Sefer Mishpatim, Hilkhot Malve VeLoveh* 3:6; *Shulḥan Arukh, Ḥoshen Mishpat* 97:19).

PERSONALITIES

Hillel the Elder – הִלֵּל הַזָּקֵן: Hillel the Elder and his colleague Shammai were the last of the *zugot*, the pairs of *tanna'im* who led the Sanhedrin toward the end of the Second Temple era. Hillel served as *Nasi* of the Sanhedrin, and Shammai was the president of the court. These leaders lived approximately one hundred years prior to the destruction of the Temple, coinciding with the beginning of Herod's reign.

Rabbi Yehoshua ben Korḥa – רַבִּי יְהוֹשֻׁעַ בֶּן קָרְחָה: Rabbi Yehoshua ben Korḥa was one of the elder *tanna'im* from the generation of Rabban Shimon ben Gamliel II. Many commentaries, including *Tosafot*, have attempted to identify him as Rabbi Yehoshua, son of Rabbi Akiva, but this is difficult to prove. Little is known about him, and only a few traditions of *halakha* and *aggada* are transmitted in his name. Rabbi Yehoshua ben Korḥa enjoyed a long life and once blessed Rabbi Yehuda HaNasi: May it be His will that you reach half of my days (*Megilla* 28a). Due to his long life, he was able to engage in halakhic dispute with Sages from several generations. He was apparently honored by all toward the end of his life, as the Sages of that time came to receive his blessing, and he took care to guide them along the right path.

אַהֲנֵי כְּתִיבָה לְגֵירָעוֹן.

The Gemara answers: The **writing** of this statement in the document **is effective for depreciation.**[N] If the collateral depreciates in value, the creditor may claim the remainder of the debt from the debtor's property.

רַבִּי יוֹסֵי הָיָה דּוֹרֵשׁ לְשׁוֹן הֶדְיוֹט; דְּתַנְיָא, רַבִּי יוֹסֵי אוֹמֵר: מָקוֹם שֶׁנָּהֲגוּ לַעֲשׂוֹת כְּתוּבָּה מִלְוָה – גּוֹבָה מִלְוָה, לִכְפּוֹל – גּוֹבָה מֶחֱצָה.

§ The Gemara continues: **Rabbi Yosei would** also **expound common language, as it is taught** in a *baraita* that **Rabbi Yosei says: In a location where they were accustomed to formulate** the terms of **a marriage contract** as one would formulate the terms of **a loan,**[NH] i.e., the precise value of the her dowry is written in the marriage contract, then upon the termination of the marriage due to divorce or the husband's death, the wife **collects** the sum of her dowry as a creditor would collect payment of **a loan.** In other words, she receives the entire sum recorded as her dowry. Conversely, in a place where the custom is **to double** the written sum of the dowry in the marriage contract to honor the bride, so that it should appear as though her father is providing her husband with a considerable dowry, she **collects** only **half** of the sum written in the marriage contract.

נְהַרְבְּלָאֵי גָּבוּ תִּילְתָּא. מָרֵימָר מַגְבֵּי נָמֵי שְׁבַחָא.

The Gemara relates: The Sages of **Neharbela**[B] **collected,** i.e., allowed the wife to collect, **one-third** of the stated sum, as the custom in their location was to write three times the actual amount of the dowry in the marriage contract. **Mareimar** would allow the wife to **collect even the added value** of those sums that the father of the bride had written in the marriage contract in honor of his daughter.

אֲמַר לֵיהּ רָבִינָא לְמָרֵימָר: וְהָתַנְיָא: לִכְפּוֹל – גּוֹבָה מֶחֱצָה! לָא קַשְׁיָא; הָא – דְּקָנֵי מִינֵּיהּ, הָא – דְּלָא קָנֵי מִינֵּיהּ.

Ravina said to Mareimar: But isn't it taught in the *baraita* that in a location where the custom is **to** record **double** the amount, she **collects** only **half?** The Gemara answers: This is **not difficult;** in **this** case, where Mareimar allowed the wife to collect the full sum, the husband **performed** an act of **acquisition** for the entire written amount **with** the father of the bride; whereas in **that** case, where the *baraita* rules that she collects only a portion of the sum written for the dowry, the husband **did not perform** an act of **acquisition** for the entire written amount **with** the father of the bride. Therefore, the wife would collect the sum of her dowry only in accordance with the regular custom.

רָבִינָא מְשַׁבַּח וְכָתֵיב לִבְרַתֵּיהּ. אָמְרוּ לֵיהּ: נִקְנֵי מִינֵּיהּ דְּמָר! אֲמַר לְהוּ: אִי מִקְנָא – לָא מִיכְפַּל, אִי מִיכְפַּל – לָא מִיקְנָא.

The Gemara relates: **Ravina wrote an enhancement** of the value of the dowry **for his daughter** in her marriage contract, in keeping with the accepted custom. The groom's family **said to** Ravina: **Let us perform** an act of **acquisition with the Master,** so that he would be required to give that entire sum as the dowry. Ravina **said to them: If** you wish to **perform** an act of **acquisition, I** will **not double** the sum of the dowry, but will record the actual sum I intend to provide; **if** you prefer that I record **double** the sum of the dowry in the marriage contract, **I** will **not** allow you to **perform** an act of **acquisition.**

הַהוּא גַּבְרָא דַּאֲמַר לְהוּ: הָבוּ לַהּ אַרְבַּע מְאָה זוּזֵי לִבְרַתִּי בִּכְתוּבָּתָהּ. שְׁלַח רַב אַחָא בְּרֵיהּ דְּרַב אַוְיָא לְקַמֵּיהּ דְּרַב אָשֵׁי: אַרְבַּע מְאָה דְּאִינּוּן תְּמָנֵי מְאָה, אוֹ אַרְבַּע מְאָה זוּזֵי דְּאִינּוּן מָאתַן? אֲמַר רַב אָשֵׁי: חָזֵינַן. אִי אֲמַר הָבוּ לַהּ – אַרְבַּע מְאָה זוּזֵי דְּאִינּוּן תְּמָנֵי מְאָה. אִי אֲמַר כְּתוּבוּ לַהּ – אַרְבַּע מְאָה זוּזֵי דְּאִינּוּן מָאתַן.

The Gemara cites a related incident: There was **a certain man who said to** his inheritors before his death: **Give four hundred dinars to my daughter in her marriage contract. Rav Aḥa, son of Rav Avya, sent** the following question to be asked **before Rav Ashi:** What was that man's intention? Did he mean an actual dowry of **four hundred** dinars, **which are** written as **eight hundred, or four hundred dinars** written in the marriage contract, **which are** actually a dowry of **two hundred** dinars? **Rav Ashi said: We examine** the matter. **If he said: Give her,** then he meant to give her **four hundred dinars, which are** written as **eight hundred.** But **if he said: Write for her,** then he meant to write **four hundred dinars, which are two hundred** in practice.

NOTES

The writing is effective for depreciation – אַהֲנֵי כְּתִיבָה לְגֵירָעוֹן: Rashi explains that if the collateral depreciates in value due to the debtor using the item, the creditor may claim more property. But most of the Sephardic scholars interpret this *halakha* in the opposite manner, that if the value of the collateral decreases the creditor may not collect from the rest of the debtor's property at all (see Ran).

To formulate a marriage contract as a loan – לַעֲשׂוֹת כְּתוּבָּה מִלְוָה: There are two fundamentally different explanations of this passage, and the meaning of the term marriage contract is different in the two explanations. Rashi explains that the term marriage contract in this context does not refer to the sum to be paid by the husband or his estate to the wife upon termination of the marriage, whether by divorce or the husband's death. Rather, it refers to the sum of the dowry provided by the father of the bride to the husband. This sum was also recorded in the marriage contract and would be returned to the wife upon termination of the marriage. In some locations, they would record the actual value of the dowry in the marriage contract, while in others, they would record an inflated value to honor the bride. Accordingly, the discussion in this passage concerns what sum the wife will receive for the return of the dowry upon the termination of her marriage: Does she receive the entire sum written in the marriage contract, or only the true value of the dowry paid by her father? Most early commentaries explain the Gemara in this manner.

By contrast, Rav Hai Gaon explains that the term marriage contract in this passage is referring to the sum that will be paid by the husband or his estate to the wife upon termination of the marriage. He explains that while generally this sum was paid only upon termination of the marriage, there were locations in which the marriage contracts would record this sum as if it were a loan from the wife to the husband. In those locations, she would be able to collect it even during their marriage (see Ra'avad and Rashash).

HALAKHA

A location where they were accustomed to formulate a marriage contract as a loan – מָקוֹם שֶׁנָּהֲגוּ לַעֲשׂוֹת כְּתוּבָּה מִלְוָה: If one marries a woman and the financial details are not specified in her marriage contract, they are assumed to have been in accordance with local custom, both with regard to the sum of the marriage contract and with regard to the dowry. Therefore, when either of the parties comes to claim the money, it is done in accordance with the local custom. If she claims he added more to the dowry than was the local custom, she must bring proof (Rema). If the husband wishes to give her less than the accepted amount for the marriage contract, he may do so as long as he does not provide less than the minimum sum required by the Sages (see *Ketubot* 54b). In some locations the custom is to use a standard formulation in all marriage contracts, even if she provided no dowry at all; if the husband does not wish to become obligated to repay the amount recorded as the dowry, she writes that she has already received it from him (Rambam *Sefer Nashim, Hilkhot Ishut* 23:11; *Shulḥan Arukh, Even HaEzer* 66:11, and in the comment of Rema).

BACKGROUND

The Sages of Neharbela – נְהַרְבְּלָאֵי: The town of Neharbela, or Neharbila, was probably located on a river, or in Hebrew, *nahar*. This river has been identified as the Baal River, or possibly the Bel or Bil River, in northern Babylonia. The Gemara (*Sanhedrin* 17b) states that the phrase: The Sages of Neharbela, refers primarily to the local scholar Rami bar Beribi, or Rav Ami bar Berukhi.

אִיכָּא דְּאָמְרִי, אֲמַר רַב אַשִׁי: חָזֵינַן. אִי אֲמַר לִכְתוּבָּתָהּ – אַרְבַּע מְאָה זוּזֵי דְּאִינּוּן תְּמָנֵי מְאָה. וְאִי אֲמַר בִּכְתוּבָּתָהּ – אַרְבַּע מְאָה זוּזֵי דְּאִינּוּן מָאתָן.

There are those who say a different version of Rav Ashi's ruling. **Rav Ashi said: We examine** the matter. **If he said: For her marriage contract** [*likhtubatah*], he meant **four hundred dinars, which are** written as **eight hundred,** because he indicated that this is the sum he wants to give for her dowry. **But if he said: In her marriage contract** [*bikhtubatah*],[H] he was clearly referring to the written amount, and it is assumed that he meant to write **four hundred dinars, which are two hundred** in practice.

וְלָא הִיא, לָא שְׁנָא דַּאֲמַר לִכְתוּבָּתָהּ וְלָא שְׁנָא דַּאֲמַר בִּכְתוּבָּתָהּ – אַרְבַּע מְאָה זוּזֵי דְּאִינּוּן מָאתָן, עַד דַּאֲמַר הֲבוּ לָהּ סְתָמָא.

The Gemara comments: **And** that **is not so.** There **is no difference whether he said: For her marriage contract, and** there **is no difference whether he said: In her marriage contract.**[N] In either case her dowry is written as **four hundred dinars, which are two hundred** in practice, **unless he** simply **said: Give her, without specification,** i.e., without mentioning the marriage contract. In that case the full sum is given as a dowry.

הַהוּא גַּבְרָא דְּקַבֵּל אַרְעָא מֵחַבְרֵיהּ. אֲמַר: אִי מוֹבַרְנָא לָהּ – יָהֵיבְנָא לָךְ אַלְפָּא זוּזֵי. אוֹבִיר תִּילְתָּא. אָמְרִי נְהַרְדְּעֵי: דִּינָא הוּא דְּיָהֵיב לֵיהּ תְּלָת מְאָה וּתְלָתִין וּתְלָתָא וְתִילְתָּא. רָבָא אֲמַר: אַסְמַכְתָּא הִיא. וְאַסְמַכְתָּא לָא קַנְיָא.

§ The Gemara relates another incident: There was **a certain man who received land from another** to cultivate. **He said: If I** fail to work the land and instead **let it lie fallow, I will give you one thousand dinars.**[H] **He let one-third** of it **lie fallow.** The Sages **of Neharde'a**[B] **said: The *halakha* is that he gives him** 333⅓ dinars, one-third of the stipulated amount, as compensation for neglecting one-third of the field. **Rava said:** This kind of agreement **is a transaction with inconclusive consent** [*asmakhta*]. **And** since **an *asmakhta***[B] **does not effect acquisition,** he need not pay.

וּלְרָבָא, מַאי שְׁנָא מֵהָא דִּתְנַן: אִם אוֹבִיר וְלָא אַעֲבִיד אֲשַׁלֵּם בְּמֵיטְבָא? הָתָם לָא קָא גָּזֵים. הָכָא כֵּיוָן דְּקָאָמַר מִילְּתָא יְתֵירְתָּא – גּוּזְמָא בְּעָלְמָא הוּא דְּקָגָזֵים.

The Gemara asks: **And according to Rava,** in **what** way **is** it **different from that which we learned** in the mishna concerning one who wrote: **If I let** the field **lie fallow and do not cultivate** it, **I will pay with best**-quality produce? The Gemara answers: **There he did not exaggerate,** but simply said he will pay for the owner's losses from best-quality produce; whereas **here, since he said something extra,** i.e., he promised to give an excessively large sum of money, **he is merely exaggerating.** It is therefore not viewed as an actual monetary obligation but an *asmakhta*.

הַהוּא גַּבְרָא דְּקַבֵּיל אַרְעָא לְשׁוּמְשְׁמֵי, זַרְעָהּ חִיטֵּי עָבְדָא חִיטֵּי כְּשׁוּמְשְׁמֵי. סָבַר רַב כָּהֲנָא לְמֵימַר: מְנַכֵּי לֵיהּ כַּחֲשָׁא דְּאַרְעָא.

§ The Gemara relates: There was **a certain man** acting as a sharecropper **who received land for** planting **sesame,**[B] which typically weakens the land but yields larger short-term profits, **but he planted it** with **wheat** instead.[H] That year, the field **produced wheat** at a value **similar to** that of **sesame.**[NB] **Rav Kahana thought to say** that the owner must **deduct** the usual amount of **the deterioration of the land** from planting sesame **from** his own share, since by planting wheat the sharecropper had spared the owner the damage to his field, while the owner had received the same profit.

HALAKHA

For her marriage contract…in her marriage contract – לִכְתוּבָּתָהּ...בִּכְתוּבָּתָהּ: If a man instructed that his daughter be provided with four hundred dinars for her marriage contract and the local custom is to record double the value at which the dowry was assessed, she may take only two hundred. It makes no difference whether he said: For her marriage contract, or: In her marriage contract. This ruling is in accordance with the conclusion of the Gemara (Rambam *Sefer Kinyan, Hilkhot Zekhiya UMattana* 11:21; *Shulḥan Arukh, Ḥoshen Mishpat* 253:15).

If I let it lie fallow I will give you one thousand dinars – אִי מוֹבַרְנָא לָהּ יָהֵיבְנָא לָךְ אַלְפָּא זוּזֵי: If one wrote that if he lets a field lie fallow he will pay the owner of the field one thousand dinars, it is considered an *asmakhta* and the owner may consequently not collect this sum. Rather, he is entitled only to his share of the amount the field would have produced (Rambam *Sefer Mishpatim, Hilkhot Sekhirut* 8:13; *Shulḥan Arukh, Ḥoshen Mishpat* 328:2).

One who plants wheat instead of sesame – הַזּוֹרֵעַ חִטִּים בִּמְקוֹם שֻׁמְשְׁמִין: If one received a field to cultivate and agreed to plant sesame and he planted wheat instead, he must pay the owner in accordance with the value of sesame it was fit to produce. If the field produced wheat equal in value to the sesame, he pays him the standard amount and he, i.e., the landowner (*Taz*; Gra), or the cultivator (*Baḥ*; *Sma*) has nothing but a grievance against him, and he does not have a monetary claim against him. If it produced more wheat than its potential value in sesame, the additional profit is divided between them in accordance with their contract, despite the fact that the owner of the field also benefited from the lack of weakening of his field due to the planting of the wheat (Rambam *Sefer Mishpatim, Hilkhot Sekhirut* 8:14; *Shulḥan Arukh, Ḥoshen Mishpat* 326:1).

NOTES

There is no difference whether he said: For her marriage contract…or: In her marriage contract – לָא שְׁנָא דַּאֲמַר לִכְתוּבָּתָהּ...בִּכְתוּבָּתָהּ: Although in tractate *Ketubot* (54b) a distinction is drawn between the expressions: For sustenance [*limzonot*], and: With sustenance [*bimzonot*], in this case, since he specified that the sum was for the purpose of the marriage contract, it is considered the same as the accepted formulation used in the marriage contract, and no distinction is made based on nuances of language (Rosh; Ran).

It produced wheat similar to sesame – עָבְדָא חִיטֵּי כְּשׁוּמְשְׁמֵי: One explanation is that the wheat crop was more successful than sesame in that particular year (*Talmid Rabbeinu Peretz*). Alternatively, Rashi indicates that the difference was simply based on the increase of the market price of wheat (see *Shita Mekubbetzet*).

BACKGROUND

Neharde'a – נְהַרְדְּעָא: A city on the Euphrates near the Malka River, Neharde'a was one of the oldest Jewish communities in Babylonia. According to tradition, Jews lived in Neharde'a as early as First Temple times, in the sixth century BCE, beginning with the exile of King Jehoiachin of Judea. One of the most important Jewish communities in Babylonia, Neharde'a was a center of Torah study from an early period and its yeshiva was the oldest in Babylonia. Many of the greatest *tanna'im* visited Neharde'a, among them Rabbi Akiva, who intercalated the year there (*Yevamot* 122a). During the life of Rav, who lived in the first half of the third century CE, the yeshiva in Neharde'a was headed by Rav Sheila and then by Shmuel. Since the city was located near the border between the Roman and the Persian Empires, it frequently suffered from the wars between the two. Pappa ben Nazer Odonathus, king of Tadmor, destroyed it entirely in 259 CE. Later, Jews resettled there, and many Torah scholars remained in Neharde'a even after its yeshiva moved to Meḥoza and Pumbedita.

Transaction with inconclusive consent [*asmakhta*] – אַסְמַכְתָּא: An *asmakhta* refers to an obligation undertaken under certain conditions that one does not expect to be required to fulfill. For example, if a seller agrees to pay exaggerated penalties if he fails to deliver merchandise by a certain time, he believes that he will certainly deliver the merchandise by that time, and will therefore never need to pay the penalty. The Sages disagreed as to whether such a commitment is binding or not. According to the opinion that such a transaction is not valid, one who forces another to fulfill such a commitment and pay the penalties is considered by rabbinic law to be a robber.

Land for sesame – אַרְעָא לְשׁוּמְשְׁמֵי: A farmer who wishes to grow sesame plants must invest much time and effort in properly preparing the soil beforehand, in caring for the sesame plants, and in harvesting the seeds at the proper time. But though the process of preparing the soil, growing the sesame, and harvesting it is difficult and time consuming, the harvest is usually much more successful and profitable than that of wheat. The factors of time and effort necessary for planting sesame on one hand and the successful harvest and higher profit on the other is the basis for the discussion in the Gemara here.

Sesame – שׁוּמְשְׁמֵי: Sesame, *Sesamum indicum*, a variety of the Pedaliaceae family, is an important plant for the production of oil and one of the earliest cultivated plants in history. Growing annually, it is pilose and grows white or pink flowers. The sesame plant sprouts in the summer, and begins to blossom within a short time, with small capsules 2–8 cm in length ripening on the stalks that enclose the sesame seeds. Sesame seeds contain a large percentage of oil as well as protein. Sesame seed oil is considered to be a high grade oil. It is used in pharmaceuticals as well as in cooking, specifically in making tahini, a smooth paste of sesame seeds. Plain sesame seeds are also frequently used as a spice. Sesame oil cakes, which are by-products of the production of sesame oil, are high in nutritional value and are used primarily as animal food. Wild sesame appears to be native to Africa, though recent studies indicate that some species originated from India. Either way, sesame subsequently spread to other warm climates, though its cultivation was limited due to the difficulty of removing the tiny seeds from their capsules.

אמר ליה רב אשי לרב כהנא: אמרי אינשי: כחשא ארעא ולא לכחוש מרה.

Rav Ashi said to Rav Kahana: People say the following proverb: Let the land be weakened, but do not weaken its owner.[N] People prefer a quick profit and discount the damage to their land. Therefore, the sharecropper is not entitled to a larger share of the yield for having spared the owner from the weakening of his field.

ההוא גברא דקביל ארעא לשומשמי, זרעא חיטי, עבדא חיטי טפי מן שומשמי. סבר רבינא למימר: יהיב ליה שבחא דביני ביני. אמר ליה רב אחא מדפתי לרבינא: אטו הוא אשבח, ארעא לא אשבחה?

The Gemara relates another incident: There was **a certain man who received land for** planting **sesame and he planted** it with **wheat.** Ultimately, it **produced more wheat than** the usual value of **sesame. Ravina thought to say** that the owner must **give** the cultivator **the added value** that is the difference **between this,** the actual value of the wheat, **and that,** the expected value of the sesame. **Rav Aḥa of Difti said to Ravina: Is that to say** that the cultivator alone **enhanced** its value, but **the land did not** help to **enhance** it? Rather, they should divide the extra sum between them.

אמרי נהרדעי: האי עיסקא, פלגא מלוה ופלגא פקדון. עבוד רבנן מילתא דניחא ליה ללוה, וניחא ליה למלוה.

§ The Gemara discusses other business arrangements. In one common type of venture, the capital or merchandise was supplied by one person and managed by another, who would receive a share, commonly half of the profits, for his efforts. This arrangement can also be viewed as one where the investor is lending half of the invested capital or merchandise to the manager, with the manager agreeing to supervise the venture in exchange for receiving the loan. In order to avoid violating the prohibition of interest, the investor agrees to accept a greater share of the possible loss, e.g., two-thirds, than of the profits, e.g., one-half. The Sages **of Neharde'a said:** With regard to its halakhic status, **this joint venture** is considered **a half-loan and half-deposit,**[NH] as the **Sages formulated** an **enactment that** would be **satisfactory for the borrower,** i.e., the manager, **and** equally **satisfactory for the lender,** i.e., the investor.

השתא דאמרינן פלגא מלוה, אי בעי למשתי ביה שכרא – שפיר דמי. רבא אמר: להכי קרו ליה עיסקא, דאמר ליה: כי יהבינא לך – לאיעסוקי ביה, ולא למשתי ביה שכרא.

Now that we have said that **half** of the capital is viewed as **a loan,** it would appear that the manager may use the money in any way he chooses: **If** he **wants to drink alcohol with it,** he may **well** do so, regardless of any objection on the part of the investor. **Rava** disagreed and **said:** It is **for this** reason that **it is called a joint venture, as** the investor can **say to** the manager: **When I gave** the money **to you** it was **to use it** for business **and not to drink alcohol with it.**[NH]

אמר רב אידי בר אבין: ואם מת – נעשה מטלטלין אצל בניו. רבא אמר: להכי קרו ליה עיסקא, דאם מת – לא יעשה מטלטלין אצל בניו.

Rav Idi bar Avin said: And according to this reasoning, **if** the manager **died,** it **becomes movable property in** the possession **of his children.** Therefore, it may not be taken from them, as movable property inherited by orphans is liened for the payment of their father's debts. **Rava** disagreed and **said:** It is **for this** reason that **it is called a joint venture, so that if he died**[H] **it does not become movable property in** the possession **of his children,** as it is considered a partnership, not a loan.

אמר רבא: חדא עיסקא ותרי שטרי – פסידא דמלוה;

Rava says: If two people conducted **one joint venture and** drafted it as separate ventures of equal value in **two** separate **documents,**[H] and they suffered a heavy loss from the venture recorded in one of the documents and had a slight gain from the other, the *halakha* is as follows: The two documents are treated as two separate agreements, and one does not calculate the profits and losses from the two ven-tures together. Therefore, this will be to **the detriment of the lender.** According to the common arrangement, he will gain half of the profits from one venture and suffer two-thirds of the loss of the other.

NOTES

Let the land be weakened, but do not weaken its owner – כחשא ארעא ולא לכחוש מרה: The commentary attributed to the Ritva notes that this principle applies only when it is advantageous to the owner, but if the cultivator planted sesame instead of wheat, in opposition to their agreement, he is liable to compensate the owner for the weakening of his field.

Half-loan and half-deposit – פלגא מלוה ופלגא פקדון: According to most early commentaries, the arrangement must, in fact, be contracted specifically as a half-loan and half-deposit, not another ratio. This arrangement also affects the obligation of the manager with regard to the money: He bears full responsibility as a borrower for the half that is considered a loan, while with regard to the other half he is merely viewed as an unpaid or paid bailee. According to the Rambam, he is an unpaid bailee, whereas others maintain that he has the status of a paid bailee, though he may conduct himself in the manner of one safeguarding his own property and is not required to provide superior safeguarding. Rav Hai Gaon interprets this statement to mean that a joint venture is in principle part loan and part deposit, meaning that it is treated as a loan in some ways and as a deposit in others, but it need not actually be divided precisely in those proportions, as half a loan and half a deposit. The Mordekhai, citing the Maharam of Rothenburg, states that the entire arrangement is in fact considered a loan with regard to certain *halakhot*, such as the *halakha* that one may not use the money to betroth a woman.

The early commentaries question the validity of such an arrangement (see *Tosafot*). Being that the manager is managing the investment on behalf of the investor while receiving a loan from him, the service provided should ostensibly be regarded as interest paid on the loan. Some explain that in order to avoid this prohibition, the investor must pay the manager for this service. The Ramban comments that absent such a payment, the prohibition of interest can be avoided by having the manager receive a larger share of the profits than the investor to serve as compensation for his efforts.

Not to drink alcohol with it – לא למשתי ביה שכרא: According to Rashi, the primary reason for this *halakha* is that the owner expects his partner to handle the joint venture in a serious, dedicated manner. Alternatively, *Tosafot* explain that the owner assumes that the money he gave for the joint venture is a fixed, guaranteed sum that may not be spent on personal needs. One of the possible differences between these two interpretations concerns a case where the manager misused a small part of the money. According to Rashi, this does not matter, whereas *Tosafot* would forbid it, as doing this would decrease the owner's capital (*Torat Ḥayyim*). Another explanation offered for this *halakha* is that had he retained the full sum he might have been capable of conducting a lucrative transaction that would have been impossible with a smaller amount, thereby causing the owner a loss (*Beit Aharon*).

HALAKHA

Joint venture a half-loan and half-deposit – עסקא, פלגא מלוה ופלגא פקדון: The Sages instituted an arrangement whereby if one provides another with money to engage in business in exchange for a share of the profits, half of the capital is considered a loan for which the manager is fully liable, while the other half is treated as a deposit, and he is therefore exempt if it is stolen or lost. The profits and losses may not be shared equally between them. Rather, the investor pays the manager a daily wage or they distribute the money between them in such a manner that the investor accepts most of the risk (Rambam *Sefer Kinyan, Hilkhot Sheluḥin VeShutafin* 6:2; *Shulḥan Arukh, Yoreh De'a* 177:2).

And not to drink alcohol with it – ולא למשתי ביה שכרא: Although the money one gives another for a joint venture is considered as a half-loan and half-deposit, the manager is not permitted to use the half that is a loan for his own personal needs or safeguard it as security. Rather, he must use all of it for commercial transactions, in accordance with the opinion of Rava (Rambam *Sefer Kinyan, Hilkhot Sheluḥin VeShutafin* 7:4; *Shulḥan Arukh, Yoreh De'a* 177:30).

The manager of a joint venture who died – מקבל עיסקא שמת: If one receives funds for a joint venture and there are witnesses that a certain sum of money or quantity of merchandise was included in this agreement, upon the manager's death the investor may claim the funds or merchandise without an oath, and creditors or the wife and heirs of the deceased are not entitled to the portion of the profit that belongs to the investor (Rambam *Sefer Kinyan, Hilkhot Sheluḥin VeShutafin* 7:5; *Shulḥan Arukh, Yoreh De'a* 177:31).

One joint venture and two documents – חדא עיסקא ותרי שטרי: If a single joint venture was recorded in two parts, each part in a separate document, they are regarded as two distinct transactions. Consequently, if the partners earned profits from one venture but suffered losses from the other, each document is treated as a separate transaction and the profits and losses are not calculated together. If they wrote one document for two joint ventures, then even if one produced profits and the other losses, they are viewed as a single transaction and any profits are shared, as stated by Rava (*Shulḥan Arukh, Yoreh De'a* 177:33).

תְּרֵי עִיסְקֵי וְחַד שְׁטָרָא – פְּסֵידָא דְּלֹוֶה.

Conversely, if two people engaged in **two joint ventures and** recorded both in **one document,** this will be to **the detriment of the borrower.** They calculate the profits and losses of the two transactions together, and therefore as long as the profits of one joint venture are greater than the losses of the other, the investor will not have to suffer a loss.

וְאָמַר רָבָא: הַאי מַאן דְּקַבֵּיל עִיסְקָא מִן חַבְרֵיה וּפְסֵיד, טָרַח וּמַלְיֵיה וְלָא אוֹדְעֵיה, לָא מָצֵי אָמַר לֵיהּ: דְּרִי מֵהַאי פְּסֵידָא בַּהֲדַאי – מִשּׁוּם דְּאָמַר לֵיהּ: לְהָכִי טְרַחְתְּ לְמַלְיוּתֵיהּ – כִּי הֵיכִי דְּלָא לִיקְרוּ לָךְ מַפְסִיד עִיסְקֵי.

And Rava says: This one, who receives merchandise for **a joint venture from another, and lost** money in the process, and then **made the effort to replace**[NH] the loss **but did not inform** the investor that he had done so, he **may not** later **say to** the investor: **Bear this** original **loss together with me.** This is **because** the investor can **say to him:** It is **for this** reason **that you made the effort to replace** the loss, **so that you should not be called a loser of ventures.** You wanted to preserve your reputation in order to improve your future business prospects but did not intend to be reimbursed.

וְאָמַר רָבָא: הָנֵי בֵּי תְּרֵי דְּעָבְדִי עִיסְקָא בַּהֲדֵי הֲדָדֵי וְרָווֹח, וְאָמַר לֵיהּ חַד לְחַבְרֵיהּ: תָּא לִיפְלוֹג, אִי אָמַר לֵיהּ אִידָּךְ נִרְווֹח טְפֵי – דִּינָא הוּא דִּמְעַכֵּב. וְאִי אָמַר לֵיהּ: הַב לִי פַּלְגָא דְּרַוְוחָא, אָמַר לֵיהּ: רַוְוחָא לְקַרְנָא מִשְׁתַּעְבֵּד.

And Rava said: With regard to **these two** managers **who engaged** in **a joint venture**[N] **together,** i.e., they both received merchandise together from an investor, **and profited** from it, **and one** of them **said to the other: Come,** let us **divide** the profits and terminate the venture, the *halakha* is as follows: **If the other said to him:** Let us wait and **profit more, the *halakha* is that** the second manager indeed **prevents** the first from executing his request. **And if,** instead of requesting the final division of the profits and the termination of the venture, one **said to** the other: At least **give me half the profits,** the latter can **say to him: The profit** is **liened to the principal,** meaning that the profits and the principal are considered a single unit, and we can earn much more if we do not set aside the profits.

וְאִי אָמַר לֵיהּ: הַב לִי פַּלְגָא רַוְוחָא וּפַלְגָא קַרְנָא, אָמַר לֵיהּ: עִיסְקָא לַהֲדָדֵי מְשׁוּעְבָּד. וְאִי אָמַר לֵיהּ: נִפְלוֹג רַוְוחָא וְנִפְלוֹג קַרְנָא, וְאִי מָטֵי לָךְ פְּסֵידָא דָּרֵינָא בַּהֲדָךְ, אָמַר לֵיהּ: לָא, מַזְּלָא דְּבֵי תְּרֵי עָדִיף.

Rava continues: **And if** one **says to** the other: **Give me half the profits and half the principal,** the latter can **say to him: The** merchandise for **the joint venture** is **liened to both** of us. As we are equal partners in this venture, you cannot force me to divide it. **And if** one **says to** the other: **Let us divide**[H] **the profits and divide the principal, and if you suffer a loss** as a result, **I will bear** the loss **with you,** his partner can **say to him: No,** I do not desire to do that, since **the luck of two** people **is better.** Consequently, I want to continue working together. In all these cases, the claims of the second manager are accepted.

מתני׳ הַמְקַבֵּל שָׂדֶה מֵחֲבֵירוֹ וְלֹא רָצָה לְנַכֵּשׁ, וְאָמַר לוֹ: מָה אִיכְפַּת לָךְ? הוֹאִיל וַאֲנִי נוֹתֵן לָךְ אֶת חֲכִירָךְ. אֵין שׁוֹמְעִין לוֹ, מִפְּנֵי שֶׁיָּכוֹל לוֹמַר לוֹ: לְמָחָר אַתָּה יוֹצֵא מִמֶּנָּה, וּמַעֲלֶת לְפָנַי עֲשָׂבִים.

MISHNA With regard to **one who received a field from another** to cultivate **and did not want to weed**[H] it, **and** he then **said to** the owner: **What do you care** if I neglect the land? You will not suffer a loss **since I will give you** the amount of produce I owe you for **your** granting me **tenancy,** regardless of the state of the field. Nevertheless, **they do not listen to him.** The reason is **because** the owner of the land **can say to him: Tomorrow you** will **depart from** the field, **and it** will **grow weeds for me,** which will remain there and disrupt the yield of the field for years to come.

גמ׳ אִי אָמַר לֵיהּ: לְבָתַר הָכִי כָּרֵיבְנָא לַהּ – אָמַר לֵיהּ: חִטֵּי מַעַלְיָיתָא בָּעֵינָא. וְאִי אָמַר לֵיהּ: זָבֵינְנָא לָךְ חִטֵּי מִשּׁוּקָא, אָמַר לֵיהּ: חִטֵּי דְּאַרְעַאי בָּעֵינָא. וְאִי אָמַר לֵיהּ: מְנַכֵּישְׁנָא לָךְ שִׁיעוּר מְנָתִיךְ, אָמַר לֵיהּ: קָא מְנַסְּבַתְּ שֵׁם רַע לְאַרְעַאי.

GEMARA If the cultivator **said to** the owner: **Afterward,** when I have reaped the field, **I will plow** it and remove the weeds, the owner can **say to him: I want superior wheat,** not wheat that sprouted among weeds. **And if he says to** the owner: **I will buy** good **wheat for you from the market,** the owner can **say to him: I want wheat from my land. And if he says to** the owner: **I will weed for you** according to the **measure of your portion,** but no more, the owner can **say to him: You are giving a bad name to my land,** as everyone will see that it is full of weeds.

NOTES

Made the effort to replace – טָרַח וּמַלְיֵיה: According to most commentaries, the manager took pains to ensure that his gains from the remaining portion of the merchandise nullified his losses. An opinion attributed to the Ra'avad maintains that this also refers to one who paid out of his own pocket or from the proceeds of other business transactions (see Rabbeinu Yehonatan).

These two who engaged in a joint venture – בֵּי תְּרֵי דְּעָבְדִי עִיסְקָא: According to Rashi, the date of the termination of this joint venture was arranged ahead of time. Rav Hai Gaon explains that there is a certain window of opportunity for the sale of each type of merchandise, and they are obligated to keep working together until that time. Rashi adds that the partners had received this merchandise from someone else; see *Tosafot*, who explain why one of them could not have accepted the merchandise from the other. The Ra'avad claims that the *halakha* concerning the termination of the partnership applies even to a case where the merchandise was supplied by one of the partners.

HALAKHA

Made the effort to replace – טָרַח וּמַלְיֵיה: One who was managing a joint venture and failed to inform the investor that he had suffered a loss but made a successful effort to replace the principal himself may not demand that the investor accept his share of the original loss. If he did inform him and stated that he, the manager, wants no further part in the agreement, he is entitled to do so, as the manager can withdraw his involvement whenever he chooses (Rambam *Sefer Kinyan, Hilkhot Sheluḥin VeShutafin* 7:2; *Shulḥan Arukh, Yoreh De'a* 177:34, and in the comment of Rema).

Let us divide – נִפְלוֹג: If two partners accepted merchandise for a joint venture from an investor for a fixed period of time, and one of them wanted to divide up the money between them before the end date, he cannot compel the other to do so (*Shulḥan Arukh, Yoreh De'a* 177:35).

One who received a field…and did not want to weed – הַמְקַבֵּל שָׂדֶה...וְלֹא רָצָה לְנַכֵּשׁ: With regard to one who accepted a field to cultivate and did not want to weed it, if the local custom is to weed fields he may not refuse to do so even if he proposes to compensate the owner with good-quality wheat, as explained by the Gemara (Rambam *Sefer Mishpatim, Hilkhot Sekhirut* 8:8; *Shulḥan Arukh, Ḥoshen Mishpat* 320:4).

HALAKHA

One who receives a field…and it did not produce – הַמְקַבֵּל שָׂדֶה וְלֹא עָשְׂתָה: If one received a field to cultivate and it failed to yield enough produce, if it produced two *se'a* more than the cost of the field's upkeep, he must continue to care for and work the field (Rambam *Sefer Mishpatim, Hilkhot Sekhirut* 8:12; *Shulḥan Arukh, Ḥoshen Mishpat* 328:1).

BACKGROUND

Winnowing shovel – רַחַת:

Winnowing shovel

Se'a – סְאָה: A *se'a* is a measure of dry volume first mentioned in Genesis (18:6). It is used by the Sages as a point of reference for all measures. Each *se'a* contains six *kav*, which equals twenty-four *log*. Estimates of the modern equivalent of a *se'a* range from 7.2 to 14.4 ℓ.

וְהָתְנַן: מִפְּנֵי שֶׁמַּעֲלַת לְפָנַי עֲשָׂבִים! אֶלָּא, מִשּׁוּם דְּאָמַר לֵיהּ: בִּזְרָא דִּנְפַל נְפַל.

The Gemara asks: **But didn't we learn** in the mishna that the reason they do not listen to him is: **Because it will grow weeds for me,** indicating that these other claims are not accepted? **Rather,** the explanation must be **because** the owner can **say to him: The seed that fell has fallen.**[N] In other words, even if the cultivator later plows the land and uproots all of the weeds, their seeds remain in the ground and will sprout in the following years.

מתני׳ הַמְקַבֵּל שָׂדֶה מֵחֲבֵירוֹ וְלֹא עָשְׂתָה, אִם יֵשׁ בָּהּ כְּדֵי לְהַעֲמִיד כְּרִי – חַיָּיב לְטַפֵּל בָּהּ. אָמַר רַבִּי יְהוּדָה: מַאי קִצְבָה בִּכְרִי? אֶלָּא, אִם יֵשׁ בָּהּ כְּדֵי נְפִילָה.

MISHNA With regard to **one who receives a field from another** to cultivate **and it did not produce**[H] a sufficient crop to cover the expenses of its upkeep, **if it has** enough produce **to form a pile**[N] he is **obligated to take care of it** and give the owner his share. **Rabbi Yehuda says: What fixed** measure **is a pile?**[N] There is no inherent measure of produce that is considered significant, as it all depends on the size of the plot of land in question. **Rather,** the relevant issue is **whether it has** a crop **equivalent to** the measure of seeds for **dropping** in a field in order to sow it.

גמ׳ תָּנוּ רַבָּנַן: הַמְקַבֵּל שָׂדֶה מֵחֲבֵירוֹ וְלֹא עָשְׂתָה, אִם יֵשׁ בָּהּ כְּדֵי לְהַעֲמִיד כְּרִי – חַיָּיב לְטַפֵּל בָּהּ, שֶׁכָּךְ כּוֹתֵב לוֹ: אֲנָא אוֹקִים וְאָנִיר וְאֶזְרַע וְאֶחֱצוֹד וַאֲעַמֵּר וְאָדוּשׁ וְאִידְרִי וְאוֹקִים כַּרְיָא קָדָמָךְ. וְתֵיתֵי אַנְתְּ וְתִיטּוֹל פַּלְגָּא, וַאֲנָא בַּעֲמָלִי וּבְנַפְקוּת יָדַי פַּלְגָּא.

GEMARA **The Sages taught:** With regard to **one who receives a field from another** to cultivate **and it did not produce** a sufficient crop, **if it has** enough produce **to form a pile** he is **obligated to take care of it** and provide the owner with his share. This is **because this** is what **he writes to him** in the cultivator's contract: **I will stand and plow and plant and reap and bind and thresh and winnow and establish a pile before you, and you will come and take half, and I, for my work and expenses,** will take the other **half.** Based on this contract, if there is sufficient produce to form a pile, the cultivator must fulfill the terms of the agreement.

וְכַמָּה ״כְּדֵי לְהַעֲמִיד בָּהּ כְּרִי״? אֲמַר רַבִּי יוֹסֵי בְּרַבִּי חֲנִינָא: כְּדֵי שֶׁתַּעֲמוֹד בּוֹ הָרַחַת. אִיבַּעְיָא לְהוּ: רַחַת הַיּוֹצֵא מֵהַאי גִּיסָא לְהַאי גִּיסָא מַאי?

The Gemara asks: **And how much** is the amount of: Enough **to form a pile?** How large must the pile be? **Rabbi Yosei, son of Rabbi Ḥanina, said:** Enough **for the winnowing shovel**[B] **to stand in it.** If the pile is big enough that the shovel can be placed there and stand independently without falling, it is considered a sufficiently large pile. **A dilemma was raised before** the Sages: With regard to **a winnowing shovel that protrudes from this side to that side,**[N] i.e., whose edges extend beyond the pile, **what** is the *halakha*? Is this considered a pile in which a winnowing shovel can stand or not?

תָּא שְׁמַע, אֲמַר רַבִּי אַבָּהוּ: לְדִידִי מְפָרְשָׁא לִי מִינֵּיהּ דְּרַבִּי יוֹסֵי בְּרַבִּי חֲנִינָא: כׇּל שֶׁאֵין כּוֹנֵס שֶׁלּוֹ רוֹאֶה פְּנֵי הַחַמָּה. אִיתְּמַר, לֵוִי אָמַר: שָׁלֹשׁ סְאִין, דְּבֵי רַבִּי יַנַּאי אָמְרִי: סָאתַיִם. אָמַר רֵישׁ לָקִישׁ: סָאתַיִם שֶׁאָמְרוּ – חוּץ מִן הַהוֹצָאָה.

The Gemara suggests: **Come** and **hear** a proof from that which **Rabbi Abbahu said:** This **was explained to me by Rabbi Yosei, son of Rabbi Ḥanina: Any** pile **in which the blade of** the winnowing shovel **cannot see the face of the sun** because it is covered by the pile is considered a significant one. **It was stated** that the *amora'im* engaged in a dispute concerning this issue: **Levi says:** This pile must be **three** ***se'a***[B] in size, while the Sages **of the school of Rabbi Yannai say: Two** ***se'a***. **Reish Lakish says: The two** ***se'a*** **of which they spoke is without** deducting **the expenses.**[N] Consequently, if he has paid the expenses and a profit of two *se'a* remains, in that case alone it is considered worthwhile to work the field. But if it cannot produce this amount, the cultivator may neglect the land if he so chooses.

NOTES

The seed that fell has fallen – בִּזְרָא דִּנְפַל נְפַל: This reason does not appear to negate the other arguments, all of which have merit, but this claim alone is sufficient to address all the concerns (*Ḥokhmat Manoaḥ*). Rabbeinu Yehonatan explains that if wheat seeds fall on weeds they will fail to sprout.

If it has enough to form a pile – אִם יֵשׁ בָּהּ כְּדֵי לְהַעֲמִיד כְּרִי: While Rabbi Yehuda clarifies his reasoning, the logic behind the ruling of the first *tanna* remains unclear. According to the *Magen Gibborim*, here too, common language is expounded, as the cultivator wrote to the owner that he would form a pile, and therefore he must do so if possible.

What fixed measure is a pile – מַאי קִצְבָה בִּכְרִי: Rashi explains that since fields differ in size, the amount of a pile does not correspond to the area of land involved. The Rambam states that the amount of a pile itself is indeterminate, as even though the Gemara says that it must be large enough that a winnowing shovel may be placed in it without falling, such vessels are also not uniform.

From this side to that side – מֵהַאי גִּיסָא לְהַאי גִּיסָא: *Tosafot* cite and explain Rabbeinu Ḥananel's version of the text, which reads: From this side or from that side. According to this version, the dilemma is whether the winnowing shovel was inserted from its wider edge or by its handle. Most early commentaries explain the Gemara in this manner, and a similar explanation can be inferred from the Jerusalem Talmud.

Without the expenses – חוּץ מִן הַהוֹצָאָה: The Jerusalem Talmud cites an amoraic dispute as to whether these deducted expenses are those of only the cultivator or those of the owner as well.

תְּנַן הָתָם: פְּרִיצֵי זֵיתִים וַעֲנָבִים, בֵּית שַׁמַּאי מְטַמְּאִין וּבֵית הִלֵּל מְטַהֲרִין.

The Gemara cites a dispute from a different area of *halakha* that discusses a similar measurement: **We learned** in a mishna **there** (*Okatzin* 3:6) concerning the *halakhot* of food impurities: With regard to **unruly olives**[NH] **and grapes, Beit Shammai** hold that they become **susceptible to ritual impurity,** as they are considered food, **and Beit Hillel** hold that they do **not** become **susceptible to ritual impurity** because they are of inferior quality and are unfit for consumption.

מַאי פְּרִיצֵי זֵיתִים? אֲמַר רַב הוּנָא: רִשְׁעֵי זֵיתִים. אֲמַר רַב יוֹסֵף: וּמַאי קְרָאָה? ״[וּבְנֵי] פָּרִיצֵי עַמְּךָ יִנַּשְּׂאוּ לְהַעֲמִיד חָזוֹן וְנִכְשָׁלוּ״. רַב נַחְמָן בַּר יִצְחָק אֲמַר מֵהָכָא: ״וְהוֹלִיד בֵּן פָּרִיץ שֹׁפֵךְ דָּם״.

The Gemara asks: **What** is the meaning of **unruly** [*peritzei*] **olives? Rav Huna said: Wicked olives,** i.e., olives that barely produce any oil. **Rav Yosef said: And what is the verse** from which it is derived? **"Also the children of the wicked** [*peritzei*] **among your people shall raise themselves up to establish the vision but they shall stumble"** (Daniel 11:14). This verse indicates that the word *peritzei* means wicked. **Rav Naḥman bar Yitzḥak said** that the meaning of this word can be derived **from here:**[N] **"If he beget a son that is a robber** [*paritz*]**, a shedder of blood"** (Ezekiel 18:10).

וְכַמָּה פְּרִיצֵי זֵיתִים? רַבִּי אֶלְעָזָר אָמַר: אַרְבַּעַת קַבִּין לְקוֹרָה, דְּבֵי רַבִּי יַנַּאי אָמְרִי: סָאתַיִם לְקוֹרָה.

The Gemara asks: **And how much** is the amount of **unruly olives?** When are olives classified as unruly? **Rabbi Elazar says:** They are classified as such if it is possible to extract only **four** ***kav***[B] of oil **from** one press of the **beam**[B] when the fruits are brought in together to the olive press. **The** Sages of the **school of Rabbi Yannai say:** They are classified as such if it is possible to extract only **two** ***se'a*** of oil **from** one press of the **beam.**

וְלָא פְּלִיגִי, הָא בְּאַתְרָא דִּמְעַיְּילֵי כּוֹרָא בְּאוּלְלָא, הָא בְּאַתְרָא דִּמְעַיְּילֵי תְּלָתָא כּוֹרִין בְּאוּלְלָא.

The Gemara comments: **And** these Sages **do not disagree** with regard to the *halakha* itself, as the difference between their rulings stems from divergent local practices. **This** statement of Rabbi Elazar is referring **to a place where** one ***kor***[B] is **brought into the press,** from which he must be able to extract four *kav*, whereas **that** *halakha* of the school of Rabbi Yannai is referring **to a place where three** ***kor*** are **brought into the baskets of the** oil **press.**[B] Since they bring in three times the amount of fruit, it must produce exactly three times as much oil.

תָּנוּ רַבָּנַן:

The Sages taught:

NOTES

Unruly olives – פְּרִיצֵי זֵיתִים: Several explanations of this category have been offered. According to Rashi, unruly olives are those that have failed to ripen. Rabbeinu Ḥananel and the *Arukh* maintain that these are hard olives that are not squeezable, while Rav Hai Gaon says that they are the leftover olives that remain after the olives are squeezed. Olive waste is generally used as animal fodder, but if olives contain sufficient oil to be squeezed they are still considered fit for human consumption. The Rambam states that these are olives burst out [*partzu*] of the basket while being squeezed, either due to their hardness or for some other reason. According to this opinion, a few olives of this kind may be disregarded, but if they amount to more than four *kav* they are significant and are susceptible to impurity.

Rav Naḥman bar Yitzḥak said from here – רַב נַחְמָן בַּר יִצְחָק אֲמַר מֵהָכָא: The reason why he finds it necessary to cite a different verse is that one might have thought that the first verse is not referring specifically to the wicked but to people who tried and failed. He therefore quotes another verse that clearly indicates that *paritzim* means wicked people (Ya'avetz; see *Ein Yehosef*).

HALAKHA

Unruly olives – פְּרִיצֵי זֵיתִים: The hard olives and grapes that are pushed out from under the beam when the fruits are squeezed are not susceptible to impurity. This *halakha* applies when there are up to four *kav* of unruly fruit for each *kor* of fruit, but if there were more than four *kav*, they are susceptible to impurity. If one gathered them in order to eat, they are susceptible to impurity even if they amount to less than four *kav* (Rambam *Sefer Tahara, Hilkhot Tumat Okhalin* 1:12).

BACKGROUND

Kav – קַב: This is a basic unit of measurement from which many other small units are derived. It is equivalent to one-sixth of a *se'a*, or 24 egg-bulks.

Beam – קוֹרָה: The beam of an olive press is a large, heavy pole that is placed in a hole in a wall above a basket of olives and weighted down on the other side in such a way that it presses down on the fruit. The olive oil that is squeezed out is collected in a hole in the ground or in special utensils prepared for this purpose.

Kor – כּוֹר: The *kor* is the largest measurement of volume mentioned in talmudic sources and contains thirty *se'a*. Due to a fundamental dispute concerning halakhic measurements, there is significant variation in opinions as to the modern measurement of a *kor*, with estimates ranging between 240 and 480 ℓ.

Baskets of the press – אוּלְלָא: During the course of the process of making olive oil, olives are placed in flat baskets and stacked on top of each other. When a certain number of baskets are placed under the beam, it is pressed down and the olives are crushed, allowing the oil to run out.

Ancient olive press in Tel Hatzor

עלו בְּאִילָן שֶׁכּוֹחוֹ רַע וּבְסוֹכָה שֶׁכּוֹחָהּ רַע – טָמֵא.

If a *zav* and a ritually pure person **climbed a tree**[N] **that has little strength,**[H] which shook as they climbed it, **or** if they climbed onto **a branch that has little strength,** the ritually pure person is **rendered ritually impure.** One of the ways a *zav* imparts impurity is by movement, and here the *zav* is viewed as having moved the pure person.

הֵיכִי דָּמֵי אִילָן שֶׁכּוֹחוֹ רַע? אָמְרִי דְּבֵי רַבִּי יַנַּאי: כׇּל שֶׁאֵין בְּעִיקָּרוֹ לַחְקוֹק רוֹבַע. הֵיכִי דָּמֵי סוֹכָה שֶׁכּוֹחָהּ רַע? אָמַר רֵישׁ לָקִישׁ: כׇּל שֶׁנֶּחְבֵּאת בְּחֵיזוֹנָה.

The Gemara asks: **What are the circumstances** of this **tree that has little strength,** i.e., how is a tree with little strength defined? The Sages of **the school of Rabbi Yannai say:** It is **any** tree **whose trunk is not**[N] broad enough **that** one can **hollow out** a vessel of **a quarter**-*kav* from it. **What are the circumstances of a branch that has little strength? Reish Lakish said:** It is **any** branch concerning **which** its circumference can **be hidden,** i.e., inserted, **in** a person's **fist.**[N] A branch of this size is generally not strong enough to hold two people without shaking.

תְּנַן הָתָם: הַמְהַלֵּךְ בְּבֵית הַפְּרָס עַל גַּבֵּי אֲבָנִים שֶׁיָּכוֹל לְהָסִיט, עַל הָאָדָם וְעַל הַבְּהֵמָה שֶׁכּוֹחָן רַע – טָמֵא.

We learned in a mishna **elsewhere** (*Oholot* 18:6): With regard to one **who walks in an area in which uncertainty exists concerning the location of a grave or corpse** [***beit haperas***],[N] if he treads **over stones that he can move** as he walks, raising concerns that he might have moved a bone of a corpse and thereby rendered himself impure, or if he was in that location, **on the back of a person or** riding **on an animal that had little strength,** he is **impure,** as he is considered to have moved the impurity himself.

הֵיכִי דָּמֵי אָדָם שֶׁכּוֹחוֹ רַע? אָמַר רֵישׁ לָקִישׁ: כׇּל שֶׁרוֹכְבוֹ וְאַרְכּוּבוֹתָיו נוֹקְשׁוֹת. הֵיכִי דָּמֵי בְּהֵמָה שֶׁכּוֹחָהּ רַע? אָמְרִי דְּבֵי רַבִּי יַנַּאי: כׇּל שֶׁרוֹכְבָהּ מְטִילָה גְּלָלִים.

The Gemara asks: **What are the circumstances** of **a person that has little strength? Reish Lakish said: Any** person **whose knees knock**[H] against each other **when** someone **rides upon him. What are the circumstances** of **an animal that has little strength?** The Sages of **the school of Rabbi Yannai say: Any** animal **that releases excrement** due to strain **when** a person **rides upon it.**

אָמְרִי דְּבֵי רַבִּי יַנַּאי: לִתְפִלָּה וְלִתְפִילִּין – אַרְבָּעָה קַבִּין.

§ As the Gemara has cited the rulings of the school of Rabbi Yannai with regard to measurements, it now cites similar *halakhot* that the Sages of **the school of Rabbi Yannai state: With regard to prayer and with regard to phylacteries,** the measure is **four** ***kav***.

לִתְפִלָּה מַאי הִיא? דְּתַנְיָא: הַנּוֹשֵׂא מַשּׂאוֹי עַל כְּתֵיפוֹ וְהִגִּיעַ זְמַן תְּפִלָּה, פָּחוֹת מֵאַרְבָּעָה קַבִּין – מַפְשִׁילִין לַאֲחוֹרָיו וּמִתְפַּלֵּל, אַרְבָּעָה קַבִּין – מַנִּיחַ עַל גַּבֵּי קַרְקַע וּמִתְפַּלֵּל.

The Gemara inquires: **What is** the relevance of this measure **with regard to prayer?** This is **as it is taught** in a *baraita*: With regard **to one who carries a load on his shoulder and the time for prayer arrives,**[H] if the load is **less than four** ***kav***, he **lowers it behind him** while still holding it **and prays,** as a light load of this size does not interfere with prayer. If the load is **four** ***kav***, **he places it on the ground and prays.**

NOTES

Climbed a tree – **עָלוּ בְּאִילָן**: The *halakhot* of ritual impurity for a *zav* include several *halakhot* that do not apply to other types of ritual impurity. One of these is ritual impurity imparted by movement. Any utensil or person that a *zav* moves from its place is rendered ritually impure, even if he does not come into direct contact with it. Consequently, if a ritually pure individual and a *zav* were sitting on a shaky surface or on an unstable tree that was then moved by the *zav*, it is as though the *zav* has moved the ritually pure individual, rendering him ritually impure.

Whose trunk is not – **שֶׁאֵין בְּעִיקָּרוֹ**: Some explain that this refers to the spot where the branches begin to separate from the trunk (*Ḥokhmat Manoaḥ*).

Hidden in a fist [*beḥezyonah*] – **נֶחְבֵּאת בְּחֵיזוֹנָה**: There are numerous versions and interpretations of this phrase. Rashi associates the term: In a fist [*beḥezyona*], with the term: In his grasp [*aḥizata*], meaning that any branch that is narrow enough to fit into one's palm is considered shaky. *Tosafot* question this approach since a slightly bigger branch would also shake if a person climbed on it. Others suggest that there is a distinction between a branch that is intrinsically weak and a branch that is not so easily movable but still gets weakened by a person's weight (see *Magen Gibborim*). The Rosh explains this statement like Rashi, but understands that the item is grasped underneath one's arm rather than in one's palm, which would refer to a thicker branch. Rabbeinu Ḥananel offers yet another interpretation, that this branch is entangled with other branches so that it has to be moved from its place in order to climb on top of it. Since it moves, it would seem that it is a branch of little strength. A similar explanation is given by the Rambam as well. Finally, some explain that the branch referred to a branch that is exceptionally small, such that it is hidden from view by the other branches of the tree and is not even visible from the outside.

One who walks in a ***beit haperas*** – **הַמְהַלֵּךְ בְּבֵית הַפְּרָס**: A *beit haperas* is a location that possibly contains ritual impurity imparted by a corpse. In this case, it appears that graves were plowed over in this location, causing bones from the corpses to be scattered across the field. Consequently, if one steps on them and moves them, he has thereby become ritually impure despite the fact that he does not know precisely where the bones are hidden. When a Jew does not come in contact with the field directly but is carried on another Jew, the one carrying him might become ritually impure (see *Tosafot*), but the one being carried does not become ritually impure. If a Jew rides on a gentile or on an animal, he also does not become ritually impure. But if he rides on a weak animal or is carried by a weak person, since his weight is a great burden to them, it is as though he himself is treading on the ground and he therefore does become ritually impure.

HALAKHA

If they climbed a tree that has little strength – **עָלוּ בְּאִילָן שֶׁכּוֹחוֹ רַע**: If a *zav* and a ritually pure individual were on a shaky surface, such as a weak tree whose trunk is not thick enough for a quarter-*kav* vessel to be carved from it, or a weak branch that would move if pushed, the ritually pure person has been rendered impure (Rambam *Sefer Tahara, Hilkhot Metamei Mishkav UMoshav* 8:7).

One who walks in a ***beit haperas***…**whose knees knock** – **הַמְהַלֵּךְ בְּבֵית הַפְּרָס...אַרְכּוּבוֹתָיו נוֹקְשׁוֹת**: If a one was riding an animal or was being carried by a person in a *beit haperas*, if the person or animal carrying him was strong enough to bear his weight he remains ritually pure. But if the person carrying him was so weak that his knees knocked together from his weight, or if the animal he was riding defecated due to the burden, he is rendered impure, as he is considered to have passed on foot (Rambam *Sefer Tahara, Hilkhot Tumat Met* 10:11).

One who carries a load and the time for prayer arrives – **הַנּוֹשֵׂא מַשּׂאוֹי...וְהִגִּיעַ זְמַן תְּפִלָּה**: With regard to a person who was carrying a burden when the time for prayer arrived, if the load was less than four *kav*, he lowers it behind him while still holding it and prays, but if it was four *kav* or more he must place it on the ground before he prays (Rambam *Sefer Ahava, Hilkhot Tefilla* 5:5; *Shulḥan Arukh, Oraḥ Ḥayyim* 97:5).

לִתְפִילִּין מַאי הִיא? דְּתַנְיָא: הָיָה נוֹשֵׂא מַשּׂאוֹי עַל רֹאשׁוֹ וּתְפִילִּין בְּרֹאשׁוֹ, אִם הָיוּ תְּפִילִּין רוֹצְצוֹת – אָסוּר, וְאִם לָאו – מוּתָּר. בְּאֵיזוֹ מַשּׂאוֹי אָמְרוּ – בְּמַשּׂאוֹי שֶׁל אַרְבַּעַת קַבִּין.

What is the relevance of this amount **with regard to phylacteries?** This is **as it is taught** in a *baraita*: If a man **was carrying a load**[N] **on his head and** he had **phylacteries on his head,**[H] **if the phylacteries were being crushed** under the load it is **forbidden** to leave them on his head, **but if** they were **not** being crushed, it is **permitted.** With regard **to which load** did the Sages **state** this *halakha*? They stated it with regard **to a load of four *kav*.**

תָּנֵי רַבִּי חִיָּיא: הַמּוֹצִיא זֶבֶל עַל רֹאשׁוֹ וּתְפִילִּין בְּרֹאשׁוֹ – הֲרֵי זֶה לֹא יְסַלְּקֵם לִצְדָדִין, וְלֹא יִקְשְׁרֵם בְּמָתְנָיו – מִפְּנֵי שֶׁהוּא נוֹהֵג בָּהֶן מִנְהַג בִּזָּיוֹן. אֲבָל קוֹשְׁרָם עַל זְרוֹעוֹ בִּמְקוֹם תְּפִילִּין.

Rabbi Ḥiyya teaches: With regard to one **who removes garbage** by carrying it **on his head and** has **phylacteries on his head, he** may **not move** the phylacteries **to the side** to prevent them from being crushed, **and** likewise he may **not tie** the phylacteries of the head **to his loins because he** thereby **treats them in a manner** of **degradation. But** he may **tie them on his arm in the location** where **the phylacteries** of the hand are placed.

מִשּׁוּם דְּבֵי שֵׁילָא אָמְרוּ: אֲפִילּוּ מִטְפַּחַת שֶׁלָּהֶן אָסוּר לְהַנִּיחַ עַל הָרֹאשׁ שֶׁיֵּשׁ בּוֹ תְּפִילִּין. וְכַמָּה? אָמַר אַבָּיֵי: אֲפִילּוּ רִבְעָא דְּרִבְעָא דְּפוּמְבְּדִיתָא.

The Sages **said in the name of the school of Sheila:** It is **forbidden to place on the head** of one **that has phylacteries on it even the scarf** in which **they** are wrapped. The Gemara asks: **And how much** does Rabbi Sheila permit one to place on his head while wearing phylacteries? **Abaye said: Even** as little as **one-quarter of one-quarter** of the smallest measurement **of Pumbedita** is still forbidden from being placed on one's head.

"אָמַר רַבִּי יְהוּדָה: מַאי קִצְבָּה בִּכְרִי? אֶלָּא אִם יֵשׁ בּוֹ כְּדֵי נְפִילָה". וְכַמָּה כְּדֵי נְפִילָה? רַבִּי אַמֵּי אָמַר רַבִּי יוֹחָנָן: אַרְבָּעָה סְאִין לְכוֹר. רַבִּי אַמֵּי דִּילֵיהּ אָמַר: שְׁמוֹנַת סְאִין לְכוֹר. אֲמַר לֵיהּ הַהוּא סָבָא לְרַב חָמָא בְּרֵיהּ דְּרַבָּה בַּר אֲבוּהּ: אַסְבְּרָה לָךְ; בִּשְׁנֵי דְּרַבִּי יוֹחָנָן הֲוָה שְׁמֵינָא אַרְעָא, בִּשְׁנֵי דְּרַבִּי אַמֵּי הֲוָה כְּחִישָׁא אַרְעָא.

§ The mishna teaches: **Rabbi Yehuda says: What fixed** measure is **a pile? Rather,** the relevant issue is **whether it has** a crop **equivalent to** the measure of seeds for **dropping** in a field in order to sow it. The Gemara asks: **And how much** is **equivalent to** the measure of seeds for **dropping** in a field in order to sow it? **Rabbi Ami says** that **Rabbi Yoḥanan** says: **Four *se'a* for** the amount of land sufficient to grow **a *kor*. Rabbi Ami himself,** though, **says eight *se'a* for** the amount of land sufficient to grow **a *kor*. A certain elder said to Rav Ḥama, son of Rabba bar Avuh: I will explain it to you: In the years of Rabbi Yoḥanan the land was fat,**[B] while **in the years of Rabbi Ami the land was lean,** and it was therefore necessary to double the amount of seed for each unit of land.

תְּנַן הָתָם: הָרוּחַ שֶׁפִּיזְּרָה אֶת הָעוֹמָרִין, אוֹמְדִים אוֹתָהּ כַּמָּה לֶקֶט רְאוּיָה לַעֲשׂוֹת, וְנוֹתֵן לַעֲנִיִּים. רַבָּן שִׁמְעוֹן בֶּן גַּמְלִיאֵל אוֹמֵר: נוֹתֵן לַעֲנִיִּים כְּדֵי נְפִילָה.

We learned in a mishna **elsewhere** (*Pe'a* 5:1): If **the wind scattered the** standing **sheaves**[H] so that it is no longer known which gleanings fell from the sheaves during the harvest and belong to the poor, one **evaluates how many gleanings**[NB] it was **fit to produce, and he gives** these **to the poor. Rabban Shimon ben Gamliel says: He gives to the poor** the amount **equivalent to** the measure of seeds **dropping** in the course of harvesting.[N]

וְכַמָּה כְּדֵי נְפִילָה? כִּי אֲתָא רַב דִּימִי אָמַר רַבִּי אֶלְעָזָר, וְאִיתֵּימָא רַבִּי יוֹחָנָן: אַרְבַּעַת קַבִּין לְכוֹר. בָּעֵי רַבִּי יִרְמְיָה: לְכוֹר זֶרַע אוֹ לְכוֹר תְּבוּאָה? לְמַפּוֹלֶת יָד אוֹ לְמַפּוֹלֶת שְׁוָורִים?

The Gemara asks: **And how much** is the amount **equivalent to** the measure of seeds **dropping** in the course of harvesting? **When Rav Dimi came** from Eretz Yisrael **he said** that **Rabbi Elazar** said, **and some say** it was **Rabbi Yoḥanan: Four *kav* for a *kor*. Rabbi Yirmeya raised a dilemma:** Does this mean **for a** field that requires a ***kor*** of **seed** to plant it, **or for a *kor* of produce?** And if it is the former, does it refer **to sowing by hand or to sowing by oxen?**[B]

NOTES

Was carrying a load – הָיָה נוֹשֵׂא מַשָּׂאוֹי: These *halakhot* were primarily relevant in talmudic times, when people would wear phylacteries all day long, even when they went to work. The Gemara therefore discusses cases in which the phylacteries must be removed so that they will not be treated in a disrespectful manner. Some of the most prominent halakhic authorities cite both the *baraita* as well as the statement of Rabbi Sheila that follows, despite the apparent contradiction between them. One explanation is that the *baraita* is referring to one whose job was to carry loads of this kind (Mahari Abuhav) or to a case where the bundle was already on his head and he now wishes to don phylacteries. By contrast, Rabbi Sheila is addressing the case of an ordinary person or one who is already wearing phylacteries and now wishes to place a load on his head.

Gleanings – לֶקֶט: The *halakhot* of gleanings are mentioned in the Torah (Leviticus 19:9), in the Book of Ruth, and in tractate *Pe'a* of the Mishna. The basic idea is that stalks that fell from the sheaves in specific ways must be left by the owner of the field for the poor. If these gleanings were inadvertently mixed with the owner's bundles by him or by the wind, he must give the poor the share to which they are entitled.

The amount equivalent to seeds dropping in the course of harvesting – נוֹתֵן...כְּדֵי נְפִילָה: Some commentaries maintain that Rabban Shimon ben Gamliel does not disagree with the first *tanna* but simply clarifies his ruling by adding that there is a fixed minimum requirement for such gleanings. By contrast, the Rambam explains in his Commentary on the Mishna that the phrase: The amount equivalent to seeds dropping in the course of harvesting, means in accordance with the amount required to seed this field, which is approximately the amount of gleanings it would produce.

HALAKHA

Carrying a load with regard to phylacteries – נוֹשֵׂא מַשָּׂאוֹי לְעִנְיַן תְּפִילִּין: If one was bearing a load on his head he must remove his phylacteries from his head until he removes the load. It is even prohibited to place the scarf in which the phylacteries are kept on his head while wearing the phylacteries. But he is permitted to wear a hat or his usual headgear while wearing phylacteries as long as it is less than four *kav* (Rema). Some later authorities contend that it is permitted even when he is wearing phylacteries if he can move the burden to the side of his head so they don't touch (*Peri Megadim*), and this is permitted as long as the load is less than four *kav* (Rambam *Sefer Ahava*, *Hilkhot Tefillin UMezuza VeSefer Torah* 4:23; *Shulḥan Arukh*, *Oraḥ Ḥayyim* 41:1, and see *Mishna Berura* there).

Wind that scattered the sheaves – הָרוּחַ שֶׁפִּיזְּרָה אֶת הָעוֹמָרִין: If the wind scattered sheaves so that the owner's harvest was mixed with the gleanings, the amount of gleanings this field was fit to produce is evaluated. This amount is determined as four *kav* for an area of a *kor*, which he must give to the poor. This ruling of the Rambam is based on the approach that Rabban Shimon ben Gamliel does not disagree with the first *tanna* but clarifies his ruling (Rambam *Sefer Zera'im*, *Mattenot Aniyyim* 4:5, and see *Kesef Mishne* and Radbaz there).

BACKGROUND

In the years of Rabbi Yoḥanan the land was fat – בִּשְׁנֵי דְּרַבִּי יוֹחָנָן הֲוָה שְׁמֵינָא אַרְעָא: There is much discussion, especially in the Jerusalem Talmud, about the sharp descent of the land's fertility in the generations of the *amora'im*. In fact, Rabbi Yoḥanan himself noted a discernible difference in the quality of the land in his own lifetime. This was apparently due to the increasingly heavy economic burden placed upon the Jewish communities in those days, which prevented farmers from investing in the upkeep of the land through techniques such as fertilizers and providing the land with fallow years. Consequently, the land was increasingly overused, which lead to a decrease in its productive capability.

Gleanings – לֶקֶט: The Torah prohibits the owner of a field from gleaning individual stalks that have fallen during the harvest (Leviticus 19:9). Rather, these stalks must be left in the field by the owner as one of the obligatory agricultural gifts given to the poor. Gleanings are defined as fewer than three stalks that fall in one location.

Sowing by hand, sowing by oxen – לְמַפּוֹלֶת יָד, לְמַפּוֹלֶת שְׁוָורִים: In the ancient world, seeds were sown by one of two methods. Some farmers would first plow the land, after which they would sow the seeds by hand. Others would affix a box filled with seeds to the plow pulled by oxen so that the seeds would automatically spill out onto the plowed furrow. This second method was less time consuming but required a far greater amount of seeds than the first one, as more seeds would fall out automatically as the plow moved than if a person carefully sowed the amount of seeds he desired.

תָּא שְׁמַע, דְּכִי אֲתָא רָבִין אָמַר רַבִּי אֲבוּהּ אָמַר רַבִּי אֶלְעָזָר, וְאָמְרִי לָהּ אָמַר רַבִּי יוֹחָנָן: אַרְבַּעַת קַבִּין לְכוֹר זֶרַע. וַעֲדַיִין תִּבְּעֵי לָךְ: לְמַפּוֹלֶת יָד אוֹ לְמַפּוֹלֶת שְׁוָורִים? תֵּיקוּ.

The Gemara answers: **Come and hear, as when Ravin came** from Eretz Yisrael **he said that Rabbi Avuh said** that **Rabbi Elazar said, and some say** that **Rabbi Yoḥanan said: Four** ***kav*** **for a** field sown with a ***kor*** **of seed.** The Gemara comments: **And** the other question should **still raise a dilemma for you:** Does this refer **to sowing** by **hand or to sowing** by **oxen?** No answer was found for this question, and the dilemma **shall stand** unresolved.

מתני׳ הַמְקַבֵּל שָׂדֶה מֵחֲבֵירוֹ וַאֲכָלָהּ חָגָב אוֹ נִשְׁדְּפָה, אִם מַכַּת מְדִינָה הִיא – מְנַכֶּה לוֹ מִן חֲכוֹרוֹ, אִם אֵינָהּ מַכַּת מְדִינָה – אֵין מְנַכֶּה לוֹ מִן חֲכוֹרוֹ. רַבִּי יְהוּדָה אוֹמֵר: אִם קִיבְּלָהּ הֵימֶנּוּ בְּמָעוֹת – בֵּין כָּךְ וּבֵין כָּךְ אֵינוֹ מְנַכֶּה לוֹ מֵחֲכוֹרוֹ.

MISHNA In the case of **one who receives a field from another** to cultivate **and grasshoppers consumed it or it was wind blasted,**[HB] **if it is a regional disaster** which affected all the fields in the area, the cultivator **subtracts from** the produce **he** owes as part of **his tenancy. If it is not a regional disaster,** the cultivator does **not subtract from** the produce **he** owes as part of **his tenancy. Rabbi Yehuda says: If** the cultivator **received it from** the owner **for** a fixed sum of **money,**[N] **whether this** way, i.e., there is a regional disaster, or **whether that** way, i.e., there was no regional disaster, **he does not subtract** the produce he owes as part of **his tenancy.**

גמ׳ הֵיכִי דָּמֵי מַכַּת מְדִינָה? אָמַר רַב יְהוּדָה: כְּגוֹן דְּאִישְׁדּוּף רוּבָּא דְּבָאגָא. עוּלָּא אָמַר: כְּגוֹן שֶׁנִּשְׁתַּדְּפוּ אַרְבַּע שָׂדוֹת מֵאַרְבַּע רוּחוֹתֶיהָ.

GEMARA The Gemara asks: **What are the circumstances of a regional disaster? Rav Yehuda said:** If, **for example, most of** that **valley** in which the field was located **was wind blasted,** it is considered a regional disaster. **Ulla said:** If, **for example, four fields were wind blasted on its four sides,** it is considered a regional disaster.

אָמַר עוּלָּא: בָּעוּ בְּמַעַרְבָא: נִשְׁדַּף תֶּלֶם אֶחָד עַל פְּנֵי כוּלָּהּ, מַאי? נִשְׁתַּיֵּיר תֶּלֶם אֶחָד עַל פְּנֵי כוּלָּהּ, מַהוּ? אַפְסִיקָא בֵּירָא, מַאי? אַסְפַּסְתָּא

Ulla also **said: They raise** the following **dilemma in the West,** Eretz Yisrael: If **one furrow was wind blasted along its entire length,** adjacent to other fields that were wind blasted, **what** is the *halakha*? Is this considered to be part of the regional disaster? Conversely, if **one furrow remained** undamaged **along its entire length, what is** the *halakha*? Does the remaining furrow mean that the entire field is not considered to be part of the regional disaster? If **a fallow** field **divided** between the cultivated fields and the fields that were wind blasted, **what** is the *halakha*? Alternatively, if there was a field of **fodder**[L] between this field and the others that were wind blasted,

מַאי? זֶרַע אַחֵר מַאי? חִיטֵּי לְגַבֵּי שְׂעוֹרִים כְּזֶרַע אַחֵר דָּמֵי אוֹ לָא? כָּל הָעוֹלָם כּוּלּוֹ בְּשִׁדָּפוֹן וְשֶׁלּוֹ בְּיֵרָקוֹן, אִי נַמִּי כָּל הָעוֹלָם כּוּלּוֹ בְּיֵרָקוֹן וְשֶׁלּוֹ בְּשִׁדָּפוֹן, מַאי? תֵּיקוּ.

what is the *halakha*? If the surrounding fields were planted with **a different** type of **seed, what** is the *halakha*? Likewise, is **wheat, in relation to barley,** considered **like a different** type of **seed or not?** Furthermore, if **the entire world,** i.e., all the surrounding fields, were blighted **by windblasts and his** was affected **by mildew;**[NH] or **alternatively,** if the fields of **the entire world** were struck **by mildew, and his** were blighted **with windblasts, what** is the *halakha*? The Gemara responds: No resolution is found to any of these dilemmas, and the dilemmas **shall stand** unresolved.

HALAKHA

One who receives a field…and grasshoppers consumed it or it was wind blasted – מְקַבֵּל שָׂדֶה...וַאֲכָלָהּ חָגָב אוֹ נִשְׁדְּפָה: If one received a field as a tenant farmer or rented it for money and it was consumed by grasshoppers or wind blasted, if this occurred to most of the fields in that city, he subtracts the amount lost from the amount he pays for his tenancy. This ruling is in accordance with the version of the text accepted by the majority of the early commentaries which reads: The majority of fields, but not in accordance with the opinion of Rabbi Yehuda, who does not agree that this is the case when he rents the field and pays the owner with money (Rambam *Sefer Mishpatim, Hilkhot Sekhirut* 8:5; *Shulḥan Arukh, Ḥoshen Mishpat* 322:1).

BACKGROUND

Wind blasted – נִשְׁדְּפָה: This blight probably refers to the plant disease caused by Ustilago smut fungi. These parasites replace the normal kernels of grain with large, distorted black tumors. These tumors, in turn, are carried by the wind and infect the surrounding plants. The Ustilago fungus can spread over great distances and cause significant damage to crops.

NOTES

If he received it from him for money – אִם קִבְּלָהּ הֵימֶנּוּ בְּמָעוֹת: According to Rabbi Yehuda, the tenant farmer is essentially viewed as one who purchased the field for a limited period. Therefore, he should not be able to subtract any amount at all from what he owes. But since the owner receives a portion of the crop itself, the tenant farmer can claim that the landowner must also bear his share of a regional disaster. Consequently, if the rental was for money, not for some of the yield, the owner is paid in full. See the later commentaries for a lengthy discussion of this issue.

LANGUAGE

Fodder [*aspasta*] – אַסְפַּסְתָּא: This word originates from the Pahlavi word aspast, which means fodder for horses.

NOTES

Windblasts and his by mildew – שִׁדָּפוֹן וְשֶׁלּוֹ בְּיֵרָקוֹן: It would appear that if the other fields were wind blasted while his was ruined due to another cause, e.g., it was consumed by locusts, it is certainly not considered to be affected by the regional disaster (Meiri).

HALAKHA

A different seed…windblasts…mildew – זֶרַע אַחֵר...שִׁדָּפוֹן...יֵרָקוֹן: Since the *halakha* is in accordance with the opinion of Rav Yehuda, not that of Ulla, none of these dilemmas have practical applications (see *Shulḥan Arukh, Ḥoshen Mishpat* 322:1 and commentaries there).

אמר ליה זרעה חיטי, ואזל הוא וזרעה שערי ואשתדוף רובא דבאגא, ואשתדוף נמי הנך שערי דיליה, מאי? מי אמרינן, דאמר ליה: אילו זרעתה חיטי הוה נמי משתדפא, או דלמא מצי אמר ליה: אילו זרעתה חיטי הוה מקיים בי: "ותגזר אמר ויקם לך"!

The Gemara poses another question: If the owner **said to** the tenant farmer: **Plant** the field with **wheat, and he went and planted** it with **barley,**[NH] **and most of the valley was wind blasted, and these** fields with **barley of his were also wind blasted, what** is the *halakha*? **Do we say that** the tenant farmer can **say to him:** Even **if I had planted it** with **wheat** it **would likewise have been wind blasted,** as all the surrounding fields suffered the same fate, **or perhaps** the owner **can say to him: Had you planted it** with **wheat,** the following verse **would have been fulfilled for me: "And you shall decree a matter**[N] **and it will be established for you,** and the light shall shine upon your ways" (Job 22:28), since you might have merited greater success by following my wishes.

מסתברא דאמר ליה: אי זרעתה חיטי – הוה מקיים בי: "ותגזר אמר ויקם לך ועל דרכיך נגה אור".

The Gemara responds: It **stands to reason that** the owner can **say to him: Had you planted it** with **wheat** it **would have fulfilled for me: "And you shall decree a matter and it will be established for you, and the light shall shine upon your ways."**

נשתדפו כל שדותיו של מחכיר, ואשתדוף נמי הא בהדייהו, ולא אשתדוף רובא דבאגא, מאי? מי אמרינן: כיון דלא אשתדוף רובא דבאגא – לא מנכי ליה? או דלמא: כיון דאשתדוף כולהו ארעתיה, מצי אמר ליה: האי משום לתך דידך הוא, דהא משתדפו כל שדותיך.

The Gemara presents another question: If **all the fields of the owner of the land were wind blasted**[H] **and this** one **was also wind blasted with them, but the majority of the valley was not wind blasted, what** is the *halakha*? **Do we say** that **since the majority of the valley was not wind blasted** the tenant farmer does **not subtract for the owner** the amount owed for his tenancy, as this is not a regional disaster, **or perhaps** could one claim that **since all the lands** of the owner **were wind blasted** the tenant **can say to** the owner: **This** happened **due to your** bad **fortune, as all your fields were wind blasted?**

מסתברא דאמר ליה: אי משום לתאי דידי – הוה משתייר לי פורתא, כדכתיב: "כי נשארנו מעט מהרבה".

The Gemara responds: It **stands to reason that** the owner can **say to** the tenant: **If** it was **due to my** bad **fortune, a little would have been left for me, as it is written: "For we are left but a few from many"** (Jeremiah 42:2), which indicates that even one suffering from misfortune does not lose all he has.

נשתדפו כל שדותיו של חוכר, ואשתדוף רובא דבאגא, ואשתדוף נמי הא בהדייהו, מאי? מי אמרינן: כיון דאשתדוף רובא דבאגא – מנכי ליה? או דלמא: כיון דאשתדוף כולהו ארעתיה מצי אמר ליה: משום לתך דידך הוא, דהא משתדפו כל שדותיך! מסתברא דאמר ליה: משום לתאך הוא.

The Gemara discusses a similar case: If **all the fields of the tenant farmer were wind blasted and most of the valley was wind blasted and this** field **was also wind blasted with them, what** is the *halakha*? **Do we say** that **since most of the valley was wind blasted** the tenant farmer **subtracts for the owner** the amount owed for his tenancy and does not pay, **or perhaps, since all** the tenant's **lands were wind blasted,** the owner **can say to the** tenant: The damage is **due to your** bad **fortune, as all your fields were wind blasted.** The Gemara responds: **It stands to reason that** the owner **can say to him:** It occurred **due to your** bad **fortune.**

אמאי? הכא נמי נימא ליה: אי משום לתאי דידי הוא – הוה משייר לי פורתא, דהוה מקיים בי: "כי נשארנו מעט מהרבה"! משום דאמר ליה: אי הוה חזית לאישתיורי לך מידי, הוה משתייר לך מדנפשך.

The Gemara asks: **Why** should this be so? **Here too, let him say** to the owner: **If** it was **due to my** bad **fortune, a little would have been left for me, as** the following verse **would have been fulfilled for me: "For we are left but a few from many."** The Gemara answers: This is not a valid claim **because** the owner can **say to** the tenant: **Had you been worthy of something being left for you,** it **would have been left from your own** private land, not the field you paid to cultivate.

NOTES

Plant it with wheat, and he…planted it with barley – **זרעה חיטי...וזרעה שערי:** The early commentaries note that this *halakha* applies both to a tenant farmer and a contractor, as the latter must also pay the value of properly grown wheat (commentary attributed to the Ritva; see also Rambam).

The following verse would have been fulfilled for me: And you shall decree a matter – **הוה מקיים בי ותגזר אומר:** All these claims based on verses must be considered in light of the underlying halakhic principles. Since the tenant promised to pay a certain sum for his use of the field, the landowner should not have to take into account any circumstances beyond his control, and he should be able to claim the full sum. But if there was a regional disaster, the tenant can claim that since this misfortune was suffered by the entire region it should be shared by the owner as well. Nevertheless, as this argument concerns an individual's fortune, the landowner may resort to any claim that enables him to escape responsibility for the disaster since the standard tenancy agreement does not make any mention of this factor whatsoever. Likewise, in any case where the tenant fails to fulfill the contract as required, the landowner has the right to enforce their agreement as written.

HALAKHA

Plant it with wheat, and he…planted it with barley – **זרעה חיטי...וזרעה שערי:** If the tenant was instructed to plant wheat and he planted barley instead, or vice versa, even if there was a regional disaster he is not entitled to subtract any amount from the produce he owes as part of his tenancy (Rambam *Sefer Mishpatim, Hilkhot Sekhirut* 8:5; *Shulḥan Arukh, Ḥoshen Mishpat* 322:2).

If the fields of the landowner or the tenant were wind blasted – **נשתדפו שדות מחכיר או חוכר:** As the *halakha* follows Rav Yehuda's opinion that a regional disaster is one that affects the majority of the fields in the valley, these questions are not relevant to the practical application of *halakha* (Rambam *Sefer Mishpatim, Hilkhot Sekhirut* 8:5; *Shulḥan Arukh, Ḥoshen Mishpat* 322:1).

מֵיתִיבֵי: הָיְתָה שְׁנַת שִׁדָּפוֹן וְיֵרָקוֹן, אוֹ שְׁבִיעִית, אוֹ שֶׁהָיוּ שָׁנִים כִּשְׁנֵי אֵלִיָּהוּ – אֵינוֹ עוֹלֶה לוֹ מִן הַמִּנְיָן.

The Gemara **raises an objection** from a mishna to the ruling that if there is a regional disaster the cultivator subtracts from the produce he owes as part of his tenancy. The *halakha* is that if one sells his field in Eretz Yisrael in a time when the *halakhot* of the Jubilee Year are in effect, he does not have the right to purchase it from the buyer until two years have passed. The mishna teaches (*Arakhin* 29b): If it **was a year of wind-blasted**[NH] crops **or mildew or** it was the **Sabbatical** Year,[B] **or** if those **years were like the years of Elijah** in which no rain fell (see 1 Kings 17:1, 18:1–2), they **do not count** as part **of his tally** of years before he may repurchase his land.

קָתָנֵי שִׁדָּפוֹן וְיֵרָקוֹן דּוּמְיָא דְּשָׁנִים כִּשְׁנֵי אֵלִיָּהוּ. מַה שְּׁנֵי אֵלִיָּהוּ – דְּלָא הֲוֵי תְּבוּאָה כְּלָל, אַף הָכָא נַמִי – דְּלָא הֲוֵי תְּבוּאָה כְּלָל. אֲבָל דְּאִיכָּא תְּבוּאָה – סָלְקָא לֵיהּ, וְלָא קָאָמְרִינַן מַכַּת מְדִינָה הִיא.

The Gemara analyzes the mishna: This *tanna* **teaches** that the cases of **windblasts and mildew** are **similar to** the case where **the years** were **like the years of Elijah. Just as the years of Elijah** is referring to a time **when there was no produce at all, so too, here,** windblasts and mildew are referring to cases **when there was no produce at all. But** by inference, one can learn that if **there was** some **produce,** it **counts** toward **his** tally of years before he may repurchase his land, **and we do not say that it is a regional disaster.**

אֲמַר רַב נַחְמָן בַּר יִצְחָק: שָׁאנֵי הָתָם, דַּאֲמַר קְרָא: "בְּמִסְפַּר שְׁנֵי תְבוּאֹת יִמְכָּר לָךְ" – שָׁנִים שֶׁיֵּשׁ בָּהֶן תְּבוּאָה בָּעוֹלָם.

The Gemara answers: **Rav Naḥman bar Yitzḥak said: There,** the case with regard to the sold field **is different, as the verse states** with regard to the sale and leasing of fields: **"According to the numbers of years of the crops he shall sell to you"** (Leviticus 25:15), which is referring to **years in which there is produce** harvested **in the world.**

אֲמַר לֵיהּ רַב אַשִׁי לְרַב כָּהֲנָא: אֶלָּא מֵעַתָּה שְׁבִיעִית תַּעֲלֶה לוֹ מִן הַמִּנְיָן, דְּהָא אִיכָּא תְּבוּאָה בְּחוּצָה לָאָרֶץ! אֲמַר לֵיהּ: שְׁבִיעִית אַפְקְעָתָא דְּמַלְכָּא הִיא.

Rav Ashi said to Rav Kahana: If that is so, the **Sabbatical** Year **should count for him** as part **of his tally** of years, **as** at least **there is produce outside of Eretz** Yisrael. Rav Kahana **said to him:** The **Sabbatical** Year **is an abrogation of the King,**[N] i.e., God. Therefore, it should not be included in the number of the years before land is repurchased.

אֲמַר לֵיהּ מָר זוּטְרָא בְּרֵיהּ דְּרַב מָרִי לְרָבִינָא: אֶלָּא מֵעַתָּה שְׁבִיעִית לֹא תַּעֲלֶה לוֹ מִן הַגֵּירוּעַ, אַלְמָה תְּנַן: נוֹתֵן סֶלַע וּפוּנְדְּיוֹן לְשָׁנָה! אֲמַר לֵיהּ: שָׁאנֵי הָתָם, דַּחֲזְיָא לְמִישְׁטְחָא בָּהּ פֵּירֵי.

Mar Zutra, son of Rav Mari, said to Ravina: If that is so, that the Sabbatical Year is entirely disregarded, then in the case of one who consecrates his field and wants to redeem it, the **Sabbatical** Year **should not count for him for the deduction**[N] of the price of the field when it is redeemed. **Why did we learn** in a mishna (*Arakhin* 25a) that the one who consecrated his field **gives a** ***sela*** **and a** ***pundeyon***[HLB] coin, which is worth 16 *perutot*, to the Temple treasury **for** each **year** remaining until the Jubilee Year, including the Sabbatical Year, in accordance with the payment prescribed by the Torah (see Leviticus 27:16–19)? The amount to be paid per year, which is fifty shekels divided by the years remaining until the Jubilee Year, should not take the upcoming Sabbatical Years into account. Ravina **said to him: There it is different, as it is suitable for laying out produce on it.** Although one may not plant the field during the Sabbatical Year, one may use it for other purposes.

NOTES

A year of wind-blasted crops – שְׁנַת שִׁדָּפוֹן: The *halakha* is that if one sells his field to another, he may not repurchase his field before the passage of the: "Years of the crops" (Leviticus 25:15), an expression that means the passage of at least two crop-yielding years. This is a Torah edict. Furthermore, the *halakha* is that the concept: Years of the crops, includes only those years during which there was no general famine and crops grew in this region, even if, due to neglect or natural causes, nothing grew in this particular field.

It is an abrogation of the King – אַפְקְעָתָא דְּמַלְכָּא הִיא: Since the Sabbatical year is an abrogation of God, who stated that one may not farm land during the Sabbatical Year, it is not considered a year of produce as required by *halakha*, as this category does not depend on the actual presence of growing produce, which could be found in the fields of gentiles in Eretz Yisrael, but rather whether this year is defined, in principle, as being suitable for crops.

Deduction – גֵּירוּעַ: The Torah (Leviticus 27:16–19) states that if an ancestral field, i.e., a field in Eretz Yisrael that had been in one's family since the initial division of the land, is consecrated to the Temple, it is evaluated for the purposes of redemption at the fixed price of a field, no matter how much of a yield it actually produces. This sum was established as fifty silver shekels for all the years through the period of one jubilee, or fifty years. When considered on a per-year basis, this equals a *sela*, the shekel of the Torah, plus a *pundeyon*, for each year. The redemption price is set at that rate, with the corresponding sum deducted for each year since the previous Jubilee Year had passed. The Torah further states that if the one who sanctified the field redeems it himself, he must add a fifth to the price of the redemption.

HALAKHA

If it was a year of wind-blasted crops – הָיְתָה שְׁנַת שִׁדָּפוֹן: A field cannot be redeemed prior to the passage of two years. If the field was wind blasted or suffered from mildew one of the years, or if one of the years was a Sabbatical Year, the year is discounted (Rambam *Sefer Zera'im, Hilkhot Shemitta VeYovel* 11:10).

He gives a *sela* and a *pundeyon* – נוֹתֵן סֶלַע וּפוּנְדְּיוֹן: If one redeems a consecrated field from the Temple treasury, he must pay a *sela* and a *pundeyon* for every year remaining until the Jubilee Year (Rambam *Sefer Hafla'a, Hilkhot Arakhin VaḤaramim* 4:6).

LANGUAGE

***Pundeyon* – פּוּנְדְּיוֹן:** From the Latin dupondium, a coin that is worth two *issar*.

BACKGROUND

The Sabbatical Year – שְׁמִיטָּה שְׁבִיעִית: The Sabbatical Year is the last year in the seven-year Sabbatical cycle. Although the *halakhot* of the Sabbatical Year are based on Torah law (Leviticus 25:1–7), some *tanna'im* maintain (*Gittin* 36a) that its observance today is by rabbinic ordinance. Commentaries explain that this is because the conditions enabling performance of the mitzva by Torah law do not currently exist. Most commentaries indeed rule that the *halakha* is in accordance with this opinion. The Hebrew term for the Sabbatical Year, *shemitta*, means abandonment or release. The meaning of the word reflects the essence of the Sabbatical Year, a year during which all agricultural land must lie fallow and working the land is prohibited unless it is necessary to keep existing crops alive. All produce that does grow is ownerless and must be left unguarded in the fields so that any creature, including people, wild animals, and birds, can have ready access to it.

A *sela* and a *pundeyon* – סֶלַע וּפוּנְדְּיוֹן: A biblical *sela*, which is equivalent to four dinars, consists of forty-eight *pundeyon*. Upon dividing fifty *sela*, which is the standard price for a field, by the forty-nine years that the field is used from one Jubilee Year to the next, the value of the field for each year individually is approximately one *sela* and one *pundeyon*.

אָמַר שְׁמוּאֵל: לֹא שָׁנוּ אֶלָּא שֶׁזְּרָעָהּ וְצָמְחָה וַאֲכָלָהּ חָגָב, אֲבָל לֹא זְרָעָהּ כְּלָל – לֹא. דְּאָמַר לֵיהּ: אִילּוּ זְרַעְתָּהּ הֲוָה מִקַּיֵּים בִּי: "לֹא יֵבֹשׁוּ בְּעֵת רָעָה וּבִימֵי רְעָבוֹן יִשְׂבָּעוּ".

Shmuel said: They taught the *halakha* that if there is a regional disaster the cultivator subtracts from the produce he owes as part of his tenancy **only if** the tenant **planted the field**[H] **and it sprouted and** then **grasshoppers consumed it,** or if he planted it with a different seed, **but if he did not plant it at all,** the tenant is **not** entitled to subtract from the amount he owes even if there was a regional disaster. This is **because** the owner can **say to him: Had you planted it,** perhaps my merit would have prevented the field from being affected by the epidemic, and the following verse **would have been fulfilled for me: "They will not be shamed in the time of evil, and in the days of famine they shall be satisfied"** (Psalms 37:19).

מְתִיב רַב שֵׁשֶׁת: רוֹעֶה שֶׁהָיָה רוֹעֶה וְהִנִּיחַ עֶדְרוֹ וּבָא לָעִיר, וּבָא זְאֵב וְטָרַף, וּבָא אֲרִי וְדָרַס – אֵין אוֹמְרִים: אִילּוּ הָיָה שָׁם הָיָה מַצִּיל. אֶלָּא אוֹמְדִין אוֹתוֹ; אִם יָכוֹל לְהַצִּיל – חַיָּיב, וְאִם לָאו – פָּטוּר. וְאַמַּאי? נֵימָא לֵיהּ: אִי הֲוֵית הָתָם – הֲוָה מִקַּיֵּים בִּי: "גַּם אֶת הָאֲרִי גַּם הַדּוֹב הִכָּה עַבְדֶּךָ"!

Rav Sheshet raises an objection from a *baraita*: In the case of **a shepherd who was herding** the animals of others, **and he left his flock and came to the town, and** in the meantime **a wolf came and tore** an animal to pieces, **or a lion came and trampled** one of the flock, **we do not say** definitively that **had he been there he would have rescued** them and therefore he is liable due to his absence. **Rather,** the court **estimates** with regard to **him: If he could** have **rescued** his animal by chasing a beast of this kind away, he is **liable,** as his departure from the scene was certainly a contributing factor to the damage. **If not,** he is **exempt** from liability. According to Shmuel's opinion, **why** is the shepherd exempt from liability? **Let** the owner **say to him: Had you been there,** the following verse **would have been fulfilled for me: "Your servant smote both the lion and the bear"** (I Samuel 17:36).

מִשּׁוּם דְּאָמַר לֵיהּ: אִי הֲוֵית חֲזֵית לְאִיתְרְחוֹשֵׁי לָךְ נִיסָּא – הֲוָה אִיתְרְחִישׁ לָךְ נִיסָּא כְּרַבִּי חֲנִינָא בֶּן דּוֹסָא, דְּמַתְיָין עִיזֵּי דּוּבֵּי בְּקַרְנַיְיהוּ. וְנֵימָא לֵיהּ: נְהִי דְּלְנִיסָּא רַבָּה לָא הֲוָה חֲזֵינָא, לְנִיסָּא זוּטָא

The Gemara answers: This is **because** the shepherd could **say to** the owner: **If you were worthy of a miracle occurring to you, a miracle would have** indeed **occurred to you as** it did to **Rabbi Ḥanina ben Dosa,**[P] **when** his **goats brought bears** impaled **on their horns** without any assistance on the part of a shepherd (see *Ta'anit* 25a). The Gemara asks: **And let** the owner **say to him: Granted that I was not worthy of a great miracle,** but **of a small miracle**

HALAKHA

They taught only if he planted the field – לֹא שָׁנוּ אֶלָּא שֶׁזְּרָעָהּ: If the cultivator did not plant the field at all, even if all the fields in the area suffered from a regional disaster, he pays the owner the full price owed for the tenancy (Rambam *Sefer Mishpatim, Hilkhot Sekhirut* 8:5; *Shulḥan Arukh, Ḥoshen Mishpat* 322:2).

PERSONALITIES

Rabbi Ḥanina ben Dosa – רַבִּי חֲנִינָא בֶּן דּוֹסָא: Rabbi Ḥanina ben Dosa was a *tanna* who lived toward the end of the Second Temple period. He was a student of Rabban Yoḥanan ben Zakkai. Very few of his statements have been recorded, but those that are recorded are mostly in the realm of *aggada*. He is known mainly through stories about his piety and his cleaving to God, as well as his righteousness, his willingness to make do with a minimum of earthly possessions, and being a miracle worker. He served as a symbol of the righteous man in all of his behaviors.

Perek **IX**
Daf **106** Amud **b**

חֲזֵינָא! קַשְׁיָא.

I was worthy.[N] The Gemara concludes: Indeed, this is **difficult.**

תָּנֵי חֲדָא: פַּעַם רִאשׁוֹנָה וּשְׁנִיָּה – זוֹרְעָהּ, וּשְׁלִישִׁית אֵינוֹ זוֹרְעָהּ. וְתַנְיָא אִידָּךְ: שְׁלִישִׁית – זוֹרְעָהּ, רְבִיעִית – אֵינוֹ זוֹרְעָהּ. לָא קַשְׁיָא; הָא – כְּרַבִּי, הָא כְּרַבָּן שִׁמְעוֹן בֶּן גַּמְלִיאֵל.

§ It **is taught** in **one** *baraita*: With regard to one who cultivates a field, **the first and second time he plants**[N] the field again if the crops were destroyed by some mishap, **but the third** time **he is not** required to **plant it** again. **And** it **is taught** in **another** *baraita* that on the **third** occasion, he must **plant it** the field again, but after the **fourth** time the crops are destroyed, **he is not** required to **plant it** again. These two *baraitot* appear to contradict one another. The Gemara explains: That is **not difficult,** as **this** *baraita* is **in accordance with** the opinion of **Rabbi** Yehuda HaNasi, whereas **that** *baraita* is **in accordance with** the opinion of **Rabban Shimon ben Gamliel.**

NOTES

Of a small miracle I was worthy – לְנִיסָּא זוּטָא חֲזֵינָא: The Rosh writes that it is evident from the rulings of the *mishnayot* with regard to bailees (see 93a–103a) that miracles are not taken into account at all. If so, Shmuel's statement would appear to be inaccurate. According to the *Minḥat HaBoker*, there is a fundamental difference between the two situations. In Shmuel's case, the tenant is liable to pay, an obligation from which he seeks to exempt himself. But with regard to bailees, there is a general principle that a bailee is not liable to pay for loss of the deposit caused by an unavoidable accident. For this and other reasons Shmuel's ruling is not rejected and is accepted as *halakha*, despite the fact that the question raised against it was left as a difficulty.

The first and second time he plants it – פַּעַם רִאשׁוֹנָה וּשְׁנִיָּה זוֹרְעָהּ: Based on the context of this statement, Rashi explains that it refers to one who planted a field that was then consumed by locusts or struck by some other disaster. According to this approach, there is a difference between the case of this *baraita* and that addressed by Reish Lakish later in this discussion. Conversely, the Ramban and the Rashba cite a *Tosefta* that indicates that this dispute also refers to one whose planting failed to sprout. In the case of the *Tosefta*, though, the field was not leased with the intention to cultivate it for a single year. Rather, it was leased for several years and planted in consecutive years without success (see the commentaries on *Shulḥan Arukh*).

הָא כְּרַבִּי, דְּאָמַר: בִּתְרֵי זִימְנֵי הָוֵי חֲזָקָה. הָא כְּרַבָּן שִׁמְעוֹן בֶּן גַּמְלִיאֵל, דְּאָמַר: בִּתְלָת זִימְנֵי הָוֵי חֲזָקָה.

The Gemara clarifies: **This** *baraita* is **in accordance with the** opinion of **Rabbi** Yehuda HaNasi **who says** that **presumptive status** is established **by two occasions,** while **that** *baraita* is **in accordance with** the opinion of **Rabban Shimon ben Gamliel, who says** that **presumptive status** is established **by three occasions.**[N]

אָמַר רֵישׁ לָקִישׁ: לֹא שָׁנוּ אֶלָּא שֶׁזְּרָעָהּ וְצָמְחָה וַאֲכָלָהּ חָגָב, אֲבָל זְרָעָהּ וְלֹא צָמְחָה – מָצֵי אָמַר לֵיהּ בַּעַל הַקַּרְקַע: כָּל יְמֵי זֶרַע זַרְעָא לָהּ וְאָזֵיל. וְעַד אֵימַת? אֲמַר רַב פַּפָּא: עַד דְּאָתוּ אֲרִיסֵי מִדַּבְרָא וְקַיְימָא כִּימָה אַרֵישַׁיְיהוּ.

Reish Lakish said: They taught that a cultivator plants a limited number of times **only if he planted** the field **and it sprouted and locusts consumed** the crops, **but if he planted it and** the crops **did not sprout** at all, **the landowner can say to him:** You should **continue planting it** on **all the days** that are fit for **planting.**[H] The Gemara asks: **And until when** does the period of planting last? The Gemara answers: **Rav Pappa said: Until** such time **that the sharecroppers come** in **from the field and** the stars of **Pleiades**[B] are **stationed over their heads,**[N] which occurs roughly during the month of *Shevat*.

מֵיתִיבֵי: רַבָּן שִׁמְעוֹן בֶּן גַּמְלִיאֵל מִשּׁוּם רַבִּי מֵאִיר אוֹמֵר, וְכֵן הָיָה רַבִּי שִׁמְעוֹן בֶּן מְנַסְיָא אוֹמֵר כִּדְבָרָיו: חֲצִי תִּשְׁרֵי, מַרְחֶשְׁוָן וַחֲצִי כִּסְלֵיו – זֶרַע;

The Gemara **raises an objection** to this from a *baraita* that discusses the verse: "While the earth remains, planting and harvest, and cold and heat, and summer and winter, and day and night shall not cease" (Genesis 8:22). The *baraita* interprets this verse as referring to six seasons of the year: **Rabban Shimon ben Gamliel says in the name of Rabbi Meir, and similarly, Rabbi Shimon ben Menasya would say in accordance with his statement:** The second **half of Tishrei,** all of **Marḥeshvan, and** the first **half of Kislev** are the days of **planting.**

חֲצִי כִּסְלֵיו, טֵבֵת וַחֲצִי שְׁבָט – חוֹרֶף; חֲצִי שְׁבָט, אֲדָר וַחֲצִי נִיסָן – קוֹר; חֲצִי נִיסָן, אִיָּיר וַחֲצִי סִיוָן – קָצִיר; חֲצִי סִיוָן, תַּמּוּז וַחֲצִי אָב – קַיִץ; חֲצִי אָב, אֱלוּל וַחֲצִי תִּשְׁרֵי – חוֹם.

The second **half of Kislev,** all of **Tevet, and** the first **half of Shevat** are **the winter** days. The second **half of Shevat,** all of **Adar, and** the first **half of** Nisan are the period of **cold;** the second **half of Nisan,** all of **Iyar, and** the first **half of Sivan** are the **harvest** period. The second **half of Sivan,** all of **Tammuz, and half of Av** are the **summer** season, while the second **half of Av,** all of **Elul, and** the first **half of Tishrei** are the season of **heat.**

רַבִּי יְהוּדָה מוֹנֶה מִתִּשְׁרֵי, רַבִּי שִׁמְעוֹן מוֹנֶה מִמַּרְחֶשְׁוָן.

The *baraita* adds: **Rabbi Yehuda** also would divide the year into these six seasons, but he **counts from** the beginning of **Tishrei** rather than from the middle. **Rabbi Shimon counts from Marḥeshvan,** so that Marḥeshvan and Kislev constitute the season of planting, and so on.

מַאן מֵיקֵל בְּכוּלְּהוּ? רַבִּי שִׁמְעוֹן, וְכוּלֵּי הַאי לָא קָאָמַר! לָא קַשְׁיָא; הָא – דְּקַבְּלָהּ מִינֵּיהּ בְּחָרְפֵי, הָא – דְּקַבְּלָהּ מִינֵּיהּ בְּאַפְלֵי.

The Gemara states its objection: **Who is the most lenient of all of them**[N] in that the period of planting occurs at the latest time of the year? It is **Rabbi Shimon, and** even he **did not say** that the planting season extends **that far** to the time when Pleiades is above their heads. The Gemara responds: That is **not difficult,** as **this** is referring to a cultivator **who accepted from** the owner the planting **of early** crops, while **that** case involves a cultivator **who accepted from** the owner the planting **of late** crops, performed at a much later date.

HALAKHA

He plants it several times – וְזוֹרְעָהּ כַּמָּה פְּעָמִים: One who accepts upon himself the duty to plant a field must continue to plant as long as the land in that location is suitable for planting, even if he fails to yield a crop numerous times. This is because the consensus among the authorities is that the dispute between Rabbi Yehuda HaNasi and Rabban Shimon ben Gamliel is irrelevant to this case, as the *halakha* follows Reish Lakish. This *halakha* applies only to a contractor, but a tenant farmer can purchase the produce he owes the owner for his tenancy on the market (Rambam *Sefer Mishpatim, Hilkhot Sekhirut* 8:5; *Shulḥan Arukh, Ḥoshen Mishpat* 322:2, and in the comment of Rema, and *Beur HaGra* there).

BACKGROUND

Pleiades – כִּימָה: If it is assumed that the workers return from their work at around sunset, as claimed by *Tosafot*, the star cluster Pleiades would be above their heads, i.e., at its highest point in the sky at the zenith of the meridian, toward the end of the month of Shevat, or, according to the solar calendar, at the end of February. Even Rabbi Shimon, who takes the most lenient approach, agrees that the planting season has already ended by the end of Tevet.

Pleiades

NOTES

How many occasions establish presumptive status – בְּכַמָּה פְּעָמִים יֵשׁ חֲזָקָה: This disagreement between Rabbi Yehuda HaNasi and Rabban Shimon ben Gamliel is a general dispute that applies to several areas of *halakha*. The issue at stake is how many times an event must transpire in order to create a presumption that it will remain or continue to occur that way. The Gemara does not provide a general ruling, but in certain cases it rules in accordance with the opinion of Rabbi Yehuda HaNasi, while in others the *halakha* follows Rabban Shimon ben Gamliel. With regard to the present issue as well, some rule in accordance with the opinion of Rabbi Yehuda HaNasi due to the similarity between this *halakha* and the other instances when the *halakha* follows his view (Meiri), whereas others claim that the *halakha* is in accordance with the opinion of Rabban Shimon ben Gamliel.

And Pleiades [*kima*] is stationed over their heads – וְקַיְימָא כִּימָה אַרֵישַׁיְיהוּ: Rashi and *Tosafot* dispute the details of this *halakha*, although they are in agreement with regard to the basic interpretation that it refers to a portion of one of the constellations that is overhead at a certain time of day. In contrast, Rabbi Yosef Tuv-Elem explains, based on the Gemara elsewhere (*Berakhot* 58b), that *kima* is the sign of the rainy season in the zodiac, whereas *kesil* is that of the summer. Consequently, the statement: *Kima* is positioned over their heads, means it is the middle of the winter, which according to his calculation is the twenty-second of Tevet.

Who is the most lenient of all of them – מַאן מֵיקֵל בְּכוּלְּהוּ: This leniency does not refer to the repeated planting of an unsuccessful cultivator, but to a regular cultivator who undertook to plant a field. Rabbi Shimon maintains that the time for planting extends until the end of Kislev, and he cannot be removed from the field if he delayed planting until this date (Ra'avad).

”רַבִּי יְהוּדָה אוֹמֵר אִם קִבְּלָהּ מִמֶּנּוּ בְּמָעוֹת”. הַהוּא גַּבְרָא דְּקַבֵּיל אַרְעָא לְמִיזְרְעָהּ בְּהוּ תּוּמֵי אַגּוּדָּא דִּנְהַר מַלְכָּא סָבָא בְּזוּזֵי. אִיסְתַּכַּר נְהַר מַלְכָּא סָבָא. אֲתָא לְקַמֵּיהּ דְּרָבָא, אֲמַר לֵיהּ: נְהַר מַלְכָּא סָבָא לָא עֲבִיד דְּמִיסְכַּר, מַכַּת מְדִינָה הִיא, זִיל נְכִי לֵיהּ.

§ The mishna teaches: **Rabbi Yehuda says: If** the cultivator **received it from** the owner **for** a fixed sum of **money,** whether a regional disaster occurred or not, he does not subtract the produce he owes as part of his tenancy. The Gemara relates: There was **a certain man who received land to plant garlic on it on the bank of the river Malka Sava**[B] in exchange **for** a specified sum of **money.** The bank of **the river Malka Sava became dammed up.** The case **came before Rava,** who **said to** the cultivator: **The river Malka Sava does not usually dam up.** Therefore, **it is** classified as **a regional disaster; go subtract** this loss from the payment you owe **to** the owner.

אֲמַרוּ לֵיהּ רַבָּנַן לְרָבָא, הָא אֲנַן תְּנַן: רַבִּי יְהוּדָה אוֹמֵר: אִם קִבְּלָהּ הֵימֶנּוּ בְּמָעוֹת - בֵּין כָּךְ וּבֵין כָּךְ אֵינוֹ מְנַכֶּה לוֹ מִן חֲכוֹרוֹ! אֲמַר לְהוּ: לֵית דְּחָשׁ לָהּ לְדְרַבִּי יְהוּדָה.

The Gemara continues the story: **The Rabbis said to Rava: Didn't we learn** in the mishna here: **If** the cultivator **received it from** the owner **for** a fixed sum of **money, whether this** way or **whether that** way, i.e., whether a regional disaster occurred or not, **he does not subtract** the produce he owes as part of **his tenancy.** Rava **said to them: There is no** one **who is concerned for** the ruling **of Rabbi Yehuda** since it is a minority opinion that is rejected.

מתני׳ הַמְקַבֵּל שָׂדֶה מֵחֲבֵירוֹ בַּעֲשָׂרָה כּוֹר חִטִּים לְשָׁנָה וְלָקְתָה - נוֹתֵן לוֹ מִתּוֹכָהּ. הָיוּ חִטֶּיהָ יָפוֹת, לֹא יֹאמַר לוֹ הֲרֵינִי לוֹקֵחַ מִן הַשּׁוּק, אֶלָּא נוֹתֵן לוֹ מִתּוֹכָהּ.

MISHNA In the case of **one who receives a field from another** to cultivate in return **for** the payment of **ten *kor* of wheat per year, and** its produce **was blighted**[H] by a crop disease or the like, the cultivator **gives** the owner the ten *kor* of wheat **from it** but does not have to provide him with high quality wheat. If the wheat stalks produced by the field **were** particularly **good** stalks of **wheat,** the cultivator **may not say to** the owner: **I will buy** regular wheat **from the market; rather,** he **gives him from inside** the field itself.

גמ׳ הַהוּא גַּבְרָא דְּקַבֵּיל אַרְעָא לְאַסְפַּסְתָּא בְּכוֹרֵי דְּשַׂעֲרֵי. עָבְדָא אַסְפַּסְתָּא, וַחֲרָשָׁהּ וּזְרָעָהּ שַׂעֲרֵי, וּלְקוּ הָנֵי שַׂעֲרֵי. שְׁלָחָהּ רַב חֲבִיבָא מִסּוּרָא דִּפְרָת לְקַמֵּיהּ דְּרָבִינָא: כִּי הַאי גַּוְנָא מַאי? כִּי לָקְתָה נוֹתֵן לוֹ מִתּוֹכָהּ דָּמֵי, אוֹ לָא?

GEMARA The Gemara relates: There was **a certain man who received land to** grow **hay** in exchange **for** paying the owner several ***kor*** **of barley.** After the field **produced hay,** the recipient **plowed and sowed it** with **barley, and that barley was blighted.** The worker sought to pay the owner from the damaged barley he had cultivated. **Rav Ḥaviva from Sura in the Euphrates sent** the following question **before Ravina: What** is the *halakha* with regard to **a case of this kind?** Is it **considered similar to** an instance of: If it **was blighted, he gives him from inside** the field, **or not?**

אֲמַר לֵיהּ: מִי דָּמֵי? הָתָם - לָא עָבְדָא אַרְעָא שְׁלִיחוּתָא דְּמָרָהּ, הָכָא - עָבְדָא אַרְעָא שְׁלִיחוּתָא דְּמָרָהּ.

Ravina **said to him: Is it comparable? There,** in the mishna, **the land did not perform its owner's mission,** and the cultivator also received blighted produce, whereas **here, the land did perform its owner's mission,** as the cultivator took the land for the purpose of growing hay, which it produced. His additional crop of barley was not part of their agreement and therefore he cannot pay his debt with blighted barley.

BACKGROUND

The river Malka Sava – **נְהַר מַלְכָּא סָבָא**: This river, named elsewhere as simply the Malka River (see *Gittin* 73a), was one of the largest canals ever built in Babylonia, connecting the Tigris with the Euphrates. It was called a river due to its size, and as it was built by the king it was named after him. It was used for irrigation as well as for transporting goods and food by boat. Damming such an important waterway was without question a rare event.

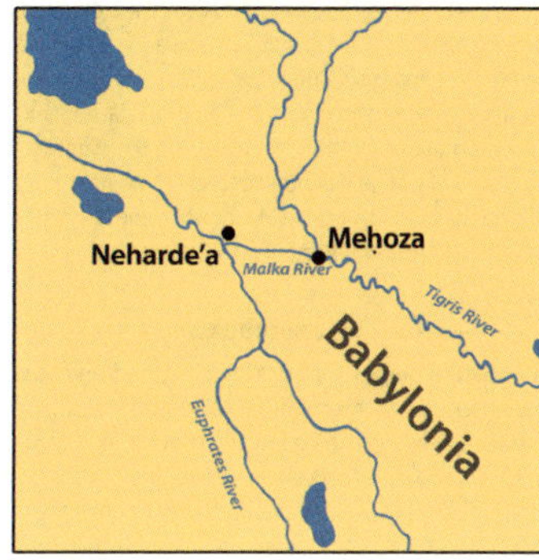

Malka River

HALAKHA

One who receives a field as a tenancy and it was blighted – **הַחוֹכֵר שָׂדֶה וְלָקְתָה**: If one receives tenancy of a field in return for a payment of ten *kor* of wheat and the wheat he grew was blighted, he may pay the owner from the produce of the field itself. If good-quality wheat grew, he may not pay the owner with other wheat that he bought from the market, but he must pay him from the crop of the field itself. The Rema adds that this *halakha* applies only if he kept to the conditions of their agreement, but if the owner stipulated that the tenant farmer should plant wheat and pay him in barley, and the tenant farmer planted barley and it was blighted, he must pay the owner with barley from the market. Similarly, if the sheaves were damaged in the field, or if the grapes went bad, he may pay the owner with them, but if the owner stipulated that he will pay him with wine, and the vineyard produced grapes but the wine went sour, the tenant farmer must pay the owner with good-quality wine, as stated by Rav Ashi (Rambam *Sefer Mishpatim, Hilkhot Sekhirut* 8:7; *Shulḥan Arukh, Ḥoshen Mishpat* 323:1–3).

NOTES

One who receives…to plant it with barley – הַמְקַבֵּל...לְזָרְעָהּ שְׂעוֹרִים: According to Rashi, this *halakha* prohibiting the cultivator from planting wheat instead of barley is limited to a case of tenancy. Since the tenant farmer pays only a set sum to the owner, the owner does not benefit from the change. Therefore, the tenant farmer is not permitted to weaken the field in order to earn more from a crop that was not part of their agreement. However, with regard to a contractor, where the owner receives a percentage of the crop, since the owner of the field also benefits from the additional produce, the recipient may use a more profitable crop that weakens the field, in accordance with the dictum: Let the land be weakened but not its owner. Conversely, the Ramban and others maintain that a contractor also has no right to make any changes, as the owner relies upon his promise to provide specifically barley or wheat.

BACKGROUND

Grain and legumes – תְּבוּאָה וְקִטְנִית: Based on nature, it would seem that the correct version should read: If one receives a field to plant legumes, he may not use it to plant grains. The reason is that certain kinds of grains spoil the soil in which they grow, while the bacteria present in the roots of legumes contribute nitrogen compounds that improve the soil. However, since the Sages' definition of legumes includes all kinds of edible seeds, it is possible that the term legume here could be referring to species that would have a deleterious effect on the soil more than grains, which would account for the version of the mishna possessed by the Rif and the Rambam.

הַהוּא גַּבְרָא דְּקַבֵּל פַּרְדֵּס מֵחַבְרֵיהּ בְּעַשַׂר דַּנֵּי חַמְרָא. תַּקִּיף הַהוּא חַמְרָא. סָבַר רַב כָּהֲנָא לְמֵימַר: הַיְינוּ מַתְנִיתִין לָקְתָה נוֹתֵן לוֹ מִתּוֹכָהּ. אֲמַר לֵיהּ רַב אַשִׁי: מִי דָּמֵי? הָתָם – לָא עָבְדָא אַרְעָא שְׁלִיחוּתָא, הָכָא – עָבְדָא אַרְעָא שְׁלִיחוּתָא.

The Gemara relates: There was **a certain man who received an orchard from another** to cultivate in exchange **for** paying the owner **ten barrels of wine,** but **that wine** produced from the orchard's grapes **turned sour. Rav Kahana thought to say** that **this is** an example of the ruling of **the mishna** that if it **was blighted he** may **give him from inside** the field. **Rav Ashi said to him: Is it comparable? There,** in the mishna, **the land did not perform** its owner's **mission,** as the crop was blighted, whereas **here, the land** did **perform** its owner's **mission,** as there was nothing wrong with the grapes themselves, and the wine turned sour in the cultivator's possession.

וּמוֹדֶה רַב אַשִׁי בְּעִינְבֵי דְּכַדּוּם, וּבְשָׂדֶה שֶׁלָּקְתָה בְּעוֹמָרֶיהָ.

The Gemara comments: **And Rav Ashi concedes with regard to grapes that shrunk** over the course of their growth **and with regard to a field whose sheaves were blighted** that since the damage occurred to the crop itself, the cultivator can pay his debt from the produce of the field.

מתני׳ הַמְקַבֵּל שָׂדֶה מֵחֲבֵירוֹ לְזׇרְעָהּ שְׂעוֹרִים – לֹא יִזְרָעֶנָּה חִטִּים. חִטִּים – יִזְרָעֶנָּה שְׂעוֹרִים. רַבָּן שִׁמְעוֹן בֶּן גַּמְלִיאֵל אוֹסֵר. תְּבוּאָה – לֹא יִזְרָעֶנָּה קִטְנִית, קִטְנִית – יִזְרָעֶנָּה תְּבוּאָה. וְרַבָּן שִׁמְעוֹן בֶּן גַּמְלִיאֵל אוֹסֵר.

MISHNA With regard to **one who receives a field from another** in order **to plant it** with **barley,**[N] he may **not plant it** with **wheat,**[H] as wheat weakens the field more than barley does. But if he receives it in order to plant **wheat,** he may **plant it** with **barley** if he wishes, but **Rabban Shimon ben Gamliel forbids** it. Similarly, if he receives it to plant **it with grain** he may **not plant it** with **legumes,**[B] as they weaken the field more than grains do, but if he receives it in order to plant **legumes** he may **plant it** with **grain, but Rabban Shimon ben Gamliel forbids** it.

גמ׳ אֲמַר רַב חִסְדָּא: מַאי טַעְמָא דְּרַבָּן שִׁמְעוֹן בֶּן גַּמְלִיאֵל? דִּכְתִיב: ״שְׁאֵרִית יִשְׂרָאֵל לֹא יַעֲשׂוּ עַוְלָה וְלֹא יְדַבְּרוּ כָזָב וְלֹא יִמָּצֵא בְּפִיהֶם לְשׁוֹן תַּרְמִית״.

GEMARA Rav Ḥisda said: **What is the reason** of the ruling of **Rabban Shimon ben Gamliel?** The landowner has apparently suffered no loss from the cultivator's actions. His reasoning is **as it is written: "The remnant of Israel shall not do iniquity, nor speak lies, neither shall a deceitful tongue be found in their mouth"** (Zephaniah 3:13). In other words, one may not retract from an obligation accepted upon oneself, even if no one suffers as a result.

מֵיתִיבֵי: מְגַבַּת פּוּרִים – לְפוּרִים, וְאֵין מְדַקְדְּקִין בַּדָּבָר. וְאֵין הֶעָנִי רַשַּׁאי לִיקַּח מֵהֶן רְצוּעָה לְסַנְדָּלוֹ, אֶלָּא אִם כֵּן הִתְנָה בְּמַעֲמַד אַנְשֵׁי הָעִיר, דִּבְרֵי רַבִּי יַעֲקֹב שֶׁאָמַר מִשּׁוּם רַבִּי מֵאִיר. רַבָּן שִׁמְעוֹן בֶּן גַּמְלִיאֵל

The Gemara **raises an objection** to this from a *baraita*: The **Purim collection is** only **for the Purim** feast, **but one does not scrutinize the matter** by limiting the allocation for the poor to the exact costs of the meal and no more. **And** it is **not permitted for a poor person to purchase** even **a strap for his sandal from it unless he stipulated in the presence of the people of the city** that he may do as he wishes with the money he receives. This is **the statement of Rabbi Ya'akov, who said it in the name of Rabbi Meir. Rabban Shimon ben Gamliel**

HALAKHA

One who receives to plant barley may not plant wheat, etc. – הַמְקַבֵּל לִשְׂעוֹרִים לֹא יִזְרַע חִטִּים וכו׳: One who receives a field to plant barley may not plant wheat in it because wheat weakens the earth more than barley. But if he receives the field to plant wheat he may plant barley. If he received it to plant legumes, he may not plant grain, but if he received it to plant grain, he may plant legumes. This ruling follows the version of the text of the mishna possessed by the Rif and the Rambam, but some authorities reverse the *halakha* concerning legumes and grain in keeping with the standard version of the text (Rema, citing *Tur*). The Rema also cites a view that a contractor may even plant a crop that weakens the soil instead of what had initially been agreed upon (Rashi; *Tur*), whereas others maintain that a contractor cannot even change the crop to one that inflicts less damage to the ground (Ramban; *Maggid Mishne*). In general, the *halakha* with regard to this issue is in accordance with the opinion of the Rabbis and not that of Rabban Shimon ben Gamliel, as is evident from the discussion of the continuation of the Gemara on the next *daf* (Rambam *Sefer Mishpatim*, *Hilkhot Sekhirut* 8:9; *Shulḥan Arukh*, *Ḥoshen Mishpat* 324:1, and in the comment of Rema).

מֵיקֵל.

is lenient,[N] as he maintains that donors are not particular in this regard. This shows that Rabban Shimon ben Gamliel is not bothered by a change of mind if no harm results.

אָמַר אַבַּיֵי: טַעְמָא דְּרַבָּן שִׁמְעוֹן כִּדְמָר, דְּאָמַר מָר: הַאי מַאן דְּנִיחָא לֵיהּ דְּתִתְבּוֹר אַרְעֵיהּ – לִיזְרְעָהּ שַׁתָּא חִטֵּי וְשַׁתָּא שְׂעָרֵי, שַׁתָּא שְׁתִי וְשַׁתָּא עֶרֶב.

Abaye said: Rabban Shimon ben Gamliel's reason is **as** explained **by the Master,**[N] Abaye's teacher Rabba, **as the Master says: One** for **whom it is preferable to** grow crops and yet have **his land** remain as fertile as if it **lay fallow should plant wheat** one **year and barley** the next **year.** In addition, he should plant one **year lengthwise and** the following **year crosswise.** In this manner, he will prevent the field from being weakened.

וְלָא אֲמָרַן אֶלָּא דְּלָא כָּרֵיב וְתָנֵי, אֲבָל כָּרֵיב וְתָנֵי – לֵית לַן בָּהּ.

The Gemara comments: **And we said** that his use of the land without following these dictates would weaken it **only where** he does **not plow and repeat** his plowing, i.e., plow the field twice before reseeding it, **but** if he **plows and repeats** his plowing, **we have no** problem **with it.** Consequently, the reasoning of Rabban Shimon ben Gamliel is that a change of crops at the wrong time can weaken the field.

״תְּבוּאָה לֹא יִזְרָעֶנָּה קִטְנִית״ [וכו׳]. מַתְנֵי לֵיהּ רַב יְהוּדָה לְרָבִין: תְּבוּאָה יִזְרָעֶנָּה קִטְנִית. אֲמַר לֵיהּ: וְהָא אֲנַן תְּנַן: תְּבוּאָה לֹא יִזְרָעֶנָּה קִטְנִית! אֲמַר לֵיהּ: לָא קַשְׁיָא; הָא – לַן וְהָא – לְהוּ.

§ The mishna states that one who receives a field to plant it with **grain may not plant it** with **legumes. Rav Yehuda taught Ravin**[N] that the *halakha* is that one who receives a field to plant it with **grain** may **plant it** with **legumes.** Ravin **said to him: But didn't we learn** in the mishna that one who receives a field to plant it with **grain may not plant it** with **legumes?** Rav Yehuda **said to him:** This is **not difficult,** as **this** *halakha* **is for us,** the residents of Babylonia, **and that** *halakha* **is for them,**[BH] the residents of Eretz Yisrael. Since what type of seed to plant depends on the quality of the land, in Eretz Yisrael, where the land is weak, there is concern that the land will be weakened. This concern does not apply to Babylonian fields.

אֲמַר לֵיהּ רַב יְהוּדָה לְרָבִין בַּר רַב נַחְמָן: רָבִין אָחִי, הָנֵי תַּחְלֵי דְּבֵי כִּתָּנָא אֵין בָּהֶן מִשּׁוּם גָּזֵל; עוֹמְדוֹת עַל גְּבוּלִין – יֵשׁ בָּהֶן מִשּׁוּם גָּזֵל.

Rav Yehuda said to Ravin bar Rav Naḥman: Ravin my brother, those cress[B] plants that grow **among flax**[H] **are not subject to** the prohibition of **robbery,** as the one taking them is effectively weeding the field, and the owner prefers that the cress not grow so as to not affect the growing flax. But if the plants **stand on the boundary** of where the flax is growing, so that their remaining there would not have a negative impact on the growing flax, **they are subject to** the prohibition of **robbery,** as it is assumed that the owner grew the plants there intentionally.

וְאִם הוּקְשׁוּ לְזֶרַע, אֲפִילּוּ דְּבֵי כִּתָּנָא נָמֵי – יֵשׁ בָּהֶם מִשּׁוּם גָּזֵל. מַאי טַעְמָא? מַאי דְּאַפְסֵיד אַפְסֵיד.

And if the cress plants were sufficiently grown to the point that they were **hardened with seed** growing inside, i.e., they were fully grown, then **even** if they were **among the flax, they are subject to** the prohibition of **robbery. What is the reason?** Concerning **that** flax **to which** they have already **caused a loss,** they have already **caused the loss.** Since the flax has already been damaged, by removing the cress now he does nothing to improve the crop and merely takes something from the owner.

NOTES

Rabban Shimon ben Gamliel is lenient – רַבָּן שִׁמְעוֹן בֶּן גַּמְלִיאֵל מֵיקֵל: The Meiri suggests that Rabban Shimon ben Gamliel rules leniently only if the poor person used a portion of the funds for a small matter, but not if he took the money and did not use it for his Purim meal at all.

His reason is as explained by the Master – טַעְמָא...כִּדְמָר: It is possible the owner planted barley the previous year and is consequently particular that wheat should be planted this year. Alternatively, perhaps he wishes to plant wheat the following year (Ra'avad).

Taught Ravin – מַתְנֵי לֵיהּ...לְרָבִין: Rashi explains that Rav Yehuda had a different version of the mishna. The Rashash suggests that Rav Yehuda taught Ravin a *baraita* that ruled differently from the mishna.

BACKGROUND

This is for us and that is for them – הָא לַן וְהָא לְהוּ: Sometimes the Gemara resolves a contradiction between two *halakhot* by suggesting that one reflects the Babylonian practice, described as: This is for us, while the other reflects the practice in Eretz Yisrael, referred to as: That is for them. The difference between the two *halakhot* reflects the different halakhic traditions or the different circumstances extant in the two countries.

Cress [*taḥlei*] – תַּחְלֵי: The Hebrew equivalent of the Aramaic term *taḥlei* is *shaḥalayim*. Today, *shaḥalayim* refers to garden cress, *Lepidium sativum*, an annual plant with bluish-green flowers that can reach up to 60 cm in height. Its seeds are usually used as a spice, and its stems can serve in salad. The plant is cut about 10 cm from the ground, and is cut a second time after it grows again. The seeds of the garden cress are ground and used for medicinal purposes. Various parts of the cress plant were used in medicine in the talmudic era by grinding them and then mixing them with wine or vinegar.

Garden cress

HALAKHA

This is for us and that is for them – הָא לַן וְהָא לְהוּ: One may plant legumes instead of grain in Eretz Yisrael, but not in Babylonia. Some authorities rule, in accordance with Rashi's version and the printed text of the Gemara, that he may plant legumes instead of grain in Babylonia but not in Eretz Yisrael (Rambam *Sefer Mishpatim, Hilkhot Sekhirut* 8:9; *Shulḥan Arukh, Ḥoshen Mishpat* 324:1).

Cress among flax – תַּחְלֵי דְּבֵי כִּתָּנָא: It is permitted for one to take cress plants that are growing in a field of flax. The reason is that the owner wants these plants to be removed due to the damage they cause to his flax, and they are consequently considered ownerless. If they have already hardened and have seeds, or were growing on the boundary of the owner's property, it is prohibited to take them (Rambam *Sefer Nezikin, Hilkhot Gezeila VaAveda* 6:4; *Shulḥan Arukh, Ḥoshen Mishpat* 273:17).

אֲמַר לֵיהּ רַב יְהוּדָה לְרָבִין בַּר רַב נַחְמָן: רָבִין אָחִי, הָנֵי דִּילִי – דִּילָךְ, וְדִילָךְ – דִּילִי. נְהוּג בְּנֵי מִצְרָא, אִילָן הַנּוֹטֶה לְכָאן – לְכָאן, וְהַנּוֹטֶה לְכָאן – לְכָאן.

Ravin bar Rav Naḥman and Rav Yehuda owned adjacent fields, and their trees leaned over the boundaries. **Rav Yehuda said to Ravin bar Rav Naḥman: Ravin my brother, these** that are **mine are yours,**[N] **and** those that are **yours are mine.** This is because it **is customary** with regard to **those** whose fields **border** on the field of their neighbors that with regard to **a tree that tilts to here,** i.e., to the property of one of them, its fruit belongs **to** the owner of the field **here,** to where it is tilting, **and** with regard to **one that tilts to there,** i.e., to the other side, its fruit belongs **to** the owner of the field **there,** as neighbors are not particular which portion of the land actually grew the fruit.

דְּאִיתְּמַר, אִילָן הָעוֹמֵד עַל הַמֵּיצַר. אָמַר רַב: הַנּוֹטֶה לְכָאן – לְכָאן, וְהַנּוֹטֶה לְכָאן – לְכָאן. וּשְׁמוּאֵל אָמַר: חוֹלְקִין.

As a dispute **was stated** about this issue between *amora'im*: With regard to **a tree that stands on the border**[H] between fields, **Rav says: That** which **tilts to here,** i.e., to this field, its fruit belongs **to** the owner of the field **here, and that** which **tilts to there** belongs **to** the owner of the field **there. And Shmuel says:** The owners of the two fields **divide** all the fruit.

מֵיתִיבֵי: אִילָן הָעוֹמֵד עַל הַמֵּיצַר – יַחֲלוֹקוּ. תְּיוּבְתָּא דְּרַב! תַּרְגְּמָא שְׁמוּאֵל אַלִּיבָּא דְּרַב: בִּמְמַלֵּא כָּל הַמֵּיצַר כּוּלּוֹ.

The Gemara **raises an objection** from a *baraita*: With regard to **a tree that stands on the border** between fields, **they divide** its fruit. This is apparently **a conclusive refutation of Rav.** The Gemara responds: **Shmuel interpreted** the *baraita* so that it should be **in accordance with** the opinion **of Rav** as referring to a case **where** the tree **fills the entire boundary,** and consequently it belongs to both of them.

אִי הָכִי, מַאי לְמֵימְרָא? לָא צְרִיכָא דְּתָלֵי טוּנֵיהּ לְחַד גִּיסָא. וְאַכַּתִּי, מַאי לְמֵימְרָא? מַהוּ דְּתֵימָא, דְּאָמַר לֵיהּ: פְּלוֹג הָכִי. קָא מַשְׁמַע לָן דְּאָמַר לֵיהּ: מַאי חָזֵית דְּפָלְגַתְּ הָכִי – פְּלוֹג הָכִי.

The Gemara asks: **If so,** this is obvious; **what** is the purpose **of** the *baraita* **stating** its ruling? The Gemara answers: **No,** it is **necessary** in a situation **where its boughs hang** more **to one side.** The Gemara asks: **But still, what** is the purpose **of stating** it? The novelty of this *halakha* remains unclear. The Gemara explains: It is necessary, **lest you say that** the owner of the field above which the boughs hang can **say to** the owner of the other field: Let us **divide** the fruit **in this** manner, where each of us receives the fruit that grows over his land. The *tanna* therefore **teaches us that** the owner of the other field may **say to him: What did you see** to make you prefer **to divide** the fruit **in this** manner, based on bisecting the tree in one direction; **divide** the fruit instead **in that** manner, i.e., based on bisecting the tree in the other direction, so that we each receive an equal share.

אֲמַר לֵיהּ רַב יְהוּדָה לְרָבִין בַּר רַב נַחְמָן: רָבִין אָחִי, לָא תִּזְבֵּין אַרְעָא דִּסְמִיכָא לְמָתָא, דְּאָמַר רַבִּי אַבָּהוּ אָמַר רַב הוּנָא אָמַר רַב: אָסוּר לוֹ לְאָדָם שֶׁיַּעֲמוֹד עַל שְׂדֵה חֲבֵירוֹ בְּשָׁעָה שֶׁעוֹמֶדֶת בְּקָמוֹתֶיהָ.

§ **Rav Yehuda said to Ravin bar Rav Naḥman: Ravin my brother, do not buy land that is near a town, as Rabbi Abbahu says that Rav Huna says that Rav says:** It is **prohibited for a person to stand by another's field**[N] **when its ripe grain is standing,** i.e., when its produce is ready for harvest, as he might harm the produce with the evil eye. Similarly, land near a town may be harmed by the people of the town watching it.

אִינִי? וְהָא אַשְׁכַּחִינְהוּ רַבִּי אַבָּא לְתַלְמִידֵיהּ דְּרַב, אֲמַר לְהוּ: מַאי אֲמַר רַב בְּהָנֵי קְרָאֵי "בָּרוּךְ אַתָּה בָּעִיר וּבָרוּךְ אַתָּה בַּשָּׂדֶה, בָּרוּךְ אַתָּה בְּבֹאֶךָ וּבָרוּךְ אַתָּה בְּצֵאתֶךָ"?

The Gemara asks: **Is that so? But when Rabbi Abba encountered Rav's students** he **said to them: What does Rav say** with regard to the meaning of **these verses** of blessing: **"Blessed shall you be in the city, and blessed shall you be in the field"** (Deuteronomy 28:3), and: **"Blessed shall you be when you enter, and blessed shall you be when you exit"** (Deuteronomy 28:6)?

וַאֲמַרוּ לֵיהּ, הָכִי אֲמַר רַב: "בָּרוּךְ אַתָּה בָּעִיר" – שֶׁיְּהֵא בֵּיתְךָ סָמוּךְ לְבֵית הַכְּנֶסֶת. "בָּרוּךְ אַתָּה בַּשָּׂדֶה" – שֶׁיְּהוּ נְכָסֶיךָ קְרוֹבִים לָעִיר. "בָּרוּךְ אַתָּה בְּבֹאֶךָ" – שֶׁלֹּא תִּמְצָא אִשְׁתְּךָ סְפֵק נִדָּה בִּשְׁעַת בִּיאָתְךָ מִן הַדֶּרֶךְ. "בָּרוּךְ אַתָּה בְּצֵאתֶךָ" – שֶׁיְּהוּ צֶאֱצָאֵי מֵעֶיךָ כְּמוֹתְךָ.

And they said to him: This is what **Rav said: "Blessed shall you be in the city"** means **that your house should be adjacent to a synagogue,**[N] and the phrase: **"Blessed shall you be in the field"** means **that your property should be near the city. "Blessed shall you be when you enter"** means **that you will not find your wife** in a state where it is **uncertain** whether she has the halakhic status of a menstruating **woman**[N] **when you come in from a journey,** which would render her forbidden to you. **"Blessed shall you be when you go out"**[N] means **that those who emerge from you,** i.e., your descendants, **should be like you.**

NOTES

Mine are yours – דִּילִי דִּילָךְ: Rabbeinu Ḥananel and Rabbeinu Meshullam explain that Rav Yehuda said to him as follows: We, as friends, are not particular about such matters, but the general custom among people is to divide the fruit as specified in the Gemara.

It is prohibited for a person to stand by another's field – אָסוּר לוֹ לְאָדָם שֶׁיַּעֲמוֹד עַל שְׂדֵה חֲבֵירוֹ: The Meiri explains that if the field is damaged for whatever reason, the owner will accuse the other of causing the damage by means of the evil eye.

Your house should be adjacent to a synagogue – יְהֵא בֵּיתְךָ סָמוּךְ לְבֵית הַכְּנֶסֶת: The reasoning of Rav is that living near the synagogue enables one to fulfill the mitzva of prayer in the best possible manner, by being among the first ten to arrive in the synagogue (*Torat Ḥayyim*; see *Berakhot* 47b).

Your wife in a state where it is uncertain whether she has the halakhic status of a menstruating woman – אִשְׁתְּךָ סְפֵק נִדָּה: Here Rashi holds that the blessing also includes the idea that one should not return from a journey and find his wife to have the definite status of a menstruating woman. By contrast, Rashi in *Sanhedrin* (103a), as well as Rabbeinu Ḥananel and others, explain that Rav's statement applies only to a woman who is uncertain whether she is menstruating, as in that situation the husband would be upset over the possibility that they may not engage in sexual intercourse despite the fact that it is not certain that it is prohibited.

When you go out – בְּצֵאתֶךָ: Neither Rav nor Rabbi Yoḥanan explain this verse in a straightforward manner as referring to one who leaves his house. The reason is that if this were the correct meaning, then the words: "When you go out," should precede the words: "When you enter." Consequently, they offer different interpretations of leaving, as referring to either children or death (*Magen Gibborim*).

HALAKHA

A tree that stands on the boundary – אִילָן הָעוֹמֵד עַל הַמֵּיצַר: If a tree is situated on the boundary between fields the owners share its fruit, even if the boughs are distributed more on one side. The *halakha* follows the opinion of Shmuel, in accordance with the explanation of *Tosafot* (Rambam *Sefer Kinyan*, *Hilkhot Shekhenim* 4:9; *Shulḥan Arukh*, *Ḥoshen Mishpat* 167:2).

וַאֲמַר לְהוּ: רַבִּי יוֹחָנָן לָא אֲמַר הָכִי, אֶלָּא: ״בָּרוּךְ אַתָּה בָּעִיר״ – שֶׁיְּהֵא בֵּית הַכִּסֵּא סָמוּךְ לְשׁוּלְחָנְךָ, אֲבָל בֵּית הַכְּנֶסֶת לֹא. וְרַבִּי יוֹחָנָן לְטַעְמֵיהּ דְּאָמַר: שְׂכַר פְּסִיעוֹת יֵשׁ.

And Rabbi Abba **said to them: Rabbi Yoḥanan did not say this, but** he interpreted the verse as follows: **"Blessed shall you be in the city,"** means **that there should be a bathroom**[B] **near your table, but** he did **not** refer to **a synagogue.** The Gemara adds: **And Rabbi Yoḥanan** conforms **to his** line of **reasoning** in this regard, **as he says: There is a reward** for **the steps** one takes to reach the location of a mitzva, and one who lives adjacent to a synagogue will not have the opportunity to earn this reward.

״בָּרוּךְ אַתָּה בַּשָּׂדֶה״ – שֶׁיְּהוּ נְכָסֶיךָ מְשׁוּלָּשִׁין: שְׁלִישׁ בִּתְבוּאָה, שְׁלִישׁ בְּזֵיתִים וּשְׁלִישׁ בִּגְפָנִים. ״בָּרוּךְ אַתָּה בְּבֹאֶךָ וּבָרוּךְ אַתָּה בְּצֵאתֶךָ״ – שֶׁתְּהֵא יְצִיאָתְךָ מִן הָעוֹלָם כְּבִיאָתְךָ לָעוֹלָם. מַה בִּיאָתְךָ לָעוֹלָם בְּלֹא חֵטְא – אַף יְצִיאָתְךָ מִן הָעוֹלָם בְּלֹא חֵטְא.

The Gemara returns to Rabbi Yoḥanan's exposition of the verses: **"Blessed shall you be in the field"** means **that your property should be** divided into **thirds:**[N] **One-third** should be invested **in grain, one-third in olives, and one-third in grapevines. "Blessed shall you be when you enter and blessed shall you be when you exit"** means **that your exit from the world should be like your entry into the world: Just as your entry into the world was without sin, so too your exit from the world** should be **without sin.**

BACKGROUND

Bathroom – בֵּית הַכִּסֵּא: There was no plumbing in talmudic times or any sewage system in the cities, and certainly not in villages. The toilet was usually located on an empty piece of land set aside for this purpose. Sometimes one's house was far from this piece of land, which made it quite inconvenient for people to relieve themselves.

NOTES

Your property should be divided into thirds – נְכָסֶיךָ מְשׁוּלָּשִׁין: Rashi explains that diversifying one's holdings in this manner will ensure that one will have a steady income even when one of his assets is not producing any profit. The *Torat Ḥayyim* explains that this will ensure he has all types of goodness in his possession.

Perek **IX**
Daf **107** Amud **b**

לָא קַשְׁיָא; הָא – דִּמְהַדַּר לֵיהּ שׁוּרָא וְרִתְקָא; הָא – דְּלָא מְהַדַּר לֵיהּ שׁוּרָא וְרִתְקָא.

In any case, it is evident that Rav approves of one whose property is located near a city. How does this accord with his statement that there is concern for the evil eye when one's field is viewed by people? The Gemara answers: This is **not difficult. This** statement is referring to **a wall and** an additional **partition** [*ritka*][L] **that surround** the plot and prevent it from being harmed by the evil eye. **That** statement is referring to a case **where a wall and** an additional **partition do not surround it.**

״וְהֵסִיר ה׳ מִמְּךָ כָּל חֹלִי״ – אָמַר רַב: זוֹ עַיִן. רַב לְטַעְמֵיהּ, דְּרַב סָלֵיק לְבֵי קִבְרֵי, עֲבַד מַאי דַּעֲבַד. אֲמַר: תִּשְׁעִין וְתִשְׁעָה בְּעַיִן רָעָה, וְאֶחָד בְּדֶרֶךְ אֶרֶץ.

§ The Gemara returns to expounding the themes of blessings and the evil eye. The Torah states: **"And the Lord will take away from you all sickness"** (Deuteronomy 7:15).[N] In interpreting this verse, **Rav says: This** verse is speaking about the evil **eye.** The Gemara comments: **Rav** conforms **to his** line of **reasoning, as Rav went to a graveyard,** and **did what** he **did,**[N] i.e., he used an incantation to find out how those buried there died, and he **said: Ninety-nine** of these died **by the evil eye, and** only **one** died **by** entirely **natural means.**

וּשְׁמוּאֵל אָמַר: זֶה הָרוּחַ. שְׁמוּאֵל לְטַעְמֵיהּ, דְּאָמַר שְׁמוּאֵל: הַכֹּל בְּרוּחַ. וְלִשְׁמוּאֵל, הָא אִיכָּא הֲרוּגֵי מַלְכוּת! הָנָךְ נַמִי, אִי לָאו זִיקָא – עָבְדִי לְהוּ סַמָּא וְחַיֵּי.

And Shmuel says: This term: "All sickness," refers to **the wind.** The Gemara comments: **Shmuel** conforms **to his** line of **reasoning, as Shmuel says: Every** injury suffered by people is due **to the wind**[B] that enters wounds and bodily cavities. The Gemara asks: **But according to Shmuel, aren't there** those **executed by the monarchy** and others killed by traumatic injury and not the wind? The Gemara responds: With regard to **these too, were it not for the wind, they would prepare a medicine for** those injured people **and** they would be healed and **live,** but the wind prevents this from happening.

רַבִּי חֲנִינָא אָמַר: זוֹ צִינָּה, דְּאָמַר רַבִּי חֲנִינָא: הַכֹּל בִּידֵי שָׁמַיִם חוּץ מִצִּנִּים פַּחִים, שֶׁנֶּאֱמַר: ״צִנִּים פַּחִים בְּדֶרֶךְ עִקֵּשׁ שׁוֹמֵר נַפְשׁוֹ יִרְחַק מֵהֶם״.

Rabbi Ḥanina says: This phrase: "All sickness," refers to **the cold,**[N] **as Rabbi Ḥanina says: All** occurrences that befall man are **at the hands of Heaven, except for** excess **cold** and **heat, as it is stated: "Cold and heat**[N] **are on the path of the perverse; he who guards his soul shall keep far from them"** (Proverbs 22:5). This indicates that cold and heat are forms of harm caused by man, from which one can protect himself.

BACKGROUND

Wind – רוּחַ: Although the precise nature of Shmuel's medical theory here is unknown, he apparently sensed that most illnesses as well as infections and complications associated with physical wounds were caused by elements in the air, which he termed: The wind. Such notions were widespread in those days with regard to certain diseases, such as malaria. One could view this as a kind of intuitive sense that infections are often caused by airborne bacteria.

LANGUAGE

Partition [*ritka*] – רִתְקָא: This word appears to come from the root *reish, tav, kuf,* which means to enclose, as in Isaiah 40:19, or to chain together.

NOTES

And the Lord will take away from you all sickness – וְהֵסִיר ה׳ מִמְּךָ כָּל חֹלִי: These interpretations of the verse are necessary since a more advantageous blessing would be for God not to bring any sickness at all upon the Jewish people. The verse in this form indicates that He will save them from an already existing affliction. The Sages consequently explain it as referring not to actual illnesses but to problems caused by natural events or by humans. Therefore, God's blessing is that He will remove such ill effects (*Torat Ḥayyim*).

Did what he did – עֲבַד מַאי דַּעֲבַד: Rabbeinu Ḥananel explains that Rav asked to be informed in a dream, and his request was granted by Heaven. The *Arukh* cites an interpretation that he planted trees by the graves and had the trees take an oath that the ones planted near people who did not die by the evil eye should sprout flowers and bear fruit.

This refers to the cold – זוֹ צִינָּה: This statement appears to contradict Rabbi Ḥanina's own statement; if this matter is not in the hands of Heaven, how can it be included in the blessing of: "And He will take away from you all sickness"? Some explain that God will provide him with clothing with which he can protect himself from the cold (*Tosafot, Avoda Zara* 3b). Alternatively, God will ensure there is no chill in the world (Maharsha).

Cold and heat [*tzinim paḥim*] – צִנִּים פַּחִים: According to *Tosafot* (*Avoda Zara* 3b), the word *paḥim* refers to heat. The Rashbam maintains that the words *tzinim paḥim* means that the cold [*tzinim*] is in fact a type of trap [*paḥim*] or obstacle for people. The commentaries discuss at length why the Gemara did not simply cite the verse without Rabbi Ḥanina's statement, as the verse itself appears to demonstrate that nature can sometimes cause illness. Some answer that according to the plain meaning of the verse, as evident from Rashi's commentary there, it is not referring to the cold at all, and only based on Rabbi Ḥanina is the verse interpreted in this manner (*Torat Ḥayyim*).

רַבִּי יוֹסֵי בַּר חֲנִינָא אָמַר: זוֹ צוֹאָה, דְּאָמַר מָר: צוֹאַת הַחוֹטֶם וְצוֹאַת הָאוֹזֶן – רוּבָּן קָשֶׁה וּמִיעוּטָן יָפֶה.

Rabbi Yosei bar Ḥanina says: This phrase: "All sickness," refers to **excrement, as the Master says:** With regard to **excrement of the nose,** i.e., mucous, **and excrement of the ear,** i.e., earwax, if a large amount is emitted, having **much of it is harmful, but** having **a bit of it is beneficial.**[B]

רַבִּי אֶלְעָזָר אָמַר: זוֹ מָרָה. תַּנְיָא נַמִּי הָכִי: מַחֲלָה – זוֹ מָרָה. וְלָמָּה נִקְרָא שְׁמָהּ מַחֲלָה? שֶׁהִיא מַחֲלָה כָּל גּוּפוֹ שֶׁל אָדָם. דָּבָר אַחֵר: מַחֲלָה שֶׁשְּׁמוֹנִים וּשְׁלֹשָׁה חֳלָאִים תְּלוּיִן בַּמָּרָה, וְכוּלָּן – פַּת שַׁחֲרִית בְּמֶלַח וְקִיתוֹן שֶׁל מַיִם מְבַטַּלְתָּן.

Rabbi Elazar says: This term: "All sickness," refers to **the gall bladder.**[N] The Gemara adds: **This is also taught** in a *baraita*: With regard to the term: **"Sickness," this** refers to **the gall bladder.**[B] **And why** is the gall bladder **called sickness?** It is **because it makes a person's entire body ill. Alternatively,** it is called **sickness because eighty-three diseases,** the numerical value of *maḥala*, sickness, **are dependent on the gall bladder.** The Gemara comments: **And** with regard to **all of them,** consuming **bread in the morning**[H] **with salt and** drinking **a large jug of water negates their** ill effects, as a simple morning meal is beneficial to the body.

תָּנוּ רַבָּנַן: שְׁלֹשָׁה עָשָׂר דְּבָרִים נֶאֶמְרוּ בְּפַת שַׁחֲרִית: מַצֶּלֶת מִן הַחַמָּה, וּמִן הַצִּנָּה, וּמִן הַזִּיקִין, וּמִן הַמַּזִּיקִין, וּמַחְכִּימַת פֶּתִי, וְזוֹכֶה בַּדִּין, לִלְמוֹד תּוֹרָה וּלְלַמֵּד, וּדְבָרָיו נִשְׁמָעִין, וְתַלְמוּדוֹ מִתְקַיֵּים בְּיָדוֹ,

§ The Gemara cites a related *baraita*: **The Sages taught** that **thirteen matters** of praise **were stated with regard to** a meal of **bread** eaten in **the morning:** It **protects** the diner **from the heat, and from the cold, and from the winds, and from the harmful spirits;** and it **makes the simple wise, and** one who consumes it will be **victorious in judgment,** he will merit **to learn Torah and to teach** it, **and his statements are heard, and his study will remain in his possession.**

וְאֵין בְּשָׂרוֹ מַעֲלֶה הֶבֶל, וְנִזְקָק לְאִשְׁתּוֹ, וְאֵינוֹ מִתְאַוֶּה לְאִשָּׁה אַחֶרֶת, וְהוֹרֶגֶת כִּינָּה שֶׁבִּבְנֵי מֵעַיִם. וְיֵשׁ אוֹמְרִים: אַף מוֹצִיא אֶת הַקִּנְאָה וּמַכְנִיס אֶת הָאַהֲבָה.

In addition, **his flesh does not generate** excess **sweat, and he engages in intercourse with his wife** at the proper time, **and he does not lust for another woman, and** this meal is so advantageous that it even **kills** any **louse in his intestines.**[B] **And some say it even removes jealousy**[N] **and brings in love.** Since he is completely healthy, he is not inclined to be angered by others.

אֲמַר לֵיהּ רַבָּה לְרָבָא בַּר מָרִי: מְנָא הָא מִילְּתָא דְּאָמְרִי אֱינָשֵׁי שִׁיתִּין רְהִיטֵי רְהוּט וְלָא מָטוּ לְגַבְרָא דְּמִצַּפְרָא כְּרַךְ – וְאָמְרוּ רַבָּנַן: הַשְׁכֵּם וֶאֱכוֹל, בַּקַּיִץ מִפְּנֵי הַחַמָּה, וּבַחוֹרֶף מִפְּנֵי הַצִּינָּה?

In relation to the above *baraita*, **Rabba said to Rava bar Mari: From where is this matter that people say** derived: **Sixty runners ran but could not catch the man who ate in the morning, and the Sages** likewise **said: Arise early and eat, in the summer due to the sun and in the winter due to the cold,** so that one's body should have the strength to withstand the climate.

אֲמַר לֵיהּ: דִּכְתִיב: "לֹא יִרְעָבוּ וְלֹא יִצְמָאוּ וְלֹא יַכֵּם שָׁרָב וָשָׁמֶשׁ". "לֹא יַכֵּם שָׁרָב וָשָׁמֶשׁ" – כֵּיוָן דְּלֹא יִרְעָבוּ וְלֹא יִצְמָאוּ.

Rava bar Mari **said to him:** It is derived from a verse, **as it is written: "They shall not hunger nor thirst, neither shall the heat nor sun smite them"** (Isaiah 49:10). Why will **the heat and the sun not smite them? Since they shall not hunger nor thirst,** as they rose early to eat.

אֲמַר לֵיהּ: אַתְּ אָמְרַתְּ לִי מֵהָתָם, וַאֲנָא אָמֵינָא לָךְ מֵהָכָא: "וַעֲבַדְתֶּם אֵת ה׳ אֱלֹהֵיכֶם וּבֵרַךְ אֶת לַחְמְךָ וְאֶת מֵימֶיךָ". "וַעֲבַדְתֶּם אֵת ה׳ אֱלֹהֵיכֶם" – זוֹ קְרִיאַת שְׁמַע וּתְפִלָּה. "וּבֵרַךְ אֶת לַחְמְךָ וְאֶת מֵימֶיךָ" – זוֹ פַּת בְּמֶלַח וְקִיתוֹן שֶׁל מַיִם. מִכָּאן וְאֵילָךְ – "וַהֲסִרֹתִי מַחֲלָה מִקִּרְבֶּךָ".

Rava **said to him: You said to me** that it is derived **from there, but I say to you** that it is derived **from here,**[N] a different verse: **"And you shall serve the Lord your God, and He will bless your bread and your water"** (Exodus 23:25), which he interprets as follows: **"And you shall serve the Lord your God," this** refers to **the recitation of** ***Shema*** and the *Amida* **prayer,** both of which constitute daily service of God. **"And He will bless your bread and your water," this** refers to **bread with salt and a large jug of water** consumed after morning prayers. **From that point onward,** the rest of the verse: **"And I will take sickness away from your midst,"** will be fulfilled.

BACKGROUND

Excrement of the nose and the ear – צוֹאַת הַחוֹטֶם וְהָאוֹזֶן: This excrement refers to mucous in the nose and to earwax. The moisture in one's nose serves to protect the sensitive membranes and ensure the proper function of the olfactory sensory neurons and to filter out dust particles inhaled through the nostrils. The increase of this natural moisture is a sign of infection, such as from the common cold or some other sickness. Similarly, the excrement of the ear is a fatty substance produced in the ear canal that helps protect the canal skin from infection. In this case as well, a large amount of discharge can indicate infection or disease and will commonly impair hearing.

NOTES

This refers to the gall bladder – זוֹ מָרָה: As the word sickness is stated in the singular, each Sage identified a different illness that he believed to be the source of many other diseases (*Hokhmat Manoaḥ*). In the Jerusalem Talmud, the following line is also added: "All sickness," this refers to worry, and some say: "All sickness," refers to the evil inclination.

Even removes jealousy – אַף מוֹצִיא אֶת הַקִּנְאָה: The Maharsha explains that one who survives merely on bread with salt and water will merit not only a healthy body. Rather, he will also be satisfied with little and not lust after money, thereby removing any jealousy or hatred from himself.

But I say to you from here – וַאֲנָא אָמֵינָא לָךְ מֵהָכָא: This proof is not from the Prophets but from the Torah.

HALAKHA

Bread in the morning – פַּת שַׁחֲרִית: It is good for one to accustom himself to eat bread in the morning (*Shulḥan Arukh, Oraḥ Ḥayyim* 155:2).

BACKGROUND

Sickness, this refers to the gall bladder – מַחֲלָה זוֹ מָרָה: Various diseases associated with digestion are caused by the gall bladder or affect its proper functioning. Nevertheless, this statement probably stems from the Greek medical theory that viewed most bodily illnesses as the result of an imbalance between the various types of bile in the gall bladder, such as white, black, green, and red.

Louse in his intestines – כִּינָּה שֶׁבִּבְנֵי מֵעַיִם: The louse referred to by the Sages does not necessarily refer to a particular type of bug, as the word is understood nowadays, but is used as a general name for small parasites. The louse referred to here is a general term for parasites that are occasionally found in human intestines, such as various types of tapeworm.

אָמַר לֵיהּ רַב יְהוּדָה לְרַב אַדָּא מְשׁוֹחָאָה: לָא תְּזַלְזֵל בְּמִשְׁחֲתָא, דְּכָל פּוּרְתָּא וּפוּרְתָּא חֲזֵי לְכוּרְכְּמָא רִישְׁקָא. אֲמַר לֵיהּ רַב יְהוּדָה לְרַב אַדָּא מְשׁוֹחָאָה: אַרְבַּע אַמּוֹת דְּאַנִּיגְרָא – זַלְזֵל בְּהוּ, דְּאַנַּהֲרָא – לָא תִּמְשְׁחִנְהוּ כְּלָל.

§ **Rav Yehuda said to Rav Adda the surveyor: Do not treat measuring lightly**[H] even for small areas of land, **as each little bit is suitable for** growing the **cultivated** [*rishka*][L] **saffron,**[B] a very expensive product. **Rav Yehuda** further **said to Rav Adda the surveyor:** With regard to the **four cubits** measured adjacent to an irrigation **channel, you may treat them lightly,**[N] and it is not necessary to provide an exact measurement of them when calculating the areas of fields. And as for the four cubits adjacent **to a river,**[H] do **not measure them at all,** but simply estimate the size and include them in the larger measurement.

רַב יְהוּדָה לְטַעְמֵיהּ, דְּאָמַר רַב יְהוּדָה: אַרְבַּע אַמּוֹת דְּאַנִּיגְרָא – לִבְנֵי אַנִּיגְרָא; דְּאַנַּהֲרָא – דְּכוּלֵּי עָלְמָא.

The Gemara comments: In this regard, **Rav Yehuda** conforms **to his** line of **reasoning, as Rav Yehuda says:** The **four cubits** adjacent **to a channel** belong **to the residents of** the houses alongside **the channel,** while the four cubits adjacent **to a river** belong **to everyone.**

מַכְרִיז רַבִּי אַמִּי: מְלֹא כַּתְפֵי נַגָּדֵי בִּתְרֵי עִבְרֵי נַהֲרָא – קוֹצוּ. רַב נָתָן בַּר הוֹשַׁעְיָא קָץ שִׁיתְסַר אַמְּתָא. אָתוּ עֲלֵיהּ בְּנֵי מַשְׁרוֹנְיָא, דְּפַנּוּהוּ. הוּא סָבַר: כִּרְשׁוּת הָרַבִּים. וְלָא הִיא, הָתָם בָּעֵינַן כּוּלֵּי הַאי. הָכָא מִשּׁוּם אַמְתּוּחֵי אַשְׁלֵיהֶן הוּא – כִּמְלֹא כַּתְפֵי נַגָּדֵי סַגִּי.

Rabbi Ami would **announce: Cut down** the trees along the width of the **full shoulders of the pullers**[B] of the boat[H] **on both sides of the river** so that the trees should not interfere with the pulling of the boats. The Gemara relates: **Rav Natan bar Hoshaya** instructed people to **cut down sixteen cubits** on each side of the river, and **the residents of Mashronya came upon him and beat him** for issuing this directive. The Gemara explains: **He holds** that any pathway must be made as wide as **like a public domain,** which is sixteen cubits wide. **But that is not so,** as **there,** in the case of a public domain, **we** do **require that much** space; **here,** however, the space **is** necessary needs to be only enough **to** enable **the stretching of the ropes** to pull the boats. Therefore, the width of the **full shoulders of the pullers is** the **sufficient** measure of space needed in order not to interfere with the pulling of the boats.

רַבָּה בַּר רַב הוּנָא הֲוָה לֵיהּ הַהוּא אָבָא אַגּוּדָּא דְּנַהֲרָא. אֲמַרוּ לֵיהּ: נִיקוֹץ מָר! אֲמַר לְהוּ: קוֹצוּ עִילָּאֵי וְתַתָּאֵי, וַהֲדַר נִיקוֹץ אֲנָא. הֵיכִי עָבֵיד הָכִי? וְהָכְתִיב: "הִתְקוֹשְׁשׁוּ וָקוֹשּׁוּ" – וְאָמַר רֵישׁ לָקִישׁ: קְשׁוֹט עַצְמְךָ וְאַחַר כָּךְ קְשׁוֹט אֲחֵרִים!

The Gemara relates another incident: **Rabba bar Rav Huna had a certain forest on the bank of a river. They said to him: Let the Master cut down** the trees on the riverbank in accordance with the above statement. Rabba bar Rav Huna **said to them:** Let **those above and below** me along the river **cut down** their trees first, **and then I will cut down** my trees. I will achieve nothing by cutting down my trees on my own. The Gemara asks: **How can he do so,** i.e., wait for others to act? **But isn't it written: "Gather yourselves together, and gather** [*hitkosheshu vakoshu*]" (Zephaniah 2:1),[N] **and Reish Lakish says** concerning this: **Adorn** [*keshot*] **yourself and afterward adorn others.** Therefore, one must first perform the required action himself before offering advice to others.

הָתָם אָבָא דְּבֵי פַּרְזָק רוּפִילָא הֲוָה, וַאֲמַר: אִי קָיְיצוּ – קָיְיצְנָא, וְאִי לָא קָיְיצוּ – אַמַּאי אֵיקוֹץ? דְּאִי מַמְתְּחֵי לְהוּ אַשְׁלַיְיהוּ – מִסְתַּגֵּי לְהוּ.

The Gemara responds: **There** it **was the forest of the house of Parzak, the general, and** it was obvious that they would pay no attention to a Jewish scholar. Rabba bar Rav Huna therefore **said:** If the workers of the Persian officer **cut down, I will cut down** as well, **and if** they do **not cut down, why should I cut down** for no purpose? **Since if** the pullers can **stretch their ropes they can go** along this side of the river,

HALAKHA

Do not treat measuring lightly – לָא תְּזַלְזֵל בְּמִשְׁחֲתָא: The measurement of land between brothers and partners must be performed in a precise manner, as even a fingerbreadth is treated as though it was filled with saffron (Rambam *Sefer Nezikin, Hilkhot Geneiva* 8:1; *Shulḥan Arukh, Ḥoshen Mishpat* 231:16).

Adjacent to a channel and adjacent to a river – דְּאַנִּיגְרָא וּדְאַנַּהֲרָא: The measurement of four cubits alongside a channel need not be performed in a precise manner, while those along a riverbank may not be measured at all, as they belong to the public (Rambam *Sefer Nezikin, Hilkhot Geneiva* 8:2; *Shulḥan Arukh, Ḥoshen Mishpat* 231:17).

Full shoulders of the pullers of the boat – מְלוֹא כַּתְפֵי נַגָּדֵי: An empty space must be left on both sides of a river that is equivalent to the width of the boat pullers. Any trees that are present in this space are immediately cut down without the need to issue a prior warning to their owners (Rambam *Sefer Nezikin, Hilkhot Nizkei Mamon* 13:26; *Shulḥan Arukh, Ḥoshen Mishpat* 417:4).

LANGUAGE

Cultivated [*rishka*] **– רִישְׁקָא:** Likely from the Middle Iranian word rēšak, which means fiber. It refers to the saffron used in the making of a hair dye.

BACKGROUND

Saffron – כּוּרְכְּמָא: Also known in Aramaic as *morika* and in Hebrew as *karkom*, saffron, or *Crocus sativus*, is a plant from the Iridaceae family that has been cultivated since ancient times. It is a perennial, bulbous plant, and its bulbs produce fresh leaves and flowers every year. These flowers have white or lilac petals that surround its crimson stigmas. It has a characteristic sweet aroma, and its flowers are used in the production of spices and perfumes as well as for concentrated yellow dye. It has also been administered as a medicine. The saffron plant is cultivated domestically, and it grows wild in many areas of Eretz Yisrael as well.

Saffron flowers with pile of crimson stigmas

Pullers – נַגָּדֵי: Boats without sails can travel easily along rivers with the current, but they require assistance to move upstream. Either oars or boat pullers, individuals who stood on the banks of a river and pulled ropes that were attached to the boat, were often employed for this purpose. Even during later periods of history, paths for these pullers were commonly found alongside rivers along which they would pull boats upstream.

Roman relief from the talmudic period depicting slaves towing a barge laden with wine barrels

NOTES

You may treat them lightly – זַלְזֵל בְּהוּ: See Rashi and *Tosafot*, who explain this as limiting the space left there. Most early commentaries, by contrast, explain this in the opposite manner: Since others are involved, the measurement must be expansive rather than limited. The four cubits alongside a river should not be measured at all, and space that is clearly larger than four cubits must be left. Some commentaries, such as the Meiri, explain that the Gemara is referring to brothers or partners who divide up their property. Since the four cubits near the irrigation channel are used by others as well, they must be measured so that neither of the pair takes more than their share. In contrast, the cubits near the river should not be measured at all, as they do not belong to either of the pair but to the public.

Gather yourselves together and gather [*hitkosheshu vakoshu*] **– הִתְקוֹשְׁשׁוּ וָקוֹשּׁוּ:** The Rashbam associates this expression with straw [*kash*]: First remove the straw from yourselves before picking it off others.

ואי לא – לא מיסתגי להו.

and if not, they will be unable to walk, but will have to cross over to the other side of the river. Therefore, no advantage exists to cutting down the trees that block part of the river.

רבה בר רב נחמן הוה קא אזיל בארבא. חזא ההוא אבא דקאי אגודא דנהרא. אמר להו: דמאן? אמרו ליה: דרבה בר רב הונא. אמר: "ויד השרים והסגנים היתה במעל הזה ראשונה". אמר להו: קוצו, קוצו!

The Gemara cites a related incident: **Rabba bar Rav Naḥman**[P] **was going on a boat** and saw **a certain forest that was located** right **on the riverbank,** as its trees had not been cut down to make room for the pullers. **He said to** those who were with him: **To whom** does this forest belong? **They said to him:** It belongs **to Rabba bar Rav Huna.**[P] Rabba bar Rav Naḥman **said:** This is reminiscent of the verse: **"And the hand of the princes and the rulers has been first in this faithlessness"** (Ezra 9:2), because a renowned scholar is acting improperly. Rabba bar Rav Naḥman **said to them: Cut down, cut down** to clear a path.

אתא רבה בר רב הונא אשכחיה דקייץ. אמר: מאן קצייה – תקוץ ענפיה. אמרי: כולהו שני דרבה בר רב הונא לא אקיים ליה זרעא לרבה בר רב נחמן.

Rabba bar Rav Huna arrived and **found that** his forest had been **cut down.** Since he was within his rights not to cut down his trees, as explained above, he grew angry and **pronounced** a curse: He **who cut down** this forest **should** have **his branches cut down.**[N] The Sages **said:** Although he was unaware of the identity of the perpetrator, the Sage's curse was nevertheless fulfilled, and consequently **all the** remaining **years that Rabba**[N] **bar Rav Huna** was alive, **the seed of Rabba bar Rav Naḥman did not last,** as his children, his branches, died in his lifetime.

אמר רב יהודה: הכל לאיגלי גפא, ואפילו מיתמי. אבל רבנן – לא. מאי טעמא? רבנן לא צריכי נטירותא. לכריא דפתיא – ואפילו מרבנן.

Rav Yehuda says: All participate in the payment **for the construction of the** city **wall, and** this sum is collected **even from orphans, but not** from **the Torah scholars.**[N] **What is the reason** for this? **The Torah scholars do not require protection,** as the merit of their Torah study protects them from harm. By contrast, money is collected **for the digging of** a river or **a well**[N] for drinking water, **even from the Torah scholars.**

ולא אמרן אלא דלא נפקא באוכלוזא, אבל לאוכלוזא – לא, דרבנן לאו בני מיפק באוכלוזא נינהו.

The Gemara adds: **And we said** this *halakha* **only if** the town inhabitants do **not go out in a crowd** to perform the work themselves but pay workers to act on their behalf. **But** if they go out **in a crowd,** Torah scholars do **not** have to join them, **as Torah scholars are not** among those **who go out in a crowd** to perform work in public view.[H]

אמר רב יהודה: לכריא דנהרא – תתאי מסייעי עילאי, עילאי לא מסייעי תתאי. וחילופא במיא דמיטרא.

Rav Yehuda says: With regard to the digging of a river, i.e., the periodic deepening of a riverbed to prevent it from blocking up, **the lower ones,** i.e., those who live by the bottom of the river, must **assist the upper ones** in digging it and fixing it, as those located at the bottom of the river stand to gain from any work performed down to their houses. But **the upper ones do not** need to **assist the lower ones,** as the reverse is not the case. **And the opposite** is true **with regard to** the digging of a ditch to remove **rainwater.** In that case, those who live higher up are interested in the operation and therefore must help the lower ones, but the latter need not aid the higher ones in doing so in the upper area.

PERSONALITIES

Rabba bar Rav Naḥman – רבה בר רב נחמן: Rabba bar Rav Naḥman was an *amora* from the third generation of Babylonian *amora'im* and a son of the great *amora* Rav Naḥman. Only a few of his statements are recorded in the Talmud, several of which are found in the Jerusalem Talmud, where he is called Abba bar Rav Naḥman. In most of these instances, he is engaged in halakhic discussions with his older colleague, Rabba bar Rav Huna.

Rabba bar Rav Huna – רבה בר רב הונא: Rabba bar Rav Huna was the son of Rav Huna, who was a leading disciple of Rav. Although Rabba bar Rav Huna studied under Rav as well, he mainly studied with his father as well as with Rav Ḥisda, of whom he was considered a disciple-colleague. He was also on close terms with Rabba bar Rav Naḥman, and delivered his harsh statement against him here only because he was unaware that his friend was the one who cut down his trees.

Rabba bar Rav Huna enjoyed a relationship with the Exilarch, and in several places the Talmud discusses his visits to the Exilarch's home. He nevertheless successfully preserved his independence, and occasionally remarked to the Exilarch: I did not receive permission to issue halakhic rulings from you, but from my father, my teacher.

He was known for his sincere humility, as he spoke of his colleagues with great respect, including those of less exalted status than he. In addition, upon the death of his father Rav Huna, he did not protest when Rav Ḥisda was appointed as the successor to his father instead of himself.

Although Rabba bar Rav Huna died in Babylonia, he was buried in Eretz Yisrael, and the poetic words of the eulogy uttered at his burial have been recorded for posterity: The shoot of an ancient line has ascended from Babylonia…He Who rides upon the clouds is happy when an innocent and righteous soul comes to Him (see *Moed Katan* 25b). He was survived by his son Rava.

NOTES

Should have his branches cut down – תקוץ ענפיה: This comparison is hinted to in the verse: "For man is a tree of the field" (Deuteronomy 20:19). Since he cut down trees, he should be punished measure for measure (*Iyyun Ya'akov*).

All the remaining years that Rabba, etc. – כולהו שני דרבה וכו׳: The Meiri infers from this account that even when it is legally permitted to cut down trees, it is improper to cut down those of a Torah scholar without his knowledge, as this might anger him. *Tosafot* indicate that Rabba bar Rav Huna was justified in not cutting down his trees that were on the riverbank. The later commentaries discuss explicitly whether Rabba bar Rav Naḥman's actions were entirely counter to *halakha* (see *Nefesh Ḥayya*).

This story is based on an idea that appears in several places in the Talmud that if a Sage feels wronged, even if he is not altogether justified, the offending party is still liable to suffer as a result.

But not from the Torah scholars – אבל רבנן לא: The Ramban maintains that with regard to this *halakha* only one who studies Torah exclusively without engaging in any other occupation is considered a Torah scholar. The commentaries discuss at length the *halakhot* concerning the exemption of Torah scholars from certain public duties (see *Shulḥan Arukh*, *Yoreh De'a* 243).

For the digging of a well – לכריא דפתיא: Some commentaries explain that this term refers to the cleaning and removal of clods of dirt and other obstacles from the streets of the city, and not to the digging of a well (*Tosafot*, *Bava Batra* 8a, citing Rabbeinu Ḥananel).

HALAKHA

The duties of town residents – חובות בני העיר: Funds needed to purchase any items required for the protection of town residents are collected from all its inhabitants, including orphans, but not from Torah scholars, as their studies protect them. Payment for repairs performed on roads, communal structures, or other items used by all are collected from everyone, including Torah scholars. If instead of hiring workers the residents go out themselves to perform the work, Torah scholars need not accompany them, nor are they obligated to hire others in their stead (Rambam *Sefer Kinyan*, *Hilkhot Shekhenim* 6:6 and *Sefer HaMadda*, *Hilkhot Talmud Torah* 6:10; *Shulḥan Arukh*, *Ḥoshen Mishpat* 163:4 and *Sma* there, *Yoreh De'a* 243:2).

תניא נמי הכי: חמש גנות המסתפקות מים ממעין אחד, ונתקלקל המעיין – כולם מתקנות עם העליונה. נמצאת התחתונה מתקנת עם כולן, ומתקנת לעצמה. וכן חמש חצרות שהיו מקלחות מים לביב אחד ונתקלקל הביב – כולן מתקנות עם התחתונה. נמצאת העליונה מתקנת עם כולן ומתקנת לעצמה.

The Gemara comments: **This is also taught** in a *baraita*: If there were **five gardens that draw** their **water** requirements **from one spring**[H] **and the spring became damaged, all** must help **fix it with** the owner of **the upper** garden, near whose garden the damage occurred. As a **result** of this ruling, the owner of **the lower** garden **fixes it with all of them** in the above case, **and fixes it for himself** if the damage occurred in the lower area. **And similarly,** if there were **five courtyards that would run off water into a single sewer**[H] **and the sewer became damaged, all** must help **fix** it **with** the owner of **the lower** courtyard, near whose courtyard the damage occurred. The **result** is that the owner of **the upper** courtyard **fixes** the sewer **with all of them and fixes it for himself** if the damage affected his courtyard alone. This is in accordance with Rav Yehuda's ruling.

אמר שמואל: האי מאן דאחזיק ברקתא דנהרא – חציפא הוי, סלוקי לא מסלקינן ליה. והאידנא דקא כתבי פרסאי קני לך עד מלי צוארי סוסיא מיא – סלוקי נמי מסלקינן ליה.

Shmuel says: One who takes possession of an open space left along **a riverbank** for the purpose of loading and unloading in order to plow and plant there during the time that it is temporarily unused **is impudent.** As for **removing** him, **we do not remove him,** as this piece of land is considered ownerless. **And nowadays, when the Persians write** to one who acquires land alongside a river: **Acquire for yourself** the field **up to** the portion of the river itself where **the water reaches a horse's neck, we even** go as far as to **remove him** from the plot of land, as it belongs to the owner of the field.

אמר רב יהודה אמר רב: האי מאן דאחזיק ביני אחי וביני שותפי – חציפא הוי, סלוקי – לא מסלקינן ליה. ורב נחמן אמר: נמי מסלקינן, ואי משום דינא דבר מצרא – לא מסלקינן ליה.

Rav Yehuda says that **Rav says: One who takes possession** of land that is located **between** the land of **brothers**[HN] **or between** the land of **partners** and causes them trouble **is impudent.** As for **removing** him, **we do not remove him,** as they have no real claim against him. **And Rav Naḥman said: We even** go as far as to **remove** him, as one should not do anything that harms another. **And if** the complaint against him is **due to the *halakha* of one** whose field **borders** the field of his neighbor,[B] as they owned fields bordering on this one, **we do not remove him.**

נהרדעי אמרי: אפילו משום דינא דבר מצרא מסלקינן ליה, משום שנאמר: "ועשית הישר והטוב בעיני ה'".

The Sages **of Neharde'a**[P] **say: Even** if his claim was **due to the *halakha* of one** whose field **borders** the field of his neighbor, **we** still **remove him,**[H] **as it is stated: "And you shall do that which is right and good**[N] **in the eyes of the Lord"** (Deuteronomy 6:18). One should not perform an action that is not right and good, even if he is legally entitled to do so.

אתא אימליך ביה, אמר ליה: איזיל איזבון? ואמר ליה: זיל זבון, צריך למיקנא מיניה או לא? רבינא אמר: לא צריך למיקנא מיניה. נהרדעי אמרי: צריך למיקנא מיניה. והלכתא: צריך למיקנא מיניה.

With the above *halakhot* in mind, the Gemara asks: If the stranger **came to consult**[H] **with** one of the owners of the fields, and **said to him:** Shall **I go** and **acquire** the field, **and** the latter **said to him, go** and **acquire** it, as I will raise no objection, is it **necessary to** perform an act of **acquisition with him** to solidify the agreement? **Or** perhaps his mere promise is sufficient and it is **not** necessary? **Ravina said:** It is **not necessary to** perform an act of **acquisition with him,** while the Sages **of Neharde'a say:** It is **necessary to** perform an act of **acquisition with him.** The Gemara concludes: **And the *halakha*** is that it is **necessary to** perform an act of **acquisition with him.**

NOTES

One who takes possession between brothers – מאן דאחזיק ביני אחי: This passage indicates that Rav Yehuda and Rav Naḥman do not accept the *halakha* of one whose field borders that of his neighbor. Such a conclusion would be surprising, as this *halakha* appears explicitly in a mishna and is unanimously accepted.

Several explanations of this discussion have been offered. Rabbeinu Tam, cited in *Tosafot*, and the Ramban maintain that the Gemara here is not speaking of one who acquired land, as in that case the *halakha* of a neighboring field would certainly apply. Rather, it refers to one who took possession of an ownerless field. Since he pays the land tax to the authorities, he is considered its owner. Therefore, one may have thought that taking ownership in this manner is akin to receiving a gift, and therefore the rights of the person whose field borders that of his neighbor do not take effect.

Rav Hai Gaon offers an entirely different interpretation of this passage. He claims that the Gemara is referring to brothers or several partners who are preparing to divide a single estate, and this buyer acquired the field from one of them. Since it is unclear prior to the division which of the brothers or partners will be his bordering neighbor, he can say that he is under no obligation to remove himself from the property.

And you shall do that which is right and good – ועשית הישר והטוב: This is a general directive of the Torah that one should act in the interest of others even when he is not obligated to do so according to the strict letter of the law. The case of one whose field borders that of his neighbor is an example of this type of *halakha*, because he will find it easier to work two contiguous plots. To this end, the Sages established several enactments that grant the neighbor certain quasi-monetary rights to the sale of any land that runs alongside his property. The disputes between the Sages concern only the specific application of these rights, and in which circumstances they may be waived.

HALAKHA

Gardens that draw water from one spring – גנות המסתפקות מים ממעין אחד: If five gardens receive their water from a single spring that became damaged, every garden owner must assist the owner of the upper garden, as each garden must help all those that are above it, but not the opposite, as stated in the *baraita* (Rambam *Sefer Kinyan, Hilkhot Shekhenim* 3:9; *Shulḥan Arukh, Ḥoshen Mishpat* 170:1).

Five courtyards…into a single sewer – חמש חצרות...לביב אחד: If the water of five courtyards runs into a single sewer, every courtyard owner must assist all the owners of the courtyards below his to fix them, but the owner of a lower one does not have to provide the owners of the courtyards above his with assistance, as stated in the *baraita* (Rambam *Sefer Kinyan, Hilkhot Shekhenim* 3:9; *Shulḥan Arukh, Ḥoshen Mishpat* 161:6; 170:1).

One who takes possession between brothers – מאן דאחזיק ביני אחי: If one of the brothers or partners sold his share to a stranger, the remaining brothers or partners may remove the buyer from the land. Some say that they may do so even if the buyer was a bordering neighbor, and the Rema rules accordingly. This is the Rambam's explanation of the Gemara, and although other interpretations of the passage have been suggested, everyone accepts the Rambam's ruling (Rambam *Sefer Kinyan, Hilkhot Shekhenim* 12:4 and *Maggid Mishne* there; *Shulḥan Arukh, Ḥoshen Mishpat* 175:5).

Due to the *halakha* of one whose field borders, we remove him – משום דינא דבר מצרא מסלקינן ליה: With regard to one who sells land to another, whether he did so himself, by means of an agent, or through the court, the owner of the adjacent field has the right to pay the buyer and remove him. This is the *halakha* even if the buyer is a Torah scholar and a close neighbor of the seller's, and the owner of the bordering field is an uneducated person who lives far away (Rambam *Sefer Kinyan, Hilkhot Shekhenim* 12:5; *Shulḥan Arukh, Ḥoshen Mishpat* 175:6).

If the buyer consulted with the bordering neighbor – נמלך הקונה במיצרן: If the potential buyer consulted with the neighbor concerning whether to buy the field and the latter told him to purchase it, the neighbor may still remove him afterward, unless the neighbor performed an act of acquisition relinquishing his rights. According to some authorities, if he relinquished his rights in the presence of witnesses, this is considered like an act of acquisition (Rambam *Sefer Kinyan, Hilkhot Shekhenim* 14:1; *Shulḥan Arukh, Ḥoshen Mishpat* 175:29).

BACKGROUND

The *halakha* of one whose field borders the field of his neighbor – דינא דבר מצרא: When someone wants to sell his field, the owner of a bordering field has the first right of purchase and can compel the seller to allow him to purchase it. This *halakha* is based on the command: "You shall do that which is right and good" (Deuteronomy 6:18).

It makes no difference to the seller who purchases his field, whereas the neighbor has a legitimate reason to want this particular field because it is easier to work and guard two contiguous plots and it would be unfair not to allow the one who would benefit the most to purchase it.

This *halakha* applies only to a sale, as in the case of a gift the owner may have specific reasons for preferring the other person.

PERSONALITIES

Sages of Neharde'a – נהרדעי: In *Sanhedrin* (17b), this anonymous term of attribution is identified as Rav Ḥama, and that is presumably the Gemara's intention here as well. Rav Ḥama was a fourth-generation *amora* in Babylonia, although it seems that he lived a long life, as he occasionally has discussions with sages of previous generations. Since he was the head of the yeshiva in Neharde'a for over twenty years, some *halakhot* of his authorship are cited as the opinion of the Sages of Neharde'a, without further identification.

הָשְׁתָּא דְּאָמְרַתְּ צָרִיךְ לְמִיקְנָא מִינֵּיהּ, אִי לָא קָנוּ מִינֵּיהּ – אִיַּיקּוּר וְזוּל בִּרְשׁוּתֵיהּ.

The Gemara adds: **Now that you have said** that it is **necessary to** perform an act of **acquisition with** the neighbor for the right to purchase the field, **if he did not** perform an act of **acquisition with him** and purchased the field, and the field **increased or decreased** in value,[H] the price fluctuation occurs **in the domain of** the owner of the bordering field. The buyer's purchase is considered a purchase on behalf of the neighbor, who then reimburses the buyer.

זַבֵּן בְּמֵאָה וְשָׁוֵי מָאתָן; חָזֵינָא, אִי לְכוּלֵּי עָלְמָא קָא מוֹזִילָא וּמְזַבֵּין – יָהֵיב לֵיהּ מְאָה וְשָׁקֵיל לֵיהּ; וְאִי לָא – יָהֵיב לֵיהּ מָאתָן וְשָׁקֵיל לֵיהּ.

Accordingly, if this buyer **bought** it **for one hundred** dinars **and** the field **was worth two hundred**[H] dinars, in order to determine how much money the neighbor must give him, **we determine** why the owner sold the field to the buyer at this price: **If he sells to everyone** at that **cheap** price,[N] the neighbor **gives** the buyer **one hundred** dinars **and takes it,** as the neighbor could have bought it for this sum himself. **But if** the owner does **not** sell to everyone at this price and this buyer was given a discount, the neighbor **gives** the buyer **two hundred** dinars, the market value of the field, **and takes it.**

זַבֵּן בְּמָאתָן וְשַׁוְיָא מְאָה, סְבוּר מִינָּהּ: מָצֵי אָמַר לֵיהּ לְתַקּוּנֵי שְׁדַרְתִּיךְ וְלָא לְעַוּוֹתֵי. אֲמַר לֵיהּ מָר קַשִּׁישָׁא בְּרֵיהּ דְּרַב חִסְדָּא לְרַב אַשִׁי: הָכִי אָמְרִי נְהַרְדְּעֵי מִשּׁוּם דְּרַב נַחְמָן: אֵין אוֹנָאָה לְקַרְקָעוֹת.

In the converse case, if **he bought** it **for two hundred** dinars **and** the field was **worth one hundred**[H] dinars, the Sages **understood** that the neighbor **can say to the** buyer: **I sent you** to act **for my benefit, but not** to act **to my detriment.** Since the field will not remain in your possession, you are effectively my agent, and I am not prepared to pay more than its market value due to your mistake. **Mar the Elder, son of Rav Ḥisda, said to Rav Ashi: This** is what the Sages **of Neharde'a say in the name of Rav Naḥman: There is no exploitation with regard to real estate,**[N] as land has no fixed value, and therefore it cannot be said that the buyer overpaid, and he is given whatever sum he spent.

זַבֵּין לֵיהּ גְּרִיוָא דְּאַרְעָא בְּמִיצְעָא נִכְסֵיהּ, חָזֵינַן: אִי עִידִּית הִיא אִי זִיבּוּרִית הִיא – זְבִינֵיהּ זְבִינֵי,

The Gemara discusses a related case: If one **sold to** another **a *beit se'a* of land**[N] **in the middle of his property**[H] so that the buyer is surrounded on all sides by the seller's fields, **we see** what type of land it is: **Whether** the land **is superior-quality** land **or whether** it **is inferior-quality** land, **his sale** is a valid **sale,** as it is a distinctive piece of land. In that case, the seller's neighbors cannot object, as their fields do not actually border on this plot.

NOTES

If he sells to everyone at that cheap price, etc. – אִי לְכוּלֵּי עָלְמָא קָא מוֹזִילָא וּמְזַבֵּין וכו׳: The Rosh asks: If the buyer received the field at a discount that was offered only to him, it would appear to be considered similar to a gift from the seller, and the *halakha* of a bordering neighbor does not apply to gifts. He answers that since there was nevertheless a purchase, the Sages did not differentiate in this regard.

There is no exploitation with regard to real estate – אֵין אוֹנָאָה לְקַרְקָעוֹת: This issue is discussed by many early commentaries: Is there indeed no exploitation with regard to land at all, or does at least the option of nullifying the transaction apply if the paid sum was far greater than the market price? The Rosh claims that the *halakha* here was stated only with regard to this particular case, where the buyer was not the actual agent of the neighbor. Consequently, the principle of: I sent you to act for my benefit, but not to act to my detriment, does not apply to him. Therefore, if the bordering neighbor wants the land for himself, he is obligated to pay for the buyer's error.

Sold to another a *beit se'a* of land – זַבֵּין לֵיהּ גְּרִיוָא דְּאַרְעָא: Rashi explains that the question is whether the rights of a bordering neighbor apply even to a plot of land in the middle of a field, which does not border the fields of others at all. Conversely, Rabbeinu Ḥananel, followed by most early commentaries, maintains that the discussion does not refer to the sold plot of land but rather to a case where the owner of the plot of land that is surrounded by land owned by someone else decides he wants to purchase an additional plot of land that is adjacent to both the first plot he purchased and the plot of the neighbor of the seller (see Rosh and *Sma*). The question is whether the initial purchase is viewed as a means of circumventing the rights of the bordering neighbor. Consequently, if the plot of land sold first possesses distinct qualities, the sale is valid, but if not, it is considered an artifice.

HALAKHA

If the buyer acquired alongside the bordering neighbor not at the market price – קָנָה הַלּוֹקֵחַ בְּצַד מֵיצַר שֶׁלֹּא בִּמְחִיר הַשּׁוּק: If one purchases a field that borders the field of another, he has the status of an agent of the latter in all regards. Accordingly, the witnesses to the sale may write a bill of sale listing the neighbor of the seller as the purchaser. If the land went up in value, the buyer must give it to the neighbor in exchange for the actual, lower, sum that he had paid, while if its value decreased, the neighbor, if he wants the field, must pay the buyer the higher amount, for which he purchased the field (Rambam *Sefer Kinyan, Hilkhot Shekhenim* 14:4; *Shulḥan Arukh, Ḥoshen Mishpat* 175:6).

If he bought it for one hundred and it was worth two hundred – זַבֵּן בְּמֵאָה וְשָׁוֵי מָאתָן: If the buyer bought the field for one hundred dinars when it was actually worth two hundred dinars, and this was the price offered to everyone, the bordering neighbor also pays one hundred dinars to the buyer in exchange for the field. If the buyer received the field at this price as a result of a discount offered specifically to him, the neighbor must pay its full value. If the neighbor contends that he too could have acquired it at the lower price, he must provide proof of this claim (Rambam *Sefer Kinyan, Hilkhot Shekhenim* 14:4; *Shulḥan Arukh, Ḥoshen Mishpat* 175:7).

If he bought it for two hundred and it was worth one hundred – זַבֵּן בְּמָאתָן וְשַׁוְיָא מְאָה: If the buyer bought the field for two hundred dinars when it was worth only one hundred dinars, a bordering neighbor who wishes to remove him must pay him two hundred dinars. In a case where the bordering neighbor claims the seller and the buyer colluded to extract the additional one hundred dinars from him, if there were witnesses to the payment he must pay the full two hundred dinars, although he can force the buyer to take an oath that he had paid two hundred dinars. If there were no witnesses, the buyer must take an oath while holding a sacred object that this was the sum he paid, and he collects two hundred dinars (*Shulḥan Arukh, Ḥoshen Mishpat* 175:9).

If a buyer purchased a plot of land in the middle of the seller's field – קָנָה בְּאֶמְצַע שָׂדֶה: If one purchased a plot of land in the middle of another's field and subsequently sought to buy another piece of land alongside the first one which was also adjacent to the property of a neighbor, if the first plot was of a distinct quality, i.e., either the highest or the lowest grade, the neighbor does not have the right of first purchase. If it was not of a distinct quality, this is viewed as an artifice and the bordering neighbor has the right of first purchase. Similarly, in any case where there is evidence of collusion, the court can intervene (Rambam *Sefer Kinyan, Hilkhot Shekhenim* 13:5; *Shulḥan Arukh, Ḥoshen Mishpat* 175:28).

וְאִי לָא – אִיעֲרוּמֵי קָא מַעֲרִים.

But if this field is **not** of any distinct quality, he is certainly trying to **employ an artifice.** His plan is to then purchase another plot of land from this owner, one that does border on the field of a neighbor. By first buying the plot in the middle, he is trying to establish himself as a neighbor so that the other neighbors will not have the first right of purchase relative to him. Therefore, the neighbors may prevent him from buying the second plot of land.

מַתָּנָה לֵית בָּהּ מִשּׁוּם דִּינָא דְּבַר מִצְרָא. אֲמַר אַמֵימָר: אִי כְּתַב לֵיהּ אַחֲרָיוּת – אִית בָּהּ מִשּׁוּם דִּינָא דְּבַר מִצְרָא.

The Gemara continues to discuss the *halakha* of one whose field borders that of his neighbor. With regard to **a gift, it is not subject to the *halakha* of one** whose field **borders** the field of his neighbor, as one can give a gift to whomever he chooses. **Ameimar said: If he wrote** a property **guarantee to** the recipient of the gift that if the field is seized for payment of a debt of the giver the giver of the gift will compensate the recipient for his loss, **it is subject to the *halakha* of one** whose field **borders** of the field of his neighbor.[H] In that case the supposed gift has the appearance of a sale, so the neighbor can force the recipient to sell the plot to him.

מָכַר כׇּל נְכָסָיו לְאֶחָד – לֵית בָּהּ מִשּׁוּם דִּינָא דְּבַר מִצְרָא. לַבְּעָלִים הָרִאשׁוֹנִים – לֵית בָּהּ מִשּׁוּם דִּינָא דְּבַר מִצְרָא. זָבַן מִנׇּכְרִי וְזַבֵּין לְנׇכְרִי – לֵית בָּהּ מִשּׁוּם דִּינָא דְּבַר מִצְרָא.

If a seller **sold all his property to a single** person,[HN] **this sale is not subject to the *halakha* of one** whose field **borders** the field of his neighbor, as the seller is not required to leave out one particular field if the buyer is acquiring all his property. Similarly, if the seller sold it back **to the previous owners,**[H] **this sale is not subject to the *halakha* of one** whose field **borders** the field of his neighbor. If a buyer **bought** a field **from a gentile**[H] **or** a seller **sold** a field **to a gentile, this** purchase or sale **is not subject to the *halakha* of one** whose field **borders** the field of his neighbor.

זָבַן מִנׇּכְרִי – דְּאָמַר לֵיהּ: אַרְיָא אַבְרַחִי לָךְ מִמִּצְרָא. זַבֵּין לְנׇכְרִי – נׇכְרִי וַדַּאי לָאו בַּר ״וְעָשִׂיתָ הַיָּשָׁר וְהַטּוֹב״ הוּא. שַׁמּוֹתֵי וַדַּאי מְשַׁמְּתִינַן לֵיהּ, עַד דִּמְקַבֵּל עֲלֵיהּ כׇּל אוֹנְסֵי דְּאָתֵי לֵיהּ מֵחֲמָתֵיהּ.

The Gemara clarifies this ruling: If a buyer **bought** the field **from a gentile** it does not apply, **as he** can **say to** the neighbor: It is better for you that I bought the field, as **I have chased away a lion**[N] **for you from the border;** since the neighbor certainly prefers having a Jewish neighbor to having a gentile neighbor. If a seller **sold** a field **to a gentile,**[H] the **gentile is certainly not bound** by the command of: **"And you shall do that which is right and good in the eyes of the Lord"** (Deuteronomy 6:18). The gentile is therefore under no obligation to refrain from purchasing this land. Nevertheless, **we certainly excommunicate**[B] the one who sold it to the gentile **until he accepts upon himself** responsibility for **all** damage resulting from **accidents**[N] **that** might **befall** the neighbor **on** the gentile's **account.**

NOTES

If he sold all his property to a single person – מָכַר כׇּל נְכָסָיו לְאֶחָד: Some commentaries explain that one does not want to deal with the documents of many people and would prefer to sell all the land to a single person (Rabbi Meir HaKohen). Alternatively, one would sell all of his property only if he was in urgent need of a significant sum of money, and therefore the *halakha* of the bordering neighbor is overlooked.

I have chased away a lion – אַרְיָא אַבְרַחִי: The Rosh asks: Even if it is accepted that he performed a commendable action by chasing away this lion, why should this exempt the buyer from his obligation of: "And you shall do that which is right and good in the eyes of the Lord," and subsequently selling the land to the bordering neighbor? Apparently this obligation applies only to the seller, and since this *halakha* was not in effect at the time the buyer purchased the field, it does not go into effect at a later stage (see *Shita Mekubbetzet* and *Beit Aharon*).

Until he accepts upon himself all accidents – עַד דִּמְקַבֵּל עֲלֵיהּ כׇּל אוֹנְסֵי: According to the Rosh this procedure is performed for the neighbor's benefit, so that he should not have to waste his time in litigation at a later stage. The Ra'avad and the Ramban maintain that if the seller did not accept this obligation upon himself beforehand and a misfortune occurred due to the gentile, the seller is considered only an indirect cause of the damage and is therefore exempt.

HALAKHA

A gift with regard to the *halakha* of one whose field borders the field of his neighbor – מַתָּנָה לְעִנְיַן בַּר מִיצְרָא: The *halakha* of one whose field borders the field of his neighbor does not apply to a gift. If the deed of gift specified that the giver guarantees that he will compensate the recipient in the event that the field is seized by the giver's creditor, the *halakha* does apply, as this is considered like a sale. In that case, the neighbor may force the recipient to leave by paying him the value of the field (Rambam *Sefer Kinyan, Hilkhot Shekhenim* 13:1; *Shulḥan Arukh, Ḥoshen Mishpat* 175:18, 24).

If he sold all his property to a single person – מָכַר כׇּל נְכָסָיו לְאֶחָד: If the owner of a field sold all his property to a single person, a bordering neighbor cannot remove the buyer from the field adjacent to his, even if he too was willing to buy all the seller's fields (Rambam *Sefer Kinyan, Hilkhot Shekhenim* 12:6; *Shulḥan Arukh, Ḥoshen Mishpat* 175:36).

If he sold it to the previous owners – מְכָרָהּ לַבְּעָלִים הָרִאשׁוֹנִים: If one sold a field to the one from whom he purchased it, the one whose field borders it may not remove him. The same *halakha* applies if he sold it to the previous owner's son, although some disagree with regard to this case. Nevertheless, if the bordering neighbor and the previous owner approached him simultaneously, the bordering neighbor receives precedence over the previous owner (Rambam *Sefer Kinyan, Hilkhot Shekhenim* 12:6, and in the comment of Rema; *Shulḥan Arukh, Ḥoshen Mishpat* 175:37).

If he bought it from a gentile – זָבַן מִנׇּכְרִי: A bordering neighbor may not remove a buyer who acquired the field from a gentile (Rambam *Sefer Kinyan, Hilkhot Shekhenim* 12:6; *Shulḥan Arukh, Ḥoshen Mishpat* 175:38).

One who sold to a gentile – הַמּוֹכֵר לְנׇכְרִי: If one sold his field to a gentile the *halakha* of a bordering neighbor does not apply, since the gentile is not obligated to abide by the command of: "And you shall do what is right and good." In such a case, the seller is excommunicated until he accepts responsibility upon himself for any damage that may result due to the gentile. Therefore, if this gentile neighbor caused any damage that a Jew would be liable for under Jewish law, the seller must compensate him. If this incident occurred in the seller's lifetime and he subsequently passed away, his son is compelled to pay from his father's estate for any damage that occurred until the time of the father's death. Some authorities maintain that if the court failed to place the seller under a ban, he cannot subsequently be forced to pay for any accident that occurs due to the gentile (Rambam *Sefer Kinyan, Hilkhot Shekhenim* 12:6–7; *Shulḥan Arukh, Ḥoshen Mishpat* 175:39–40, and in the comment of Rema).

BACKGROUND

We certainly excommunicate – שַׁמּוֹתֵי וַדַּאי מְשַׁמְּתִינַן: There are several degrees of excommunication the community or a rabbinic leader can impose on an individual who acts sinfully or inappropriately. The partial or complete expulsion of someone from the Jewish people is a punishment or a means of exerting pressure upon him to alter his conduct. One who is completely excommunicated is no longer considered a member of the community. He is neither included in a prayer quorum nor in any other religious activities. It is prohibited to stand within four cubits of him or to have commercial dealings with him.

NOTES

The mortgage [*mashkanta*] resides [*shekhuna*] with him – מַשְׁכַּנְתָּא דִּשְׁכוּנָה גַּבֵּיהּ: The early commentaries disagree as to whether the one to whom the field is mortgaged is considered fully in possession of the land to the extent that he even has the first right of purchase over the bordering neighbor. Some say the neighbor does not have the first right of purchase relative to the one to whom the field is mortgaged, but the latter has the first right of purchase relative to the neighbor. Others explain that the idea of: It resides with him, is that the bordering neighbors cannot force the owner of the field to mortgage his field to one of them (Ra'avad).

Partners – שׁוּתָּפֵי: Some commentaries maintain that these partners must be bordering neighbors, but the consensus among the commentaries is that the same *halakha* applies even if they were not bordering neighbors at all (Rabbeinu Tam; Ramban). The *ge'onim* likewise state that partners to a deal take precedence over others. Another reason for this *halakha* is that partners rely on each other (*Torat Ḥayyim*). According to the Meiri, this refers to partners of a field that had not yet been parceled out, and therefore they are not considered bordering neighbors.

מַשְׁכַּנְתָּא לֵית בָּהּ מִשּׁוּם דִּינָא דְּבַר מִצְרָא, דַּאֲמַר רַב אַשִׁי: אֲמַרוּ לִי סָבֵי דְּמָתָא מְחַסְיָא: מַאי מַשְׁכַּנְתָּא? דִּשְׁכוּנָה גַּבֵּיהּ. מַאי נָפְקָא מִינָּהּ? לְדִינָא דְּבַר מִצְרָא.

The Gemara continues: If he sold a field previously given as a **mortgage** to the one to whom it was mortgaged, **this sale is not subject to the *halakha* of one** whose field **borders** the field of his neighbor,[H] **as Rav Ashi said: The elders of** the town of **Mata Meḥasya said to me: What** is the meaning of the word **mortgage** [***mashkanta***]? It means **that it resides** [***shekhuna***] **with** the one to whom it was mortgaged.[N] The Gemara asks: **What difference does it make** what the word means? The Gemara answers: It is relevant **with regard to the *halakha* of one** whose field **borders** the field of his neighbor in that the person to whom the field is mortgaged has more rights than bordering neighbors, as he lays claim to a measure of ownership over the land.

לְמִכּוֹר בְּרָחוֹק וְלִגְאוֹל בְּקָרוֹב, בְּרַע וְלִגְאוֹל בְּיָפָה – לֵית בָּהּ מִשּׁוּם דִּינָא דְּבַר מִצְרָא.

If one sought **to sell a distant** field **and to redeem,** i.e., purchase for himself, **a close** one, or if he sold **a bad** one **to redeem a good** one,[H] **this** sale **is not subject to the *halakha* of one** whose field **borders** the field of his neighbor. Rather, he may sell his field whenever he has the opportunity.

לְכַרְגָּא וְלִמְזוֹנֵי וְלִקְבוּרָה – לֵית בָּהּ מִשּׁוּם דִּינָא דְּבַר מִצְרָא. דְּאָמְרִי נְהַרְדְּעָא: לְכַרְגָּא, לִמְזוֹנֵי וְלִקְבוּרָה מְזַבְּנִינַן בְּלָא אַכְרְזְתָּא. לְאִשָּׁה וְלִיתְמֵי וּלְשׁוּתָּפֵי – לֵית בָּהּ מִשּׁוּם דִּינָא דְּבַר מִצְרָא.

Likewise, if he sells his field to pay for necessities, such as **for taxes, for** his wife and daughters' **sustenance, or for** the **burial**[H] of one of his family members, **this** sale **is not subject to the *halakha* of one** whose field **borders** the field of his neighbor. This is **because** the Sages of **Neharde'a said: For taxes, for sustenance, and for burial we sell** a field **without a proclamation,**[H] as such matters are pressing and urgent and should not be delayed out of consideration for the rights of a bordering neighbor. Similarly, if he sold the field **to a woman,** who does not usually chase after vendors, **or to orphans, or to his partners,**[NH] **this** sale **is not subject to the *halakha* of one** whose field **borders**[H] the field of his neighbor.

HALAKHA

A mortgage and the *halakha* of one whose field borders the field of his neighbor – מַשְׁכַּנְתָּא וְדִין בַּר מִצְרָא: If one mortgaged his field and subsequently sold it to the one to whom the field had been mortgaged, the bordering neighbor cannot force the buyer to leave. If, however, the field was sold to someone else, the one to whom the field had been mortgaged cannot claim the right of the bordering neighbor. Others disagree and hold that the one to whom the field had been mortgaged can claim the right of the bordering neighbor (Rambam *Sefer Kinyan, Hilkhot Shekhenim* 12:9; *Shulḥan Arukh, Ḥoshen Mishpat* 175:57, and in the comment of Rema).

To redeem a close one…to redeem a good one – לִגְאוֹל בְּקָרוֹב...לִגְאוֹל בְּיָפָה: With regard to one who sells a bad field to purchase a good one or who sells a distant one to buy a closer one, since he is interested in this particular transaction he need not wait to sell to the bordering neighbor (Rambam *Sefer Kinyan, Hilkhot Shekhenim* 12:9; *Shulḥan Arukh, Ḥoshen Mishpat* 175:42).

For taxes, for sustenance, or for burial – לְכַרְגָּא לִמְזוֹנֵי וְלִקְבוּרָה: If one sells a field to obtain money to pay his taxes to the government, to bury a relative, or to provide sustenance for his wife and daughters, the *halakha* of a bordering neighbor does not apply. The Rema maintains that this *halakha* includes one who had to buy food for himself as well. This *halakha* also applies to one who borrowed money for one of these purposes and paid back the debt with his land (Rambam *Sefer Kinyan, Hilkhot Shekhenim* 12:9; *Shulḥan Arukh, Ḥoshen Mishpat* 175:43).

We sell without a proclamation – מְזַבְּנִינַן בְּלָא אַכְרְזְתָּא: A proclamation is issued even before selling a field belonging to orphans in order to obtain a better price. If it is sold to pay for a tax debt, pay for a burial, or to provide sustenance for a wife and daughters, no proclamation is required (Rambam *Sefer Nashim, Hilkhot Ishut* 12:16, 18:20, and *Sefer Mishpatim, Hilkhot Malve VeLoveh* 12:11; *Shulḥan Arukh, Ḥoshen Mishpat* 109:3 and *Even HaEzer* 70:5, 93:25).

The *halakha* of a bordering neighbor does not apply to a partner – שֻׁתָּף אֵין בּוֹ דִּין מִיצְרָנוּת: If one sells his field to his business partner he takes precedence over the bordering neighbor, even if he is not his partner with regard to land. Some say that if a buyer is in desperate need of the land while the neighbor merely wants it to improve his comfortable estate, the *halakha* of one whose field borders the field of his neighbor does not apply (Ba'al HaMaor; *Tosafot*). Others, such as the Ramban, dispute this claim (Rambam *Sefer Kinyan, Hilkhot Shekhenim* 12:5; *Shulḥan Arukh, Ḥoshen Mishpat* 175:49).

If he sold to a woman or to orphans…this sale is not subject to the *halakha* of one whose field borders – לְאִשָּׁה וְלִיתְמֵי...לֵית בָּהּ מִשּׁוּם דִּינָא דְּבַר מִצְרָא: If one sold his field to minor orphans or to a woman, the *halakha* of a bordering neighbor does not apply. According to the Rema, this exception does not apply either to adult orphans or to minors who are not orphans. In addition, it applies only to a woman who is unmarried or who owns property that she administers (Rema, citing *Nimmukei Yosef*). The same exception for women applies as well to a *tumtum* and a hermaphrodite, as they are possibly considered women. Furthermore, some authorities maintain that the *halakha* of a bordering neighbor also does not apply to a man who purchases a field from a woman (Rambam *Sefer Kinyan, Hilkhot Shekhenim* 12:13–14; *Shulḥan Arukh, Ḥoshen Mishpat* 175:47).

שְׁכֵינֵי הָעִיר וּשְׁכֵינֵי שָׂדֶה – שְׁכֵינֵי הָעִיר קוֹדְמִין.

If various individuals have equal rights to the field, such as both are bordering neighbors, but some of them are **neighbors** whose fields are adjacent to his on the side **of the city,** i.e., their fields are between the city and the field being sold; **and** others are **neighbors** whose fields are adjacent to his on the side **of the field,** i.e., their fields are between the field being sold and the area further from the city, the **neighbors** whose fields are adjacent to his on the side **of the city** receive **precedence.**

שָׁכֵן וְתַלְמִיד חָכָם – תַּלְמִיד חָכָם קוֹדֵם. קָרוֹב וְתַלְמִיד חָכָם – תַּלְמִיד חָכָם קוֹדֵם. אִיבַּעְיָא לְהוּ: שָׁכֵן וְקָרוֹב מַאי? תָּא שְׁמַע: ״טוֹב שָׁכֵן קָרוֹב מֵאָח רָחוֹק״.

If one is a regular **neighbor and** the other is **a Torah scholar,**[N] **the Torah scholar** receives **precedence.** If one is **a relative and** the other is **a Torah scholar,** here too, **the Torah scholar** receives **precedence. A dilemma was raised before** the Sages: With regard to **a neighbor and a relative,**[H] **what** is the *halakha*? Which of them takes precedence? The Gemara suggests: **Come** and **hear** an answer from the following verse: **"Better a neighbor who is near than a brother who is far"** (Proverbs 27:10).

הָנֵי זוּזֵי טָבֵי וְהָנֵי זוּזֵי תְּקוּלֵי – לֵית בֵּיהּ מִשּׁוּם דִּינָא דְּבַר מִצְרָא. הָנֵי צַיְירֵי וְהָנֵי שְׁרֵי – לֵית בֵּיהּ מִשּׁוּם דִּינָא דְּבַר מִצְרָא.

If two people sought to acquire a field, and **these** coins that the first produces for payment are **good dinars, and those** coins that the second uses are **weighed**[N] **dinars,** which are preferable to the good dinars, **this** sale **is not subject to the *halakha* of** one whose field **borders** the field of his neighbor, as the owner can say he prefers the superior quality coins. If **these** coins were **wrapped up and those** were **loose,**[NH] **this** sale **is not subject to the *halakha* of** one whose field **borders** on the field his neighbor, as he may sell his field to the one whose money is ready to be counted.

אֲמַר: אֵיזִיל וְאֶטְרַח וְאַיְיתֵי זוּזֵי – לָא נָטְרִינַן לֵיהּ. אֲמַר: אֵיזִיל אַיְיתֵי זוּזֵי, חָזֵינַן; אִי גַּבְרָא דַּאֲמִיד הוּא, דְּאָזֵיל וּמַיְיתֵי זוּזֵי – נָטְרִינַן לֵיהּ. וְאִי לָא – לָא נָטְרִינַן לֵיהּ.

If the neighbor **said: I will go and expend effort**[H] **and bring money, we do not wait for him,** despite his status as a bordering neighbor, if someone else is available who is prepared to pay immediately. If **he said: I will go bring money, we see** what his financial status is: **If he is a person who is assessed** as one **who can go and bring money** without delay, **we wait for him, but if not, we do not wait for him.**

NOTES

A neighbor and a Torah scholar, etc. – שָׁכֵן וְתַלְמִיד חָכָם וכו׳: According to some commentaries this means that they are both bordering neighbors and the question is which of them receives precedence (*Tosafot*). Others maintain that this inquiry does not concern the *halakha* of a bordering neighbor at all, but rather the question is who gets precedence when there is no such neighbor (Rashi).

Good and weighed – טָבֵי וּתְקוּלֵי: The Ra'avad explains that good coins are ones that are used easily as currency, whereas weighed coins weigh the proper amount but are not used easily as currency.

Wrapped up and…loose – צַיְירֵי וּ...שְׁרֵי: The Rosh maintains that neither of these types is invariably preferable to the other, as one sometimes wants wrapped-up money while at other times he prefers loose coins. According to the Rashba this refers to coins that were bound together as a type of deposit, which the recipient may not spend until the owner of the deposit comes and agrees to that particular usage (see Ra'avad).

HALAKHA

A neighbor, a Torah scholar, a relative – שָׁכֵן, תַּלְמִיד חָכָם, קָרוֹב: If two people want to buy a field and neither is a bordering neighbor, but one is a neighbor from the city while the other is a neighbor from the field, the former takes precedence. A Torah scholar takes precedence over both a neighbor and a family relative. If a neighbor and a relative both wish to purchase, the neighbor takes precedence. Rabbeinu Yeruḥam maintains that only a neighbor who is also a friend is included in this *halakha*, but some commentaries disagree (Rambam *Sefer Kinyan, Hilkhot Shekhenim* 14:5; *Shulḥan Arukh, Hoshen Mishpat* 175:50).

Good and weighed; wrapped up and loose – טָבֵי וּתְקוּלֵי, צַיְירֵי וּשְׁרֵי: If the bordering neighbor and the other buyer both brought money to purchase the field and the coins of the latter were superior to those of the neighbor or can be used more easily as currency, the *halakha* of the bordering neighbor does not apply. The *halakha* is the same if these coins were wrapped up while the others were loose. Moreover, the Rema adds that in any case that involves a loss to the seller, he need not relinquish his rights due to the bordering neighbor (Rambam *Sefer Kinyan, Hilkhot Shekhenim* 14:1; *Shulḥan Arukh, Ḥoshen Mishpat* 175:53).

I will go and expend effort, etc. – אֵיזִיל וְאֶטְרַח וכו׳: If the bordering neighbor said to the seller: Wait for me while I expend effort in finding money to pay, the seller is not obligated to wait for him and he has forfeited his rights. In a case where he simply said: I will go and get the money, if he is assessed as one who can do so without delay then they wait for him to bring the money, but if not, the seller need not wait. Some say that if the bordering neighbor was unaware of the sale but when he found out he expressed a desire to buy the field, they wait for him to bring the money (Rambam *Sefer Kinyan, Hilkhot Shekhenim* 14:1; *Shulḥan Arukh, Ḥoshen Mishpat* 175:25).

אַרְעָא דְּחַד וּבָתֵּי דְּחַד – מָרֵי אַרְעָא מְעַכֵּב אַמָּרֵי בָתֵּי, מָרֵי בָתֵּי לָא מְעַכֵּב אַמָּרֵי דְּאַרְעָא. אַרְעָא דְּחַד וְדִיקְלֵי דְּחַד – מָרֵי דְּאַרְעָא מָצֵי מְעַכֵּב אַמָּרֵי דִּקְלֵי, מָרֵי דִּיקְלֵי לָא מָצֵי מְעַכֵּב אַמָּרֵי דְּאַרְעָא.

If the **land** belonged **to one** person **and the houses** on the land belonged **to another one,**[H] **the owner of the land prevents the owner of the houses** from selling his houses to someone else, as he has the first right of purchase. By contrast, **the owner of the houses does not prevent the owner of the land** from selling his land, as one can change his place of residence with relative ease, so he is not considered tied to the land. Similarly, if the **land** belonged **to one and** its **palm trees to** another **one, the owner of the land can prevent the owner of the palm trees** from selling the trees to another, but **the owner of the palm trees cannot prevent the owner of the land** from selling his land to another.

אַרְעָא לְבָתֵּי וְאַרְעָא לְזַרְעָא – יִשּׁוּב עָדִיף, וְלֵית בָּהּ מִשּׁוּם דִּינָא דְּבַר מִצְרָא.

If two people wanted to purchase the land, but one desired the **land** for building **houses**[N] **and** the other wished to purchase **the land for planting,**[H] **the settling** of the land through construction of houses is **preferable, and this** sale **is not subject to the *halakha* of one** whose field **borders** the field of his neighbor. Therefore, he may sell to the one who wants to build a house there, even if he is not a bordering neighbor and the other potential buyer is.

אַפְסֵיק מְשׁוּנִיתָא אוֹ רִיכְבָא דְּדִיקְלָא, חָזֵינָא: אִם יָכוֹל לְהַכְנִיס בָּהּ אֲפִילּוּ תֶּלֶם אֶחָד – אִית בָּהּ מִשּׁוּם דִּינָא דְּבַר מִצְרָא; וְאִי לָא – לֵית בָּהּ מִשּׁוּם דִּינָא דְּבַר מִצְרָא.

If **a jagged edge of rock**[NH] **or a row of palm trees served as a barrier** between two bordering fields, **we see** whether any open space exists. **If** the owner of the adjacent field **can insert even a single furrow there** that comes into contact with the other field, **this** sale **is subject to the *halakha* of one** whose field **borders** the field of his neighbor. **But if** sufficient space for a furrow does **not** exist, **this** sale **is not subject to the *halakha* of one** whose field **borders** the field of his neighbor.

הָנֵי אַרְבָּעָה בְּנֵי מִצְרָנֵי, דְּקַדֵּים חַד מִינַּיְיהוּ וּזְבַן – זְבִינֵיהּ זְבִינֵי. וְאִי כּוּלְּהוּ אָתוּ בַּהֲדֵי הֲדָדֵי – פַּלְגוּ לַהּ בְּקַרְנָזִיל.

In a case of **those four bordering neighbors**[H] who surround a field that is for sale from all four sides, if **one of them preceded** the others **and purchased** it, **his purchase** is a valid **purchase** and the others cannot object. **And if they all came simultaneously** to purchase it, then **they divide** the plot of land, **with** two bisecting **diagonal**[L] lines[B] so that each receives a portion near his field.

NOTES

Land for houses – אַרְעָא לְבָתֵּי: This passage apparently refers to houses whose proprietors do not have any right of ownership over the land. Rabbeinu Tam, in a lengthy discussion in *Sefer HaYashar*, maintains that the *halakha* of one whose field borders the field of his neighbor does not apply to houses at all.

Jagged edge of rock [*meshunita*] – מְשׁוּנִיתָא: Other interpretations of *meshunita* include a high range of hills, a ditch or cleft, and non-fruit-bearing trees (Rabbeinu Ḥananel).

LANGUAGE

Diagonal [*karnazil*] – קַרְנָזִיל: This word is written either as *karnezol* or as *karnazil*. It has been interpreted as a form of the word *keren*, horn, possibly a reference to an angle [*keren zavit*] or a diagonal [*karna azil*] or the like. Modern Hebrew has accepted the use of *alakhson*, a word of Greek etymology, to denote a diagonal.

BACKGROUND

They divide it with diagonal lines – פַּלְגוּ לַהּ בְּקַרְנָזִיל:

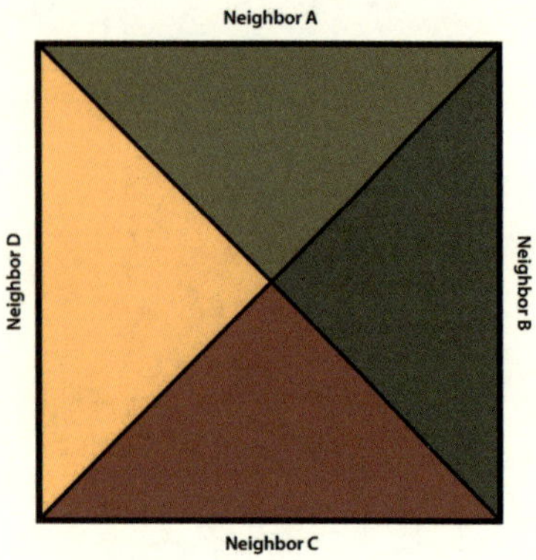

Lot split evenly between the four neighbors

HALAKHA

The land belonged to one person and the houses to another one – אַרְעָא דְּחַד וּבָתֵּי דְּחַד: In a case where the land itself belonged to one person while the building or trees were owned by another, if the owner of the building or the trees, respectively, had rights to use the land, both the owner of the land and the owner of the building or trees, respectively, are considered bordering neighbors. Consequently, if any of them sells his share, the other can force the buyer out, even if the buyer is himself a bordering neighbor. If the owner of the building or the trees had no rights to use the land at all, he does not retain the rights of a bordering neighbor. The owner of the land is still considered a bordering neighbor relative to the building.

With regard to a case of a house and an upper story, each owned by a different person, the Rema rules that each of them is considered a bordering neighbor. The *Sma* and the *Taz* disagree, and the *Netivot HaMishpat* rules likewise (Rambam *Sefer Kinyan, Hilkhot Shekhenim* 12:16; *Shulḥan Arukh, Ḥoshen Mishpat* 175:51).

For building and for planting – לְבִנְיָה וְלִזְרִיעָה: If the bordering neighbor wished to purchase the land in order to plant, while the other potential buyer sought to purchase it to build a house there, the latter takes precedence due to the importance of settling the land. Some say that if the bordering neighbor wants to plant trees specifically, he retains his right, as this type of planting is considered more important (Rambam *Sefer Kinyan, Hilkhot Shekhenim* 14:1; *Shulḥan Arukh, Ḥoshen Mishpat* 175:26).

A jagged edge of rock – מְשׁוּנִיתָא: With regard to a case of an uninterrupted row of palm trees that serve as a barrier between one field and another, or a barrier formed by a tall building or a trench, if it is possible to insert even a single furrow into the space between the fields so that the fields can be joined, the owners of the neighboring fields are considered bordering neighbors, but if this cannot be done, they are not considered bordering neighbors (Rambam *Sefer Kinyan, Hilkhot Shekhenim* 12:17; *Shulḥan Arukh, Ḥoshen Mishpat* 175:27).

Four bordering neighbors – אַרְבָּעָה בְּנֵי מִצְרָנֵי: If the field for sale was surrounded on four sides by four bordering neighbors, they each have equal rights to it, and they each have the right to purchase part of it by means of dividing the field with bisecting diagonals. If there were two bordering neighbors located on the same side, they receive one portion that they share between them. These *halakhot* apply only if they all arrived simultaneously to acquire the field, but if one of the bordering neighbors arrived before the others and acquired the field, it belongs entirely to him. The *Maggid Mishne* holds he should sell it to all of them together *ab initio*, although some authorities dispute this ruling (Rambam *Sefer Kinyan, Hilkhot Shekhenim* 12:5; *Shulḥan Arukh, Ḥoshen Mishpat* 175:11).

מתני׳ הַמְקַבֵּל שָׂדֶה מֵחֲבֵירוֹ לְשָׁנִים מוּעָטוֹת – לֹא יִזְרָעֶנָּה פִּשְׁתָּן, וְאֵין לוֹ בְּקוֹרוֹת שִׁקְמָה. קִיבְּלָהּ הֵימֶנּוּ לְשֶׁבַע שָׁנִים – שָׁנָה רִאשׁוֹנָה יִזְרָעֶנָּה פִּשְׁתָּן, וְיֵשׁ לוֹ בְּקוֹרוֹת שִׁקְמָה.

MISHNA One **who receives a field**[N] **from another** to cultivate **for a few years,**[H] i.e., fewer than seven, **may not plant flax**[B] **in it,** as flax greatly weakens the soil, **and** if a sycamore tree was growing in the field, **he does not have** rights **to** the **beams** fashioned from the branches of the **sycamore**[B] tree. Therefore, he may not cut down its branches for his own use, as it takes many years for new ones to grow. If **he received** the field **from him for seven years,** in **the first year he** may **plant flax in it, and he does have** rights **to** the **beams** fashioned from the branches of the **sycamore** tree.

גמ׳ אָמַר אַבָּיֵי: בְּקוֹרוֹת שִׁקְמָה – אֵין לוֹ, בְּשֶׁבַח שִׁקְמָה – יֵשׁ לוֹ. וְרָבָא אָמַר: אֲפִילּוּ בְּשֶׁבַח שִׁקְמָה נָמֵי אֵין לוֹ.

GEMARA **Abaye says:** Although **he does not have** rights **to the beams** fashioned from the branches of the **sycamore tree, he does have** rights **to** the value of **the enhancement of the sycamore** tree, i.e., the value of its growth that occurred while he was cultivating the field. **And Rava says: He does not even have** rights **to** the value of **the enhancement of the sycamore** tree.

מֵיתִיבֵי: הַמְקַבֵּל שָׂדֶה מֵחֲבֵירוֹ וְהִגִּיעַ זְמַנּוֹ לָצֵאת – שָׁמִין לוֹ. מַאי לָאו – שָׁמִין לוֹ בְּשֶׁבַח שִׁקְמָה? לָא, שָׁמִין לוֹ יַרְקָא וְסִילְקָא.

The Gemara **raises an objection** to Rava's opinion from a *baraita*: With regard to **one who receives a field from another** to cultivate **and his time to leave arrives,** the court **appraises** its value **for him. What, is it not** that the court **appraises for him** the value of **the enhancement of the sycamore** or other trees? The Gemara responds: **No,** the court **appraises for him** the value of **the vegetables and beets**[NH] left in the field.

יַרְקָא וְסִילְקָא, נֶעֱקוֹר וְנִשְׁקוֹל! בִּדְלָא מְטָא יוֹמָא דְשׁוּקָא.

The Gemara challenges: If it is referring to **vegetables and beets, let him uproot and take** them. The Gemara explains: It is referring to a case **where the market day has not** yet **arrived,** so that if he uproots them now he will not be able to sell them. He therefore leaves them for the owner of the land and receives money instead.

תָּא שְׁמַע: הַמְקַבֵּל שָׂדֶה מֵחֲבֵירוֹ וְהִגִּיעַ שְׁבִיעִית – שָׁמִין לוֹ. שְׁבִיעִית – מִי קָא מַפְקְעָא אַרְעָא! אֶלָּא אֵימָא: הַמְקַבֵּל שָׂדֶה מֵחֲבֵירוֹ וְהִגִּיעַ יוֹבֵל – שָׁמִין לוֹ.

The Gemara suggests: **Come** and **hear** another proof from a *baraita*: In the case of one **who receives a field from another** to cultivate **and the Sabbatical** Year **arrived,** the court **appraises** it **for him.** The Gemara first expresses puzzlement over the *baraita* itself: **Does** the **Sabbatical** Year **release land** from the one who contracted to cultivate it? The arrangement is in effect it during this time, so why is there a need for an appraisal? The Gemara responds: **Rather, say** that the *baraita* reads as follows: In the case of one **who receives a field from another** to cultivate **and the Jubilee** Year[B] **arrived,**[H] the court **appraises** it **for him.**

BACKGROUND

Flax – פִּשְׁתָּן: Cultivated flax, *Linum usitatissimum* L., is an annual plant that grows erect to a height of 40–120 cm, and whose flowers are blue or white. Its stiff stalks contain flax fibers, and oil is extracted from its seeds. After the plant is cut, the stalks are soaked in water, called *mei mishra* in the language of the Sages, for several days. Various bacteria then cause the materials that attach the fibers to the stalks to decompose. Following that, the shell is beaten and opened, and the fibers are extracted for the purpose of weaving linen, known as *bad* or *sheish* in the language of the Torah. The flax plant has been cultivated since ancient times, especially in ancient Egypt.

Sycamore – שִׁקְמָה: The sycamore tree, *Ficus sycomorus*, is a tall, broad species related to the common fig. Although the fruit of the sycamore are edible, it is mostly grown for its wood, as beams fashioned from sycamore branches are large, wide, and relatively lightweight. The sycamore tree must be left to grow for several years until it reaches sizeable dimensions, at which point the wood is cut, while part of its trunk is left for a few more years to allow the branches to grow back and more wood to be harvested.

Old sycamore with a hollow trunk

NOTES

One who receives a field, etc. – הַמְקַבֵּל שָׂדֶה וכו׳: According to Rashi this mishna refers only to a tenant farmer, but a contractor may plant whatever he wants. The Ramban disagrees, as he maintains that even a contractor may not alter the terms of the agreement. The Ran explains in accordance with Rashi and adds that a contractor may plant whatever he chooses because the owner of the field did not specify what he must plant.

The court appraises for him the vegetables and beets – שָׁמִין לוֹ יַרְקָא וְסִילְקָא: The Gemara explains that this refers to a situation where the market day had not yet arrived. In that case, if the vegetables are not yet fully ripe the owner of the field retains a portion of them, as his land is still nurturing their growth. By contrast, the phrase: The court appraises its value for him, indicates that the tenant receives the entire value of the vegetables. The Rashba maintains that there is no difference in this regard, and that the Gemara merely offered an example. With regard to the *halakha*, everyone agrees that the cultivator is entitled to part of the vegetables even if they are not fully grown.

HALAKHA

One who receives a field…for a few years – הַמְקַבֵּל שָׂדֶה...לְשָׁנִים מוּעָטוֹת: One who receives a field from another for a few years may not plant flax there. In addition, he does not have the right to take the branches of the sycamore trees, nor the value of any enhancements to trees that grew of their own accord. He is entitled to compensation for the loss of produce resulting from the growth of the trees in the area he was cultivating, provided that the trees grew in a place suitable for the growth of the crop he planted. Others, such as the Rosh, maintain that if he claims that he would have planted trees there even had they not sprouted on their own he is entitled to the value of a portion of the trees as though he planted them. If he received the field for a period of at least seven years, he may plant flax in the first year, and he is entitled to the branches from the sycamore tree (Rambam *Sefer Mishpatim*, *Hilkhot Sekhirut* 8:3; *Shulḥan Arukh*, *Ḥoshen Mishpat* 325:1).

The court appraises for him the vegetables and beets – שָׁמִין לוֹ יַרְקָא וְסִילְקָא: If the time arrived for the cultivator of a field to leave and there were vegetables that had not yet fully grown, or if the market day had not yet arrived, the court appraises them for him and he collects this sum from the owner of the land (Rambam *Sefer Mishpatim*, *Hilkhot Sekhirut* 8:3; *Shulḥan Arukh*, *Ḥoshen Mishpat* 327:1).

One who purchases a field and the Jubilee arrives – הַלּוֹקֵחַ שָׂדֶה וְהִגִּיעַ יוֹבֵל: If one bought an ancestral field and planted trees there which flourished, when the field is returned in the Jubilee Year, the value of the improvement of the trees is evaluated and the buyer collects this sum (Rambam *Sefer Zera'im*, *Hilkhot Shemitta VeYovel* 11:8).

BACKGROUND

Jubilee Year – יוֹבֵל: The Jubilee Year is the fiftieth year following seven Sabbatical cycles of seven years. Its status is unique in a number of ways. First, all of the agricultural *halakhot* that are followed in the Sabbatical Year must be observed in the Jubilee Year. In addition, all Hebrew slaves, including those who agreed to continue in servitude beyond their initial obligation, are emancipated, and ancestral fields that have been sold are returned to their original owners (see Leviticus 25). The emancipation of the slaves and the restoration of the fields takes place after Yom Kippur. The Jubilee Year is observed only when the majority of the Jewish people are living in Eretz Yisrael. Consequently, its observance was discontinued toward the close of the First Temple period and was never renewed.

וְאַכַּתִּי, יוֹבֵל מִי מַפְקְעָא קַבְּלָנוּת? ״לִצְמִיתֻת״, אֲמַר רַחֲמָנָא! אֶלָּא אֵימָא: הַלּוֹקֵחַ שָׂדֶה מֵחֲבֵירוֹ וְהִגִּיעַ יוֹבֵל – שָׁמִין לוֹ.

The Gemara asks: **But still,** this is difficult; **does the Jubilee** Year **release** the term of **a contractor? The Merciful One states: "Permanently"** (Leviticus 25:23), which indicates that only land that was permanently sold returns to its owner, whereas land that was rented does not revert to the owner at the Jubilee Year. **Rather, say** that the *baraita* reads as follows: In the case of **one who purchases a field from another and the Jubilee** Year **arrives,** the court **appraises** it **for him.**

וְכִי תֵּימָא הָכִי נַמִי שָׁמִין לוֹ בְּיַרְקָא וְסִילְקָא, סִילְקָא וְיַרְקָא בְּיוֹבֵל הֶפְקֵירָא הוּא! אֶלָּא לָאו – שְׁבַח שִׁקְמָה!

And if you would say that **so too** here it means that the court **appraises it for him with regard to vegetables and beets,** this cannot be, as **vegetables and beets in the Jubilee** Year **are ownerless.** This is because the Jubilee is like the Sabbatical Year in that any produce that grows is ownerless and may be taken by anyone. **Rather,** is the *baraita* **not** referring to **the enhancement of** the value of **the sycamore that occurred** during the time he had owned the field? It must be referring to this, and therefore presents a difficulty to Rava.

תַּרְגְּמָא אַבַּיֵי אַלִּיבָּא דְּרָבָא: שָׁאנֵי הָתָם דְּאָמַר קְרָא: ״וְיָצָא מִמְכַּר בַּיִת״, מִמְכָּר – חוֹזֵר, שְׁבָח – אֵינוֹ חוֹזֵר. וְנִגְמַר מִינֵּיהּ! הָתָם זְבִינֵי מְעַלְּיָא הוּא, וְיוֹבֵל אַפְקְעָתָא דְּמַלְכָּא הִיא.

Abaye interpreted the *baraita* so that it is **in accordance with** the opinion **of** his disputant **Rava: There it is different, as the verse states: "Then the house that was sold shall go out**… in the Jubilee" (Leviticus 25:33), which teaches that the house or field that was **sold returns** to its owner, but the value of its **enhancement** does **not return,** but remains with the buyer. The Gemara asks: If so, **let us derive from it** a general *halakha* that the value of enhancement need not be returned. The Gemara answers: The two cases are dissimilar, as **there,** in the *baraita*, it is **a full-fledged sale,**[N] **and the Jubilee** released it, as it **is a release of the King,** a Divine decree. Since the buyer had been in full ownership of the field, he keeps the value of the enhancement that occurred while it was his. By contrast, one who receives a field to cultivate is not an owner.

רַב פַּפָּא קַבֵּיל אַרְעָא לְאַסְפַּסְתָּא. קָדְחוּ בָּהּ תָּאלֵי. כִּי קָא מִסְתַּלֵּק אֲמַר לְהוּ: הֲבוּ לִי שִׁבְחָא! אֲמַר לֵיהּ רַב שֵׁישָׁא בְּרֵיהּ דְּרַב אִידִי לְרַב פַּפָּא: אֶלָּא מֵעַתָּה, דִּיקְלָא וְאַלֵּים – הָכִי נַמִי דְּבָעֵי מָר שִׁבְחֵיהּ? אֲמַר לֵיהּ: הָתָם לָאו אַדַּעְתָּא דְּהָכִי נָחֵית, אֲנָא הָכָא אַדַּעְתָּא דְּהָכִי נְחֵיתְנָא.

The Gemara relates: **Rav Pappa received land** as a contractor **for** growing **hay.** During the time he was cultivating it, **palm trees sprouted in** the ground. **When he left** the land **he said to** the owners of the field: **Give me** the value of **the enhancement** to the field from the palm trees. **Rav Sheisha, son of Rav Idi, said to Rav Pappa: If that is so,** i.e., if your claim is justified, then in a situation where there was **a palm tree and it grew thick,**[N] **so too would the Master,** i.e., Rav Pappa, **want** to be paid for the value of the tree's **enhancement?** Rav Pappa **said to him: There,** in that theoretical case, the cultivator **did not descend** to the field **with that** possibility **in mind,** as the cultivator considered only the consumption of the date palm's fruit, not its growth. **Here,** in my case, **I did** indeed **descend** to the field **with this in mind,** as I anticipated receiving compensation for any growth of the field.

כְּמַאן? כְּאַבַּיֵי, דְּאָמַר: בִּשְׁבַח שִׁקְמָה יֵשׁ לוֹ? אֲפִילּוּ תֵּימָא כְּרָבָא. הָתָם – לֵית לֵיהּ פְּסֵידָא, הָכָא – אִיכָּא פְּסֵידָא.

The Gemara asks: **In accordance with whose** opinion did he make this statement? Is it not **in accordance with** the opinion of **Abaye, who says** that **he does have** rights **to** the value of **the enhancement of the sycamore?** The Gemara refutes this claim: **You** may **even say** that he holds **in accordance with** the opinion of **Rava,** as **there** the cultivator suffers **no loss** when the sycamore grows in the field, so he is not entitled to the value of the enhancement as compensation. By contrast, **here there is a loss,** as the palm trees that sprouted occupied space designated for hay.

אָמַר לֵיהּ: מַאי פְּסַדְתִּיךְ? יָדָא דְּאַסְפַּסְתָּא. שְׁקוֹל יָדָא דְּאַסְפַּסְתָּא וְזִיל! אָמַר לֵיהּ: אֲנָא כּוּרְכְּמָא רִישְׁקָא רַבַּאי. אָמַר לֵיהּ: גַּלֵּית אַדַּעְתָּךְ דִּלְמִשְׁקַל וְאִסְתַּלּוּקֵי עָבְדַתְּ. שְׁקַל כּוּרְכְּמָא רִישְׁקָא וְזִיל, אֵין לְךָ אֶלָּא דְּמֵי עֵצִים בִּלְבָד.

Rav Sheisha **said to Rav Pappa:** But here too, the owner of the field can say: **What loss have I caused you?** I have caused you to lose **a handful of hay. Take a handful of hay and go.** Rav Pappa **said to him:** I claim that **I grew garden saffron** there. He claimed that he lost land that he could have used for the cultivation of expensive produce, not only hay. Rav Sheisha **said to him:** Even so, you admit that you wanted the land for other plantings, not to plant palm trees, and **you** have thereby **revealed your intention that you acted** so as **to take**[N] the produce **and leave. Take** your **garden saffron and leave,** as **you have** rights **only** to **the value of wood alone.** Since you did not mean to grow these trees, you are entitled only to the price you could have received for the palm trees had you uprooted them and sold them as wood during the time you cultivated the field.

NOTES

A full-fledged sale – זְבִינֵי מְעַלְּיָא: Since this was a full-fledged sale, the *halakha* is that the buyer receives all rights to the item unless it was specified to the contrary. Although the field will eventually be returned in the Jubilee Year, the transaction is not viewed as a temporary deal but as a complete sale that is later revoked.

A palm tree and it grew thick – דִּיקְלָא וְאַלֵּים: The difference between the thickening of the tree and the palm trees that sprouted is that the cultivator is entitled to anything that will be cut and removed. With regard to the additional thickness of a date palm, which remains attached to the ground, he has no rights at all (Rid).

You have revealed your intention that you acted to take, etc. – גַּלֵּית אַדַּעְתָּךְ דִּלְמִשְׁקַל...עָבְדַתְּ וכו׳: Most commentaries agree that the determining factor here is what he intended to plant. If he sought to plant trees he is entitled to the improvement of the trees when they grow of their own accord, but since he wanted to grow produce that could be entirely removed he does not retain any rights to the improvement of the trees. Although Rav Pappa could have made the former claim, he was one who "speaks truth in his heart" (Psalms 15:2; see *Makkot* 24a) and would not state a claim that was not true (Rashba).

Some commentaries maintain that it makes no difference what he intended to grow, be it hay, saffron, or anything else; the determining factor is the purpose for which he initially accepted the land. Since in this case he did so to plant hay, it is not relevant whether he intended to plant trees (Rid). This is also the ruling of the Rambam.

רַב בֵּיבָי בַּר אַבַּיֵי קַבֵּיל אַרְעָא וְאַהֲדַר לֵיהּ מְשׁוּנִיתָא. קְדַחוּ בֵּיהּ וַרְדָּתָא. כִּי קָא מִיסְתַּלֵּק אֲמַר לְהוּ: הֲבוּ לִי שְׁבָחַאי. אֲמַר רַב פַּפִּי: מִשּׁוּם דְּאָתִיתוּ מִמּוּלָאֵי אָמְרִיתוּ מִילֵּי מוּלְיָיתָא? אֲפִילּוּ רַב פָּפָּא לָא אֲמַר אֶלָּא דְּאִית לֵיהּ פְּסֵידָא. הָכָא – מַאי פְּסֵידָא אִית לָךְ?

The Gemara relates another incident: **Rav Beivai bar Abaye**[P] **received land** to cultivate **and** he **surrounded it** with **a fence** made **of earth.** In the meantime, **trees sprouted in it. When he left** the field **he said to** the owners: **Give me my** value of the **enhancement** of the trees that sprouted. **Rav Pappi said:** Is it **because you come from unfortunate people**[N] that **you say unfortunate** and unsound **words?** Abaye's family came from the family of Eli, whose descendants were sentenced to die at a young age. Rav Pappi explains: **Even Rav Pappa said only** that he is entitled to the value of the enhancement of the palm trees **when** he **has** suffered **a loss,** as they take up part of the field. **Here,** by contrast, **what loss do you have?** As the trees sprouted in a place that would have been left unplanted, you have not lost anything and you are not entitled to compensation.

רַב יוֹסֵף הֲוָה לֵיהּ הַהוּא שְׁתָלָא. שְׁכֵיב וּשְׁבַק חֲמִשָּׁה חַתְנְוָתָא. אֲמַר: עַד הָאִידָּנָא – חַד, הַשְׁתָּא – חֲמִשָּׁה. עַד הָאִידָּנָא לָא הָווּ סָמְכוּ אַהֲדָדֵי וְלָא מַפְסְדוּ לִי. הַשְׁתָּא חֲמִשָּׁה, סָמְכוּ אַהֲדָדֵי וּמַפְסְדוּ לִי. אֲמַר לְהוּ: אִי שָׁקְלִיתוּ שְׁבָחַיְיכוּ וּמִסְתַּלְּקִיתוּ – מוּטָב; וְאִי לָא – מְסַלֵּיקְנָא לְכוּ בְּלָא שְׁבָחָא.

§ The Gemara relates: **Rav Yosef had a certain planter** whose job it was to plant trees, similar to a sharecropper. **He died**[H] **and left** behind **five sons-in-law.** Rav Yosef **said: Until now** I had to deal with only **one** person; **now** there are **five.**[N] **Until now they did not rely on each other** to plant the trees **and did not cause me a loss,** as the responsibility was their father-in-law's, but **now** that they are **five they will rely on each other** to plant the trees **and cause me a loss.** In light of these considerations, he decided to discontinue the agreement with them. Rav Yosef **said to them: If you take** the value of **your enhancement** that you brought to the field **and remove** yourselves, all is **well, but if not, I will remove you without** giving you the value of **the enhancement.**

דְּאָמַר רַב יְהוּדָה, וְאִיתֵּימָא רַב הוּנָא, וְאִיתֵּימָא רַב נַחְמָן: הַאי שְׁתָלָא דְּשָׁכֵיב – יוֹרְשִׁים דִּילֵיהּ מִסְתַּלְּקִין לְהוּ בְּלָא שְׁבָחָא. וְלָאו מִילְּתָא הִיא.

Rav Yosef explains his statement: **As Rav Yehuda says, and some** say it was **Rav Huna, and some say** it was **Rav Naḥman:** With regard to **this planter who died, his heirs may be removed without** receiving the value of the **enhancement.** The Gemara comments: **But this is not correct,**[N] as the *halakha* is not in accordance with this opinion.

הַהוּא שַׁתָּלָא דַּאֲמַר לְהוּ: אִי מַפְסַדִינָא מְסַלַּקְנָא. אַפְסִיד. אֲמַר רַב יְהוּדָה: מִסְתַּלֵּק בְּלָא שְׁבָחָא. רַב כָּהֲנָא אֲמַר: מִסְתַּלֵּק וְשָׁקֵיל שְׁבָחָא. וּמוֹדֶה רַב כָּהֲנָא דְּאִי אֲמַר אִי פָּסֵידְנָא מִסְתַּלַּקְנָא בְּלָא שְׁבָחָא – מִסְתַּלֵּק בְּלָא שְׁבָחָא. רָבָא אֲמַר: אַסְמַכְתָּא הִיא, וְאַסְמַכְתָּא לָא קָנְיָא.

The Gemara relates another incident. There was **a certain planter who said to** the owner: **If I cause a loss** to the vineyard by ruining its plants **I will leave** the field. Ultimately, he indeed **caused a loss** to the plants, but some enhancement from the time he began did still exist.[H] **Rav Yehuda said: He leaves without** receiving payment for **the enhancement,** while **Rav Kahana said: He leaves and takes the** payment for the **enhancement** resulting from his work. **And Rav Kahana concedes that if he said: If I cause a loss I will leave without** receiving payment for **the enhancement, he** indeed **leaves without** receiving payment for **the enhancement.** Conversely, **Rava said:** A promise of this kind, which he does not expect to have to fulfill, **is a transaction with inconclusive intent** [*asmakhta*], **and** the *halakha* is that **an** *asmakhta* **does not effect acquisition** and is therefore not legally binding.

וּלְרָבָא, מַאי שְׁנָא מֵהָא דִּתְנַן: אִם אוֹבִיר וְלָא אַעֲבִיד אֲשַׁלֵּם בְּמֵיטְבָא? הָתָם מַאי דְּאַפְסֵיד מְשַׁלֵּם. הָכָא – מַאי דְּאַפְסֵיד מְנַכִּינַן לֵיהּ, וְאִידָּךְ יָהֲבִינַן לֵיהּ.

The Gemara asks: **And according to Rava,** in **what** way **is it different from that which we learned** in a mishna (104a) that the recipient of the field stipulates: **If I let** the field **lie fallow and do not cultivate** it **I will pay with the best**-quality produce, in which case he is obligated to fulfill his promise? The Gemara answers: **There, he pays for** the **loss he caused,** while **here, we deduct from him the loss that he caused, and we give him the other** portion of the money. He does not forfeit all that was due to him just because some of his plantings were unsuccessful.

PERSONALITIES

Rav Beivai bar Abaye – רַב בֵּיבָי בַּר אַבַּיֵי: Rav Beivai was a fifth-generation Babylonian *amora* and apparently the son of Abaye, Rava's friend and colleague. There is no available information with regard to the identity of his teachers. Presumably, he studied with his father and the other Sages of the previous generation. He engaged in halakhic discussions primarily with Rav Pappa and Rav Huna, son of Rav Yehoshua. Apparently, he lived in Pumbedita and worked with his father as a farmer. His statements appear throughout the Talmud, although he never headed his own yeshiva. Rav Beivai engaged in the study of esoterica, and many of his statements in that area are found in the Talmud.

NOTES

Come from unfortunate people [*mimmula'ei*] – **אָתִיתוּ מִמּוּלָאֵי:** Various interpretations have been offered for this expression, which appears in several places in the Talmud. One opinion is that the word *mula'ei* means truncated and flawed, an allusion to Rav Beivai's ancestry from the family of Eli, who were cursed to die at a young age (see I Samuel 2:32–33). Others maintain that *Memala* is the name of the place where Eli's descendants lived (based on *Bereshit Rabba*). By contrast, the *Arukh* cites an explanation that *memala* means exalted and great, and this statement therefore means: Since you come from great people like Abaye and Rabba, you teach great ideas.

Now five – הַשְׁתָּא חֲמִשָּׁה: The Ramban writes that these are considerations of piety, as according to the letter of the law the agreement with the original planter does not transfer to his children by inheritance. Rav Yosef was supplying a rational basis for his decision that they would understand and accept.

But this is not correct – וְלָאו מִילְּתָא הִיא: The Rivan (cited in *Tosafot*, 109b) maintains that the statement attributed to Rav Yehuda was never stated at all, and Rav Yosef said so only as a threat to the heirs. *Tosafot* raise several difficulties with this interpretation. Other commentaries contend that although the actual statement was not formulated in the precise manner in which it was transmitted, the ruling *halakha* is essentially accurate, and the Rambam rules accordingly.

HALAKHA

Planter died – שַׁתָּלָא שְׁכֵיב: If someone received a field for a fixed period of time and subsequently died and left behind a son, the owner may not demand payment for what the father ate. Similarly, the son is not entitled to everything that was agreed upon with his father. Instead, the court appraises the value of what he did until his death and this sum is given to his son (*Shulḥan Arukh*, *Ḥoshen Mishpat* 329:1).

Planter…who caused a loss – שַׁתָּלָא...אַפְסִיד: In a location where the custom is that one who plants trees receives half of the value of the enhancement and his planting resulted in both losses and enhancements, half of the enhancement is calculated, from which the amount of the loss he caused is deducted, and he receives the remainder of the sum. Even if the planter stipulated that if he causes a loss he should receive nothing, this condition is disregarded as an *asmakhta*, and he forfeits only the actual loss, in accordance with the opinion of Rava (Rambam *Sefer Mishpatim*, *Hilkhot Sekhirut* 10:6; *Shulḥan Arukh*, *Ḥoshen Mishpat* 330:2).

רוניא שתלא דרבינא הוה. אפסיד, סלקיה. אתא לקמיה דרבא, אמר ליה: חזי מר מאי קא עביד לי! אמר ליה: שפיר עביד. אמר ליה: הא לא התרה בי! אמר ליה: לא צריכא להתרות. רבא לטעמיה, דאמר רבא: מקרי דרדקי, שתלא, טבחא, ואומנא,

The Gemara relates that **Runya was the planter of Ravina. He caused a loss,** and Ravina **removed him** from his field. Runya **came before Rava** and **said to him:** Let **the Master see what** Ravina **has done to me.** Rava **said to him:** Ravina **did well,** as you caused him a loss. Runya **said to him: But** Ravina **did not warn me** beforehand. How can he force me to leave without prior warning? Rava **said to him:** In this case it **is not necessary to provide a warning.** The Gemara comments: **Rava** conforms **to his** line of **reasoning, as Rava said:** With regard to **a teacher of children,**[N] **a planter, a ritual slaughterer,**[N] **and a bloodletter,**

NOTES

A teacher of children – מקרי דרדקי: According to Rashi the reason is that his students will absorb his errors, which will be hard to correct later. Other commentaries question this interpretation, as it is apparently the opposite of Rava's own opinion (see *Bava Batra* 21a). Some differentiate between mistakes the children make on their own and those of the teacher. The Rif maintains that this refers to a teacher who beats his pupils or is unable to control them. *Tosafot* (*Bava Batra* 21b) offer a third explanation, that the irretrievable loss is the lost time.

A ritual slaughterer – טבחא: It is clear that if a ritual slaughterer renders the animal meat forbidden he must pay for the damage. There is an additional loss that might be incurred if, for example, the ritual slaughterer rendered the meat forbidden, and as a result a host is unable to honor his guests properly by serving them meat. This would be cause for the ritual slaughterer's dismissal (Rabbeinu Yona). With regard to the *halakha* itself, the Ra'avad maintains that the offender is not removed from his post immediately, but only after several incidents of this kind.

וספר מתא – כולן כמותרין ועומדין דמי. כללא דמילתא: כל פסידא דלא הדר – כמותרין ועומדין דמי.

and a town scribe[N] who drafts documents on behalf on the local residents, **all of these are considered forewarned.**[H] Therefore, any loss incurred due to them is deducted from their wages, and they are fined without the need for prior warning. **The principle of** this **matter** is: With regard to **any loss that is not recoverable they are considered forewarned.**

ההוא שתלא דאמר להו: הבו לי שבחאי, דבעינא למיסק לארעא דישראל. אתא לקמיה דרב פפא בר שמואל. אמר להו: הבו ליה שבחיה. אמר ליה רבא: איהו אשבח, ארעא לא אשבח? אמר ליה: אנא פלגא דשבחא קאמינא לך. אמר ליה: עד האידנא הוה שקיל בעל הבית פלגא ושתלא פלגא, השתא בעי למיתב מנתא לאריסא! אמר ליה: ריבעא דשבחא קאמינא.

§ The Gemara relates: There was **a certain planter who said to** the owner of the field: **Give me** the value of **my enhancement because I wish to ascend to Eretz Yisrael.**[NH] The owner **came** for a ruling **before Rav Pappa bar Shmuel,** who **said to him: Give** the planter **the value of his enhancement. Rava said to** Rav Pappa bar Shmuel: Did **he** alone **enhance** the field, while **the land did not enhance it?** He cannot be credited with all the improvement. Rav Pappa bar Shmuel **said to** Rava: **I am telling you** that he is entitled to **half** the value of **the enhancement. Rava said to him: Until now the owner of the land would take half and the planter** would take **half,** while the planter would work the field. **Now** the owner **also needs to give a portion to the sharecropper,** so that the sharecropper will continue working the field. Rav Pappa bar Shmuel **said to him: I am telling you** to give him **one-quarter of** the value **of the enhancement,** half of the sum to which he is entitled.

סבר רב אשי למימר: ריבעא דהוא דנקא, דאמר רב מניומי בריה דרב נחומי: באתרא דשקיל שתלא פלגא ואריסא תילתא, האי שתלא דבעי לאסתלוקי יהבינן ליה שבחא ומסלקינן ליה, כי היכי דלא נמטייה הפסד לבעל הבית.

Rav Ashi thought to say that when he referred to one-quarter he meant **one-quarter that is one-sixth,** i.e., one-quarter of the sum due to the owner, as the sum due to the owner is two-thirds of the entire yield. This payment would therefore amount to one-sixth of the total. **As Rav Minyumi, son of Rav Naḥumi, said: In a location where the planter takes half** the fruit **and the sharecropper** takes **one-third, with regard to a planter who wants to leave, we give him** his share of the value of **the enhancement and remove him** in such a manner **so that the homeowner should suffer no loss.**

אי אמרת בשלמא ריבעא דהוא דנקא – שפיר. אלא אי אמרת ריבעא ממש – קא מטי ליה פסידא לבעל הבית פלגא דנקא!

Granted, if you say that he meant **one-quarter that is one-sixth,** this is **well** and the calculations are in order, **but if you say** he referred to **an actual quarter, the homeowner suffers the loss of half of one-sixth.** This is because if the owner had paid the planter initially he would have given him only one-half, whereas now he must give the planter one-quarter and the sharecropper one-third. He thereby pays an extra twelfth.

NOTES

A town scribe [*safar*] – ספר מתא: Some commentaries cite an explanation, based on Rashi (97a), that this refers to a barber [*sapar*], as a bad haircut that causes shame is also considered a loss that cannot be undone (Rabbeinu Yehonatan of Lunel).

To ascend to Eretz Yisrael – למיסק לארעא דישראל: If he does not have a good enough reason for leaving he may not do so without the owner's consent, and if he leaves regardless, he is not entitled to the value of the enhancement (Rid).

HALAKHA

Are considered forewarned – כמותרים ועומדים: With regard to a planter who caused a loss, a ritual slaughter who invalidated the animals he slaughtered, a bloodletter who injured someone, a scribe who erred in writing documents, and a teacher who taught improperly, in all these cases, where the loss cannot be restored, they are removed from their posts. The Rema, citing the *Tur*, states that the same *halakha* applies when these professionals work for a private individual. Some authorities maintain that although they must certainly pay for the loss immediately and no warning is required, they are not removed from their posts until they have made enough mistakes to establish a presumption of error (Rambam *Sefer Mishpatim, Hilkhot Sekhirut* 10:7; *Shulḥan Arukh, Ḥoshen Mishpat* 306:8, and in the comment of Rema).

A planter who leaves – שתל המסתלק: If a planter planted trees and left with the permission of the landowner (Rema, citing *Nimmukei Yosef*), so that the owner of the land had to hire the services of a sharecropper, the owner takes half the crop as before, the sharecropper receives the usual amount of a sharecropper, and the planter is entitled to the rest. This ruling is in accordance with Rav Ashi, as most authorities, including the Rif, the Rambam, the Ra'avad, and the Rosh rule in accordance with his view (Rambam *Sefer Mishpatim, Hilkhot Sekhirut* 10:6; *Shulḥan Arukh, Ḥoshen Mishpat* 330:3).

אֲמַר לֵיהּ רַב אַחָא בְּרֵיהּ דְּרַב יוֹסֵף לְרַב אַשִׁי: וְלֵימָא לֵיהּ: אַנְתְּ מְנָתָא דִּילָךְ הַב לֵיהּ לַאֲרִיסָא, וַאֲנָא – מְנָתָא דִּילִי מַאי דְּבָעֵינָא עָבֵידְנָא בֵּיהּ! אֲמַר: כִּי מָטֵית לִשְׁחִיטַת קָדָשִׁים תָּא וְאַקְשִׁי לִי.

Rav Aḥa, son of Rav Yosef, said to Rav Ashi: Let the planter **say to** the owner: **You give your portion to the sharecropper,**[N] **and I will do what I wish with my portion.** I performed my half of the work properly, so why should I suffer a loss because you want to pay the sharecropper? Rav Ashi **said** to him: **When you reach** the tractate of: **The slaughter of sacrificial** animals,[N] i.e., tractate *Zevaḥim*, **come and ask** this difficulty **to me.** In other words, your question is a good one, worthy of a difficult tractate full of complex reasoning such as *Zevaḥim*.

גּוּפָא, אֲמַר רַב מִנְיוּמִי בְּרֵיהּ דְּרַב נַחוּמִי: בְּאַתְרָא דְּשָׁקֵיל שָׁתָלָא פַּלְגָא וַאֲרִיסָא תִּילְתָּא, הַאי שָׁתָלָא דְּבָעֵי אִיסְתַּלּוֹקֵי – יָהֲבִינַן לֵיהּ שְׁבָחֵיהּ וּמְסַלְּקִינַן לֵיהּ, כִּי הֵיכִי דְּלָא לִיפְסוֹד בַּעַל הַבַּיִת. אֲמַר רַב מִנְיוּמִי בְּרֵיהּ דְּרַב נַחוּמִי: קוֹפָא סָבָא – פַּלְגָא; שָׁטְפָה נַהֲרָא – רִיבְעָא.

With regard to **the** matter **itself, Rav Minyumi, son of Rav Naḥumi, said:**[N] **In a location where the planter takes half** the fruit **and the sharecropper one-third,** with regard to **a planter who wants to leave, we give him** his share of the value of **the enhancement and remove him** in such a manner **so that the homeowner should suffer no loss. Rav Minyumi, son of Rav Naḥumi,** further **said:** With regard to **an old vine**[N] in a vineyard, the planter receives **half.** Although he did not plant the vine, since he was placed in charge of the entire vineyard, he receives a portion of that which was there before. If **a river flooded**[H] the vineyard and the owner and the planter come to divide the trees that fell down, the planter receives **one-quarter.**

הַהוּא גַּבְרָא דְּמַשְׁכֵּין פַּרְדֵּיסָא לְחַבְרֵיהּ לַעֲשַׂר שְׁנִין, וְקַשׁ לְחָמֵשׁ שְׁנִין. אַבַּיֵי אֲמַר: פֵּירָא הָוֵי. רָבָא אֲמַר: קַרְנָא הָוֵי, וְיִלָּקַח בּוֹ קַרְקַע וְהוּא אוֹכֵל פֵּירוֹת.

§ The Gemara relates: There was **a certain man who mortgaged an orchard to another,** i.e., the creditor, **for ten years** in order that the latter should use the profits gained from the orchard as repayment of the debt. **But** the orchard **aged**[H] **after five years** and no longer produced quality fruit. Consequently, the only way to proceed was to cut down its trees and sell them as wood. **Abaye said:** This wood **is** considered as **produce**[N] of the orchard, and therefore the creditor is entitled to cut them down and sell them. **Rava said:** The wood **is** classified as **principal**[N] and is therefore viewed as part of the orchard itself. Consequently, the creditor has no rights to the wood itself, **but** other **land** is **purchased with** the profits from the sale of the wood **and** the creditor **consumes the produce** of that land until the debt is repaid.

מֵיתִיבֵי: יָבֵשׁ הָאִילָן אוֹ נִקְצַץ – שְׁנֵיהֶם אֲסוּרִים בּוֹ. כֵּיצַד יַעֲשׂוּ? יִמָּכְרוּ לְעֵצִים, וְיִלָּקַח בָּהֶן קַרְקַע, וְהוּא אוֹכֵל פֵּירוֹת. מַאי לָאו יָבֵשׁ דּוּמְיָא דְּנִקְצַץ? מַה נִּקְצַץ – בִּזְמַנּוֹ, אַף יָבֵשׁ – בִּזְמַנּוֹ. וְקָתָנֵי: יִלָּקַח בָּהֶן קַרְקַע וְהוּא אוֹכֵל פֵּירוֹת. אַלְמָא: קַרְנָא הָוֵי!

The Gemara **raises an objection** against this from a *baraita* that discusses the *halakhot* of a mortgage: If **the tree dried up or was chopped down,** it is **forbidden** for **both** the creditor and the debtor to take **it** for themselves. **How should they proceed?** It **is sold for wood, and land should be purchased with** the proceeds, **and he,** i.e., the creditor, **consumes the produce** from that land. The Gemara clarifies: **What, is it not** referring to **a dry** tree that is **similar** to one **that was chopped down,** in that **just as** the tree **was chopped down at its** proper **time, so too,** the tree **dried at its** proper **time? And** yet the *tanna* **teaches** that **land should be purchased with** the money **and** the creditor **consumes the produce. Apparently,** the wood **is** considered part of the **principal,** not the profits. This supports Rava's opinion and presents a difficulty to Abaye.

HALAKHA

An old vine…a river flooded – קוֹפָא סָבָא...שָׁטְפָה נַהֲרָא: A planter who takes half the fruit is also entitled to half of the old vines. If the vineyard was flooded by a river or uprooted in the wind he receives only one-quarter. The Gra and the *Arukh HaShulḥan* accept the ruling of the *Tur* that in the latter case he receives only one-sixth, in accordance with Rav Ashi (*Shulḥan Arukh*, *Ḥoshen Mishpat* 330:4).

Mortgaged an orchard…but it aged – מַשְׁכֵּין פַּרְדֵּיסָא...וְקַשׁ: If one received an orchard as a mortgage for ten years and it dried up during this time, its wood should be sold. The proceeds from the sale should be used for the purchase of land, whose produce the creditor consumes until the end of the mortgage period. It is prohibited for both individuals to use the trees themselves, out of concern for interest. The Ra'avad maintains that the reason it is prohibited for the creditor is to ensure that the principal should not be consumed, while it is prohibited for the debtor because it is currently on lien to the debtor. The same *halakhot* apply in the case of one who rents an orchard from another. The *halakha* here follows Rava in opposition to Abaye, as in almost all of their disputes (Rambam *Sefer Mishpatim*, *Hilkhot Sekhirut* 7:5 and *Maggid Mishne* there).

NOTES

You give your portion to the sharecropper – אַנְתְּ מְנָתָא דִּילָךְ הַב לֵיהּ לַאֲרִיסָא: The commentaries discuss the opinions of Rav Ashi and Rav Aḥa, son of Rav Yosef, at length. One explanation of Rav Aḥa's opinion is as follows: The planter says to the owner that he should give his share to the sharecropper, but the planter believes that with regard to his own share, perhaps he can find a sharecropper to work the field for a smaller payment (Rabbeinu Ḥananel). The Rosh explains that according to Rav Aḥa the planter has certain rights to the land itself (see *Tosafot*), and he is consequently entitled to his half even if he is evicted (see Gra).

When you reach the tractate of the slaughter of sacrificial animals – כִּי מָטֵית לִשְׁחִיטַת קָדָשִׁים: Rashi explains this reaction as a praise of Rav Aḥa's question, and the Ra'ah and the Ba'al HaMaor seem to concur. Most commentaries, including Rabbeinu Ḥananel and the *Arukh*, maintain that this cannot be the case, especially in light of the well-known consideration that the tractates of *Nezikin* are more analytical than tractate *Zevaḥim*, which mainly consists of traditions handed down through the generations (Ramban). Consequently, they understand this expression as a rejection of the difficulty: When you have learned much of the Talmud and reach tractate *Zevaḥim* in the order of *Kodashim*, you will realize that your question is not problematic at all. From the ruling of the Rambam, it appears that he also understood the Gemara this way.

With regard to the matter itself Rav Minyumi…said – גּוּפָא אָמַר רַב מִנְיוּמִי: The commentaries are puzzled as to why the Gemara repeats this statement of Rav Minyumi, as it neither analyzes nor adds anything to the previous discussion. The Rosh explains that it is mentioned only as an introduction to Rav Minyumi's second statement. Another possibility is that the Rif had a different version of the Gemara, according to which there is a difference between the original version of Rav Minyumi's statement and the second version that appears here.

An old vine [*kofa*] – קוֹפָא סָבָא: Rabbeinu Ḥananel and the *Arukh* explain that here the planter exerted himself to plant entirely new vines as replacements for the old one, which is the reason he receives half. Conversely, if the ground of the vineyard was made soft due to an overflowing river, the land is ready for planting, and the planter need not toil as much. Therefore, he is entitled to only one-quarter. The *Sma*, citing Rashi, suggests an alternative explanation of the difference between the two cases: The aging of a vine is a natural occurrence, and the planter initially undertook the job in order to receive the wood. By contrast, the river overflowing is not an event that can be anticipated ahead of time, and therefore he receives only one-quarter.

The Ra'avad interprets the word *kofa* as a beam, and explains that it refers to the beam of a vine that became wormy over time and must be replaced. In this case, the planter is entitled to half the value of the beam.

It is produce – פֵּירָא הָוֵי: Even according to Rav's opinion (see 79a) that the principal may not be entirely consumed, here the *halakha* is different, as they knew the plants would grow old and had the wood in mind when they made their agreement, as opposed to that case, when the donkey died unexpectedly (Rosh, 79a).

It is classified as principal – קַרְנָא הָוֵי: Similar to the previous note, even Shmuel, who rules in the case of a donkey (see 79a) that the principal may be destroyed, might agree here that the wood is treated as principal. The difference is that there they have no possibility of buying another donkey for the value of its carcass and consequently the principal is irretrievably lost; here they can purchase a certain amount of land that will bear produce (Rosh, 79a). Alternatively, in this case the planter intended to take only the produce, and therefore has no rights to the principal at all (Ran).

HALAKHA

If she had old vines and olive trees bequeathed to her – נָפְלוּ לָהּ גְּפָנִים וְזֵיתִים זְקֵנִים: With regard to the case of a wife who inherited olive trees and vines, if she did not inherit the land on which the trees and vines were growing, and they cover the cost of their upkeep, then they should not be sold because they are assets of her paternal family. This ruling, which is accepted by the Rif and the Rosh, is based on the Jerusalem Talmud. If the trees and vines do not produce enough profit to justify their maintenance, they should be sold for wood and the proceeds used for the purchase of land for the woman, with her husband retaining the right to consume its produce (Rambam *Sefer Nashim*, *Hilkhot Ishut* 22:23; *Shulḥan Arukh*, *Even HaEzer* 85:14).

לָא, נִקְצַץ דּוּמְיָא דְּיָבֵשׁ. מָה יָבֵשׁ בְּלֹא זְמַנּוֹ – אַף נִקְצַץ בְּלֹא זְמַנּוֹ.

The Gemara rejects this argument: **No,** the **chopped-down** tree mentioned in the *baraita* **is similar to** the **dry** one: **Just as** that tree **dried up before its time, so too,** this one **was chopped down before its time.** Since this did not occur naturally, the wood is classified as produce; had the orchard dried up at the expected time, its trees would be considered as part of the land.

תָּא שְׁמַע: נָפְלוּ לָהּ גְּפָנִים וְזֵיתִים זְקֵנִים

The Gemara suggests: **Come** and **hear** a proof to Rava's opinion from a mishna (*Ketubot* 79b): If a woman after her marriage had **old vines and olive** trees that were **bequeathed to her**[H] by means of inheritance,

Perek **IX**
Daf **110** Amud **a**

NOTES

Say, and they grew old – אֵימָא: וְהִזְקִינוּ: Rashi explains that the trees aged before their time, and an alternate version of the text actually states this explicitly. The other commentaries, though, question how this is implied by the language found in the standard text. One answer offered is that she did not inherit old trees but rather trees that grew old, and therefore did not have this outcome in mind when the trees came into her possession (*Torat Ḥayyim*). According to this opinion it makes no difference whether or not the trees aged before their time.

יִמָּכְרוּ לְעֵצִים וְיִלָּקַח בָּהֶן קַרְקַע, וְהוּא אוֹכֵל פֵּירוֹת! אֵימָא: וְהִזְקִינוּ.

such trees **are sold as wood and land is acquired with them, and** her husband **consumes the produce,** while the land itself belongs to the wife. The Gemara answers that the text should be emended to **say: And they grew old,**[N] meaning that the trees were not old when she inherited them but they aged with the passage of time.

וְאִיבָּעֵית אֵימָא: לָאו מִי אוֹקִימְנָא לְהַהִיא כְּגוֹן שֶׁנָּפְלוּ לָהּ בְּשָׂדֶה אַחֶרֶת, דְּקָא כָלְיָא קַרְנָא.

And if you wish, say: Did we not already **establish that** mishna as referring to a case **where** the vines or olive trees **were bequeathed to her in a different field** that did not belong to her? Since in **that** case she inherited only the trees but not the land itself, they are considered the principal. Consequently, the husband taking all of it **would consume the principal** entirely. Therefore, they must be sold as wood, with the proceeds used for the purchase of land.

הַהוּא שְׁטָרָא דַּהֲוָה כְּתִיב בֵּיהּ שְׁנִין סְתָמָא. מַלְוֶה אָמַר: שָׁלֹשׁ, לֹוֶה אָמַר: שְׁתַּיִם. קְדֵים מַלְוֶה וְאַכְלִינְהוּ לְפֵירֵי. מִי נֶאֱמָן? רַב יְהוּדָה אָמַר: קַרְקַע בְּחֶזְקַת בְּעָלֶיהָ קָיְימָא. רַב כָּהֲנָא אָמַר: פֵּירוֹת בְּחֶזְקַת אוֹכְלֵיהֶן קָיְימִי.

§ The Gemara relates: There was **a certain** mortgage **document in which it was written** that the land was granted to the creditor for **an unspecified** number of **years.** The **creditor said** it was for **three** years, whereas **the debtor said** it was for **two** years.[H] While the issue was being adjudicated, the **creditor arose and consumed the produce** of the field in the third year. **Which** of them is **deemed credible** and accepted? **Rav Yehuda said:** The *halakha* is that **land remains in its owner's possession.** Therefore, the debtor has the presumptive right to the land, while the creditor, who owns the document, must provide proof for his claim. **Rav Kahana said:** The **produce remains in the possession of** the one who **consumed it,** and therefore the creditor's claim is accepted.

וְהִלְכְתָא כְּוָותֵיהּ דְּרַב כָּהֲנָא, דְּאָמַר: פֵּירוֹת בְּחֶזְקַת אוֹכְלֵיהֶן קָיְימִי. וְהָא קַיְימָא לַן דְּהִלְכְתָא כְּוָותֵיהּ דְּרַב נַחְמָן, דְּאָמַר: קַרְקַע בְּחֶזְקַת בְּעָלֶיהָ עוֹמֶדֶת!

The Gemara states: **And the** ***halakha*** **is in accordance with** the opinion **of Rav Kahana, who said** that the **produce remains in the possession of** the one who **consumed it.** The Gemara asks: **But don't we maintain that the** ***halakha*** **is in accordance with** the opinion **of Rav Naḥman, who said** with regard to uncertainty concerning a rental during the extra month of a leap year that **land remains in its owner's possession,** and he has the rights to that month? These two rulings appear to contradict each other.

הָתָם מִילְּתָא דְּלָא עֲבִידָא לְאִיגַּלּוּיֵי הִיא; הָכָא – מִילְּתָא דַּעֲבִידָא לְאִיגַּלּוּיֵי הִיא, וְאַטְרוּחֵי בֵּי דִינָא תְּרֵי זִימְנֵי לָא מַטְרְחִינַן.

The Gemara answers: **There it is a matter that will not be revealed** because it is impossible to clarify the uncertainty concerning whether the extra month is included. By contrast, **here it is a matter that will be revealed,** as the witnesses who signed the document may eventually reveal what it stated, **and we do not trouble the court** to convene **twice.** Therefore, the produce should remain in the possession of the one who consumed it until the matter is resolved.

HALAKHA

The creditor said three and the debtor said two – מַלְוֶה אָמַר שָׁלֹשׁ לֹוֶה אָמַר שְׁתַּיִם: If a rental document or mortgage stated: Years, without specifying how many, and the creditor claims it was for three years, while the landowner, i.e., the debtor, says it was for only two years, if the former went ahead and consumed the produce it is considered in his possession unless the landowner provides proof to the contrary. Some authorities maintain that if the court sees this matter will not be clarified, the creditor is forced to pay for the produce he consumed during the third year (Rambam *Sefer Mishpatim*, *Hilkhot Sekhirut* 7:6; *Shulḥan Arukh*, *Ḥoshen Mishpat* 150:7; 317:3).

מַלְוֶה אוֹמֵר חָמֵשׁ, לֹוֶה אוֹמֵר שָׁלֹשׁ. אֲמַר לֵיהּ: אַיְיתִי לִי שְׁטָרָךְ! אֲמַר לֵיהּ: שְׁטָרָא אִירְכַּס לִי. אֲמַר רַב יְהוּדָה: מַלְוֶה נֶאֱמָן, מִגּוֹ דְּאִי בָּעֵי אָמַר לְקוּחָה הִיא בְּיָדַי.

The Gemara analyzes another case involving mortgaged land. The **creditor says** the mortgage was for **five** years while the **debtor** who owned the land **says** it was for **three.**[H] The debtor **said to** the creditor: **Give me your document** so that we can see what is written there. The creditor **said to him: I lost the document. Rav Yehuda said:** The **creditor is deemed credible** and accepted in this case **since he could have made a more advantageous claim** [***miggo***].[B] As the mortgage document is missing and even according to the claim of the debtor he could be in control of the land for the three years required for presumptive ownership, **if** he **wants** to lie he could **say:** The land was **purchased by me.** Since he did not submit this superior claim, his claim should be accepted.

אֲמַר לֵיהּ רַב פַּפָּא לְרַב אַשִׁי: רַב זְבִיד וְרַב עֲוִירָא לָא סְבִירָא לְהוּ הָא דְּרַב יְהוּדָה. מַאי טַעְמָא? הַאי שְׁטָרָא כֵּיוָן דִּלְגוּבַיְינָא קָאֵי – מִיזְהַר זָהֵיר בֵּיהּ, וּמִיכְבַּשׁ הוּא דִּכְבַשֵׁיהּ לִשְׁטָרֵיהּ. סָבַר: אוֹכְלָהּ תַּרְתֵּין שְׁנִין יְתֵירָתָא.

Rav Pappa said to Rav Ashi: Rav Zevid and Rav Avira do not hold of **this** opinion **of Rav Yehuda. What is the reason** for this? **Since this document stands** ready **for collecting** the debt, the creditor would certainly have been **careful with regard to it.** Since he wants to ensure his money is returned it is unlikely he actually lost it. Rather, **he is** merely **hiding his document,** as he **thinks: I will consume** the produce of the field for **two extra years.**

אֲמַר לֵיהּ רָבִינָא לְרַב אַשִׁי: אֶלָּא מֵעַתָּה, הַאי מַשְׁכַּנְתָּא דְּסוּרָא דְּכָתְבִי הָכִי: בְּמִישְׁלַם שְׁנַיָּא אִלֵּין תֵּיפּוֹק אַרְעָא דָּא בְּלָא כְּסַף – הֵיכָא דִּכְבַשֵׁיהּ לִשְׁטַר מַשְׁכַּנְתָּא וַאֲמַר לְקוּחָה הִיא בְּיָדַי, הָכִי נַמִי דִּמְהֵימָן? וְכִי מְתַקְּנִי רַבָּנַן מִילְּתָא דְּאָתֵי בָּהּ [לִידֵי] פְּסֵידָא? אֲמַר לֵיהּ: הָתָם תַּקִּינוּ לֵיהּ רַבָּנַן דְּמָרֵי אַרְעָא יָהֵיב טַסְקָא וְכָרֵי כַּרְיָא.

The Gemara analyzes Rav Yehuda's opinion. **Ravina said to Rav Ashi: If that is so,** that Rav Yehuda is correct, then with regard to **this mortgage according to** the custom practiced in **Sura,**[N] a city in Babylonia, in **which they write this: Upon the completion of these years** of the mortgage **this land shall leave** the creditor's possession and return to its owner **without** the debtor paying any **money** (see 67b), in a case **where** the creditor **hid the mortgage document**[H] **and said** that the land was **purchased by me, so too** is it possible **that he is deemed credible?**[N] **Would the Sages institute a matter that** might **cause a loss?** Rav Ashi **said to him: There,** in the mortgage of Sura, **the Sages instituted for** the landowner, i.e., the debtor, **that the landowner,** i.e., the debtor, **pays the** land **taxes and digs the trenches** for the irrigation of the field. In this manner, his ownership is preserved and established.

אַרְעָא דְּלֵית לָהּ כַּרְיָא וְלָא יָהֵיב טַסְקָא מַאי? אֲמַר לֵיהּ: אִיבָּעֵי לֵיהּ לְמַחוּיֵי. לָא אִימְחָא מַאי? אִיהוּ הוּא דְּאַפְסֵיד אַנַּפְשֵׁיהּ.

Ravina asks further: With regard to **land that has no** need for **trenches and** for which he **does not pay taxes, what** could he have done? Rav Ashi **said to him: He should have protested**[B] before the three years needed for presumptive status had passed by announcing that the land was his. Ravina again inquires: If he **did not protest, what** is the *halakha*? Rav Ashi replied: In that case, **he caused his own loss** by failing to take the necessary precautions.

HALAKHA

The creditor says five while the debtor says three – מַלְוֶה אוֹמֵר חָמֵשׁ לֹוֶה אוֹמֵר שָׁלֹשׁ: If one took possession of a field as a mortgage and stayed there for three years, and there are no witnesses that he took it as a mortgage, if he claims that the terms of the mortgage allowed him to retain the field for an additional two years he is deemed credible, as he could have claimed that he had purchased it. This applies even if he says he had the mortgage document and lost it. This is the ruling of the Rif, the Rambam, and the Rosh, in accordance with Rav Yehuda, as Rav Ashi apparently accepts his opinion.

According to the *Shakh*, since the *Ba'al Halakhot Gedolot*, the Ramban, Rabbeinu Yona and others all dispute this ruling and maintain that the *halakha* is in accordance with the opinion of Rav Zevid and Rav Avira, this should be considered an uncertain case of monetary law, and should be treated accordingly (Rambam *Sefer Mishpatim*, *Hilkhot Sekhirut* 7:6; *Shulḥan Arukh*, *Ḥoshen Mishpat* 150:7; 317:4).

Mortgage according to the custom practiced in Sura… where he hid the mortgage document – ...מַשְׁכַּנְתָּא דְּסוּרָא דִּכְבַשֵׁיהּ: If one took possession of a field as a mortgage he does not obtain presumptive ownership over it after three years, as long as the facts of the case remain known. Nevertheless, it is advisable for the debtor to lodge a protest at the end of every three years, in case the creditor hides the mortgage document and waits for the matter to be forgotten before claiming that he had purchased the field (*Shulḥan Arukh*, *Ḥoshen Mishpat* 150:1).

BACKGROUND

Since he could have made a more advantageous claim [*miggo*] – מִגּוֹ: This concept refers to an important legal argument, used to support the claim of one of the parties in a dispute. If one of the litigants could have made a claim more advantageous to his cause than he actually did, it is assumed that he is telling the truth. The *miggo* argument may be expressed in the following manner: Had he wanted to lie he would presumably have put forward the claim most advantageous to himself. Since he could have made a superior claim but did not do so, he therefore must be telling the truth.

There are certain limitations governing the application of this principle. For example, there is no *miggo* where there are witnesses (see *Ketubot* 27b). In other words, *miggo* is not effective where witnesses contradict the litigant's claim. The principle of *miggo* is the subject of profound legal analysis in the Talmud and its commentaries.

He should have protested – אִיבָּעֵי לֵיהּ לְמַחוּיֵי: If one has been physically in possession of property for a period of time, it serves as proof that the person in possession is in fact, as he claims, the legal owner. The period varies according to the nature of the property, e.g., real estate requires three years. One who is able to prove uninterrupted possession for the necessary period is no longer required to produce documentary evidence of his legal title to the property. In order to preclude the one using the property from claiming ownership after three years, the previous owner must lodge a protest during that period.

NOTES

If that is so, this mortgage according to the custom practiced in Sura – אֶלָּא מֵעַתָּה הַאי מַשְׁכַּנְתָּא דְּסוּרָא: The Ramban explains that the Gemara cited the example of the mortgage of Sura because Rav Ashi maintains that the creditor is permitted to consume the produce of the land in payment for the debt only with regard to a mortgage of this kind. Alternatively, the question is less problematic concerning other types of mortgages that were not instituted by the Sages, and there is no concern that it leads to a distortion of justice. The Ran discusses this idea more at length. The Ra'avad contends that concerning other types of mortgages the owner of the land can evict the creditor at any time, whereas a mortgage of Sura applies for a predetermined period.

So too is it possible that he is deemed credible, etc. – הָכִי נַמִי דִּמְהֵימָן וכו׳: The commentaries engage in a dispute concerning the meaning of Ravina's question as well as to which of the opinions it is directed. Some maintain, based on Rashi, that the difficulty lies in the opinion of Rav Yehuda. Rav Zevid and Rav Avira hold that one would not dare lie about a mortgage when the truth is likely to come out. By contrast, since Rav Yehuda deems the creditor credible when he says he purchased the field, this concern does apply to a mortgage of Sura (Rid).

Others contend that the question is relevant to the opinion of Rav Zevid as well, as he too agrees that the claim that the creditor purchased the field is valid in principle. Nevertheless, if the creditor said he lost the document, this is effectively a *miggo* that is contradicted by witnesses, as one would certainly not treat a document of this kind in such a careless manner. Consequently, if there is no clear counterargument of this kind, the creditor's claim that he purchased the field would be accepted.

The assumption behind the question, then, is that apparently people in general are aware of the need to lodge a protest only if their land has been seized by a robber, but if it was given to someone as a mortgage they do not realize that a protest is required or is even effective (Rosh).

אָרִיס אוֹמֵר: לְמֶחֱצָה יָרַדְתִּי, וּבַעַל הַבַּיִת אוֹמֵר: לִשְׁלִישׁ הוֹרַדְתִּיו, מִי נֶאֱמָן? רַב יְהוּדָה אָמַר: בַּעַל הַבַּיִת נֶאֱמָן. רַב נַחְמָן אָמַר: הַכֹּל כְּמִנְהַג הַמְּדִינָה.

§ The Gemara discusses another case. If **a sharecropper says: I descended** to the field **for half** the produce,[N] as this was the agreement that we made, **and the homeowner says: I sent him down for** only **one-third** of the produce,[H] **who is deemed credible** and his claim consequently accepted? **Rav Yehuda says: The homeowner is deemed credible** and his claim is consequently accepted, while **Rav Naḥman says: All** matters are **in accordance with the regional custom.**[N] As the terms of their agreement are unknown, this sharecropper should have the same status as other sharecroppers in that location.

סְבוּר מִינָּהּ: לָא פְּלִיגִי; הָא – בְּאַתְרָא דְּשָׁקֵיל אֲרִיסָא פַּלְגָּא, הָא – בְּאַתְרָא דְּשָׁקֵיל אֲרִיסָא תִּילְתָּא.

They **understood from** the above discussion that these two Sages **do not disagree,** but were referring to different cases: **This** one, Rav Naḥman, stated his ruling **with regard to a location where the sharecropper takes half,** in which case the sharecropper is believed, while **that** one, Rav Yehuda, stated his ruling **with regard to a location where the sharecropper takes one-third,** in which case the homeowner is believed.

אֲמַר לְהוּ רַב מָרִי בְּרֵהּ דְּבַת שְׁמוּאֵל: הָכִי אֲמַר אַבָּיֵי: אֲפִילּוּ בְּאַתְרָא דְּשָׁקֵיל אֲרִיסָא פַּלְגָּא פְּלִיגִי. רַב יְהוּדָה אָמַר: בַּעַל הַבַּיִת נֶאֱמָן, דְּאִי בָּעֵי אָמַר שְׂכִירִי וְלָקִיטִי הוּא.

Rav Mari, son of the daughter of Shmuel, said to them: This is what **Abaye said:** They **even disagree with regard to a location where the sharecropper** usually **takes half.** In that case, **Rav Yehuda said** that here too **the homeowner is deemed credible** and his claim is consequently accepted, **as if he wants** to lie he could **say:** The other is not a sharecropper at all but merely **my hired worker,** who received a stipulated wage, **or my gleaner,** who performs occasional work for me but has no prearranged share of the crop at all.

יְתוֹמִים אוֹמְרִים: אָנוּ הִשְׁבַּחְנוּ, וּבַעַל חוֹב אוֹמֵר: אֲבִיכֶם הִשְׁבִּיחַ – עַל מִי לְהָבִיא רְאָיָה?

The Gemara addresses another issue: If a field was on lien for a loan and the debtor died, and **the orphans** who inherited the field **say: We enhanced**[N] the land after we inherited it, and therefore the creditor does not have a right to the value of that enhancement, **and the creditor says: Your father enhanced it,** and I am entitled to the land as it is, **upon whom** does the burden **to bring proof** fall?

Perek **IX**
Daf **110** Amud **b**

סָבַר רַבִּי חֲנִינָא לְמֵימַר: אַרְעָא בְּחֶזְקַת יַתְמֵי קַיְימָא, וְעַל בַּעַל חוֹב לְהָבִיא רְאָיָה. אֲמַר לְהוּ הַהוּא סָבָא, הָכִי אָמַר רַבִּי יוֹחָנָן: עַל הַיְתוֹמִים לְהָבִיא רְאָיָה. מַאי טַעְמָא? אַרְעָא, כֵּיוָן דִּלְגוּבַיְינָא קַיְימָא, כְּמַאן דְּגַבְיָא דַּמְיָא, וְעַל הַיְתוֹמִין לְהָבִיא רְאָיָה.

Rabbi Ḥanina thought to say that the **land remains in the orphans' possession,** as they are currently in control of it, **and** therefore the responsibility falls **upon the creditor to bring proof.**[N] **A certain elder said to them: This** is what **Rabbi Yoḥanan says:** The responsibility falls **upon the orphans to bring proof.**[H] **What is the reason** for this? **Since** this **land stands** ready **for collection,** it is **considered as though it has** already **been collected** and is in the creditor's possession. Consequently, the responsibility falls **upon the orphans to bring proof.**

NOTES

A sharecropper says…for half – אָרִיס אוֹמֵר לְמֶחֱצָה: It would appear that the same question applies even if the sharecropper had already consumed half the crops: Is the value of that which he unlawfully consumed removed from him? (*Ma'ayanei HaḤokhma*).

All matters are in accordance with the regional custom – הַכֹּל כְּמִנְהַג הַמְּדִינָה: The early commentaries infer from here that a *miggo* is not accepted if it contradicts an established custom, as this is considered a *miggo* against witnesses (Ramban, citing *Ge'onim*). Other commentaries contend that no principle may be deduced from here, as Rav Naḥman rejects this particular *miggo* as a weak argument, whereas in other cases he might accept a *miggo* even if it runs counter to the local custom (*Urim VeTummim*).

The orphans say we enhanced – יְתוֹמִים אוֹמְרִים אָנוּ הִשְׁבַּחְנוּ: The early commentaries note that this refers only to a field that the debtor, the orphans' father, set aside as designated repayment, as in other cases a different *halakha* applies to a buyer and orphans (*Tosafot*, *Ketubot* 96b; Rosh).

HALAKHA

A sharecropper says…for half and the homeowner says…for one-third – אָרִיס אוֹמֵר לְמֶחֱצָה...וּבַעַל הַבַּיִת אוֹמֵר לִשְׁלִישׁ: If a sharecropper claims that the owner agreed he is entitled to half the produce, while the owner says he stipulated that he should receive only one-third, the regional custom is followed, as the *halakha* is in accordance with Rav Naḥman in cases of monetary law (Rambam *Sefer Kinyan*, *Hilkhot Sheluḥin VeShutafin* 8:5; *Shulḥan Arukh*, *Ḥoshen Mishpat* 330:5).

HALAKHA

Orphans and a creditor with regard to enhancement – יְתוֹמִים וּבַעַל חוֹב בְּשֶׁבַח: If a creditor seized a field from orphans and the land had been enhanced through labor, and the orphans claimed to have enhanced the land themselves while the creditor says their deceased father was responsible, the burden of proof falls upon the orphans. This ruling is in accordance with the opinion of the Rambam. Other authorities maintain that it is the creditor who must bring proof, unless the field was the designated repayment for the debt (Rema, citing *Tur* and Rosh). The *Shakh* rules in accordance with the first opinion (Rambam *Sefer Mishpatim*, *Hilkhot Malve VeLoveh* 21:7; *Shulḥan Arukh*, *Ḥoshen Mishpat* 115:5).

NOTES

Orphans and a creditor – יְתוֹמִים וּבַעַל חוֹב: Behind the various explanations and rulings with regard to this issue lies a fundamental dispute between the early commentaries with regard to the standing of orphans vis-à-vis their deceased father's creditor concerning enhancement of property the latter is given as payment for the debt. The Rif, *Tosafot*, and the Ra'avad maintain that such orphans are considered as if they purchased the land from their father. Consequently, they are treated in the same manner as anyone who purchased land from a debtor and then has that land seized by the creditor, and are not entitled to payment for the enhancement to the land in the interim, even if it resulted from their labor. An exception to this would be if the field was set aside as designated repayment for the debt, in which case they are considered like one who enhanced another's field without asking the owner first, who is entitled to receive some compensation (*Tosafot*).

The Gemara here is somewhat difficult to understand according to this explanation, as these commentaries are forced to explain that the entire discussion is relevant only in the case of field set aside as designated repayment.

By contrast, Rashi, the Rambam, the Ramban, and the Rashba maintain that the orphans are considered as if they received the land as a gift from their father. Accordingly, the creditor has rights only to the land itself but not to the enhancement, except for any enhancement that resulted from natural causes, not due to efforts expended by the orphans. The passage here fits well with this explanation, although certain difficulties arising from another passage must still be addressed (see *Bekhorot* 52a). See the Rashba, who discusses this issue and offers a resolution to these problems.

The reasoning behind the first explanation is apparently that orphans replace their father in all respects. Consequently, just as the creditor had the right to take the enhanced field from the father as payment for the debt, he has the right to take the enhanced field from the orphans. For more on this, see the Ra'avad and *Tosafot* (15a). As for the second explanation, the commentary attributed to the Ritva states that orphans are comparable to recipients of a gift, as they too have no one from whom they can collect their loss, as opposed to a buyer, who can return to claim his expenses from the seller.

אמר אביי: אף אנן נמי תנינא: ספק זה קדם וספק זה קדם – קוצץ ואינו נותן דמים.

Abaye said: We learn a similar *halakha* in the mishna (*Bava Batra* 24b) **as well,** with regard to a tree planted adjacent to a city. Such a tree must be chopped down in any event, regardless of what preceded what. If the city preceded the tree, the owner is not entitled to compensation, but if the tree was there first, he receives payment for the tree. If it is **uncertain** whether **this** one was **first**[H] or **that** one was **first,** the owner of the tree **cuts it down and** the people of the city **do not give money** to the owner.

אלמא: כיון דלמיקץ קיימא – אמרינן ליה: אייתי ראיה ושקול. הכי נמי, האי שטרא כיון דלגוביינא קיימא – כמאן דגביא דמיא, ועל היתומים להביא ראיה.

Apparently, since this tree is **standing to be chopped down,** as it is chopped down regardless of whether it or the town was there first, **we say to** the owner of the tree: You must **bring proof** to support your claim that the tree was there before the town **and** only then you may **take** its value, although the tree is currently in his possession and has not yet been cut down. **So too,** with regard to **this document** recording the lien on the land, **since it** is **ready for collection,** it is **considered as though it has been collected and** the responsibility falls **upon the orphans to bring proof.**

אייתו יתמי ראיה דאינהו אשבחו. סבר רבי חנינא למימר: כי מסלקינן להו בארעא מסלקינן להו.

In the case where **the orphans brought proof that they** indeed **enhanced** the land, **Rabbi Ḥanina thought to say: When we remove them, we remove them by** giving them part of **the land** equivalent to the value of their enhancement.

ולא היא, בדמי מסלקינן להו, מדרב נחמן. דאמר רב נחמן אמר שמואל: שלשה שמין להם את השבח, ומעלין אותן בדמים, ואלו הן: בכור לפשוט,

The Gemara comments: **But** that **is not** so, as **we remove them** by paying them **with money,**[H] as derived **from** a statement **of Rav Naḥman. As Rav Naḥman says** that **Shmuel says:** In **three** cases the court **appraises the enhanced** value **for** the parties involved in enhancing a field, **and they are paid in money**[H] rather than by being given a portion of the property. **And these are they:** The first is a **firstborn** son who makes payment **to an ordinary,** i.e., non-firstborn, son.[H] This is a case where two sons, one firstborn and the other not, inherit a field from their father. Before it is divided, they both work and enhance the field. When the time comes to divide the field, the firstborn son, who receives a double portion, must pay his brother for the enhancement that the latter contributed to the former's portion. This payment is given in money rather than land.

ובעל חוב וכתובת אשה ליתומים, ובעל חוב ללקוחות.

And the second case is that of payment taken by **a creditor or** the payment of **a marriage contract** by someone who is obligated **to** reimburse **orphans,** i.e., a creditor or widow who collects land from the orphans of the deceased debtor or husband, respectively. He or she must pay the orphans for any enhancements they made after their father's death. This payment is also given in money rather than land. **And** the third case is that of **a creditor** who is obligated **to purchasers,** i.e., a creditor who collects the debt from lands that were sold by the debtor. He pays money to the purchaser for the enhancements generated by the purchaser but does not pay him in land.

אמר ליה רבינא לרב אשי: למימרא דסבר שמואל בעל חוב ללקוחות? ומאי אית ליה שבחא ללוקח? והאמר שמואל: בעל חוב גובה את השבח! וכי תימא: לא קשיא, כאן בשבח המגיע לכתפים; כאן בשבח שאין מגיע לכתפים – והא מעשים בכל יום, וקא מגבי שמואל אפילו בשבח המגיע לכתפים!

Ravina said to Rav Ashi: Is this **to say that Shmuel maintains** that **a creditor** must pay the value of the enhancement **to the buyers? And what** type of **enhancement is there** that is given **to a buyer** according to Shmuel? **But doesn't Shmuel say: A creditor collects** even **the enhancement,** not only the land itself? **And if you would say** that this is **not difficult,** as **here** it is referring **to enhancement** that is so great **that** it **reaches the shoulders,**[N] meaning it is large enough to be carried away on porters' shoulders, whereas **there** it is referring **to enhancement that does not reach the shoulders,** that is still difficult. **But aren't there incidents every day** where **Shmuel would collect** everything on behalf of a creditor, **even enhancement that reaches the shoulders?**

לא קשיא; הא – דמסיק ביה כשיעור ארעא ושבחא; הא – דלא מסיק ביה שיעור ארעא ושבחא.

The Gemara responds: It is **not difficult; this** is referring to a case **where** the debtor **owed him the amount** of the value of **the land and the enhancement** combined, and therefore the creditor does not leave the buyers with anything, whereas **that** involves a case **where he did not owe him the amount** of the value of **the land and the enhancement.** Since he has taken more than the sum to which he is entitled, he pays the buyers for the improvement.

HALAKHA

If it is uncertain whether this one was first – ספק זה קדם: All trees must be planted at least twenty-five cubits away from a city, while carob trees and fig trees must be positioned at a distance of fifty cubits. If trees were found closer than this and the city preceded the trees, they are chopped down and the owner is not entitled to compensation. If the tree came first, it is chopped down but the owner is paid. If it is uncertain which came first, he does not receive compensation. According to the *Maggid Mishne*, this *halakha* is in force only in Eretz Yisrael (*Shulḥan Arukh, Ḥoshen Mishpat* 155:22, and in the comment of Rema).

How is the enhancement paid to orphans – כיצד משלמים שבח ליתומים: If a field was set aside as designated repayment for a loan and the orphans brought proof that they were responsible for its enhancement, if the creditor seizes the land he must compensate them either for the enhancement or for their expenses incurred in enhancing the field, whichever is less. The Rema, citing the *Tur*, states that this *halakha* applies only if the debt did not amount to the sum of the field and the enhancement, but if it was equal in value to both of them he does not have to pay them anything. The later commentaries reject this view (*Arukh HaShulḥan*, citing *Sma*). In a case where the field was not set aside as designated repayment, the orphans may either pay off the debt to the creditor by giving him money or give him the land and claim the value of the enhancement by keeping a portion of the land itself (Rambam *Sefer Mishpatim, Hilkhot Malve VeLoveh* 21:7; *Shulḥan Arukh, Ḥoshen Mishpat* 115:6).

Appraises the enhanced value…in money – שמין להם את השבח...בדמים: In the case of a wife's marriage contract, a creditor, or a buyer, when the recipient is obligated to pay for the enhancement he pays it in the form of money, not land (Rambam *Sefer Mishpatim, Hilkhot Naḥalot* 3:4; *Shulḥan Arukh, Ḥoshen Mishpat* 115:1, 6).

A firstborn to an ordinary son with regard to enhancement – בכור לפשוט בשבח: A firstborn is entitled to a double portion of the enhancement of inherited property after the father's death only if it became enhanced of its own accord, such as a tree that grew. If the enhancement marked a change in the item, such as a fruit that sprouted, and certainly if it came about as a result of labor, the enhancement is evaluated and he must compensate the other brothers (Rambam *Sefer Mishpatim, Hilkhot Naḥalot* 3:4; *Shulḥan Arukh, Ḥoshen Mishpat* 278:6).

NOTES

Enhancement that reaches the shoulders – שבח המגיע לכתפים: This phrase may be understood in several different ways. Most commentaries interpret it to mean produce that is fully grown and ready to be harvested and carried on the shoulders of laborer (Rabbeinu Ḥananel; Rif; Rashi). Rashi qualifies this interpretation, stating that the produce is clearly not completely ready to be harvested, as if that were the case it would not be liened to debts at all.

A second interpretation is that the phrase is referring to any produce that will eventually be harvested and removed from the land. This category excludes enhancements to the field itself, such as enrichment of the soil or growth of its trees (*Tosafot, Bava Kamma* 95b; Rabbeinu Tam, *Sefer HaYashar*). A third interpretation is that it is referring to an enhancement that is the result of manual labor, rather than enhancements that occur without intervention (Rashba, citing Rabbeinu Tam; Ra'avad, citing Rav Hai Gaon).

וְכִי לָא מַסֵּיק שִׁיעוּר אַרְעָא וְשִׁבְחָא – דְּיָהֵיב לֵיהּ זוּזֵי לַלּוֹקֵחַ וּמְסַלֵּק לֵיהּ. הָנִיחָא לְמַאן דְּאָמַר אִי אִית לֵיהּ זוּזֵי לַלּוֹקֵחַ – לָא מָצֵי מְסַלֵּק לֵיהּ לְבַעַל חוֹב – שַׁפִּיר. אֶלָּא לְמַאן דְּאָמַר אִית לֵיהּ זוּזֵי לַלּוֹקֵחַ מָצֵי מְסַלֵּק לֵיהּ לְבַעַל חוֹב, וְנֵימָא לֵיהּ: אִי הָווּ לִי זוּזֵי – הֲוָה מְסַלֵּיקְנָא לָךְ מִכּוּלָּא אַרְעָא. הָשְׁתָּא דְּלֵית לִי זוּזֵי – הַב לִי גְּרִיוָא דְּאַרְעָא בְּאַרְעַאי שִׁיעוּר שִׁבְחַאי!

The Gemara asks: **And if he did not owe** him **the amount** of the value **of the land and the enhancement,** it was stated **that** the creditor **gives the buyer money and removes him. This works out well according to the one who says** that even **if the buyer has money he cannot remove the creditor** by paying him his debt in cash, as the creditor has the right to claim land. According to this opinion, it works **well. But according to the one who says** that if **the buyer has money he may remove the creditor** by paying him cash and keep the land for himself, **let him say to him** as follows: **If I had money** prepared **I would remove you from the entire land; now that I do not have money** equal to the value of the entire land, since you must repay me for the enhancement, at least **give me a plot of earth in my land** corresponding to the **amount** of the value **of my enhancement.**

הָכָא בְּמַאי עָסְקִינַן – כְּגוֹן דְּשַׁוְיָא נִיהֲלֵיהּ אַפּוֹתֵיקִי, דַּאֲמַר לֵיהּ: לֹא יְהֵא לְךָ פֵּרָעוֹן אֶלָּא מִזּוֹ.

The Gemara responds: **Here we are dealing with** a case **where** the debtor **set aside** this land as **designated repayment** [*apoteiki*][L] **for** the creditor, **as he said to him: You shall be able to collect from only this** land, but no other. Consequently, the creditor wants to take the entire land, as his lien applies only to this field, and if it turns out that he has other claims he will be unable to collect them from elsewhere.

מתני׳ הַמְקַבֵּל שָׂדֶה מֵחֲבֵירוֹ לְשָׁבוּעַ אֶחָד בְּשֶׁבַע מֵאוֹת זוּז – הַשְּׁבִיעִית מִן הַמִּנְיָן. קִבְּלָהּ הֵימֶנּוּ שֶׁבַע שָׁנִים בְּשֶׁבַע מֵאוֹת זוּז – אֵין הַשְּׁבִיעִית מִן הַמִּנְיָן.

MISHNA In the case of one **who receives a field from another** to cultivate **for one** Sabbatical **cycle** of seven years culminating with the Sabbatical Year **for seven hundred dinars, the Sabbatical** Year is included **in the tally,**[N] despite the fact that he is unable to work the land during that year. If he **received it from him** to cultivate **for seven years**[H] **for seven hundred dinars, the Sabbatical** Year is **not** included **in the number,** and he may keep the field for an additional year to take the place of the Sabbatical Year, during which he could not work the land.

שְׂכִיר יוֹם גּוֹבֶה כָּל הַלַּיְלָה, שְׂכִיר לַיְלָה גּוֹבֶה כָּל הַיּוֹם. שְׂכִיר שָׁעוֹת גּוֹבֶה כָּל הַלַּיְלָה וְכָל הַיּוֹם. שְׂכִיר שַׁבָּת, שְׂכִיר חֹדֶשׁ, שְׂכִיר שָׁנָה, שְׂכִיר שָׁבוּעַ – יָצָא בַּיּוֹם, גּוֹבֶה כָּל הַיּוֹם; יָצָא בַּלַּיְלָה – גּוֹבֶה כָּל הַלַּיְלָה וְכָל הַיּוֹם.

The *tanna* addresses a different issue, the *halakha* of the payment of workers. **A day laborer collects** his wages from his employer **all night**[N] following his work shift. **A night laborer**[H] **collects** his wages **all the** following **day,** while **an hourly laborer**[H] **collects** his wages **all night and all day.** With regard to **a weekly laborer, a monthly laborer,**[H] **a yearly laborer,** or **a laborer** for a Sabbatical **cycle** of seven years, if he **left** upon the completion of his work **in the day, he collects** his wages **all day;** if he **left at night, he collects** his wages **all night and all day.**

גמ׳ תָּנוּ רַבָּנַן: מִנַּיִן לִשְׂכִיר יוֹם שֶׁגּוֹבֶה כָּל הַלַּיְלָה? תַּלְמוּד לוֹמַר: ״לֹא תָלִין פְּעֻלַּת שָׂכִיר אִתְּךָ עַד בֹּקֶר״. וּמִנַּיִן לִשְׂכִיר לַיְלָה שֶׁגּוֹבֶה כָּל הַיּוֹם? שֶׁנֶּאֱמַר: ״בְּיוֹמוֹ תִתֵּן שְׂכָרוֹ״.

GEMARA **The Sages taught: From where** is it derived **concerning a day laborer that** he **collects** his wages **all night? The verse states: "The wages of a hired laborer shall not remain with you all night until the morning"** (Leviticus 19:13). This indicates that he must pay him by the morning, and he has therefore not transgressed the prohibition of delaying the payment of wages until that time. **And from where** is it derived **concerning a night laborer that** he **collects** his wages **all day? As it is stated: "On the same day you shall give him his wages"** (Deuteronomy 24:15).

וְאֵימָא אִיפְּכָא! שְׂכִירוּת אֵינָהּ מִשְׁתַּלֶּמֶת אֶלָּא בַּסּוֹף.

The Gemara asks: **But** why not **say the opposite,** i.e., that a night laborer may be paid all night, while a day laborer receives his wages all day? The Gemara responds: **The obligation to pay** a person's **wage** is incurred **only at the end** of the period for which he was hired.

תָּנוּ רַבָּנַן: מִמַּשְׁמָע שֶׁנֶּאֱמַר: ״לֹא תָלִין פְּעֻלַּת שָׂכִיר אִתְּךָ״ אֵינִי יוֹדֵעַ שֶׁ״עַד בֹּקֶר״? מַה תַּלְמוּד לוֹמַר ״עַד בֹּקֶר״ – מְלַמֵּד שֶׁאֵינוֹ עוֹבֵר אֶלָּא עַד בֹּקֶר רִאשׁוֹן בִּלְבַד.

The Sages taught: From the indication of that which is stated in the verse: **"The wages of a hired laborer shall not remain with you all night** [*lo talin*]," **do I not know that** this means: **"Until the morning,"** as this is the meaning of: "Remain with you all night [*talin*]"? **Why** must **the verse state: "Until the morning"?** It **teaches that he transgresses** the prohibition of withholding payment **only until the first morning alone,** but does not transgress this prohibition another time for any further delay.

LANGUAGE

Designated repayment [*apoteiki*] – אַפּוֹתֵיקִי: From the Greek ὑποθήκη, *hupothēkē*, meaning mortgage, or property with a lien. The Sages saw in it the phrase *apo tehei kai*, meaning: On this it will stand, i.e., this property is under a mortgage agreement. It was usually a precisely defined property used as a guarantee for a certain payment. When a property became an *apoteiki*, the one responsible for payment had the right to pay from this property before paying other creditors. It was agreed between the two parties that the property with an *apoteiki* status was the only guarantee for payment of the debt, and the debt could not be collected from other properties.

NOTES

The Sabbatical Year is included in the tally – הַשְּׁבִיעִית מִן הַמִּנְיָן: Based on the Gemara on 109a, Rabbeinu Yehonatan of Lunel states that although it is prohibited to grow anything in one's field during the Sabbatical Year, since the recipient may use the land for other purposes it is still considered to be in his possession.

A day laborer collects all night – שְׂכִיר יוֹם גּוֹבֶה כָּל הַלַּיְלָה: The Rosh cites this *halakha* as proof that according to Torah law a laborer must work right up to the night, and therefore he may be paid until the next morning. Laborers who do not work literally all day are considered as hourly laborers.

HALAKHA

One who receives a field for one Sabbatical cycle of seven years – מְקַבֵּל שָׂדֶה לְשָׁבוּעַ לְשֶׁבַע שָׁנִים: If one rented or received a field to cultivate for seven years, he may use it for seven years excluding the Sabbatical Year, but if he took it for a Sabbatical cycle of seven years [*shavua*], his term includes the Sabbatical Year (Rambam *Sefer Mishpatim*, *Hilkhot Sekhirut* 8:3).

A day laborer and a night laborer – שְׂכִיר יוֹם וּשְׂכִיר לַיְלָה: A day laborer must be paid the following night, and if his employer neglects to do so he transgresses the prohibition of: "The wages of a hired laborer shall not remain with you all night until the morning." A night laborer may be paid the entire next day, but if he was not paid by evening, his employer transgresses the mitzva of: "On his day you shall give him his wages." Nowadays, when laborers do not work until nightfall, they must be paid by sunset (Rambam *Sefer Mishpatim*, *Hilkhot Sekhirut* 11:2; *Shulḥan Arukh*, *Ḥoshen Mishpat* 339:3, and in the comment of Rema).

An hourly laborer – שְׂכִיר שָׁעוֹת: A worker who was hired to work for several hours during the day must be paid that day, and if he worked at night he must receive his wages that night, as explained by Rav in the Gemara (Rambam *Sefer Mishpatim*, *Hilkhot Sekhirut* 11:2; *Shulḥan Arukh*, *Ḥoshen Mishpat* 339:4).

A weekly laborer, a monthly laborer – שְׂכִיר שַׁבָּת, שְׂכִיר חֹדֶשׁ: With regard to a worker who was hired for a longer period than a day, if his term of employment ends in the day he must be paid that day; if it ends at night he receives his wages that night, in accordance with the opinion of Rav (Rambam *Sefer Mishpatim*, *Hilkhot Sekhirut* 11:2; *Shulḥan Arukh*, *Ḥoshen Mishpat* 339:5).

מִכָּאן וְאֵילָךְ מַאי? אָמַר רַב: עוֹבֵר מִשּׁוּם בַּל תְּשַׁהֶא. אָמַר רַב יוֹסֵף: מַאי קְרָאָה? "אַל תֹּאמַר לְרֵעֲךָ לֵךְ וָשׁוּב וּמָחָר אֶתֵּן וְיֵשׁ אִתָּךְ".

The Gemara asks: **From that** point **forward, what** is the *halakha*? **Rav said:** Although one no longer transgresses the prohibition of delaying payment of wages, one **violates** the prohibition **of: Do not delay,**[NH] by delaying his wages. **Rav Yosef said: What is the verse** from which it is derived? **"Do not say to your neighbor: Go and come again, and tomorrow I will give, when you have it with you"** (Proverbs 3:28).

תָּנוּ רַבָּנַן: הָאוֹמֵר לַחֲבֵירוֹ צֵא שְׂכוֹר לִי פּוֹעֲלִים – שְׁנֵיהֶן אֵין עוֹבְרִין מִשּׁוּם בַּל תָּלִין, זֶה – לְפִי שֶׁלֹּא שְׂכָרָן,

The Sages taught: Concerning one **who says to another: Go out and hire workers for me, both of them do not violate the prohibition of delaying** payment of wages if they fail to pay immediately. **This** one, the employer, is exempt **because he did not hire them** himself, and strictly speaking they are not his hired workers.

Perek **IX**
Daf **111** Amud **a**

וְזֶה לְפִי שֶׁאֵין פְּעוּלָּתוֹ אֶצְלוֹ. הֵיכִי דָּמֵי? אִי דְּאָמַר לְהוּ שְׂכַרְכֶם עָלַי – שְׂכָרוֹ עָלָיו הוּא, דְּתַנְיָא: הַשּׂוֹכֵר אֶת הַפּוֹעֵל לַעֲשׂוֹת בְּשֶׁלּוֹ וְהֶרְאָהוּ בְּשֶׁל חֲבֵירוֹ – נוֹתֵן לוֹ שְׂכָרוֹ מִשָּׁלֵם, וְחוֹזֵר וְנוֹטֵל מִבַּעַל הַבַּיִת מַה שֶּׁהֶהֱנָה אוֹתוֹ!

And that one, the middleman, is exempt **because his work is not** performed **for him.** The Gemara asks: **What are the circumstances** of this case? **If** the middleman **said to them: Your wages** are incumbent **upon me, his wages are** indeed **upon him,** as the one who hired the workers bears full responsibility. **As it is taught** in a *baraita*: With regard to **one who hires a laborer to perform** work **in his own** field, **and** the employer inadvertently **showed** the laborer a field **belonging to another** in which he should work, the employer **must give** the laborer **his full wages; and** in addition, the employer **goes back and takes from the owner** of the field in which he worked the value of **the benefit** that owner **received from** the laborer. The employer is entitled to claim from the owner of the field the profit that owner gained from the work, but not the entire wages of the laborer. This indicates that one who says: Your wage is incumbent upon me, is responsible for the arrangement.

לָא צְרִיכָא, דַּאֲמַר לְהוּ: שְׂכַרְכֶם עַל בַּעַל הַבַּיִת.

The Gemara explains: **No,** it is **necessary** to state this *halakha* **where** the middleman **said to them:** The obligation to pay **your wages** is incumbent **upon the employer,** in which case they share responsibility for the payment and neither violates the prohibition.[H]

יְהוּדָה בַּר מָרֵימָר אֲמַר לֵיהּ לְשַׁמָּעֵיהּ: זִיל אֲגִיר לִי פּוֹעֲלִים, וְאֵימָא לְהוּ: שְׂכַרְכֶם עַל בַּעַל הַבַּיִת. מָרֵימָר וּמָר זוּטְרָא אָגְרִי לַהֲדָדֵי.

The Gemara relates: **Yehuda bar Mareimar** would **say to his attendant: Go hire workers for me**[N] **and say to them: Your wages are upon the employer.** Yehuda bar Mareimar instructed the attendant to do this in order to avoid violating the prohibition of delaying payment of wages. **Mareimar**[P] **and Mar Zutra would hire** workers **for each other** for the same reason.

אָמַר רַבָּה בַּר רַב הוּנָא: הָנֵי שׁוּקָאֵי דְּסוּרָא לָא עָבְרִי מִשּׁוּם בַּל תָּלִין; מֵידַע יָדְעִי דְּעַל יוֹמָא דְשׁוּקָא סָמְכִי, אֲבָל מִשּׁוּם בַּל תְּשַׁהֶא – וַדַּאי עוֹבֵר.

Rabba bar Rav Huna said: Those marketplace workers of Sura[H] **do not violate the prohibition** by Torah law **of delaying** payment of wages, in the event that they do not pay their employees immediately. This is because everyone **knows that they rely on the market day**[N] to earn their money, and the employees are aware that they will not be paid on the same day that they worked. **But he certainly violates the prohibition** by rabbinic law **of: Do not delay,** if he withholds payment any later than the market day.

NOTES

Do not delay – בַּל תְּשַׁהֶא: This is a quasi-biblical formulation of a rabbinic law, as the Sages decreed that any further delay of wages constitutes the violation of a rabbinic prohibition. The verse from Proverbs is cited as proof that the Torah itself condemns one who puts off his creditor with false claims. See Rashi and the later commentaries for more on this point.

Hire workers for me – אֲגִיר לִי פּוֹעֲלִים: According to *Tosafot*, Yehuda bar Mareimar was worried he would be preoccupied when the time came to pay the workers and would thereby violate the prohibition of delaying payment of wages. The Rosh (cited in *Shita Mekubbetzet*) and the commentary attributed to the Ritva add that although he would nevertheless transgress the rabbinic prohibition of delaying payment, this is a minor infringement in comparison to the Torah prohibition.

They rely on the market day – עַל יוֹמָא דְשׁוּקָא סָמְכִי: Some commentaries maintain that in this type of case it does not matter when they claim their wages, as even if they demand payment immediately he does not transgress until the market day. With regard to the *halakha* after the market day, some say that at that point if he does not compensate them he violates the prohibition of delaying payment of wages. Others claim that in this case the Torah prohibition is no longer in effect. Since these merchants rely on the market day, even if they have available money they need not pay immediately, as they can say they need the money to conduct business on the market day (attributed to the Ritva).

HALAKHA

Delayed payment – תַּשְׁלוּם לְאַחַר זְמַן: If an employer fails to pay his employee on the first day following the completion of the work he has violated the prohibition of: "The wages of a hired laborer shall not remain with you all night until the morning." If he continues to delay payment he does not transgress this mitzva a second time. He is still obligated to pay immediately, and he transgresses the rabbinical prohibition of: Do not delay, as well (Rambam *Sefer Mishpatim*, *Hilkhot Sekhirut* 11:5; *Shulḥan Arukh*, *Ḥoshen Mishpat* 339:8).

Hiring workers through another – שְׂכִירַת פּוֹעֲלִים עַל יְדֵי אַחֵר: If one says to a middleman: Go and hire workers for me, and upon hiring them the middleman informed them that the employer was responsible for their wages, neither of them transgresses the prohibition of delaying payment of wages. Nevertheless, the employer is in violation of the verse: "Do not say to your neighbor, go and come again" (Proverbs 3:28) if he is not busy and is merely putting them off. If the middleman neglected to say that the employer was responsible for their wages, even if he did not say: Your wages are upon me, he is obligated to pay their wages and he transgresses the prohibition of delaying payment of wages if he fails to do so. The Rema maintains that even in that case, if the workers are aware that they are not working for the middleman, he does not transgress unless he specifically stated that he was responsible for their wages (Rambam *Sefer Mishpatim*, *Hilkhot Sekhirut* 11:4; *Shulḥan Arukh*, *Ḥoshen Mishpat* 339:7, and in the comment of Rema).

The marketplace workers of Sura – שׁוּקָאֵי דְּסוּרָא: If the worker was aware that the employer does not usually have money until the day of the market, the employer does not transgress the prohibition of delaying the payment of wages even if he did have money available at the time. Once the market day arrives, any delay of payment causes him to transgress the verse: "Do not say to your neighbor, go and come again." Similarly, those who do not pay until they have completed their business dealings do not violate the prohibition until such time arrives (*Shulḥan Arukh*, *Ḥoshen Mishpat* 339:9, and in the comment of Rema).

PERSONALITIES

Mareimar – מָרֵימָר: Mareimar was an *amora* from the generation of Rav Ashi. Very little is known about his personality other than that he was a student-colleague of Mar Zutra and a colleague of Rav Ashi. It is likely that he lived in Sura, as its scholars followed his ruling. In addition, the later Ravina (see *Ketubot* 100b), who is assumed to be the last of the *amora'im*, was probably a student of his.

After the passing of Rav Ashi, Mareimar eventually became the head of the yeshiva in Sura, and he and the earlier Ravina continued the work of editing the Talmud. His son, Rav Yehuda bar Mareimar, was also an important Sage of the next generation.

״שְׂכִיר שָׁעוֹת גּוֹבֶה כׇּל הַלַּיְלָה וְכׇל הַיּוֹם״. אָמַר רַב: שְׂכִיר שָׁעוֹת דְּיוֹם – גּוֹבֶה כׇּל הַיּוֹם; שְׂכִיר שָׁעוֹת דְּלַיְלָה – גּוֹבֶה כׇּל הַלַּיְלָה. וּשְׁמוּאֵל אָמַר: שְׂכִיר שָׁעוֹת דְּיוֹם – גּוֹבֶה כׇּל הַיּוֹם, וּשְׂכִיר שָׁעוֹת דְּלַיְלָה – גּוֹבֶה כׇּל הַלַּיְלָה וְכׇל הַיּוֹם.

§ The mishna teaches that **an hourly laborer collects** his wages **all night and all day. Rav says: An hourly laborer** who worked **by day collects** his wages **all** that **day,** while **an hourly laborer** who worked **by night collects** his wages **all** that **night. And Shmuel says: An hourly laborer** who worked **by day** indeed **collects** his wages **all** that **day, but an hourly laborer by night collects** his wages **all** that **night and all** the following **day.**

תְּנַן: שְׂכִיר שָׁעוֹת גּוֹבֶה כׇּל הַלַּיְלָה וְכׇל הַיּוֹם. תְּיוּבְתָּא דְּרַב! אָמַר לָךְ רַב: לִצְדָדִין קָתָנֵי; שְׂכִיר שָׁעוֹת דְּיוֹם – גּוֹבֶה כׇּל הַיּוֹם, שְׂכִיר שָׁעוֹת דְּלַיְלָה – גּוֹבֶה כׇּל הַלַּיְלָה.

We learned in the mishna: **An hourly laborer collects** his wages **all night and all day.** This is apparently **a conclusive refutation of Rav.** The Gemara answers: **Rav** could have **said to you** that **he teaches** the mishna **disjunctively**[N] in the following manner: **An hourly laborer by day collects** his wages **all day,** while **an hourly laborer by night collects** his wages **all night.**

תְּנַן: הָיָה שְׂכִיר שַׁבָּת, שְׂכִיר חֹדֶשׁ, שְׂכִיר שָׁנָה, שְׂכִיר שָׁבוּעַ, יוֹצֵא בַּיּוֹם – גּוֹבֶה כׇּל הַיּוֹם, יוֹצֵא בַּלַּיְלָה – גּוֹבֶה כׇּל הַלַּיְלָה וְכׇל הַיּוֹם!

We learned in the mishna: If **he was a weekly laborer, a monthly laborer, a yearly laborer,** or **a laborer** for a Sabbatical **cycle** of seven years, if he **left** upon the completion of his work **in the day, he collects** his wages **all day;** if he **left at night, he collects** his wages **all night and all day.**[N] This indicates that one who finishes his work at night can be paid throughout the following day as well.

אָמַר לָךְ רַב: תַּנָּאֵי הִיא; דְּתַנְיָא: שְׂכִיר שָׁעוֹת דְּיוֹם – גּוֹבֶה כׇּל הַיּוֹם; שְׂכִיר שָׁעוֹת דְּלַיְלָה – גּוֹבֶה כׇּל הַלַּיְלָה, דִּבְרֵי רַבִּי יְהוּדָה. רַבִּי שִׁמְעוֹן אוֹמֵר: שְׂכִיר שָׁעוֹת דְּיוֹם – גּוֹבֶה כׇּל הַיּוֹם; שְׂכִיר שָׁעוֹת דְּלַיְלָה – גּוֹבֶה כׇּל הַלַּיְלָה וְכׇל הַיּוֹם.

The Gemara replies: **Rav** could have **said to you** that it **is** a dispute between ***tanna'im*****, as it is taught** in a *baraita*: **An hourly laborer by day collects** his wages **all day,** while **an hourly laborer by night collects** his wages **all night;** this is **the statement of Rabbi Yehuda. Rabbi Shimon says: An hourly laborer by day collects** his wages **all day,** while **an hourly laborer by night collects** his wages **all night and all day.**

מִכָּאן אָמְרוּ: כׇּל הַכּוֹבֵשׁ שְׂכַר שָׂכִיר עוֹבֵר בַּחֲמִשָּׁה שֵׁמוֹת הַלָּלוּ, וַעֲשֵׂה: מִשּׁוּם בַּל תַּעֲשֹׁק אֶת רֵעֲךָ, וּמִשּׁוּם בַּל תִּגְזֹל, וּמִשּׁוּם בַּל תַּעֲשֹׁק שָׂכִיר עָנִי, וּמִשּׁוּם בַּל תָּלִין, וּמִשּׁוּם בְּיוֹמוֹ תִתֵּן שְׂכָרוֹ, וּמִשּׁוּם לֹא תָבֹא עָלָיו הַשֶּׁמֶשׁ.

The *baraita* continues. **From here** the Sages **stated: Anyone who withholds**[N] **the wages of a hired laborer**[H] **violates these five** negative **prohibitions and one positive mitzva.**[N] He **violates** the prohibition **of: "Do not oppress your neighbor"** (Leviticus 19:13), **and** the prohibition **of: "Do not steal"** (Leviticus 19:13), **and** the **prohibition of: "You should not oppress a hired laborer who is poor"** (Deuteronomy 24:14), **and the prohibition of delaying** payment of wages (Leviticus 19:13), **and** he has not fulfilled the positive mitzva **of: "On the same day you shall give him his wages"** (Deuteronomy 24:15), **and** he has violated the prohibition **of: "The sun shall not set upon him"** (Deuteronomy 24:15).

HALAKHA

One who withholds the wages of a laborer – הַכּוֹבֵשׁ שְׂכַר שָׂכִיר: Whoever refuses to pay a hired laborer his wages violates five prohibitions and a positive mitzva. The commentaries disagree as to the precise identity of these prohibitions (Rambam *Sefer Mishpatim, Hilkhot Sekhirut* 11:2; *Shulḥan Arukh, Ḥoshen Mishpat* 339:2).

NOTES

He teaches the mishna disjunctively – לִצְדָדִין קָתָנֵי: In other words, this clause of the mishna should not be read as a single phrase, despite the connecting word: And, in the phrase: By day and by night. Instead, it refers to two separate cases. Therefore, there is no need to adjust the wording of the text, but merely to read the sentence in a different manner so that it addresses two separate sets of circumstances.

The commentaries point out that although this answer explains the language of the first part of the mishna, the second clause concerning a weekly and monthly laborer still contradicts the opinion of Rav, as the Gemara notes in the following line. What, then, is the point of suggesting this answer?

One explanation is that Rav maintained this second clause of the mishna is in accordance with the opinion of Rabbi Shimon. Some even suggest that perhaps Rav holds the entire mishna is in accordance with the opinion of Rabbi Shimon, which would mean that it is no longer necessary to employ the answer that the mishna is disjunctive (Maharshal; *Tosefot Yom Tov*). Alternatively, Rav might explain the last clause disjunctively as well, as everything depends on when the laborer finished his work. If he completed his work by day he must be paid that day, and if his work ended at night he receives his wages at night (see *Torat Ḥayyim*).

He collects all night and all day – גּוֹבֶה כׇּל הַלַּיְלָה וְכׇל הַיּוֹם: Some commentaries explain Rabbi Shimon's opinion on the basis of his general opinion that one derives *halakhot* based on the reason for the mitzva (see 115a). The logic here that a night laborer can be paid the next day as well may be because his employer does not always have cash available at night, and it is difficult to find someone to lend him money at such a late hour. Consequently, he is granted the whole of the subsequent day as well (*Ḥokhmat Manoaḥ*).

From here they stated, anyone who withholds – מִכָּאן אָמְרוּ כׇּל הַכּוֹבֵשׁ: The connection between the first part of the *baraita* and its conclusion is unclear, and several explanations have been proposed. Some early commentaries maintain that once the *baraita* states that the employer transgresses the prohibition of delaying payment of wages even in the case of one who worked for several hours, clearly the employer would violate the prohibition when withholding wages from any other type of laborer as well (Ra'avad; Ran).

Others suggest that this *halakha* does not relate specifically to the previous case in the *baraita*, but is rather based on the principle that since there is a fixed time for payment, any postponement is not merely a delay of wages but also oppression and robbery (*Ḥokhmat Manoaḥ*). Yet others contend that the connecting link is specifically within Rabbi Shimon's opinion that in certain cases the obligation applies with regard to both day and night. This indicates that he transgresses both the prohibitions of: "On the same day," and: "The sun shall not set" (*Ein Yehosef*; *Ma'ayanei HaḤokhma*).

Five prohibitions and one positive mitzva – חֲמִשָּׁה שֵׁמוֹת וַעֲשֵׂה: The commentaries disagree as to the precise identity of these prohibitions. Rashi maintains, in accordance with the standard version of the text, that he violates the five prohibitions of: "Do not oppress your neighbor," "Do not steal," "You should not oppress a hired laborer who is poor," the prohibition of delaying payment of wages, the negative prohibition of: "The sun shall not set upon him," and the positive mitzva of: "On the same day you shall give him his wages." By contrast, the Rif, the Rambam, and the Rosh, following a different version of the text, count only five altogether, as they do not list two prohibitions of oppression, just that of: "You shall not oppress a hired laborer."

With regard to the actual counting of the mitzvot, most authorities do not consider the prohibition of delaying payment of wages and that of: "The sun shall not set upon him," as two separate mitzvot, but as particular applications of the same general mitzva (Rambam, *Sefer HaḤinnukh*). Others list only two prohibitions out of all these: "Do not steal," and "The wages of a hired laborer shall not remain with you all night until the morning," as well as the positive mitzva of: "On his day you shall give him his wages" (*Sefer Mitzvot Katan*).

הָנֵי דְּאִיכָּא בִּימָמָא – לֵיכָּא בְּלֵילְיָא, דְּאִיכָּא בְּלֵילְיָא – לֵיכָּא בִּימָמָא? אָמַר רַב חִסְדָּא: שֵׁם שְׂכִירוּת בְּעָלְמָא.

The Gemara asks: But these five prohibitions do not all take effect at the same time, since **those that are** applicable **by day are not** in effect **by night,** while those **that are** applicable **by night are not** relevant **by day.** How can he be in violation of them all? **Rav Ḥisda said:** It means **merely** that **the general concept** of withholding the **wages** of a hired laborer includes all these prohibitions and one positive mitzva.

אֵיזֶה הוּא עוֹשֵׁק וְאֵיזֶהוּ גּוֹזֵל? אָמַר רַב חִסְדָּא: לֵךְ וָשׁוּב, לֵךְ וָשׁוּב – זֶה הוּא עוֹשֵׁק. יֵשׁ לְךָ בְּיָדִי וְאֵינִי נוֹתֵן לְךָ – זֶה הוּא גּוֹזֵל.

§ The Gemara asks: **What is** defined as **oppression and what is** defined as **stealing,** and what is the difference between them?[NH] **Rav Ḥisda said:** If he told him: **Go and return, go and return** (see Proverbs 3:28), avoiding paying him while saying that he will pay him at some point, **this is oppression.** If he says to him: **You have** money owed to you **in my possession but I will not give it to you, this is stealing.**

מַתְקִיף לַהּ רַב שֵׁשֶׁת: אֵיזֶהוּ עוֹשֵׁק שֶׁחִיְּיבָה עָלָיו תּוֹרָה קָרְבָּן? דּוּמְיָא דְּפִקָּדוֹן, דְּקָא כָּפַר לֵיהּ מָמוֹנָא! אֶלָּא אָמַר רַב שֵׁשֶׁת: נְתַתִּיו לְךָ – זֶהוּ עוֹשֵׁק; יֵשׁ לְךָ בְּיָדִי וְאֵינִי נוֹתֵן לְךָ – זֶה הוּא גּוֹזֵל.

Rav Sheshet objects to this from a *baraita*: **What is** the type of **oppression for which the Torah obligated him** to bring **an offering?** It is **similar to** the case of one who had been entrusted with money as **a deposit, where he** then **denies** that he accepted it, thereby keeping **the money.** This contradicts Rav Ḥisda's claim that oppression is referring to one who admits that he owes him. **Rather, Rav Sheshet said** that the difference is as follows: If he said to him: **I gave it to you, this is** defined as **oppression.** If he tells him: **You have** money owed to you **in my possession but I am not giving** it **to you, this is** defined as **stealing.**

מַתְקִיף לַהּ אַבָּיֵי: אֵיזֶה הוּא גּוֹזֵל שֶׁחִיְּיבָה עָלָיו תּוֹרָה קָרְבָּן? דּוּמְיָא דְּפִקָּדוֹן בָּעֵינַן, דְּקָא כָּפַר לֵיהּ מָמוֹנָא! אֶלָּא אָמַר אַבָּיֵי: לֹא שְׂכַרְתִּיךָ מֵעוֹלָם – זֶה הוּא עוֹשֵׁק; נְתַתִּיו לְךָ – זֶה הוּא גּוֹזֵל.

Abaye objects to this: What is the type of **stealing for which the Torah obligated him** to bring **an offering? We require** it to be **similar to** the case of one who had been entrusted with money as **a deposit, where he** then **denies** that he accepted it, thereby keeping **the money.** That is unlike the example of stealing given by Rav Ḥisda and Rav Sheshet, where the party withholding the money concedes that he owes it. **Rather, Abaye said:** If he said to him: **I never hired you, this is oppression;** if he claimed: **I gave it to you, this is stealing.**

וּלְרַב שֵׁשֶׁת, מַאי שְׁנָא עוֹשֵׁק דְּקַשְׁיָא לֵיהּ, וּמַאי שְׁנָא גּוֹזֵל דְּלָא קַשְׁיָא לֵיהּ? אָמַר לָךְ: גּוֹזֵל – דִּגְזַלֵיהּ וַהֲדַר כְּפָרֵיהּ.

The Gemara asks: **And according to Rav Sheshet, what is different** about **oppression that he raised a difficulty** against Rav Ḥisda concerning it, **and what is different** about **stealing that he did not raise a difficulty,** although Abaye's question was similar to his. The Gemara explains: Rav Sheshet could have **said to you: Stealing** means **that** he first **stole from him** by stating that he will not give him the money, **and later denied** owing it.

אִי הָכִי, אֲפִילּוּ עוֹשֵׁק נָמֵי דַּהֲדַר כְּפָרֵיהּ! הָכִי הַשְׁתָּא? בִּשְׁלָמָא הָתָם כְּתִיב: "אוֹ בְגָזֵל" – מִכְּלָל דְּאוֹדֵי לֵיהּ מֵעִיקָּרָא. אֲבָל גַּבֵּי עוֹשֵׁק מִי כְּתִיב: "אוֹ בְעוֹשֶׁק"? "אוֹ עָשַׁק" כְּתִיב – שֶׁעֲשָׁקוֹ כְּבָר.

The Gemara challenges: **If so,** then **even** with regard to **oppression as well,** the case can be **that** he first conceded that he owes the wages **and** then **later denied it.** Why does Rav Sheshet say that the case must be where the employer said to the laborer: I gave it to you? The Gemara responds: **How can** these cases **be compared? Granted, there it is written:** "And if he deals falsely with his neighbor in a matter of deposit, or of pledge, **or of robbery**" (Leviticus 5:21), which **by inference** indicates **that he admitted to him at the outset. But with regard to oppression is it written: Or by oppression? It is written: "Or he oppressed,"** which does not refer back to his previous denial but is referring to the actual sin, indicating **that he had already oppressed him.**

רָבָא אָמַר: זֶה הוּא עוֹשֵׁק זֶהוּ גּוֹזֵל. וְלָמָּה חִלְּקָן הַכָּתוּב? לַעֲבוֹר עָלָיו בִּשְׁנֵי לָאוִין.

Rava said: There is no need for such an artificial distinction, as **oppression is the same as stealing,** and no practical difference exists between the two categories. **And why,** then, **did the verse divide them**[N] into two categories? It did this **so that he will violate two prohibitions,** stealing and oppression.

HALAKHA

Stealing and oppression – גָּזֵל וְעוֹשֶׁק: A robber is one who forcibly takes money from another, for example one who snatches an item out of someone's hand or enters their field and takes their produce. By contrast, oppression is defined as one taking possession of another's money with their consent but then retaining possession of it and refusing to return it when requested. With regard to stealing from and oppression of hired workers, other *halakhot* apply (Rambam *Sefer Nezikin, Hilkhot Gezeila VaAveda* 1:3–4 and *Maggid Mishne* there; *Shulḥan Arukh, Ḥoshen Mishpat* 359:7–8).

NOTES

What is oppression and what is stealing – אֵיזֶה הוּא עוֹשֵׁק וְאֵיזֶהוּ גּוֹזֵל: Numerous commentaries struggle to explain why there is such a basic question as to what is oppression and what is stealing, as these terms are used in other contexts without comment. It seems that many of the commentaries on the Rambam, the *Tur*, and the *Shulḥan Arukh* accept an interpretation mentioned briefly by the commentary attributed to the Ritva. He contends that the Gemara's question here refers only to the *halakhot* of stealing and oppression involving the hiring of workers, but does not concern these categories in general (*Derisha*; *Sma*; Gra; *Maggid Mishne*; *Mishne LaMelekh*; *Parashat Derakhim*).

And why did the verse divide them – וְלָמָּה חִלְּקָן הַכָּתוּב: Although there are a number of alternative versions of the text, the early commentaries write that the standard version is preferable, as the main problem is not the use of two distinct terms, but rather the repetition itself, which would be problematic even if the Torah had used the same expression twice. See the commentary attributed to the Ritva and others for further elaboration.

מתני׳ אֶחָד שְׂכַר אָדָם וְאֶחָד שְׂכַר בְּהֵמָה וְאֶחָד שְׂכַר כֵּלִים – יֵשׁ בּוֹ מִשּׁוּם בְּיוֹמוֹ תִתֵּן שְׂכָרוֹ, וְיֵשׁ בּוֹ מִשּׁוּם לֹא תָלִין פְּעֻלַּת שָׂכִיר אִתְּךָ עַד בֹּקֶר. אֵימָתַי? בִּזְמַן שֶׁתְּבָעוֹ. לֹא תְבָעוֹ – אֵינוֹ עוֹבֵר עָלָיו. הִמְחָהוּ אֵצֶל חֶנְוָנִי אוֹ אֵצֶל שׁוּלְחָנִי – אֵינוֹ עוֹבֵר עָלָיו.

MISHNA **Whether** referring to **a person's wages** that he receives **or the renting of an animal or the renting of utensils,**[H] are all **subject to** the prohibition **of: "On the same day**[N] **you shall give him his wages"** (Deuteronomy 24:15), **and** are **subject to** the prohibition of: **"The wages of a hired laborer shall not remain with you all night until the morning"** (Leviticus 19:13). **When** does he transgress these prohibitions? He transgresses them **when** the one owed the money **claimed** the payment from **him.** If he **did not claim** his payment from **him** the other **does not transgress** the prohibitions. **If** the one who owes the money **transferred his** payment by leaving instructions **with a storekeeper or with a money changer** to pay him, **he does not transgress** the prohibitions.

שָׂכִיר בִּזְמַנּוֹ – נִשְׁבָּע וְנוֹטֵל. עָבַר זְמַנּוֹ – אֵינוֹ נִשְׁבָּע וְנוֹטֵל. אִם יֵשׁ עֵדִים שֶׁתְּבָעוֹ בִּזְמַנּוֹ – הֲרֵי זֶה נִשְׁבָּע וְנוֹטֵל.

The mishna discusses other related *halakhot*: If **a hired laborer** requests payment **at** the proper **time** and the employer claims he already paid him, the laborer **takes an oath** that he did not receive his wages **and** then **takes** the wages from the employer. If **the time had passed,** he does **not take an oath and take** the wages. **If there are witnesses** who testify **that he claimed** the money from **him at** the proper **time, he takes an oath and takes** the money.

גֵּר תּוֹשָׁב – יֵשׁ בּוֹ מִשּׁוּם בְּיוֹמוֹ תִתֵּן שְׂכָרוֹ וְאֵין בּוֹ מִשּׁוּם לֹא תָלִין פְּעוּלַּת שָׂכִיר אִתְּךָ עַד בֹּקֶר.

One who hires **a gentile who resides in Eretz Yisrael and observes the seven Noahide mitzvot** [*ger toshav*][B] **is subject to** the prohibition of: **"On the same day you shall give him his wages," but is not subject to** the negative mitzva **of: "The wages of a hired laborer shall not remain with you all night until the morning."**[H]

גמ׳ מַנִּי מַתְנִיתִין? לָא תַּנָּא קַמָּא דְּמֵאַחֶיךָ וְלָא רַבִּי יוֹסֵי בְּרַבִּי יְהוּדָה! מַאי הִיא? דְּתַנְיָא:

GEMARA The Gemara asks: **Whose** opinion is expressed in **the mishna?** It is **not** that of **the first *tanna*** of the *baraita*, who interprets the phrase: **"From your brothers"** (Deuteronomy 24:14), **and** it is **not Rabbi Yosei, son of Rabbi Yehuda.** The Gemara clarifies: **What is** this *baraita* that is referred to here? The Gemara explains: **As it is taught** in a *baraita*:

Perek **IX**
Daf **111** Amud **b**

״מֵאַחֶיךָ״ – פְּרָט לַאֲחֵרִים; ״גֵּרְךָ״ – זֶה גֵּר צֶדֶק; ״בִּשְׁעָרֶיךָ״ – זֶה אוֹכֵל נְבֵילוֹת.

The verse states: "You shall not oppress a hired laborer who is poor and needy, whether he be from your brothers or from your stranger that is in your land within your gates" (Deuteronomy 24:14), which is interpreted as follows: The term **"from your brothers"** serves **to exclude others,**[N] i.e., gentiles, who are not your brothers. As for the term **"your stranger," this** is referring to **a righteous convert.**[B] As for the term **"within your gates," this** is referring to a *ger toshav* who lives in Eretz Yisrael and **eats unslaughtered animal carcasses** because he has not accepted Judaism upon himself.

אֵין לִי אֶלָּא שְׂכַר אָדָם. מִנַּיִן לְרַבּוֹת בְּהֵמָה וְכֵלִים? תַּלְמוּד לוֹמַר: ״בְּאַרְצְךָ״, כָּל שֶׁבְּאַרְצְךָ. וְכוּלָּן עוֹבְרִים בְּכָל הַשֵּׁמוֹת הַלָּלוּ.

I have derived **only** that the prohibitions of delaying wages apply to **the hire of people. From where** do I know **to include** payment for the rental of **animals and utensils** in the prohibition of delaying wages? **The verse states: "In your land,"** which includes **all that is in your land.**[N] **And in all of** the above cases of delaying payment they **transgress all of these prohibitions** which apply to delaying payment.

HALAKHA

The prohibition of delaying payment of wages – **אִיסּוּר הֲלָנַת שָׂכָר**: It is a positive mitzva to pay a hired worker on time, and one who delays his payment transgresses a negative mitzva. This *halakha* applies to the hire of people, renting animals, and renting utensils. With regard to rental of real estate, some say that the renter does not violate this prohibition (Rambam *Sefer Mishpatim*, *Hilkhot Sekhirut* 11:1; *Shulḥan Arukh*, *Ḥoshen Mishpat* 339:1).

Delaying payment of wages of a *ger toshav* – **הֲלָנַת שְׂכַר גֵּר תּוֹשָׁב**: One who delays the payment of a *ger toshav* violates the positive mitzva of: "On the same day you shall give him his wages," but he has not transgressed a negative mitzva (Rambam *Sefer Mishpatim*, *Hilkhot Sekhirut* 11:1).

NOTES

Are subject to: On the same day, etc. – **יֵשׁ בּוֹ מִשּׁוּם בְּיוֹמוֹ**: The *tanna* did not find it necessary to list all the relevant prohibitions, but merely listed the positive mitzva and one prohibition, which includes all the rest (Ran).

To exclude others – **פְּרָט לַאֲחֵרִים**: Some early commentaries are puzzled as to why both opinions require a verse to demonstrate that this *halakha* does not apply to gentiles, since the specific inclusion of converts clearly indicates that the *halakha* does not extend to gentiles (*Tosafot*). Some later commentaries answer that two expositions were necessary to include both a *ger toshav* and a convert, because otherwise one might have thought that a convert is mentioned not to equate him with those who must be paid on time, but to place him in a special category such that one who delays his wages violates an additional command (*Torat Ḥayyim*). This would be similar to the prohibition against verbal mistreatment, where one who verbally mistreats a convert transgresses not only the prohibition against verbal mistreatment, which applies to all Jews, but also violates the additional prohibition against mistreating a convert.

All that is in your land – **כָּל שֶׁבְּאַרְצְךָ**: It is not possible to derive from this phrase that this prohibition applies only in Eretz Yisrael, as the difference between inside and outside Eretz Yisrael concerns only mitzvot that pertain to the ground, not those that apply to the person, such as this one.

The Ramah, citing the Jerusalem Talmud, derives a different *halakha* from this phrase. The Gemara there learns from here that this *halakha* includes only items that come into direct contact with the land, i.e., animals and vessels, but it does not apply to use of the land itself (see Rosh).

BACKGROUND

A gentile who resides in Eretz Yisrael and observes the seven Noahide mitzvot [*ger toshav*] – **גֵּר תּוֹשָׁב**: A gentile who seeks to reside permanently in Eretz Yisrael is required to accept certain mitzvot. There are several opinions with regard to the extent of the commitment required. Some authorities require only acceptance of the prohibition against idol worship. Others require him to observe virtually all the prohibitions with the exception of those prohibiting consumption of certain foods. Most opinions require him to observe the seven Noahide mitzvot.

Righteous convert – **גֵּר צֶדֶק**: A righteous convert is a gentile who has accepted Judaism upon himself. After circumcision, immersion in a ritual bath for the purpose of conversion, and acceptance of the mitzvot of the Torah in the presence of a court, he is considered a Jew in all respects. In Temple times, conversion was not completed until the convert brought a burnt-offering. Even if he later returns to his previous faith, his conversion to Judaism remains in effect and his status is that of an apostate Jew.

The Torah specifically commands Jews to love a convert (Deuteronomy 10:19), not to cause him distress by reminding him of his past (Exodus 22:20), and to support him in every sense. By Torah law, a convert is like a newborn child. He is considered to have no legal familial ties to his biological parents or relatives.

מכאן אמרו: אחד שכר אדם ואחד שכר בהמה ואחד שכר כלים – יש בו משום ביומו תתן שכרו ויש בהן משום בל תלין פעלת שכיר. רבי יוסי ברבי יהודה אומר: גר תושב יש בו משום ביומו תתן שכרו ואין בו משום לא תלין. בהמה וכלים אין בהן אלא משום בל תעשק בלבד.

From here the Sages **stated: Whether** referring to **the hire of a person or the rental of an animal or the rental of utensils,** all are **subject to** the prohibition **of: "On the same day you shall give him his wages"** (Deuteronomy 24:15), **and they are** likewise **subject to the prohibition of delaying** the payment of wages of a **hired laborer** (Leviticus 19:13). **Rabbi Yosei, son of Rabbi Yehuda,**[P] **says:** One who hires a ***ger toshav***[N] **is subject to** the prohibition **of: "On the same day you shall give him his wages," but is not subject to the prohibition of delaying** payment of wages, and the payment of rent of **an animal or vessels is included only in** the prohibition **of: "Do not oppress" alone.**

מני? אי תנא קמא ד"מאחיך" – קשיא גר תושב. אי רבי יוסי – קשיא בהמה וכלים!

The Gemara returns to its initial question: In accordance with **whose** opinion is the mishna? **If** it is in accordance with the opinion of **the first *tanna* of** the *baraita*, who interprets the verse: **"From your brothers,"** the *halakha* of **a *ger toshav*** is **difficult,** as he equates a *ger toshav* with a Jew, unlike the mishna. **If** it is in accordance with the opinion of **Rabbi Yosei,** son of Rabbi Yehuda, the *halakha* of the rental payment of **animals and vessels** is **difficult,** as Rabbi Yosei maintains they are not included in any of the prohibitions except for: Do not oppress.

אמר רבא: האי תנא – תנא דבי רבי ישמעאל הוא. דתנא דבי רבי ישמעאל: אחד שכר אדם ואחד שכר בהמה ואחד שכר כלים – יש בו משום ביומו תתן שכרו ומשום לא תלין. גר תושב יש בו משום ביומו תתן שכרו ואין בו משום בל תלין.

Rava said: This *tanna* of the mishna **is a *tanna* from the school of Rabbi Yishmael, as the school of Rabbi Yishmael taught: Whether** in the case of **the hire of a person, the rental of an animal, or the rental of vessels,** all of these payments are **subject to** the mitzva **of: "On the same day you shall give him his wages," and the prohibition of delaying** payment of wages. **A *ger toshav*** is **subject to** the mitzva **of: "On the same day you shall give him his wages," but** he **is not subject to the prohibition of delaying** payment of wages.

מאי טעמא דתנא קמא ד"מאחיך"? גמר "שכיר", "שכיר". ורבי יוסי ברבי יהודה לא גמר "שכיר", "שכיר".

Until this point, the Gemara has discussed the source of the ruling of the first *tanna*. It now analyzes the reasons behind the different opinions. **What is the reason of the first *tanna* of** the *baraita*, who interprets the verse: **"From your brothers"?** He **derives** it by verbal analogy comparing the words: "You shall not oppress **a hired laborer,"** and the verse: "The wages of a **hired laborer** shall not remain with you all night until the morning." Just as the former verse includes a Jew, a *ger toshav*, the rental of an animal, and the rental of utensils, so too, the latter verse includes all of the above. **And Rabbi Yosei, son of Rabbi Yehuda, does not derive** this verbal analogy of: **"Hired laborer"** and **"hired laborer."**

נהי דלא גמר "שכיר", "שכיר", בהמה וכלים משום "ביומו תתן שכרו" נמי ניחייב! תני רבי חנניא: אמר קרא "ולא תבא עליו השמש כי עני הוא". מי שהן באין לידי עניות ועשירות, יצאו בהמה וכלים שאינן באין לידי עניות ועשירות.

The Gemara challenges: **Although** Rabbi Yosei, son of Rabbi Yehuda, does **not derive** the verbal analogy of the words: **"Hired laborer"** and **"hired laborer,"** one **should** still **also be liable** in the case of **animals or vessels due to** the injunction **of: "On the same day you shall give him his wages."** From where does he derive that such items are not included in this prohibition? **Rabbi Ḥananya teaches** in a *baraita* that **the verse states:** "On his day you shall give him his wages, **and the sun shall not set upon him, for he is poor"** (Deuteronomy 24:15). This verse clearly is referring to **one who** can **enter into** a state of **poverty and wealth,** which **excludes animals and vessels, which cannot enter into** a state of **poverty and wealth.**

ותנא קמא, האי "כי עני הוא" מאי עביד ליה? ההוא מיבעי להקדים עני לעשיר. ורבי יוסי ברבי יהודה? ההוא מ"לא תעשק שכיר עני ואביון" נפקא.

The Gemara asks: **And** with regard to **the first *tanna*,** who does not address **this** verse of: **"For he is poor," what** does he **do with it?** The Gemara answers: **That** verse is **necessary to give precedence to a poor person over a wealthy person** if the employer does not have enough money to pay all his workers. **And** how does **Rabbi Yosei, son of Rabbi Yehuda,** derive that *halakha*? In his opinion **that** *halakha* **is derived from: "You shall not oppress a hired laborer who is poor and needy"** (Deuteronomy 24:14).

PERSONALITIES

Rabbi Yosei, son of Rabbi Yehuda – רבי יוסי ברבי יהודה: Rabbi Yosei, son of Rabbi Yehuda, was a *tanna* from the last generation of *tanna'im* and the son of the *tanna* Rabbi Yehuda bar Elai. Rabbi Yosei was apparently the preeminent disciple of his father, though he does occasionally disagree with him on matters of *halakha*. He was also a friend of Rabbi Yehuda HaNasi, with whom he collaborated on several matters, and in addition, he engaged in halakhic discussions with other Sages of his generation.

His halakhic decisions were apparently tied to those of Rabbi Yehuda HaNasi, and his statements are found a number of times in the mishna, as well as frequently in the *Tosefta* and other sources. He was also a master of *aggada*, and a number of famous statements were transmitted in his name. He apparently died before Rabbi Yehuda HaNasi, as he instructed the latter with regard to certain matters before his death.

NOTES

Ger toshav – **גר תושב:** The biblical term *ger* includes two separate categories of people, and it is sometimes necessary to consider the context to help determine which of them is the subject of the verse. The first type is the righteous convert, a full-fledged convert who is obligated in all Torah laws after circumcision, ritual immersion, and the acceptance of all the mitzvot. He has the status of a full-fledged Jew, apart from various issues such as certain appointments and some prohibitions that apply to him. The other is a gentile who resides in Eretz Yisrael and observes the seven Noahide commandments.

The definition of who qualifies as the second type of *ger* is subject to a dispute among *tanna'im*. Some say that he has to accept upon himself only not to worship idolatry, while others maintain that he must agree to observe all the *mitzvot* apart from the consumption of animal carcasses.

The consensus among the ruling authorities is that a *ger toshav* is one who has accepted upon himself the observance of the seven Noahide commandments. Since he has accepted these Torah laws he is considered a righteous member of the nations, and Jews are therefore obligated to support him, to provide him with a livelihood, and to care for his welfare. Naturally, it is prohibited to steal from a *ger toshav*, to oppress him, or to exploit him, which includes delaying his wages. Nevertheless, with regard to certain mitzvot that involve a particular emphasis on the special affinity of Jews to each other, he has the status of a gentile.

NOTES

To give a poor person precedence over a destitute person – לְהַקְדִּים עָנִי לְאֶבְיוֹן: The Rambam and others do not cite this statement as *halakha*. They apparently rely on the *Sifrei* that derives from the verse: "You shall not oppress a hired laborer who is poor and needy" that one who delays the payment of wages to any poor person has transgressed a special prohibition, and God will hasten to punish him. See also the Ramban's Commentary on the Torah concerning this point.

From your brothers…your neighbor, etc. – מֵאַחֶיךָ...רֵעֲךָ וכו׳: The early commentaries point out that the phrase: "Your neighbor," presents a difficulty also to Rabbi Yosei, son of Rabbi Yehuda. Nevertheless, it is more problematic for the first *tanna*, as Rabbi Yosei, son of Rabbi Yehuda, derives from here that the verbal analogy of "hired laborer" and "hired laborer" must be rejected, because a *ger toshav* is not called "your neighbor" (Ramban).

Stealing from a gentile and oppressing him – גָּזֵל נָכְרִי וְעוֹשְׁקוֹ: According to the Meiri, this statement is in accordance with the opinion that stealing from a gentile is permitted under certain circumstances. He adds that the *halakha* is that it is prohibited to steal even from a gentile, and it is certainly prohibited to exploit or oppress him. It is likewise prohibited to delay paying his wages deliberately if he never intended to pay him on time. The principal issue at hand is whether these prohibitions against stealing apply with regard to all people, or whether, like taking interest, they are considered unique *halakhot* that result from the special unity of the Jewish people.

וְתַנָּא קַמָּא? חַד לְהַקְדִּים עָנִי לְעָשִׁיר, וְחַד לְהַקְדִּים עָנִי לְאֶבְיוֹן.

The Gemara asks: **But** if so, why does **the first *tanna*** require another verse? The Gemara explains: He maintains that **one** verse serves **to give a poor person precedence over a wealthy person,** while the other **one** serves **to give a poor person precedence over a destitute person,**[N] i.e., a complete pauper who owns nothing.

וּצְרִיכָא, דְּאִי אַשְׁמְעִינַן אֶבְיוֹן – מִשּׁוּם דְּלָא כָּסֵיף לְמִתְבְּעֵיהּ, אֲבָל עָשִׁיר דְּכָסֵיף לְמִתְבְּעֵיהּ – אֵימָא לָא. וְאִי אַשְׁמְעִינַן עָשִׁיר – מִשּׁוּם דְּלָא צָרִיךְ לֵיהּ, אֲבָל אֶבְיוֹן דְּצָרִיךְ לֵיהּ – אֵימָא לָא. צְרִיכָא.

The Gemara adds: **And** both verses are **necessary, as had** the Torah **taught us** only that a poor person comes before one who is **destitute** one could have said that this is **because** a destitute person is **not ashamed to demand** his money; he is so needy he is not embarrassed to ask for money. **But** with regard to **a wealthy person, who is ashamed to demand** his wages, one might **say** that a poor person does **not** receive precedence over him. **And** conversely, **had** the Torah **taught us** only that this *halakha* applies to **a wealthy person** one could have said that it is **because** he **does not need** his wages right away, **but** with regard to **a destitute person, who does need it** immediately, **say** that it does **not** apply. It was therefore **necessary** for both verses to be stated.

וְתַנָּא דִּידַן: מַה נַּפְשָׁךְ, אִי יָלֵיף "שָׂכִיר", "שָׂכִיר" – אֲפִילּוּ גֵּר תּוֹשָׁב נָמֵי! אִי לָא יָלֵיף "שָׂכִיר", "שָׂכִיר" – בְּהֵמָה וְכֵלִים מְנָא לֵיהּ?

The Gemara asks: **And** with the regard to the ruling of **the *tanna* of our** mishna, **whichever way you** look at it, it requires clarification. **If he derives** the verbal analogy of the words: **"Hired laborer"** and **"hired laborer,"** then **even a *ger toshav*** should be included. **If** he does **not derive** the verbal analogy of the words: **"Hired laborer"** and **"hired laborer," from where does he** derive that this *halakha* applies **to animals and vessels?**

לְעוֹלָם לָא יָלֵיף "שָׂכִיר", "שָׂכִיר", וְשָׁאנֵי הָתָם דְּאָמַר קְרָא: "וְלֹא תָלִין פְּעֻלַּת שָׂכִיר אִתְּךָ עַד בֹּקֶר" – כׇּל שֶׁפְּעוּלָּתוֹ אִתְּךָ. אִי הָכִי, אֲפִילּוּ גֵּר תּוֹשָׁב נָמֵי! אָמַר קְרָא: "רֵעֲךָ" – "רֵעֲךָ" וְלֹא גֵּר תּוֹשָׁב.

The Gemara answers: **Actually,** he does **not derive** the analogy of: **"Hired laborer"** and **"hired laborer," and there it is different, as the verse states: "The wages of [*pe'ulat*] a hired laborer shall not remain with you all night until the morning"** (Leviticus 19:13). This verse is referring to **any** case **where its work [*pe'ulato*] is with you,** which includes animals and vessels. The Gemara asks: **If so,** then **even a *ger toshav*** should be included, as he too performs work for you. The Gemara responds: The initial section of **the verse states: "Your neighbor,"** which refers to **your neighbor** who is Jewish, **and not a *ger toshav*,** who is not called a neighbor.

אִי הָכִי, אֲפִילּוּ בְּהֵמָה וְכֵלִים נָמֵי! הָא כְּתִיב "אִתְּךָ". מָה רָאִיתָ לְרַבּוֹת בְּהֵמָה וְכֵלִים וּלְהוֹצִיא גֵּר תּוֹשָׁב? מִסְתַּבְּרָא, בְּהֵמָה וְכֵלִים הֲוָה לֵיהּ לְרַבּוֹת – שֶׁכֵּן יֶשְׁנָן בִּכְלַל מָמוֹן רֵעֲךָ, גֵּר תּוֹשָׁב אֵינוֹ בִּכְלַל מָמוֹן רֵעֲךָ.

The Gemara asks: **If so,** then **even animals and utensils** should not be included, as they too are not called: Your neighbor. The Gemara replies: It is **written: "With you,"** which includes all items that work with you. The Gemara asks: **What did you see** to decide **to include animals and utensils, and to exclude a *ger toshav*?** The Gemara answers: **It stands to reason** that **he should include animals and utensils, as they are** at least **included in** the category of **your neighbor's money,** whereas **a *ger toshav* is not included in your neighbor's money.**

וְתַנָּא קַמָּא דְּ"מֵאַחֶיךָ" הַאי "רֵעֲךָ" מַאי עָבֵיד לֵיהּ? הַהוּא מִיבְּעֵי לֵיהּ לִכְדְתַנְיָא: "רֵעֲךָ" וְלֹא נׇכְרִי. נׇכְרִי מֵ"אַחֶיךָ" נָפְקָא!

The Gemara asks: **And the first *tanna* of** the *baraita*, who interprets: **"From your brothers," what does he do with this** verse: **"Your neighbor"?**[N] The Gemara explains: **That** verse **is necessary for him for that which is taught** in a *baraita*: **"Your neighbor," and not a gentile.** The Gemara challenges: The exclusion of **a gentile** is **derived from: "Your brothers,"** and no additional verses are necessary for this purpose.

חַד לְמִשְׁרָא עוֹשְׁקוֹ, וְחַד לְמִשְׁרָא גְּזֵלוֹ. וּצְרִיכִי. דְּאִי אַשְׁמְעִינַן גְּזֵלוֹ – מִשּׁוּם דְּלָא טָרַח בֵּיהּ, אֲבָל עוֹשְׁקוֹ דְּטָרַח בֵּיהּ – אֵימָא לָא. וְאִי אַשְׁמְעִינַן עוֹשְׁקוֹ – מִשּׁוּם דְּלָא אֲתָא לִידֵיהּ, אֲבָל גְּזֵלוֹ דַּאֲתָא לִידֵיהּ – אֵימָא לָא. צְרִיכָא.

The Gemara answers: **One** verse serves **to permit** one who **oppresses him, and** the other **one** serves **to permit stealing from him,**[N] **and** both are **necessary. Because had** the Torah **taught us** this *halakha* only with regard to **stealing from him,** one could have said that this is **because** the gentile **did not toil for him, but** one who **oppresses him, where he** has **toiled for him,** you might **say** that he is **not** permitted to oppress him. **And** conversely, **had** the Torah **taught us** only that the practice of he who **oppresses him** is permitted, it might have been said that this is **because** the money has **not** yet **reached his hand, but** with regard to **stealing from him,** when he takes money **that** has already **reached his hand, say** that this *halakha* does **not** apply. Therefore, both cases are **necessary.**

וְרַבִּי יוֹסֵי בְּרַבִּי יְהוּדָה, הַאי "לֹא תָלִין פְּעֻלַּת שָׂכִיר אִתְּךָ עַד בֹּקֶר" מַאי עָבֵיד לֵיהּ? מִיבְּעֵי לֵיהּ לְכִדְרַב אַסִי. דְּאָמַר רַב אַסִי: אֲפִילּוּ לֹא שְׂכָרוֹ אֶלָּא לִבְצוֹר לוֹ אֶשְׁכּוֹל אֶחָד שֶׁל עֲנָבִים – עוֹבֵר מִשּׁוּם בַּל תָּלִין.

The Gemara asks: **And what** does **Rabbi Yosei, son of Rabbi Yehuda, do with this** verse: **"The wages of a hired laborer shall not remain with you all night until the morning"?** The Gemara answers: It **is necessary for him for that which Rav Asi** teaches, **as Rav Asi says: Even** if one **hired** the laborer **to harvest only one cluster**[N] **of grapes for him,** one **violates the prohibition of delaying** payment of wages.

וְאִידָּךְ? מִ"וְאֵלָיו הוּא נֹשֵׂא אֶת נַפְשׁוֹ" נָפְקָא, דָּבָר הַמּוֹסֵר נַפְשׁוֹ עָלָיו.

The Gemara asks: **And** from where does **the other** Sage, i.e., the first *tanna*, derive this *halakha*? The Gemara answers: He **derives** it **from** the phrase: **"For he sets his soul upon it"** (Deuteronomy 24:15). This indicates that one is liable for delaying the payment of wages due for any work; as a laborer obligates himself to perform the work, it is **something for which he gives his soul.**

NOTES

Hired him to harvest only one cluster – שְׂכָרוֹ אֶלָּא לִבְצוֹר לוֹ אֶשְׁכּוֹל אֶחָד: According to the Meiri, this passage indicates that the prohibition of delaying payment of wages applies no matter how small the sum, as even if he hired him to perform work worth less than the value of one *peruta* he must pay him on time despite the fact that this amount is not considered a halakhically significant sum of money. This interpretation resolves several difficulties raised by the early commentaries, and several later commentaries explain similarly.

Perek **IX**
Daf **112** Amud **a**

וְאִידָּךְ? הַהוּא מִיבְּעֵי לֵיהּ לְכִדְתַנְיָא: "וְאֵלָיו הוּא נֹשֵׂא אֶת נַפְשׁוֹ", מִפְּנֵי מָה עָלָה זֶה בַּכֶּבֶשׁ וְנִתְלָה בָּאִילָן וּמָסַר אֶת עַצְמוֹ לְמִיתָה? לֹא עַל שְׂכָרוֹ?

The Gemara asks: **And** what does **the other** Sage, the second *tanna*, derive from this verse? The Gemara responds: **That** verse is **necessary for that which is taught** in a *baraita*: The expression **"for he sets his soul upon it"** explains why one must be so precise when paying a laborer his wages: **For what** reason did **this** laborer **ascend on** a tall **ramp or suspend** himself **from a tree and risk death to himself?**[N] Was it **not for his wages?** How, then, can his employer delay his payment?

דָּבָר אַחֵר: "וְאֵלָיו הוּא נֹשֵׂא אֶת נַפְשׁוֹ" – כָּל הַכּוֹבֵשׁ שְׂכַר שָׂכִיר כְּאִילּוּ נוֹטֵל נַפְשׁוֹ מִמֶּנּוּ. רַב הוּנָא וְרַב חִסְדָּא – חַד אָמַר: נַפְשׁוֹ שֶׁל גַּזְלָן, וְחַד אָמַר: נַפְשׁוֹ שֶׁל נִגְזָל.

Alternatively,[N] the words **"for he sets his soul upon it"**[N] teach that concerning **one who withholds the wages of a hired laborer,**[H] it is **as though he takes his soul from him. Rav Huna and Rav Ḥisda** disagreed over the meaning of this statement. **One says** it is referring to **the soul of the robber,** meaning that one who steals from a hired laborer by delaying payment of his wages causes Heaven to remove his own soul, **and one says** that he takes **the soul of the robbery victim,** meaning that one who steals from a hired worker causes the death of the worker.

מַאן דְּאָמַר נַפְשׁוֹ שֶׁל גַּזְלָן – דִּכְתִיב: "אַל תִּגְזָל דָּל כִּי דַל הוּא וְאַל תְּדַכֵּא עָנִי בַשָּׁעַר", וּכְתִיב: "כִּי ה' יָרִיב רִיבָם וְקָבַע אֶת קֹבְעֵיהֶם נָפֶשׁ". וּמַאן דְּאָמַר נַפְשׁוֹ שֶׁל נִגְזָל – דִּכְתִיב: "כֵּן אָרְחוֹת כָּל בֹּצֵעַ בָּצַע, אֶת נֶפֶשׁ בְּעָלָיו יִקָּח".

The Gemara cites proof for these two opinions. **The one who says** it is referring to **the soul of the robber** bases his opinion on a verse, **as it is written: "Do not rob from the weak because he is weak, nor crush the poor in the gate"** (Proverbs 22:22), **and** it **is written** immediately afterward: **"For the Lord will plead their cause, and spoil the soul of those who spoil them"** (Proverbs 22:23). This indicates that God will take the soul of one who steals from a poor person. **And the one who says** it is referring to **the soul of the robbery victim** bases his opinion on a verse, **as it is written: "So are the ways of everyone who is greedy for gain; it takes away the life of its owners"** (Proverbs 1:19). A robber is considered as if he removed the very soul of his victim.

וְאִידָּךְ נַמִי, הָכְתִיב: "אֶת נֶפֶשׁ בְּעָלָיו יִקָּח"! בְּעָלָיו דְּהָשְׁתָּא. וְאִידָּךְ נַמִי, הָכְתִיב: "וְקָבַע אֶת קֹבְעֵיהֶם נָפֶשׁ"! מַה טַּעַם קָאָמַר; מַה טַּעַם קָבַע אֶת קֹבְעֵיהֶם? מִשּׁוּם דְּנָטְלוּ נֶפֶשׁ.

The Gemara asks: **And** according to **the other** Sage **too, isn't it written: "It takes away the life of its owners"?** How does he interpret this verse? The Gemara answers: This is referring to **its current owner,** i.e., the robber, who took the money and now owns it. The Gemara asks: **And** according to **the other** Sage **too, isn't it written: "And spoil the soul of those who spoil them"?** How does he interpret this verse? The Gemara answers: This verse employs the style know as: **What is the reason,** as follows: **What is the reason** that God will **spoil those who spoil them? Because they took** someone's **soul,** for which He will exact retribution.

NOTES

And risk death to himself – וּמָסַר אֶת עַצְמוֹ לְמִיתָה: The *Noda BiYehuda* rules, based on this Gemara, that although there is a mitzva to protect oneself from harm (see Deuteronomy 4:15), one is permitted to engage in an occupation even if in doing so one will need to place oneself in a situation of danger.

Alternatively, etc. – דָּבָר אַחֵר וכו׳: This additional exposition is necessary because the first exposition refers only to a laborer who performs a hard, life-threatening job. The Gemara therefore cites this second verse, indicating that an employer who does not pay a laborer has transgressed a severe prohibition even if the laborer performs an easy task (*Iyyun Ya'akov*).

For he sets his soul upon it [*elav*] – וְאֵלָיו הוּא נוֹשֵׂא אֶת נַפְשׁוֹ: The Ra'avad explains that the term *elav* is interpreted as: For it [*alav*]. In other words, God punishes him for the sin of delaying payment of wages.

HALAKHA

One who withholds the wages of a hired laborer – הַכּוֹבֵשׁ שְׂכַר שָׂכִיר: Anyone who neglects to pay a laborer's wages is considered as though he took his very soul (Rambam *Sefer Mishpatim*, *Hilkhot Sekhirut* 11:2; *Shulḥan Arukh*, *Ḥoshen Mishpat* 339:2).

״אֵימָתַי? בִּזְמַן שֶׁתְּבָעוֹ. לֹא תְּבָעוֹ אֵינוֹ עוֹבֵר עָלָיו״. תָּנוּ רַבָּנַן: ״לֹא תָלִין פְּעֻלַּת שָׂכִיר״. יָכוֹל אֲפִילּוּ לֹא תְּבָעוֹ – תַּלְמוּד לוֹמַר: ״אִתְּךָ״, לְדַעְתְּךָ.

§ The mishna teaches: **When** does he transgress these prohibitions? He transgresses them **when** the one owed the money **claimed** the payment from **him.** If he **did not claim** his payment from **him,** the other **does not transgress** the prohibitions. **The Sages taught:** With regard to the verse: **"The wages of a hired laborer shall not remain** with you all night until the morning" (Leviticus 19:13), one **might** have thought that he should be liable **even** if the laborer **did not claim** his wages from **him. The verse states "with you,"** meaning the prohibition is not transgressed unless it is **with your knowledge** and consent that you have not paid him. But if he did not even request his wages yet, the prohibition has not been violated.

יָכוֹל אֲפִילּוּ אֵין לוֹ – תַּלְמוּד לוֹמַר: ״אִתְּךָ״, שֶׁיֵּשׁ אִתְּךָ. יָכוֹל אֲפִילּוּ הִמְחָהוּ אֵצֶל חֶנְוָנִי וְאֵצֶל שׁוּלְחָנִי – תַּלְמוּד לוֹמַר: ״אִתְּךָ״ – וְלֹא שֶׁהִמְחָהוּ אֵצֶל חֶנְוָנִי וְאֵצֶל שׁוּלְחָנִי.

Furthermore, one **might** have thought that the employer is liable **even** if he **does not have** the money to pay him. Therefore, **the verse states "with you,"** indicating **that there is** money **with you.**[N] One **might** have thought that **even** if the employer **transferred** his payment **to a storekeeper or to a money changer,** he still violates the prohibition of delaying payment of wages. Therefore, **the verse states "with you,"** indicating that it applies only if the payment is your obligation, **but not if** he **transferred it to a storekeeper or to a money changer,** as then the payment of the laborer's wages is no longer his responsibility.[H]

״הִמְחָהוּ אֵצֶל חֶנְוָנִי וְאֵצֶל שׁוּלְחָנִי אֵינוֹ עוֹבֵר״. אִיבַּעְיָא לְהוּ: חוֹזֵר אוֹ אֵינוֹ חוֹזֵר? רַב שֵׁשֶׁת אָמַר: אֵינוֹ חוֹזֵר, וְרַבָּה אָמַר: חוֹזֵר.

§ The mishna teaches: **If** the one who owes the money **transferred his** payment by leaving instructions **with a storekeeper or with a money changer** to pay him, **he does not transgress** the prohibitions. **A dilemma was raised before** the Sages: If the storekeeper or money changer neglected to pay the wages, may the laborer **return** to the employer and claim his money from him, **or** may he **not return,**[NH] as the storekeeper or money changer is now his exclusive address for complaints? **Rav Sheshet says he may not return, and Rabba says he may return.**

אָמַר רַבָּה: מְנָא אָמִינָא לָהּ – מִדְּקָתָנֵי: אֵינוֹ עוֹבֵר עָלָיו. מֵעֲבַר הוּא דְּלָא עָבַר, הָא מִיהְדַּר הָדַר. וְרַב שֵׁשֶׁת אָמַר: מַאי אֵינוֹ עוֹבֵר? אֵינוֹ בְּתוֹרַת לַעֲבוֹר.

Rabba said: From where do I state my opinion? **From** the fact **that** the mishna **teaches: He does not transgress** the prohibition, from which it may be inferred: **He does not transgress** the prohibition, **but** the laborer **may** still **return** to him to collect his wages. **And Rav Sheshet said: What** is the meaning of the ruling that he does **not transgress** the prohibition? It means that he **is not** included **in the category of transgressing,** as his transfer of the payment exempts him from all responsibility.

בָּעוּ מִינֵּיהּ מֵרַב שֵׁשֶׁת: קַבְּלָנוּת עוֹבֵר עָלָיו מִשּׁוּם בַּל תָּלִין אוֹ אֵין עוֹבֵר מִשּׁוּם בַּל תָּלִין?

The Sages **inquired of Rav Sheshet:** If the laborer worked as a **contractor,** who is paid for a completed job rather than by the hour, does the employer **violate** the prohibition **of delaying** payment of wages **or** does he **not violate** the prohibition **of delaying** payment of wages?

אוּמָּן קוֹנֶה בְּשֶׁבַח כְּלִי – וְהַלְוָאָה הִיא? אוֹ אֵין אוּמָּן קוֹנֶה בְּשֶׁבַח כְּלִי וּשְׂכִירוּת הִיא?

The resolution to this inquiry depends on how a craftsman's wages are classified. Does **a craftsman,** who is a type of contractor, **acquire** ownership rights **through enhancement of the vessel?**[NH] This would mean that the craftsman is considered to have acquired the vessel through his work, which enhances its value, and it remains in his possession until he returns it to the owners, who are then considered to have purchased the enhanced item from him. **And** accordingly, his payment **is** akin to **a loan** in that it will not be subject to the prohibition of delaying the payment of wages. **Or** perhaps **a craftsman does not acquire** ownership rights **through enhancement of the vessel, and** the obligation of the owner to pay him is similar to the obligation to pay wages to any laborer, in which case the money **is** classified as **a wage,** and is subject to the prohibition of delaying wages.

אֲמַר לְהוּ רַב שֵׁשֶׁת: עוֹבֵר. וְהָתַנְיָא: אֵינוֹ עוֹבֵר! הָתָם שֶׁהִמְחָהוּ אֵצֶל חֶנְוָנִי וְאֵצֶל שׁוּלְחָנִי.

Rav Sheshet said to them: He does **violate** the prohibition. They asked Rav Sheshet: **But isn't it taught** in a *baraita* that a contractor **does not violate** the prohibition? Rav Sheshet replied: **There** it is referring to a case **where** he **transferred** the wages **to a storekeeper or to a money changer.**

NOTES

That there is with you – שֶׁיֵּשׁ אִתְּךָ: According to an opinion cited by the commentary attributed to the Ritva, one may derive from here that even if the employer owns movable property, or other kinds of property, he need not sell them to pay his laborer's wages, as he is obligated to use only money available in his possession.

May he return or may he not return – חוֹזֵר אוֹ אֵינוֹ חוֹזֵר: According to *Tosafot*, the word return means that the prohibition of delaying payment reverts back to the employer. Most commentaries interpret the question as relating to whether the employee may claim his wages from his employer despite the transfer of the debt (see Meiri).

Does a craftsman acquire ownership rights through enhancement of the vessel – אוּמָּן קוֹנֶה בְּשֶׁבַח כְּלִי: The early commentaries note that this distinction was not stated by Rav Sheshet himself, as he holds that a craftsman does acquire ownership rights through enhancement of the vessel. It was added by the Gemara, which maintains that the matter of whether one violates the prohibition of delaying the payment of wages is connected to the matter of whether a craftsman acquires ownership rights through enhancement of the vessel. The conclusion is that the two matters are not related, and a contractor is equivalent to a hired laborer regardless of whether a craftsman acquires ownership rights through the enhancement of a vessel (see Ran and *Shakh*).

HALAKHA

When does one not transgress the prohibition of delaying payment of wages – מָתַי אֵינוֹ עוֹבֵר בְּהַלָנַת שָׂכָר: An employer is in violation of the prohibition of delaying payment of wages only if the laborer claimed his wages. If the laborer claimed his wages but the employer had no available cash or had transferred the debt to a storekeeper or a money changer, who accepted the obligation of payment, the employer has not violated the prohibition (*Shulḥan Arukh, Ḥoshen Mishpat* 339:10).

May he return or may he not return – חוֹזֵר אוֹ אֵינוֹ חוֹזֵר: Even if the employer transferred the responsibility of payment to a third party, if the laborer prefers, he may return to the employer to claim his salary, as the *halakha* is in accordance with the opinion of Rabba. The Rema adds, citing the Rosh, that if an act of acquisition was performed formalizing the transfer of the debt, the laborer may no longer return to the employer to claim his salary (*Shulḥan Arukh, Ḥoshen Mishpat* 339:10, and in the comment of Rema).

Does a craftsman acquire ownership rights through enhancement of the vessel – אוּמָּן קוֹנֶה בְּשֶׁבַח כְּלִי: If one gave a craftsman wood to prepare a vessel and it broke after it was fashioned, he must pay the owner the full value of the vessel, as a craftsman does not acquire ownership rights through enhancement of the vessel (Rambam *Sefer Mishpatim, Hilkhot Sekhirut* 10:4; *Shulḥan Arukh, Ḥoshen Mishpat* 306:2, and see *Sma* there).

נֵימָא מְסַיְּיעָא לֵיהּ: הַנּוֹתֵן טַלִּיתוֹ לְאוּמָּן, גְּמָרָהּ וְהוֹדִיעוֹ – אֲפִילּוּ מִכָּאן וְעַד עֲשָׂרָה יָמִים אֵינוֹ עוֹבֵר מִשּׁוּם בַּל תָּלִין. נְתָנָהּ לוֹ בַּחֲצִי הַיּוֹם – מִשֶּׁשָּׁקְעָה עָלָיו חַמָּה עוֹבֵר מִשּׁוּם בַּל תָּלִין.

The Gemara suggests: **Let us say** that the following *baraita* **supports** the opinion of Rav Sheshet: With regard to **one who gave his garment to a craftsman,** and the craftsman **concluded** the work **and notified** the owner that the work was complete, **even** if the owner delays paying the craftsman **from now until ten days** henceforth, **he does not violate** the **prohibition of delaying** the payment of wages. If the craftsman **gave** the garment **to him at midday,** then **once the sun has set** and the **owner** has not paid him, the owner **does violate** the **prohibition of delaying** the payment of wages.[H]

וְאִי אָמְרַתְּ אוּמָּן קוֹנֶה בִּשְׁבַח כְּלִי, אַמַּאי עוֹבֵר?

The Gemara concludes: **And if it enters your mind** to say that a **craftsman acquires** ownership rights **through** the **enhancement of the vessel, why does** the owner **violate** the prohibition of delaying the payment of wages? It is as if the craftsman acquired the garment, and the payment is considered to be a purchase of the garment by the owner, rather than a wage.

אֲמַר רַב מָרִי בְּרֵיהּ דְּרַב כָּהֲנָא: בְּגַרְדָּא דְּסַרְבְּלָא. לְמַאי יְהָבָהּ נִיהֲלֵיהּ? לְרַכּוֹכֵי, הַיְינוּ שְׁבָחֵיהּ!

Rav Mari, son of Rav Kahana, said: There is no proof from here, as the *baraita* is stating the *halakha* **with regard to the laundering of a thick garment, where there is no enhancement** of the garment. Therefore, the craftsman does not acquire it. The Gemara asks: Ultimately, **to what** end **did** the owner of the garment **give it to** the craftsman? He gave it to him in order **to soften** it. Once he has softened it, **that is its enhancement,** and the craftsman has therefore acquired it.

לָא צְרִיכָא, דְּקָא אַגְרֵיהּ מִינֵּיהּ לְבַטּוּשֵׁי, בַּטְשָׁא וּבַטְשָׁא בְּמָעֲתָא.

The Gemara responds: **No,** it is **necessary** to teach this *halakha* in a case **where** the owner **hired** the craftsman **for treading,** i.e., to forcefully tread on the garment in water until it softens, with the owner paying the craftsman **a *ma'a***[B] coin **for each tread.**[BN] Accordingly, this is considered hired labor, where the craftsman is paid based on the amount of times he performed an action, and not contractual labor, where he is paid based on the outcome, in this case, a softened garment, and the prohibition of delaying payment of wages does apply to this case.

HALAKHA

The prohibition of delaying payment with regard to a contractor – בַּל תָּלִין בְּקַבְּלָנוּת: If one gave a craftsman a vessel to fix, and hired the craftsman as a contractor, as long as the vessel is in the craftsman's possession, the owner has not transgressed the prohibition of delaying payment of wages. Once the craftsman has returned the vessel to its owner, the owner is immediately obligated to pay him, and any delay violates the prohibition of delaying payment of wages, as a contractor is considered like a hired laborer in this regard, as stated by Rav Sheshet (Rambam *Sefer Mishpatim, Hilkhot Sekhirut* 11:3; *Shulḥan Arukh, Ḥoshen Mishpat* 339:6).

BACKGROUND

***Ma'a* – מָעָה:** The *ma'a* is a small silver coin generally identified, both in weight and significance, with the *gera*, the smallest denomination of currency mentioned in the Torah. Originally, the biblical sacred shekel, equal in worth to the mishnaic *sela*, was worth twenty *ma'a*, but the *sela* was later increased by 20 percent to twenty-four *ma'a*. The mishnaic shekel, half of a biblical shekel, was worth twelve *ma'a*.

Each tread – בַּטְשָׁא וּבַטְשָׁא: In talmudic times, new garments, particularly thick ones, were often too rigid to wear immediately after weaving. To make them suitable for wearing, they were given to craftsmen who would tread on them inside a vessel full of water mixed with softeners and cleaning agents.

Roman fresco depicting adults and children treading on laundry in tubs

NOTES

A *ma'a* for each tread – בַּטְשָׁא וּבַטְשָׁא בְּמָעֲתָא: Rashi in tractate *Bava Kamma* (99a) explains that in this case he is not a contractor because he receives payment for each stage of the work. Others are puzzled by this interpretation, as the definition of a hired laborer is one who works for a specific amount of time, whereas anyone whose agreement concerns the quality of the work is called a contractor (*Tosafot* in *Bava Kamma*). Rashi here explains that the reason he is considered a laborer and not a contractor is that the owner does not pay attention to the enhancement but to the amount of times the laborer trod on the garment. According to *Tosafot* in tractate *Bava Kamma* (99a), the first times he treads on the garment do not improve it, and therefore they do not serve to acquire the item for him. Others explain that this refers to the very first strikes on the vessel before it is assembled or washed, which do not result in the vessel's improvement (*Arukh*).

HALAKHA

A hired laborer at his proper time takes an oath and receives the wages – שָׂכִיר בִּזְמַנּוֹ נִשְׁבָּע וְנוֹטֵל: The Sages instituted that at the proper time for receiving his wages, a hired laborer should take an oath while holding a sacred item and receive his wages from his employer (Rambam *Sefer Mishpatim*, *Hilkhot Sekhirut* 11:6; *Shulḥan Arukh*, *Ḥoshen Mishpat* 89:1).

״שָׂכִיר בִּזְמַנּוֹ נִשְׁבָּע וְנוֹטֵל״ וכו׳. שָׂכִיר אַמַּאי תַּקִּינוּ לֵיהּ רַבָּנַן לְמִשְׁתַּבַּע וְשָׁקֵיל?

The mishna teaches: If **a hired laborer** requests payment **at** the proper **time** and the employer claims he already paid him, the laborer **takes an oath** that he did not receive his wages **and** then **receives** the wages from the employer.[H] The Gemara asks: **Why** did **the Sages institute** for **a hired laborer,** who is the plaintiff, **to take an oath and receive** his wages, in opposition to the principle that in the case of a monetary dispute between two parties, the defendant takes an oath that he is not liable and thereby exempts himself from payment?

אָמַר רַב יְהוּדָה אָמַר שְׁמוּאֵל: הֲלָכוֹת גְּדוֹלוֹת שָׁנוּ כָּאן. הָנֵי הִלְכְתָא נִינְהוּ? הָנֵי תַּקָּנוֹת נִינְהוּ! אֶלָּא, אָמַר רַב יְהוּדָה אָמַר שְׁמוּאֵל: תַּקָּנוֹת גְּדוֹלוֹת שָׁנוּ כָּאן. גְּדוֹלוֹת מִכְּלָל דְּאִיכָּא קְטַנּוֹת?

Rav Yehuda says that **Shmuel says: They taught great *halakhot* here.** The Gemara is puzzled by this choice of words: **Are these *halakhot*?**[N] **They are ordinances** designed for the proper running of business transactions, not *halakhot* that apply to everyone at all times. The Gemara emends the above statement: **Rather, Rav Yehuda says** that **Shmuel says: They taught great ordinances here.** The Gemara is still unsatisfied with the terminology: Does the word **great** indicate **by inference that there are minor** ordinances? Which ordinances are considered of minor importance?

אֶלָּא אָמַר רַב נַחְמָן אָמַר שְׁמוּאֵל: תַּקָּנוֹת קְבוּעוֹת שָׁנוּ כָּאן. שְׁבוּעָה דְּבַעַל הַבַּיִת הִיא וַעֲקַרוּהָ רַבָּנַן לִשְׁבוּעָה דְּבַעַל הַבַּיִת וְשַׁדְיוּהָ אַשָּׂכִיר, מִשּׁוּם כְּדֵי חַיָּיו דְּשָׂכִיר. וּמִשּׁוּם כְּדֵי חַיָּיו דְּשָׂכִיר מַפְסְדִינָא לֵיהּ לְבַעַל הַבַּיִת?

Rather, Rav Naḥman says that **Shmuel says: They taught fixed ordinances here** that are necessary for practical life. The reason is that taking the **oath is** actually the duty **of the employer, but the Sages transferred the oath of the employer**[N] **and imposed it upon the hired laborer due to the livelihood of the hired laborer.** The laborer requires his wages to survive, and therefore if the employer is allowed to exempt himself by taking an oath, the laborer will be left with nothing. The Gemara asks: **And simply due to the livelihood of the hired laborer** should **we cause the employer** to **lose out?** If the employer is entitled to take an oath to exempt himself, why should he suffer due to the laborer's needs?

בַּעַל הַבַּיִת גּוּפֵיהּ נִיחָא לֵיהּ דְּמִשְׁתַּבַּע שָׂכִיר וְשָׁקֵיל, כִּי הֵיכִי דְּלִיתַּגְרוּ לֵיהּ פּוֹעֲלִים. שָׂכִיר גּוּפֵיהּ נִיחָא לֵיהּ דְּמִשְׁתַּבַּע בַּעַל הַבַּיִת וְיִפָּקַע, כִּי הֵיכִי דְּלִיגְרוּהוּ! בַּעַל הַבַּיִת עַל כָּרְחֵיהּ אָגַר. שָׂכִיר נַמִי בְּעַל כָּרְחֵיהּ אִיתַּגַּר!

The Gemara answers: It is **preferable for the employer himself that the hired laborer should take an oath and receive** his wages **so that laborers will hire themselves out to him** with the knowledge that their wages are secure. The Gemara asks: Why not argue the reverse, that it is **preferable for the hired laborer himself that the employer should take an oath and be exempt so that he should be hired?** If the terms of labor are too imposing, people will not hire laborers. The Gemara responds: The **employer must perforce** find a laborer to **hire.** The Gemara retorts: **A hired laborer, too, must perforce** allow himself to **be hired out.**

NOTES

Are these *halakhot* – הָנֵי הִלְכְתָא נִינְהוּ: Rashi explains that the Gemara means to question whether these laws are *halakhot* transmitted to Moses from Sinai. Others add that the word *halakhot* indicates a law similar to a *halakha* transmitted to Moses from Sinai in the sense that it is an established law without a given reason, and the Gemara's question is that this is an ordinance of the Sages, for which they certainly provided a justification (*Ein Yehosef*).

But the Sages transferred the oath of the employer – וַעֲקַרוּהָ רַבָּנַן לִשְׁבוּעָה דְּבַעַל הַבַּיִת: The Ramban is troubled by the statement of the Gemara that the obligation to take an oath would have been upon the employer, as in this case he is denying the claim of the laborer, and by Torah law a defendant takes an oath only if he admits to part of the claim. In addition, at the time of the mishna, the Sages had not yet instituted the rabbinic ordinance requiring an oath of inducement to be taken by the employer in a case where he completely denies the claim of the laborer. Therefore, the employer would not have been obligated to take any oath. The Ramban explains that although generally speaking a defendant who completely denies the claim of the plaintiff is exempt from taking an oath, there are strong grounds for the Sages to institute an oath in this particular case, for several reasons. One is that there are witnesses that he hired the laborer. Furthermore, it can be assumed that the laborer is more exact in keeping track of the payment of the wages than the employer. It is concerning this oath by rabbinic law that the Gemara states that the Sages transferred the oath that would have been imposed upon the employer and imposed it on the employee.

אֶלָּא, בַּעַל הַבַּיִת טָרוּד בִּפוֹעֲלִים הוּא. אִי הָכִי נֵיתַב לֵיהּ בְּלָא שְׁבוּעָה! כְּדֵי לְהָפִיס דַּעְתּוֹ שֶׁל בַּעַל הַבַּיִת.

The Gemara now retracts the previous explanation: **Rather, the employer is preoccupied with** many **laborers,**[N] and it is more likely that he forgot and mistakenly believed that he already paid this laborer's wages. The Gemara asks: **If so,** i.e., if it is reasonable that the employer forgot, we **should give** the laborer his wages **without** him taking **an oath,** as there are grounds to presume that the employer erred. The Gemara responds: The laborer takes an oath **in order to alleviate the concerns of the employer,** as, if he is not required to take an oath, the employer will feel that he has been cheated.

וְנֵיתַב לֵיהּ בְּעֵדִים! טְרִיחָא לְהוּ מִילְּתָא. וְנֵיתַב לֵיהּ מֵעִיקָּרָא! שְׁנֵיהֶם רוֹצִים בְּהַקָּפָה.

The Gemara asks: **But** why not **have** the employer instead **give him** his wages **in** the presence of **witnesses** each time, which would remove any uncertainty? The Gemara answers: **The matter** would be **an inconvenience to them** both if they needed to find witnesses before each payment. The Gemara asks: **But** why not **have** the employer **give him** the wages **at the outset,** before he starts working, when he is less preoccupied? The Gemara answers: **Both of them want** the payment to be in the form **of credit,**[N] i.e., that the wages not be paid in advance. The employer prefers this arrangement in case he has no ready cash at his disposal, while the laborer also prefers to be paid at the end of the day so that he does not lose his money in the meantime.

אִי הָכִי, אֲפִילּוּ קָצַץ נַמִי. אַלְמָה תַּנְיָא: אוּמָּן אוֹמֵר שְׁתַּיִם קָצַצְתָּ לִי, וְהַלָּה אוֹמֵר לֹא קָצַצְתִּי לְךָ אֶלָּא אַחַת – הַמּוֹצִיא מֵחֲבֵירוֹ עָלָיו הָרְאָיָה! קְצִיצָה וַדַּאי מִידְכַּר דְּכִירֵי לָהּ אֱינָשֵׁי.

The Gemara asks: **If so,** then **even** if the dispute between them concerns **a fixed** amount of payment[H] **as well,** the laborer should take an oath. **Why did we learn** in a *baraita*: If **the craftsman says: You fixed two**[N] coins **for me** as my payment, **and the other,** i.e., the employer, **says: I fixed only one** coin **for you,** then **the burden of proof rests upon the claimant.** Why is it not assumed that the employer was preoccupied and forgot, as in the previous case? The Gemara answers: **The fixing** of wages is **certainly** an event that **people remember,** and there is no concern that the employer forgot how much he stipulated.

אִי הָכִי, אֲפִילּוּ עָבַר זְמַנּוֹ נַמִי. אַלְמָה תְּנַן: עָבַר זְמַנּוֹ אֵינוֹ נִשְׁבָּע וְנוֹטֵל! חֲזָקָה אֵין בַּעַל הַבַּיִת עוֹבֵר מִשּׁוּם בַּל תָּלִין.

The Gemara asks: **If so,** i.e., if the concern exists that the employer might have forgotten, then **even** if **his time had passed** for claiming his wages, the laborer should be entitled to take an oath and claim his wages. **Why did we learn** in the mishna: If **the time had passed** he does **not take an oath and receive** the wages? The Gemara answers: The reason in that case is that **a presumption**[B] exists that **an employer does not** generally **violate** the prohibition **of delaying** payment of wages.

וְהָא אָמְרַתְּ בַּעַל הַבַּיִת טָרוּד בִּפוֹעֲלָיו הוּא! הָנֵי מִילֵּי מִקַּמֵּיהּ דְּלִימְטְיֵיהּ זְמַן חִיּוּבֵיהּ,

The Gemara asks: **But didn't you say** that **the employer is preoccupied with his laborers?** The Gemara answers: **This statement** applies only **before the time of his obligation** to pay **arrives,** as it is possible that his preoccupation with other matters caused him to forget whether he had already paid him,

NOTES

Preoccupied with laborers – טָרוּד בִּפוֹעֲלִים: According to the Rif in tractate *Shevuot*, there are two reasons for the ruling that it is the laborer who takes the oath: The employer is distracted, and the laborer's livelihood is at stake. With regard to the claim that the employer is preoccupied with his laborers, Rashi explains that since he has many laborers, some of whom have been paid, he may wrongly assume that he has paid the others as well. It is explained in the Jerusalem Talmud that an employer is busy with his large workload, and the concern exists that this will cause him to overlook paying wages, even if he has only one laborer.

Both of them want the payment to be in the form of credit – שְׁנֵיהֶם רוֹצִים בְּהַקָּפָה: Rashi explains that the employer wants payment to be in the form of credit because he occasionally lacks sufficient cash to pay the employee at the start of the day. The employee wants payment to be in the form of credit because he is concerned that he may lose the money over the course of the day while he is working. Rashi in tractate *Shevuot* (45a) suggests another reason that the employee prefers payment in the form of credit: He does not want to risk spending the money during the day on non-essential purchases. Others add an additional reason, with regard to the employer: He is reluctant to pay in advance, in case the employee decides to stop working early (*Nefesh Ḥayya*).

If the craftsman says you fixed two – אוּמָּן אוֹמֵר שְׁתַּיִם קָצַצְתָּ: Many commentaries are bothered by the fact that, in this case, the employer has made a partial admission. Therefore, by Torah law, he should have to take an oath. Some early commentaries, such as the Rambam, rule that this is the case (see *Tosafot*). The Ri Migash suggests that this refers to a situation where the employer had already paid the laborer the amount that he felt was due, or he told him: Here it is, in which case the *halakha* of an admission to part of a claim no longer applies (see 4a). The Ramban suggests another reason for this ruling: Part of the reason for the ordinance of the employer taking an oath was due to the necessity of the laborer receiving a livelihood. As the sum needed to cover one's basic expenses is known, it is not likely that the agreement would have been for the employer to pay less than that. Therefore, the sum subject to their dispute is presumably concerning an amount greater than that needed to cover one's basic expenses, and is similar to a standard claim.

HALAKHA

A dispute over a fixed amount of payment – מַחְלוֹקֶת בִּקְצִיצָה: In this case, an individual gave a vessel to a craftsman who in turn claims that his payment was two coins, while the owner says he agreed to pay him only one. If the vessel is still in the craftsman's possession, and the circumstances are such that he could claim it belongs to him, the craftsman takes an oath while holding a sacred item, attesting to the truth of his claim, and collects his money. If the vessel is no longer in the craftsman's possession or if he could not claim it as his, the burden of proof rests upon the craftsman, since he is the claimant. If he fails to bring proof, the employer takes an oath and is exempt (Rambam *Sefer Mishpatim, Hilkhot Sekhirut* 11:8; *Shulḥan Arukh, Ḥoshen Mishpat* 89:5).

BACKGROUND

Presumption – חֲזָקָה: This term, which is frequently used in *halakha*, has different meanings depending on the context. In general, it means an assumption that is widely accepted based on facts, circumstances, custom, or general behavioral tendencies. One example of a presumption is: An agent performs his assigned agency. Another example is: Children who are treated as family members are, in fact, their parents' offspring. Unless the facts prove otherwise, these presumptions are accepted as truth. At times, even corporal punishment may be administered based on these presumptions.

HALAKHA

If there are witnesses that he claimed the money from him, etc. – אִם יֵשׁ עֵדִים שֶׁתְּבָעוֹ כו׳: A hired laborer takes an oath and receives his wages if there are witnesses who testify that he was hired and performed work for the employer. If there are no witnesses, since his employer could have claimed that he never hired the laborer, the employer is deemed credible when he claims to have paid, although he must take an oath of inducement, which is an oath by rabbinic law. If he admits to part of the claim, he must take an oath by Torah law. The Rema, citing the *Tur*, states that even when the employer denies everything, if he hired the laborer in the presence of one witness, the employer must take an oath by Torah law. Similarly, if the laborer claimed his money after the time for payment was due, even if the laborer was hired in the presence of witnesses, the burden of proof rests upon the claimant, and if he is unable to provide proof, the employer takes an oath of inducement.

How long does the period for a laborer claiming his wages last? In the case of a day laborer, he may do so the entire night following the day he worked. Similarly, a night laborer may claim his wages any time throughout the following day. If the laborer brings proof that he claimed his money within this time, he may take an oath and receive his wages one day after the time for payment. From that point onward, the burden of proof rests upon the claimant. If the laborer provides proof that he has continually been claiming his wages, he may take an oath the following day and receive his wages. This ruling is the consensus among the authorities, including the *Taz* (Rambam *Sefer Mishpatim*, *Hilkhot Sekhirut* 11:6; *Shulḥan Arukh*, *Ḥoshen Mishpat* 89:3, and see *Sma* there).

אֲבָל מְטָא זְמַן חִיּוּבֵיהּ – רָמֵי אַנַּפְשֵׁיהּ וּמִידְכַּר.

but when **the time of his obligation** to pay **arrives, he applies himself and remembers**[N] all the details, so as not to violate the prohibition of delaying payment of the laborer's wages.

וְכִי שָׂכִיר עוֹבֵר מִשּׁוּם בַּל תִּגְזוֹל? הָתָם תְּרֵי חֲזָקֵי, הָכָא חֲדָא חֲזָקָה. גַּבֵּי בַּעַל הַבַּיִת אִיכָּא תְּרֵי חֲזָקֵי: חֲדָא דְּאֵין בַּעַל הַבַּיִת עוֹבֵר מִשּׁוּם בַּל תָּלִין, וַחֲדָא דְּאֵין שָׂכִיר מַשְׁהֶא שְׂכָרוֹ. וְהָכָא – חֲדָא חֲזָקָה.

The Gemara asks: Why would one rely upon the presumption that the employer would not transgress? **But is the hired laborer** suspected of **violating** the **prohibition of stealing?**[N] The Gemara replies: **There,** concerning the credibility of an employer, there are **two presumptions,** whereas **here,** concerning the credibility of a laborer, there is only **one presumption.** The Gemara explains: **Concerning** the credibility of **an employer there are** the following **two presumptions: One is that the employer does not violate** the **prohibition of delaying** payment of wages, **and** the other **one** is **that a hired laborer does not delay** the request for **his wages. But here,** concerning the credibility of the laborer, there is only **one presumption,** i.e., that the laborer does not violate the prohibition of stealing.

״אִם יֵשׁ עֵדִים שֶׁתְּבָעוֹ הֲרֵי זֶה נִשְׁבָּע וְנוֹטֵל״. וְהָא קָתְבָעוֹ לְקַמָּן! אָמַר רַבִּי אַסִי: שֶׁתְּבָעוֹ בִּזְמַנּוֹ. וְדִלְמָא לְבָתַר הָכִי פָּרַע! אָמַר אַבַּיֵי: שֶׁתְּבָעוֹ כׇּל זְמַנּוֹ.

The mishna teaches: **If there are witnesses** who testify **that he claimed** the money from **him,**[H] **he takes an oath and receives** the money. The Gemara asks: **But** what need is there for witnesses that he lodged a claim, when **he is claiming** it from **him in front of us? Rabbi Asi said:** The *tanna* is referring to witnesses **that** testified that he **claimed** it from **him at its** proper **time.** The Gemara challenges: Even if the laborer claimed the money at the proper time, **perhaps** the employer **paid** him **afterward. Abaye said:** The witnesses testify **that he claimed** it from **him the entire time,** i.e., from the time he completed his labor until the end of that day.

וּלְעוֹלָם לָא פָּרַע לֵיהּ? אָמַר רַב חָמָא בַּר עוּקְבָא: כְּנֶגֶד אוֹתוֹ הַיּוֹם שֶׁל תְּבִיעָה.

The Gemara continues: **And** is it **always** assumed that the employer **did not pay** the laborer? Why does the fact that he claimed his money at the proper time mean that his claim against his employer is always accepted? **Rav Ḥama bar Ukva said:** The *tanna* means that he is given another day **corresponding to that day of his claim**[N] during which the laborer can claim that he has not been paid.

NOTES

He applies himself and remembers – רָמֵי אַנַּפְשֵׁיהּ וּמִידְכַּר: Commentaries raise the following question: Since the employer is capable of remembering whether or not he paid the laborer in order to avoid violating the prohibition of delaying the payment of his wages, why did the Sages not impose the oath on the employer before the time of his obligation to pay arrives, which could also result in his applying himself to remember? One answer suggested in the *Shita Mekubbetzet* is that an employer will apply himself in order to avoid violating the prohibition because he is always aware that he must pay the wages. By contrast, an oath imposed suddenly upon him in the case of a dispute with the laborer will not help him remember.

But is the hired laborer suspected of transgressing the prohibition of stealing – וְכִי שָׂכִיר עוֹבֵר מִשּׁוּם בַּל תִּגְזוֹל: Early commentaries ask whether this same reasoning can be applied to the hired laborer's employer: Is the employer actually suspected of stealing? One explanation is that there is a difference between the two cases: An employer who fails to pay has not actually stolen anything, as he always has the option of paying later, whereas an employee who takes more than his due has actively stolen money (Rosh, cited in *Shita Mekubbetzet*).

Corresponding to that day of his claim – כְּנֶגֶד אוֹתוֹ הַיּוֹם שֶׁל תְּבִיעָה: There is a dispute with regard to this issue in the Jerusalem Talmud. According to one opinion, since the witnesses testified that the employer did not pay on time and the employer claimed he had paid, the laborer may take an oath and receive his wages at any time, as the employer is no longer considered to be credible. Conversely, Rabbi Yosei, son of Rabbi Bun, maintains that the laborer receives one extra day following the time of the claim, per the Gemara's conclusion here. If the witnesses testified that he continued to claim his wages without response, he receives one day from the final time he stated his claim to take an oath and take his wages. The early commentaries maintain positions similar to those found in the Jerusalem Talmud (see *Shita Mekubbetzet*).

מתני׳ הַמַּלְוֶה אֶת חֲבֵירוֹ – לֹא יְמַשְׁכְּנֶנּוּ אֶלָּא בְּבֵית דִּין. וְלֹא יִכָּנֵס לְבֵיתוֹ לִיטּוֹל מַשְׁכּוֹנוֹ, שֶׁנֶּאֱמַר: ״בַּחוּץ תַּעֲמֹד״. הָיוּ לוֹ שְׁנֵי כֵלִים – נוֹטֵל אֶחָד וּמַנִּיחַ אֶחָד.

MISHNA With regard to one **who lends** money to **another** and the debtor fails to repay it at the end of the term of the loan, the creditor **may take collateral from him** to ensure payment **only by means of** an agent of **the court,**[H] not of his own accord. **And he may not enter** the debtor's **house to take his collateral, as it is stated:** "When you lend your neighbor any manner of loan, you shall not go into his house to take his collateral. **You shall stand outside,** and the man to whom you lend shall bring forth the collateral to you outside" (Deuteronomy 24:10–11). If the debtor **had two utensils**[H] of the same kind, the creditor **takes one and leaves** the other **one**[N] in the debtor's possession.[N]

וּמַחֲזִיר אֶת הַכַּר בַּלַּיְלָה וְאֶת הַמַּחֲרֵישָׁה בַּיּוֹם. וְאִם מֵת – אֵינוֹ מַחֲזִיר לְיוֹרְשָׁיו. רַבָּן שִׁמְעוֹן בֶּן גַּמְלִיאֵל אוֹמֵר: אַף לְעַצְמוֹ אֵינוֹ מַחֲזִיר אֶלָּא עַד שְׁלֹשִׁים יוֹם, וּמִשְּׁלֹשִׁים יוֹם וּלְהַלָּן מוֹכְרָן בְּבֵית דִּין.

And in addition, the creditor **must return a pillow at night,**[N] as the debtor requires it for sleeping, **and a plow,** which is needed for his daytime work, **by day.**[H] If the debtor **died,** he is **not** required to **return** it **to** the debtor's **heirs. Rabban Shimon ben Gamliel says: Even to** the debtor **himself** he needs to **return** the collateral each day **only until thirty days** have passed, **and from thirty days onward,** the creditor can **sell them in court,** with the proceeds going toward payment of the debt.

גמ׳ אָמַר שְׁמוּאֵל: שְׁלִיחַ בֵּית דִּין, מִנְתַּח נַתּוּחֵי – אִין, אֲבָל מַשְׁכּוּנֵי – לָא. וְהָתְנַן: הַמַּלְוֶה אֶת חֲבֵירוֹ לֹא יְמַשְׁכְּנֶנּוּ אֶלָּא בְּבֵית דִּין – מִכְּלָל דִּבְבֵית דִּין מְמַשְׁכְּנִין!

GEMARA **Shmuel says: An agent** of **the court** who was granted permission to appropriate items from a debtor up to the sum of the loan **may seize**[N] these items from him in the marketplace, **but** is **not** permitted to enter the debtor's house and **take collateral.** The Gemara asks: **But didn't we learn** in the mishna that one **who lends** money to **another may take collateral from him only by means of** an agent of **the court,** which proves **by inference that** when it is taken **by means of** an agent of **the court** the agent of the court may enter the debtor's house and **take collateral?**

אָמַר לָךְ שְׁמוּאֵל: אֵימָא לֹא יְנַתְּחֶנּוּ אֶלָּא בְּבֵית דִּין. הָכִי נַמִי מִסְתַּבְּרָא, דְּקָתָנֵי סֵיפָא: לֹא יִכָּנֵס לְבֵיתוֹ לִיטּוֹל מַשְׁכּוֹנוֹ. מַנִּי? אִילֵימָא בַּעַל חוֹב – מֵרֵישָׁא שְׁמַע מִינָּהּ; אֶלָּא לָאו שְׁלִיחַ בֵּית דִּין.

The Gemara responds: **Shmuel** could have **said to you: Say** that the mishna meant as follows: **He may seize it** forcibly from him **only by means of** an agent of **the court.** The Gemara adds: **So, too, it is reasonable** that this is correct, **as the latter clause** of the mishna **teaches:** And **he may not enter** the debtor's **house**[N] **to take his collateral. Who is** the *tanna* referring to here? **If we say** it is referring to **the creditor,** this clause is not needed, as this *halakha* can be **concluded from the first clause** of the mishna, which states that a creditor has no right to take collateral himself. **Rather, is it not** referring **to the court agent?** Accordingly, this teaches that even an agent of the court may not enter the debtor's house to take the collateral.

HALAKHA

He may take collateral from him only by means of the court – **לֹא יְמַשְׁכְּנֶנּוּ אֶלָּא בְּבֵית דִּין**: A creditor who wishes to take collateral from the debtor's property after the loan was granted may not do so himself and, if he does, he violates a Torah prohibition. According to the Rema, even if the creditor wishes to enter the debtor's house to take an inventory of his property, the court does not grant such a request. Instead, the court sends its own agent, who, like the creditor, may not enter the debtor's house. The agent of the court may take from the debtor any item that he finds outside the debtor's house, even if the agent has to use force. After the agent takes an item, he delivers it to the creditor.

Tur, citing Rabbeinu Tam, rules that the prohibition against entering the debtor's house applies only to collateral that the creditor wants as a security against his loan. However, if the time for payment arrived and the debtor does not wish to pay, the court agent may enter the debtor's house to take collateral, and the court may use all means at its disposal to compel the debtor to repay his debt (Rambam *Sefer Mishpatim*, *Hilkhot Malve VeLoveh* 3:4; *Shulḥan Arukh*, *Ḥoshen Mishpat* 97:6, 15).

If he had two utensils, etc. – **הָיוּ לוֹ שְׁנֵי כֵלִים כו׳**: If the debtor had two vessels of the same type, the creditor takes one as collateral and leaves him the other. In that case, the creditor is not obligated to return the item at any particular time. If the collateral item is not needed by the debtor, the creditor may keep it for thirty days, after which time he may sell it through the court (Rambam *Sefer Mishpatim*, *Hilkhot Malve VeLoveh* 3:6; *Shulḥan Arukh*, *Ḥoshen Mishpat* 97:18, and *Beur HaGra* there).

The return of collateral – **הַחְזָרַת הָעֲבוֹט**: If one takes collateral from another, whether through the court or illegally, by force, it is a mitzva for him to give the debtor back his collateral when he needs it. Therefore, a creditor should restore the debtor's pillow to him by night, and should restore the debtor's plow to him by day, when he requires it for work. These *halakhot* apply only to collateral that was not taken at the time of the loan. If he took the item at the time of the loan, he is not obligated to return it. Although the court has the right to compel the restoration of the collateral taken at the time of the loan, it is not required to do so, although some authorities disagree (Rambam *Sefer Mishpatim*, *Hilkhot Malve VeLoveh* 3:5; *Shulḥan Arukh*, *Ḥoshen Mishpat* 97:16, and in the comment of Rema and *Sma* there).

NOTES

He takes one and leaves one – **נוֹטֵל אֶחָד וּמַנִּיחַ אֶחָד**: According to *Tosafot* and the Ran, this refers to a creditor who unlawfully took collateral from the debtor. According to the Rambam, the same *halakha* applies if collateral was taken with the sanction of the court.

The return of collateral – **הַחְזָרַת הָעֲבוֹט**: There are various types of collateral. One is an item taken by the creditor at the time of the loan as a guarantee of payment. Since the debtor gives this collateral of his own free will, the *halakhot* of returning the collateral that are stated here do not apply to that case at all. Another type of collateral is an item taken from the debtor as a form of payment for his debt. Rabbeinu Tam and the Ra'avad maintain that here, too, the *halakhot* of the return of collateral are not in effect. A third type of collateral is defined in the mishna here, and refers to collateral taken during the period of a loan to ensure repayment of the loan. All the *halakhot* stated in the mishna apply to collateral of this sort, both with regard to the limitations upon the type of item as well as with regard to which items must be returned.

He must return a pillow at night – **מַחֲזִיר אֶת הַכַּר בַּלַּיְלָה**: This *halakha* is questioned by *amora'im* and leading early commentaries. What is the point of taking the collateral in the first place if the creditor must return it whenever the debtor requires it? The reason given in the Gemara is that the collateral ensures that the Sabbatical Year will not cancel this loan. Furthermore, if the debtor dies, the creditor need not return the collateral to his heirs. *Tosafot*, citing Rabbeinu Elḥanan, suggest an alternative answer: The feelings of trouble and shame that the debtor must experience at having the collateral taken multiple times compel him to repay his debt.

May seize – **מִנְתַּח נַתּוּחֵי**: According to some commentaries, the court agent has the right to physically force the debtor to his house and compel him to bring out the collateral (Ra'avad; Meiri).

He may not enter his house, etc. – **לֹא יִכָּנֵס לְבֵיתוֹ וכו׳**: The early commentaries disagree as to whether the creditor may take collateral from the debtor outside of the debtor's house. According to the Rambam and the *Tur*, the creditor is prohibited by Torah law from doing so. According to *Tosafot* and the Rosh, he is permitted to do so by Torah law, but the Sages prohibited the practice lest he enter the debtor's house, which everyone agrees is prohibited by Torah law.

אִי מִשּׁוּם הָא לָא אִירְיָא. הָכִי קָאָמַר: הַמַּלְוֶה אֶת חֲבֵירוֹ לֹא יְמַשְׁכְּנֶנּוּ אֶלָּא בְּבֵית דִּין. מִכְּלָל דִּבְבֵית דִּין – מְמַשְׁכְּנִים. וּבַעַל חוֹב אֲפִילּוּ נַתּוּחֵי נַמִי לָא, שֶׁלֹּא יִכָּנֵס לְבֵיתוֹ לִיטּוֹל מַשְׁכּוֹנוֹ.

The Gemara refutes the above claim: **If** the argument to understand the mishna in that manner **is due to that** reason, **there is no** conclusive **argument**, as it is possible that **this** is what the mishna **is saying:** One **who lends** money **to another may take collateral from him** by entering the debtor's house **only by means of** an agent of **the court,** which proves **by inference that** it is permitted to **take collateral** by entering the debtor's house **by means of** an agent of **the court.** One can then infer: **But** as for the **creditor** himself, he may **not even seize** collateral outside the debtor's house. This is a rabbinic decree so **that** he should **not enter** the debtor's **house to take his collateral.**

מְתִיב רַב יוֹסֵף: ״לֹא יַחֲבֹל רֵיחַיִם וָרָכֶב״, הָא דְּבָרִים אֲחֵרִים – חָבֵל. ״לֹא תַחֲבֹל בֶּגֶד אַלְמָנָה״, הָא שֶׁל אֲחֵרִים – תַּחֲבֹל. מַאן? אִי נֵימָא בַּעַל חוֹב – הָא כְּתִיב: ״לֹא תָבֹא אֶל בֵּיתוֹ לַעֲבֹט עֲבֹטוֹ״. אֶלָּא לָאו שְׁלִיחַ בֵּית דִּין!

Rav Yosef raises an objection to Shmuel's statement from a *baraita*: The Torah states: **"He may not take the lower or upper millstone as collateral"** (Deuteronomy 24:6). **But** it may be inferred that **other items** may be **taken as collateral.** Similarly, it states: **"You may not take a widow's garment as collateral"** (Deuteronomy 24:17), **but** clothing that **belongs to others you may take as collateral.** The Gemara analyzes these statements: **Who** is permitted to do so? **If we say** that **the creditor** may take these items, that cannot be, as it **is written: "You shall not go into his house to take his collateral"** (Deuteronomy 24:10). **Rather, is it not** referring to **the agent of the court,** which indicates that the agent of the court may enter the debtor's house and take collateral, although the Torah places limits on which item he can take?

תַּרְגְּמָהּ רַב פַּפָּא בְּרֵיהּ דְּרַב נַחְמָן קַמֵּיהּ דְּרַב יוֹסֵף, וְאָמְרִי לַהּ רַב פַּפָּא בְּרֵיהּ דְּרַב יוֹסֵף קַמֵּיהּ דְּרַב יוֹסֵף: לְעוֹלָם בְּבַעַל חוֹב, וְלַעֲבוֹר עָלָיו בִּשְׁנֵי לָאוִין.

Rav Pappa, son of Rav Naḥman, interpreted the *baraita* **before** Rav Yosef; **and some say** it was **Rav Pappa, son of Rav Yosef,** who interpreted the *baraita* **before Rav Yosef: Actually,** it is referring **to a creditor, and** the Torah's additional prohibition against appropriating certain items is given **so that he will violate two prohibitions** for this action. For example, if he took the lower or upper millstone he violates both the command: "You shall not go into his house," as well as the more specific prohibition.

תָּא שְׁמַע: מִמַּשְׁמָע שֶׁנֶּאֱמַר ״בַּחוּץ תַּעֲמֹד״ אֵינִי יוֹדֵעַ שֶׁ״הָאִישׁ אֲשֶׁר אַתָּה נֹשֶׁה בוֹ יוֹצִיא״? אֶלָּא מַה תַּלְמוּד לוֹמַר ״וְהָאִישׁ״? לְרַבּוֹת שְׁלִיחַ בֵּית דִּין. מַאי לָאו – שְׁלִיחַ בֵּית דִּין כְּלֹוֶה?

The Gemara suggests: **Come** and **hear** a different *baraita* that contradicts Shmuel: **From the implication of that** which **is stated: "You shall stand outside," do I not know that: "And the man to whom you lend shall bring forth outside"** (Deuteronomy 24:11)? **Rather, why** must **the verse state** the inclusive phrase **"And the man** to whom you lend shall bring forth outside"? This serves **to include the agent of the court.** The Gemara comments: **What, is it not** that **the agent of the court** has the same status **as the debtor** himself, indicating that just as the debtor may enter his own house at any time, the court agent may act likewise?

Perek **IX**
Daf **113** Amud **b**

לָא, שְׁלִיחַ בֵּית דִּין כְּמַלְוֶה.

The Gemara responds: **No, the agent** of **the court** is considered **like** the **creditor,** who must wait outside for the debtor to deliver his collateral.

תָּא שְׁמַע: ״אִם חָבֹל תַּחְבֹּל שַׂלְמַת רֵעֶךָ״ – בִּשְׁלִיחַ בֵּית דִּין הַכָּתוּב מְדַבֵּר. אַתָּה אוֹמֵר בִּשְׁלִיחַ בֵּית דִּין הַכָּתוּב מְדַבֵּר, אוֹ אֵינוֹ אֶלָּא בְּבַעַל חוֹב? כְּשֶׁהוּא אוֹמֵר: ״לֹא תָבֹא אֶל בֵּיתוֹ לַעֲבֹט עֲבֹטוֹ״ – הֲרֵי בַּעַל חוֹב אָמוּר. הָא מָה אֲנִי מְקַיֵּים ״אִם חָבֹל תַּחְבֹּל שַׂלְמַת רֵעֶךָ״? בִּשְׁלִיחַ בֵּית דִּין הַכָּתוּב מְדַבֵּר!

The Gemara attempts a further proof. **Come** and **hear** that which the Sages taught: The verse states: **"If you take as collateral your neighbor's garment,** you shall restore it to him until the sun goes down" (Exodus 22:25). **The verse is speaking of an agent of the court.** Do you say that **the verse is speaking of an agent of the court, or** perhaps **it is** referring **only to a creditor? When it says: "You shall not go into his house to take his collateral"** (Deuteronomy 24:10), the case of **a creditor is** thereby **stated. How** then **do I realize** the meaning of the verse: **"If you take as collateral your neighbor's garment"? The verse is speaking of an agent of the court.** This indicates that an agent of the court has permission to take collateral.

תַּנָּאֵי הִיא; דְּתַנְיָא: שְׁלִיחַ בֵּית דִּין שֶׁבָּא לְמַשְׁכְּנוֹ – לֹא יִכָּנֵס לְבֵיתוֹ לְמַשְׁכְּנוֹ, אֶלָּא עוֹמֵד מִבַּחוּץ וְהַלָּה מוֹצִיא לוֹ מַשְׁכּוֹן, שֶׁנֶּאֱמַר: ״בַּחוּץ תַּעֲמֹד וְהָאִישׁ״.

The Gemara responds: This issue **is a** dispute between ***tanna'im***, **as it is taught** in a *baraita*: **An agent of the court who comes to take collateral** from a debtor **may not enter**[N] **his house to take the collateral from him. Rather,** the agent **stands outside and the other,** i.e., the debtor, **brings out** the **collateral to him, as it is stated: "You shall stand outside, and the man** to whom you lend shall bring forth the collateral" (Deuteronomy 24:11). According to this *tanna*, the agent of the court has the same status as the creditor.

וְתַנְיָא אִידַּךְ: בַּעַל חוֹב שֶׁבָּא לְמַשְׁכְּנוֹ – לֹא יִכָּנֵס לְבֵיתוֹ לְמַשְׁכְּנוֹ, אֶלָּא עוֹמֵד בַּחוּץ, וְהַלָּה נִכְנָס וּמוֹצִיא לוֹ מַשְׁכּוֹנוֹ, שֶׁנֶּאֱמַר: ״בַּחוּץ תַּעֲמֹד״. וּשְׁלִיחַ בֵּית דִּין שֶׁבָּא לְמַשְׁכְּנוֹ – הֲרֵי זֶה נִכְנָס לְבֵיתוֹ וּמְמַשְׁכְּנוֹ.

And it is taught in **another** *baraita*: **A creditor who comes to take collateral from** the debtor **may not enter his house to take his collateral. Rather,** he **stands outside, and the other,** i.e., the debtor, **enters and brings out the collateral to him, as it is stated: "You shall stand outside,** and the man to whom you lend shall bring forth the collateral" (Deuteronomy 24:11). **But** as for **an agent of the court who comes to take collateral from** the debtor, **this** agent **may enter his house and take his collateral.**

וְלֹא יְמַשְׁכְּנֶנּוּ דְּבָרִים שֶׁעוֹשִׂין בָּהֶן אוֹכֶל נֶפֶשׁ. וְנוֹתֵן מִטָּה, וּמִטָּה וּמַצָּע – לְעָשִׁיר. מִטָּה, וּמִטָּה וּמַפָּץ – לְעָנִי. לוֹ, אֲבָל לֹא לְאִשְׁתּוֹ, וְלֹא לְבָנָיו וְלִבְנוֹתָיו.

The *baraita* continues: The agent of the court may **not take** as **collateral from** the debtor **items that** people **use in the preparation of food,**[H] as the debtor needs such items, and the Torah explicitly forbade their removal. **And** the agent **gives,** i.e., leaves behind, **a bed, and** a second **bed, and blankets, for a wealthy person;** and **a bed, and** a second **bed, and a mat, for a poor person.** These items are left **for** the debtor himself, **but not for his wife, and not for his sons or for his daughters,**[H] as the Torah did not obligate the creditor to care for the debtor's family.

כְּדֶרֶךְ שֶׁמְּסַדְּרִין לְבַעַל חוֹב כָּךְ מְסַדְּרִין בָּעֲרָכִין. כְּלַפֵּי לְיָיא? עִיקַּר סִידּוּר בָּעֲרָכִין כְּתִיב! אֶלָּא אֵימָא: כְּדֶרֶךְ שֶׁמְּסַדְּרִין בָּעֲרָכִין – כָּךְ מְסַדְּרִין בְּבַעַל חוֹב.

The *tanna* adds: **In the manner that arrangements are made for a debtor** to be left with certain necessary utensils, **so arrangements are made for** one obligated to give money to the Temple treasury resulting from a vow in the category of **valuations.**[B] If one vowed to give a certain valuation to the Sanctuary as specified in the Torah (see Leviticus 27) but does not have sufficient money to pay that sum immediately, a similar arrangement is made for him. The Gemara is puzzled by this last clause: **Isn't it the opposite?** The **primary** discussion of **arrangements is stated** in the Torah **with regard to valuations,** from which the *halakha* of other debts is derived. **Rather, say** that **in the manner that arrangements are made for valuations**[H] as explained by the Torah, **so arrangements are made for a debtor.**[N]

אָמַר מָר: נוֹתֵן מִטָּה וּמִטָּה וּמַצָּע לְעָשִׁיר, מִטָּה וּמִטָּה וּמַפָּץ לְעָנִי. לְמַאן? אִילֵימָא לְאִשְׁתּוֹ וּלְבָנָיו וְלִבְנוֹתָיו – הָא אָמְרַתְּ: לוֹ, אֲבָל לֹא לְאִשְׁתּוֹ וּלְבָנָיו וְלִבְנוֹתָיו! אֶלָּא, אִידֵי וְאִידֵי לְדִידֵיהּ.

§ **The Master said** above: He **gives a bed, and** a second **bed, and blankets, for a wealthy person;** and **a bed, and** a second **bed, and a mat, for a poor person.** The Gemara asks: **For whom** is this extra bed? **If we say** it is **for his wife, for his sons, or for his daughters, didn't you** expressly **say** that these items are left **for him, but not for his wife, for his sons, or for his daughters? Rather,** both **this** bed **and that** bed **are for him.**

תַּרְתֵּי לָמָּה לִי? חֲדָא דְּאָכֵיל עֲלַהּ, וַחֲדָא דָּגֵן עֲלַהּ. כִּדְשְׁמוּאֵל, דְּאָמַר שְׁמוּאֵל: כָּל מִילֵּי יָדַעְנָא אַסְוָתַיְיהוּ, לְבַר מֵהָנֵי תְּלָת: מַאן דְּאָכֵיל אֲהִינָא מְרִירָא אַלִּיבָּא רֵיקָנָא; מַאן דְּאָסַר מִיתְנָא דְּכִיתָּנָא רְטִיבָא אַחַרְצֵיהּ; וּמַאן דְּאָכֵיל נַהֲמָא וְלָא מַסְגֵּי אַרְבְּעָה גַּרְמִידֵי.

The Gemara asks: **Why does** the debtor **need two** beds when one should suffice for all his needs? The Gemara answers: **One** is for him to **eat on it and one** is for him to **sleep on it,** and this is **in accordance** with the opinion **of Shmuel. As Shmuel,** who was a doctor by profession, **said:** With regard to **all items** that cause illness, **I know their cure, apart from these three: One who eats a bitter date** [*ahina*][L] **on an empty stomach, one who girds a wet linen belt around his loins, and one who eats bread and does not walk four cubits** afterward. It is for this reason that one requires two beds, so that he should not eat and sleep on the same bed without having to walk a little distance between them after his meal.

NOTES

An agent of the court…may not enter – שְׁלִיחַ בֵּית דִּין לֹא יִכָּנֵס: The early commentaries ask: If even a court agent is prohibited from entering the debtor's house, how is it possible to fulfill the mitzvot of "If you take as collateral" and of returning collateral? After all, it is prohibited to take his items in the first place. One explanation is that this *tanna* maintains that the mitzva of returning collateral refers to an item confiscated from outside of the house. Alternatively, it refers to items taken at the time of the loan (Ran). This issue is related to the dispute between Abaye and Rava in tractate *Temura* (4b) with regard to whether, in the case of one who violates a prohibition, his action is nevertheless legally effective, where the Rambam and the *Shulḥan Arukh* rule that the *halakha* of returning the collateral applies even if the collateral was illegally appropriated.

Arrangement and the collection of collateral – סִדּוּר וּגְבִיַּת מַשְׁכּוֹן: The early commentaries disagree as to when making arrangements applies in the case of a debtor. According to *Tosafot* and the Rosh, when collateral is seized as a guarantee of the debtor's loan after the loan was granted but not as payment of the debt, no arrangement is made at all, and the creditor may seize whatever he wishes. Nevertheless, the creditor is obligated to return the items required by the debtor whenever the debtor needs them. By contrast, the Rambam maintains that even if the creditor takes collateral that is not payment for the loan, he must leave the debtor with a few items, such as a cushion, pillows, and his work tools, as stated in the *baraita*. The Ramban and the Rashba contend that even if the collateral was not taken at the time of the loan, the same arrangement is made on behalf of the debtor as for one repaying his debts. According to the Gra, they essentially agree with the opinion of the Rambam.

HALAKHA

The agent of the court may not take as collateral from the debtor items that people use in the preparation of food – לֹא יְמַשְׁכְּנֶנּוּ דְּבָרִים שֶׁעוֹשִׂין בָּהֶן אוֹכֶל נֶפֶשׁ: If a court agent comes to take collateral from a debtor, he may not seize items the debtor cannot afford to give him, such as the clothes he is wearing or the utensils he uses in the preparation of food. He must also leave him beds and blankets, or a mat if he is a poor person. He may confiscate all other items. In addition, he must give back, by day, the vessels the debtor needs during the day as well as his work tools; and he must return, at night, the items the debtor uses during the night (Rambam *Sefer Mishpatim*, *Hilkhot Malve VeLoveh* 3:2, 6; *Shulḥan Arukh*, *Ḥoshen Mishpat* 97:6, 17, 23).

But not for his wife, and not for his sons or for his daughters – אֲבָל לֹא לְאִשְׁתּוֹ וְלֹא לְבָנָיו וְלִבְנוֹתָיו: When a debtor's debt is collected from his movable property, he must be left with enough clothes for twelve months and other basic needs. All this applies only to items he needs himself, but he need not be left with items for his wife and children, even if they rely on him for their sustenance (Rambam *Sefer Mishpatim*, *Hilkhot Malve VeLoveh* 1:7; *Shulḥan Arukh*, *Ḥoshen Mishpat* 97:23).

That arrangements are made for valuations – שֶׁמְּסַדְּרִין בָּעֲרָכִין: One who consecrated a valuation to the Temple but cannot afford to pay the stipulated sum must allow all of his possessions to be sold in order to pay off his debt. He is left with certain items, such as his phylacteries, sandals, a bed, blankets, a thirty-day supply of food, and clothing for a twelve-month period. This allowance applies to his own needs, but he is not left with any items for the needs of his household (Rambam *Sefer Hafla'a*, *Hilkhot Arakhin* 3:14).

BACKGROUND

Valuations – עֲרָכִין: The *halakhot* of valuations are listed in Leviticus (27:1–8), and are clarified in tractate *Arakhin*. A valuation [*erekh*] is a special type of consecration by which a fixed sum is given for each individual in accordance with his age and sex, regardless of importance or actual monetary worth as a slave.

LANGUAGE

Bitter date [*ahina*] – אֲהִינָא: This Aramaic word means an unripe date and, by extension, all kinds of unripe fruits. Sometimes these dates would be left to ripen after they were plucked, while at other times they would be cooked. Like all unripe fruits, such dates contain tannin, which can cause abdominal pain.

תָּנֵי תַּנָּא קַמֵּיהּ דְּרַב נַחְמָן: כְּדֶרֶךְ שֶׁמְּסַדְּרִין בַּעֲרָכִין – כָּךְ מְסַדְּרִין בְּבַעַל חוֹב. אֲמַר לֵיהּ: הַשְׁתָּא זַבּוּנֵי מְזַבְּנִינַן לֵיהּ, סַדּוּרֵי מְסַדְּרִינַן לֵיהּ? וּמִי מְזַבְּנִינַן לֵיהּ? וְהָתְנַן: מַחֲזִיר אֶת הַכַּר בַּלַּיְלָה וְאֶת הַמַּחֲרֵישָׁה בַּיּוֹם!

§ A *tanna* taught a *baraita* **before Rav Naḥman: In the manner in which arrangements are made for valuations, so arrangements are made for a debtor.** Rav Naḥman **said to him: Now** that it states in the mishna that **we sell** his collateral, **do we arrange for him** to keep part of it? The Gemara asks: **And do we sell it? But didn't we learn** in the mishna that **he returns a pillow at night and a plow by day,** which demonstrates that such items are not sold?

תָּנָא כְּרַבָּן שִׁמְעוֹן בֶּן גַּמְלִיאֵל תְּנָא קַמֵּיהּ, וְהָכִי קָאָמַר לֵיהּ: הַשְׁתָּא לְרַבָּן שִׁמְעוֹן בֶּן גַּמְלִיאֵל זַבּוּנֵי מְזַבְּנִינַן לֵיהּ, סַדּוּרֵי מְסַדְּרִינַן לֵיהּ? דִּתְנַן, רַבָּן שִׁמְעוֹן בֶּן גַּמְלִיאֵל אוֹמֵר: אַף לְעַצְמוֹ אֵינוֹ מַחֲזִיר אֶלָּא עַד שְׁלֹשִׁים יוֹם, מִכָּאן וְאֵילָךְ מוֹכְרָן בְּבֵית דִּין.

The Gemara answers: **The *tanna*** taught the *baraita* **before him in accordance with** the opinion of **Rabban Shimon ben Gamliel, and this is what** Rav Naḥman **was saying to him: Now,** since **according to Rabban Shimon ben Gamliel we sell** the collateral, **do we make arrangements for him** to keep it? **As we learned** in the mishna: **Rabban Shimon ben Gamliel says: Even to the debtor himself** he needs to **return** the collateral each day **only until thirty days** have passed, **and from that point onward,** the creditor can **sell them in court,** with the proceeds going toward payment of the debt.

וּמִמַּאי דְּכִי קָאָמַר רַבָּן שִׁמְעוֹן בֶּן גַּמְלִיאֵל זַבּוּנֵי לְגַמְרֵי קָאָמַר? דִּלְמָא הָכִי קָאָמַר: עַד שְׁלֹשִׁים יוֹם – הָדַר לֵיהּ בְּעֵינֵיהּ; מִכָּאן וְאֵילָךְ – מִיהֲדַר לֵיהּ לְמַאי דַּחֲזֵי לֵיהּ, וּמְזַבְּנִינַן מַאי דְּלָא חֲזֵי לֵיהּ.

The Gemara asks: **And from where** is it known **that when Rabban Shimon ben Gamliel said** that he **sells** the collateral, he **was saying** that there may be **a complete** sale? **Perhaps this** is what he **is saying: Until thirty days,** the creditor **returns** it **to** the debtor **as is; from that** point **onward,** the creditor **returns to him that which is fit for him, and we sell what is not fit for him.**

אִי סָלְקָא דַּעְתָּךְ אִית לֵיהּ לְרַבָּן שִׁמְעוֹן בֶּן גַּמְלִיאֵל הַאי סְבָרָא – לֵיכָּא מִידֵּי דְּלָא חֲזֵי לֵיהּ. דַּאֲמַר אַבַּיֵי: רַבָּן שִׁמְעוֹן בֶּן גַּמְלִיאֵל וְרַבִּי שִׁמְעוֹן וְרַבִּי יִשְׁמָעֵאל וְרַבִּי עֲקִיבָא, כּוּלְּהוּ סְבִירָא לְהוּ: כָּל יִשְׂרָאֵל בְּנֵי מְלָכִים הֵן.

The Gemara rejects this suggestion: **If it enters your mind** that **Rabban Shimon ben Gamliel maintains this reasoning, there is nothing that is unfit for him. As Abaye said: Rabban Shimon ben Gamliel and Rabbi Shimon and Rabbi Yishmael and Rabbi Akiva all hold** that **all Israel are the children of kings.**[N] In other words, a Jew is never deemed unfit to use a certain item, even if it is a luxury item.

רַבָּן שִׁמְעוֹן בֶּן גַּמְלִיאֵל דִּתְנַן: לֹא אֶת הַלּוּף וְלֹא אֶת הַחַרְדָּל. רַבָּן שִׁמְעוֹן בֶּן גַּמְלִיאֵל מַתִּיר בַּלּוּף, מִפְּנֵי שֶׁהוּא מַאֲכָל לָעוֹרְבִין.

The Gemara cites the cases in which the *tanna'im* apply the above principle. **Rabban Shimon ben Gamliel** applies this principle, **as we learned** in a mishna (*Shabbat* 126b): One may **not** move either raw **arum**[B] **or** raw **mustard** on Shabbat,[H] as these are unfit for consumption when they are raw, and are therefore set-aside [*muktze*]. **In the case of arum, Rabban Shimon ben Gamliel permits** moving it **because it is** considered **food for ravens,** which wealthy Jews would breed for purposes of ornamentation and amusement. As Rabban Shimon ben Gamliel permits all people to move arum, not only the rich, it is evident that he maintains that all Jews are considered wealthy in this regard.

רַבִּי שִׁמְעוֹן – דִּתְנַן: בְּנֵי מְלָכִים סָכִין שֶׁמֶן וֶורֶד עַל גַּבֵּי מַכּוֹתֵיהֶן בְּשַׁבָּת, שֶׁכֵּן דַּרְכָּן לָסוּךְ בַּחוֹל. רַבִּי שִׁמְעוֹן אוֹמֵר: כָּל יִשְׂרָאֵל בְּנֵי מְלָכִים הֵן.

Rabbi Shimon applies this principle **as we learned** in a mishna (*Shabbat* 111a): **Princes may smear rose oil on their wounds on Shabbat,** even though most people use this oil for medicinal purposes, and healing oneself using oil is prohibited on Shabbat. The reason is **that it is the usual manner** of princes **to smear** rose oil on themselves for pleasure **during the week. Rabbi Shimon says: All of the Jewish people are princes,** and it is permitted for them to smear rose oil on themselves on Shabbat.[H]

NOTES

All Israel are the children of kings – כָּל יִשְׂרָאֵל בְּנֵי מְלָכִים הֵן: As the descendants of Abraham, Isaac, and Jacob, who were like kings in all respects, all Jews are considered of royal descent (*Torat Ḥayyim*). The point of this statement is that one who is accustomed to luxuries suffers when they are no longer available. Although in fact not all Jews are accustomed to luxuries, their quasi-royal status renders the items fit for them nonetheless. The above notwithstanding, it is agreed that when arrangements are made, a wealthy individual is left with higher-quality items than a poor person.

BACKGROUND

Arum [*luf*] – לוּף: *Luf* is generally identified as *Arum palestinium*, which is a member of the Araceae family. This plant has a bulb that is located in the ground, from which large leaves sprout. The arum inflorescence has a unique structure, and is covered with a special type of leaf, or spathe. All parts of the plant contain calcium oxalate, or $Ca(COO)_2$, which is poisonous and causes extreme itching to any skin with which it comes into contact. Consequently, arum is not eaten by humans in its raw state, but it is considered potential nourishment for a few animals. In order to be used as human food, the bulb and leaves must be cooked or roasted. The plant grows wild in all areas of Israel.

Arum

HALAKHA

Moving arum and mustard on Shabbat – טִלְטוּל לוּף וְחַרְדָּל בְּשַׁבָּת: Any food items that are suitable for consumption by common animals or fowl may be moved on Shabbat. If a food item is suitable for consumption by rare animals but not by common animals, one may move the food only if he owns rare animals. If he does not own rare animals, he is prohibited from moving these food items, even if wealthy people or other individuals often own them. Examples of food that is suitable for consumption by rare animals but not by common animals are arum and mustard that has not been prepared for human consumption. This ruling is not in accordance with the opinion of Rabban Shimon ben Gamliel (Rambam *Sefer Zemanim, Hilkhot Shabbat* 26:16; *Shulḥan Arukh, Oraḥ Ḥayyim* 308:29).

One may not smear with rose oil – אֵין סָכִין בְּשֶׁמֶן וֶורֶד: One who feels pain in his loins may not smear himself on Shabbat with oil and vinegar together, as this is a medicinal balm, but he may smear himself with oil alone, as this is practiced even by people who are not sick. The Rema adds that if the custom in a particular location is that only those who are ill smear themselves with oil on Shabbat, it is prohibited for one to do so. One may not smear oneself with rose oil, as this is clearly performed for curative purposes, unless it is commonly done in that location. This ruling is not in accordance with the opinion of Rabbi Shimon (Rambam *Sefer Zemanim, Hilkhot Shabbat* 21:23; *Shulḥan Arukh, Oraḥ Ḥayyim* 327:1).

רַבִּי יִשְׁמָעֵאל וְרַבִּי עֲקִיבָא, דְּתַנְיָא: הֲרֵי שֶׁהָיוּ נוֹשִׁין בּוֹ אֶלֶף זוּז וְלָבוּשׁ אִיצְטְלָא בַּת מֵאָה מָנֶה – מַפְשִׁיטִין אוֹתָהּ מִמֶּנּוּ, וּמַלְבִּישִׁים אוֹתוֹ אִיצְטְלָא הָרְאוּיָה לוֹ. וְתָנָא מִשּׁוּם רַבִּי יִשְׁמָעֵאל, וְתָנָא מִשּׁוּם רַבִּי עֲקִיבָא: כָּל יִשְׂרָאֵל רְאוּיִן לְאוֹתָהּ אִיצְטְלָא.

Rabbi Yishmael and Rabbi Akiva also hold this opinion, **as it is taught** in a *baraita*: If creditors **were claiming one thousand dinars** from someone, **and** he was **wearing a cloak** [*itztela*][HL] **worth ten thousand dinars,**[B] the court **strips it from him** and sells it for his debt, **and dresses him** in **a cloak appropriate for him,** as one who is in debt does not have the right to withhold payment while possessing such an expensive garment. **And** it was **taught in the name of Rabbi Yishmael, and** it was similarly **taught in the name of Rabbi Akiva: All of the Jewish people are fit for that cloak.** One's clothing is not sold to pay a debt, and since all Jews are worthy of wearing the finest garments, this *halakha* applies to an expensive cloak as well.

וּלְמַאי דְּסָלֵיק אַדַּעְתִּין מֵעִיקָּרָא, דְּיָהֵיב לֵיהּ מַאי דַּחֲזֵי לֵיהּ, וּמְזַבְּנִינַן מַאי דְּלָא חֲזֵי לֵיהּ – בִּשְׁלָמָא כַּר וָכֶסֶת חֲזֵי לֵיהּ דְּבֵינֵי בֵּינֵי. אֶלָּא מַחֲרֵישָׁה לְמַאי חַזְיָא? אֲמַר רָבָא בַּר רַבָּה: מַחֲרֵישָׁה דְּכַסְפָּא.

The Gemara returns to the issue at hand: **And with regard to what entered our minds initially, that** according to the opinion of Rabban Shimon ben Gamliel, the creditor **returns to him that which is fit for him and we sell what is not fit for him,** there is a difficulty, as the examples given in the mishna are bedding and a plow. **Granted,** this is understandable with regard to a pillow or cushion, as it can mean that the court sells these items only if the difference in cost **between** the ones he has and less expensive ones that are also **fit for him** suffices to repay the debt. **But for what is a plow fit?** In other words, how can there be a difference in price in this case? **Rava bar Rabba said:** This is referring to **a silver plow,**[NB] which is an ornament and not used for work.

מַתְקִיף לָהּ רַב חַגָּא: וְלֵימָא לֵיהּ לָאו עֲלַי קָרָמֵית! אֲמַר לֵיהּ אַבָּיֵי:

Rav Ḥagga objects to this entire opinion concerning the arrangement made for a debtor: **Let** the creditor **say to** the debtor: **Your** needs **are not cast upon me.**[N] In other words, why should I, who lent you money, make allowances for your livelihood? **Abaye said to him:**

NOTES

A silver plow – מַחֲרֵישָׁה דְּכַסְפָּא: It is clear that this plow is not a work utensil, as it cannot be used for plowing. Rather, this is a type of ornament. Rabbeinu Ḥananel (cited in *Tosafot* 113a) explains that it is a tool used for scraping the body after smearing it with oil, while according to the *Arukh* it is a kind of comb. Rabbeinu Ḥananel's approach is consistent with his opinion that a special prohibition exists to take utensils used in the preparation of food or that serve the body in other ways, and that this prohibition does not apply to work tools.

Your needs are not cast upon me – לָאו עֲלַי קָרָמֵית: According to Rashi, this point is being raised with regard to the obligation to return any collateral. According to *Tosafot*, this inquiry concerns only the opinion that all Israel are considered to be the children of kings. According to the *Torat Ḥayyim*, the question refers to the *halakha* of making arrangements: Rav Ḥagga wanted to know why the obligation to make arrangements for the debtor is the responsibility of the creditor.

HALAKHA

A debtor who has an expensive cloak – לְוֶה שֶׁיֵּשׁ לוֹ אִיצְטְלָה יְקָרָה: When an arrangement is made for a debtor, he is not left with the clothes he owns. Rather, his expensive garments are sold and he is given simpler ones appropriate for him (Rambam *Sefer Mishpatim*, *Hilkhot Malve VeLoveh* 1:7; *Shulḥan Arukh*, *Ḥoshen Mishpat* 97:23).

LANGUAGE

Cloak [*itztela*] – אִיצְטְלָא: From the Greek στολή, *stolē*, which means a garment or cape.

BACKGROUND

Ten thousand dinars – מֵאָה מָנֶה: A *maneh* is a coin worth one hundred dinars. The dinar coin in turn was worth ten *issar*, and was widely used in the Roman Empire.

Silver plow – מַחֲרֵישָׁה דְּכַסְפָּא: According to Rabbeinu Ḥananel, the *Arukh*, and *Tosafot*, the silver plow mentioned in the Gemara is a scraping tool made from silver, also known as a strigil, an implement mentioned elsewhere in the Talmud.

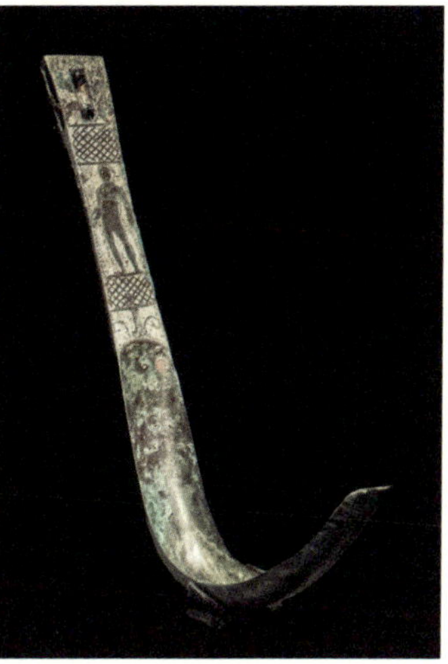

Silver Roman strigil used to scrape oil off bathers

Perek **IX**
Daf **114** Amud **a**

אִיבְרָא, עֲלֵיהּ קָרָמֵי, מִשּׁוּם שֶׁנֶּאֱמַר: ״וּלְךָ תִּהְיֶה צְדָקָה״.

Indeed, the debtor's needs are **cast upon him, because it is stated** in connection with this same issue of returning the collateral: **"And it shall be righteousness to you"** (Deuteronomy 24:13), which indicates that there is an obligation for the creditor to act toward the debtor with righteousness.

אִיבַּעְיָא לְהוּ: מַהוּ שֶׁיְּסַדְּרוּ בְּבַעַל חוֹב? מִי גָּמַר ״מִיכָה״, ״מִיכָה״ מֵעֲרָכִין אוֹ לָא?

§ **A dilemma was raised before** the Sages: **What is the** *halakha* with regard to **making arrangements for the debtor**[N] so that he will retain some of his possessions so that he may continue living as before, albeit at a slightly lower standard? The issue on which this is based is **whether or not** a verbal analogy is **derived from** the usage of the term **"poor"** written in the context of a debtor (Leviticus 25:35) and the term **"poor"** written in the context of **valuations** (Leviticus 27:8), as the Gemara will discuss further at the end of the *amud*.

NOTES

What is the *halakha* with regard to making arrangements for the debtor – מַהוּ שֶׁיְּסַדְּרוּ בְּבַעַל חוֹב: According to the Ramban and the Ran, this discussion reflects the same disagreement between the Rabbis and Rabban Shimon ben Gamliel that was discussed previously in the mishna and the Gemara, and the focus here is what is followed as practical *halakha*. By contrast, the opinion of *Tosafot* is that this arrangement is a separate issue that is unconnected to the restoration of collateral discussed in the mishna. Rather, this arrangement relates to how the actual collection of the debt is performed.

תָּא שְׁמַע, דִּשְׁלַח רָבִין בְּאִגַּרְתֵּיהּ: דָּבָר זֶה שְׁאַלְתִּי לְכׇל רַבּוֹתַי וְלֹא אָמְרוּ לִי דָּבָר. בְּרַם כָּךְ הָיְתָה שְׁאֵלָה: הָאוֹמֵר הֲרֵי עָלַי מָנֶה לְבֶדֶק הַבַּיִת מַהוּ שֶׁיְּסַדְּרוּ?

The Gemara suggests: **Come** and **hear** a proof, **as Ravin sent** a message **in his letter** from Eretz Yisrael: **I asked all my teachers** concerning **this matter, but they did not tell me anything. But there was this question** concerning a similar matter that I heard them discuss: With regard to **one who says:** It is incumbent **upon me** to bring **one hundred dinars for the Temple maintenance, what** is the *halakha* as to whether **they make arrangements** for him? Although an arrangement is explicitly taught only with regard to the specific type of donation of valuations, is it applicable here as well?

רַבִּי יַעֲקֹב מִשְּׁמֵיהּ דְּבַר פַּדָּא, וְרַבִּי יִרְמְיָה מִשְּׁמֵיהּ דְּאִילְפָא אָמְרִי: קַל וָחוֹמֶר מִבַּעַל חוֹב. וּמַה בַּעַל חוֹב שֶׁמַּחֲזִירִין – אֵין מְסַדְּרִין, הֶקְדֵּשׁ שֶׁאֵין מַחֲזִירִין – אֵינוֹ דִּין שֶׁאֵין מְסַדְּרִין? וְרַבִּי יוֹחָנָן אָמַר: ״נֶדֶר בְּעֶרְכְּךָ״ כְּתִיב, מַה עֲרָכִין מְסַדְּרִין – אַף הֶקְדֵּשׁ מְסַדְּרִין.

Rabbi Ya'akov in the name of bar Padda, and Rabbi Yirmeya in the name of Ilfa, each say: It is an ***a fortiori*** inference **from** the *halakhot* of **a debtor: And if** for **a debtor, to** whom one **returns** his collateral, they do **not make arrangements** for the payment of his debt, then in the case of **consecration, where** they do **not return** his collateral, **is it not logical that** they should **not make arrangements** for the payment of his debt? **And Rabbi Yoḥanan says:** It is **written:** "When a man shall clearly utter **a vow according to your valuation**" (Leviticus 27:2). In this verse, all vows of consecrated property are juxtaposed to valuations, teaching that **just as** they **make arrangements** for the payment of a debt with regard to **valuations, so too** they **make arrangements** for the payment of a debt with regard to any vow of **consecration.**[H]

וְאִידָּךְ? הַהוּא לְנִידּוֹן בִּכְבוֹדוֹ הוּא דַּאֲתָא. מַה עֲרָכִין נִידּוֹן בִּכְבוֹדוֹ – אַף הֶקְדֵּשׁ נִידּוֹן בִּכְבוֹדוֹ.

The Gemara asks: **And** what do **the other** Sages, i.e., Rabbi Ya'akov and Rabbi Yirmeya, derive from this juxtaposition between vows and valuations? The Gemara replies: They maintain **that** this juxtaposition **comes to** teach the *halakha* that a vow of consecration is **judged by its significance.**[N] If one stated a vow of valuation concerning a vital part of his body, e.g., that he will donate the value of his heart, he is obligated to pay not only the value of that organ, but the valuation of his entire self. Consequently, the phrase "a vow according to your valuation" indicates that **just as valuations are judged by their significance,**[H] **so too consecrated** property is **judged by its significance.**

וִיסַדְּרוּ בְּבַעַל חוֹב קַל וָחוֹמֶר מֵעֲרָכִין: וּמַה עֲרָכִין שֶׁאֵין מַחֲזִירִין – מְסַדְּרִין; בַּעַל חוֹב שֶׁמַּחֲזִירִין – אֵינוֹ דִּין שֶׁמְּסַדְּרִין? אָמַר קְרָא: ״וְאִם מָךְ הוּא מֵעֶרְכֶּךָ״ – ״הוּא״ וְלֹא בַּעַל חוֹב.

The Gemara asks: **But they should make arrangements for a debtor** based on an ***a fortiori*** inference **from** the *halakhot* of **valuations,** as follows: **And if** in the case of **valuations** the *halakha* is **that** they do **not return**[H] his collateral and yet they do **make arrangements** for the payment of his debt, then with regard to **a debtor,** where the *halakha* is **that** one does **return** his collateral, **is it not logical that** they should **make arrangements** for the payment of his debt? The Gemara responds: **The verse states: "But if he is too poor for your valuation**…and the priest shall value him, according to the means of the one that vowed shall the priest value him" (Leviticus 27:8). The Torah emphasizes that this *halakha* is applicable only to **"he"** who makes a valuation, **but not** to **a debtor.**

וְאִידָּךְ? הַאי – עַד שֶׁיְּהֵא בְּמָכוּתוֹ מִתְּחִילָּתוֹ וְעַד סוֹפוֹ.

The Gemara asks: **And** according to **the other** opinion, which maintains that they do make arrangements for a debtor, how is the word "he" interpreted? The Gemara answers: This word teaches that the *halakha* does not apply **unless** he **remains in his** state of **poverty**[HN] **from the beginning to the end.**[N] If he was rich at the outset, or grew wealthy at some later stage, arrangements are not made for him.

HALAKHA

Making arrangements for vows of consecration – סִדּוּר בְּהֶקְדֵּשׁ: The court makes arrangements in a range of situations, including valuations as well as in other cases of consecration, such as that of one who consecrated a certain sum to the Temple. In any of these cases, the arrangement involves not taking all of the debtor's money, but leaving him enough for his livelihood (Rambam *Sefer Hafla'a, Hilkhot Arakhin VaḤaramim* 3:15).

Judged by their significance – נִדּוֹן בִּכְבוֹדוֹ: One who says he will consecrate the valuation of his hand or foot is not obligated to give anything. If he consecrated the valuation of his heart, liver, or any other limb that he cannot live without, he must give the valuation of his entire body (Rambam *Sefer Hafla'a, Hilkhot Arakhin VaḤaramim* 2:1).

In the case of valuations they do not return – עֲרָכִין שֶׁאֵין מַחֲזִירִין: The court forcibly takes collateral from those who owe money for consecrating by valuation or other methods. Furthermore, the court does not have to return this collateral by day or night in the manner of a creditor (Rambam *Sefer Hafla'a, Hilkhot Arakhin VaḤaramim* 3:14).

Unless he remains in his state of poverty – עַד שֶׁיְּהֵא בְּמָכוּתוֹ: If a wealthy person made a valuation and subsequently became poor, or if he made a valuation as a poor person and then became wealthy, he is obligated to give the amount of a valuation of a wealthy individual (Rambam *Sefer Hafla'a, Hilkhot Arakhin VaḤaramim* 3:5).

NOTES

Judged by its significance [*bikhvodo*] **– נִדּוֹן בִּכְבוֹדוֹ:** An alternative version cited by Rabbeinu Ḥananel reads: By his liver [*bikhveido*]. According to this version, the Gemara is saying that if someone consecrates the valuation of his liver, he must give the valuation of his entire body, as the liver is one of those organs without which one cannot survive.

Remains in his state of poverty – שֶׁיְּהֵא בְּמָכוּתוֹ: Despite the fact that there are fixed amounts for valuations, the Torah states: "But if he be too poor for your valuation, then he shall be set before the priest, and the priest shall value him; according to the means of him that vowed shall the priest value him" (Leviticus 27:8). Consequently, if the one who takes a vow in this manner is poor, he is not obligated to pay the full sum. This is a unique *halakha* that applies to valuations alone but not to other types of consecrations.

From the beginning to the end – מִתְּחִילָּתוֹ וְעַד סוֹפוֹ: This issue is a dispute among *tanna'im*. Rabbeinu Tam and others explain that according to this opinion, one who was poor when he vowed, became wealthy, and once again descended into poverty is excluded from this verse. Since he did not remain in a state of poverty the entire time, he is not entitled to the dispensation given to a poor person.

וְיַחֲזִירוּ בְּהֶקְדֵּשׁ קַל וָחוֹמֶר מִבַּעַל חוֹב: וּמַה בַּעַל חוֹב שֶׁאֵין מְסַדְּרִין – מַחֲזִירִין, הֶקְדֵּשׁ שֶׁמְּסַדְּרִין אֵינוֹ דִּין שֶׁמַּחֲזִירִין? אָמַר קְרָא: ״וְשָׁכַב בְּשַׂלְמָתוֹ וּבֵרְכֶךָּ״ – יָצָא הֶקְדֵּשׁ שֶׁאֵין צָרִיךְ בְּרָכָה.

The Gemara asks an additional question: **And** once it is established that arrangements are not made for a debtor, **they should return** the collateral **in** the case of **consecration** based on **an *a fortiori*** inference **from** the *halakhot* of **a debtor: And if** in the case of a **debtor, where** they do **not make arrangements** for him, the creditor nevertheless **returns**[N] his collateral, with regard to **consecration, where** they do **make arrangements** for the payment of his debt, **is it not logical that** they should **return** his collateral to him? The Gemara answers: **The verse states** with regard to a regular loan: "You shall restore to him the collateral… **and he will sleep in his garment and he will bless you**" (Deuteronomy 24:13), **excluding consecration, where** there is **no need** for **a blessing,** and therefore it is not included in the *halakha* of returning the collateral.

וְלָא? וְהָכְתִיב: ״וְאָכַלְתָּ וְשָׂבָעְתָּ וּבֵרַכְתָּ״ וגו׳! אֶלָּא אָמַר קְרָא: ״וּלְךָ תִּהְיֶה צְדָקָה״ – מִי שֶׁצָּרִיךְ צְדָקָה, יָצָא הֶקְדֵּשׁ שֶׁאֵין צָרִיךְ צְדָקָה.

The Gemara is puzzled by this claim: **And** is consecrated property **not** in need of a blessing? **But isn't it written: "And you shall eat and be satisfied, and bless** the Lord your God" (Deuteronomy 8:10), indicating that consecrated property also requires a blessing? **Rather,** the reason is that **the verse states** with regard to the restoration of collateral: **"And it shall be righteousness [*tzedaka*] for you"** (Deuteronomy 24:13), which is referring to caring for **one who requires charity [*tzedaka*], excluding consecrated** property, **which** does **not require charity.**

אַשְׁכְּחֵיהּ רַבָּה בַּר אֲבוּהּ לְאֵלִיָּהוּ דְּקָאֵי בְּבֵית הַקְּבָרוֹת שֶׁל נׇכְרִים. אֲמַר לֵיהּ: מַהוּ שֶׁיְּסַדְּרוּ בְּבַעַל חוֹב? אֲמַר לֵיהּ: גָּמַר ״מִיכָה״, ״מִיכָה״ מֵעֲרָכִין; גַּבֵּי עֲרָכִין כְּתִיב: ״וְאִם מָךְ הוּא מֵעֶרְכֶּךָ״, גַּבֵּי בַּעַל חוֹב כְּתִיב: ״וְכִי יָמוּךְ אָחִיךָ״.

§ The Gemara relates: **Rabba bar Avuh**[P] **found Elijah**[N] **standing in a graveyard of gentiles.** Rabba bar Avuh **said to him: What is** the *halakha* with regard to **making arrangements for the debtor?**[H] Elijah **said to him:** A verbal analogy is **derived from** the usage of the term **"poor"** written in the context of a debtor and the term **"poor"** written in the context of **valuations.** With regard **to valuations, it is written: "But if he is too poor [*makh*] for your valuation"** (Leviticus 27:8), and **with regard to a creditor,** it **is written: "But if your brother be poor [*yamukh*]"** (Leviticus 25:35).

NOTES

They make arrangements and return – מְסַדְּרִין וּמַחֲזִירִין: According to *Tosafot*, the *halakha* of returning the collateral applies only to collateral taken to ensure future payment of the debt, whereas an arrangement is made at the time the debt is repaid. These are two separate *halakhot*, despite the fact that both ensure that the debtor is not left without any possessions. According to other early commentaries, the *halakha* of returning the collateral refers to one who has several vessels used for the preparation of food that must all be returned, and if an arrangement is made, only those items the debtor really needs are restored. The same applies to an expensive garment (Ramban; Ran).

He found Elijah – אַשְׁכְּחֵיהּ...לְאֵלִיָּהוּ: The Talmud often mentions that Elijah appeared to righteous men. The question is what is the reason is for Elijah's appearance and what weight does it carry in the halakhic sense. According to *Shabbat* 104a, a prophet cannot issue halakhic rulings through prophecy. He is entitled to issue a halakhic ruling in the capacity of a Sage. The early commentaries note that, for this reason, Elijah's statement carries no more weight than those of disputing *amora'im* (see Ran).

The commentaries discuss the sequence of questions Rabba bar Avuh asked Elijah. According to some commentaries, the first two questions he asked him were only preliminary inquiries, leading up to his main question, which was about Elijah's presence in a cemetery (see the *Iyyun Ya'akov*). Others explain the relationship of the questions as follows: With regard to valuations, the *halakha* is that one may value a gentile in the same manner as a Jew. Similarly, with regard to the *halakhot* of distancing oneself from nakedness in order to recite blessings, the status of a gentile is equivalent to that of a Jew. If gentiles are treated as Jews in these areas, then why was Elijah permitted to enter a gentile cemetery? Elijah replied that there is a special derivation with regard to this *halakha* (*Minḥat HaBoker*).

PERSONALITIES

Rabba bar Avuh – רַבָּה בַּר אֲבוּהּ: Rabba bar Avuh was an *amora* from the second generation of Babylonian *amora'im*. He was the preeminent disciple of Rav, and many of his statements are transmitted in the name of Rav. Rabba bar Avuh lived in the town of Meḥoza, where he spread his knowledge of Torah. His foremost disciple was Rav Naḥman, who apparently was his son-in-law as well and transmitted many statements in his name. Rabba bar Avuh descended from the family of the Exilarch, yet he himself was quite poor for most of his days, and he was reluctant to use his stature to obtain a livelihood. The Talmud relates that Elijah the prophet revealed himself to him on several occasions, and he took the opportunity to ask Elijah questions. Rabba bar Avuh had a son who was a Torah scholar, Rav Ḥama, and his descendants include the great *ge'onim* of Babylonia, Rav Sherira Gaon and Rav Hai Gaon.

HALAKHA

Making arrangements for the debtor – יְסַדְּרוּ בְּבַעַל חוֹב: When the time for payment arrives and the possessions of a debtor are seized for his debt, the court makes an arrangement for him. How is this done? They instruct him to bring all his movable property, including utensils used for preparing food (Rema, citing *Nimmukei Yosef*), and they give him sufficient food for thirty days and clothing for twelve months, a bed, and any blankets or other items necessary for sleeping that he requires. If he is a craftsman, they leave him two of each of the tools of his trade. This ruling is in accordance with the conclusion of the Gemara (113b) that the court makes an arrangement for a debtor, as well as with the opinion of Elijah here, in opposition to Ravin (*Shulḥan Arukh*, *Ḥoshen Mishpat* 97:23).

מִנַּיִן לְעָרוֹם שֶׁלֹּא יִתְרוֹם? דִּכְתִיב: "וְלֹא יִרְאֶה בְךָ עֶרְוַת דָּבָר".

Rabba bar Avuh now asks Elijah another question: **From where** is it derived with regard **to a naked person that he may not separate** ***teruma*****?**[H] He replied: **As it is written: "And He see no unseemly thing in you"** (Deuteronomy 23:15). This verse indicates that one may not recite any words of sanctity, including the blessing upon separating *teruma*, in front of one who is naked.

אֲמַר לֵיהּ: לָאו כֹּהֵן הוּא מָר? מַאי טַעְמָא קָאֵי מָר בְּבֵית הַקְּבָרוֹת? אֲמַר לֵיהּ: לָא מַתְנֵי מָר טְהָרוֹת? דְּתַנְיָא, רַבִּי שִׁמְעוֹן בֶּן יוֹחַי אוֹמֵר: קִבְרֵיהֶן שֶׁל נׇכְרִים אֵין מְטַמְּאִין, שֶׁנֶּאֱמַר: "וְאַתֵּן צֹאנִי צֹאן מַרְעִיתִי אָדָם אַתֶּם" – אַתֶּם קְרוּיִין אָדָם, וְאֵין נׇכְרִים קְרוּיִין אָדָם.

The *amora* proceeded to ask Elijah a different question and **said to him: Is not the Master a priest?**[N] **What is the reason** that **the Master** is **standing in a cemetery?** Elijah **said to him: Has the Master not studied** the mishnaic order of ***Teharot*****? As it is taught** in a *baraita*: **Rabbi Shimon ben Yoḥai says that the graves of gentiles**[H] **do not render** one **impure,**[N] **as it is stated: "And you, My sheep, the sheep of My pasture, are man"** (Ezekiel 34:31), which teaches that **you,** i.e., the Jewish people, **are called "man," but gentiles are not called "man."**[N] Since the Torah states with regard to ritual impurity imparted in a tent: "If a man dies in a tent" (Numbers 19:14), evidently impurity imparted by a tent does not apply to gentiles.

אֲמַר לֵיהּ: בְּאַרְבָּעָה לָא מָצֵינָא, בְּשִׁיתָּא מָצֵינָא? אֲמַר לֵיהּ: וְאַמַּאי? אֲמַר לֵיהּ: דְּחִיקָא לִי מִילְּתָא. דַּבְרֵיהּ וְעַיְילֵיהּ לְגַן עֵדֶן. אֲמַר לֵיהּ: פְּשׁוֹט גְּלִימָךְ, סְפֵי שְׁקוֹל מֵהָנֵי טַרְפֵי. סְפָא שְׁקַל.

Rabba bar Avuh **said to him:** How could I be familiar with that *baraita*? If I **cannot** be proficient **in** the more commonly studied **four** orders of the Mishna, **can I** be knowledgeable **in all six?**[N] Elijah **said to him: Why** are you not learned in them all? Rabba bar Avuh **said to him: The matter** of a livelihood is **pressing for me,** and I am therefore unable to study properly. Elijah **led him and brought him into the Garden of Eden**[N] and **said to him: Remove your cloak, gather up** and **take** some **of these leaves** lying around. Rabba Bar Avuh **gathered** them **up** and **took** them.

כִּי הֲוָה נָפֵיק שְׁמַע דְּקָאָמַר: מַאן קָא אָכֵיל לְעָלְמֵיהּ כְּרַבָּה בַּר אֲבוּהּ! נְפַץ שַׁדְנְהוּ. אֲפִילּוּ הָכִי, אַתְיֵיהּ לִגְלִימֵיהּ, סְחַט גְּלִימָא רֵיחָא, זַבְנֵיהּ בִּתְרֵיסַר אַלְפֵי דִּינָרֵי, פַּלְגִינְהוּ לְחַתְנָוָותֵיהּ.

When he **was exiting,** he **heard** a voice **that declared: Who** else **consumes his World**-to-Come **like Rabba bar Avuh,** who takes his merit of the next world for his use in the present one? **He spread** out his cloak and **threw away** the leaves. **Even so,** when he **brought his cloak** back, he discovered that **the cloak** had **absorbed** such a good **scent** from those leaves that he **sold it for twelve thousand dinars.** Since he knew that this was taken from his portion in the World-to-Come, he did not want to benefit from it himself, and he therefore **divided** the sum **among his sons-in-law.**

HALAKHA

A naked person that he may not separate *teruma* – עָרוֹם שֶׁלֹּא יִתְרוֹם: It is forbidden for an unclothed person to separate *teruma*, as he cannot recite the blessing. If he did so his separation is valid (Rambam *Sefer Zera'im*, *Hilkhot Terumot* 4:4).

The graves of gentiles – קִבְרֵיהֶן שֶׁל נׇכְרִים: Gentile corpses impart ritual impurity by contact and by carrying, but not by being under the same roof. This is the ruling of most early commentaries, as opposed to *Tosafot* and the Rosh. Nevertheless, it is appropriate for a priest to be stringent and avoid walking on the graves of gentiles (Rambam *Sefer Tahara*, *Hilkhot Tumat Met* 1:13; *Shulḥan Arukh*, *Yoreh De'a* 372:2, and in the comment of Rema).

NOTES

Is not the Master a priest – לָאו כֹּהֵן הוּא מָר: Some commentaries point out that it is not at all clear that Elijah is a priest, as the Torah is silent with regard to origins. It simply states: "Elijah the Tishbite, who was of the settlers of Gilead" (I Kings 17:1), which does not even prove that he came from Gilead, but merely that this was his place of residence (*Tosafot*). There are many conflicting statements in the Midrash with regard to the identity of Elijah's tribe.

Another question discussed in *Tosafot* is that if Elijah was a priest, how could he resurrect a child (see I Kings 17:21), as this necessitated contact with the dead. The answer suggested by *Tosafot* is that since it was clear to Elijah that he would successfully resuscitate him, it was permitted for him to come in contact with the child due to the need to save a life. Some later commentaries offer a slightly different explanation: The child was still considered to be halakhically alive since Elijah was certain that he would be resuscitated (*Beit Aharon*). Other commentaries suggest that the child was not deceased, but dying (*Talmid Rabbeinu Peretz*). Alternatively, this was a special dispensation by divine command (Rosh).

The graves of gentiles do not render one impure – קִבְרֵיהֶן שֶׁל נׇכְרִים אֵין מְטַמְּאִין: According to *Tosafot*, Elijah's answer, in which he cites Rabbi Shimon bar Yoḥai, does not reflect his true halakhic opinion. In reality, Elijah believed that the graves of gentiles impart ritual impurity to one who is under the same roof, but the reason why Elijah was permitted to enter the graveyard of the gentiles had to do with the manner in which the bodies were buried there (see *Tosafot* and *Nimmukei Yosef* for further elaboration). Other early commentaries maintain that Elijah did follow the opinion of Rabbi Shimon bar Yoḥai, and ruled that gentile graves do not impart ritual impurity to one who is under the same roof (Rambam; *Sefer Yere'im*).

Gentiles are not called "man" – אֵין נׇכְרִים קְרוּיִין אָדָם: The Ramban in tractate *Yevamot* (61a) explains at length that this does not mean that gentiles are not called man at all, as certain verses clearly refer to gentiles as men. Rather, since in this context the word man is used in reference to Jews alone, apparently the term applies only to Jews with regard to the portions of *halakha* in the Torah. Rabbeinu Tam demonstrates that there is a difference between the term "man [*adam*]," which includes only Jews in halakhic contexts, and the term "the man [*ha'adam*]," which applies to all people, gentile and Jew alike. Either way, everyone agrees that the discussion about the term man here is a technical one in the context of *halakha*, not an abstract discussion about the essence of what defines a man.

In four, in six – בְּאַרְבָּעָה, בְּשִׁיתָּא: The Maharsha explains that Rabba bar Avuh meant the following: It is evident from my question about a debtor that I am not even proficient in the fourth order, *Nezikin*. How, then, can you expect me to know the sixth order, *Teharot*?

Rashi's opinion is that the four orders that Rabba bar Avuh had in mind are: *Moed*, *Nezikin*, *Nashim*, and *Kodashim*. It would seem that this choice is based on the fact that the Babylonian Talmud includes only these four orders in their entirety. Others claim that the four orders are the first ones: *Zera'im*, *Moed*, *Nashim*, and *Nezikin*, which apply nowadays. The other two, *Kodashim* and *Teharot*, which were applicable only during the times of the Temple, were not studied as much then. According to *Tosafot*, the Sages were proficient in the six orders of the Mishna themselves, but they were not expert in all of the additional *baraitot* that pertain to each order.

He led him and brought him into the Garden of Eden – עַיְילֵיהּ לְגַן עֵדֶן: According to some commentaries, this story illustrates the great reward in store for the righteous, as even the slight odor of the leaves of the Garden of Eden was precious and valuable (*Torat Ḥayyim*). Other commentaries have explained the entire episode homiletically: Elijah showed Rabba bar Avuh his future portion in the World-to-Come so that he should not suffer from his present hardships. The trees of the Garden of Eden represent the mitzvot he performed, along the lines of the statement: One consumes the profits of his good deeds in this world, and the principal remains intact for him in the World-to-Come. The voice he heard was hinting to him that even the smallest portion of such profit, as symbolized by its leaves in accordance with the verse: "And whose leaf does not wither" (Psalms 1:3), is better for the righteous to leave for the World-to-Come. Nevertheless, the odor of the fruit, which symbolizes the positive impact of his good deeds upon others and is also a great gift, represents the reward granted in this world (*Minḥat HaBoker*; *Ein Eliyahu*).

תָּנוּ רַבָּנַן: ״וְאִם אִישׁ עָנִי הוּא לֹא תִשְׁכַּב בַּעֲבֹטוֹ״, הָא עָשִׁיר – שְׁכֵיב. מַאי קָאָמַר? אֲמַר רַב שֵׁשֶׁת: הָכִי קָאָמַר: וְאִם אִישׁ עָנִי הוּא לֹא תִשְׁכַּב וַעֲבוֹטוֹ אֶצְלְךָ, הָא עָשִׁיר – שְׁכֵיב וַעֲבוֹטוֹ אֶצְלְךָ.

§ **The Sages taught** with regard to the verse: **"If he be a poor man, you shall not sleep with his collateral"** (Deuteronomy 24:12), **but if** he is **wealthy,** one may **lie down.**[N] The Gemara asks: **What is the** *tanna* **saying? Rav Sheshet said** that **this** is what he **is saying: And if he be a poor man, you shall not sleep while his collateral is with you;** rather, you must restore it to him before the sun sets. **But if** he is **a wealthy** man, you may **lie down while his collateral is with you.**[H]

תָּנוּ רַבָּנַן: הַמַּלְוֶה אֶת חֲבֵירוֹ אֵינוֹ רַשַּׁאי לְמַשְׁכְּנוֹ, וְאֵינוֹ חַיָּיב לְהַחֲזִיר לוֹ, וְעוֹבֵר בְּכָל הַשֵּׁמוֹת הַלָּלוּ. מַאי קָאָמַר? אֲמַר רַב שֵׁשֶׁת, הָכִי קָאָמַר: הַמַּלְוֶה אֶת חֲבֵירוֹ אֵינוֹ רַשַּׁאי לְמַשְׁכְּנוֹ, וְאִם מִשְׁכְּנוֹ – חַיָּיב לְהַחֲזִיר לוֹ; וְעוֹבֵר בְּכָל הַשֵּׁמוֹת הַלָּלוּ – אַסֵּיפָא.

The Sages taught: One **who lends** money **to another is not permitted to take collateral from him, and is not obligated to return** it **to him, and transgresses all of these labels** [*shemot*][L] of prohibitions. The meaning of this *baraita* is unclear, and the Gemara asks: **What is** the *tanna* **saying? Rav Sheshet said: This** is what he **is saying:** One **who lends** money to **another is not permitted to take collateral from him, and if** he did **take collateral from him,** he is **obligated to return** it **to him.** As for the clause: **And** he **transgresses all of these labels** of prohibitions, this is referring **to the latter clause,** i.e., the case implicit in the *baraita,* where the creditor took collateral from the debtor and did not return it, and the *baraita* explains that such a person violates all of the Torah prohibitions that apply to this situation.

רָבָא אֲמַר: הָכִי קָאָמַר: הַמַּלְוֶה אֶת חֲבֵירוֹ אֵינוֹ רַשַּׁאי לְמַשְׁכְּנוֹ, וְאִם מִשְׁכְּנוֹ – חַיָּיב לְהַחֲזִיר לוֹ. בַּמֶּה דְּבָרִים אֲמוּרִים – שֶׁמִּשְׁכְּנוֹ שֶׁלֹּא בִּשְׁעַת הַלְוָאָתוֹ, אֲבָל מִשְׁכְּנוֹ בִּשְׁעַת הַלְוָאָתוֹ – אֵינוֹ חַיָּיב לְהַחֲזִיר לוֹ. וְעוֹבֵר בְּכָל הַשֵּׁמוֹת הַלָּלוּ – אַרֵישָׁא.

Rava said: This is what the *tanna* **is saying:** One **who lends** money to **another is not permitted to take collateral from him, and if** he did **take collateral from him,** he is **obligated to return** it **to him. In what** case **is this statement said?** It is referring to **where he took collateral from him when** it was **not at the time of the loan,** but rather as a means of ensuring payment. **But if** he **took collateral from him at the time of the loan,** in which case the collateral serves as a guarantee of the loan, **he is not obligated to return** it **to him.** According to this interpretation, the statement: **And** he **transgresses of all these labels** of prohibitions, is referring **to the first clause** of the *baraita,* concerning the prohibition against taking collateral.

תָּנֵי רַב שֵׁיזְבִי קַמֵּיהּ דְּרָבָא: ״עַד בֹּא הַשֶּׁמֶשׁ תְּשִׁיבֶנּוּ לוֹ״ – זוֹ כְּסוּת לַיְלָה; ״הָשֵׁב תָּשִׁיב לוֹ אֶת הָעֲבוֹט כְּבוֹא הַשֶּׁמֶשׁ״ – זוֹ כְּסוּת יוֹם. אֲמַר לֵיהּ: דִּימָמָא בְּלֵילְיָא לָמָּה לִי, וּדְלֵילְיָא בִּימָמָא לָמָּה לִי?

Rav Sheizevi taught the following *baraita* **before Rava:** With regard to the verse: "And if you take as collateral your neighbor's garment, **you shall restore it to him until the sun goes down"** (Exodus 22:25), **this** is referring to **a garment** worn at **night** and teaches that the garment is returned during the day; and with regard to the verse: **"You shall restore to him the collateral when the sun goes down"** (Deuteronomy 24:13), **this** is referring to **a garment** worn during the **day.** Rava **said to him:** This statement is puzzling, as with regard to a garment worn **in the day, why do I** need it **at night, and** as for a garment worn **at night, why do I** need it **in the day?** What purpose is served by giving back the garments at such times?

אֲמַר לֵיהּ: אִיסַמְיֵיהּ? אֲמַר לֵיהּ: לָא, הָכִי קָאָמַר: ״עַד בֹּא הַשֶּׁמֶשׁ תְּשִׁיבֶנּוּ לוֹ״ – זוֹ כְּסוּת יוֹם שֶׁנִּיתְּנָה לַחֲבוֹל בַּלַּיְלָה; ״הָשֵׁב תָּשִׁיב לוֹ אֶת הָעֲבוֹט כְּבוֹא הַשֶּׁמֶשׁ״ – זוֹ כְּסוּת לַיְלָה שֶׁנִּיתְּנָה לַחֲבוֹל בַּיּוֹם.

Rav Sheizevi **said to him:** Do you think this *baraita* is so corrupt that I should **erase it,**[N] i.e., no longer teach it? Rava **said to him: No,** do not erase it, because **this** is what it **is saying:** With regard to the verse **"You shall restore it to him until when the sun goes down," this** is referring to **a garment** worn during the **day, which may be taken as collateral by night** but must be returned to the debtor for the day. With regard to the verse **"You shall restore to him the collateral when the sun goes down," this** is referring to **a garment** worn at **night, which may be taken as collateral by day.**

אָמַר רַבִּי יוֹחָנָן: מִשְׁכְּנוֹ וּמֵת – שׁוֹמְטוֹ מֵעַל גַּבֵּי בָּנָיו. מֵיתִיבֵי, אָמַר רַבִּי מֵאִיר: וְכִי מֵאַחַר שֶׁמְּמַשְׁכְּנִין לָמָּה מַחֲזִירִין? לָמָּה מַחֲזִירִין? רַחֲמָנָא אֲמַר אַהֲדַר! אֶלָּא: מֵאַחַר שֶׁמַּחֲזִירִין,

§ **Rabbi Yoḥanan said:** If he **took collateral from him,** returned it, and then the debtor **died,**[H] the creditor may **take** the collateral **from** the debtor's **children** and is under no obligation to leave it with them. The Gemara **raises an objection** to this from a *baraita*: **Rabbi Meir said: But since** one **takes collateral, why does** he **return** it? The Gemara expresses surprise at this question: **Why does** he **return** it? **The Merciful One states** to **return** it. **Rather,** the question is as follows: **Since** he must **return** it,

NOTES

But if he is wealthy one may lie down – **הָא עָשִׁיר שְׁכֵיב**: According to the *Sifrei*, this prohibition includes a wealthy person as well, but one who treats a poor person unfairly is punished more severely. According to the Rosh and *Talmid Rabbeinu Peretz*, the wealthy person mentioned in the *Sifrei* is a landowner who requires his everyday tools since he possesses only a few. Conversely, the wealthy person referred to by the Gemara is one who owns extensive properties and does not need to spend all his time tending to his fields.

I should erase it – **אִיסַמְיֵיהּ**: The *amora'im* who recited *mishnayot* and *baraitot* were experts in these statements, and they would serve as living libraries by reciting these quotations from memory before the Sages. The Sages would then elucidate and clarify the *baraitot* and place them in context. Occasionally, when they encountered a text of a *baraita* that was corrupt, the Sage would instruct the one who taught it not to repeat it anymore, as it was not considered definitive enough to use as a source for practical *halakha*.

HALAKHA

The restoration of collateral to a wealthy person and a poor person – **הֲשָׁבַת הָעֲבוֹט לְעָשִׁיר וְעָנִי**: When a creditor takes an item as collateral that the debtor requires for his basic needs, the creditor must return it to him during the time that the debtor requires it for use. If the debtor does not need the item, the creditor is not obligated to give it back. This *halakha* applies to one who seized collateral after the time of the loan, but if the creditor took the collateral when he granted the loan, he does not have to return it (Rambam *Sefer Mishpatim, Hilkhot Malve VeLoveh* 3:5; *Shulḥan Arukh, Ḥoshen Mishpat* 97:16).

LANGUAGE

Labels [*shemot*] – **שֵׁמוֹת**: The word *shemot* as used here and in other places in the Talmud signifies something slightly different from its literal meaning, i.e., names. Here, *shem*, the singular form, means a concept or an issue.

HALAKHA

If he took collateral from him and he died – **מִשְׁכְּנוֹ וּמֵת**: If a creditor took collateral from the debtor, returned the collateral, and then the debtor subsequently died, the creditor may take the collateral from his children without having to return it to them (Rambam *Sefer Mishpatim, Hilkhot Malve VeLoveh* 3:6; *Shulḥan Arukh, Ḥoshen Mishpat* 97:19).

לָמָּה חוֹזְרִין וּמְמַשְׁכְּנִין? שֶׁלֹּא תְּהֵא שְׁבִיעִית מְשַׁמַּטְתּוֹ, וְלֹא יֵעָשֶׂה מִטַּלְטְלִין אֵצֶל בָּנָיו.

why does one **go back and take the collateral** again, as the creditor must anyway restore it to the debtor the following day? The Gemara replies: Any loan that is secured by collateral is not canceled by the Sabbatical Year, in contrast to other debts, which are canceled. Therefore, this ensures **that the Sabbatical** Year **should not cancel it.**[H] **And** an additional reason is so that the collateral **should not become movable property** in the possession **of his children,** as one generally cannot claim such items from orphans to pay for their father's debt.

טַעְמָא – דַּהֲדַר וּמַשְׁכְּנֵיהּ, הָא לָא הֲדַר וּמַשְׁכְּנֵיהּ – לָא!

The Gemara infers: The **reason** these exceptions apply is **that** he **goes back and takes it as collateral; but** if he did **not go back and take it as collateral,** these exceptions do **not** apply. This *baraita* therefore contradicts the opinion of Rabbi Yoḥanan, who held that the initial seizing of collateral is sufficient to grant the creditor full rights to it.

אֲמַר רַב אַדָּא בַּר מַתָּנָא: וְלָאו תֵּרוּצֵי קָא מְתָרְצַתְּ לָהּ? תְּרֵיץ הָכִי: וְכִי מֵאַחַר שֶׁמַּחֲזִירִין לָמָּה מְמַשְׁכְּנִין מֵעִיקָּרָא? שֶׁלֹּא תְּהֵא שְׁבִיעִית מְשַׁמַּטְתּוֹ, וְלֹא יֵעָשֶׂה מִטַּלְטְלִין אֵצֶל בָּנָיו.

Rav Adda bar Mattana said: And did you not resolve this *baraita* once already by adjusting its wording slightly? **Answer** it by changing its formulation again in **this** manner: **And since** one must **return** the collateral, **why** does one **take collateral at the outset?** It is done so **that the Sabbatical** Year **should not cancel** the debt, **and** so that it **should not become movable property** in the possession **of his children.** This version is in accordance with the opinion of Rabbi Yoḥanan, as it teaches that one who has taken collateral even on a single occasion may confiscate it from the debtor's heirs.

תָּנוּ רַבָּנַן: ״לֹא תָבֹא אֶל בֵּיתוֹ לַעֲבֹט עֲבֹטוֹ״. לְבֵיתוֹ אִי אַתָּה נִכְנָס, אֲבָל אַתָּה נִכְנָס לְבֵיתוֹ שֶׁל עָרֵב. וְכֵן הוּא אוֹמֵר: ״לְקַח בִּגְדוֹ כִּי עָרַב זָר״ וגו׳.

§ **The Sages taught:** The verse states: "When you lend your neighbor any manner of loan, **you shall not go into his house to take his collateral**" (Deuteronomy 24:10). This verse indicates that **you may not enter his house, but you** may **enter the house of a guarantor**[HN] to take collateral from him. **And similarly it states: "Take his garment**[N] **that is a surety for a stranger"** (Proverbs 20:16).

וְאוֹמֵר: ״בְּנִי אִם עָרַבְתָּ לְרֵעֶךָ תָּקַעְתָּ לַזָּר כַּפֶּיךָ, נוֹקַשְׁתָּ בְאִמְרֵי פִיךָ נִלְכַּדְתָּ בְּאִמְרֵי פִיךָ, עֲשֵׂה זֹאת אֵפוֹא בְּנִי וְהִנָּצֵל כִּי בָאתָ בְכַף רֵעֶךָ לֵךְ הִתְרַפֵּס וּרְהַב רֵעֶיךָ״.

And it further **states** with regard to the same issue: **"My son, if you are a guarantor for your neighbor, if you have struck your hands for a stranger, you are ensnared by the words of your mouth; you are caught by the words of your mouth. Do this, now, my son, and deliver yourself, when you have come into the hand of your friend; go humble yourself and strengthen your friend"** (Proverbs 6:1–3).[N]

אִם מָמוֹן יֵשׁ לוֹ בְּיָדְךָ – הַתֵּר לוֹ פִּיסַּת יָד; וְאִם לָאו – הַרְבֵּה עָלָיו רֵעִים.

This passage in Proverbs is interpreted as follows: The phrase "You are snared by the words of your mouth" is referring to a guarantor who obligated himself to pay or one who upset his friend with his comments. In such a case, one should do the following: **If he has money in your hand,** "go humble yourself [*hitrapes*]," which is expounded as: **Release for him the palm of your hand** [***hatter lo pissat yad***] to give him his money. **And if** it is **not** money that you owe him, but rather you have "become ensnared by the words of your mouth" and owe him an apology for a personal slight, **gather together many neighbors** through which to seek **his** forgiveness.

HALAKHA

That the Sabbatical Year should not cancel it, etc. – **שֶׁלֹּא תְּהֵא שְׁבִיעִית מְשַׁמַּטְתּוֹ וכו׳**: The Sabbatical Year does not cancel any loan for which collateral has been taken. Similarly, if the debtor dies, the creditor need not return the collateral to his children (Rambam *Sefer Mishpatim, Hilkhot Malve VeLoveh* 3:5; *Shulḥan Arukh, Ḥoshen Mishpat* 97:16).

You may enter the house of a guarantor – **אַתָּה נִכְנָס לְבֵיתוֹ שֶׁל עָרֵב**: Although it is prohibited to seize collateral from a debtor, one may do so from the guarantor of the loan. An exception is when the guarantor is an unconditional guarantor, who has the status of a debtor himself. No permission is required from the court in order to take collateral from a guarantor, and one may forcibly enter his house and seize it. The Rema cites an opinion that even so, it is forbidden to take any utensil used for the preparation of food as collateral from a guarantor (Rambam *Sefer Mishpatim, Hilkhot Malve VeLoveh* 3:7; *Shulḥan Arukh, Ḥoshen Mishpat* 97:14).

NOTES

You may enter the house of a guarantor – **אַתָּה נִכְנָס לְבֵיתוֹ שֶׁל עָרֵב**: As for why it is permitted to enter the house of the guarantor but not that of the debtor to take collateral, several explanations have been offered. One of them is that the guarantor does not feel as much shame as does the debtor himself when the creditor enters his house (*Iyyun Ya'akov*; see also Rabbeinu Yehonatan of Lunel).

Take his garment – **לְקַח בִּגְדוֹ**: The Rashbam (*Bava Batra* 173b) explains this as a directive to the creditor, that he may take the guarantor's garment. Others maintain that the interpretation here is based on the end of the verse: "And hold him in pledge that is surety for an alien woman" (Proverbs 20:16), which indicates that one may even enter a guarantor's house to seize collateral. The purpose of the second verse cited from Proverbs by the Gemara is to illustrate that the guarantor replaces the debtor with regard to the obligation to repay the debt itself as well as with regard to the collateral (*Torat Ḥayyim*).

Strengthen [*rehav*] your friend – **וּרְהַב רֵעֶיךָ**: According to the Gemara's interpretation, the word *rehav* should be understood to mean increase [*harbeh*], through metathesis. Alternatively, it may be understood to mean great [*rabba*], in the sense that one should exalt his friend in an effort to placate him by having other friends and close acquaintances honor him (Rabbeinu Yehonatan of Lunel).

לְצַד שֵׁנִי: לְבֵיתוֹ אִי אַתָּה נִכְנָס, אֲבָל אַתָּה נִכְנָס לִשְׂכַר כַּתָּף, לִשְׂכַר חַמָּר, לִשְׂכַר פּוּנְדָּק, לִשְׂכַר דְּיוֹקְנָאוֹת. יָכוֹל אֲפִילּוּ זְקָפָן עָלָיו בְּמִלְוֶה – תַּלְמוּד לוֹמַר: ״מַשַּׁאת מְאוּמָה״.

The verse "When you lend your neighbor any manner of loan, you shall not go into his house to take his collateral" can be interpreted **in a different direction,** i.e., in another manner: **You may not enter his house** to take collateral for the loan, **but** if he owes wages, **you may enter** and take collateral **for a porter's wages, for a donkey driver's wages, for an innkeeper's payment,** or **for the wages for** one who made **drawings** [***diyokanaot***][L] for him.[H] One **might** have thought that this applies **even** if the one owed the money **establishes it as a loan for** the one who owes the money after he was already liable for such payment. Therefore, **the verse states: "Any manner** of loan" (Deuteronomy 24:10), which demonstrates that once the debt has been converted into a loan, it is like any other loan, and therefore one may not take collateral against the debtor's will.

מתני׳ אַלְמָנָה, בֵּין שֶׁהִיא עֲנִיָּה בֵּין שֶׁהִיא עֲשִׁירָה – אֵין מְמַשְׁכְּנִין אוֹתָהּ, שֶׁנֶּאֱמַר: ״וְלֹא תַחֲבֹל בֶּגֶד אַלְמָנָה״.

MISHNA With regard to **a widow, whether she is** poor or **whether she is wealthy,** one **may not take collateral from her,**[N] **as it is stated: "And you may not take the garment of a widow**[N] **as collateral"** (Deuteronomy 24:17).[H]

גמ׳ תָּנוּ רַבָּנַן: אַלְמָנָה, בֵּין שֶׁהִיא עֲנִיָּה בֵּין שֶׁהִיא עֲשִׁירָה – אֵין מְמַשְׁכְּנִין אוֹתָהּ, דִּבְרֵי רַבִּי יְהוּדָה.

GEMARA **The Sages taught:** With regard to **a widow, whether she is poor** or **whether she is** wealthy, one **may not take collateral from her.** This is **the statement of Rabbi Yehuda.**

רַבִּי שִׁמְעוֹן אוֹמֵר: עֲשִׁירָה – מְמַשְׁכְּנִין אוֹתָהּ, עֲנִיָּה – אֵין מְמַשְׁכְּנִין אוֹתָהּ, שֶׁאַתָּה חַיָּיב לְהַחֲזִיר לָהּ וְאַתָּה מַשִּׂיאָהּ שֵׁם רַע בִּשְׁכֵנוֹתֶיהָ.

Rabbi Shimon says: With regard to **a wealthy** widow, one may **take collateral from her.** But with regard to **a poor** widow, one may **not take collateral from her,**[N] because **you are obligated to return** it **to her,** in accordance with the *halakha* that the collateral of a poor person must be returned to him whenever he needs it. **And** since you will be entering every day to return the collateral to her, **you** will thereby **give her a bad name**[N] **among her neighbors,** as they will suspect her of developing an inappropriate relationship with you. By contrast, in the case of a wealthy widow, since there is no obligation to return her collateral, it is permitted to take collateral from her.

לְמֵימְרָא דְּרַבִּי יְהוּדָה לָא דָּרֵישׁ טַעְמָא דִּקְרָא, וְרַבִּי שִׁמְעוֹן דָּרֵישׁ טַעְמָא דִּקְרָא? וְהָא אִיפְּכָא שָׁמְעִינַן לְהוּ,

The Gemara asks: Is this **to say that Rabbi Yehuda does not interpret the rationale** behind the mitzva **in the verse** and draw halakhic conclusions based on that interpretation, and **Rabbi Shimon does interpret the rationale** behind the mitzva **in the verse? But** haven't we **heard them** holding **the reverse** opinions elsewhere?

דְּתַנְיָא: ״וְלֹא יַרְבֶּה לּוֹ נָשִׁים״ – רַבִּי יְהוּדָה אוֹמֵר: מַרְבֶּה הוּא, וּבִלְבַד שֶׁלֹּא יְהוּ מְסִירוֹת אֶת לִבּוֹ. רַבִּי שִׁמְעוֹן אוֹמֵר: אֲפִילּוּ אַחַת וְהִיא מְסִירָה אֶת לִבּוֹ הֲרֵי זֶה לֹא יִשָּׂאֶנָּה. אִם כֵּן מָה תַּלְמוּד לוֹמַר ״וְלֹא יַרְבֶּה לּוֹ נָשִׁים״ – אֲפִילּוּ כַּאֲבִיגַיִל!

As it is taught in a mishna (*Sanhedrin* 21a) concerning the mitzvot of a king: **"And he should not multiply wives for himself,** that his heart not turn away" (Deuteronomy 17:17). **Rabbi Yehuda says: He** may **accumulate many** wives **for himself, provided that they are not** like those who **turn his heart** from reverence for God. **Rabbi Shimon says: Even one who turns his heart away, he should not marry her. If so, why is it stated: "He shall not multiply wives for himself"?** This teaches that **even** with regard to wives **like Abigail,**[N] who was righteous and prevented David from sin (see I Samuel chapter 25), he is forbidden to have many. In this case, Rabbi Shimon does not interpret the rationale of the verse, while Rabbi Yehuda does interpret its rationale.

LANGUAGE

Drawings [*diyokanaot*] – דְּיוֹקְנָאוֹת: The origin of this word is not entirely clear. Some claim that it is derived from the Greek **δείκανον**, *deikanon*, meaning a form or woven figure. Others maintain that it comes from the word **εἰκών**, *eikon*, which means a statue or image, with the letter *dalet* added as a prefix.

HALAKHA

Collateral for payment of wages – מַשְׁכּוֹן עֲבוּר שְׂכִירוּת: If one owes wages to another, either for a service the other performed or a rental payment for the use of his animal or vessels, the one demanding the money may enter his house and take collateral even without the authorization of the court. If the debtor established it as a loan for the creditor, it is like any other loan, and therefore he may not enter his house (Rambam *Sefer Mishpatim, Hilkhot Malve VeLoveh* 3:7; *Shulḥan Arukh, Ḥoshen Mishpat* 97:14).

A widow's collateral – מַשְׁכּוֹן אַלְמָנָה: No collateral may be taken from a widow even by a court agent, regardless of whether she is poor or wealthy, unless it is taken at the time of the loan. If the creditor nevertheless took the garment of a widow, he is compelled to return it. According to the *Taz*, it is prohibited to take collateral from any unmarried woman, while according to the *Sma*, it is permitted in the case of an unmarried woman who is still under the jurisdiction of her father. According to the *Shakh*, the *Urim VeTummim*, and the *Arukh HaShulḥan*, only a widow is included in this prohibition (Rambam *Sefer Mishpatim, Hilkhot Malve VeLoveh* 3:1–2; *Shulḥan Arukh, Ḥoshen Mishpat* 97:14).

NOTES

With regard to a widow…one may not take collateral from her – אַלְמָנָה...אֵין מְמַשְׁכְּנִין אוֹתָהּ: The Rambam explains the reason for this *halakha*: Since he enters her house, and she too has to visit him to deal with the collateral, her reputation may be ruined and she may be lead to temptation. This logic applies to a wealthy woman as well and is apparently the reason why several commentaries extend this *halakha* to any unmarried woman who conducts her own business. Others maintain that this *halakha* applies only to a widow, as one must be careful to act with more sensitivity toward her than toward other women and not increase her misery in any way. See the later commentaries who discuss this point.

The garment of a widow – בֶּגֶד אַלְמָנָה: Some claim that this *halakha* applies only to articles of clothing, but not to other utensils (Riaz).

A wealthy or poor widow – אַלְמָנָה עֲשִׁירָה וַעֲנִיָּה: In the Jerusalem Talmud the dispute is recorded in a slightly different manner. The Gemara there attributes the mishna's statement to Rabbi Meir, while Rabbi Yehuda claims that one may not take collateral from a poor widow at all, while with regard to a rich widow, one may seize collateral and does not need to return it.

Give her a bad name – מַשִּׂיאָהּ שֵׁם רַע: Even if the collateral is seized by a court agent, this too will give her a bad reputation. Although in theory the mission may be performed by a female agent, the Sages did not take that unique possibility into account when formulating the *halakha* (*Ḥokhmat Manoaḥ*).

Even like Abigail – אֲפִילּוּ כַּאֲבִיגַיִל: Abigail is cited as the prototype of a good wife, since she prevented David from sinning, as he himself said to her: "And blessed be your discretion and blessed be you, who has kept me this day from shedding blood" (I Samuel 25:33).

HALAKHA

The prohibition against taking the lower and upper millstone as collateral – אִיסּוּר חֲבָלַת רֵיחַיִם וָרֶכֶב: If collateral is taken from the debtor not at the time of the loan, the creditor may not take vessels used in the preparation of food, such as the lower and upper millstones. This prohibition applies even if he does not enter her house but takes them from outside (Rambam *Sefer Mishpatim, Hilkhot Malve VeLoveh* 3:1–2; *Shulḥan Arukh, Hoshen Mishpat* 97:6).

Liability for taking the lower and upper millstones as collateral – חִיּוּבֵי חֲבָלַת רֵיחַיִם וָרֶכֶב: If a creditor took as collateral many vessels used in the preparation of food, he is flogged for each item separately. This *halakha* applies even to two utensils that are used together for a single task, such as the lower and upper millstones, in accordance with the opinion of Rav Yehuda (Rambam *Sefer Mishpatim, Hilkhot Malve VeLoveh* 3:3).

BACKGROUND

Flogged with two sets of lashes – לוֹקֶה שְׁתַּיִם: These lashes are a form of punishment and are performed by tying the victim to a post in a leaning position and whipping him on his back and his chest. Although the straightforward understanding of the verse indicates that forty lashes are normally administered per transgression, the Sages interpreted the verse: "Forty lashes he may give him, he may not exceed" (Deuteronomy 25:3), to mean that the number of lashes actually given is only thirty-nine. If the victim cannot survive that number of lashes, he receives only the number he can bear. Transgression of prohibitions is, as a rule, punishable by lashes, although there are several exceptions. The administration of lashes is limited to cases where there are two witnesses to the transgression, the sinner was forewarned immediately prior to his transgression, and a court of three determines that he should be flogged.

לְעוֹלָם רַבִּי יְהוּדָה לָא דָּרֵישׁ טַעְמָא דִּקְרָא, וְשָׁאנֵי הָכָא דִּמְפָרֵשׁ קְרָא: ״וְלֹא יַרְבֶּה לּוֹ נָשִׁים וְלֹא יָסוּר״. מַאי טַעְמָא לֹא יַרְבֶּה לּוֹ נָשִׁים? מִשּׁוּם דְּ״לֹא יָסוּר״.

The Gemara answers: **Actually, Rabbi Yehuda does not** generally **interpret the rationale of the verse, and it is different here,** with regard to a king, **as the verse** itself **specifies** the reason: **"And he should not multiply wives for himself, that** his heart **not turn away." What is the reason** that **he may not multiply wives for himself?** It is **because** he must ensure **that** his heart **will not turn away.**

וְרַבִּי שִׁמְעוֹן: מִכְּדִי בְּעָלְמָא דָּרְשִׁינַן טַעְמָא דִּקְרָא – לִכְתּוֹב רַחֲמָנָא ״לֹא יַרְבֶּה״ וְלָא בָּעֵינַן ״לֹא יָסוּר״, וַאֲנָא יָדַעְנָא: מַאי טַעְמָא ״לֹא יַרְבֶּה״? מִשּׁוּם דְּ״לֹא יָסוּר״. ״לֹא יָסוּר״ דִּכְתַב רַחֲמָנָא לָמָּה לִי? אֲפִילּוּ אַחַת וּמְסִירָה אֶת לִבּוֹ – הֲרֵי זֶה לֹא יִשָּׂאֶנָּה.

And Rabbi Shimon maintains: **Since we generally interpret the rationale in the verse,** there is no need for the verse itself to supply the rationale for the prohibition. **Let the Merciful One state: "He may not multiply," and we do not need** the Torah to add "that his heart **not turn away," and I** would already **know** the answer to the question: **What is the reason** that **he may not accumulate** many wives? It is **because** of the concern that his heart **not turn away.** If so, **why do I** need the phrase "His heart **not turn away" that the Merciful One writes?** It must certainly be necessary in order to increase the scope of the prohibition: **Even** if there is **one** woman who **turns his heart away, he may not marry her.** Therefore, the verse includes two *halakhot*: A general stricture against a king's marrying too many women, and a further *halakha* that a king may not marry even one woman who will lead him astray.

מתני׳ הַחוֹבֵל אֶת הָרֵיחַיִם עוֹבֵר מִשּׁוּם לֹא תַעֲשֶׂה, וְחַיָּיב מִשּׁוּם שְׁנֵי כֵלִים, שֶׁנֶּאֱמַר: ״לֹא יַחֲבֹל רֵיחַיִם וָרָכֶב״. וְלֹא רֵיחַיִם וָרֶכֶב בִּלְבַד אָמְרוּ, אֶלָּא כָּל דָּבָר שֶׁעוֹשִׂין בּוֹ אוֹכֶל נֶפֶשׁ, שֶׁנֶּאֱמַר: ״כִּי נֶפֶשׁ הוּא חֹבֵל״.

MISHNA One **who takes a millstone as collateral**[N] **violates a prohibition, and** he is **liable** for taking **two vessels,** i.e., both millstones in the pair, **as it is stated: "He shall not take the lower or upper millstone as collateral"** (Deuteronomy 24:6).[H] The *tanna* adds: **Not only** did the Sages **say** that it is prohibited to take **the lower or upper millstone**[N] as collateral, **but** they also said that one may not take **anything that** people **use in the preparation of food** [*okhel nefesh*], **as it is stated: "For he takes a man's life** [*nefesh*] **as collateral"** (Deuteronomy 24:6).

גמ׳ אָמַר רַב הוּנָא: חָבַל רֵיחַיִם – לוֹקֶה שְׁתַּיִם, מִשּׁוּם ״רֵיחַיִם״ וּמִשּׁוּם ״כִּי נֶפֶשׁ הוּא חֹבֵל״. רֵיחַיִם וָרֶכֶב – לוֹקֶה שָׁלֹשׁ, מִשּׁוּם ״רֵחַיִם וָרֶכֶב״, וּמִשּׁוּם ״כִּי נֶפֶשׁ הוּא חֹבֵל״.

GEMARA **Rav Huna says:** One who **took a lower millstone as collateral is flogged** with **two** sets of lashes:[B] One set is **due to** violating the prohibition of taking the **lower millstone** as collateral, **and** the second is **due to: "For he takes a man's life as collateral,"** since he took an item used in the preparation of food. If he took **the lower and upper millstone,** he **is flogged** with **three** sets of lashes: Two sets are **due to** violating the prohibitions of taking **a lower millstone and an upper millstone** as collateral, **and** the third is **due to** violating the prohibition: **"For he takes a man's life as collateral."**[N]

וְרַב יְהוּדָה אָמַר: חָבַל רֵיחַיִם – לוֹקֶה אַחַת; ״וָרֶכֶב״ – לוֹקֶה אַחַת; ״רֵיחַיִם וָרֶכֶב״ – לוֹקֶה שְׁתַּיִם. ״כִּי נֶפֶשׁ הוּא חֹבֵל״

And Rav Yehuda says: If he **took a lower millstone as collateral he is flogged** with **one** set of lashes, if he took **an upper millstone he is flogged** with **one** set of lashes, and if he took both **the lower and upper millstones** together as collateral **he is flogged** with **two** sets of lashes.[H] With regard to the verse: **"For he takes a man's life as collateral,"**

NOTES

One who takes a millstone as collateral – הַחוֹבֵל אֶת הָרֵיחַיִם: This passage is difficult to understand, as taking an item as collateral involves entering the debtor's house, which as was seen above is clearly prohibited. Some explain that this refers to a court agent who seizes the millstone outside the debtor's house (Rid). The Rambam maintains that it is prohibited to take the lower or upper millstone as collateral even at the time of the loan, when it is permitted to enter the house. Most ruling authorities reject this view.

Not only did the Sages say that it is prohibited to take the lower or upper millstone – וְלֹא רֵיחַיִם וָרֶכֶב בִּלְבַד אָמְרוּ: The phrase: Not only did they say, is problematic, as it was not the Sages but the Torah itself that mentioned these items. Some commentaries answer that it means the following: Not only did the Sages say that the lower and upper millstones should be considered two separate vessels for which he violates two transgressions, but they say that this *halakha* also applies to any similar pair of utensils (*Melekhet Shlomo*).

Rav Huna's reasoning – סְבָרַת רַב הוּנָא: Rav Huna maintains that the same applies to all utensils used in the preparation of food, which he derives from the verse: "He shall not take the lower or upper millstone as collateral," using hermeneutical principles. He therefore reads the verse: "For he takes a man's life as collateral" (Deuteronomy 24:6), as an additional prohibition (*Torat Ḥayyim*).

לִשְׁאָר דְּבָרִים הוּא דַּאֲתָא.

it comes to teach **about** the prohibition **against** taking as collateral **other items** used in the preparation of food.

לֵימָא אַבַּיֵּי וְרָבָא בִּפְלוּגְתָּא דְּרַב הוּנָא וְרַב יְהוּדָה קָמִיפַּלְגִי;

§ The Gemara suggests: **Shall we say** that **Abaye and Rava,** in another dispute, **disagree with regard to** the issue that is the subject of this **dispute between Rav Huna and Rav Yehuda** concerning the collateral? The Torah commands with regard to the preparation of the Paschal offering: "Do not eat of it raw, nor cooked in water, but roasted with fire, its head with its legs and with the innards thereof" (Exodus 12:9). Abaye and Rava engage in a dispute concerning the case of one who ate the meat when it was not properly roasted.

דְּאָמַר רָבָא: אָכַל נָא – לוֹקֶה שְׁתַּיִם, מִשּׁוּם "נָא", וּמִשּׁוּם "כִּי אִם צְלִי אֵשׁ". מְבוּשָּׁל – לוֹקֶה שְׁתַּיִם, מִשּׁוּם "מְבוּשָּׁל" וּמִשּׁוּם "כִּי אִם צְלִי אֵשׁ". נָא וּמְבוּשָּׁל – לוֹקֶה שָׁלֹשׁ: מִשּׁוּם "נָא", וּמִשּׁוּם "מְבוּשָּׁל", וּמִשּׁוּם "לֹא תֹאכְלֶנּוּ כִּי אִם צְלִי אֵשׁ".

As Rava says: If he **ate** an olive-bulk of it **raw,** he **is flogged** with **two** sets of lashes. One set of lashes is **due to** the prohibition: "Do not eat of it raw," **and** the other is **due to** the prohibition: **"But roasted with fire."** If he ate an olive-bulk of a Paschal offering that had been **cooked,** he also **is flogged** with **two** sets of lashes: One set of lashes is **due to** the prohibition against it being **cooked** in water, **and** the second is **due to** the injunction: **"But roasted with fire."** If he ate an olive-bulk of both **raw** meat **and cooked**[H] meat, he **is flogged** with **three** sets of lashes: One set of lashes is **due to** the prohibition against it being **raw, and** the second is **due to** the prohibition against it being **cooked, and** the third is **due to** the prohibition: **"Do not eat of it…but roasted with fire."**

אַבַּיֵּי אָמַר: אֵין לוֹקִין עַל לָאו שֶׁבִּכְלָלוֹת. לֵימָא אַבַּיֵּי דְּאָמַר כְּרַב יְהוּדָה, וְרָבָא דְּאָמַר כְּרַב הוּנָא!

Conversely, **Abaye says:** The prohibition "Do not eat of it…but roasted with fire" is not referring exclusively to this issue, but includes many cases, and one **is not flogged for** violating **a general prohibition.**[N] In this case, Abaye and Rava apparently disagree over the same matter as do Rav Huna and Rav Yehuda. **Shall we say that Abaye states** his opinion **in accordance with** the opinion of **Rav Yehuda, and Rava states** his opinion **in accordance with** the opinion of **Rav Huna?**

אָמַר לָךְ רָבָא: אֲנָא דַּאֲמַרִי – אֲפִילּוּ כְּרַב יְהוּדָה. עַד כָּאן לָא קָאָמַר רַב יְהוּדָה הָתָם אֶלָּא דְּ"כִי נֶפֶשׁ הוּא חֹבֵל" לָא מַשְׁמַע רֵיחַיִם וָרֶכֶב. הִלְכָּךְ לִשְׁאָר דְּבָרִים הוּא דַּאֲתָא.

The Gemara responds: **Rava** could have **said to you: I state** my opinion **even in accordance with** the opinion of **Rav Yehuda,**[N] as there is a difference between the two cases: **Rav Yehuda states** his opinion **only there,** with regard to collateral, **because** the phrase: **"For he takes a man's life as collateral"** (Deuteronomy 24:6), **does not** itself **indicate** that the verse is referring to **the lower and upper millstones.** Rather, it is a general statement, and **therefore it comes to** teach **about** the prohibition **against** taking as collateral **other items** used in the preparation of food, not to add a prohibition to take as collateral the lower and upper millstones.

אֲבָל הָכָא "כִּי אִם צְלִי אֵשׁ" לְמַאי אֲתָא? שְׁמַע מִינָּהּ – לְלָאו.

But here, the phrase **"but roasted with fire" comes for what** purpose? It excludes only raw or cooked meat, which were already mentioned. Therefore, **learn from** it that it comes **to** include another **prohibition** in addition to those specific directives referring to raw and cooked meat.

וְאַבַּיֵּי אָמַר לָךְ: אֲנָא דַּאֲמַרִי אֲפִילּוּ לְרַב הוּנָא. עַד כָּאן לָא קָאָמַר רַב הוּנָא הָתָם אֶלָּא דְּ"כִי נֶפֶשׁ הוּא חֹבֵל"

And Abaye could have **said to you: I state** my opinion **even in accordance with** the opinion of **Rav Huna.** This is because **Rav Huna states** his opinion **only there,** with regard to collateral, **because** the prohibition **"For he takes a man's life as collateral"**

NOTES

A general prohibition – לָאו שֶׁבִּכְלָלוֹת: The definition of a general prohibition is not at all clear, and there are several opinions among the early commentaries as to the meaning of this term. Moreover, the Meiri concludes that there appear to be a few categories of prohibitions that are called general prohibitions and yet are governed by different *halakhot*. One type is a general Torah prohibition that includes a variety of prohibitions from different areas of the *halakha*, none of which are explicitly stated in the Torah. A prohibition of this kind, such as: "You shall not eat with the blood" (Leviticus 19:26), is certainly a general prohibition, and everyone agrees that no lashes are administered for the violation of this prohibition. Furthermore, some prohibitions of this kind are not even counted by those commentaries who list the mitzvot written in the Torah, as their details are not specified in the Torah at all.

Another type of general prohibition is one that is stated in general terms, but all or some of its details are specified in the Torah. Examples of this include the prohibitions mentioned here: "Do not eat of it raw," and the stricture against taking the lower and upper millstones as collateral. In all these cases, the Rambam holds that one does not receive an additional set of lashes for each specific detail, due to the fact that it is stated as one general prohibition. According to the Ramban all these details are considered distinct prohibitions, and one who violated two of them at once, such as if he ate an olive-bulk of the Paschal offering that was raw and another olive-bulk that was cooked, is flogged with two sets of lashes. He is not flogged with a third set of lashes for the general prohibition. The Rambam concedes, though, that there are certain prohibitions of this kind for which one is flogged with a separate set of lashes for each detail due to an exposition of the verses or a tradition to this effect. See the Rambam's *Sefer HaMitzvot* for more discussion about this point.

If there was a general prohibition but the Torah subsequently listed each case individually, one is flogged separately for each one, and the fact that they are included in one prohibition on one occasion is disregarded. An example of this would be the prohibition: "You shall eat neither any fat nor any blood" (Leviticus 3:17). In this case, one is flogged for each of these, as both forbidden fat and blood are treated separately elsewhere in the Torah. According to *Tosafot*, if a specific prohibition is mentioned in connection with one of the detailed cases, this demonstrates that one is liable to receive lashes for each of them separately. According to the Ramban, if the general prohibition includes *halakhot* that belong to the same overall category, one is flogged separately for every item listed. According to Rashi, one is also flogged for each specific situation in cases where there are superfluous words in the Torah in that context (see Ran).

I state even in accordance with Rav Yehuda – אֲנָא דַּאֲמַרִי אֲפִילּוּ כְּרַב יְהוּדָה: The difference between the verse that is the subject of the dispute between Abaye and Rava and the verse that is the subject of the dispute between Rav Yehuda and Rav Huna is that the phrase "for he takes a man's life as collateral" is the Torah's explanation of the aforementioned prohibitions. In the case of the Paschal offering, the general statement is not an explanation of the earlier prohibitions, and therefore it is possible that one is liable to receive lashes for it (Rosh).

HALAKHA

One who ate raw and cooked – אָכַל נָא וּמְבוּשָּׁל: If one ate an olive-bulk of raw or cooked meat of the Paschal offering on Passover night, he is flogged. If he ate an olive-bulk of raw meat and an olive-bulk of cooked meat, he is flogged with only one set of lashes, as one is not flogged for a general prohibition. This is the ruling of the Rambam. The Ra'avad and the Ramban are puzzled as to why the Rambam rules in accordance with Abaye in opposition to Rava, which contravenes the accepted rules of *halakha*. According to the *Kesef Mishne*, the Rambam's version of the text had the opinions reversed from how they appear in the standard version of the text. The Ramban rules that he is flogged with two sets of lashes, in accordance with the opinion of Rava as it appears in the standard version of the text (Rambam *Sefer Korbanot*, *Hilkhot Korban Pesaḥ* 8:4 and *Sefer Shofetim*, *Hilkhot Sanhedrin* 18:3).

LANGUAGE

Scissors [*zog*] – זוֹג: This word originates from the Greek word ζυγόν, *zugon*, which refers to items that come in pairs. It was then borrowed by the Sages to refer to utensils that come in pairs, especially scissors.

יְתֵירָא הוּא, כֵּיוָן דִּיתֵירָא הוּא – שַׁדְיֵיהּ אַרֵיחַיִם וָרֶכֶב.

is superfluous[N] and therefore includes other utensils as well. **Since it is superfluous, apply it** as another prohibition **upon the lower and upper millstones.**

אֲבָל הָכָא "כִּי אִם צְלִי אֵשׁ" לָאו יְתֵירָא הוּא. דְּמִבָּעֵי לֵיהּ לְכִדְתַנְיָא: בְּשָׁעָה שֶׁיֶּשְׁנוֹ בְּקוּם אֱכוֹל צָלִי – יֶשְׁנוֹ בְּבַל "תֹּאכַל נָא"; בְּשָׁעָה שֶׁאֵינוֹ בְּקוּם אֱכוֹל צָלִי – אֵינוֹ בְּ"בַל תֹּאכַל נָא".

But here, with regard to the Paschal offering, the phrase **"but roasted with fire" is not superfluous, as he requires it for that which is taught** in a *baraita*: **At the time when one is included in** the mitzva **to arise** and **eat the roasted** Paschal offering,[H] **he is** also **included in** the prohibition **not to eat** of it **raw,** but **at a time when one is not included in** the mitzva **to arise** and **eat the roasted** Paschal offering, **he is not** included **in** the prohibition **not to eat** of it **raw** either. Consequently, one who eats the Paschal offering at that time is not liable to receive lashes.

תַּנְיָא כְּוָותֵיהּ דְּרַב יְהוּדָה: חָבַל זוֹג שֶׁל סַפָּרִים וְצֶמֶד שֶׁל פָּרוֹת – חַיָּיב שְׁתַּיִם. זֶה בְּעַצְמוֹ וְזֶה בְּעַצְמוֹ – אֵינוֹ חַיָּיב אֶלָּא אַחַת.

§ The Gemara returns to the dispute concerning the lower and upper millstones. It **is taught** in a *baraita* **in accordance with** the opinion **of Rav Yehuda:**[N] If one **took as collateral barbers' scissors** [*zog*][LN] **or a pair of cows,** he is **liable** to receive **two** sets of lashes. If he took **this** one blade of the pair of scissors **by itself** or **that** one cow **by itself,** he is **liable** to receive **only one** set of lashes. According to this *tanna,* he is not liable for the general prohibition.

וְתַנְיָא אִידָּךְ: חָבַל זוֹג שֶׁל סַפָּרִים וְצֶמֶד שֶׁל פָּרוֹת, יָכוֹל לֹא יְהֵא חַיָּיב אֶלָּא אַחַת – תַּלְמוּד לוֹמַר: "לֹא יַחֲבֹל רֵיחַיִם וָרָכֶב". מַה רֵיחַיִם וְרֶכֶב שֶׁהֵן מְיוּחָדִין, שְׁנֵי כֵלִים וְעוֹשִׂין מְלָאכָה אַחַת וְחַיָּיב עַל זֶה בִּפְנֵי עַצְמוֹ וְעַל זֶה בִּפְנֵי עַצְמוֹ – אַף כָּל דְּבָרִים שֶׁהֵן שְׁנֵי כֵלִים מְיוּחָדִים, וְעוֹשִׂין מְלָאכָה אַחַת – חַיָּיב עַל זֶה בִּפְנֵי עַצְמוֹ וְעַל זֶה בִּפְנֵי עַצְמוֹ.

And it is taught in **another** *baraita*: If one **took as collateral barbers' scissors or a pair of cows,** one **might** have thought that he is **liable** to receive **only one** set of lashes. Therefore, **the verse states: "He may not take as collateral the lower or upper millstone,"** which indicates that **just as the lower and upper millstones are unique** in that they are **two** distinct **vessels and** they **perform one task** together, and nevertheless one is **liable separately for this and separately for that, so too,** with regard to **all items that are** composed of **two individual vessels,** such as barbers' scissors or a pair of cows, **and they perform one task,** he is **liable separately for this and separately for that.**[H]

NOTES

Is superfluous – יְתֵירָא הוּא: Although Abaye here explained his opinion in accordance with the opinion of Rav Huna, it is clear that they generally maintain conflicting views, as according to Abaye one is not flogged for violating a general prohibition, whereas Rav Huna rules that one is flogged for violating such a prohibition (Rosh).

It is taught in a *baraita* in accordance with Rav Yehuda – תַּנְיָא כְּוָותֵיהּ דְּרַב יְהוּדָה: The commentaries point out that the proof from the *baraita* is refutable, which is why the Gemara does not present the *baraita* as a difficulty against the opinion of Rav Huna. Rav Huna could claim that these *baraitot* teach that one is liable twice for any vessel comprising two parts, but the *tanna* is not addressing the issue of exactly how many other prohibitions are involved (*Ein Yehosef*).

Barbers' [*shel sapparim*] scissors – זוֹג שֶׁל סַפָּרִים: Rabbeinu Tam altered the text here to read: Scissors used for cutting [*tisporet*], and explains that this refers to scissors used for cutting leaves of edible vegetables. This interpretation accords with his opinion, and that of most commentaries, that this prohibition applies only to utensils actually used in the preparation of food. The Ran maintains that the prohibition includes work tools required for the owner's main occupation and source of livelihood as well. According to this view, the Gemara may be understood in its straightforward sense, i.e., that it refers to a barber's scissors.

HALAKHA

At the time when one is included in the mitzva to arise and eat the roasted Paschal offering – בְּשָׁעָה שֶׁיֶּשְׁנוֹ בְּקוּם אֱכוֹל צָלִי: If one ate raw or cooked meat from the Paschal offering before the time for eating it had arrived, he is not liable to receive lashes, as he violates the prohibition only when the mitzva to eat it is in effect (Rambam *Sefer Korbanot*, *Hilkhot Korban Pesaḥ* 5:4).

One who took many vessels as collateral – חָבַל כֵּלִים הַרְבֵּה: If one seized several utensils used in the preparation of food as collateral, he is liable for every utensil. Even if he took two items that are joined together for the performance of one task, such as scissors used for cutting vegetables, he is liable for transgressing two prohibitions (Rambam *Sefer Mishpatim*, *Hilkhot Malve VeLoveh* 3:3; *Shulḥan Arukh*, *Ḥoshen Mishpat* 97:10).

הַהוּא גַּבְרָא דַּחֲבַל סַכִּינָא דְּאַשְׁכַּבְתָּא מֵחַבְרֵיהּ. אֲתָא לְקַמֵּיהּ דְּאַבַּיֵּי, אֲמַר לֵיהּ: זִיל אַהַדְרֵיהּ, דְּהָוֵי לֵיהּ כְּלִי שֶׁעוֹשִׂים בּוֹ אוֹכֶל נֶפֶשׁ, וְתָא קוּם בְּדִינָא עֲלָהּ. רָבָא אֲמַר: לָא צְרִיךְ לְמֵיקַם בְּדִינָא עֲלָהּ, וְיָכוֹל לִטְעוֹן עַד כְּדֵי דְּמֵיהֶן.

§ The Gemara relates: There was **a certain man who took as collateral a slaughtering knife**[N] **from another. He came before Abaye** to ask him what to do. Abaye **said to him: Go and return it,**[N] **as it is a vessel used in the preparation of food,**[H] and it is therefore forbidden to take as collateral, **and go stand in judgment,** i.e., litigate with the debtor in court, **concerning** how much money he owes you. **Rava said:** He does **not have to stand in judgment for this.**[H] Since the knife is in his possession, **he can claim** the amount of the debt **up to its value.**[N]

וְאַבַּיֵּי לֵית לֵיהּ הַהִיא סְבָרָא? מַאי שְׁנָא מֵהָנְהוּ עִיזֵּי דְּאָכְלִי חוּשְׁלָא בִּנְהַרְדְּעָא, וַאֲתָא מָרָא דְּחוּשְׁלָא וּתְפַס לְהוּ וְקָא טָעֵין טוּבָא. וַאֲמַר אֲבוּהּ דִּשְׁמוּאֵל: יָכוֹל לִטְעוֹן עַד כְּדֵי דְּמֵיהֶן.

The Gemara asks: **And does Abaye not accept that reasoning,** that one who seized an item belonging to a debtor may claim the sum owed to him up to the value of the item? In **what way is** it **different from** the incident involving **those goats that ate peeled barley** [*ḥushla*][L] **in Neharde'a, and the owner of the peeled barley came and seized** the goats and **claimed** that their owner was indebted to him for **a large** amount, **and Shmuel's father,** who acted as a judge in this case, **said** that **he can claim** a sum **up to their value?**

הָתָם לָאו מִידֵּי דְּעָבְדָא לְאוֹשׁוּלֵי וּלְאוֹגוּרֵי הוּא; הָכָא – מִידֵּי דַּעֲבִיד לְאוֹשׁוּלֵי וּלְאוֹגוּרֵי הוּא. דִּשְׁלַח רַב הוּנָא בַּר אָבִין: דְּבָרִים הָעֲשׂוּיִין לְהַשְׁאִיל וּלְהַשְׂכִּיר, וְאָמַר לְקוּחִין הֵן בְּיָדִי – אֵינוֹ נֶאֱמָן.

The Gemara answers that there is a difference between the two cases: **There,** a goat **is an item that is not usually lent**[H] out **or rented.** Consequently, the one who possesses them has a presumptive right of ownership upon which he can base his claim. Conversely, **here,** the slaughtering knife is **an item that** is **usually lent**[H] out **or rented.** Therefore, he is not deemed credible without proof that it is his merely by virtue of its being in his possession. The Gemara supports this distinction: **As Rav Huna bar Avin sent** the following ruling: In a case of **items that are usually lent** out **or rented,**[H] **and** one in possession of them **says: They were acquired by me, he is not deemed credible** by this claim alone. He must provide further proof, as he might have borrowed or rented them.

NOTES

A slaughtering [*ashkavta*] knife – סַכִּינָא דְּאַשְׁכַּבְתָּא: According to most authorities, this refers to a knife used for slaughtering, which is a utensil used in the preparation of food. A version of the text cited in the *Arukh* reads *ashkafta*, which would refer to a sandal maker's knife. This version is in accordance with the opinion that any tool that is vital for the performance of work is included in this prohibition.

Go and return it – זִיל אַהַדְרֵיהּ: The early commentaries explain that everyone agrees that one who retains possession of such vessels transgresses a prohibition each and every moment that he maintains them in his domain. This is the *halakha* even according to Abaye, who maintains (see *Temura* 4b) that if one transgressed a prohibition, the action is still legally effective (Mordekhai). One reason given for this *halakha* is that the verse states: "For he takes a man's life as collateral," in the present tense, which indicates that it is considered as though he takes it each and every moment (*Ma'ayanei HaḤokhma*).

Up to its value – עַד כְּדֵי דְּמֵיהֶן: The Ra'ah notes that he does not have to claim its full value, as he can demand less, but the Gemara refers to the usual case where a creditor in this situation would presumably claim the total value of the item. The *ge'onim* add that the creditor must still take an oath by Torah law, as the concern exists, since he is in possession of the items, that perhaps he will be brazen and claim more than the amount owed to him.

LANGUAGE

Peeled barley [*ḥushla*] – חוּשְׁלָא: This word refers to barley after its husks have been removed. In addition, elsewhere (*Yoma* 79a) it is indicated that this is the meaning of the word *ushla*, which is closely related to the word *ḥushla*. According to the *Arukh*, *ḥushla* is the correct version of the text there as well.

HALAKHA

The return of a vessel used in the preparation of food – הַחְזָרַת כְּלִי אוֹכֶל נֶפֶשׁ: If a creditor took as collateral a utensil used for the preparation of food, such as a millstone or a slaughtering knife, the court forces him to give it back. It is permitted to take other work tools as collateral (Rambam *Sefer Mishpatim, Hilkhot Malve VeLoveh* 3:3; *Shulḥan Arukh, Ḥoshen Mishpat* 97:8).

He does not have to stand in judgment for this – לָא צְרִיךְ לְמֵיקַם עֲלָהּ בְּדִינָא: If a creditor came to court holding collateral that he wanted to sell to receive compensation for the money owed him, the court does not obligate him to wait for the debtor to arrive and issue his claim, as the creditor can say he acquired the item. Instead, they offer him the advice that he should sell it in the presence of witnesses. In a case where there is a dispute between the creditor and the debtor concerning the sum of the debt, if the creditor is in possession of collateral in a manner that would enable him to claim ownership of it without the debtor being able to contest that claim, he is deemed credible when he says he lent the debtor up to the value of the item. In this case, he must take an oath while holding a sacred item. This ruling is in accordance with Rava, which is also the conclusion of the Gemara (Rambam *Sefer Mishpatim, Hilkhot Malve VeLoveh* 13:3 and *Hilkhot To'en VeNitan* 8:2; *Shulḥan Arukh, Ḥoshen Mishpat* 72:17).

An item that is not usually lent – לָאו מִידֵּי דְּעָבְדָא לְאוֹשׁוּלֵי: If the creditor had seized collateral that he cannot claim as his, and the debtor maintains that the creditor lent him less money than the latter contends, the debtor takes an oath, pays the amount that he admits he owes, and receives his collateral (Rambam *Sefer Mishpatim, Hilkhot To'en VeNitan* 8:3; *Shulḥan Arukh, Ḥoshen Mishpat* 72:18–19).

An item that is usually lent – מִידֵּי דַּעֲבִיד לְאוֹשׁוּלֵי: Items that are regularly lent or rented are always considered to be the possessions of their last known owners. Even if this particular owner often sells his vessels, in a case where there are witnesses that this specific item is lent regularly, the court removes it from the one currently holding it, unless he can provide proof that it was sold or given to him (Rambam *Sefer Mishpatim, Hilkhot To'en VeNitan* 8:3; *Shulḥan Arukh, Ḥoshen Mishpat* 90:11–13, 133:5).

Items that are usually lent or rented – דְּבָרִים הָעֲשׂוּיִין לְהַשְׁאִיל וּלְהַשְׂכִּיר: The early commentaries disagree over the definition of this category. According to the Rambam, it refers to items manufactured for this purpose, while the Rif and Rabbeinu Tam maintain that all items are included in this category apart from those that people are particular not to lend. The Rema, citing the *Tur*, states that in all such cases the local custom and the particular circumstances of the case at hand are both considered in rendering a decision (Rambam *Sefer Mishpatim, Hilkhot To'en VeNitan* 8:3; *Shulḥan Arukh, Ḥoshen Mishpat* 72:19, and in the comment of Rema).

וְרָבָא לֵית לֵיהּ הַאי סְבָרָא? וְהָא רָבָא אַפֵּיק זוּגָא דְּסַרְבְּלָא וְסִפְרָא דְּאַגַּדְתָּא מִיַּתְמֵי בִּדְבָרִים הָעֲשׂוּיִין לְהַשְׁאִיל וּלְהַשְׂכִּיר! אָמַר לָךְ רָבָא: הַאי נַמִּי, כֵּיוָן דְּמִיפַּגְמָא – קָפְדֵי אֱינָשֵׁי וְלָא מוֹשְׁלֵי.

הדרן עלך המקבל

The Gemara asks: **And does Rava not accept this reasoning? But didn't Rava** himself **remove scissors** used **for wool**[NB] **and a scroll of *aggada***[NB] **from** the possession of **orphans as items that are usually lent**[N] out **or rented?** The Gemara answers: **Rava** could have **said to you:** With regard to **this** slaughtering knife **too, since** it is likely to **be damaged, people are particular and do not lend** it out. Therefore, it is not considered an item that is typically lent out, and the one in possession of it can claim the money owed to him up to the value of the knife.

NOTES

Scissors for wool [*zugga desarbela*] – זוּגָא דְּסַרְבְּלָא: The *Arukh* records an alternative version of the text that reads: A pair of overalls [*zuza desarbela*].

A scroll of *aggada* – סִפְרָא דְּאַגַּדְתָּא: Rashi in tractate *Shevuot* (46b) explains that since these scrolls were not read on a regular basis but were opened only at rare intervals, they were not usually lent out.

Items that are usually lent – דְּבָרִים הָעֲשׂוּיִין לְהַשְׁאִיל: According to the Rambam, this refers to items that were manufactured for the purpose of being rented out. An example of such an item is a large vat, which was not used for private purposes but was rented out for feasts and the like. Other commentaries, by contrast, maintain that the term: Usually, indicates that the owner is not particular about the items and does not mind lending them.

BACKGROUND

Scissors for wool – זוּגָא דְּסַרְבְּלָא:

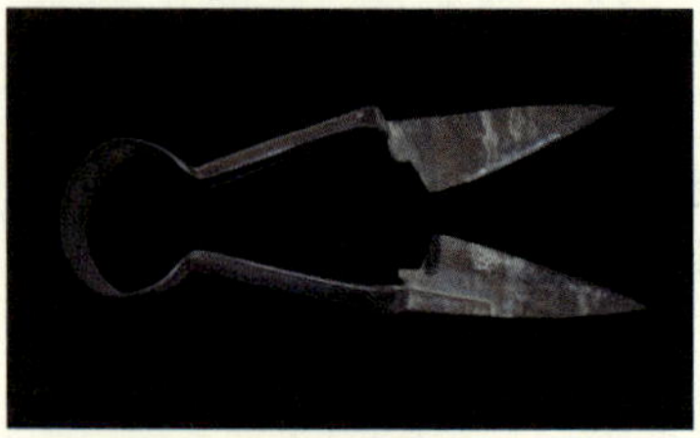

Reconstruction of Roman wool shears

A scroll of *aggada* – סִפְרָא דְּאַגַּדְתָּא: Generally, the term *aggada* is used for all sections of the Talmud that are not halakhic in nature and that are therefore not subject to any final, definitive ruling. Therefore, all the theological and philosophical discussions, stories about individuals, ethical guidance, and other such matters are included in this category, which is by no means homogeneous. Although Torah transmitted by oral tradition was generally not written down in scrolls that were copied and distributed, some individuals took notes in order to remember this material, or kept personal notes in private manuscripts. The scroll mentioned here was a set of notes of the Sages' expositions in *aggada* that may have been the basis for a collection of *aggada* such as the *Midrash Rabba*.

Summary of **Perek IX**

The first section of this chapter included discussions concerning the *halakha* that one does not deviate from the local custom, and any matter that is not addressed directly in the contract is presumed to be in accordance with the local custom. In addition, although the formulation of contracts is determined by the custom of the people in that location and the local vernacular, the Sages nevertheless attach special significance to the wording of these agreements and derive certain halakhic details from them. This is true not only of contracts concerning an agreement between a landowner and a cultivator but also for other cases where it is accepted to use a fixed text for the contract.

The Sages generally interpret the conditions of an agreement in the simplest manner and require the cultivator to abide by them, yet they do permit him to change the conditions in certain situations where the potential profit can also benefit the landowner. In addition, when a natural regional disaster occurs, the cultivator is exempt from his obligations. In any other situation, including circumstances beyond his control, the cultivator must abide by the rules of the agreement.

Following the discussion with regard to fields and the obligations of the cultivator to the landowner, the Gemara explored another topic that is related to the ownership of fields. The *halakha* known as the law of one whose field borders the field of his neighbor is based on the principle: "You shall do that which is right and good" (Deuteronomy 6:18), and dictates that when a field is put up for sale, those whose fields directly border it have the right of first refusal. This obligation is rooted in the concept that the court coerces individuals that exhibit conduct characteristic of Sodom; i.e., one may not prevent another from benefiting if no loss is suffered on his part. Therefore, the limitations to the law of one whose field borders the field of his neighbor are simple: In any case where the seller would suffer a loss of either money or time if he were to sell the property to his neighbor, he is not obligated to do so.

In the second section of the chapter, which addressed the *halakhot* of delaying payment of wages, it was established that for many type of payments, including wages for one's own labor and a rental fee of one's animal or utensils, the obligation of giving the payments takes effect immediately upon the completion of the term. If the employee demands his wages, the employer violates at least one prohibition and sometimes more if he delays the payment of wages for more than twelve hours, and in some exceptional cases if he delays for more than twenty-four hours. As an extension of the mitzva to pay a worker on time, the Sages instituted that in a case where there is some doubt as to whether the wages were paid or not, the employee may take an oath and receive his salary.

The Torah provides additional protection for the poor through the *halakhot* of taking collateral. It is prohibited for the creditor to enter the house of the debtor to take collateral. Rather, he must request that the debtor bring the collateral outside to him. In addition, if the debtor does not own other items similar to the collateral, the creditor must return the collateral to him at any time that he needs it, even daily. This is the *halakha* with regard to collateral that was appropriated to be used as security to ensure that the loan will be returned. These *halakhot* do not apply if the creditor takes items to be used as payment of the debt. Even in such cases, the court makes arrangements to help the debtor so that his most important utensils and critical work tools are not taken away.

The Torah renders it prohibited to take collateral in two situations: First, it is prohibited to take collateral from a widow. According to the practical halakhic conclusion, this is true for both a wealthy widow as well as a poor one. Second, it is prohibited to appropriate utensils that are used for the preparation of food. One who violates the latter of these prohibitions is liable for each utensil taken, and if the utensil consists of a pair of items, one is liable for both parts. Aside from the heavenly punishment received for this transgression, the court also forces him to return any item that he took without sanction.

Introduction to **Perek X**

This short chapter primarily deals with issues that arise from one situation: A house of two or more stories that belonged to different people and that collapsed entirely or partially.

If the house collapsed entirely, questions include how to divide the stones from the collapsed structure and what the owner of the upper story should do if the owner of the lower story refuses to rebuild his part.

In a case where only part of the structure collapsed, there are several questions as well. If the resident of the collapsed upper story is a renter, to what degree is he responsible to find another residence and to what degree is this the responsibility of the owner. Other questions pertain to a case where the floor separating two stories broke, and the repair work is divided between the residents of the upper and lower stories. These questions are not limited to a house, but to any case of two stories where one is built on top of the other, such as in the case of a garden that was built on top of another structure.

The cases of a structure that collapses into the property of someone else and one that collapses in the public domain are also discussed. In these situations, questions include who is obligated to clear away the debris, and whether or not it is permitted to pay the one who cleared the area with the materials that he cleared. A related discussion pertains to the proper use of the public domain for the sake of building, shipping, delivery, or any other use. In a case of materials that were delivered to the public domain, who is liable: the owner or the one that made the delivery? A related question concerns two adjacent gardens that are not on the same level. In such a case, to whom does the wall of soil between the two gardens belong, and who owns the vegetables that grow out of it?

These issues, as well as related topics that are connected to the discussions, are the subjects of this chapter.

מתני׳ הַבַּיִת וְהָעֲלִיָּיה שֶׁל שְׁנַיִם שֶׁנָּפְלוּ, שְׁנֵיהֶם חוֹלְקִין בָּעֵצִים וּבָאֲבָנִים וּבֶעָפָר, וְרוֹאִין אֵלּוּ אֲבָנִים הָעֲשׂוּיוֹת לְהִשְׁתַּבֵּר. אִם הָיָה אֶחָד מֵהֶן מַכִּיר מִקְצָת אֲבָנָיו – נוֹטְלָן, וְעוֹלוֹת לוֹ מִן הַחֶשְׁבּוֹן.

MISHNA In the case of **the house and the upper story belonging to two** people, i.e., the lower story was owned by one individual, while the upper story belonged to someone else, **that collapsed, the two of them divide**[H] **the timber and the stones**[N] **and the earth** of the collapsed structure. **And the** court **considers which stones were likely to break,** those of the lower or upper story, and gives those broken stones to the one who presumably owned them. **If one of them recognized some of his stones**[H] he may **take them** for himself, **and they count toward his amount** of stones, and the other party takes other stones accordingly. They do not divide the remaining stones equally.

גמ׳ מִדְּקָתָנֵי רוֹאִין – מִכְּלָל דְּאִיכָּא לְמֵיקַם עֲלַיְיהוּ אִי בַּחֲבָסָא נְפֵיל אִי בַּחֲבָטָא נָפֵיל.

GEMARA **From** the fact **that** the mishna **teaches** that the court **considers** which stones were likely to break, it can be understood **by inference** that the case is one in **which it is possible to establish with regard to** the stones, by looking at the debris, how the accident occurred: **Whether it fell with pressure** [*ḥavasa*],[L] i.e., the lower story collapsed, and the upper story followed, or **whether it fell with a blow,** i.e., the upper story collapsed, and caused the lower story to follow suit. In the first instance, it is the stones of the lower story that were likely to break, in the latter instance, the stones of the upper story.

אִי הָכִי, רֵישָׁא אַמַּאי חוֹלְקִין? נֶחֱזֵי: אִי בַּחֲבָטָא נָפֵיל – עִלָּיְיתָא אִיתְּבוּר; אִי בַּחֲבָסָא נָפֵיל – תַּתָּיְיתָא אִיתְּבוּר!

The Gemara asks: **If that is so,** that it is possible to ascertain how the collapse occurred, then **why,** in **the first clause** of the mishna, do they **divide** the stones without taking the circumstances into consideration? **Let us see: If** the house **fell with a blow,** it means that **the** stones of the **upper** story **broke,** and the owner of the lower story takes the unbroken stones. And **if it fell with pressure,** it means that the stones of **the lower** story **broke,** and the owner of the upper story takes the unbroken stones.

לָא צְרִיכָא, דְּנָפֵיל בְּלֵילְיָא. וְלֶחֱזֵינְהוּ בְּצַפְרָא! דְּפַנִּינְהוּ. וְלֶיחֱזֵי מַאן פַּנִּינְהוּ וְלִשַׁיְּילֵיהּ? דְּפַנִּינְהוּ בְּנֵי רְשׁוּת הָרַבִּים וְאָזְלוּ לְעָלְמָא.

The Gemara rejects this analysis: **No,** it is **necessary** to state the ruling of the mishna in a case **when** the house **collapsed at night,** and no one saw how it fell. The Gemara challenges: **But** in such a case, **let them see** the stones **in the morning** to ascertain how the house collapsed. The Gemara answers: The first clause of the mishna is referring to a case **where they had cleared** away the stones, and consequently there is no way to determine what occurred. The Gemara challenges: **But** even in such a case, **let them see who cleared them** away, **and let them ask them** what happened. The Gemara explains: The ruling of the first clause of the mishna is stated with regard to a case **where the general public cleared them** away **and left,** so that they cannot be asked.

NOTES

They divide the timber and the stones – חוֹלְקִין בָּעֵצִים וּבָאֲבָנִים: Older versions of Rashi's commentary indicate that the difference in size of the two stories is not taken into account in the division of materials, since there is no way of knowing which material came from which part of the house. Other commentaries explain that the materials are divided based on the size of the stories (Ramban; Rashba; see *Minḥat HaBoker*).

LANGUAGE

Pressure [*ḥavasa*] – חֲבָסָא: This is an Aramaic word related to the Aramaic *ḥavatz*, which refers to breaking an item by smashing it.

HALAKHA

The house and the upper story…the two of them divide – הַבַּיִת וְהָעֲלִיָּיה...שְׁנֵיהֶם חוֹלְקִים: If a house belonged to one individual and its upper story to another, and they both collapsed, the two owners divide the timber, stones, and earth. If one of the stories was taller than the other, that owner takes a proportionately larger share of the timber and stones (Rema, citing *Tur*). If some of the stones broke, the court determines whether they are from the lower story or from the upper story by looking at how the house collapsed. If it cannot be determined how it collapsed, they both divide both the unbroken and broken stones, in accordance with the mishna and the explanation of the Gemara (Rambam *Sefer Kinyan, Hilkhot Shekhenim* 4:2; *Shulḥan Arukh, Ḥoshen Mishpat* 164:3).

If one of them recognized some of his stones – אִם הָיָה אֶחָד מֵהֶן מַכִּיר מִקְצָת אֲבָנָיו: In the case where one of the two owners recognizes his stones and they are unbroken, if the other concedes to his claim, or if he concedes to part of his claim and with regard to the rest he says he doesn't know, the first party may take the stones that he recognizes. The second one is entitled to take a proportionate number of unbroken stones for himself, but he cannot object if the stones that the first recognized and took were of better quality, in accordance with the conclusion of Abaye. It would appear that if there were not enough unbroken stones left over equal to the amount that the first one took, then the second party suffers the loss (*Shulḥan Arukh, Ḥoshen Mishpat* 164:4 and *Sma* there).

NOTES

You have in my possession only fifty dinars – **אֵין לְךָ בְּיָדִי אֶלָּא חֲמִשִּׁים**: If one claims that another owes him money and the defendant admits that he owes part of the sum, then the defendant is obligated to take an oath that he owes no additional money and is then exempt from paying any more than he admitted. If he refuses to take the oath, he must pay the full amount of the claim. In the case of Rav Naḥman, the individual cannot take an oath that he does not owe the remainder of the claim, since he himself is unsure about it.

וְלֶיחֱזֵי בִּרְשׁוּת דְּמַאן יָתְבָן, וְלֶיהֱוֵי אִידָּךְ הַמּוֹצִיא מֵחֲבֵירוֹ עָלָיו הָרְאָיָה! לָא צְרִיכָא, דְּיָתְבָן בְּחָצֵר דְּתַרְוַיְיהוּ. אִי נַמִּי: בִּרְשׁוּת הָרַבִּים. וְאִיבָּעֵית אֵימָא: שׁוּתָּפִין בְּכִי הַאי גַּוְונָא לָא קָפְדֵי אַהֲדָדֵי.

The Gemara challenges: **But** even in such a case, **let them see in whose domain** the stones **are situated. And** once this is determined, the *halakha* will be that **the burden of proof rests upon the claimant**, i.e., the owner of the stones situated in the other's domain. The Gemara answers: **No,** it is **necessary** to state the ruling of the mishna in a case **where** the stones **are situated in a courtyard that** belongs to **both of them,** or **alternatively,** if the stones fell **into the public domain. And if you wish, say** that **partners in cases like this are not particular with each other** about dividing the courtyard in such a way that the one cannot leave his belongings on the other's side of the courtyard, and therefore the presence of the stones in the area of the courtyard belonging to one of them does not substantiate a claim for the stones.

״אִם הָיָה אֶחָד מֵהֶן מַכִּיר״ כו׳. וְהַלָּה מַה טוֹעֵן? אִי דְּקָאָמַר אִין – פְּשִׁיטָא! וְאִי לָא אֲמַר אִין – לָמָּה נוֹטֵל? אֶלָּא, דַּאֲמַר לֵיהּ: אֵינִי יוֹדֵעַ.

§ The mishna teaches: **If one of them recognized** his stones he may take them. The Gemara asks: **And the other, what** does **he claim? If he says: Yes,** they belong to the other, this *halakha* is **obvious,** so why would the mishna need to state this? **And if he does not say yes, why** does the one that recognizes the stones **take** them? What proof does he have that they are his? **Rather,** it must be **that** the other **says to him: I don't know** whose stones they are, and consequently, the one who stated a definitive claim is deemed credible.

לֵימָא תֶּהֱוֵי תְּיוּבְתָּא דְּרַב נַחְמָן? דְּאִיתְּמַר: מָנֶה לִי בְּיָדְךָ וְהַלָּה אוֹמֵר אֵינִי יוֹדֵעַ, רַב הוּנָא וְרַב יְהוּדָה אָמְרִי: חַיָּיב. רַב נַחְמָן וְרַבִּי יוֹחָנָן אָמְרִי: פָּטוּר.

The Gemara suggests: **Shall we say that it is a conclusive refutation** of the opinion **of Rav Naḥman?** As **it was stated** that the *amora'im* disagreed about the following case: With regard to one who approaches another and says: **I have one hundred dinars in your possession, and the other says: I don't know, Rav Huna and Rav Yehuda say:** The respondent is **liable** to pay, because he did not deny the claim. **Rav Naḥman and Rabbi Yoḥanan say:** He is **exempt** from payment. It appears from the mishna that the response: I don't know, is tantamount to an admission.

כִּדְאָמַר רַב נַחְמָן: כְּגוֹן שֶׁיֵּשׁ עֵסֶק שְׁבוּעָה בֵּינֵיהֶן – הָכָא נַמִּי כְּגוֹן שֶׁיֵּשׁ עֵסֶק שְׁבוּעָה בֵּינֵיהֶן.

The Gemara refutes this contention: Just **as Rav Naḥman says** in that context: He is liable to pay only in a case **where there is a matter of an oath between them, here too,** it is a case **where there is a matter of an oath between them.** In that case, Rav Naḥman rules that he is liable to pay only if he is already liable to take an oath concerning his denial of part of the claim. Since he does not know if he owes this sum, and he is therefore unable to take the oath he is liable to take, he must pay. In this case as well, the mishna is discussing a case where the one who says he does not know is liable to take an oath.

הֵיכִי דָּמֵי עֵסֶק שְׁבוּעָה? כִּדְרָבָא. דְּאָמַר רָבָא: מָנֶה לִי בְּיָדְךָ וְהַלָּה אוֹמֵר אֵין לְךָ בְּיָדִי אֶלָּא חֲמִשִּׁים וְהַשְּׁאָר אֵינִי יוֹדֵעַ, מִתּוֹךְ שֶׁאֵינוֹ יָכוֹל לִישָּׁבַע – יְשַׁלֵּם.

The Gemara asks: **What are the circumstances** of a **matter of an oath?** The Gemara explains: This **in accordance with** the statement **of Rava, as Rava says:** One who approaches another and says: **I have one hundred dinars in your possession, and the other says: You have in my possession only fifty** dinars[N] that I am sure about, **and** as for **the rest, I don't know.** As one who admitted to part of a claim, he is liable, by Torah law, to take an oath that he does not owe the other fifty dinars. **Since he cannot take an oath** to that effect, as he is unsure if he owes it, **he must pay.**

״וְעוֹלוֹת לוֹ מִן הַחֶשְׁבּוֹן״. סָבַר רָבָא לְמֵימַר: לְפִי חֶשְׁבּוֹן שְׁבוּרוֹת. אַלְמָא, כֵּיוָן דַּאֲמַר אֵינִי יוֹדֵעַ – רִיעַ טְפֵי.

§ The mishna teaches: If one of them recognized some of his stones he may take them for himself, **and they count toward his amount** of stones, and the other party takes other stones accordingly. **Rava thought to say** that this means they count **toward** his **amount** of his **broken** stones. In other words, the first party takes the unbroken stones he recognized, in place of a similar amount of broken stones, and the other party takes an amount of broken stones corresponding to the amount of unbroken stones claimed by the first person. **Apparently, since he said: I don't know,** his legal status **is worse.**

אֲמַר לֵיהּ אַבַּיֵּי: אַדְּרַבָּה, הָא רִיעַ טְפֵי. מִדְּהָנֵי יָדַע, טְפֵי לָא יָדַע – תּוּ לֵית לֵיהּ, וְאִידָּךְ כּוּלְּהוּ – דְּהֵיאַךְ נִינְהוּ.

Abaye said to him: On the contrary, this one, the one who recognizes some of his stones, **is worse** off. He is worse off **because since he knows** and recognizes **these** stones, **he** evidently **does not know** anything about any **more** stones, and therefore **he has no** rights to any **more** unbroken stones, **and all the others are** the property **of the other** party.

אֶלָּא אָמַר אַבָּיֵי: לְפִי חֶשְׁבּוֹן שְׁלֵימוֹת. אִי הָכִי מַאי קָמְהַנֵּי לֵיהּ? לְמַלְבְּנָא רְווֹחָא, אִי נַמִי טִינָא דִּמְעַבְדָא.

Rather, Abaye said that it means they count **toward** his **amount** of his **unbroken** stones. In other words, the first party takes the unbroken stones he recognized, in place of a similar amount of unbroken stones, and the other party takes an amount of unbroken stones corresponding to the amount of unbroken stones claimed by the first person. The Gemara asks: **If so, what did** the first party **gain** from recognizing his own stones? The Gemara answers: He gains with regard **to** bricks from the structure made in **a wide brick mold.**[B] If his bricks were constructed from a wider mold, he is entitled to these slightly larger ones. **Alternatively,** if the **clay** from which his bricks were formed was **processed** better, he gains by obtaining superior bricks.

מתני׳ הַבַּיִת וְהָעֲלִיָּיה, נִפְחֲתָה הָעֲלִיָּיה וְאֵין בַּעַל הַבַּיִת רוֹצֶה לְתַקֵּן – הֲרֵי בַּעַל הָעֲלִיָּיה יוֹרֵד וְדָר לְמַטָּה, עַד שֶׁיְּתַקֵּן לוֹ אֶת הָעֲלִיָּיה.

MISHNA If there was **a house and an upper story** owned by one person, and the upper story was rented out to another, if the floor of **the upper story was broken,**[N] i.e., it fell in or collapsed, **and the owner of the house does not want to repair it,**[H] **the resident of the upper story can go down and live** in the house **below until the** owner **repairs the upper story for him.**

רַבִּי יוֹסֵי אוֹמֵר: הַתַּחְתּוֹן נוֹתֵן אֶת הַתִּקְרָה, וְהָעֶלְיוֹן אֶת הַמַּעֲזִיבָה.

Rabbi Yosei says: With regard to a house of two stories owned by two people, i.e., the lower level was owned by one and the upper level by the other, in which the ceiling collapsed; the owner of **the lower** story **provides the ceiling** of beams or stones, **and** the owner of **the upper** story provides **the plaster.**

גמ׳ נִפְחֲתָה, בְּכַמָּה? רַב אָמַר: בְּרוּבָּהּ, וּשְׁמוּאֵל אָמַר: בְּאַרְבָּעָה.

GEMARA The Gemara asks: In the case of the floor of an upper story that **was broken, to what extent** did it break? What is the extent of damage that permits the upper resident to say that he is no longer able to live there? **Rav says: Most of it** was damaged, **and Shmuel says:** A break **of four** handbreadths occurred.

רַב אָמַר: בְּרוּבָּהּ, אֲבָל בְּאַרְבָּעָה – לָא, אָדָם דָּר חֶצְיוֹ לְמַטָּה וְחֶצְיוֹ לְמַעְלָה. וּשְׁמוּאֵל אָמַר: בְּאַרְבָּעָה, אֵין אָדָם דָּר חֶצְיוֹ לְמַטָּה וְחֶצְיוֹ לְמַעְלָה.

The Gemara analyzes their opinions. **Rav says: Most of it** was damaged, **but** if the break is only **of four** handbreadths, this *halakha* does **not** apply, since the owner of the upper story can use the lower story to place the item that would normally be placed in the area of the hole, and **a person** can **reside partially** on a level **below and partially** on a level **above.** In other words, the upper story remains inhabitable even if he must use the lower story to house some of his belongings. **And Shmuel says** a break **of four** handbreadths is sufficient for the *halakha* to apply, since **a person cannot reside partially** on a level **below and partially** on a level **above.**

הֵיכִי דָמֵי? אִי דַּאֲמַר עֲלִיָּיה זוֹ – אָזְדָא. אֶלָּא דַּאֲמַר לֵיהּ עֲלִיָּיה סְתָם – לוֹגַר לֵיהּ אַחֲרִיתִי!

The Gemara asks: **What are the circumstances** of the case in the mishna? **If** the owner **said** at the time of the rental that he is renting **this upper story** to the tenant, the tenant has rights only to this upper story, and he has **lost** the ability to live there. **Rather,** the owner **said to him** that he wants to rent **an upper story** to him, **without specifying** which one. If so, the renter is certainly entitled to functional living quarters, and the owner **must rent him** an upper story in **a different** house belonging to this owner where he can live.

אָמַר רָבָא: לָא צְרִיכָא, דַּאֲמַר לֵיהּ עֲלִיָּיה זוֹ שֶׁאֲנִי מַשְׂכִּיר לְךָ, כִּי סָלְקָא – סְלֵיק בַּהֲדָהּ, וְכִי נָחֵית – חוּת בַּהֲדָהּ. אִי הָכִי, מַאי לְמֵימְרָא?

The Gemara answers: **Rava says: No,** it is **necessary** to state the ruling of the mishna in a case **where** the owner **said to him: This upper story that I am renting to you, when it is up,** i.e., functional, live **up there in it, and when it descends,** i.e., it is no longer functional, **descend with it** and live in the lower story. The Gemara asks: **If so, what** is the purpose **of** the mishna **stating** this ruling, as there was an explicit condition to this effect?

אֶלָּא אָמַר רַב אַשִׁי: דַּאֲמַר לֵיהּ עֲלִיָּיה זוֹ שֶׁעַל גַּבֵּי בַּיִת זֶה אֲנִי מַשְׂכִּיר לְךָ, דְּהָא שַׁעְבֵּיד בַּיִת לַעֲלִיָּיה.

The Gemara answers: **Rather, Rav Ashi said:** This is a case **where** the owner **said to him: I am renting to you this** particular **upper story, which is on top of this** particular **house.**[H] As by emphasizing that the upper story is above that particular house, the owner thereby **rendered the house as liened with regard to the upper story,** although he did not explicitly state that the renter will have the right to live in the house were the upper story to become non-functional.

BACKGROUND

A wide brick mold [*malbena*] – מַלְבְּנָא רְווֹחָא: During the time of the Talmud, bricks were produced by hand using molds in order to make the bricks of uniform size. A brick mold, the *malben*, was a box into which clay was poured. It was generally rectangular in shape but occasionally other shapes were used according to the type of brick needed. The clay was first mixed with cut straw for reinforcement. The mixture was then pressed into the *malben* and then removed to dry in the sun or in an oven.

NOTES

A house and an upper story, if the floor of the upper story was broken – הַבַּיִת וְהָעֲלִיָּיה נִפְחֲתָה הָעֲלִיָּיה: It is clear from the context and from the Gemara that this case is referring to an upper story that was rented out, although the subsequent *mishnayot* revert back to discussing the case of a house and upper story owned by two people. Since this *halakha* of a rented place is similar to the case of a house and upper story owned by two people and it fits in well with the overall topic, the *tanna* mentions it here (Ramban).

HALAKHA

If the floor of the upper story was broken and he did not want to repair it – נִפְחֲתָה הָעֲלִיָּיה וְלֹא רָצָה לְתַקֵּן: If someone rented an upper story to another and the floor broke, if it has a hole an area of four handbreadths or more, the owner must fix it. The renter may descend and live with the owner in his apartment until it is fixed, in accordance with the opinion of Shmuel, as the *halakha* follows Shmuel in his disputes with Rav with regard to monetary law (Rambam *Sefer Kinyan*, *Hilkhot Sekhirut* 5:8; *Shulḥan Arukh*, *Ḥoshen Mishpat* 312:18).

This upper story which is on top of this house – עֲלִיָּיה זוֹ שֶׁעַל גַּבֵּי בַּיִת זֶה: If one rents an upper story to a tenant without specifying which upper story, and the one he was living in collapsed, the owner is obligated to provide the tenant with another upper story in which to live. If the owner had said: This upper story, i.e., he specified one particular upper story, and it collapsed, he does not have to provide him with another one, and the tenant pays him for the time that he lived there (*Sma*, citing *Tur*). If the owner said: This upper story that is on top of this house, he is obligated to fix it, in accordance with the statement of Rav Ashi (Rambam *Sefer Kinyan*, *Hilkhot Sekhirut* 5:8; *Shulḥan Arukh*, *Ḥoshen Mishpat* 312:18).

וְכִי הָא דַּאֲמַר רָבִין בַּר רַב אַדָּא אֲמַר רַבִּי יִצְחָק: מַעֲשֶׂה בְּאֶחָד שֶׁאָמַר לַחֲבֵירוֹ דָּלִית שֶׁעַל גַּבֵּי פַּרְסֵק זֶה אֲנִי מוֹכֵר לְךָ, וְנֶעֱקַר הַפַּרְסֵק, וּבָא מַעֲשֶׂה לִפְנֵי רַבִּי חִיָּיא וַאֲמַר: חַיָּיב אַתָּה לְהַעֲמִיד לוֹ פַּרְסֵק, כׇּל זְמַן שֶׁהַדָּלִית קַיְּימָא.

The Gemara adds: **And this is in accordance with that** which **Ravin bar Rav Adda said** that **Rabbi Yitzḥak said:** There was **an incident involving one who said to another: I am selling to you the vine that is on top of this peach tree** [*parsek*],[HL] **and** then **the peach tree was uprooted. And the incident came before Rabbi Ḥiyya, and he said: You are obligated to erect for him a peach tree** to support the vine, **as long as the vine exists.**

בָּעֵי רַבִּי אַבָּא בַּר מֶמֶל:

§ **Rabbi Abba bar Memel raised a dilemma:**

LANGUAGE

Peach tree [*parsek*] – פַּרְסֵק: From the Greek μῆλον Περσικον, *melon persikon*, sometimes just called Περσικον, *persikon*, which means peach. The word is phonetically related to Persia, as this fruit was widely cultivated there.

HALAKHA

A vine that is on top of a peach tree – דָּלִית שֶׁעַל גַּבֵּי פַּרְסֵק: An incident occurred in which one said to another that he is renting him this vine hanging on this peach tree, and the tree was subsequently uprooted. When the case came before the Sages they obligated the owner to provide him with a peach tree to support the vine. If the peach tree was completely chopped down, he does not have to provide him with another (Rambam *Sefer Kinyan*, *Hilkhot Sekhirut* 5:8; *Shulḥan Arukh*, *Ḥoshen Mishpat* 312:20, and in the comment of Rema).

Perek **X**
Daf **117** Amud **a**

כְּשֶׁהוּא דָּר, לְבַדּוֹ הוּא דָּר כִּדְמֵעִיקָּרָא? אוֹ דִּלְמָא שְׁנֵיהֶם דָּרִין, דְּאָמַר לֵיהּ: אַדַּעֲתָא לְאַפְּקִינַן – לָא אָגְרִי לָךְ?

With regard to a resident of the upper story who is entitled to move into the lower story, **when he resides** there,[H] does **he reside alone as** he did **at the outset** when he occupied the upper story, and the owner of the house has no choice but to move out? **Or perhaps they both reside** there together, as the owner can **say to him: I did not rent** the upper story to you **with the intention of being removed** from my domicile.

אִם תִּמְצָא לוֹמַר שְׁנֵיהֶם דָּרִין בּוֹ, כְּשֶׁהוּא מִשְׁתַּמֵּשׁ – דֶּרֶךְ פְּתָחִים מִשְׁתַּמֵּשׁ אוֹ דֶּרֶךְ גַּגִּין מִשְׁתַּמֵּשׁ? מִי אָמַר: כִּדְמֵעִיקָּרָא, מָה מֵעִיקָּרָא – דֶּרֶךְ גַּגִּין, הָשְׁתָּא נַמִי – דֶּרֶךְ גַּגִּין. אוֹ דִּלְמָא מָצֵי אָמַר לֵיהּ: עֲלִיָּיה – קַבִּילִי עֲלַאי, עֲלִיָּיה וִירִידָה – לָא קַבִּילִי עֲלַאי.

If you **say** that **they both reside there, when** the upper-story resident **uses** the house, does he **use** it by **way of** its **entrances,** like the owner, **or** must he **use** it by **way of** the **roofs?** Must he climb the stairs and enter the upper story, and then descend to the house from there? **Can** the owner **say:** The tenant must act **as** he did **at the outset; just as at the outset** he entered by **way of the roofs, now too,** he must enter by **way of the roofs? Or perhaps** the renter **can say to him: I accepted upon myself an ascent** and agreed to climb the stairs to the upper story, but **I did not accept upon myself an ascent and a descent,** which would be necessary if I entered by way of the roofs.

אִם תִּמְצָא לוֹמַר, מָצֵי אָמַר לֵיהּ: עֲלִיָּיה וִירִידָה לָא קַבִּילִי עֲלַאי, שְׁתֵּי עֲלִיּוֹת זוֹ עַל גַּב זוֹ מַהוּ? אִיפְּחִית עֶלְיוֹנָה – נָחֵית וְדָר בַּתַּחְתּוֹנָה. אִיפְּחִית תַּחְתּוֹנָה מַהוּ לְמִיסְלַק לְגַמְרֵי בָּעֶלְיוֹנָה?

If you **say** that the tenant **can say to** the owner: **I did not accept upon myself an ascent and a descent,** in a case where there were **two upper stories, this one on top of that** one,[H] **what is** the *halakha*? The Gemara clarifies the circumstances of this case: **If the** floor of the **higher** upper story **was broken,** clearly he may **descend and reside in the lower** one, but if **the** floor of the **lower** upper story **was broken, what is** the *halakha*? Is he required **to ascend** the **full** way and reside **in the higher** upper story, or does he go down to reside on the ground floor?

מִי אָמְרִינַן, דְּאָמַר לֵיהּ: שֵׁם עֲלִיָּיה קַבֵּילִית עֲלָךְ? אוֹ דִּלְמָא: חַד עֲלִיָּיה – קַבֵּיל עֲלֵיהּ, שְׁתֵּי עֲלִיּוֹת – לָא קַבֵּיל עֲלֵיהּ? תֵּיקוּ.

Do we say that the owner of the house can **say to** the tenant: **You accepted upon yourself the term: An upper story,** and I have provided one for you? **Or perhaps** one says that the tenant **accepted upon himself one ascent, but he did not accept upon himself two ascents.** No answer was found for these questions, and the Gemara concludes: These dilemmas **shall stand** unresolved.

״רַבִּי יוֹסֵי אוֹמֵר הַתַּחְתּוֹן נוֹתֵן אֶת הַתִּקְרָה״ כו׳. מַאי תִּקְרָה? רַבִּי יוֹסֵי בַּר חֲנִינָא אָמַר: קִינִּים וּסְנָאִין. וּסְטִינִי אָמַר רַבִּי שִׁמְעוֹן בֶּן לָקִישׁ: לְווֹחִים. וְלָא פְּלִיגִי, מָר כִּי אַתְרֵיהּ וּמָר כִּי אַתְרֵיהּ.

§ The mishna teaches: **Rabbi Yosei says: The lower** resident **provides the ceiling** and the upper resident provides the plaster. The Gemara asks: **What is** the word **ceiling** referring to[N] in this context? **Rabbi Yosei bar Ḥanina says: Mats and beams. And** the Sage **Setini**[L] **says** that **Rabbi Shimon ben Lakish says: Wide wooden planks.** The Gemara comments: **And** these two opinions **do not disagree** over the basic *halakha*; rather, this **Sage** rules **in accordance with** the custom of **his locale and** this **Sage in accordance with** the custom of **his locale,** and they each were describing the necessary materials for a ceiling, according to the local building conventions.

HALAKHA

When he resides there – כְּשֶׁהוּא דָּר: If an upper story collapsed and the owner of the house was deemed liable to rebuild it, in the meantime the former tenant of the upper story may reside with the owner in his house, but the tenant cannot evict the owner of the house from his own home. While living there he may enter and exit in the usual manner, and he does not have to come in through the upper story (Rambam *Sefer Mishpatim*, *Hilkhot Sekhirut* 5:8; *Shulḥan Arukh*, *Ḥoshen Mishpat* 312:18).

Two upper stories, this one on top of that one – שְׁתֵּי עֲלִיּוֹת זוֹ עַל גַּב זוֹ: If there were two upper stories, and the higher one collapsed, its tenant may move into the lower one, i.e., the middle floor. If the lower story of the two upper stories collapsed, i.e., the middle floor, it is uncertain whether he moves into the higher one, i.e., the third floor, or the house below, i.e., the ground floor. Therefore, he may not live in the house below. If he does move into the ground floor, he cannot be evicted, as this dilemma is left unresolved in the Gemara (Rambam *Sefer Mishpatim*, *Hilkhot Sekhirut* 5:8; *Shulḥan Arukh*, *Ḥoshen Mishpat* 312:19).

NOTES

What is the word ceiling [*tikra*] referring to – מַאי תִּקְרָה: According to the version of the Gemara cited by the *Arukh*, the question is: What is plaster [*ma'aziva*]? In the *Musaf HeArukh* it is explained that it was well known what the term *tikra* refers to, whereas with regard to the term *ma'aziva* it was necessary to clarify what exactly is included. Is only the upper coating included or is the base upon which it rests also considered part of it?

LANGUAGE

Setini – סְטִינִי: There are various opinions as to the correct text of the Gemara. According to one reading, the word is *vetina*, meaning: And clay, where the word *tin* or *tit* means clay. According to that explanation, this word is a continuation of the previous sentence and indicates that to build a roof, first reeds were placed, which were subsequently covered with clay.

According to other readings, Setini is the name of a Sage who stated the subsequent opinion. The name Setini is a shortened form of the Latin name Justinus, meaning a righteous man who acts with justice, similar to the Hebrew Shoftaya. The Jerusalem Talmud occasionally cites this name in the abbreviated form, Yosta.

הָנְהוּ בֵּי תְּרֵי דְּהָווּ דָּיְירִי, חַד עִילַּאי וְחַד תַּתַּאי. אִיפְּחִית מַעֲזִיבָה. כִּי מָשֵׁי מַיָּא עִילַּאי – אָזְלִי וּמַזְּקִי לְתַתַּאי. מִי מְתַקֵּן? רַבִּי חִיָּיא בַּר אַבָּא אָמַר: הָעֶלְיוֹן מְתַקֵּן, וְרַבִּי אֶלְעַאי מִשּׁוּם רַבִּי חִיָּיא בְּרַבִּי יוֹסֵי אָמַר: הַתַּחְתּוֹן מְתַקֵּן. וְסִימָן "וְיוֹסֵף הוּרַד מִצְרָיְמָה".

§ The Gemara relates: An incident occurred with **these two** people **who were residing** in the same house, **one** in the **upper** story, **and** the other **one** in the **lower** story. The **plaster** of the floor of the upper story **broke,** so that **when** the resident of **the upper** apartment would **wash** with **water,** it would **run down**[H] **and** cause **damage to the lower** story. The question was: **Who** must **repair** the ceiling? **Rabbi Ḥiyya bar Abba says: The upper** resident **repairs** it, **and Rabbi Elai says in the name of Rabbi Ḥiyya, son of Rabbi Yosei: The lower** resident **repairs** it. The Gemara comments: **And** the following verse can serve as **a mnemonic** device to remember who issued which ruling: **"And Joseph was brought down to Egypt"** (Genesis 39:1). Rabbi Ḥiyya, son of Rabbi Yosei, indicated by Joseph, is the Sage who maintains that the owner of the lower story, indicated by: Brought down, must repair the ceiling.

לֵימָא רַבִּי חִיָּיא בַּר אַבָּא וְרַבִּי אֶלְעַאי בִּפְלוּגְתָּא דְּרַבִּי יוֹסֵי וְרַבָּנַן קָמִיפַּלְגִי? לְמַאן דְּאָמַר הָעֶלְיוֹן מְתַקֵּן – קָסָבַר: עַל הַמַּזִּיק לְהַרְחִיק אֶת עַצְמוֹ מִן הַנִּיזָּק, וּמַאן דְּאָמַר תַּחְתּוֹן מְתַקֵּן – קָסָבַר: עַל הַנִּיזָּק לְהַרְחִיק אֶת עַצְמוֹ מִן הַמַּזִּיק.

The Gemara suggests: **Shall we say** that **Rabbi Ḥiyya bar Abba and Rabbi Elai disagree with regard to the** matter subject to **dispute** between **Rabbi Yosei and the Rabbis** in the mishna? The explanation of the dispute would then be as follows: **According to the one who says** that **the upper** resident **repairs** it, **he holds** that the responsibility is **on the one** potentially **responsible for the damage to distance himself from the** one whose property is potentially **damaged.** This accounts for the opinion of Rabbi Yosei in the mishna, who holds that the resident of the upper story must provide the plaster, because his water is clearly causing damage below. **And the one who says** that **the lower** resident **repairs** it, **he holds** like the Rabbis, who say that the responsibility is **on the** one whose property is potentially **damaged to distance himself from the one** potentially **responsible for the damage.**

וְתִיסְבְּרָא רַבִּי יוֹסֵי וְרַבָּנַן לְעִנְיַן נְזָקִין פְּלִיגִי? וְהָא אִיפְּכָא שָׁמְעִינַן לְהוּ, דִּתְנַן: מַרְחִיקִין אֶת הָאִילָן מִן הַבּוֹר עֶשְׂרִים וְחָמֵשׁ אַמָּה. וּבֶחָרוּב וּבַשִּׁקְמָה – חֲמִשִּׁים אַמָּה, בֵּין מִלְמַעְלָה בֵּין מִן הַצַּד. אִם הַבּוֹר קָדַם – קוֹצֵץ וְנוֹתֵן דָּמִים; אִם הָאִילָן קָדַם – לֹא יָקוֹץ. סָפֵק זֶה קָדַם סָפֵק זֶה קָדַם – לֹא יָקוֹץ.

The Gemara asks: **And** how can **you understand** it that way? Do **Rabbi Yosei and the Rabbis disagree** in the mishna **with regard to** distancing oneself from **damages? But haven't we heard them** say **the opposite? As we learned** in a mishna (*Bava Batra* 25b): **One must distance a tree twenty-five cubits from a pit,** because its roots damage the pit, **and** in the case **of a carob or sycamore** tree, whose roots spread far, one must distance it by **fifty cubits.** This is the *halakha* **whether** the pit or tree **is** located **above or to the side** of the other. **If the pit preceded** the tree, the owner of the pit **may cut down** the tree **and pay** its **monetary** value. **If the tree preceded** the pit, then **he may not cut** it **down.** If it is **uncertain** whether **this** tree **preceded** that pit, and it is **uncertain** whether **that** pit **preceded** this tree, **he may not cut down** the tree.

רַבִּי יוֹסֵי אוֹמֵר: אַף עַל פִּי שֶׁהַבּוֹר קוֹדֶמֶת לָאִילָן – לֹא יָקוֹץ, שֶׁזֶּה חוֹפֵר בְּתוֹךְ שֶׁלּוֹ, וְזֶה נוֹטֵעַ בְּתוֹךְ שֶׁלּוֹ. אַלְמָא, רַבִּי יוֹסֵי סָבַר: עַל הַנִּיזָּק לְהַרְחִיק אֶת עַצְמוֹ, וְרַבָּנַן סָבְרִי: עַל הַמַּזִּיק לְהַרְחִיק אֶת עַצְמוֹ.

Rabbi Yosei says: Even if the pit preceded the tree, he may not cut it **down.** Why is that? **As this one digs in his own** property, **and that one plants in his own** property. Consequently, the owner of the pit cannot complain about the damage, and if he wants to avoid it, he can dig his pit elsewhere. **Apparently,** this mishna indicates that **Rabbi Yosei holds** that the responsibility is **on the** one whose property is potentially **damaged to distance himself**[H] from the one potentially responsible for the damage, **and the Rabbis hold** that the responsibility is **on the one** potentially **responsible for the damage to distance himself** from the one whose property is potentially damaged.

HALAKHA

Water from the upper story that runs down – מַיִם מֵהָעֲלִיָּיה שֶׁיּוֹרְדִים לְמַטָּה: In a case where water from the upper story was leaking and causing damage to the lower story, if it was falling directly into the lower story, then the owner of the upper story is obligated to repair the leak, since it is like an arrow shot by the one responsible for the damage. If the water was not falling directly into the lower story, but was absorbed by the plaster before making its way downward, the owner of the upper story is not obligated to repair the leak. The Rema, citing the Mordekhai, writes that it depends on the case: If there is only a small amount of water that evaporates soon after entering the lower story, the owner of the upper story is not obligated to repair the leak; but if there is a constant flow of water, then even if it descends by way of the plaster, he must repair the leak (Rambam *Sefer Kinyan, Hilkhot Shekhenim* 10:6; *Shulḥan Arukh, Ḥoshen Mishpat* 155:4).

Responsibility is on the one whose property is potentially damaged to distance himself – עַל הַנִּיזָּק לְהַרְחִיק אֶת עַצְמוֹ: If one has a tree in his field next to his neighbor's pit, or if he wants to plant a tree there, the owner of the pit cannot object. This is because it is not the responsibility of the one potentially responsible for the damage to distance himself from causing any damage that does not immediately occur as a result of his actions. This applies to all similar cases, in accordance with the opinion of Rabbi Yosei (Rambam *Sefer Kinyan, Hilkhot Shekhenim* 10:5; *Shulḥan Arukh, Ḥoshen Mishpat* 155:31–32).

אֶלָּא, אִי אִיכָּא לְמֵימַר פְּלִיגִי – בִּפְלוּגְתָּא דְּרַבִּי יוֹסֵי וְרַבָּנַן דְּהָתָם קָמִיפַּלְגִי.

Rather, if it can be said that these *amora'im* **disagree** with regard to the issue that is the subject of the dispute between these *tanna'im*, then **they disagree in the dispute between Rabbi Yosei and the Rabbis there,** concerning the question of who is obligated to distance himself from the damage, but it has nothing to do with the dispute in the mishna here.

וְרַבִּי יוֹסֵי וְרַבָּנַן דְּהָכָא בְּמַאי פְּלִיגִי? בְּחוֹזֶק תִּקְרָה קָמִיפַּלְגִי. רַבָּנַן סָבְרִי: מַעֲזִיבָה אַחְזוּקֵי תִּקְרָה הוּא, וְאַחְזוּקֵי תִּקְרָה עַל הַתַּחְתּוֹן בָּעֵי לְאַחֲזוּקֵי. וְרַבִּי יוֹסֵי סָבַר: מַעֲזִיבָה אַשְׁוּוּיֵי גּוּמּוֹת הוּא, וְאַשְׁוּוּיֵי גּוּמּוֹת עַל הָעֶלְיוֹן לְאַשְׁוּוּיֵי.

The Gemara asks: **And with regard to what** principle **do Rabbi Yosei and the Rabbis of** the mishna **here disagree?** The Gemara answers: **They disagree with regard to the strength of a ceiling. The Rabbis hold** that the function of the **plaster is** to **strengthen the ceiling, and strengthening the ceiling** is the obligation **of the lower** resident, as he is **required to strengthen** it.[H] **And Rabbi Yosei holds** that the function of the **plaster is** to **level out** any **holes,** so that the surface of the ceiling will be flat, **and leveling out holes** it is the obligation **of the upper** resident, as he is required **to level** them **out.**

אִינִי? וְהָאָמַר רַב אַשִׁי: כִּי הֲוֵינָא בֵּי רַב כָּהֲנָא הֲוָה אָמְרִינַן: מוֹדֶה רַבִּי יוֹסֵי בְּגִירֵי דִּילֵיהּ!

The Gemara challenges the above conclusion: **Is that so? But didn't Rav Ashi say: When I was in the school of Rav Kahana we would say** that **Rabbi Yosei concedes** in a case **of his arrows.** Although Rabbi Yosei holds that the responsibility is on the one whose property is potentially damaged to distance himself from the one potentially responsible for the damage, that is only if the one causing the damage is not performing a direct action that is causing the damage, as in the case of the tree and the pit. But if he is performing an action that causes damage from a distance, as in this case, where the water he pours damages the resident of the lower story, he is like someone shooting arrows, who is certainly obligated to ensure that he does not cause any damage.

דְּפָסְקֵי מַיָּא וְהָדַר נָפְלֵי.

The Gemara answers: This is a case in **which the water** flow **stops** in one place, as the hole in the floor is not directly in the place where the water was poured, **and subsequently** it **falls** into the lower story once it flows to the opening in the floor. Consequently, even in this case, the upper resident does not directly cause the damage.

מתני׳ הַבַּיִת וְהָעֲלִיָּיה שֶׁל שְׁנַיִם שֶׁנָּפְלוּ, אָמַר בַּעַל הָעֲלִיָּיה לְבַעַל הַבַּיִת לִבְנוֹת וְהוּא אֵינוֹ רוֹצֶה לִבְנוֹת – הֲרֵי בַּעַל הָעֲלִיָּיה בּוֹנֶה אֶת הַבַּיִת וְדָר בְּתוֹכָהּ, עַד שֶׁיִּתֵּן לוֹ אֶת יְצִיאוֹתָיו.

MISHNA In the case of **the house and the upper story belonging to two** different people, and **that** house and upper story **collapsed,** and **the owner of the upper story told the owner of the house to build** the lower story in order to enable him to rebuild the upper story, **and he does not want to build** it,[H] **the owner of the upper story** may **build the house and reside in it, until** the other **gives him his expenses** for the construction of the house, and he then rebuilds his upper story.

רַבִּי יְהוּדָה אוֹמֵר: אַף זֶה דָּר בְּתוֹךְ שֶׁל חֲבֵירוֹ, צָרִיךְ לְהַעֲלוֹת לוֹ שָׂכָר. אֶלָּא, בַּעַל הָעֲלִיָּיה בּוֹנֶה אֶת הַבַּיִת וְאֶת הָעֲלִיָּיה, מְקָרֶה אֶת הָעֶלְיוֹנָה וְיוֹשֵׁב בַּבַּיִת עַד שֶׁיִּתֵּן לוֹ אֶת יְצִיאוֹתָיו.

Rabbi Yehuda says: This one too, i.e., the owner of the upper story, who is meanwhile **residing inside** the property **of the other, must pay him rent.** Since he derived benefit by living in the house of the other, as he had no other place in which he could live, he must pay rent. This solution is therefore flawed. **Rather, the owner of the upper story builds the house and the upper story,** and he **roofs the upper** story, i.e., he completes the entire construction of the upper story, **and he** may then **sit in the house,** i.e., the lower story, **until** the other **gives him his expenses** for the building of the house, at which point he returns to his upper story. Since in any event he could have lived in the upper story, he is not considered to have derived any benefit by living in the lower story, and is not obligated to pay rent.

HALAKHA

Is the plaster the obligation of the lower resident or the upper one – **מַעֲזִיבָה חוֹבַת תַּחְתּוֹן אוֹ עֶלְיוֹן:** The plaster is part of the support of the ceiling. Therefore, if it develops a hole of four handbreadths, the owner of the lower story is obligated to repair it, in accordance with the opinion of the Rabbis (Rambam *Sefer Mishpatim*, *Hilkhot Sekhirut* 6:4; *Shulḥan Arukh*, *Ḥoshen Mishpat* 314:1).

The house and the upper story belonging to two…and he does not want to build – **הַבַּיִת וְהָעֲלִיָּיה שֶׁל שְׁנַיִם...וְהוּא אֵינוֹ רוֹצֶה לִבְנוֹת:** If a house and its upper story, which belonged to two different people, collapsed, and the owner of the upper story told the owner of the house to rebuild his house so that he can rebuild his upper story, and the latter was unwilling to do so, the owner of the upper story may rebuild the house and live there until the owner of the house reimburses him for all of his expenses. Then, the owner of the upper story rebuilds the upper story (Rambam *Sefer Mishpatim*, *Hilkhot Sekhirut* 4:3; *Shulḥan Arukh*, *Ḥoshen Mishpat* 164:5).

גמ׳ אָמַר רַבִּי יוֹחָנָן: בִּשְׁלֹשָׁה מְקוֹמוֹת שָׁנָה לָנוּ רַבִּי יְהוּדָה אָסוּר לְאָדָם שֶׁיֵּהָנֶה מִמָּמוֹן חֲבֵירוֹ. חֲדָא – הָא דְּתְנַן.

GEMARA **Rabbi Yoḥanan says: In three places Rabbi Yehuda taught us** the principle that it is **forbidden for a person to derive benefit from the property of another** without his full awareness and consent, even if the other does not suffer a loss. **One** of the places where we are taught this principle is **that which we learn** in the mishna, that Rabbi Yehuda does not allow one to reside in another's property without paying him rent.

אִידָךְ מַה הִיא? דִּתְנַן: הַנּוֹתֵן צֶמֶר לְצַבָּע לִצְבּוֹעַ לוֹ אָדוֹם וּצְבָעוֹ שָׁחוֹר, שָׁחוֹר וּצְבָעוֹ אָדוֹם, רַבִּי מֵאִיר אוֹמֵר: נוֹתֵן לוֹ דְּמֵי צַמְרוֹ. רַבִּי יְהוּדָה אוֹמֵר: אִם הַשֶּׁבַח יוֹתֵר עַל הַהוֹצָאָה – נוֹתֵן לוֹ הַיְּצִיאָה וְאִם הַהוֹצָאָה יְתֵירָה עַל הַשֶּׁבַח – נוֹתֵן לוֹ אֶת הַשֶּׁבַח.

What is another place where we are taught this principle from Rabbi Yehuda's statements? **As we learned** in a mishna (*Bava Kamma* 100b): If **one gives wool to a dyer**[B] to dye it **red for him and** instead **he dyed it black,**[H] or to dye it **black and he dyed it red, Rabbi Meir says:** The dyer **gives** the owner of the wool **the value of his wool. Rabbi Yehuda says: If** the value of **the enhancement exceeds the** dyer's **expenses,** the owner of the wool **gives** the dyer **the expenses. And if the expenses exceed the enhancement, he gives him** the value of **the enhancement.** But the dyer may not keep the dyed wool for himself, as it is forbidden for one to benefit from another's property.

וְאִידָךְ מַאי הִיא? דִּתְנַן: מִי שֶׁפָּרַע מִקְצָת חוֹבוֹ וְהִשְׁלִישׁ אֶת שְׁטָרוֹ, וְאָמַר לוֹ: אִם אֵין אֲנִי נוֹתֵן לָךְ מִכָּאן וְעַד זְמַן פְּלוֹנִי – תֵּן לוֹ שְׁטָרוֹ. הִגִּיעַ זְמַן וְלֹא נָתַן, רַבִּי יוֹסֵי אוֹמֵר: יִתֵּן. רַבִּי יְהוּדָה אוֹמֵר: לֹא יִתֵּן.

And what is the other, third place where we are taught this principle from Rabbi Yehuda's statements? **As we learned** in a mishna (*Bava Batra* 168a): In a case of a debtor **who repaid part of his debt, and he deposited** the promissory **note with a third party**[H] serving as a trustee, to ensure that the creditor not collect the full amount, **and** the debtor **said to** the trustee: **If I do not give you** the balance **from now until such and such a time, give** the creditor **his** promissory **note,** thereby enabling him to collect the full amount stated in the note; if the stipulated **time arrived and** the debtor **has not given** the balance to the trustee, **Rabbi Yosei says:** The trustee **shall give** the promissory note to the creditor, in accordance with the debtor's stipulation. **Rabbi Yehuda says:** The trustee **shall not give** it, as the stipulation is void. Here too, the reason is that the creditor is forbidden to benefit from the property of another.

אַמַּאי? דִּלְמָא עַד כָּאן לָא קָאָמַר רַבִּי יְהוּדָה הָכָא – אֶלָּא מִשּׁוּם דְּאִיכָּא שַׁחֲרוּרִיתָא.

The Gemara refutes these proofs as to the general applicability of Rabbi Yehuda's rulings. **Why** is it necessary to explain in this manner? **Perhaps Rabbi Yehuda** is **saying** this **only here,** with regard to the case of the mishna concerning a house and an upper story, **only because there is** the **blackening** of the walls. By using the house, the owner of the upper story causes its walls to blacken, thereby lowering its value, and yet he will ultimately claim the value of a new house that he built. Therefore, he is prohibited from using the house without paying.

אִי נַמִי לִצְבּוֹעַ לוֹ אָדוֹם וּצְבָעוֹ שָׁחוֹר – מִשּׁוּם דְּקָא מְשַׁנֶּה, וְהָתְנַן: כׇּל הַמְשַׁנֶּה יָדוֹ עַל הַתַּחְתּוֹנָה.

Alternatively, if one attempts to prove a general principle from the case where one instructed a dyer **to dye** the wool **for him red and he dyed it black,** it can be explained that the reason for the ruling of Rabbi Yehuda is **due to** the fact that the dyer **is changing** and deviating from the owner's instructions, **and didn't we learn** in a mishna (76a) that **whoever changes** the terms accepted by both parties **is at a disadvantage?**

וּמִי שֶׁפָּרַע מִקְצָת חוֹבוֹ נַמִי, הָוֵי אַסְמַכְתָּא, וְשָׁמְעִינַן לֵיהּ לְרַבִּי יְהוּדָה דְּאָמַר לָא קָנֵי.

And as for the case of **one who repaid part of his debt,** there **too,** the reason the trustee may not transfer the promissory note is not as explained above. Rather, it is due to the fact that the transfer of the promissory note and subsequent collection of the entire sum if he does not repay on time **is** considered **a transaction with inconclusive intent** [*asmakhta*], a condition that an individual accepts upon himself as an exaggerated measure that he does not expect to have to fulfill, **and we heard Rabbi Yehuda who says** that an ***asmakhta* does not effect acquisition.** There is therefore no proof that Rabbi Yehuda holds that it is forbidden for one to benefit from the money of another.

BACKGROUND

If one gives wool to a dyer – הַנּוֹתֵן צֶמֶר לְצַבָּע: In mishnaic times, wool was ordinarily dyed, as opposed to being bleached or used in its natural color. Most often, professional dyers would receive laundered fleece and would dye the wool according to the customer's specifications. Occasionally, it would occur that even an expert dyer might produce wool that had a darker hue than was ordered. A reason for this could be that the pot used for the dying had been used previously and there was some remnant of the dye absorbed in the pot. Alternatively, the usage of a pot made of certain material could itself affect the color of the final product. The mishna refers to this undesired darker hue as black. If the shade of the wool turned out to be unacceptable to the owner of the wool, the final product may end up being worthless, or, at any rate, worth less than the cost of the dye that was used.

HALAKHA

If one gives wool to a dyer to dye it red for him, and he dyed it black – הַנּוֹתֵן צֶמֶר לְצַבָּע לִצְבּוֹעַ לוֹ אָדוֹם וּצְבָעוֹ שָׁחוֹר: If one gives wool to a dyer to dye it red for him and instead he dyed it black, if the value of the enhancement exceeds the dyer's expenses, the owner of the wool gives the dyer the expenses. If the expenses exceed the enhancement, he gives him the value of the enhancement, in accordance with the opinion of Rabbi Yehuda, as the *halakha* follows Rabbi Yehuda when in opposition to Rabbi Meir (Rambam *Sefer Mishpatim*, *Hilkhot Sekhirut* 10:4; *Shulḥan Arukh*, *Ḥoshen Mishpat* 306:3).

One who repaid part of his debt and he deposited the promissory note with a third party – מִי שֶׁפָּרַע מִקְצָת חוֹבוֹ וְהִשְׁלִישׁ אֶת שְׁטָרוֹ: If one paid his debt in part, and deposited the promissory note with a third party with the instruction that if he fails to pay the remaining sum by a certain date, the third party should give the document to the creditor; the third party may not hand over the document on that date, as a condition of this kind is an *asmakhta* (Rambam *Sefer Kinyan*, *Hilkhot Mekhira* 11:5; *Shulḥan Arukh*, *Ḥoshen Mishpat* 55:1, 207:12).

אָמַר רַב אַחָא בַּר אַדָּא מִשְּׁמֵיהּ דְּעוּלָּא: תַּחְתּוֹן הַבָּא לְשַׁנּוֹת בְּגְוִיל – שׁוֹמְעִין לוֹ; בְּגָזִית – אֵין שׁוֹמְעִין לוֹ;

§ **Rav Aḥa bar Adda says in the name of Ulla:** In the case of a resident of the **lower** story who wishes to rebuild the collapsed house, **who comes to change**[H] the structure and now seeks to rebuild it **with untrimmed stones** that are larger than the original ones, the court **listens to him** and accepts his wishes, since an adjustment of this kind only serves to benefit the owner of the upper story. But if the house was previously built with large untrimmed stones and he now wants to rebuild it **with hewn stones,**[B] which are smaller, the court **does not listen to him,**[N] as this reduces the strength of the building.

בִּכְפִיסִין – שׁוֹמְעִין לוֹ; בִּלְבֵנִים – אֵין שׁוֹמְעִין לוֹ. לְסַכֵּךְ בַּאֲרָזִים – שׁוֹמְעִין לוֹ; בְּשִׁקְמִים – אֵין שׁוֹמְעִין לוֹ.

Similarly, if the house was formerly built with bricks, and he wants to rebuild it **with girders,**[B] the court **listens to him,** as this type of wall is very stable. But if the house was previously built with girders, and he now wants to rebuild it **with bricks,** the court **does not listen to him.** If he wants **to roof** it **with** strong **cedar wood,** the court **listens to him,** but if he wants to roof it **with sycamore** wood, instead of cedar, the court **does not listen to him.**

לְמַעֵט בַּחַלּוֹנוֹת – שׁוֹמְעִין לוֹ; לְהַרְבּוֹת בַּחַלּוֹנוֹת – אֵין שׁוֹמְעִין לוֹ; לְהַגְבִּיהַּ – אֵין שׁוֹמְעִין לוֹ; לְמַעֵט – שׁוֹמְעִין לוֹ.

If he wants **to reduce** the number **of windows,** the court **listens to him,** as this will strengthen the walls, but if he wants **to increase** the number **of windows,** the court **does not listen to him.** If he wants **to heighten** the building, the court **does not listen to him,** as it might be less stable than before, but if he wants **to reduce** its height, the court **listens to him.**

עֶלְיוֹן שֶׁבָּא לְשַׁנּוֹת בְּגָזִית – שׁוֹמְעִין לוֹ; בְּגְוִיל – אֵין שׁוֹמְעִין לוֹ;

The *halakha* is the same in the reverse: In the case of a resident of the **upper** story **who comes to change**[H] the structure, and wishes to rebuild the upper story **with hewn stones** instead of large untrimmed stones, the court **listens to him,** as this reduces the weight on the lower floor. But if he wants to change from smaller hewn stones and rebuild **with** larger **untrimmed stones,** the court **does not listen to him,** as this would make the upper story heavier.

בִּכְפִיסִין – אֵין שׁוֹמְעִין לוֹ; בִּלְבֵנִים – שׁוֹמְעִין לוֹ; בַּאֲרָזִים – אֵין שׁוֹמְעִין לוֹ; בְּשִׁקְמָה – שׁוֹמְעִין לוֹ. לְרַבּוֹת בַּחַלּוֹנוֹת – שׁוֹמְעִין לוֹ; לְמַעֵט בַּחַלּוֹנוֹת – אֵין שׁוֹמְעִין לוֹ; לְהַגְבִּיהַּ – אֵין שׁוֹמְעִין לוֹ; לְמַעֵט – שׁוֹמְעִין לוֹ.

Likewise, if he wants to rebuild it **with girders** instead of bricks, the court **does not listen to him,** but if it was previously built with girders, and he now wants to rebuild it **with bricks,** the court **listens to him.** If he wants to roof it **with** heavy **cedar wood,** the court **does not listen to him,** but if he wants to roof it **with sycamore** wood instead of cedar, the court **listens to him.** If he wants **to increase** the number **of windows,** which would lessen the weight of the construction, the court **listens to him,** but if he wants **to reduce the** number **of windows,** the court **does not listen to him.** If he wants **to heighten** the building, the court **does not listen to him,** as this increases the weight of the building, but if he wants **to reduce** its height, the court **listens to him.**

NOTES

The court does not listen to him – אֵין שׁוֹמְעִין לוֹ: Rabbeinu Yeruḥam maintains that this applies only if the change is solely the wish of the one rebuilding. But if it was the local custom to build in this manner, he may make the change even if the previous structure was built differently. The logic is that he can claim that since the house was previously built in an improper fashion he cannot be compelled to restore it to its prior state.

HALAKHA

A lower resident who comes to change – תַּחְתּוֹן הַבָּא לְשַׁנּוֹת: If a house and its upper story collapsed, and the owner of the house wants to rebuild it in a manner different from its former state, he is allowed to do so only if the changes would strengthen the construction of the house, such as by widening the walls or decreasing the number of windows. But if the proposed changes would not strengthen the house, his request is not accepted (Rambam *Sefer Kinyan, Hilkhot Shekhenim* 4:5; *Shulḥan Arukh, Ḥoshen Mishpat* 164:6).

An upper resident who comes to change – עֶלְיוֹן שֶׁבָּא לְשַׁנּוֹת: If the owner of the upper story wants to rebuild the upper story in a manner different from its former state, he can make changes only if they lessen the weight of the building, but not changes that would increase its weight. The Rema, citing the *Tur,* adds that if his proposed changes to the building were in line with the local custom, he may rebuild it in that manner regardless (Rambam *Sefer Kinyan, Hilkhot Shekhenim* 4:5; *Shulḥan Arukh, Ḥoshen Mishpat* 164:7).

BACKGROUND

Untrimmed stones, hewn stones – גְּוִיל, גָּזִית: Both of these types of stones were used for building purposes but there was a difference in their form. Hewn stones were dressed and straightened, and were typically two and a half handbreadths wide. Untrimmed stones, although also cut square, were not trimmed on all sides and would bulge out in some directions. Their standard width was three handbreadths.

Girders – כְּפִיסִים: This word, possibly with a different meaning, appears in this verse: "For the stone shall cry out of the wall, and the beam [*vekhafis*] out of the timber shall answer it" (Habakkuk 2:11). In rabbinic Hebrew, it refers to half-bricks arranged in two parallel rows, generally separated by the space of about one handbreadth, which was filled with stones and limestone. A wall of this kind was much stronger than a plain brick one.

אֵין לוֹ לָזֶה וְלֹא לָזֶה, מַאי? תַּנְיָא: אֵין לוֹ לֹא לָזֶה וְלֹא לָזֶה – אֵין לוֹ לְבַעַל עֲלִיָּיה בַּקַּרְקַע כְּלוּם.

§ The Gemara poses a question: If they are so poor that **neither this one nor that one has**[NH] enough money to rebuild it, and they are prepared to sell the land, **what** is the *halakha*? The Gemara answers: It **is taught** in a *baraita*: If **neither this one nor that one has** the money to rebuild the house, **the owner of** the **upper story does not have any** rights **to the land,** and all rights of the land belong to the owner of the lower story.

תַּנְיָא – רַבִּי נָתָן אוֹמֵר: תַּחְתּוֹן נוֹטֵל שְׁנֵי חֲלָקִים, וְהָעֶלְיוֹן שְׁלִישׁ. וַאֲחֵרִים אוֹמְרִים: תַּחְתּוֹן נוֹטֵל שְׁלֹשָׁה חֲלָקִים, וְהָעֶלְיוֹן נוֹטֵל רְבִיעַ. אָמַר רַבָּה: נְקוֹט דְּרַבִּי נָתָן בִּידָךְ, דְּדַיָּינָא הוּא וְנָחֵית לְעוּמְקָא דְּדִינָא. קָא סָבַר: כַּמָּה מַפְסִיד עֲלִיָּיה בַּבַּיִת? תִּילְתָּא; הִלְכָּךְ אִית לֵיהּ תִּילְתָּא.

It **is taught** in a different *baraita*: **Rabbi Natan**[P] **says:** The resident of the **lower** story **takes two shares** of the land, **and the** resident of the **upper** story takes **one-third. And others say:** The resident of the **lower** story **takes three shares, and the** resident of the **upper** story **takes one-quarter. Rabba says: Take** the statement **of Rabbi Natan in your hand, because he is a judge, and he descends to the depths of the law. He maintains: How much** does the presence of the **upper story depreciate** the value[N] **of the house? One-third. Therefore he has one-third,** i.e., he is entitled to one-third of the total sum that they receive for the land.

מתני׳ וְכֵן בֵּית הַבַּד שֶׁהוּא בָנוּי בַּסֶּלַע, וְגִינָּה אַחַת עַל גַּבָּיו וְנִפְחַת – הֲרֵי בַעַל הַגִּינָּה יוֹרֵד וְזוֹרֵעַ לְמַטָּה, עַד שֶׁיַּעֲשֶׂה לְבֵית בַּדּוֹ כִּיפִּין.

MISHNA **And likewise,** in the case of **an olive press that is built** inside a cave **in a rock,**[N] **and one garden,** belonging to another person, was planted **on top of it,**[B] **and** the roof of the olive press **broke,**[H] which caused the garden to collapse inward, in such a case, **the owner of the garden** may **descend and sow below until** the other one **constructs for his olive press** sturdy **arches** to support the roof, so that the owner of the garden can once again sow above him.

הַכּוֹתֶל וְהָאִילָן שֶׁנָּפְלוּ לִרְשׁוּת הָרַבִּים וְהִזִּיקוּ – פָּטוּר מִלְּשַׁלֵּם. נָתְנוּ לוֹ זְמַן לָקוֹץ אֶת הָאִילָן וְלִסְתּוֹר אֶת הַכּוֹתֶל וְנָפְלוּ, בְּתוֹךְ הַזְּמַן – פָּטוּר; לְאַחַר הַזְּמַן – חַיָּיב.

The mishna continues: In the case of **a wall or a tree that fell into the public domain and caused damage,**[H] the owner is **exempt**[N] **from** having **to pay,** as it was an accident. If the court saw that the wall was shaky, or that the tree was tilting, and **they gave him time to cut down the tree or to dismantle the wall, and** then **they fell** down, if this occurred **during the** allotted **time,** he is **exempt,** but if they collapsed **after the time** given to him had elapsed, he is **liable** to pay, since he was warned against this very occurrence.

NOTES

Neither this one nor that one has – אֵין לוֹ לָזֶה וְלֹא לָזֶה: According to Rashi, this refers to a case where the owner of the land wants to sell the property. He can therefore claim that the owner of the upper story has no actual right to the land itself, but only to the airspace above the lower floor, and consequently he has no say in the sale of the property. Other commentaries maintain that this refers even to a case where the owner of the lower story wanted to sell the land for the purpose of building a house, but the purchaser does not want to construct an upper story. The idea is that since the owner of the upper story cannot build himself, it would be conduct characteristic of Sodom were he to prevent the construction of the house. *Tosafot* disagree and explain that this is a case where the owner of the land wishes to sow the land, and the owner of the upper story wishes to sow part of the land too.

How much does the upper story depreciate the value – כַּמָּה מַפְסִיד עֲלִיָּיה: Rav Amram Gaon, cited by the *Arukh*, explains that the upper story is the cause of the shortening of the lifespan of the house by one-third. Consequently, the evaluation of the value of the upper story is based on this ratio and the rights of the owner to the land are calculated accordingly.

An olive press that is built in a rock – בֵּית הַבַּד שֶׁהוּא בָּנוּי בַּסֶּלַע: According to Rashi, this refers to an olive press and a garden that belong to two separate people. *Tosafot* maintain that the one using the garden was a renter. With regard to the *halakha* itself, the consensus among the authorities is that there is no difference between partners and a renter (see *Tur*).

A wall or a tree that fell into the public domain and caused damage, he is exempt – הַכּוֹתֶל וְהָאִילָן שֶׁנָּפְלוּ לִרְשׁוּת הָרַבִּים וְהִזִּיקוּ פָּטוּר: He is exempt from payment for all forms of damage caused, both for direct damage caused by the collapse, as well as any harm caused by the resulting stumbling block. This cannot be compared to a pit that one dug, since a pit by definition is a potential source of harm, whereas a wall and a tree are not initially dangerous. Consequently, if the wall was initially erected in an unsafe manner, he would be liable for all damage that it caused when it fell (*Nimmukei Yosef*).

HALAKHA

Neither this one nor that one has – אֵין לוֹ לָזֶה וְלֹא לָזֶה: If two people own a house and an upper story that collapsed, and they cannot afford to rebuild it, the owner of the house takes two-thirds of the land, while the owner of the upper story takes one-third. The same *halakha* applies if they agreed to sell the land, that the owner of the house takes two-thirds of the money received, while the owner of the upper story takes one-third, in accordance with the opinion of Rabbi Natan (Rambam *Sefer Mishpatim, Hilkhot Shekhenim* 4:4; *Shulḥan Arukh, Ḥoshen Mishpat* 164:5, and in the comment of Rema).

An olive press that is built in a rock and one garden was planted on top of it, and the roof broke – בֵּית הַבַּד שֶׁהוּא בָּנוּי בַּסֶּלַע, וְגִינָּה אַחַת עַל גַּבָּיו וְנִפְחַת: If an olive press was built into a rock, with a garden belonging to someone else above it, and the olive press collapsed, the owner of the garden may descend and sow below until the owner of the olive press builds arches to support it, at which point the owner of the garden returns above, fixes the ground, and sows his plants (Rambam *Sefer Mishpatim, Hilkhot Shekhenim* 4:8; *Shulḥan Arukh, Ḥoshen Mishpat* 165:1).

A wall or a tree that fell into the public domain and caused damage – הַכּוֹתֶל וְהָאִילָן שֶׁנָּפְלוּ לִרְשׁוּת הָרַבִּים וְהִזִּיקוּ: If a wall or a tree fell into the public domain and caused harm, the owner is exempt from payment. The Rema adds, citing *Tosafot*, that this *halakha* applies only if it was initially built or planted properly. If the tree or wall was in danger of falling, and the court set a time period for him to chop down the tree or to dismantle the wall, and the tree or wall fell before the court's deadline, the owner is exempt. But if the tree or the wall collapsed after the deadline, he is liable for all damage caused by the collapse. This *halakha* applies only if the court itself warned him, but not if he was told by others (Rambam *Sefer Nezikin, Hilkhot Nizkei Mamon* 13:19; *Shulḥan Arukh, Ḥoshen Mishpat* 416:1, and in the comment of Rema).

PERSONALITIES

Rabbi Natan – רַבִּי נָתָן: This is Rabbi Natan HaBavli, one of the great *tanna'im* of the generation preceding the redaction of the Mishna. Rabbi Natan was the son of the Exilarch of Babylonia, whose family traced their descent back to King David. Due to his greatness in Torah and prestigious lineage, Rabbi Natan was appointed *Av Beit Din*, the head of the court, the second highest position in the Sanhedrin. Along with Rabbi Meir, Rabbi Natan tried to change the procedure for the inheritance of the position of *Nasi*, i.e., the president of the Sanhedrin, and to become the new *Nasi*. The attempt failed, and as a sort of punishment, his name is omitted from the Mishna and his opinion is prefaced with the anonymous moniker: There are those who say (see *Horayot* 13b). In reality, this principle is not always upheld in the Mishna. Rabbi Natan compiled several collections of *mishnayot*, and the tractate *Avot DeRabbi Natan* is named for him. He had many disciples, the most noted of which was Rabbi Yehuda HaNasi.

BACKGROUND

An olive press and a garden on top of it – בֵּית הַבַּד וְגִינָּה עַל גַּבָּיו:

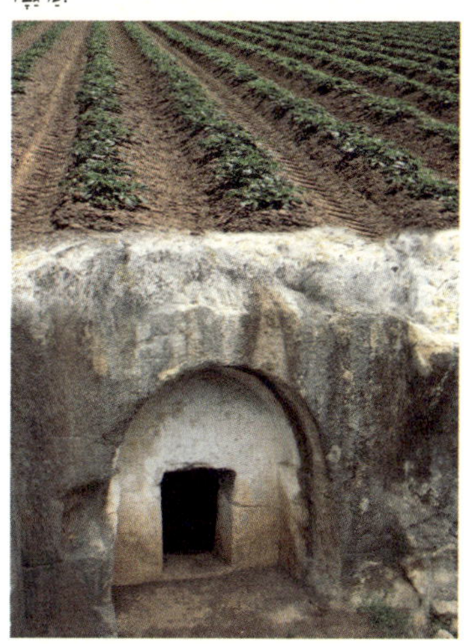

Garden situated atop a cave, which houses an olive press

מִי שֶׁהָיָה כּוֹתְלוֹ סָמוּךְ לְגִינַּת חֲבֵירוֹ וְנָפַל, וְאָמַר לוֹ: פַּנֵּה אֲבָנֶיךָ, וְאָמַר לוֹ:

In the case of **one whose wall was adjacent to another's garden,**[H] **and** the wall **fell, and** the owner of the garden **said to him: Clear** away **your stones, and** the owner of the stones **said to him:**

HALAKHA

One whose wall was adjacent to another's garden – מִי שֶׁהָיָה כּוֹתְלוֹ סָמוּךְ לְגִינַּת חֲבֵירוֹ: If one's wall fell into his neighbor's garden, the owner of the wall is obligated to clear away the stones. If he said to the owner of the garden: Remove the stones and they are yours, the court does not listen to him. If the owner of the garden agreed and cleared away the stones, and the owner of the wall subsequently changed his mind and wanted his stones, for which he would pay him the expense of their removal, the court does not listen to him. But if the owner of the garden hasn't yet removed them, even if the owner of the wall had told him: Remove the stones and they are yours, and they are in his courtyard, he has not acquired ownership of the stones (Rambam *Sefer Kinyan*, *Hilkhot Shekhenim* 3:8; *Shulḥan Arukh*, *Ḥoshen Mishpat* 166:1).

HALAKHA

One who hires a laborer…take what you have worked with as your wages – הַשּׂוֹכֵר אֶת הַפּוֹעֵל...טוֹל מַה שֶּׁעָשִׂיתָ בִּשְׂכָרְךָ: If one hires a laborer to work with his property, or to gather up ownerless property, he cannot tell him: Take what you accomplished as your wages. If the laborer accepted these terms, and the employer later wishes to retract, the court does not listen to him if the worker has performed an act of acquisition by pulling or lifting, or if the items were in his domain (Rambam *Sefer Mishpatim*, *Hilkhot Sekhirut* 9:10; *Shulḥan Arukh*, *Ḥoshen Mishpat* 336:2).

הַגִּיעוּךְ – אֵין שׁוֹמְעִין לוֹ. מִשֶּׁקִּבֵּל עָלָיו, אָמַר לוֹ: הֵילָךְ אֶת יְצִיאוֹתֶיךָ, וַאֲנִי אֶטּוֹל אֶת שֶׁלִּי – אֵין שׁוֹמְעִין לוֹ.

They are yours, as I hereby declare them ownerless, and you can take them for yourself; the court **does not listen to him,** since he cannot force the other to acquire the stones. If **after** the owner of the garden voluntarily **accepted** ownership of the stones **upon himself,** the owner of the wall **said to him: Here you are,** take **your expenditures** for the removal of the stones, **and I will take** the stones that are **mine;** the court **does not listen to him,** as they had already been acquired by the owner of the garden.

הַשּׂוֹכֵר אֶת הַפּוֹעֵל לַעֲשׂוֹת עִמּוֹ בְּתֶבֶן וּבְקַשׁ, וְאָמַר לוֹ: תֵּן לִי שְׂכָרִי, וְאָמַר לוֹ: טוֹל מַה שֶּׁעָשִׂיתָ בִּשְׂכָרְךָ – אֵין שׁוֹמְעִין לוֹ. מִשֶּׁקִּבֵּל עָלָיו, וְאָמַר לוֹ: הֵילָךְ שְׂכָרְךָ וַאֲנִי אֶטּוֹל אֶת שֶׁלִּי – אֵין שׁוֹמְעִין לוֹ.

The mishna continues: In the case of **one who hires a laborer to do** work **with him with hay or with straw, and** after he finished the task, the laborer **said to** the employer: **Give me my wages, and** the employer **said to him: Take what you have worked with as your wages,**[H] i.e., take some of the hay or straw as payment, the court **does not listen to him.** Although debts can be paid with any item of value, even hay or straw, the wages of a laborer must be paid in accordance with the initial agreement between the laborer and the employer. But if **after** the laborer **accepted upon himself** to keep the hay or straw as payment, the employer changed his mind **and said to him: Here you are,** take **your wages and I will take** what is **mine;** the court **does not listen to him,** since the laborer had already acquired the hay.

גמ׳ נִפְחֲתָה – רַב אָמַר: בְּרוּבָּהּ, וּשְׁמוּאֵל אָמַר: בְּאַרְבַּע. רַב אָמַר: בְּרוּבָּהּ, אֲבָל בְּאַרְבַּע – אָדָם זוֹרֵעַ חֶצְיוֹ לְמַטָּה וְחֶצְיוֹ לְמַעְלָה. וּשְׁמוּאֵל אָמַר: בְּאַרְבַּע. אֵין אָדָם זוֹרֵעַ חֶצְיוֹ לְמַטָּה וְחֶצְיוֹ לְמַעְלָה.

GEMARA With regard to the case of the roof of the olive press that **was broken,** the Gemara cites a dispute with regard to the amount that collapsed: **Rav says: Most of it** must have collapsed, **and Shmuel says:** Even a hole **of four** handbreadths is sufficient for the ruling of the mishna to apply. **Rav says: Most of it** must have collapsed, **but** if it is only a hole **of four** handbreadths, there is no basis for a claim, since **a person** can **sow partially** on a level **below, and partially** on a level **above. And Shmuel says:** It is enough if it is a hole **of four** handbreadths, as **a person cannot sow partially** on a level **below, and partially** on a level **above.**

וּצְרִיכָא. דְּאִי אַשְׁמוּעִינַן דִּירָה – בְּהָא קָאָמַר שְׁמוּאֵל, מִשּׁוּם דְּלָא עָבְדִי אֱינָשֵׁי דְּדָיְירִי פּוּרְתָּא הָכָא וּפוּרְתָּא הָכָא, אֲבָל לְעִנְיַן זְרִיעָה – עָבְדִי אֱינָשֵׁי דְּזָרְעִי הָכָא פּוּרְתָּא וְהָכָא פּוּרְתָּא, אֵימָא מוֹדֶה לֵיהּ לְרַב. וְאִי אִיתְּמַר בְּהָךְ – בְּהָךְ קָאָמַר רַב, אֲבָל בְּהָא – אֵימָא מוֹדֶה לֵיהּ לִשְׁמוּאֵל. צְרִיכָא.

The Gemara comments: **And** it is **necessary** for the dispute between Rav and Shmuel to be stated both here and with regard to the case of an upper story of a house that collapsed (116b). **As had** the Gemara **taught us only** that they disagree with regard to **a residence,** one would have said: It is only **in this** case that **Shmuel is saying** his ruling, **because people do not tend to live a little here and a little there, but with regard to sowing, people** do **tend to sow a little here and a little there.** Therefore, one might **say** that he **concedes to Rav** in the case of the olive press. **And if** this dispute **was stated** only **with regard to this** case of the olive press, one would have said that it is only **with regard to this** case that **Rav is saying** his opinion, **but with regard to that** case involving the house, one might **say** that he **concedes to Shmuel.** Therefore, it is **necessary** to state that their dispute applies to both cases.

"נָתְנוּ לוֹ זְמַן". וְכַמָּה זְמַן בֵּית דִּין? אָמַר רַבִּי יוֹחָנָן: שְׁלֹשִׁים יוֹם.

§ The mishna teaches: If the court saw that the wall was shaky, or that the tree was tilting, and **they gave him time** to cut down the tree or to dismantle the wall, and then they fell down, if this occurred during the allotted time, he is exempt, but if they collapsed after the time given to him had elapsed, he is liable to pay. The Gemara asks: **And how much time** will **a court** usually allot[HN] for this purpose? **Rabbi Yoḥanan says:** The standard period is **thirty days.**

"מִי שֶׁהָיָה כּוֹתְלוֹ" כו'. הָא מִדְּקָתָנֵי סֵיפָא הֵילָךְ יְצִיאוֹתֶיךָ – מִכְּלָל דְּפַנִּינְהוּ עָסְקִינַן. טַעְמָא – דְּפַנִּינְהוּ, הָא לָא פַּנִּינְהוּ – לָא.

§ The mishna teaches: In the case of **one whose wall** was located next to his friend's garden and it fell, if the owner of the wall told the owner of the garden to keep the stones, he cannot retract. The Gemara comments: **But from the fact that the last clause** of the mishna **teaches** that if the owner of the fallen wall says: **Here you are,** take **your expenditures,** the court does not listen to him, it can be understood **by inference** that **we are dealing with** a case **where** the owner of the garden **cleared** away the stones. It can therefore be deduced that the **reason** the owner of the fallen wall cannot retract his offer is **that** the owner of the garden **cleared them** away,[N] **but** if **he did not clear them** away, the stones are **not** considered his, and they remain in the possession of the owner of the wall.

אַמַּאי? וְתִקְנֶה לֵיהּ שָׂדֵהוּ, דְּאָמַר רַבִּי יוֹסֵי בְּרַבִּי חֲנִינָא: חֲצֵירוֹ שֶׁל אָדָם קוֹנָה לוֹ שֶׁלֹּא מִדַּעְתּוֹ!

The Gemara asks: **Why** do they remain in the possession of the owner of the wall? **But shouldn't** the owner of the garden's **field effect acquisition** of the stones on **his** behalf? **As Rabbi Yosei, son of Rabbi Ḥanina, says: The courtyard of a person effects acquisition for him** of those items that enter it, even **without his knowledge.**

הָנֵי מִילֵּי – הֵיכָא דְּקָא מִיכַּוֵּין לְאַקְנוּיֵי לֵיהּ, אֲבָל הָכָא – אִישְׁתַּמּוֹטֵי הוּא דְּקָא מִישְׁתַּמֵּיט לֵיהּ.

The Gemara answers: **This statement** applies only in a case **where** the giver **intends to transfer them to him,** in which case the field can effect acquisition of the stones for the receiver without an additional act of acquisition, **but here,** the owner of the fallen wall **is** seeking only to **evade** the owner of the garden. He wants the owner of the garden to take care of the stones, at which point he can collect them from him without much effort on his part, and he does not intend to give the stones to him.

"הַשּׂוֹכֵר לַעֲשׂוֹת עִמּוֹ בְּתֶבֶן" כו'. וּצְרִיכָא.

§ The mishna teaches: In the case of **one who hires** a laborer **to do** work **with him with hay,** the employer cannot force him to accept his wages in the form of some of the hay.[N] The Gemara comments: **And** it is **necessary** to mention this *halakha* with regard to both cases.

דְּאִי אַשְׁמוֹעִינַן לְהָךְ קַמַּיְיתָא, דְּכִי קָאָמַר לֵיהּ הֲגִיעוּךָ אֵין שׁוֹמְעִין לוֹ – מִשּׁוּם דְּלֵית אַגְרָא גַּבֵּיהּ, אֲבָל הָכָא דְּאִית לֵיהּ אַגְרָא גַּבֵּיהּ – אֵימָא שׁוֹמְעִין לוֹ. דְּאָמְרִי אֱינָשֵׁי: מִמָּרֵי רַשְׁוָתֵיךְ – פָּארֵי אִפְרַע.

As had it taught us only **with regard to this first** case of the stones that fell **that when** the owner of the fallen wall **says to** the owner of the garden: **They are yours,** the court **does not listen to him,** one would have said that this is the *halakha* **because he does not have a wage** owed **by him,** as they had no prior business dealings together, and the owner of the stones does not owe the owner of the garden anything. **But here,** in the case of a laborer working with hay, in **which** the laborer **does have a wage** owed **by** the employer, one might **say** that the court **listens to him, as people say** the following proverb: When collecting a debt **from your debtor,** allow yourself to be **repaid** even in **bran** [*parei*],[L] i.e., take whatever you can as payment of a loan.

HALAKHA

Time allotted by the court – **זְמַן בֵּית דִּין**: If one's wall is unstable, the court allots him a period of thirty days to dismantle it. The Rema, citing the Rashba, adds that if there is an urgent need for it to be dismantled, or if it poses immediate danger, he can be forced to remove it without delay (Rambam *Sefer Nezikin, Hilkhot Nizkei Mamon* 3:19; *Shulḥan Arukh, Ḥoshen Mishpat* 416:6).

LANGUAGE

Bran [*parei*] – **פָּארֵי**: It is unclear whether or not this word comes from a non-Semitic source, but in Syriac and in rabbinic Hebrew it means bran.

NOTES

And how much time will a court allot – **וְכַמָּה זְמַן בֵּית דִּין**: The early commentaries learn from here that the standard time provided by the court, not only for dismantling a wall but also for other court-ordered actions without a fixed time, is thirty days (see Ran).

That he cleared them away – **דְּפַנִּינְהוּ**: The Gemara concludes that the owner of the garden does not acquire the stones unless he actually removes them. But before he actually clears them, it is assumed that the owner of the stones is trying only to avoid clearing them, and did not intend to give them away. The *Tur* writes that, by contrast, with regard to a laborer he acquires the hay as soon as the employer states that he may keep it. The difference is explained in the *Nimmukei Yosef*: Since it is uncommon to immediately clear away the stones, the owner supposes that he still has time to retract; he did not intend to transfer ownership of the stones, and is seeking only to avoid clearing them. But with regard to the hay, since the laborer is expected to take his wages home with him immediately, if the employer agreed to give it away, he promptly transfers ownership. The *Tosefot Yom Tov* explains the case of the hay differently: Since the employer fears transgressing the prohibition of delaying the wages of a worker, it is therefore assumed that he promptly transfers ownership of the hay.

Non-monetary payment – **תַּשְׁלוּם שֶׁלֹּא בְּכֶסֶף**: The early commentaries explain that there are three categories with regard to this matter: The first is a creditor, who collects money from the debtor if he has any. Otherwise, he may take anything that the debtor owns. The second is one who is liable for damage, who must give what he has, but if he pays in land he must give the injured party his best-quality land. The third is an employer, who is obligated to pay his laborer with money, and even if he has none, he must obtain some. The Ran explains that the laborer was expecting money at the end of the day, and it never occurred to him that he would receive payment in a manner that would necessitate the trouble of selling it before he could make use of his wages. The *Mordekhai*, citing the Maharam of Rothenburg, states that if the employer paid the worker with foodstuff that the laborer worked with, he has fulfilled his duty if he has no other money.

HALAKHA

If he hired him to safeguard ownerless property – **שְׂכָרוֹ לִשְׁמוֹר דְּבַר הֶפְקֵר**: If a laborer was hired to safeguard ownerless property, his employer can tell him to take part of it as his wages, as the employer has not yet acquired it (*Shulḥan Arukh*, *Ḥoshen Mishpat* 336:3).

NOTES

With ownerless property – **בְּשֶׁל הֶפְקֵר**: The logic is that since the worker knows that the items he is working with do not belong to the employer, he doesn't rely on him, and initially relies on the ownerless items with which he is working to serve as his compensation (*Torat Ḥayyim*).

There with regard to viewing [*habata*] – **כָּאן בְּהַבָּטָה**: An alternative version, cited by the *Arukh*, reads: *Ḥabata*. As hinted by Rashi, this means that his job is to throw down items. The Meiri includes both versions as part of the Gemara, and explains that *ḥabata* refers to work such as threshing, which does not involve lifting the items. According to all explanations, the point is that his work does not involve an act of acquisition by lifting.

וְאִי אַשְׁמוּעִינַן הָדָא – הָכָא שֶׁמְּשַׁקְבֵּל עָלָיו אֵין שׁוֹמְעִין לוֹ – מִשּׁוּם דְּאִית לֵיהּ אַגְרָא גַּבֵּיהּ, אֲבָל הָכָא דְּלֵית לֵיהּ אַגְרָא גַּבֵּיהּ – אֵימָא שׁוֹמְעִין לוֹ. צְרִיכָא.

And had it taught us only over **here** with regard to the hay, one would have said that it is only **here that after** the laborer **has** already **accepted** ownership **upon himself,** the court **does not listen to** the employer who desires to retract, **because** the laborer **has a wage** owed **by him,** and therefore there is reason to say that he receives the hay. **But here,** with regard to the stones, **where** the owner of the garden **does not have a wage** owed **by** the owner of the fallen wall, one might **say** that the court **listens to him** and he can retract. It is therefore **necessary** for the mishna to teach both cases.

״אֵין שׁוֹמְעִין לוֹ״. וְהָתַנְיָא: שׁוֹמְעִין לוֹ! אָמַר רַב נַחְמָן: לָא קַשְׁיָא. כָּאן – בְּשֶׁלּוֹ, כָּאן – בְּשֶׁל חֲבֵירוֹ.

§ The mishna teaches that if an employer seeks to pay his laborer with straw, the court **does not listen to him.** The Gemara asks: **But isn't it taught** in a *baraita* that the court **does listen to him?** The Gemara answers: **Rav Naḥman said:** This is **not difficult.** The ruling of the mishna **here,** that the court does not listen to him, is stated **with regard to** a case of work done with the employer's **own** property. And the ruling of the *baraita* **there,** that the court does listen to him, is stated **with regard to** work done with the property **of another,** and there the employer's request is accepted.

אֲמַר לֵיהּ רָבָא לְרַב נַחְמָן: בְּשֶׁלּוֹ מַאי טַעְמָא? דְּאָמַר לֵיהּ: אַגְרָא עֲלָךְ; בְּשֶׁל חֲבֵירוֹ נַמִי שְׂכָרוֹ עָלָיו! דְּתַנְיָא: הַשּׂוֹכֵר אֶת הַפּוֹעֵל לַעֲשׂוֹת בְּשֶׁלּוֹ וְהֶרְאָהוּ בְּשֶׁל חֲבֵירוֹ – נוֹתֵן לוֹ שְׂכָרוֹ מִשָּׁלֵם, וְחוֹזֵר וְנוֹטֵל מִבַּעַל הַבַּיִת מַה שֶּׁהֶהֱנָה אוֹתוֹ.

Rava said to Rav Naḥman: In a case where he is working with **his own** property, **what is the reason** that the court does not listen to him? **As** the laborer can **say to** the employer: The responsibility of paying my **wage is on you.** But if he was working **with** the property **of his friend,** the responsibility of paying **his earnings is also on** the employer, **as it is taught** in a *baraita*: With regard to **one who hires a laborer to perform** work **in his own** field, **and** the employer inadvertently **showed** the laborer the field **belonging to another** in which he should work, the employer **must give** the laborer **his full wages, and** in addition, the employer **goes back and takes from the owner** of the field in which he worked the value of **the benefit** that owner **received from** the laborer. The payment of the wages is incumbent upon the employer, not the owner of the field.

אֶלָּא אָמַר רַב נַחְמָן: לָא קַשְׁיָא. כָּאן – בְּשֶׁלּוֹ, כָּאן – בְּשֶׁל הֶפְקֵר.

Rather, Rav Naḥman said a different explanation: It is **not difficult.** The ruling of the mishna **here,** that the court does not listen to him, is stated **with regard to** work done with the employer's **own** property. And the ruling of the *baraita* **there,** that the court does listen to him, is stated **with regard to** work done with **ownerless** property,[HN] e.g., the employer hired him to gather ownerless hay, and later told him to keep some of the hay as his wages. In that case, he can force the laborer to accept the hay as payment.

אֵיתִיבֵיהּ רָבָא לְרַב נַחְמָן: מְצִיאַת פּוֹעֵל – לְעַצְמוֹ. אֵימָתַי – בִּזְמַן שֶׁאָמַר לוֹ בַּעַל הַבַּיִת נַכֵּשׁ עִמִּי הַיּוֹם, אוֹ עֲדוֹר עִמִּי הַיּוֹם. אֲבָל אִם אָמַר לוֹ עֲשֵׂה עִמִּי מְלָאכָה הַיּוֹם – מְצִיאָתוֹ לְבַעַל הַבַּיִת.

Rava raised an objection to Rav Naḥman: It was taught in a *baraita*: **The found item of** a salaried **laborer** belongs **to himself. When** is this so? **When the employer told him** to perform a specific task, for example if he said: **Weed with me today, or** if he said: **Hoe with me today.** If the laborer finds lost property while performing that task, then the item belongs to him. **But if** the employer **says to** the laborer: **Work with me today,** without specifying what labor he wants him to perform, **his found item** belongs **to the employer,** as acquiring found items can be considered part of his terms of employment. In the case of Rav Naḥman, since the employer instructed the laborer to gather ownerless hay, the acquisition of the hay is certainly part of the terms of his employment, and belongs to the employer. Since it is the employer's property, he is not able to force the laborer to accept the hay as payment.

אֶלָּא אָמַר רַב נַחְמָן: לָא קַשְׁיָא. כָּאן – בְּהַגְבָּהָה, כָּאן – בְּהַבָּטָה.

Rather, Rav Naḥman said: Both the ruling of the mishna and the ruling of the *baraita* are stated with regard to a laborer hired to work with ownerless property, but it is **not difficult.** The ruling of the mishna **here,** that the court does not listen to him, is stated **with regard to** a case where the laborer's task was to **lift** up the hay and gather it, and he is therefore considered the employer's agent and acquires the hay for him. Since the hay then belongs to the employer, he cannot force the laborer to accept it as payment. And the ruling of the *baraita* **there,** that the court does listen to him, is stated **with regard to** a case where his work merely consisted of **viewing,**[N] e.g., he hired him to make sure that no one takes the ownerless hay. In that case, even the employer does not acquire the straw, and it remains ownerless. Consequently, the employer can tell the laborer to take some hay as payment.

אָמַר רַבָּה: הַבָּטָה בְּהֶפְקֵר תַּנָּאֵי הִיא. דִּתְנַן: שׁוֹמְרֵי סְפִיחֵי שְׁבִיעִית נוֹטְלִין שְׂכָרָן מִתְּרוּמַת הַלִּשְׁכָּה. רַבִּי יוֹסֵי אוֹמֵר: הָרוֹצֶה מִתְנַדֵּב הוּא, וְשׁוֹמֵר חִנָּם. אָמְרוּ לוֹ: אַתָּה אוֹמֵר כֵּן – אֵין בָּאִין מִשֶּׁל צִבּוּר!

Rabba says: The issue of whether, **in** the case of **ownerless** property, **viewing** effects acquisition of it **is** a dispute between ***tanna'im*****. As we learned** in a mishna (*Shekalim* 9b): The **watchmen of** the ***sefiḥim***, grain that grew without being purposely planted, **of the Sabbatical** Year[H] ensured that people did not take this ownerless grain, so that it remained available to be used for the *omer* offering and the two loaves, i.e., the public offering on *Shavuot* of two loaves from the new wheat. These watchmen **take their wages from** the **collection of the** Temple treasury **chamber,** as they are employed by the Temple treasury. **Rabbi Yosei says: One who** so **desires** can **volunteer** his services and safeguard the grain, **and** he has the status of **an unpaid bailee.** The Rabbis **said to him:** Do **you say so?** But according to your view, the *omer* and the two loaves **do not come from communal** funds as required, since in reality they come from a private individual, i.e., the bailee.

מַאי לָאו בְּהָא קָמִיפַּלְגִי: דְּתַנָּא קַמָּא סָבַר: הַבָּטָה בְּהֶפְקֵר קָנֵי, וְאִי יְהִיבֵי לֵיהּ אַגְרָא – אִין, וְאִי לָא – לָא. וְרַבִּי יוֹסֵי סָבַר: הַבָּטָה בְּהֶפְקֵר לָא קָנֵי, וְכִי אָזְלִי צִבּוּר וּמַיְיתִי – הָשְׁתָּא הוּא דְּקָא זָכֵי בֵּיהּ.

The Gemara suggests: **What, is it not with regard to this that they disagree: The first *tanna*** holds that **in** the case of **ownerless** property, **viewing effects acquisition** of it, and so the watchman, although he did not lift up the grain, acquires the grain by viewing it. **And** therefore, **if he is given a wage** from communal funds, then **yes,** he is safeguarding it on behalf of the community, and he acquires it for them. **But if** he is **not** paid, he has **not** acquired it for the community, but for himself. **And,** conversely, **Rabbi Yosei holds** that **in** the case of **ownerless** property, **viewing does not effect acquisition** of it, **and when** the **community goes and brings** the grain for the *omer* offering and the two loaves, **it is** only **now,** at this stage, **that they acquire it.**

וּמָה אַתָּה אוֹמֵר – הָכִי קָאָמְרִי לֵיהּ: מִדְּבָרֶיךָ לִדְבָרֵינוּ אֵין עוֹמֶר וּשְׁתֵּי לֶחֶם בָּאִין מִשֶּׁל צִבּוּר.

And what, according to this explanation, is the meaning of the phrase: Do **you say** so? **This is what they were saying to him:** If the opinion **from your statement** that one may volunteer as an unpaid bailee is applied **to our statement** that in the case of ownerless property, viewing effects acquisition, the result is that the ***omer***[B] **offering and the two loaves**[B] **do not come from communal** funds as required.

אֲמַר רָבָא: לָא. דְּכוּלֵּי עָלְמָא הַבָּטָה בְּהֶפְקֵר קָנֵי, וְהָכָא – חָיְישִׁינַן שֶׁמָּא לֹא יִמְסְרֵם יָפֶה יָפֶה קָמִיפַּלְגִי; דְּרַבָּנַן סָבְרִי: יָהֲבִינַן לֵיהּ אַגְרָא, וְאִי לָא חָיְישִׁינַן שֶׁמָּא לֹא יִמְסְרֵם יָפֶה יָפֶה.

Rava said: No; the dispute can be explained differently. It can be explained **that everyone** agrees that **in** the case of **ownerless** property, **viewing effects acquisition, and here they disagree** with regard to the question of whether **we are concerned** that **perhaps he will not give** the grain **over wholeheartedly** to the community. **As the Rabbis hold** that **we give** the watchman **a wage, and if** we do **not** pay him, but allow him to act as a volunteer, **we are concerned** that **perhaps he will not give** the grain **over wholeheartedly** to the community, as deep down he might feel that the grain really belongs to him and that he is offering it from his own pocket, which means that the *omer* offering and two loaves are not properly offered by the community.

רַבִּי יוֹסֵי סָבַר: לָא חָיְישִׁינַן שֶׁמָּא לֹא יִמְסְרֵם יָפֶה יָפֶה. וּמַה אַתָּה אוֹמֵר – הָכִי קָאָמְרִי לֵיהּ: מִדְּבָרֶיךָ לִדְבָרֵינוּ, דְּחָיְישִׁינַן שֶׁמָּא לֹא יִמְסְרֵם יָפֶה יָפֶה – אֵין עוֹמֶר וּשְׁתֵּי לֶחֶם בָּאִין מִשֶּׁל צִבּוּר.

Conversely, **Rabbi Yosei holds** that **we are not concerned** that **perhaps he will not hand** the grain **over wholeheartedly** to the community. **And what** is the meaning of the phrase: Do **you say** so? **This is what they were saying to him:** If the opinion **from your statement** that one may volunteer as an unpaid bailee is applied **to our statement that we are concerned** that **perhaps he will not give** the grain **over wholeheartedly,** the result is that the ***omer*** **offering and** the **two loaves do not come from communal** funds as required.

אִיכָּא דְּאָמְרִי, רָבָא אֲמַר: דְּכוּלֵּי עָלְמָא הַבָּטָה בְּהֶפְקֵר לָא קָנֵי, וְהָכָא בְּחָיְישִׁינַן לְבַעֲלֵי זְרוֹעוֹת קָמִיפַּלְגִי. דְּתַנָּא קַמָּא סָבַר: דְּתַקִּינוּ רַבָּנַן לְמֵיתַב לֵיהּ אַרְבַּע זוּזֵי, כִּי הֵיכִי דְּלִישְׁמְעִי בַּעֲלֵי זְרוֹעוֹת וְלִיפְרְשׁוּ מִינַּיְיהוּ. וְרַבִּי יוֹסֵי סָבַר: לָא תַּקִּינוּ.

There are those **who say** that there is a different version of this discussion: **Rava said:** It can be explained **that everyone** agrees that **in** the case of **ownerless** property, **viewing does not effect acquisition** of it, **and here,** concerning the *omer* offering, **they disagree with regard to** the question of whether **we are concerned about violent people** that may come and seize the grain for themselves. **As the first *tanna*** **holds that the Sages instituted** a directive **to give him four dinars,** or whatever payment is appropriate for his services as a watchman, **so that violent people should hear** of this **and keep away from** the grain, since when they hear that the Temple is paying the watchmen, they will certainly not take the grain. **And Rabbi Yosei holds** that the Sages **did not institute** this directive, since there is no concern about violent people.

HALAKHA

Watchmen of the *sefiḥim* of the Sabbatical Year – שׁוֹמְרֵי סְפִיחֵי שְׁבִיעִית: In the Sabbatical Year, the court hires watchmen to secure the grain from which they will bring the *omer* offering and the two loaves. These watchmen take their wages from the Temple treasury. Even if one wants to volunteer as an unpaid bailee, the court does not listen to him, as there is a concern that violent men will seize the grain from him, in accordance with the opinion of the Rabbis (Rambam *Sefer Zemanim*, *Hilkhot Shekalim* 4:5–6).

BACKGROUND

***Omer* – עוֹמֶר:** Technically, an *omer* is a measure of grain, one-tenth of an ephah. In general, though, the term is used to refer to the measure of barley offered in the Temple on the sixteenth of Nisan, the second day of Passover. The *omer* offering was brought whether the sixteenth of Nisan was a Shabbat or a weekday. The *omer* offering consisted of newly ripe barley that was prepared as roasted flour. The barley was harvested on the night following the first day of Passover. A handful of the flour was burned on the altar and the rest was eaten by the priests. In addition to the flour offering, a male sheep was sacrificed as a burnt-offering, together with a wine libation and two-tenths of an ephah of wheat flour as a meal-offering. Once the *omer* offering had been sacrificed, grain from the new harvest could be eaten. The Torah further commands that forty-nine days be counted from the time the *omer* is brought until the holiday of *Shavuot*. This period itself became known as the *omer*, as it began at the time of the offering; the counting of the days between the second day of Passover and Shavuot is referred to as: The counting of the *omer*.

Two loaves – שְׁתֵּי לֶחֶם: Two loaves of bread were brought as a communal offering on the festival of *Shavuot* (Leviticus 23:17). In contrast to most of the other meal-offerings, these loaves were leavened. Two lambs, the communal peace-offering, were brought together with these two loaves. Both the loaves and the lambs were first ceremonially waved. Afterward, the loaves were divided among the priests and eaten in the Temple courtyard, and the lambs were sacrificed as a peace-offering.

״וּמָה אַתָּה אוֹמֵר״ – הָכִי קָאָמְרִי לֵיהּ: מִדְּבָרֶיךָ לִדְבָרֵינוּ אֵין בָּאִין מִשֶּׁל צִבּוּר. וְכֵן כִּי אֲתָא רָבִין אָמַר רַבִּי יוֹחָנָן: חוֹשְׁשִׁין לְבַעֲלֵי זְרוֹעוֹת אִיכָּא בֵּינַיְיהוּ.

And what is the meaning of the phrase: Do **you say** so? **This is what they were saying to him:** If we apply the opinion **from your statement** that one may volunteer as an unpaid bailee, **to our statement** that the Sages instituted a directive to give him four dinars, the result is that communal offerings **do not come from communal** funds as required. **And likewise, when Ravin came** from Eretz Yisrael to Babylonia, he said that **Rabbi Yoḥanan says:** The question of whether or not **we are concerned about violent people is** the difference **between** the opinions of the Rabbis and Rabbi Yosei, i.e., that is the crux of their dispute.

מתני׳ הַמּוֹצִיא זֶבֶל לִרְשׁוּת הָרַבִּים, הַמּוֹצִיא – מוֹצִיא, וְהַמְזַבֵּל – מְזַבֵּל. אֵין שׁוֹרִין טִיט בִּרְשׁוּת הָרַבִּים, וְאֵין לוֹבְנִים לְבֵנִים. אֲבָל גּוֹבְלִין טִיט בִּרְשׁוּת הָרַבִּים, אֲבָל לֹא לְבֵנִים.

MISHNA In the case of **one who takes manure out to the public domain,**[NH] in order for it to be transported to fertilize a field, he **who takes it out** from his property **takes it out, and** immediately, he **who** takes it to **fertilize** the field takes it to **fertilize** the field. They must relocate the manure immediately without allowing it to sit around in the public domain. Similarly, **one may not soak clay in the public domain**[H] before it is kneaded, **and one may not mold bricks** in the public domain since this takes a long time and inhibits use of the public domain by others. **But one may knead clay in the public domain,** as this process does not take long, **but not bricks.**[N]

הַבּוֹנֶה בִּרְשׁוּת הָרַבִּים – הַמֵּבִיא אֲבָנִים מֵבִיא, וְהַבּוֹנֶה בּוֹנֶה. וְאִם הִזִּיק – מְשַׁלֵּם מַה שֶּׁהִזִּיק. רַבָּן שִׁמְעוֹן בֶּן גַּמְלִיאֵל אוֹמֵר: אַף מְתַקֵּן הוּא אֶת מְלַאכְתּוֹ לִפְנֵי שְׁלֹשִׁים יוֹם.

With regard to **one who builds** a structure, keeping the building materials **in the public domain,**[H] he **who brings** the **stones brings** them, **and** immediately, he **who builds** the structure **builds** with them, and may not leave them there. **And** if the stones **cause damage**[H] before he had a chance to build them into the structure, **he** must **pay** for **what he damaged. Rabban Shimon ben Gamliel says:** One may **even prepare his work thirty days beforehand;** he may keep the building materials in the public domain for that duration.

גמ׳ לֵימָא מַתְנִיתִין דְּלָא כְּרַבִּי יְהוּדָה, דְּתַנְיָא: רַבִּי יְהוּדָה אוֹמֵר: בִּשְׁעַת הוֹצָאַת זְבָלִים אָדָם מוֹצִיא זְבָלוֹ לִרְשׁוּת הָרַבִּים, וְצוֹבְרוֹ כָּל שְׁלֹשִׁים יוֹם, כְּדֵי שֶׁיְּהֵא נִישּׁוֹף בְּרַגְלֵי אָדָם וּבְרַגְלֵי בְהֵמָה, שֶׁעַל מְנָת כֵּן הִנְחִיל יְהוֹשֻׁעַ לְיִשְׂרָאֵל אֶת הָאָרֶץ.

GEMARA The Gemara suggests: **Let us say that the mishna is not in accordance with the** opinion of **Rabbi Yehuda? As it is taught** in a *baraita* (*Tosefta* 11:8): **Rabbi Yehuda says: When it is** the **time** for the **manure** to be **taken out, a person** may **take his manure out into the public domain and** may **pile it** up for **all thirty days, so that it will be trodden on by the feet of people and by the feet of animals,** to prepare it for use as fertilizer, **since** it was **on this condition** that **Joshua bequeathed Eretz** Yisrael **to the Jewish people.** In other words, it is universally accepted that some will relinquish certain rights for the sake of others, and although it may be a nuisance for certain people, this practice is allowed.

אֲפִילּוּ תֵּימָא רַבִּי יְהוּדָה. מוֹדֶה רַבִּי יְהוּדָה שֶׁאִם הִזִּיק – חַיָּיב לְשַׁלֵּם. וְהָתְנַן: מוֹדֶה רַבִּי יְהוּדָה בְּנֵר חֲנוּכָּה שֶׁהוּא פָּטוּר, מִפְּנֵי שֶׁהוּא עוֹשֶׂה בִּרְשׁוּת. מַאי לָאו – רְשׁוּת דְּבֵית דִּין? לָא, רְשׁוּת דְּמִצְוָה.

The Gemara responds: **You** may **even say** that the mishna is in accordance with the opinion of **Rabbi Yehuda,** since **Rabbi Yehuda concedes that** although he acted within his rights, **if** the manure **caused damage,** the one who placed it there is **liable to pay.** The Gemara asks: **But didn't we learn** in a mishna (*Bava Kamma* 62b): **Rabbi Yehuda concedes with regard to a Hanukkah lamp** placed in the public domain that ignited a fire and caused damage **that he is exempt, because he acts with permission? What,** is the reason he is exempt **not** that he acted with the **permission of the court** to use the public domain in this manner, which indicates that one who acts with court permission is exempt from liability for damage? The Gemara rejects this suggestion: **No,** it means that he has the **permission of a mitzva.** Since it is a mitzva to place the Hanukkah lamp outside, he is exempt from paying for the damage it caused. The mere right to place the item in the public domain does not exempt the owner from liability.

NOTES

One who takes manure out to the public domain – הַמּוֹצִיא זֶבֶל לִרְשׁוּת הָרַבִּים: The Rid has an alternative version of the text that reads: One who takes manure out to the public domain for those who fertilize. He explains accordingly that this excludes one who takes manure out to the public domain in order to clean his house, as it is permitted for one to place manure in the public domain only when it is necessary in order to transport it to fertilize his field, but he may not do so to clean his premises.

But not bricks – אֲבָל לֹא לְבֵנִים: The commentaries are puzzled by this clause, as it was already stated that one may not mold bricks in the public domain. One explanation is that one clause refers to placing the bricks there for use, while the other refers to their preparation (*Ḥeshek Shlomo*). According to other versions of the text, it should read: But not for bricks, which then means that one may not knead clay for the purpose of making bricks. The ruling of the *Shulḥan Arukh* reflects this understanding.

HALAKHA

One who takes manure out to the public domain – הַמּוֹצִיא זֶבֶל לִרְשׁוּת הָרַבִּים: It is permitted for everyone to take manure and animal droppings and place them in the public domain at the set time for removal of manure. At other times one is allowed to do so only if he will remove it from there immediately (Rema, citing the *Tur*). At the set time for removal of manure, it is permitted to leave the manure in the public domain for thirty days so that it will be well trodden. If the manure caused damage, the owner must pay, in accordance with the opinion of the unattributed view in the mishna, and not the opinion of Rabbi Yehuda (Rambam *Sefer Nezikin, Hilkhot Nizkei Mamon* 13:15; *Shulḥan Arukh, Ḥoshen Mishpat* 414:2, and in the comment of Rema).

Clay in the public domain – טִיט בִּרְשׁוּת הָרַבִּים: One may not soak clay in the public domain with the intention of leaving it there for a long time, nor may one mold bricks in the public domain. It is permitted to knead clay for immediate placement in a building, but not for molding bricks (Rambam *Sefer Nezikin, Hilkhot Nizkei Mamon* 13:16; *Shulḥan Arukh, Ḥoshen Mishpat* 417:5).

One who builds in the public domain – הַבּוֹנֶה בִּרְשׁוּת הָרַבִּים: One who builds in the public domain may not leave the stones lying there. Rather, he must build them into the structure without delay (Rambam *Sefer Nezikin, Hilkhot Nizkei Mamon* 13:17; *Shulḥan Arukh, Ḥoshen Mishpat* 417:6).

And if the stones cause damage – וְאִם הִזִּיק: If one placed stones in, or took manure out, to the public domain, even if he acted in a permitted manner, he is liable to pay for any damage that resulted (Rambam *Sefer Nezikin, Hilkhot Nizkei Mamon* 13:17; *Shulḥan Arukh, Ḥoshen Mishpat* 417:7).

והתניא: כל אלו שאמרו מותרין לקלקל ברשות הרבים, אם הזיק – חייב לשלם, ורבי יהודה פוטר! אלא מחוורתא, מתניתין דלא כרבי יהודה.

The Gemara asks: **But isn't it taught** in a *baraita*: With regard to **all these** cases in **which** the Sages **said** that **it is permitted** for people **to place obstacles in the public domain, if they caused damage,** these people **are liable to pay, and Rabbi Yehuda exempts** them? Evidently, according to Rabbi Yehuda, if one has the permission of the court to put an item in the public domain, he is exempt from paying damages. **Rather, it is clear** that **the mishna is not in accordance with** the opinion **of Rabbi Yehuda.**

אמר אביי: רבי יהודה ורבן שמעון בן גמליאל ורבי שמעון כולהו סבירא להו: כל מקום שנתנו לו חכמים רשות והזיק – פטור. רבי יהודה – הא דאמרן. רבן שמעון בן גמליאל – דתנן: רבן שמעון בן גמליאל אומר: אף מתקן הוא את מלאכתו לפני שלשים יום.

Abaye said: Rabbi Yehuda and Rabban Shimon ben Gamliel and Rabbi Shimon all hold that **wherever the Sages gave** someone **permission** to perform an action, **and** in performing this action **he causes damage,** he is **exempt** from payment. The Gemara cites the sources for this assertion: It is clear that **Rabbi Yehuda** is of that opinion based on **that which we** just **said.** It is clear that **Rabban Shimon ben Gamliel** is of that opinion, **as we learned** in the mishna: **Rabban Shimon ben Gamliel says:** One may **even prepare his work thirty days beforehand.**

רבי שמעון – דתנן: היה מעמידו בעלייה – צריך שיהא תחתיו מעזיבה שלשה טפחים, ובכירה – טפח. ואם הזיק – משלם מה שהזיק. רבי שמעון אומר: לא אמרו כל השיעורים הללו אלא שאם הזיק פטור מלשלם.

It is clear that **Rabbi Shimon** is of that opinion, **as we learned** in a mishna (*Bava Batra* 20b): If **one was setting up** an oven **in the upper story,**[NH] **there must be a plaster floor beneath it,** which serves as the ceiling of the lower story, at least **three handbreadths** thick, so that the ceiling below does not burn. **And** in the case **of a stove** the plaster floor must be at least one **handbreadth** thick. **And if** he **causes damage** after having taken the necessary precautions, **he pays** compensation for that **which he damaged. Rabbi Shimon says:** The Sages **said all of these measurements** to teach **only that if he causes damage he is exempt from paying,** as he took all reasonable precautions.

תנו רבנן: החצב שמסר לסתת – הסתת חייב. הסתת שמסר לחמר – החמר חייב. החמר שמסר לכתף – הכתף חייב. הכתף שמסר לבנאי – הבנאי חייב. הבנאי שמסר לאדריכל – אדריכל חייב. ואם הניח אבן על הדימוס והזיקה – כולן חייבין לשלם.

§ **The Sages taught:** Once **the stonecutter** has **delivered** the stones **to the chiseler,** from that point on, **the chiseler** is **liable** for any damage caused by them. Once **the chiseler** has **delivered** the stones **to the donkey driver** to transport them, **the donkey driver** is **liable.** Once **the donkey driver** has **delivered** the stones **to a porter** to carry them to the building site, **the porter** is **liable.** Once **the porter** has **delivered** the stones **to the builder, the builder** is **liable.** Once **the builder** has **delivered** them **to the master builder** [*adrikhal*],[L] who places and straightens the stones on the structure, **the master builder** is **liable.**[H] **And if he placed a stone upon the row** [*dimos*][L] of stones **and** the stone fell off and **caused damage,** then **they are all liable to pay.**[N]

והתניא: אחרון חייב וכולן פטורים! לא קשיא: כאן – בשכירות, כאן – בקבלנות.

The Gemara asks: **But isn't it taught** in a *baraita*, that only the **last one,** the master builder, is **liable, and all of them are exempt?** The Gemara answers: This is **not difficult,** as the ruling **here,** in this *baraita*, is stated **with regard to** a case of **hiring,** and therefore only the last one is liable, whereas the ruling **there,** in that *baraita*, is stated **with regard to** a case of **contracting,** in which they all agreed to perform the work together, and therefore they are all liable to pay.

NOTES

If one was setting up an oven in the upper story – היה מעמידו בעלייה: Rashi in tractate *Bava Kamma* (61b) explains that not only can the owner of the residence below object, but neighbors can also object to the construction of an oven or a stove that poses a fire hazard to the public.

They are all liable to pay – כולם חייבין לשלם: Rashi explains that since the stone fell off after it was placed, no one can be held directly responsible for the damage caused, and so they are all liable to pay, considering their partnership in the work. The Ra'avad explains this ruling differently: Usually the stone is heavy, and so the porter and the builder will typically help the master builder place it, and they are therefore all responsible when it falls from their hands. But even according to this opinion, this general liability applies only to contractors; in a case of hired workers, even if they help each other, it is only the one in charge of that particular job that is responsible.

LANGUAGE

Master builder [*adrikhal*] – אדריכל: The original version of this word is seemingly *ardikhal*. Many claim that this word comes from the Akkadian *arad-ekalli*, which literally translates as: Servant of the chamber, and was perhaps used as a nickname for the head builder. In rabbinic Hebrew it refers to the master builder, whose job was to straighten the stones in the building and ensure their correct placement.

Row [*dimos*] – דימוס: From the Greek δόμος, *domos*, meaning a house, or a row of stones or bricks in a structure.

HALAKHA

An oven in a house that has an upper story above it – תנור בבית שעלייה על גביו: If a house and its upper story belonged to two different people, the owner of the house may place an oven in his house only if there is a distance of four cubits between the top of the oven and the ceiling. Similarly, the owner of the upper story may position his oven only above a layer of plaster a minimum of three handbreadths thick. In the case of a stove, one handbreadth is sufficient. One must also ensure that it poses no danger to the neighbors. In any case, even if he kept the proper distance, if it caused a fire that caused damage, he is liable to pay (Rambam *Sefer Kinyan, Hilkhot Shekhenim* 9:11; *Shulḥan Arukh, Ḥoshen Mishpat* 155:1).

Damage caused by building stones – נזקי אבני בניה: If the stonecutter delivered the stone to the chiseler and the stone caused damage, the chiseler is liable. Once the chiseler has handed the stone over to the donkey driver, the donkey driver is liable. When the donkey driver delivers the stone to the porter, the porter is liable; when the porter gives it to the builder, the builder is liable. Once the builder has delivered the stone to the master builder, who straightens the stones on the structure, the master builder is liable. In a case where the stone caused damage after it was set in its place, if they all share the work as contractors, they are all liable. If they were hired workers, the last one is liable (Rambam *Sefer Nezikin, Hilkhot Nizkei Mamon* 13:18; *Shulḥan Arukh, Ḥoshen Mishpat* 384:4).

HALAKHA

Two gardens, one above the other – שְׁתֵּי גִּנּוֹת זוֹ עַל גַּב זוֹ: If there were two adjacent gardens, one higher than the other, and vegetables grew out of the wall of soil between the gardens, any vegetable that the owner of the upper garden can reach by hand and take belongs to him, and the rest belongs to the owner of the lower garden, in accordance with the opinion of Rabbi Shimon. An exception to this ruling is a case of vegetables that are growing within three handbreadths of the ground: These always belong to the owner of the lower garden (Rambam *Sefer Kinyan, Hilkhot Shekhenim* 4:9; *Shulḥan Arukh, Ḥoshen Mishpat* 167:1, and in the comment of Rema).

That which sprouts from the trunk belongs to the owner of the tree, etc. – מִן הַגֶּזַע שֶׁל בַּעַל הָאִילָן וכו׳: If one owned two trees in another's field, and another tree sprouted from the trunk, when it is chopped down, it belongs to the owner of the tree. That which grows from the roots and does emerge above the soil belongs to the owner of the field, since the *halakha* is in accordance with the opinion of Rabbi Yehuda when in opposition to Rabbi Meir (Rambam *Sefer Kinyan, Hilkhot Mekhira* 24:7; *Shulḥan Arukh, Ḥoshen Mishpat* 216:10).

NOTES

Rabbi Meir said: Since the two of them can object – אָמַר רַבִּי מֵאִיר מֵאַחַר שֶׁשְּׁנֵיהֶן יְכוֹלִין לִמְחוֹת: This statement shows that Rabbi Meir's previous explanation was not the main reason for his opinion, as his ruling is primarily based on the issue of the source of the plant's nourishment (*Tosafot* in tractate *Gittin* 25a). By contrast, the Meiri's version of the text reads: Rabbi Yosei said, and this is a new opinion of a different *tanna*.

מתני׳ שְׁתֵּי גִּנּוֹת זוֹ עַל גַּב זוֹ וְהַיָּרָק בֵּינְתַיִם, רַבִּי מֵאִיר אוֹמֵר: שֶׁל עֶלְיוֹן. רַבִּי יְהוּדָה אוֹמֵר: שֶׁל תַּחְתּוֹן. אָמַר רַבִּי מֵאִיר: אִם יִרְצֶה הָעֶלְיוֹן לִיקַּח אֶת עֲפָרוֹ – אֵין כָּאן יָרָק! אָמַר רַבִּי יְהוּדָה: אִם יִרְצֶה הַתַּחְתּוֹן לְמַלְּאוֹת אֶת גִּנָּתוֹ – אֵין כָּאן יָרָק!

MISHNA In the case of **two gardens** that were located **one above the other,**[HB] i.e., a garden on a plateau that borders another garden below, **and vegetables** grew **in-between,** out of the wall of soil resulting from the difference in height between the two gardens, **Rabbi Meir says:** These vegetables belong **to** the owner of the **upper** garden. **Rabbi Yehuda says:** They belong **to** the owner of the **lower** one. **Rabbi Meir said** in explanation of his ruling: **If the** owner of the **upper** garden would **want to** dig and **take his dirt** and does so, **no vegetables** would grow **here,** as that wall made of soil would not exist. The vegetables therefore belong to him. In response, **Rabbi Yehuda said: If the** owner of the **lower** garden would **want to fill his garden** with dirt and does so, thereby raising its level, **no vegetables** would grow **here,** as that wall made of soil would not exist. The vegetables therefore belong to him.

אָמַר רַבִּי מֵאִיר: מֵאַחַר שֶׁשְּׁנֵיהֶן יְכוֹלִין לִמְחוֹת זֶה עַל זֶה – רוֹאִין מֵהֵיכָן יָרָק זֶה חַי. אָמַר רַבִּי שִׁמְעוֹן: כָּל שֶׁהָעֶלְיוֹן יָכוֹל לִפְשׁוֹט אֶת יָדוֹ וְלִיטּוֹל – הֲרֵי הוּא שֶׁלּוֹ, וְהַשְּׁאָר שֶׁל תַּחְתּוֹן.

Rabbi Meir said: Since the two of them can object[N] **to each other,** as they each have the ability to prevent the vegetable growth, nothing can be decided based on such considerations. Instead, the court **considers from where this vegetable lives** and derives nourishment, whether from above or from below. **Rabbi Shimon said: Any** vegetables **that the** owner of the **upper** garden **can stretch out his hand and take, those** vegetables **are his, and the rest** belong **to the** owner of the **lower** garden.

גמ׳ אָמַר רָבָא: בְּעִיקָּרוֹ – כּוּלֵּי עָלְמָא לָא פְּלִיגִי דְּעֶלְיוֹן הָוֵי. כִּי פְּלִיגִי – בְּנוֹפוֹ. רַבִּי מֵאִיר סָבַר: שְׁדֵי נוֹפוֹ בָּתַר עִיקָּרוֹ, וְרַבִּי יְהוּדָה סָבַר: לָא אָמְרִינַן שְׁדֵי נוֹפוֹ בָּתַר עִיקָּרוֹ.

GEMARA Rava says: With regard to the root of the vegetable growing out of the wall of soil, **everyone agrees** that **it is** the property of the owner **of the upper** garden, since the ground belongs to him. **When they disagree,** it is **with regard to its leaves,** which grow above the airspace of the lower garden. **Rabbi Meir holds: Cast its leaves after its root,** and consider that they too belong to the owner of the upper garden. **And Rabbi Yehuda holds: We do not say: Cast its leaves after its root.**

וְאָזְדָא לְטַעְמַיְיהוּ, דְּתַנְיָא: הַיּוֹצֵא מִן הַגֶּזַע וּמִן הַשָּׁרָשִׁין – הֲרֵי אֵלּוּ שֶׁל בַּעַל הַקַּרְקַע, דִּבְרֵי רַבִּי מֵאִיר. רַבִּי יְהוּדָה אוֹמֵר: מִן הַגֶּזַע – שֶׁל בַּעַל הָאִילָן, וּמִן הַשָּׁרָשִׁין – שֶׁל בַּעַל הַקַּרְקַע.

The Gemara comments: **And they follow their** line of **reasoning, as it is taught** in a *baraita* with regard to a tree belonging to one individual that grew on land owned by another: **That which sprouts from the trunk and from the roots,**[B] **these** belong **to the owner of the land.** This is **the statement of Rabbi Meir. Rabbi Yehuda says:** That which sprouts **from the trunk** belongs **to the owner of the tree,**[H] **and** anything that grows **from the roots** belongs **to the owner of the land.** This statement demonstrates that according to Rabbi Yehuda, ownership of the sprouts is not determined exclusively based on the ownership of the roots.

BACKGROUND

Two gardens one above the other – שְׁתֵּי גִּנּוֹת זוֹ עַל גַּב זוֹ:

Farming plots situated on terraces, one above the other

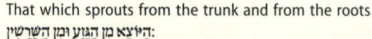

That which sprouts from the trunk and from the roots – הַיּוֹצֵא מִן הַגֶּזַע וּמִן הַשָּׁרָשִׁין:

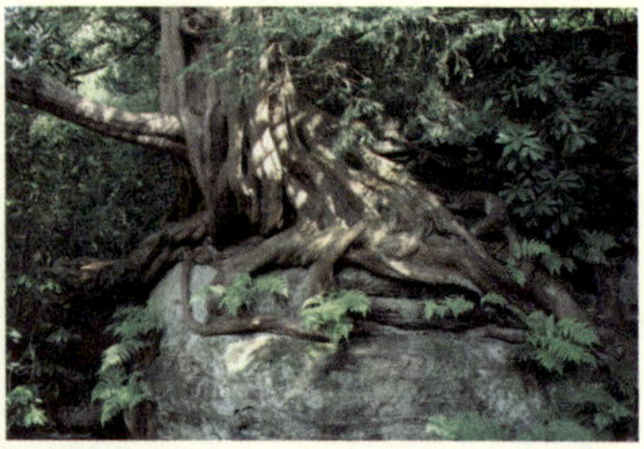

Above: New growth from roots

Left: New growth from a trunk

וּתְנַן נַמִּי גַּבֵּי עָרְלָה כִּי הַאי גַּוְונָא: אִילָן הַיּוֹצֵא מִן הַגֶּזַע וּמִן הַשָּׁרָשִׁין – חַיָּיב בְּעָרְלָה, דִּבְרֵי רַבִּי מֵאִיר. רַבִּי יְהוּדָה אוֹמֵר מִן הַגֶּזַע – פָּטוּר, מִן הַשָּׁרָשִׁין – חַיָּיב.

And we also learned a case like this in a *baraita* (*Tosefta*, *Orla* 1:4), **with regard to** the prohibition against eating **the fruit of a tree during the first three years after its planting** [*orla*]:[B] In the case **of a tree that sprouts from the trunk and from the roots** of an old tree, its owner is **obligated in *orla*,**[H] since it is considered like a new tree, and the *orla* years must be counted anew. This is **the statement of Rabbi Meir. Rabbi Yehuda says:** If it sprouts **from the trunk,** the owner is **exempt,** since it is considered like a branch of the old tree, but if it grows **from the roots,** the owner is **obligated.**

וּצְרִיכִי, דְּאִי אַשְׁמוֹעִינַן קַמַּיְיתָא – בְּהָא קָאָמַר רַבִּי יְהוּדָה, מִשּׁוּם דְּמָמוֹנָא. אֲבָל גַּבֵּי עָרְלָה דְּאִיסּוּרָא – אֵימָא מוֹדֵי לֵיהּ לְרַבִּי מֵאִיר. וְאִי אִיתְּמַר בְּהָא – בְּהָא קָאָמַר רַבִּי מֵאִיר, אֲבָל בְּהַהִיא אֵימָא מוֹדֵי לֵיהּ לְרַבִּי יְהוּדָה. צְרִיכִי.

The Gemara comments: **And** both cases **are necessary** to be stated although they are both based on the same principle. **As had** it **taught us** only the **first** *halakha*, that of ownership, one could say that it is only **with regard to this** case that **Rabbi Yehuda said** his ruling, **due to** the fact **that** it pertains to **monetary matters, but with regard to *orla*, which is** a matter of **a prohibition,** one could **say** that **he concedes to Rabbi Meir. And if it was stated** only **with regard to this** case of *orla*, one could say that it is only **with regard to this** case that **Rabbi Meir said** his stringent ruling, **but with regard to that** case, one could **say** that **he concedes to Rabbi Yehuda.** It is therefore **necessary** to state both disputes.

״אָמַר רַבִּי שִׁמְעוֹן: כָּל שֶׁהָעֶלְיוֹן יָכוֹל לִפְשׁוֹט״ [וכו׳]. אָמְרִי דְּבֵי רַבִּי יַנַּאי: וּבִלְבַד שֶׁלֹּא יֵאָנֵס.

§ The mishna teaches: **Rabbi Shimon**[N] **said: Any** vegetables **that the** owner of the **upper** garden **can stretch out** his hand and take, those vegetables are his, and the rest belong to the owner of the lower garden. In **the school of Rabbi Yannai they say: And** this is only so **provided that he does not force** himself,[HN] but simply stretches out his hand in the usual manner.

BACKGROUND

Orla – עָרְלָה: It is prohibited to eat or derive benefit from fruit that grows during the first three years after a tree has been planted (see Leviticus 19:23). This prohibition applies only to the fruit but not to the other parts of the tree. In addition, the prohibition does not apply to trees planted as a fence for property or as a wind buffer, and not for their fruit.

HALAKHA

The trunk and roots with regard to *orla* – גֶּזַע וְשָׁרָשִׁים בְּעָרְלָה: In the case of a tree that sprouts from the trunk of an older tree, the owner is exempt from *orla*, but with regard to any tree that sprouts from the roots, he is liable, since the *halakha* follows Rabbi Yehuda when in opposition to Rabbi Meir (Rambam *Sefer Zera'im*, *Hilkhot Ma'aser Sheni* 10:19).

Provided that he does not force himself – וּבִלְבַד שֶׁלֹּא יֵאָנֵס: Although the *halakha* is in accordance with the opinion of Rabbi Shimon that any growth within reach of the owner of the upper garden belongs to him, this applies only if he can take it with ease, but not if he has to exert himself to reach it, as stated by Rabbi Yannai (Rambam *Sefer Kinyan*, *Hilkhot Shekhenim* 4:9; *Shulḥan Arukh*, *Ḥoshen Mishpat* 166:1).

NOTES

Rabbi Shimon's opinion – שִׁיטַת רַבִּי שִׁמְעוֹן: According to Rashi's explanation, Rabbi Shimon agrees with Rabbi Meir that in principle it all belongs to the owner of the upper garden. But since it is inconvenient for the owner of the upper garden to descend to the lower one, Rabbi Shimon holds that he renounces ownership of anything that he cannot reach by hand, and the owner of the lower garden may take it. By contrast, the Rambam maintains that Rabbi Shimon agrees with Rabbi Yehuda that the owner of the lower garden is entitled to all the plants; but he renounces ownership of the upper plants, and the owner of the upper garden may take them.

Provided that he does not force himself – וּבִלְבַד שֶׁלֹּא יֵאָנֵס: In accordance with Rashi's explanation of the opinion of Rabbi Shimon, it can be explained that since the owner of the upper garden may not descend into the lower one to collect the plants without permission, if he takes something he can barely reach, the owner of the lower garden will suspect him of entering his property (*Torat Ḥayyim*).

בָּעֵי רַב עָנָן וְאִיתֵימָא רַבִּי יִרְמְיָה: מַגִּיעַ לְנוֹפוֹ וְאֵין מַגִּיעַ לְעִיקָּרוֹ, מַגִּיעַ לְעִיקָּרוֹ וְאֵין מַגִּיעַ לְנוֹפוֹ, מַאי? תֵּיקוּ.

Rav Anan, and some say it was **Rabbi Yirmeya, raised a dilemma:** If the owner of the upper garden can **reach its leaves, but** he **cannot reach its roots,** or if he can **reach its roots but** he **cannot reach its leaves,**[H] **what** is the *halakha*? Is the plant considered to be within his reach or not? No answer was found for this question, and the Gemara concludes: The dilemma **shall stand** unresolved.

אָמַר אֶפְרַיִם סָפְרָא תַּלְמִידוֹ שֶׁל רֵישׁ לָקִישׁ מִשּׁוּם רֵישׁ לָקִישׁ: הֲלָכָה כְּרַבִּי שִׁמְעוֹן. אֲמַרוּהָ קַמֵּיהּ דִּשְׁבוּר מַלְכָּא. אֲמַר לְהוּ: אַפִּרְיוֹן נִמְטְיֵיהּ לְרַבִּי שִׁמְעוֹן.

Efrayim the scribe, a student of Reish Lakish, says in the name of Reish Lakish: The *halakha* **is in accordance with** the opinion of **Rabbi Shimon. They stated** this case **before** the Persian **King Shapur,**[N] who expressed an interest in this legal issue, and **he said to them: Let us offer praise** [*apiryon*][L] **to Rabbi Shimon.**[N] He too felt that this was the best resolution.

הדרן עלך הבית והעלייה
וסליקא לה מסכת בבא מציעא

HALAKHA

If he can reach its leaves but he cannot reach its roots or if he can reach its roots but he cannot reach its leaves – מַגִּיעַ לְנוֹפוֹ וְאֵין מַגִּיעַ לְעִיקָּרוֹ מַגִּיעַ לְעִיקָּרוֹ וְאֵין מַגִּיעַ לְנוֹפוֹ: If the owner of the upper garden can reach the leaves of a plant but not its roots, or vice versa, he may not take it, but if he did the court does not remove it from him. The reason is that this dilemma is left unresolved by the Gemara. The *Tur* states that they should divide these plants between them *ab initio* (Rambam *Sefer Kinyan, Hilkhot Shekhenim* 4:9; *Shulhan Arukh, Ḥoshen Mishpat* 166:1, and in the *Sma* there).

NOTES

They stated before King Shapur – אֲמַרוּהָ קַמֵּיהּ דִּשְׁבוּר מַלְכָּא: King Shapur, or Shavor Malka, was the name of several Persian kings, among whom there were some who had great interest in Jewish law and tradition. Rashi and most commentaries maintain that this story relates to one of these kings. The *Ye'arot Devash* explains that although it is generally forbidden to teach Torah to gentiles, here it was permitted to teach them these *halakhot* since they pertain to monetary law, and descendants of Noah are also obligated to observe monetary laws. Other commentaries suggest that in this context King Shapur is used as a nickname for one of the Sages, perhaps Shmuel or Rabba, both of whom are referred to by this name elsewhere in the Talmud.

Let us offer praise [*apiryon*] to Rabbi Shimon – אַפִּרְיוֹן נִמְטְיֵיהּ לְרַבִּי שִׁמְעוֹן: The *Arukh* associates *apiryon* with *periya ureviya*, to be fruitful and multiply, similar to "Joseph is a fruitful vine [*ben porat*]" (Genesis 49:22), a blessing that there should be many more Sages like Rabbi Shimon.

LANGUAGE

Praise [*apiryon*] – אַפִּרְיוֹן: From the Middle Persian term āfrīn, meaning blessing or praise.

Summary of **Perek X**

Although this chapter discussed somewhat limited topics, in order to clarify the questions concerning the relationship of two residents of a house that collapsed, it was necessary to examine some fundamental points that have wider ramifications.

This chapter discussed the *halakha* that if one of the residents of a house that collapsed recognizes his stones, he may take them. In the case of a house and an upper story that was rented out, and the floor of the upper story broke, the renter can force the owner to make the necessary repairs, and in the meantime, the renter may live in the owner's house. If a house owned by two people collapsed entirely, they both must rebuild it as it previously stood, and any change that may negatively affect the sturdiness of the building may be implemented only with mutual consent. If the resident of the lower story refuses to rebuild, the owner of the upper story may rebuild the lower story and reside in it until the other pays his expenses, at which time he rebuilds the upper story.

In this chapter it was determined that if someone is performing an action in his own domain that can potentially be harmful to someone else or someone else's property, the one who may be damaged is responsible to distance himself from the damage, and one cannot compel another to refrain from actions that can cause harm indirectly. If the damage is a direct result, or if it includes an act on the part of the perpetrator that directly causes damage to the injured party, the one who causes the damage is obligated to distance himself.

The question of whether one may make use of the public domain was also discussed. It was concluded that anyone may place his items in the public domain temporarily in order to ship them elsewhere, but may not keep them there for an extended period of time. Likewise, one may not use the public domain to do work there. Also, the right to leave things temporarily in the public domain does not exempt the owner, or the one responsible for the shipping of the goods, from paying for damage that may occur from the items placed there.

Another issue discussed in this chapter was the manner in which one pays wages to his laborers. It was concluded that only in specific scenarios is it permitted to pay the laborer with the materials that he cleared; generally speaking, payment must be made with money, unless specifically stipulated otherwise.

The discussion of vegetables growing out of a wall of soil between two adjacent gardens that are not on the same level digressed to the broader questions of whether a plant is defined by its leaves or its roots, and whether the ownership of a tree is decided by its physical location or by its source of nourishment. The *Tur* writes that in a situation where the *halakha* is unclear the vegetables should be divided equally, as this prevents disagreement and increases peace in the world.

Image **Credits**

All images are copyright © Koren Publishers Jerusalem Ltd., except:

p273 © Almog; **p280** © Bob Familiar; **p283** © Rainer Zenz; **p287** top image © Gts, www.shutterstock.com; **p295** © Eitan f; **p313** © brightasafig; **p320** © Eitan f; **p321** © Mary Harrsch; **p332** © Audrius Meskauskas; **p352** left image © Agricmarketing; **p352** center image © John O'Neill; **p352** right image © Marco Schmidt.

My Notes

My Notes

My Notes

My Notes

My Notes

תלמוד בבלי

— מהדורות נאה —

בבא מציעא חלק ו

Steinsaltz Center

KOREN

Please note that the number ranges that appear at the bottom of each daf of the Vilna pages indicate the corresponding pages of the Koren Talmud Bavli translation and commentary.

תלמוד בבלי

הוצאת קורן ירושלים

— מהדורת נאה —

מסכת בבא מציעא
דף קג. עד דף קיט.

COMMENTARY BY
Rabbi Adin Even-Israel
Steinsaltz

EDITOR-IN-CHIEF
Rabbi Dr Tzvi Hersh Weinreb

EXECUTIVE EDITOR
Rabbi Joshua Schreier

•

STEINSALTZ CENTER
KOREN PUBLISHERS JERUSALEM

*[א]שָׂכִיר בִּזְמַנּוֹ נִשְׁבָּע וְנוֹטֵל. שָׂכִיר הוּא דְּרָמוּ רַבָּנַן שְׁבוּעָה עֲלֵיהּ, [ב]מִשּׁוּם דְּבַעַל הַבַּיִת טָרוּד בְּפוֹעֲלָיו. אֲבָל [ג]הָכָא — שׂוֹכֵר מְהֵימַן בִּשְׁבוּעָה. אָמַר רָבָא אָמַר רַב נַחְמָן: [ד]הַאי מַאן דְּאוֹגַר לֵיהּ בֵּיתָא לְחַבְרֵיהּ לְעֶשֶׂר שְׁנִין, וּכְתַב לֵיהּ שְׁטָרָא, וְא"ל: נְקִיטַתְּ חָמֵשׁ שְׁנִין — מְהֵימַן. א"ל רַב אַחָא מִדִּפְתִּי לְרָבִינָא: אֶלָּא מֵעַתָּה אוֹזְפֵיהּ מְאָה זוּזֵי בִּשְׁטָרָא, וְא"ל פְּרַעְתִּיךְ פַּלְגָא — ה"נ דִּמְהֵימַן? א"ל: הָכִי הַשְׁתָּא? הָתָם — שְׁטָר לְגוּבַיְנָא קָאֵי, אִם אִיתָא דִּפְרָעֵיהּ — אִיבָּעֵי לֵיהּ לְמִכְתְּבָא אַגַּבֵּיהּ, א"נ מִיכְתַּב עֲלֵיהּ תַּבְרָא. אֲבָל הָכָא, אָמַר לֵיהּ: הַאי דִּכְתִיבִי לָךְ שְׁטָרָא — כִּי הֵיכִי דְּלָא [א] תֶּחֱזַק עֲלֵיהּ. אָמַר רַב נַחְמָן: [ה]שׁוֹאֵל אָדָם בְּטוּבוֹ לְעוֹלָם. אָמַר רַב מָרִי בְּרֵהּ דְּבַת שְׁמוּאֵל: [ו]וְהוּא דְּקָנֵי מִינֵּיהּ. אָמַר רַב מָרִי בְּרֵיהּ דְּרַב אַשִׁי: [ז]וּמְהַדַּר לֵיהּ קַתֵּיהּ. אָמַר רָבָא: [ח]הַאי מַאן דְּאָמַר לֵיהּ לְחַבְרֵיהּ: אוֹשְׁלַן מָרָא לְמִירְפַּק בֵּיהּ הַאי פַּרְדֵּיסָא — רָפֵיק בֵּיהּ הַהוּא פַּרְדֵּיסָא. פַּרְדֵּיסָא — רָפֵיק בֵּיהּ כָּל פַּרְדֵּיסָא דְּבָעֵי. פַּרְדֵּיסֵי — רָפֵיק וְאָזֵיל כָּל פַּרְדֵּיסֵי דְּאִית לֵיהּ, וּמְהַדַּר לֵיהּ קַתֵּיהּ. אָמַר רַב פָּפָּא: [ט]הַאי מַאן דְּאָמַר לֵיהּ לְחַבְרֵיהּ אוֹשְׁלַן הַאי גַּרְגּוּתָא וְנָפְלָה — לָא בָּנֵי לָהּ. גַּרְגּוּתָא וְנָפְלָה — בָּנֵי לָהּ. בֵּי גַּרְגּוּתָא — כָּרֵי וְאָזֵיל כַּמָּה גַּרְגּוּתֵי בְּאַרְעֵיהּ עַד דְּמִתְרַמֵּי לֵיהּ. וְצָרִיךְ לְמִיקְנֵי מִינֵּיהּ.§

מתני' [י]הַמַּשְׂכִּיר בַּיִת לַחֲבֵירוֹ וְנָפַל — חַיָּיב לְהַעֲמִיד לוֹ בַּיִת. הָיָה קָטָן — לֹא יַעֲשֶׂנּוּ גָּדוֹל, גָּדוֹל — לֹא יַעֲשֶׂנּוּ קָטָן. אֶחָד — לֹא יַעֲשֶׂנּוּ שְׁנַיִם, שְׁנַיִם — לֹא יַעֲשֶׂנּוּ אֶחָד. לֹא יִפְחוֹת מִן הַחַלּוֹנוֹת וְלֹא יוֹסִיף עֲלֵיהֶם, אֶלָּא מִדַּעַת שְׁנֵיהֶם.§ **גמ'** הֵיכִי דָמֵי? אִי דְּאָמַר לֵיהּ בַּיִת זֶה — נָפַל אֲזַל לֵיהּ! אִי דְּאָמַר לֵיהּ בַּיִת סְתָם — אֶחָד [כ]אַמַּאי לֹא יַעֲשֶׂנּוּ שְׁנַיִם, קָטָן אַמַּאי לֹא יַעֲשֶׂנּוּ גָּדוֹל? אָמַר רֵישׁ לָקִישׁ: דְּאָמַר לֵיהּ: בַּיִת שֶׁאֲנִי מַשְׂכִּיר לָךְ מִדַּת אָרְכּוֹ כָּךְ וְכָךְ. אִי הָכִי, מַאי לְמֵימְרָא? אֶלָּא, כִּי אֲתָא רָבִין אֲמַר רֵישׁ לָקִישׁ: דְּאָמַר לֵיהּ [ל]בַּיִת כָּזֶה אֲנִי מַשְׂכִּיר לָךְ. וְאַכַּתִּי מַאי לְמֵימְרָא? [מ]לָא צְרִיכָא דְּקָאֵי אַגּוּדָּא דְּנַהֲרָא. מַהוּ דְּתֵימָא: מַאי כָּזֶה — דְּקָאֵי אַגּוּדָּא דְּנַהֲרָא. קמ"ל.§

הדרן עלך השואל

הַמְקַבֵּל שָׂדֶה מֵחֲבֵירוֹ, [נ]מָקוֹם שֶׁנָּהֲגוּ לִקְצוֹר — יִקְצוֹר, לַעֲקוֹר — יַעֲקוֹר, לַחֲרוֹשׁ (א) אַחֲרָיו — יַחֲרוֹשׁ, הַכֹּל כְּמִנְהַג הַמְּדִינָה. [ס]כְּשֵׁם שֶׁחוֹלְקִין בַּתְּבוּאָה כָּךְ חוֹלְקִין בַּתֶּבֶן וּבַקַּשׁ, כְּשֵׁם שֶׁחוֹלְקִין בַּיַּיִן כָּךְ חוֹלְקִין בַּזְּמוֹרוֹת

רש"י

שָׂכִיר בִּזְמַנּוֹ נִשְׁבָּע וְנוֹטֵל. אִם בַּיּוֹם שֶׁיָּצָא מִמְּלַאכְתּוֹ תְּבָעוֹ — נִשְׁבָּע שֶׁלֹּא קִיבֵּל, וְנוֹטֵל. שֶׁזֶּה אֶחָד מִן הַנִּשְׁבָּעִים וְנוֹטְלִין הָאֲמוּרִים בְּמַסֶּכֶת שְׁבוּעוֹת (דף מד:) שֶׁתִּקְּנוּ לוֹ חֲכָמִים. דְּהַקְלוּהָ לִשְׁבוּעָה מִבַּעַל הַבַּיִת וְהִטִּילוּהָ אַשָּׂכִיר, מִשּׁוּם דְּבַעַל הַבַּיִת טָרוּד בְּפוֹעֲלָיו, וּכְסָבוּר שֶׁנָּתַן לָזֶה כְּשֶׁנָּתַן לַחֲבֵירוֹ. (ב) אֲבָל. בְּעָלְמָא, אֲפִי' בְּיוֹם זְמַנּוֹ נֶאֱמָן לוֹמַר: פְּרַעְתִּיךָ כְּבָר! וּבִשְׁבוּעַת הֶיסֵּת שֶׁהִטִּילוּ חֲכָמִים — עַל מִי שֶׁאֵינוֹ מוֹדֶה בְּמִקְצָת. וּכְתַב לֵיהּ. מַשְׂכִּיר לַשּׂוֹכֵר שְׁטָר שֶׁהִשְׂכִּירָהּ לוֹ לְעֶשֶׂר שָׁנִים, וְלֹא נִכְתַּב בַּשְּׁטָר זְמַן. וּלְאַחַר זְמַן בָּא לִפְנֵי ב"ד, וְאָמַר: כְּבָר דַּרְתָּ בָּהּ חָמֵשׁ שָׁנִים. וְזֶה אָמַר: לֹא דַּרְתִּי אֶלָּא שָׁלֹשׁ. מְהֵימַן. בַּעַל הַבַּיִת. דְּקַרְקַע בְּחֶזְקַת בְּעָלֶיהָ עוֹמֶדֶת, עַל כָּל דָּבָר סָפֵק הַבָּא לְפָנֵינוּ. תַּבְרָא. שׁוֹבֵר. דְּלָא תֶּחֱזַק בָּהּ. דְּלֹא תֹּאמַר: לְקוּחָה הִיא בְּיָדִי. וְלֹא שֶׁתּוּכַל לִתְבּוֹעַ עֶשֶׂר שָׁנִים לְעוֹלָם. שׁוֹאֵל אָדָם בְּטוּבוֹ לְעוֹלָם. אִם רָאָה אָדָם כְּלִי לַחֲבֵירוֹ, וְאָמַר: הַשְׁאִילֵנִי בְּטוּבוֹ, וא"ל: הֵן — שׁוֹאֲלוֹ לוֹ לְעוֹלָם, כָּל זְמַן שֶׁהוּא רָאוּי לִמְלָאכָה. דְּהַאי "בְּטוּבוֹ" מַשְׁמַע לָן: כָּל זְמַן שֶׁהוּא *טוּבוֹ, אֲפִילוּ מַחֲזִירוֹ — חוֹזֵר וְנוֹטְלוֹ כְּשֶׁיִּצְטָרֵךְ. וְהוּא דְּקָנֵי מִינֵּיהּ. דִּבְעָלִים, אֲבָל לֹא קָנֵי —[ב] מָצֵי מַהְדְּרֵיהּ דְּלָתָה קִנְיָיה דְּמַשִׁיכָה רִאשׁוֹנָה. וּמְהַדַּר לֵיהּ קַתֵּיהּ. וּכְשֶׁיִּפְחוֹת, שֶׁלֹּא יְהֵא רָאוּי — יַחֲזִיר לוֹ שְׁבָרָיו. דְּהָא לָאו בְּמַתָּנָה יְהָבֵיהּ אֶלָּא שְׁאֵלָה הֲוַאי, [ג] וּבְטוּבוֹ (ג) הוּא, וְהַאי לָאו טוּב הוּא. פַּרְדֵּיסָא. סְתָמָא. רָפֵיק בֵּיהּ. חַד פַּרְדֵּיסָא. כָּל דְּבָעֵי. אֲפִילוּ [ד] גָּדוֹל כְּאַנְטוֹכְיָא. וְאִי א"ל פַּרְדֵּיסֵי. רָפֵיק בֵּיהּ, כָּל פַּרְדֵּיסֵי דְּאִית לֵיהּ, וְלָא אָמְרִינַן: תְּרֵי פַּרְדֵּיסֵי הוּא דְּקָאָמַר לֵיהּ, דַּאֲפִי' טוּבָא נַמִּי מַשְׁמַע. אוֹשְׁלַן. הַשְׁאִילֵנִי. גַּרְגּוּתָא. בְּאֵר מַיִם חַיִּים לְהַשְׁקוֹת שָׂדוֹת. לָא בָּנֵי לָהּ. אִם בָּא לִבְנוֹתוֹ וְלוֹמַר: עוֹד שְׁאוֹל לִי — לְעוֹלָם זֶה מְעַכֵּב עָלָיו, וְאוֹמֵר: לֹא הִשְׁאַלְתִּיךָ אֶלָּא אוֹתוֹ, וְלֹא כְּשֶׁנַּעֲשָׂה אַחֵר. בָּנֵי לָהּ. וַהֲרֵי הִיא שְׁאוּלָה לוֹ עַד שֶׁיַּשְׁקֶה כָּל שְׂדוֹתָיו. בֵּי גַּרְגּוּתָא. אָמַר לוֹ בַּלָּשׁוֹן הַזֶּה: הַשְׁאִילֵנִי בֵּי גַּרְגּוּתָא — הַשְׁאִילֵנִי מָקוֹם לַחְפּוֹר בּוֹ בְּאֵר קָאָמַר לֵיהּ. וְכָרֵי וְאָזֵיל כַּמָּה גַּרְגּוּתֵי בְּאַרְעֵיהּ. אִם לֹא יִמְצָא כָּאן יַחְפּוֹר בְּמָקוֹם אַחֵר, עַד דְּמִתְרַמֵּי לֵיהּ מָקוֹם הָרָאוּי. וְצָרִיךְ לְמִיקְנֵי מִינֵּיהּ. מֵעִיקָּרָא, וְאִי לָא קָנָה מִינֵּיהּ — דִּיבּוּרָא בְּעָלְמָא הוּא, וּמָצֵי לְמֶהְדַּר בֵּיהּ. **מתני'** חַיָּיב לְהַעֲמִיד לוֹ בַּיִת. בִּימֵי שְׂכִירוּתוֹ. לֹא יַעֲשֶׂנּוּ קָטָן. הַשּׂוֹכֵר מְעַכֵּב עָלָיו: אִי אֶפְשִׁי בְּבַיִת גָּדוֹל, וְאִי אֶפְשִׁי בְּבַיִת קָטָן. **גמ'** וְאִי דְּאָמַר לֵיהּ בַּיִת זֶה. אֲנִי מַשְׂכִּיר לָךְ. אָזְדָא לֵיהּ. הָלַךְ לוֹ, מַזָּלוֹ גָּרַם, וְאַמַּאי חַיָּיב לְהַעֲמִיד לוֹ בַּיִת? וְלִיטְעֲמִיהּ. ל"ג. מַהוּ דְּתֵימָא מַאי כָּזֶה דְּקָאֵי אַגּוּדָּא דְּנַהֲרָא. שֶׁהוּא חָשׁוּב, וַאֲגוּדָּא דְּנַהֲרָא הוּא דְּמַתְנֵי בַּהֲדֵיהּ, שֶׁדֶּרֶךְ בְּנֵי אָדָם מַקְפִּידִין בְּכָךְ. אֲבָל אָרְכּוֹ וְרָחְבּוֹ לָא אַתְנֵי בַּהֲדֵיהּ. קמ"ל. דְּאַכּוּלָּהּ מִילְּתָא אַתְנֵי.

הדרן עלך השואל

הַמְקַבֵּל . אוֹ בַּאֲרִיסוּת: לְמֶחֱצָה וְלִשְׁלִישׁ וְלִרְבִיעַ, אוֹ בַּחֲכִירוּת: בְּכָךְ וְכָךְ כּוֹרִים לְשָׁנָה. לַחֲרוֹשׁ אַחֲרָיו. אַחַר הַקְּצִירָה, אוֹ הָעֲקִירָה, כְּדֵי לַהֲפוֹךְ שָׁרָשִׁים שֶׁל עֲשָׂבִים רָעִים שֶׁבּוֹ, וְיָמוּתוּ, וְלֹא יַחְזְרוּ וְיִצְמְחוּ לִכְשֶׁתִּזָּרַע. בַּזְּמוֹרוֹת

תוספות

נקיטת חמש שנין. פר"ח, לשון אחד, וכן בקונטרס: שאין כתוב בשטר לא תחילת השנים ולא סופן. והשטר ביד השוכר. ואומר משכיר לשוכרך כבר דרת ה' שנים. ופריך: בשטר מלוה — מי נאמן לומר פרעתי פלגא?! ומשני: הכא א"ל: האי דכתבי לך שטרא — כי היכי דלא תחזק, פירוש: עיקר השטר נכתב בשבילי. שלא תאמר: לקוח הוא בידי, ואין השטר בידך אלא כדי שלא אכחש לך חשבו השנים כמה היו, מכל מקום, עיקר השטר — בשבילי נכתב, שע"י כן יש קול שבמשכנתא הוא אצלך, אע"פ שהשטר בידך. ולשון שני פר"ח, וזה לשונו: יש אומרים שכתוב בשטר: בזמן כך וכך שכרתי אצרו של פלוני עשר שנים בק' דינרים, י' דינרים בכל שנה, ואחר ה' שנים טוען השוכר ואמר למשכיר: נקיטת שכירות חמש שנין כו' ואסיקנא דהשוכר נאמן, ובשבועה. ומסתברא כי האי פירושא בתרא. עכ"ל. ולשון זה נראה עיקר. הדא, דבנאמנות השוכר האומר שפרע השכירות — איירי נמי לעיל מיניה, בסמוך, ומשמע דבהכי נמי איירי. (ד) ועוד, דהשתא ניחא טפי מה שאמר במסקנא. שלא נעשה שטר לגוביינא אלא כדי שלא יחזיק השוכר, דלפי זה השטר ישנו ביד המשכיר. **שואל** אדם בטובו. בערוך בערך "שואל, מפרש: בטובו — בטובה שמחזיק השואל להמשאיל, יכול השואל להשתמש לעולם בכליו של משאיל. ואין נראה. **פרדיסי** רפיק ביה כל פרדיסי דאית ליה. וא"ת: דאמר בריש "המוכר את הבית" (ב"ב דף סא: ושם ד"ה ארעתא): ארעתא — תרתי משמע, ואין לומר: דהתם נמי אי אמר "ארעאי" — הוה משמע כולה כמו פרדיסי, דהא אמר התם בסוף פרק (דף סט:): דיקלי — יהיב ליה תרי דיקלי, ותו לא. וי"ל: דהיינו דוקא גבי מכר, דאין לנו לומר שמכר כל קרקעותיו אלא הפחות, אבל בשאלה אינו מקפיד, דמשאיל לכל צרכו. (ה) ועוד י"ל: דהתם — יד לוקח על התחתונה, שהמוכר מוחזק. והכא — יד המשאיל על התחתונה, שהשואל מוחזק. וכ"ת לא מקרי שוא "מוחזק", כיון שסופו להחזיר ואין נשאר בידו, כדאמר לעיל: קרקע בחזקת בעליה עומדת ואפי' בסוף החדש — לא דמי: דדוקא קרקע, שאין יכול להגניע לשמטו מיד בעלה — אזלינן בתר חזקה קמא, אבל במטלטלין, — אזלינן בתר מאן דתופס השתא, היכא דליכא חזקת קרקע כנגדה.

הדרך עלך השואל

המקבל . בתבן ובקש. אותו שנקצץ עם השבולת קרוי תבן, והנשאר בארץ קרוי קש, שקורין אישטובל"א כדכתיב (בראשית כד): "גם תבן גם מספוא רב עמנו" ואותו שנשאר בקרקע אין נותנין לבהמות לאכול, וכתיב נמי (שמות ה): "לקושש קש לתבן" — שהיו מלוקטים בשדות הקש הנשאר שם תחת התבן, כי התבן כבר הוליכוהו הבעלים איש לביתו. וכן אמרינן בפרק "שואל" (שבת דף קנ:): בשלמא קש משכחת לה במחובר, אלא תבן — במחובר היכי משכחת לה?! ובגמרא דקאמר: (ו) בעינא דתיתבן ארעאי — הוה ליה למימר: דתתקש, אלא משום שרגילות הוא לעשות אשפה מן התבן ולזבל השדה, ולהכי קאמר: דתיתבן, כלומר: שיהא הקש במקום הזבל העושין מן התבן. והא דקאמר נמי: בעינא תיבנא, התם לפי שעוקר הכל, ודש את הכל במוריגים, ומתרכך — נקרא הכל תבן. [וע"ע תוספות שבת נו: ד"ה כירה]: ואזיל

[לקמן קיח.] שבועות מה:

נ"ל טוב ואפילו. יעב"ץ ועי' רש"ש

עין משפט נר מצוה

קב א ב מיי' פי"א מהל' שכירות הל' ו סמג עשין צ טוש"ע ח"מ סי' פט סעיף ב וסעיף ג:
קג ג מיי' שם פ"ז הל' ג ועיין במגדל עוז ובמ"מ סמג שם טוש"ע ח"מ סי' שיז סעיף א:
קד ד מיי' שם הלכה ד טוש"ע שם סעיף ב:
קה ה ו ז מיי' פ"א מהל' שאלה ופקדון הלכה ח סמג לאוין נב טוש"ע ח"מ סי' שמא סעיף ו:
קו ח מיי' שם הלכה ז טוש"ע שם סעיף ז:
קז ט מיי' שם הלכה ט טוש"ע שם סעיף ח:
קח י כ ל מ מיי' פ"ה מהלכות שכירות הלכה ז סמג עשין פט טוש"ע ח"מ סי' שיב סעיף יז:
א נ מיי' שם פ"ח הל' ו סמג שם טוש"ע ח"מ סי' שכ סעיף ד:
ב ס מיי' שם הלכה י סמג שם טוש"ע ח"מ סי' שכז סעיף ב:

הגהות הב"ח

(א) במשנה לחרוש אחריו יחרוש: (ב) רש"י ד"ה שכיר וד"ה אבל הד"א: (ג) ד"ה ומהדר וכו' ובטובו הוא והאי: (ד) תוס' ד"ה נקיטת וכו' דבהכי נמי איירי הכא ועוד: (ה) ד"ה פרדיסי וכו' ועוד י"ל. נ"ב ובריש המוכר [את] הבית דחו התוס' פירוש זה: (ו) תוס' ד"ה המקבל וכו' ובגמרא דקאמר האי אמר בעינא דתיתבן:

הגהות הגר"א

[א] גמ' תחזק. נ"ב גירסת ר"ח אחזיק עלך. בעל העיטור ועי' בתוס' (ולשון שני פר"ח כו'): [ב] רש"י ד"ה והוא דקני. מכי כו'. נ"ב ורי"ף ורמב"ם מפרשים אפי' לא אהדריה ועי' רא"ש והג"א: [ג] שם ד"ה ומהדר. ובטובו כו'. נ"ב ר"ל שאינו יכול לתקנו: [ד] שם ד"ה כל דבעי אפי' כו'. נ"ב ורמב"ם פי' אפי' אינו שלו:

בַּזְּמוֹרוֹת וּבַקָּנִים, וּשְׁנֵיהֶם מְסַפְּקִין אֶת הַקָּנִים.§
גמ' תָּנָא: מָקוֹם שֶׁנָּהֲגוּ לִקְצוֹר — אֵינוֹ רַשַּׁאי לַעֲקוֹר, לַעֲקוֹר — אֵינוֹ רַשַּׁאי לִקְצוֹר, [א]וּשְׁנֵיהֶם מְעַכְּבִין זֶה עַל זֶה. "לִקְצוֹר אֵינוֹ רַשַּׁאי לַעֲקוֹר" — הַאי אָמַר: בָּעֵינָא דְּתִתְבַּן לִי אַרְעַאי, וְהַאי אָמַר: לָא מָצֵינָא. "לַעֲקוֹר אֵינוֹ רַשַּׁאי לִקְצוֹר" — הַאי אָמַר: בָּעֵינָא דְּתִינָּקֵר אַרְעַאי, וְהַאי אָמַר: בָּעֵינָא תִּיבְנָא. "וּשְׁנֵיהֶם מְעַכְּבִין זֶה עַל זֶה". לָמָּה לִי? מַה טַּעַם קָאָמַר; מַה טַּעַם לִקְצוֹר אֵינוֹ רַשַּׁאי לַעֲקוֹר, לַעֲקוֹר אֵינוֹ רַשַּׁאי לִקְצוֹר? מִשּׁוּם דִּשְׁנֵיהֶם מְעַכְּבִין זֶה עַל זֶה.§ "לַחֲרוֹשׁ אַחֲרָיו יַחֲרוֹשׁ".§ פְּשִׁיטָא! [ב]לָא צְרִיכָא, בְּאַתְרָא דְּלָא מְנַכְּשֵׁי, וַאֲזַל אִיהוּ וְנָכֵישׁ. מַהוּ דְּתֵימָא? אֲמַר לֵיהּ: הַאי דְּנָכֵישְׁנָא — אַדַּעְתָּא דְּלָא כְּרֵיבְנָא לָהּ, קמ"ל [א] [ג]דְּאִיבָּעֵי לֵיהּ לְפָרוֹשֵׁי לֵיהּ.§ "הַכֹּל כְּמִנְהַג הַמְּדִינָה".§ "הַכֹּל" לְאֵתוֹיֵי מַאי? לְאֵתוֹיֵי הָא דְּת"ר: [ד]מָקוֹם שֶׁנָּהֲגוּ לְהַשְׂכִּיר אִילָנוֹת עַל גַּבֵּי קַרְקַע — מַשְׂכִּירִין, מָקוֹם שֶׁאֵין נָהֲגוּ לְהַשְׂכִּיר — אֵין מַשְׂכִּירִין. "מָקוֹם שֶׁנָּהֲגוּ לְהַשְׂכִּיר מַשְׂכִּירִין". פְּשִׁיטָא! [ה]לָא צְרִיכָא, דְּכ"ע יָהֲבִי בְּתִילְתָּא וַאֲזַל אִיהוּ וִיהָבֵיהּ בְּרִיבְעָא. מַהוּ דְּתֵימָא? דְּאָמַר לֵיהּ: הַאי דְּבָצְרִי לָךְ — אַדַּעְתָּא דְּלָא יָהֵיבְנָא לָךְ בְּאִילָנוֹת, קמ"ל דְּאִיבָּעֵי לֵיהּ לְפָרוֹשֵׁי לֵיהּ.§ "מָקוֹם שֶׁנָּהֲגוּ שֶׁלֹּא לְהַשְׂכִּיר אֵין מַשְׂכִּירִין".§ פְּשִׁיטָא! [ו]לָא צְרִיכָא, דְּכ"ע מְקַבְּלֵי (א) בְּרִיבְעָא, וַאֲזַל אִיהוּ וְקִיבְּלָהּ בְּתִילְתָּא. מַהוּ דְּתֵימָא? א"ל: הַאי דְּטַפַּאי לָךְ — אַדַּעְתָּא דִּיהַבְתְּ לִי בְּאִילָנוֹת. קמ"ל דְּאִיבָּעֵי לֵיהּ לְפָרוֹשֵׁי לֵיהּ.§ "כְּשֵׁם שֶׁחוֹלְקִין בַּתְּבוּאָה כָּךְ חוֹלְקִין בַּתֶּבֶן וּבַקַּשׁ".§ אֲמַר רַב יוֹסֵף: בְּבָבֶל נְהִיגוּ דְּלָא יָהֲבִי תִּיבְנָא לַאֲרִיסָא. לְמַאי נָפְקָא מִינָּהּ? דְּאִי אִיכָּא אִינִישׁ דְּיָהֵיב — עַיִן יָפָה הוּא, וְלָא גָּמְרִינַן מִינֵּיהּ. אֲמַר רַב יוֹסֵף: [ז]בּוּכְרָא וְטַפְתָּא וְאַרְכַּבְתָּא וְקָנֵי דְּחִיזְרָא — דְּבַעַל הַבַּיִת, וְחִיזְרָא גּוּפֵיהּ דַּאֲרִיסָא. [ח]כְּלָלָא דְּמִילְּתָא: כָּל עִיקַּר [ב] *בַּלְמָא — דְּבַעַל הַבַּיִת, נְטִירוּתָא יְתֵירְתָּא — דַּאֲרִיסָא. וַאֲמַר רַב יוֹסֵף: [ג] [ט]מָרָא וּזְבִילָא וְדַוְולָא וְזַרְנוּקָא — דְּבַעַל הַבַּיִת; אֲרִיסָא עָבֵיד בֵּי יְאוֹרֵי.§ "כְּשֵׁם שֶׁחוֹלְקִין בְּיַיִן כָּךְ חוֹלְקִין בַּזְּמוֹרוֹת וּבַקָּנִים".§ (ב) קָנִים מַאי עֲבִידְתַּיְיהוּ? אָמְרִי דְּבֵי רַבִּי יַנַּאי: קָנִים הַמּוּחְלָקִין, שֶׁבָּהֶן מַעֲמִידִין אֶת הַגְּפָנִים.§ "וּשְׁנֵיהֶם מְסַפְּקִין אֶת הַקָּנִים".§ לָמָּה לִי? מַה טַּעַם קָאָמַר; מַה טַּעַם שְׁנֵיהֶם חוֹלְקִין בַּקָּנִים? מִשּׁוּם דִּשְׁנֵיהֶם מְסַפְּקִין אֶת הַקָּנִים.§

מתני' [א]הַמְקַבֵּל שָׂדֶה מֵחֲבֵירוֹ וְהִיא בֵּית הַשְּׁלָחִין אוֹ בֵּית הָאִילָן, יָבַשׁ הַמַּעְיָן וְנִקְצַץ הָאִילָן — אֵינוֹ מְנַכֶּה לוֹ מִן חֲכוֹרוֹ. [ב]אִם אָמַר לוֹ חֲכוֹר לִי שְׂדֵה בֵּית הַשְּׁלָחִין זוֹ אוֹ שְׂדֵה בֵּית הָאִילָן זֶה יָבַשׁ הַמַּעְיָן וְנִקְצַץ הָאִילָן — מְנַכֶּה לוֹ מִן חֲכוֹרוֹ.§ **גמ'** הֵיכִי דָּמֵי? אִילֵימָא דְּיָבַשׁ נַהֲרָא רַבָּה — אַמַּאי אֵינוֹ מְנַכֶּה לוֹ מִן חֲכוֹרוֹ? [ד] [ל]נֵימָא לֵיהּ: מַכַּת מְדִינָה הִיא! אֲמַר רַב פָּפָּא: [מ]דְּיָבֵשׁ נַהֲרָא זוּטָא, דְּאָמַר לֵיהּ: אִיבָּעֵי

רש"י

בִּזְמוֹרוֹת. הַקְּלוּלִין מִן הַגְּפָנִים. בְּקָנִים. מְפָרֵשׁ בַּגְּמָ': קָנִים הַמַּעֲמִידִים אֶת הַגְּפָנִים, שֶׁקּוֹרִין פוֹסי"ל. וּשְׁנֵיהֶם מְסַפְּקִין אֶת הַקָּנִים. הַחֲדָשִׁים, בְּכָל שָׁנָה, שֶׁאֵין עַל הָאָרִיס אֶלָּא לַעֲבוֹד וְלִשְׁמוֹר, אֲבָל שְׁאָר דְּבָרִים עַל שְׁנֵיהֶן. וְסֵיפָא דְּמַתְנִיתִין לֵיתָא אֶלָּא בְּקַבְּלָנוּת, דְּאִי בַּחֲכָרָנוּת — לָא שַׁיְיכָא חֲלוּקָה. **גמ'** וּשְׁנֵיהֶן מְעַכְּבִין. לְשַׁנּוֹת מִן הַמִּנְהָג. הַאי אָמַר. בַּעַל הַקַּרְקַע — אִי אֶפְשִׁי שֶׁתַּעֲקוֹר, דְּבָעֵינָא דְּתֵיתְבַּן אַרְעַאי — שֶׁיִּשָּׁאֲרוּ בָּהּ מִן הַקַּשִּׁין וִיהֵא לָהּ לְזֶבֶל לִזְרִיעָתָהּ לַשָּׁנָה הַבָּאָה. וְהַאי אָמַר. אִם בַּעַל הַבַּיִת אָמַר: עֲקוֹר, מָצֵי הַאי לְמֵימַר לֵיהּ: לָא מָצֵינָא מִיטְרַח, שֶׁהַקְּצִירָה נוֹחָה מִן הָעֲקִירָה. דְּתִינָּקֵר. שֶׁתְּהֵא נְקִיָּה שֶׁאֵינָהּ צְרִיכָה לְזֶבֶל. בָּעֵינָא תִּיבְנָא. אֲנִי צָרִיךְ תֶּבֶן לִבְהֵמוֹתַי, וְאִי אֶפְשִׁי שֶׁתִּשָּׁאֵר בַּקַּרְקַע. שְׁנֵיהֶן מְעַכְּבִין זֶה עַל זֶה לָמָּה לִי. כֵּיוָן דִּתְנַן בִּתְרַוַיְיהוּ: אֵינוֹ רַשַּׁאי — מִכְּלָל דְּזִימְנִין דְּנִיחָא לֵיהּ לְמָר בְּהָכִי וּלְמָר בְּהָכִי, וְזִימְנִין אִיפְּכָא. מִשּׁוּם דִּשְׁנֵיהֶם מְעַכְּבִין. כְּלוֹמַר: מִפְּנֵי שֶׁשְּׁנֵיהֶן יֵשׁ לָהֶם טַעֲנָה לְכָאן וּלְכָאן. וַאֲזַיל אִיהוּ וְנָכֵישׁ. בְּעוֹד שֶׁהַתְּבוּאָה מְחוּבֶּרֶת, וְתָלַשׁ מִמֶּנָּה עֲשָׂבִים רָעִים. אֶלָּא שֶׁלְּאַחַר מִכָּאן חָזְרוּ וְגָדְלוּ בָּהֶן קְצָת מֵהֶן. דְּלָא כְּרֵיבְנָא לֵיהּ. שֶׁלֹּא אֶחֱרוֹשׁ עוֹד אַחֲרֶיהָ, שֶׁהַנִּיכּוּשׁ בִּמְקוֹם חֲרִישָׁה שֶׁלְּאַחַר הַקְּצִירָה הִיא, לִמְנוֹעַ עֲשָׂבִים הָרָעִים. שֶׁנָּהֲגוּ לְהַשְׂכִּיר אִילָנוֹת. עִם שְׂדֵה לָבָן, שֶׁיִּטּוֹל הָאָרִיס חֶלְקוֹ בְּפֵירוֹת הָאִילָן, אע"פ שֶׁאֵינוֹ טוֹרֵחַ בָּהֶן, שֶׁאֵינָן צְרִיכִין לַעֲבוֹדָה. מַשְׂכִּירִין. כְּלוֹמַר: מִסְתָּמָא הֵן מוּשְׂכָּרִין. יָהֲבִי בְּתִילְתָּא. נוֹתְנִין קַרְקָעוֹת לַאֲרִיסִין ע"מ שֶׁיִּטְּלוּ הֵן חֵלֶק שְׁלִישִׁי, וְאָרִיס שְׁנֵי חֲלָקִים. וַאֲזַל אִיהוּ וְיָהֵיב בְּרִיבְעָא. שֶׁלֹּא יִטּוֹל הוּא אֶלָּא רְבִיעַ, וְהָאָרִיס שְׁלֹשָׁה חֲלָקִים. דְּבָצְרִי לָךְ. שֶׁאֲנִי נוֹטֵל פָּחוֹת מִשְּׁאָר בַּעֲלֵי בָתִּים. מְקַבְּלֵי בְּרִיבְעָתָא. ע"מ לִיתֵּן לְבַעַל הַקַּרְקַע רְבִיעַ בַּתְּבוּאָה. בּוּכְרָא וְטַפְתָּא וְאַרְכַּבְתָּא וְקָנֵי דְּחִיזְרָא דְּבַעַל הַבַּיִת. סְבִיבוֹת הַשָּׂדֶה עוֹשִׂין חָרִיץ וְנוֹתְנִין הֶעָפָר עַל הַמֵּיצַר לְהַגְבִּיהַּ סְבִיבוֹתָיו. וּלְאַחַר זְמַן, כְּשֶׁנִּידַּשׁ, חוֹזֵר הוּא וּמוֹסִיף עָלָיו עָפָר שֵׁנִית, וְכֵן שְׁלִישִׁית. רִאשׁוֹן — קָרֵי בּוּכְרָא, וְהַשֵּׁנִי — טַפְתָּא, לְשׁוֹן רִיבּוּי — דִּמְטַפֵּי לָהּ, וְהַשְּׁלִישִׁי קָרֵי אַרְכַּבְתָּא. קָנֵי דְּחִיזְרָא. קָנִים שֶׁנּוֹטְעִים בָּאָרֶץ לֶאֱרוֹג בּוֹ קוֹצִים אוֹ נְסָרִים סְבִיבוֹת הַשָּׂדֶה. דְּבַעַל הַבַּיִת. עָלָיו יְלִיאָה זֹאת לַעֲשׂוֹת. חִיזְרָא גּוּפֵיהּ. הַקּוֹצִים שֶׁאוֹרְגִין בּוֹ סָבִיב הַקָּנִים — דְּאָרִיסָא. עִיקַּר בַּלְמָא. עִיקַּר שְׁמִירָה, שֶׁאִי אֶפְשָׁר בְּלֹא הִיא. נְטִירוּתָא יְתֵירְתָּא דַּאֲרִיסָא. עָלָיו לְהוֹצִיא, שֶׁאֵינוֹ עוֹשֶׂה אֶלָּא לְהָקֵל מֵעָלָיו, שֶׁלֹּא יִצְטָרֵךְ לִטְרוֹחַ כָּל כָּךְ בִּשְׁמִירָתָהּ. מָרָא. פוסוי"ר בְּלַעַ"ז. וּזְבִילָא. (ג) פאל"א. וְדַוְולָא. דְּלִי לְהַשְׁקוֹת שָׂדֶה. וְזַרְנוּקָא. נוֹד לְמַלְאוֹת, בְּמָקוֹם שֶׁנּוֹהֲגִין לִדְלוֹת בְּנוֹדוֹת. אֲרִיסָא עָבֵיד בֵּי יְאוֹרֵי. עָלָיו לַעֲשׂוֹת חֲרִיצִין מִשְּׂפַת הַנָּהָר עַד סוֹף הַשָּׂדֶה, חֲרִיצִין הַרְבֵּה, שֶׁכְּשֶׁדּוֹלִין הַמַּיִם מִן הַנָּהָר — שׁוֹפְכִין בַּחֲרִיצִין, וְהַחֲרִיצִין מוֹלִיכִין עַד סוֹף הַשָּׂדֶה, וְהִיא שׁוֹתָה מֵאֵלֶיהָ. מוּחְלָקִין. שֶׁנִּיטְּלָה קְלִיפָּתָן, מֵחֲשׁוֹף הַלָּבָן שֶׁעֲלֵיהֶן. שְׁנֵיהֶם מְסַפְּקִין לָמָּה לִי. פְּשִׁיטָא! כֵּיוָן דִּתְנָא דְּלִשְׁנֵיהֶן הֵן, וְחוֹלְקִין בָּהֶן — מִמֵּילָא שָׁמְעִינַן דִּשְׁנֵיהֶן מְסַפְּקִין אֶת הַחֲדָשִׁים, דְּאִי לָא יָהֵיב מְעִיקָּרָא — אַמַּאי פָּלֵיג בִּישָׁנִים? **מתני'** בֵּית הַשְּׁלָחִין. קַרְקַע יְבֵשָׁה דְּלֹא דַּיָּיהּ בְּמֵי הַגְּשָׁמִים, וּמִמַּעְיָין שֶׁבָּהּ מַשְׁקֶה אוֹתָהּ. אוֹ בֵּית הָאִילָן. וּבִשְׁבִיל הָאִילָן הַהוּא חֲבִיבָה עַל הָאָרִיס, שֶׁנּוֹטֵל חֵלֶק בְּפֵירוֹת בְּלֹא טוֹרַח. מִן חֲכוֹרוֹ. אִם קִיבְּלָהּ מִמֶּנּוּ בַּחֲכִירוֹת בְּכָךְ וְכָךְ כּוֹרִין לְשָׁנָה, דִּמְעִיקָּרָא לָא גַּלֵּי דַּעְתֵּיהּ דְּמִשּׁוּם מַעְיָין אוֹ אִילָן טָפֵי לֵיהּ בַּחֲכִירוּתֵיהּ. חֲכוֹר לִי בֵּית הַשְּׁלָחִין זוֹ. גַּלֵּי דַּעְתֵּיהּ, דְּבִשְׁבִיל שֶׁהוּא בֵּית הַשְּׁלָחִין — טָפֵי לֵיהּ, וַחֲכָרָהּ מִמֶּנּוּ. **גמ'** נַהֲרָא רַבָּה. שֶׁהַכֹּל מַשְׁקִין מִמֶּנּוּ. נֵימָא לֵיהּ מַכַּת מְדִינָה הִיא. וּתְנַן לְקַמָּן בְּפִירְקִין (דף קה:): הַמְקַבֵּל שָׂדֶה מֵחֲבֵירוֹ וַאֲכָלָהּ חָגָב, אוֹ שֶׁנִּשְׁדְּפָה, אִם מַכַּת מְדִינָה הִיא — מְנַכֶּה מִן הַחֲכִירוּת. נַהֲרָא זוּטָא. אַמַּת הַמַּיִם שֶׁהִמְשִׁיכוּ מִן הַנָּהָר הַגָּדוֹל אֵצֶל הַבִּקְעָה, לְהַשְׁקוֹת מִמֶּנָּה.
מַשְׁכַּחַתְּ

[גי' הערוך ערך כלס בלמי פי' סייג לסתום הפרלות]

תוספות

ואזל הוא ויהיב בריבעא. תימה: דהכא משמע דבעל הבית שקיל פחות מן האריס, ובכל דוכתי משמע — שהאריס נוטל פחות, כדאמרינן ב"מי שאחזו" (גיטין דף עד:): כ"ע דלו תלת ושקלי ריבעא, ואת דלי ארבעה ושקיל תילתא. ולקמן בפירקין (דף קי.) נמי אמרינן: אריס אומר: למחצה ירדתי, ובעל הבית אומר: לשליש הורדתיו. משמע שאריס רגיל ליטול פחות?! ולא יותר. וי"ל: דהכא איירי — שהאריס נותן זרע, אבל בכל דוכתי איירי שבעל הבית נותן זרע, או בכרמים ופרדסים שאין צריך זרע. דאיכא אתרא דעבדי הכי, דאריסא יהיב בזרא, ואיכא אתרא דעבדי הכי, דמרי ארעא יהיב בזרא. כדאמר לעיל בסוף "איזהו נשך" (דף עד:).

בוכרא וטפתא. פר"ח: חריץ ובן חריץ, שכך רגילים לעשות סביבות השדה מחוץ לגדר, כדאמרינן בסוף פרק "בית כור" (ב"ב דף קח.). ובערוך [ערך ארכבתא] פי' כפירוש הקונטרס. **בלמא** · פירוש: שמירה, כמו "פיו בלום" (בכורות דף מ:) — פירוש: סגור. וכן: בולס עלמו בשעת מריבה, שילהי "כיסוי הדם" (חולין דף פט.). אבל "אוכר בלוס" דסוף פרק "התקבל" (גיטין דף סז. ושם ד"ה בלוס) — הוא בסמ"ך (ג) כמו "עיסה בלוסה" — מעורב, בפרק "כלל גדול" (שבת דף עו:) "ואוכרות בלוסין" בב"ר (פרשה ט).

מנכה לו מחכורו. בין בחכירות בין בקבלנות איירי, כדאמר בגמרא. ואע"ג דתנן לקמן (דף קה:): המקבל שדה מחבירו ואכלה חגב, אם מכת מדינה היא — מנכה לו מחכירותו, ולא איירי אלא בחכירות, דבקבלנות — אינו מנכה לו, אלא נוטל שליש או רביע כמו שהתנה, כדפירש לקמן בקונטרס. מ"מ, הכא בסיפא — מנכין לו, כיון דא"ל: בית השלחין, דלא איבעי ליה למימר, כיון דקאי בגווה. מדאמר "זו" כדאמר בגמרא — ש"מ שרולה לומר: כל זמן שתהא בית השלחין כמו שהיא עכשיו, שיש בה מעין.
דאפשר

עין משפט נר מצוה

ג א ב ג מיי' פ"ח מהל' שכירות הל' ו סמג עשין פט טוש"ע ח"מ סי' שכ סעיף ד:
ד ד ה ו מיי' שם טור ש"ע שם סעיף ה:
ה ז ח ט מיי' שם הל' ב טוש"ע שם סעיף ג:
ו י מיי' שם הל' ד סמג שם טוש"ע ח"מ סי' שכא סעיף א:
ז כ מיי' שם טוש"ע שם סעיף ב:
ח ל מ מיי' שם ועיין במ"מ טוש"ע שם סעיף א:

הגהות הב"ח

(א) גמ' מקבלי בריבעתא ואזל איהו: (ב) שם קנים מאי עבידתייהו. נ"ב עיין פ' המוכר את הבית ד' ס"ט פרשב"ם קנים מאי עבידתייהו מה לריכים לכרם קנים הגדילים בקרקע דקנים סתמא משמע ליה במקום גידולן כמו חילת הקנים קנים המחולקין מפוללין שמעמידין תחת הגפנים כדי שיהיו הגפנים זקופין והאשכולות תולין באויר ולא יתקלקל בקרקע וקורין להו פאשיל"ש: (ג) רש"י ד"ה וזבילא פאל"א. נ"ב בלשון אשכנז מיש"ט גאב"ל: (ד) תום' ד"ה בלמא וכו' הוא בסמ"ך. נ"ב וכן פי' רשב"ם פ' ח"ה דף נ"ח ע"א:

הגהות הגר"א

[א] גמ' דאיבעי כו'. נ"ב ר"ל דכה"ג מהני אף אם שתק בע"ה. הרמ"ה: [ב] שם בלמא. נ"ב פי' סייג. לשון הרי"ף: [ג] שם מרא וזבילא. נ"ב מרא. וזבילא. לשון הרמב"ם הקרדום שחופרין בו הארץ. והכלים שנושאין בהם העפר ומפרש דכל זה ה"ה בחוכר והטור חלק עליו בזה וכן ב"ה ורא"יה ממה שמליין על סיפא דמתני' כשם כו': [ד] שם נימא כו'. נ"ב ר"ל בחכירות ועי' רש"י כאן ולקמן ק"ה ב' במתני' ועיין תוס' ד"ה מנכה כו'. מ"מ דלא כטור (ועמ"ש רבינו בח"מ סי' שכ"א ס"ק ב'):

משכחת לה בין בחכירות ובין בקבלנות. דכולן יש לומר: לקצור יקצור, לעקור יעקור. דכל מה שיש לו לטעון בקבלנות יש לו לטעון בחכירות. וגבי יבש המעיין, אם אמר "חכור לי שדה [בית] שלחין זו" כי היכי דבחכירות כי יבש המעיין מנכה לו — הכי נמי בקבלנות, אם קבלה בשליש ולמחצה — הכל לפי מה שנפסד. **מכאן ואילך כו'.** כל אחת אפרשנה במקומה. **שמא בעלמא.** כך היא נקראת, אבל לא בשביל המעיין העליתי בחכירותך. **לתך.** חצי כור. לפי חשבון סאתים בחצר המשכן, חמשים על חמשים הוי בית סאה. אע"פ שאין בו גפנים גרסינן, וגבי פרדס אע"פ שאין בו רימונים גרסינן. **אמר לו מחכיר לחוכר.** שדה בית השלחין אני מחכיר לך יכול לומר שמא בעלמא אמרי. **מתני' הובירה.** שלא חרשה ולא זרעה. **שמין אותה.** כגון בקבלנות, שקבל למחצה ולשליש ולרביע. אבל בחכרנות לא שייכא הא, דמאי שמין איכא? חכירותו יתן לו. **אם אוביר.** אעשנה בורה. **ולא אעביד.** ולא אעשה בה פעולה הראויה לה. **גמ' דורש לשון הדיוט.** שהרגילו הדיוטות לכתוב שלא כתקנת חכמים, היה דורש הלשון לפסוק הדין אחריו. **אדם מביא קרבן עשיר על אשתו.** שהוא חייב בקרבן לידתה וצרעתה. ואם הוא עשיר אין יכול לומר: היא אין לה כלום, ותיפטר בקרבן עני. **כל הקרבנות שהיא חייבת.** שלא בנדר ונדבה, כגון קרבן זיבתה ואשם וחטאת שעליה. ה"ג לה (א) בת"כ: א"ר יהודה: לפיכך אם פטרה אינו חייב בהן, שכן היא כותבת לו אחראין (ב) דאיתא לי עלך מן קדמת דנא. והכי פירושה: לפיכך, אם גירשה ונתן לה כתובתה, ועדיין קרבנותיה עליה — אינו חייב בהן, שכך כותבת לו בתוך השובר שכותבת לו על קבלת כתובתה: התקבלתי כתובתי, ואחראין דאית לי עלך מן קדמת דנא = וכל אחריות שהיה לי עליך מלפני היום הזה. ולשון הספרים איני יודע לפרשו כראוי. **כתובת אמן.** שכותבין להן ביום אירוסין. **לכשתכנסי לחופה.** וקדושיהן ע"מ כן. ולא חלו קדושין בה עד שתיכנס לחופה, והרי חטפה קודם לכן. **לא ימשכננו.** ע"י שליח בית דין, במשכון שהוא יתר על חובו. שכך הוא כותב לו תשלומתא דאית לך עלי כל קבל דיכי. אם משיב לו את העבוט לזמן מרובה שמין את המשכון, וכותב לו זה בשטר: יהיו לך כל תשלומין עלי ליפרע ממני דמי משכון זה, ואם משכנו יותר על חובו — נמצא גובה שלא כדין. **טעמא דכתב ליה הכי.** כלומר: למה ליה למיכתב ליה? והאמר ר' יוחנן: משכנו והשיב לו את העבוט, ומת הלוה — שומטו המלוה מעל בניו. ולא הוו כשאר מטלטלי דיתמי דלא משתעבדי לבעל חוב. דכיון דמשכני' — קנייה כי דידיה לגוביינא. אהני

איבעי לך לאתויי בדוולא. אמר רב פפא: [א]הני תרתי מתניתא קמייתא משכחת לה בין בחכרנותא בין בקבלנותא. מכאן ואילך, דאיתא בקבלנותא — ליתא בחכרנותא, ודאיתא בחכרנותא — ליתא בקבלנותא.§ "אם אמר לו חכור לי שדה בית השלחין זה [וכו']§ ואמאי? לימא ליה: שמא בעלמא אמרי לך. מי לא תניא: *[ב]האומר לחבירו בית כור עפר אני מוכר לך, אע"פ שאין בו אלא לתך — הגיעו, שלא מכר לו אלא שמא, והוא דמתקרי בית כור. [ג]כרמא אני מוכר לך אע"פ שאין בו גפנים — הגיעו, שלא מכר לו אלא שמא, והוא דמתקרי כרמא. [ד]פרדס אני מוכר לך אע"פ שאין בו רמונים — הגיעו, שלא מכר לו אלא שמא, והוא דמתקרי פרדסא. אלמא אמר ליה: שמא בעלמא אמרי לך; הכא נמי נימא ליה: שמא בעלמא אמרי לך! אמר שמואל: לא קשיא; [ה]הא דאמר ליה מחכיר לחוכר, הא דאמר ליה חוכר למחכיר. אמר ליה מחכיר לחוכר — שמא בעלמא א"ל. א"ל חוכר למחכיר — קפידא. רבינא אמר: אידי ואידי דא"ל מחכיר לחוכר. מדקאמר זה — מכלל [ו]דקאי בגוה עסקינן. בית השלחין למה ליה למימר? דקאמר ליה: בית השלחין כדקיימא השתא.§ **מתני'** [ז]המקבל שדה מחבירו והובירה — שמין אותה כמה ראויה לעשות, ונותן לו. שכך כותב לו: *אם אוביר ולא אעביד אשלם במיטבא.§ **גמ'** ר"מ היה [ח]דורש לשון הדיוט; דתניא, *ר"מ אומר: אם אוביר ולא אעביד אשלם במיטבא. רבי יהודה היה דורש לשון הדיוט; *דתניא, ר' יהודה אומר: [ט]אדם מביא קרבן עשיר על אשתו, וכן כל קרבן וקרבן שהיא חייבת, *שכך כותב לה: אחריות דאית ליך עלי מן קדמת דנא. *הלל הזקן היה דורש לשון הדיוט; דתניא: *)אנשי אלכסנדריא היו מקדשין את נשותיהם, ובשעת כניסתן לחופה באין אחרים וחוטפים אותם מהן, ובקשו חכמים לעשות בניהם ממזרים. אמר להן הלל הזקן: הביאו לי כתובת אמכם. הביאו לו כתובת אמן, ומצא שכתוב בהן: לכשתכנסי לחופה הוי לי לאינתו, ולא עשו בניהם ממזרים. ר"י בן קרחה היה דורש לשון הדיוט; דתניא, *ר"י בן קרחה אומר: המלוה את חבירו לא ימשכננו יותר מחובו, שכך כותב לו: תשלומתא דאית לך עלי כל קבל דיכי. טעמא — דכתב ליה הכי, הא אי לא כתב ליה הכי — לא קניא? והא אמר רבי *יוחנן: משכנו והשיב לו המשכון ומת — שומטו מעל גבי בניו! אהני

*) תוספתא דכתובות פ"ד

דאפשר לאתויי בדוולא. וא"ת: אפילו לא אפשר נמי, אמאי מנכין לו? דכיון דלא יבש נהרא רבה — תו לא הוי מכת מדינה! וי"ל: דנקט האי טעמא לאשמועינן דאפילו יבשו נמי שאר יאורי שדות אחרים, דהשתא הוי מכת מדינה — אפילו הכי אינו מנכה לו, כיון דאפשר לאתויי בדוולא מנהרא רבה. דדוקא באכלה חגב או נשדפה שאין יכול לתקן הקלקול ע"י שום טורח — מנכה לו. אי נמי, יש לומר: דודאי בחכירות לא היה צריך לטעם זה, אפילו בלא אפשר לאתויי — אתי שפיר. אבל משום קבלנות איצטריך, שלא יוכל לומר לא אתעסק בה, ואפ"ה לא אשלם במיטבא, לפי שאינו מחוייב להביא מנהרות אחרים הרחוקים ביותר, ועל כן הוצרך לומר דלא יבש נהרא רבא, ומצי לאתויי בדוולא — ולכך מחוייב לעשות בקבלנותו.

הני תרי מתני' קמייתא איתנהו בין בחכרנותא כו'. ואע"ג דכסס שחולקין בתבואה ליתא בחכירות — מ"מ עיקר מילתא, דהיינו רישא, מיירי בין בחכירות בין בקבלנות. **אידי** ואידי דאמר ליה מחכיר לחוכר. לכאורה משמע דבא"ל חוכר למחכיר הוי קפידא בלאו האי טעמא, מדלא קאמר אידי ואידי בין אמר ליה חוכר למחכיר בין אמר ליה מחכיר לחוכר. [א] אבל אי אפשר לומר כן, דהא מתני' בדא"ל חוכר למחכיר איירי, דקתני: א"ל חכור לי שדה בית השלחין, ואפ"ה משום האי טעמא דוקא הוי קפידא. ולאו דוקא נקט מחכיר לחוכר דה"ה חוכר למחכיר, אלא משום דשמואל לא משכח קפידא במחכיר לחוכר קאמר רבינא דבמחכיר לחוכר נמי הוה קפידא, בכה"ג דאיירי מתני'.

היה דורש לשון הדיוט. לשונות שלא תיקנו חכמים לכתוב, אלא הדיוטות הורגלו לכותבן, היה דורש. ואפילו לא כתב — כאילו נכתב. דאי דוקא כשכתב — מה היה דורש? פשיטא שיש לו לקיים כמו שהתנה, דהא לאו אסמכתא היא.

הכי גרסינן בתוספתא דכתובות: (ג) אדם מביא קרבן עשיר על אשתו, וכן כל קרבנות שהיא חייבת, שכך כתב לה "אחריות דאית ליה עלי מן קדמת דנא". פי': כל קרבנות שהיתה חייבת קודם שנשאתו לו — יביא בעבורה, שכתב לה 'אחריות דאית ליך' = שאתה חייבת, יהא עלי מן קדמת דנא — אפילו חובות שקדמו לנישואין. ודוקא בקרבנות שהן חובה לכפרתה כגון לידה וזיבה וצרעת, או להכשירה לאכול בתרומה או לשתות ביין אם היא נזירה. והכי איתא בירושלמי בכתובות בפרק "נערה", דקתני התם: אפילו אכלה חלב או חיללה שבת. משמע דוקא בהני שצריכה להביא, אבל קרבנות שנדרה ונדבה קודם ניסואין, או לוותה ואכלה — לא ישלם. ועד כאן לא מיבעיא לן בס"פ "יש נוחלין" (ב"ב דף קלט.) בלוותה ואכלה ועמדה ונשאת אי כלוקח הוי אי כיורש הוי. אי כלוקח הוי — ואין המלוה מוציא מיד הבעל, אי כיורש הוי — ומוציא, אלא בנכסים שהכניסה לו. אבל מנכסי הבעל — פשיטא דלא גבי. וה"ה לוותה כשהיא תחתיו לצורך מה שאינו משועבד לה, דלא משלם. ובלא שום ראיה דבר פשוט הוא, דאל"כ, אם יקניטוה — תלוה ותשליך לאיבוד, ותחייבנו ק' מנה בכל יום. אבל בנזירות — אין לחוש שתדור ותפסידו. ובנדרים ובנדבות נמי, אם היה חייב לשלם — היתה מפסדת לו כמה וכמה, דאפילו יוכל להפר דחשיב כדברים שבינו לבינה משום הפסד ממונו — יש לחוש שמא תדור ותפרע קודם שישמע, ואפילו ישמע — זימנין דמיטרד, כדאמר בנדרים בפ' "נערה" (דף עג.). ודלא *כרב אחא שהורה שהבעל חייב לפרוע חובת אשתו שלוותה קודם שנשאה מכח דר' יהודה דהכא. **לא** ימשכננו יותר מחובו. *דאף על גב דאין משלם לו הגירעון אלא בכתב, מכל מקום לא ימשכננו יותר מחובו.

טעמא דכתב ליה הכי והא אמר רבי יוחנן כו'. ותימה: והא כיון דדריש לשון הדיוט, אפילו לא כתב נמי, כדפרישית לעיל, ומאי פריך לרבי יוחנן? וי"ל: דאם איתא דרבי יוחנן דאמר שומטו מעל גבי בניו, דמכח לשון הדיוט קאמר — היה לו לפרש. אהני

ט א עיין בטור ש"ע ח"מ סי' שכא סעיף א בהג"ה:
י ב מיי' פכ"ח מהל' מכירה הלכה יד סמג עשין פב טוש"ע ח"מ סי' ריח סעיף יז:
יא ג ד מיי' שם טוש"ע שם סעיף יח:
יב ה ו מיי' פ"ח מהל' שכירות הלכה ד סמג עשין פט טוש"ע ח"מ סי' שכא סעיף ב בהג"ה:
יג ז מיי' שם הלכה יג סמג שם טוש"ע ח"מ סי' שכח סעיף ב:
יד ח טוש"ע ח"מ סי' מב סעיף טו:
טו ט מיי' פ"י מהל' שגגות הלכה ו סמג עשין רעג:
טז י מיי' פ"ג מהלכות מלוה ולוה הלכה ו סמג לאוין קפח טוש"ע ח"מ סי' נז סעיף יט:

הגהות הב"ח
(א) רש"י ד"ה לה בת"כ. נ"ב בפרקא מצורע במגילת מצורע סוף פ"ד: (ב) בא"ד אחראין דאית כצ"ל ואות א' נמחק: (ג) תוס' ד"ה ה"ג בתוספתא דכתובות פ"ד אדם:

[סיומא דמילתא שכך כותב לה וכו' ליתא במשנה לכך שפיר גרסינן דתניא והיינו תוס' בכתובות פ"ד ע"ש]

הגהות הגר"א
[א] תוס' ד"ה אידי. אבל כו'. נ"ב ורמ"ה חולק:

ב"ב ז.
לעיל עג: [לקמן קט.]
[תוספתא דכתובות פ"ד]
נדרים לה: נזיר כד. נגעים פי"ד [מי"ב]
[עי' תוס' יבמות קז. ד"ה בית הלל ותוס' כתובות נג. ד"ה שאין]
[תוספתא דכתובות פ"ד]
[לקמן קיד: ושם הגי' משכנו ומת שומטו כו' וכ"ה גי' הערוך ערך שמט א' וע"ש ברש"י]
פי' הוא רב אחאי גאון ויש גורסין כרב אחד. רש"ל
[עי' מהר"ם ורש"ש ורש"א]

— אהני כתיבה לגירעון. ר' יוסי היה דורש לשון הדיוט; דתניא, *רבי יוסי אומר: [א]מקום שנהגו לעשות כתובה מלוה — גובה מלוה, לכפול — גובה מחצה. נהרבלאי גבו תילתא. מרימר מגבי נמי שבחא. א"ל רבינא למרימר: והתניא: לכפול — גובה מחצה! לא קשיא; הא — דקני מיניה, הא — דלא קני מיניה. רבינא משבח וכתיב לברתיה. אמרו ליה: נקני מיניה דמר! אמר להו: אי מקנא — לא מיכפל, אי מיכפל — לא מיקנא. ההוא גברא דאמר להו: הבו לה ארבע מאה זוזי לברתי בכתובתה. שלח רב אחא בריה דרב אויא לקמיה דרב אשי: ארבע מאה דאינון תמני מאה, או ארבע מאה זוזי דאינון מאתן? אמר רב אשי: חזינן. אי אמר הבו לה — ארבע מאה זוזי דאינון תמני מאה. אי אמר כתובו לה — ארבע מאה זוזי דאינון מאתן. איכא דאמרי, אמר רב אשי: חזינן. אי אמר לכתובתה — ארבע מאה זוזי דאינון תמני מאה. ואי אמר בכתובתה — ארבע מאה זוזי דאינון מאתן. [ב]ולא היא, *לא שנא דאמר לכתובתה ולא שנא דאמר בכתובתה — ארבע מאה זוזי דאינון מאתן, עד דאמר הבו לה סתמא. ההוא גברא דקביל ארעא מחבריה. אמר: אי מוברנא לה — יהיבנא לך אלפא זוזי. אוביר תילתא. אמרי נהרדעי: דינא הוא דיהיב ליה תלת מאה ותלתין ותלתא ותילתא. רבא אמר: *[ג]אסמכתא היא, ואסמכתא לא קניא. ולרבא, מ"ש מהא *דתנן: אם אוביר ולא אעביד אשלם במיטבא? התם לא קא גזים. הכא כיון דקאמר מילתא יתירתא — גוזמא בעלמא הוא דקגזים. ההוא גברא דקביל ארעא לשומשמי, זרעה חיטי, עבדא חיטי כשומשמי. סבר רב כהנא למימר: מנכי ליה כחשא דארעא. אמר ליה רב אשי לרב כהנא: [ד]אמרי אינשי: כחשא ארעא ולא לכחוש מרה. ההוא גברא דקביל ארעא לשומשמי, זרעא חיטי, עבדא חיטי טפי מן שומשמי. סבר רבינא למימר: יהיב ליה שבחא דביני ביני. אמר ליה רב אחא מדפתי לרבינא: [ה]אטו הוא אשבח, ארעא לא אשבחה? *אמרי נהרדעי: [ו]האי עיסקא, פלגא מלוה ופלגא פקדון. עבוד רבנן מילתא דניחא ליה ללוה, וניחא ליה למלוה. השתא דאמרינן פלגא מלוה, אי בעי למשתי ביה שכרא — שפיר דמי. רבא אמר: [ז]להכי קרו ליה עיסקא, דאמר ליה: כי יהבינא לך — לאיעסוקי ביה, ולא למשתי ביה שכרא. אמר רב אידי בר אבין: ואם מת — נעשה מטלטלין אצל בניו. רבא אמר: [ח]להכי קרו ליה עיסקא, דאם מת — לא יעשה מטלטלין אצל בניו. אמר רבא: [ט]חדא עיסקא ותרי שטרי — פסידא דמלוה;
תרי

אהני כתיבה לגירעון. וא"ת: היכי משמע לומר מה שכתב לו "תשלומין דאית ליך עלי כל קבל דיכי" שיהא מהני לשומטו מע"ג בניו, שיהא טועה המקשה לומר שלכך כתב לו כן? ויש לומר דהכי משמע ליה למקשה: תשלומין דאית ליך עלי – לא מכח תחילת המלוה שכבר נפרעת בנתינת המשכון, כי הקניתיו לך והשאלתו לי, ועל שאילה זו יש לך תשלומין *עליו. וע"כ מקשה: למה צריך לכתוב לו כך כדי לשומטו מע"ג בניו? בלאו הכי נמי הוא שומטו, דממילא קני ליה המשכון, ואפילו לא יקנה לו הלוה. וא"ת: וכיון שאם לא כתב לו הוא פטור מן הגירעון – א"כ מלוה הוא שלא יקחנו, והיאך הוא מותר על ידי כתיבה זו? וי"ל: שמדעתו מקנה לו הלוה, לפי שמחזירו לו ימים רבים, וכיון שמקנה לו – אינו עוד בידו בתורת השבת העבוט אלא בתורת שאלה. א"נ: רבנן הוא דתקון שיכתוב, כדי שלא ימנע המלוה מלהחזיר, כמו שתקן הלל פרוזבול לפי שראה שהיו נמנעים מלהלוות (שביעית פ"י מ"ג).

סבר רב כהנא למימר מנכה ליה כחשא דארעא. ומתני' דקתני אומדין כמה היתה ראויה ליעשות גבי מקבל שדה והובירה – היינו בר מכחשא דארעא. א"נ: הכא דוקא גבי שומשמי, דמכחשי יותר, סבר דמנכה לו. ואפילו מאן דחייש לכחש גופנא בפ' "הכונס" (ב"ק דף נט.) – הכא מודה לרב אשי דלא חיישינן.

האי עיסקא פלגא מלוה ופלגא פקדון. ממתני' ד"איזהו נשך" (לעיל דף סח.) דאין מושיבין חנוני למחצית שכר אא"כ נותן כו' לא שמעינן דהוה פלגא מלוה ופלגא פקדון, דה"א דטפי מפלגא פקדון הוי, ואפ"ה בעי שכר עמלו, כיון דליכא תרי תילתי פקדון. **דלא** למישתי ביה שכרא. שכשמוליכה מפסיד המלוה, שאין קרן שלו קיים, ואין לו על מה לסמוך.
הני

אהני כתיבה לגירעון. השטר מועיל לפחות דמיו, אם יפחתו דמי המשכון שנשתמש בו הלוה – יפרע משאר נכסיו ככל הכתוב בשטר. מקום שנהגו לעשות כתובה מלוה. שכל מה שכתוב בשטר כתובתה: ודין נדוניא דהנעלת ליה מבי נשא לבית בעלה וכו' – נפרעת ממנו כשנתארמלה או נתגרשה, כדרך שבעל חוב נפרע, ככל הכתוב בשטר מלוה. כגון שכותבין בה כמו שאנו כותבין אחריות דנא קבילת עלאי. גובה מלוה. בעל גובה מאבי הבת כל מה שכתוב בכתובתה, כאילו הלוהו. מקום שנהגו לכפול. לשום את מה שמכנסת לו כפליים בדמיו בשביל כבוד, ולכתוב כפליים בכתובתה, וכשהיא יוצאה אינה נפרעת אלא החצי. גובה. החתן מחמיו מחצה. מגבי שבחא. כל מה שהיה כותב וכופל היה גובה מאבי הבת. הא דקנו מיניה. מאבי הבת. ההוא דאמר להו. מלוה מחמת מיתה היה. (א) שלח רב אחא כו'. האי "לכתובתה", אכתובה קאי או אגובריינא? מקום שנהגו לכפול היה. הבו לה ארבע מאה. קאמר שיכתבו אותן תמני מאה בכתובתה, או ד' מאה דכתובה קאמר, דאינון מאתים לגבייה? אי אמר לכתובתה. לגובריינא קאמר. ואי אמר בכתובתה. לכתוב לה בשטר כתובה קאמר. לא גזים. אינו מקבל עליו דבר גוזמא אלא כמשפט. ולאו אסמכתא היא, דהכי אפסדיה. דקביל ארעא לשומשמי. קבלנות היתה לזורעה שומשמין, והן יקרין מן החטין, ומכחישין הקרקע יותר מן החטין. ועבדה חטין כשומשמי. הצליח זריעתו, ואף החטין הוקרו. ונמצא שלא הפסיד בעל הבית במה ששינה זה, ונשתכר כחש הקרקע שהיה נכחש בשומשמין יותר מן החטין. מנכה ליה. בעל הקרקע מחלקו דמי כחשא דארעא, מה שהיתה מכחשת אם היה זורעה שומשמין יותר משזרעה חטין, ולא יטול בה חטין שיעור שומשמין – שהרי לא הכחישה כל כך מחמת החטין. אמר ליה אמרי אינשי כחוש ארעא כו'. כלומר: היה לו לזרוע שומשמין אפילו היתה מכחשת קרקע יותר, ולא יכחוש מרה, ליטול עכשיו פחות וירעב הוא וביתו. טפי משומשמין. הוקרו החטין והצליחה אותה שנה זריעת חטין יותר משל שומשמין. יהיב ליה. בעל הקרקע מנכה לו מחכירתו, ולא יטול אלא כדי שיעור דמי שומשמין שהיא ראויה להעשות, לפי שזה גרם זה השבח. האי עיסקא פלגא מלוה ופלגא פקדון. המקבל פרגמטיא מבעל הבית ושמה לו כפי דמיה שהיא שוה כאן, והוא מוליכה למקום היוקר למחצית השכר – חצי אחריות אונסים עליו כמלוה, וחצי אחריותה על בעלים כפקדון. תקון רבנן הך תקנתא. דניחא להו לתרוייהו. ואי בעי למישתי ביה שכרא. אם רצה להוציא חציה בהוצאת ביתו – מוציא, שהרי מלוה עליו היא. לאיעסוקי ביה. דמתוך שתשתכר בשלך, תטרח ותעסוק בה יפה. ואם מת. הלוה, והעיסקא קיימת ביד בניו – הרי חצייה שהיא מלוה נעשית מטלטלין אצל בניו, ואין הבעלים גובין ממנה, דמטלטלי דיתמי לא משתעבדי לבעל חוב. להכי קרו ליה עיסקא. שתהא קיימת תמיד, ומתעסק בה, ויסמכו עליה בעליה שלא תינתן להוציאה. ואם מת לוה – יגבה, ולא תיעשה כמטלטלין שלהן. דכיון דצריכה להיות קיימת – סמיכתו עליה כמקרקעי. דטעמא דלא קא משתעבדי מטלטלי דיתמי לב"ח – משום דמעיקרא לאו עלייהו סמך, דלאו למיגבי מינייהו אוזפיה, שהרי בידו להוציאן. אבל הני – אין בידו להוציאן, וסמך עלייהו. חד עיסקא ותרי שטרי פסידא דמלוה. משום דסתם עיסקא תילתא באגר לבעל הבית ופלגא בהפסד, כדאמר ב"איזהו נשך" (לעיל דף סח:) גבי שטרא דרב עיליש. דאי לא – מתחזי כרבית. דכיון דפלגא מלוה, אי לאו דשקיל מנתא באגרא דפלגא פקדון – אישתכח דקא טרח בפקדון משום רבית דמלוה, הלכך מאן דיהיב עיסקא שני חבילות בגדים במנה – נכתוב שטר של מנה, אי מפסיד באחת מן החבילות מדמי הקרן מחמשים ה' דינרים, ומשתכר בחבירתה ט"ו דינרין – אין כאן חשבון להפסד לבד ולשכר לבד, אלא נשתכר בפרגמטיא זו י' דינרין. *(וישלמו (ב) תחילת חבילה החסירה בה' דינרין של ט"ו דינרים שהרויח בחבילה אחרת וי' דינרין הנותרים הן הן ריוח, ויטול מהן. דיהיב עיסקא תילתא באגר והמקבל תרי תילתי), ויטלו בעליו מאותם י' דינרים שליש שהן ג' דינרים ושליש דינר, והמקבל יטול שני שלישים, אי כתב עלייהו שני שטרות כל חבילה שטר של חמשים – נמצא חשבון של כל אחד לבדו, ויקבל עליו המלוה בהפסד החצי שהוא שני דינרים וחצי, ובשכר של חבירתה לא יטול אלא שליש, ולא נמצא לחלקו שכר אלא שלשים מעות – דהיינו חמשה דינרים. דדינר ו' מעות כסף פשיטי הן, הרי פסידא דמלוה.
תרי

יז א מיי' פכ"ג מהלכות אישות הלכה יא סמג עשין מח טוש"ע אה"ע סי' סו סעיף יא:
יח ב מיי' פי"א מהל' זכיה ומתנה הלכה כא טוש"ע ח"מ סי' רנג סעיף טו:
[בדפו"י הגי' עלי]
יט ג מיי' פ"ח מהלכות שכירות הלכה יג סמג עשין פט טוש"ע ח"מ סי' שכח סעיף ב:
כ ד ה מיי' שם הלכה יד סמג שם טור ש"ע ח"מ סי' שכו:
כא ו מיי' פ"ו מהלכות שלוחין ושותפין הלכה ב ועיין בהשגות ובכ"מ סמג עשין פב טור ש"ע י"ד סי' קעז סעיף ב:
כב ז מיי' שם פ"ו הלכה ד סמג שם טוש"ע י"ד שם סעיף ל:
כג ח מיי' שם הלכה ט סמג שם טוש"ע שם סעיף לא:
כד ט טוש"ע שם סעיף לג:

הגהות הב"ח
(א) רש"י ד"ה שלח וכו' הכא הכי הס"ד: (ב) ד"ה חד עיסקא וכו' וישלמו תחילה חבילה וכו' הכיינו ה' דינרים דדינר כסף שש מעות הרי פסידא דמלוה כצ"ל ותיבת פשיטי הן נמחק:

[תוספתא דכתובות פ"ד]
[עי' תוס' כתובות נג: ד"ה למזונות]
[לעיל סו. וש"נ]
לעיל ע"א עג: [לקמן קט.]
ב"ב ע:
רש"ל מ"ז

תרי עיסקי וחד שטרא – פסידא דלוה. ואמר רבא: [א]האי מאן דקביל עיסקא מן חבריה ופסיד, טרח ומלייה ולא אודעיה, לא מצי אמר ליה: דרי מהיאך פסידא בהדאי – משום דאמר ליה: להכי טרחת למליותיה – כי היכי דלא ליקרו לך מפסיד עיסקי. ואמר רבא: *[ב]הני בי תרי דעבדי עיסקא בהדי הדדי ורווח, וא"ל חד לחבריה: תא ליפלוג, אי א"ל אידך נרווח טפי – דינא הוא דמעכב. (א) ואי א"ל: הב לי פלגא דרווחא, אמר ליה: רווחא לקרנא משתעבד. ואי א"ל: הב לי פלג' רווחא ופלגא קרנא, אמר ליה: עיסקא להדדי משועבד. ואי א"ל: נפלוג רווחא ונפלוג קרנא, ואי מטי לך פסידא דרינא בהדך, א"ל: לא, מזלא דבי תרי עדיף.§

מתני' [ג]המקבל שדה מחבירו ולא רצה לנכש, ואמר לו: מה איכפת לך? הואיל ואני נותן לך את חכירך. אין שומעין לו, מפני שיכול לומר לו: למחר אתה יוצא ממנה, ומעלת לפני עשבים.§

גמ' [ד]אי א"ל: לבתר הכי כריבנא לה – אמר ליה: חטי מעלייתא בעינא. ואי א"ל: זביננא לך חטי משוקא, א"ל: חטי דארעאי בעינא. ואי א"ל: מנכישנא לך שיעור מנתיך, א"ל: קא מנסבת שם רע לארעאי. והתנן: מפני שמעלת לפני עשבים! אלא, משום דא"ל: בזרא דנפל נפל.§

מתני' המקבל שדה מחבירו ולא עשתה, אם יש בה כדי להעמיד כרי – חייב לטפל בה. א"ר יהודה: מאי קצבה בכרי? אלא, אם יש בה כדי נפילה.§

גמ' ת"ר: [ה]המקבל שדה מחבירו ולא עשתה, אם יש בה כדי להעמיד כרי – חייב לטפל בה, שכך כותב לו: אנא אוקים ואניר ואזרע ואחצוד ואעמר ואדוש ואידרי ואוקים כריא קדמך. ותיתי אנת ותיטול פלגא, ואנא בעמלי ובנפקות ידי פלגא. וכמה "כדי להעמיד בה כרי"? א"ר יוסי בר' חנינא: כדי שתעמוד בו הרחת. איבעיא להו: רחת היוצא מהאי גיסא להאי גיסא מאי? ת"ש, א"ר אבהו: לדידי מפרשא לי מיניה דר' יוסי בר' חנינא: כל שאין כונס שלו רואה פני החמה. איתמר, לוי אמר: שלש סאין, דבי רבי ינאי אמרי: [ו]סאתים. אמר ר"ל: סאתים שאמרו – [ז]חוץ מן ההוצאה. תנן התם: *פריצי זיתים וענבים, ב"ש מטמאין וב"ה [ח]מטהרין. מאי פריצי זיתים? אמר רב הונא: רשעי זיתים. אמר רב יוסף: ומאי קראה? °"[ובני] פריצי עמך ינשאו להעמיד חזון ונכשלו". ר"נ בר יצחק אמר מהכא: °"והוליד בן פריץ שופך דם". וכמה פריצי זיתים? ר' אלעזר אמר: [ט]ארבעת קבין לקורה, דבי ר' ינאי אמרי: סאתים לקורה. ולא פליגי, הא באתרא דמעיילי כורא באוללא, הא באתרא דמעיילי תלתא כורין באוללא. תנו רבנן:

עלו

תרי עיסקי וחד שטרא פסידא דלוה. קבל היום ממנו במנה ולמחר במנה, וכתב שטר על מאתים – הפסיד הלוה, כמה דפרישית. שאם יהא הפסד בזה ושכר בזה – לא יחשבו כל אחד לבדו אלא השכר ימלא הקרן תחילה, ואח"כ יחלוקו המותר. ואם כתב ב' שטרות כמשפט הזה מחשב הפסד של זה לבד, והשכר של זה לבד, ויקבל הבעלים עליו בהפסד החצי ובשכר השליש. ועלה טובה קמ"ל רבא דבחד עיסקא לכתוב חד שטרא, ובתרי עסקי נכתוב ב' שטרי, ויהא הדבר שקול. ולא מצי למימר ליה. לבתר דמלייה. דרי מהיאך פסידא קמא בהדאי. וקבל עליך חצי הפסד, ובשכר טול שליש, ונמלאת פוחת מן הקרן. דא"ל להכי טרחת ומליי' וכו'. דמדלא אודעתן מעיקרא – נכלם היית בדבר, ואדעתא דמלוי קרנא טרחת. בי תרי דעבוד עיסקא בהדי הדדי ורווח. שני קבלנים שקבלו עיסקא מבעל הבית בשותפות, שימכרוהו ויסחרו במעות עד זמן פלוני ויחלקו ביניהם ובין בעה"ב כמשפט, ונשתמשו חצי הזמן ונשתכרו. דמעכב. עליה עד שיגיע הזמן שקבעו לבעה"ב, שיחזרו לו את שלו, והמותר יחלוקו. אי אמר ליה ניפלוג רווחא. השתא מפרש ואזיל מ"ט אית ליה דניעכב? אי א"ל האי: פלוג רווחא והקרן ניתפוס עדיין להרויח בו עד הזמן – מצי א"ל אידך: רווחא לקרנא משתעבד, שמא בסחורה שנעשה עוד נפסיד, וצריך שיהא הריוח קיים להשתכר בו עוד כדי למלאות הקרן. ואי אמר ניפלוג. תרווייהו, מצי א"ל: עיסקא להדדי משתעבד, ואם ניפלוג – שמא אני אפסיד בסחורה שאקנה, שהרי קבלתי אני להתעסק בה עד אותו הזמן, ואם אפסיד – שמא חלק השני ישתכר וימלא חסרון, והנו יחד קבלנו ונשתעבדו החלקים זה לזה. **מתני'** ולא רצה לנכש. התבואה. אתן לך חכירך. כך וכך כורין שפסקתי עמך, ומה איכפת לך אם יחסר חלקי, שהעשבים (ב) מכחישים השבלים – אין זה אלא עלי. אין שומעין לו. והא ליתא אלא בחכרנותא. דאי בקבלנותא – פשיטא, מי מצי א"ל מאי איכפת לך? **גמ'** ואי א"ל כריבנא וכו'. השתא מפרש אמאי אין שומעין לו. אי אמר לו אני אחרוש אחר הקצירה, ואהפוך שרשי העשבים שנותרו בה וימותו, ולא תעלה לפניך עשבים – מאי מהדר ליה. א"ל אנא חטי מעליא בעינא. אותו חכירות שפסקת לי אני רוצה שיהו בריאים ולא כחושים. מנסבת שם רע לארעאי. הרואים סבורים שניכשת, ואעפ"כ היא מלאה עשבים, ואתה מוציא שם רע לארעאי. ומחר, אם באתי למכור או להוריד לזה אריס אחר – לא יהיה יורד. והא תנן וכו'. הרי לא שנה במתני' אלא טענה אחת, ובשבילה קאמר אין שומעין לו, ע"כ דהא תליא כולה. אלא משום דא"ל בזרא דנפל נפל. כל טענתו אינה אלא שמעלת עשבים לשנה הבאה, וטענתו לעולם עומדת. דכי א"ל כריבנא לאחר הקצירה, א"ל האי: נהי דעקרת לשרשים, סוף סוף העשבים שהניח בה עכשיו עד שיזרעו יפלו הזרעים לארץ, ויצמחו לשנה הבאה, ולזו לא תועיל החרישה. **מתני'** המקבל שדה מחבירו ולא עשתה. תבואה אלא מעט, ובא לו האריס למנוע מלהתעסק בה עוד, שאין בה עוד כדי טרחו. אם יש בה כדי לעשות. מתבואתה כרי. ובגמרא מפרש מאי שיעוריה. חייב ליטפל בה. בעל כרחו. והא ליתא אלא בקבלנותא, דאי בחכרנותא – מה לו לבעל השדה אם יחדל לו? סוף סוף חכירו הוא נותן לו. מה קצבה בכרי. מה קצבה יש אם קצבתם לו כרי לשיעור חיוב טיפול שדה גדולה לשיעור כרי, ושדה קטנה לשיעור כרי. אלא אם יש בה כדי נפילה. שיכול לחזור ולזורעה לשנה הבאה מתבואת שנה זו. נפילה. זרע שמפזרים לה במפולת יד. **גמ'** אקום ואניר. אעמוד ואחרוש. ואדרי. אזרה המוץ ברחת או בנפה. בעמלאי ובנפקות ידי. בהוצאתי. הרחת. פל"א, שזורין המוץ ברוח מתוך התבואה. שתעמוד בה. כשתוחבין אותה בתוכו. מהאי גיסא ומהאי גיסא. אם נראין חודיה משני צדדין. כונס שלו. פלדי"ן בלע"ז. הרחת שמכניסין אותה *לגבות התבואה עליה לזרות שאין רואה פני החמה, ולצדדין נמי בכלל כונס הם. תנן התם. במס' עוקצין וכו'. משום אמרי דבי ר' ינאי דמפרשי שיעורא בכולהו הנך מתני' נקט להו גבי מתני' דמפרשי בה דבי ר' ינאי שיעורא. פריצי זיתים. כדמפרש: רשעי זיתים וענבים, שהן לעולם בוסר, שאין בישולן נגמר לעולם. מטהרים. מן טומאת אוכלין, דלא חזי לאכילה. וכמה פריצי. כמה הן מבושלין ועדיין פריצין הן. ארבעת קבין לקורה. שמכניסין בבית הבד מהן כדי שיעור טעינת הקורה בפעם אחת, ואין מוציאין אלא ארבעה קבין שמן. באוללא. בתפוסה אחת שקורין ש"ק. ויש מקום שבתי בד שלהן גדולין ומכניסין שלשת כורים יחד, ויש מקום שאין מכניסין אלא כור זיתים בטעינת קורה. וישער רבי אלעזר בקטנים, ורבי ינאי בגדולים. וסאתים הוי תלתא זימני ארבעה קבין.

עלו

הני בי תרי דקבלו עיסקא בהדי הדדי. מאדם אחד. וא"ת: ואמאי נקט בכי האי גוונא ולא נקט האי מאן דקביל עיסקא מחבריה? וי"ל: לפי שהמקבל יכול לחזור קודם הזמן ולומר: לו אטרח עוד ואטול מה שיגיע לידי עד הנה. דפועל יכול לחזור אפילו בחצי היום. אבל בעל העיסקא – יכול להיות שאין יכול לחזור, שהרי פלגא הוה מלוה ביד המקבל, וגם פלגא דפקדון נתן לו זכות והשליטו להשתכר בו עד הזמן. וזה לא היה שום חידוש להשמיענו דמעכב המקבל, דטעם פשוט כדפרישית, ולהכי לא נקט בכי האי גוונא. **מזלא** דבי תרי עדיף. בכולהו הוה מצי למימר בהו הכי, אלא דעדיפא מיניה קאמר בהו.

ר"ח גרים: מהאי גיסא או מהאי גיסא. פירוש: כדי להעמיד לד הרחב שלמטה, שאז אין צריך תבואה כל כך, שבדבר מועט עומד ואינו נופל. או מהאי גיסא של מעלה, שאינו רחב, שאז צריך תבואה הרבה. ופשיט ליה מדקאמר כל שאין כונס שלו רואה פני חמה – דהיינו לד הרחב, שיש בו בית קיבול קצת לקבל תבואה.

כל

כה א מיי' פ"ז מהלכות שלוחין ושותפין הלכה ב סג עשין פב טוש"ע י"ד סי' קעז סעיף לד:

כו ב טוש"ע שם סעיף לה:

כז ג ד מיי' פ"ח מהל' שכירות הלכה ח סמג עשין פט טוש"ע ח"מ סי' שכ סעיף ד:

כח ה ו ז מיי' שם הלכה יב סמג שם טוש"ע ח"מ סי' שכח סעיף א:

כט ח ט מיי' פ"א מהל' טומאת אוכלין הלכה יב:

הגהות הב"ח

(א) גמ' הוא דמעכב אי כצ"ל ואות ו' נמחק: (ב) רש"י ד"ה אתן וכו' שמכחישים כצ"ל:

[עי' תוס' גיטין לא: ד"ה לשותפי]

עוקצין פ"ג [מ"ו]

דניאל יא

יחזקאל יח

ל"ל לקבל יעב"ץ

ל א ב ג מיי' פ"ח מהל' מטמאי משכב ומושב הלכה ז סג עשין רג:
לא ד ה ו מיי' פ"י מהלכות טומאת מת הלכה יא:
לב ז מיי' פ"ה מהלכות תפלה הלכה ה סמג עשין יט טוש"ע א"ח סי' צז סעיף ה [רב אלפס ברכות פ"ג יז.]:
לג ח ט מיי' פ"ד מהל' תפילין הלכה כג סמג עשין יט טוש"ע א"ח סי' מא ובהג"ה [רב אלפס שם ובהלכות תפילין עה.]
לד י כ מיי' פ"ד מהלכות מתנות עניים הלכה ה:
לה ל מ מיי' פ"ח מהל' שכירו' הלכה ה סמג עשין פט טוש"ע ח"מ סי' שכב סעיף א:

כל שנחבאת בחזיונה. תימה: אמאי קרי אין כחו רע לפי שאינה נחבאת באגרופו? והלא היא רותת תחתיהן. **על** אדם שכחו רע שיכול להסיטו טמא. תימה: אפילו אין כחו רע, שאין יכול להסיטו, אמאי טהור? הלא יטמא התחתון לעליון! ועוד: הטומאה בחיבורים הוא, וטמא טומאת שבעה, כדאמר בפרק "אין מעמידין" (ע"ז דף לז: ושם)! וי"ל: כגון שתחתון גוי, שאינו מקבל טומאה, וטהור העליון מטומאה דאורייתא. א"נ, אפילו התחתון ישראל. וכגון שלובשין הרבה בגדים, דטומאה בחיבורים לא מטמא אלא אדם אחד או בגד אחד, אבל שני – אין טמא אלא טומאת ערב, ואין מטמא אדם וכלים. ואפילו יטמא טומאה מדרבנן, כמו שפי' ר"י בפ"ק דשבת (דף יז.) גבי מרדע – מ"מ שלישי לא הוי אלא ראשון, ולא יטמא אדם.
מטפחת שלהן. ר"ח גריס: של לאס. וכן נראה, דלא אשכחן שנותנין תפילין במטפחת, כי אם בכיס או בתיק.
ארבעת סאין לכור. פי' במקום שראוי לצמוח כור, ולא גדל רק ארבע סאין – דהיינו כדי נפילה. דבמקום שזורעים ד' סאין רגילות לצמוח כור. ובשני דר' אמי צריך לזרוע ח' סאין לצמוח כור. ובסמוך גבי לקט – מיירי בכור זרע.

*אעָלוּ בְּאִילָן שֶׁכּוֹחוֹ רַע וּבְסוּכָה שֶׁכּוֹחָהּ רַע – טָמֵא. הֵיכִי דָּמֵי אִילָן שֶׁכּוֹחוֹ רַע? אָמְרִי דְּבֵי ר' יַנַּאי: בכָּל שֶׁאֵין בְּעִיקָּרוֹ לָחוֹק רוֹבַע. הֵיכִי דָּמֵי סוֹכָה שֶׁכּוֹחָהּ רַע? אָמַר ר"ל: גכָּל שֶׁנֶּחְבֵּאת (א) בְּחֶזְיוֹנָהּ. תְּנַן הָתָם: *דהַמְהַלֵּךְ בְּבֵית הַפְּרָס עַל גַּבֵּי אֲבָנִים שֶׁיָּכוֹל לְהָסִיט, עַל הָאָדָם וְעַל הַבְּהֵמָה שֶׁכּוֹחָן רַע – טָמֵא. ה"ד אָדָם שֶׁכּוֹחוֹ רַע? אָמַר ר"ל: הכָּל שֶׁרוֹכְבוֹ וְאַרְכּוּבוֹתָיו נוֹקְשׁוֹת. ה"ד בְּהֵמָה שֶׁכּוֹחָהּ רַע? אָמְרִי דְּבֵי ר' יַנַּאי: וכָּל שֶׁרוֹכְבָהּ מַטִּילָה גְּלָלִים. אָמְרִי דְּבֵי ר' יַנַּאי: לִתְפִלָּה וְלִתְפִילִּין – ד' קַבִּין. לִתְפִלָּה מַאי הִיא? דְּתַנְיָא: זהַנּוֹשֵׂא מַשְּׂאוֹי עַל כְּתֵפוֹ וְהִגִּיעַ זְמַן תְּפִלָּה, פָּחוֹת מִד' קַבִּין – (ב) מַפְשִׁילִין לַאֲחוֹרָיו וּמִתְפַּלֵּל, אַרְבָּעָה קַבִּין – מַנִּיחַ ע"ג קַרְקַע וּמִתְפַּלֵּל. לִתְפִילִּין מַאי הִיא? דְּתַנְיָא: חהָיָה נוֹשֵׂא מַשְּׂאוֹי עַל רֹאשׁוֹ וּתְפִילִּין בְּרֹאשׁוֹ, אִם הָיוּ תְּפִילִּין רוֹצְצוֹת – אָסוּר, וְאִם לָאו – מוּתָּר. בְּאֵיזוֹ מַשְּׂאוֹי אָמְרוּ – בְּמַשְּׂאוֹי שֶׁל אַרְבַּעַת קַבִּין. תָּנֵי רַבִּי חִיָּיא: הַמּוֹצִיא זֶבֶל עַל רֹאשׁוֹ וּתְפִילִּין בְּרֹאשׁוֹ – ה"ז לֹא יְסַלְּקֵם לִצְדָדִין, וְלֹא יִקְשְׁרֵם בְּמָתְנָיו – מִפְּנֵי שֶׁהוּא נוֹהֵג בָּהֶן מִנְהַג בִּזָּיוֹן. אֲבָל קוֹשְׁרָם עַל זְרוֹעוֹ בִּמְקוֹם תְּפִילִּין. מִשּׁוּם דְּבֵי שֵׁילָא אָמְרוּ: טאֲפִילּוּ מִטְפַּחַת שֶׁלָּהֶן אָסוּר לְהָנִיחַ עַל הָרֹאשׁ שֶׁיֵּשׁ בּוֹ תְּפִילִּין. וְכַמָּה? אֲמַר אַבַּיֵי: אֲפִילּוּ רִבְעָא דְּרִבְעָא דְּפוּמְבְּדִיתָא. § "אָמַר ר' יְהוּדָה: מַאי קִצְבָה בְּכָרֵי? אֶלָּא אִם יֵשׁ בּוֹ כְּדֵי נְפִילָה". § וְכַמָּה כְּדֵי נְפִילָה? ר' אַמִּי אָמַר רַבִּי יוֹחָנָן: אַרְבָּעָה [א] סְאִין לְכוֹר. רַבִּי אַמִּי דִּילֵיהּ אָמַר: שְׁמוֹנַת [ב] סְאִין לְכוֹר. אֲמַר לֵיהּ הַהוּא סָבָא לְרַב חָמָא בְּרֵיהּ דְּרַבָּה בַּר אֲבוּהּ: אַסְבְּרָה לָךְ; בִּשְׁנֵי דְּרַבִּי יוֹחָנָן הֲוָה שְׁמִינָה אַרְעָא, בִּשְׁנֵי דְּרַבִּי אַמִּי הֲוָה כְּחִישָׁא אַרְעָא. תְּנַן הָתָם: *יהָרוּחַ שֶׁפִּיזְּרָה אֶת הָעוֹמָרִין, אוֹמְדִים אוֹתָהּ כַּמָּה לֶקֶט רְאוּיָה לַעֲשׂוֹת, וְנוֹתֵן לַעֲנִיִּים. רשב"ג אוֹמֵר: נוֹתֵן לַעֲנִיִּים כְּדֵי נְפִילָה. וְכַמָּה כְּדֵי נְפִילָה? כִּי אֲתָא רַב דִּימִי אָמַר ר' אֶלְעָזָר, וְאִיתֵּימָא ר' יוֹחָנָן: כאַרְבַּעַת קַבִּין לְכוֹר. בָּעֵי רַבִּי יִרְמְיָה: לְכוֹר זֶרַע אוֹ לְכוֹר תְּבוּאָה? לְמַפּוֹלֶת יָד אוֹ לְמַפּוֹלֶת שְׁוָורִים? ת"ש, דְּכִי אָתֵי רָבִין א"ר אֲבוּהּ א"ר אֶלְעָזָר, וְאָמְרִי לַהּ אָמַר ר' יוֹחָנָן: אַרְבַּעַת קַבִּין לְכוֹר זֶרַע. וַעֲדַיִין תִּיבָּעֵי לָךְ: לְמַפּוֹלֶת יָד אוֹ לְמַפּוֹלֶת שְׁוָורִים? תֵּיקוּ. § **מתני'** להַמְקַבֵּל שָׂדֶה מֵחֲבֵירוֹ וַאֲכָלָהּ חָגָב אוֹ נִשְׁדְּפָה, אִם מַכַּת מְדִינָה הִיא – מְנַכֶּה לוֹ מִן חֲכוֹרוֹ, אִם אֵינָהּ מַכַּת מְדִינָה – אֵין מְנַכֶּה לוֹ מִן חֲכוֹרוֹ. ר' יְהוּדָה אוֹמֵר: אִם קִיבְּלָהּ הֵימֶנּוּ בְּמָעוֹת – בֵּין כָּךְ וּבֵין כָּךְ אֵינוֹ מְנַכֶּה לוֹ מֵחֲכוֹרוֹ. § **גמ'** ה"ד מַכַּת מְדִינָה? אָמַר רַב יְהוּדָה: מכְּגוֹן דְּאִישְׁדּוּף רוּבָּא דְּבָאגָא. עוּלָּא אֲמַר: כְּגוֹן שֶׁנִּשְׁתַּדְּפוּ אַרְבַּע שָׂדוֹת מֵאַרְבַּע רוּחוֹתֶיהָ. אֲמַר עוּלָּא: בָּעוּ בְּמַעַרְבָא: נִשְׁדַּף תֶּלֶם אֶחָד עַל פְּנֵי כּוּלָּהּ, מַאי? נִשְׁתַּיֵּיר תֶּלֶם אֶחָד עַל פְּנֵי כּוּלָּהּ, מַהוּ? אַפְסִיקָא בֵּירָא, מַאי? אַסְפַּסְתָּא
מַאי

עָלוּ. זָב וְטָהוֹר לְאִילָן שֶׁכֹּחוֹ רַע, אוֹ לְסוּכָה = עֲנַף אִילָן – שֶׁכּוּחָהּ רַע. טָמֵא. הַטָּהוֹר, שֶׁכֵּיוָן שֶׁהָאִילָן אוֹ הַסּוּכָה כֹּחָהּ רַע נִכְפֶּפֶת תַּחְתֵּיהֶן, וְכָבֵד הָעֶלְיוֹן עַל הַתַּחְתּוֹן וְנִשְׁעָן עָלָיו מִכֹּחוֹ שֶׁל עֶלְיוֹן, וּבֵין זָב שֶׁנִּשְׁעַן עַל הַטָּהוֹר וּבֵין טָהוֹר שֶׁנִּשְׁעַן עַל הַזָּב – טָמֵא. שֶׁאֵין בְּעִיקָּר לָחוֹק. בִּרְחָבּוֹ רוֹבַע הַקַּב. שֶׁנֶּחְבֵּאת (ג) בְּחֶזְיוֹנָהּ. שֶׁנִּטְמֶנֶת בַּאֲחִיזָתָהּ, שֶׁהָאוֹחֵז בָּהּ טוֹמְנָהּ בְּכַף יָדוֹ. הַמְהַלֵּךְ בְּבֵית הַפְּרָס. שָׂדֶה שֶׁנֶּחֱרַשׁ בָּהּ קֶבֶר, חָשׁוּ לְעֶצֶם כִּשְׂעוֹרָה שֶׁמְּטַמֵּא בְּמַגָּע וּבְמַשָּׂא וְאֵינוֹ מְטַמֵּא בְּאֹהֶל, וְהָיוּ שָׁם אֲבָנִים שֶׁאֵינָן תְּקוּעוֹת וּקְבוּעוֹת בָּאָרֶץ, וְהֵן נִסָּטוֹת מֵחֲמַת הָעוֹבֵר עֲלֵיהֶן, וְעֶצֶם כִּשְׂעוֹרָה נִיסָּט מִכֹּחוֹ. אוֹ רָכַב מִי שֶׁרוֹצֶה לֶאֱכוֹל טְהָרוֹת עַל אָדָם אוֹ בְּהֵמָה שֶׁכּוֹחָן רַע, וְהוֹלִיכוּהוּ עֲלֵיהֶן – טָמֵא הָרוֹכֵב. לָא מִיבַּעְיָא נִרְכָּב דְּטָמֵא, דְּבְלָאו הֶיסֵּט אֲבָנִים נַמִי טָמֵא הַמְהַלֵּךְ בְּבֵית הַפְּרָס, אֶלָּא אַף הָרוֹכֵב טָמֵא. דְּכֵיוָן דְּכֹחַ הַתַּחְתּוֹן רַע – מֵחֲמַת מַשָּׂא הָעֶלְיוֹן נִיסָּטוּ, וַהֲרֵי כְּאִילּוּ מְסִיטוֹ הוּא. וְכֹחַ הַתַּחְתּוֹן אֵינוֹ מוֹעִיל לְהַבִּילוֹ אא"כ כֹּחוֹ יָפֶה. אֲבָל אִם הָיָה כֹּחוֹ יָפֶה – לָא חֲשִׁיב מַשָּׂא הָעֶלְיוֹן, וְאֵינוֹ כְּמַסִּיטוֹ. נוֹקְשׁוֹת. זוֹ לָזוֹ. אַרְבָּעָה קַבִּין. הָוֵי שִׁיעוּר מַשּׂוֹי. מַפְשִׁילָן לַאֲחוֹרָיו. שֶׁאֵין כּוֹבְדָן מוֹנֵעַ מִלְּהִתְכַּוֵּין לִבּוֹ. רוֹצְצוֹת. מִתְמַעֲכוֹת תַּחַת הַמַּשָּׂא. וְאִם לָאו. שֶׁהוּא קַל אוֹ שֶׁאֵינוֹ מוּטָּל עֲלֵיהֶן. בְּאֵיזֶה מַשְּׂאוֹי. הָוֵי רְגִילָה. בִּמְקוֹם תְּפִילִּין. אֵצֶל תְּפִילִּין שֶׁל יָד. אֲפִילּוּ מִטְפַּחַת שֶׁלָּהֶן. שֶׁכּוֹרְכִין בָּהּ תְּפִילִּין בַּלַּיְלָה. אָסוּר. לְהַנִּיחַ לְשֵׁם מַשּׂוֹי עַל הָרֹאשׁ בְּשָׁעָה שֶׁתְּפִילִּין בִּמְקוֹמָן מוּנָּחִין. וְכַמָּה. יְהֵא בַּמַּשּׂוֹי וִיהֵא אָסוּר לְהַנִּיחוֹ עַל הָרֹאשׁ – אַלִּיבָּא דְּר' שֵׁילָא. רִיבְעָא דְּרִיבְעָא. רְבִיעַ לִיטְרָא, דָּבָר מוּעָט הוּא. *ד' סְאִין [זֶרַע] לְכוֹר. לְבֵית קַרְקַע כּוֹר, וְהוּא אֶלֶף וַחֲמֵשׁ מֵאוֹת אַמָּה אוֹרֶךְ שֶׁל נ' אַמָּה רוֹחַב. דַּחֲצַר הַמִּשְׁכָּן הָוֵי סָאתַיִם וְהוּא מֵאָה עַל נ' וְכוֹר ל' סְאִין, וּבֵין מְרוּבָּע וּבֵין אָרוֹךְ וְקָצָר, לְפִי חֶשְׁבּוֹן זֶה שִׁיעוּרוֹ. אַסְבְּרָא לָךְ. לָאו דְּרַבִּי אַמִּי פָּלֵיג אַדְּרַבִּי יוֹחָנָן רַבֵּיהּ, אֶלָּא שֶׁהָעוֹלָם מִתְקַלְקֵל וְהוֹלֵךְ. בִּימֵי ר' יוֹחָנָן הֲוָה שְׁמֵינָה אַרְעָא. וְדַיּוֹ לְבֵית כּוֹר בְּד' סְאִין, וּבִשְׁנֵי דְּר' אַמִּי כְּבָר הוּכְחֲשָׁה, וּצְרִיכָה ח' סְאִין. הָרוּחַ שֶׁפִּיזְּרָה אֶת הָעוֹמָרִים. בַּשָּׂדֶה, וְכִיסּוּ אֶת הַלֶּקֶט שֶׁל עֲנִיִּים הַמְפוּזָּר בַּשָּׂדֶה, וְאֵין יָדוּעַ כַּמָּה לֶקֶט הָיָה שָׁם לְמַטָּה מִן הָעוֹמָרִים, שָׁמִין אוֹתוֹ ב"ד, הוֹלְכִין עָלֶיהָ וְשָׁמִין כַּמָּה לֶקֶט שָׂדֶה זוֹ רְאוּיָה לְהֵעָשׂוֹת בְּכָל שָׁנָה. רשב"ג אוֹמֵר. אֵין הַדָּבָר צָרִיךְ אוֹמֶד; כְּבָר קָצוּב כְּדֵי נְפִילָה וְעוֹמֵד וְנוֹתֵן לַעֲנִיִּים כְּדֵי נִיפּוּל, לֶקֶט הַקָּצוּב, וּלְקַמָּן מְפָרֵשׁ לְהוּ. לְכוֹר זֶרַע. לְשָׂדֶה שֶׁזָּרְעוּ בָּהּ כּוֹר, אוֹ לְשָׂדֶה שֶׁלּוֹקֵט בָּהּ כּוֹר תְּבוּאָה. וְאִם תִּמְצָא לוֹמַר – לְכוֹר זֶרַע. לְמַפּוֹלֶת יָד אוֹ לְמַפּוֹלֶת שְׁוָורִים. יֵשׁ מָקוֹם שֶׁזּוֹרְעִין אֶת הַתְּבוּאָה בַּיָּד, וְיֵשׁ מָקוֹם שֶׁנּוֹתְנִין הַזֶּרַע בָּעֲגָלָה מְנוּקֶּבֶת וּמוֹלִיכִין הַשְּׁוָורִים אֶת הָעֲגָלָה עַל הַמַּחֲרֵישָׁה, וְהַזֶּרַע הוּא נוֹפֵל וְהוֹלֵךְ. וְהַרְבֵּה זֶרַע צָרִיךְ לְמַפּוֹלֶת שְׁוָורִים יוֹתֵר מִמַּפּוֹלֶת יָד. וְקָא מִיבַּעְיָא לָן: לְשָׂדֶה שֶׁל זֶרַע כּוֹר לְמַפּוֹלֶת יָד שֶׁלֹּא שִׁיעֲרוּ בַּלֶּקֶט שֶׁלָּהּ אַרְבַּעַת קַבִּין, אוֹ לְכוֹר זֶרַע לְמַפּוֹלֶת שְׁוָורִים. **מתני'** מַכַּת מְדִינָה. מְפָרֵשׁ בַּגְּמָ'. וְהָא לֵיתָא אֶלָּא בַּחֲכִירוּתָא, דְּאִי בְּקַבְּלָנוּתָא – מַאי מְנַכֶּה אִיכָּא? מַה שֶּׁיִּמְצָאוּ – יַחֲלוֹקוּ. אֵינוֹ מְנַכֶּה. דְּאָמַר לוֹ: מַזָּלְךָ גָּרַם. בֵּין כָּךְ וּבֵין כָּךְ. אֲפִילּוּ הִיא מַכַּת מְדִינָה אֵינוֹ מְנַכֶּה: שֶׁעַל הַמָּעוֹת לֹא נִגְזְרָה גְּזֵירָה, הִלְכָּךְ לָא עָלֶיהָ הָיְתָה פּוּרְעָנוּת זוֹ. **גמ'** רוּבָּא דְּבָאגָא. [ג] רוֹב הַבִּקְעָה שֶׁזּוֹ בְּתוֹכָהּ. נִשְׁדַּף תֶּלֶם אֶחָד. וְלֹא יוֹתֵר, מִשָּׂדוֹת שֶׁהֵן סְבִיבוֹתֶיהָ. וְאוֹתוֹ תֶּלֶם כָּל סְבִיבוֹת שָׂדֶה זוֹ. תֶּלֶם. = שׁוּרוֹת הַמַּעֲנָה. נִשְׁתַּיֵּיר תֶּלֶם אֶחָד. כָּל סְבִיבוֹתֶיהָ, שֶׁלֹּא נִשְׁדַּף, וְאַרְבַּע שָׂדוֹת שֶׁסְּבִיבוֹתֶיהָ נִשְׁדְּפוּ, וְגַם זוֹ נִשְׁדְּפָה. מַהוּ. מִי אָמְרִינַן: דְּכֵיוָן דְּנִשְׁתַּיֵּיר תֶּלֶם אֶחָד עַל פְּנֵי כּוּלָּהּ שֶׁלֹּא לָקְתָה – אֵין זוֹ מַכַּת מְדִינָה, אֶלָּא מַזָּלוֹ, אוֹ דִּלְמָא: הַאי שִׁיּוּרָא לָאו כְּלוּם הִיא. אִיפְסִיק בֵּירָא מַהוּ. אִם הָיוּ אַרְבַּע שָׂדוֹת שֶׁהֵן סְבִיבוֹתֶיהָ בּוּרוֹת, וּשְׁאָר שָׂדוֹת סָבִיב סָבִיב נִשְׁדְּפוּ, מִי אָמְרִינַן: ד' שָׂדוֹת שֶׁסְּבִיבוֹתֶיהָ לֹא נִשְׁדְּפוּ, א"ד אָמַר לֵיהּ: אִם הָיוּ זְרוּעוֹת – אַף הֵם נִשְׁדְּפוּ. אִיפְסִיק בֵּירָא. שָׂדֶה בּוּר הִפְסִיק בֵּין הַשְּׁדוּפוֹת לָזוֹ. אַסְפַּסְתָּא. הָיוּ אוֹתָן שֶׁסְּבִיבוֹתֶיהָ זְרוּעוֹת שַׁחַת לְמַאֲכַל בְּהֵמָה, וְלֹא נִשְׁדְּפוּ, וְהֵן הִפְסִיקוּ בֵּין הַשְּׁדוּפוֹת לָזוֹ.
מַאי

הגהות הב"ח
(א) גמ' שנחבאת באחיזונה תנן התם המהלך בבית הפרס על גבי אבנים שאינו יכול להסיטן על האדם ועל הבהמה שכוחן יפה טהור על גבי אבנים שיכול: (ב) שם מפשילן כצ"ל ואות י' נמחק: (ג) רש"י ד"ה שנחבאת באחיזונה וכו' כשאוחז בה:

הגהות הגר"א
[א ב] גמ' סאין צ"ל קבין: [ג] רש"י ד"ה רובא דבאגא רוב כו'. נ"ב אבל הרמב"ם כתב רוב השדות של אותה העיר וכגירסת הרא"ש רובא דבאגי:

זבין פ"ג [מ"א]
אהלות פי"ח [מ"ז]
פאה פ"ה [מ"א]
נ"א ד' סאין לבית כור קרקע זרע ועיין רש"א

מַאי? זֶרַע אַחֵר מַאי? חִיטֵּי לְגַבֵּי שְׂעוֹרִים כְּזֶרַע אַחֵר דָּמֵי אוֹ לָא? כָּל הָעוֹלָם כּוּלּוֹ בְּשִׁדָּפוֹן וְשֶׁלּוֹ בְּיֵרָקוֹן, אִי נַמִי כָּל הָעוֹלָם כּוּלּוֹ בְּיֵרָקוֹן וְשֶׁלּוֹ בְּשִׁדָּפוֹן, מַאי? תֵּיקוּ. אֲמַר לֵיהּ זַרְעָהּ חִיטֵּי, וַאֲזַל הוּא וּזְרָעָהּ שְׂעָרֵי וְאִשְׁתַּדּוּף רוּבָּא דְּבָאגָא, וְאִשְׁתַּדּוּף נַמִי הָנָךְ שְׂעָרֵי דִּילֵיהּ, מַאי? מִי אָמְרִינַן, דְּאָמַר לֵיהּ: אִילּוּ זַרְעְתָּהּ חִיטֵּי הֲוָה נַמִי מִשְׁתַּדְּפָא, אוֹ דִּלְמָא מָצֵי אָמַר לֵיהּ: אִילּוּ זַרְעְתָּהּ חִיטֵּי הֲוָה מְקַיֵּים בִּי: °"וְתִגְזַר אוֹמֶר וְיָקָם לָךְ"! [א]מִסְתַּבְּרָא דְּאָמַר לֵיהּ: אִי זַרְעְתָּהּ חִיטֵּי — הֲוָה מְקַיֵּים בִּי: "וְתִגְזַר אוֹמֶר וְיָקָם לָךְ וְעַל דְּרָכֶיךָ נָגַהּ אוֹר". נִשְׁתַּדְּפוּ כָּל שְׂדוֹתָיו שֶׁל מַחְכִּיר, וְאִשְׁתַּדּוּף נַמִי הָא בַּהֲדַיְיהוּ, וְלָא אִשְׁתַּדּוּף רוּבָּא דְּבָאגָא, מַאי? מִי אָמְרִינַן: כֵּיוָן דְּלָא אִשְׁתַּדּוּף רוּבָּא דְּבָאגָא — לָא מְנַכֵּי לֵיהּ? אוֹ דִּלְמָא: כֵּיוָן דְּאִשְׁתַּדּוּף כּוּלְּהוּ אַרְעָתֵיהּ, מָצֵי אָמַר לֵיהּ: הַאי מִשּׁוּם לָתָךְ דִּידָךְ הוּא, דְּהָא מִשְׁתַּדְּפוּ כָּל שְׂדוֹתֶיךָ. [ב]מִסְתַּבְּרָא דְּאָמַר לֵיהּ: אִי מִשּׁוּם לַתַּאי דִּידִי — הֲוָה מִשְׁתַּיֵּיר לִי פּוּרְתָּא, כִּדְכְתִיב: °"כִּי נִשְׁאַרְנוּ מְעַט מֵהַרְבֵּה". נִשְׁתַּדְּפוּ כָּל שְׂדוֹתָיו שֶׁל חוֹכֵר, וְאִשְׁתַּדּוּף רוּבָּא דְּבָאגָא, וְאִשְׁתַּדּוּף נַמִי הָא בַּהֲדַיְיהוּ, מַאי? מִי אָמְרִינַן: כֵּיוָן דְּאִשְׁתַּדּוּף רוּבָּא דְּבָאגָא — מְנַכֵּי לֵיהּ? אוֹ דִּלְמָא: כֵּיוָן דְּאִשְׁתַּדּוּף כּוּלְּהוּ אַרְעָתֵיהּ מָצֵי אָמַר לֵיהּ: מִשּׁוּם לָתָךְ דִּידָךְ הוּא, דְּהָא מִשְׁתַּדְּפוּ כָּל שְׂדוֹתֶיךָ! [ג]מִסְתַּבְּרָא דְּאָמַר לֵיהּ: מִשּׁוּם לָתָאךְ הוּא. אַמַּאי? הָכָא נַמִי נֵימָא לֵיהּ: אִי מִשּׁוּם לַתַּאי דִּידִי הוּא — הֲוָה מְשַׁיֵּיר לִי פּוּרְתָּא, דַּהֲוָה מְקַיֵּים בִּי: "כִּי נִשְׁאַרְנוּ מְעַט מֵהַרְבֵּה"! מִשּׁוּם דְּאָמַר לֵיהּ: אִי הֲוָה חֲזֵית לְאִישְׁתַּיּוּרֵי לָךְ מִידֵּי, הֲוָה מִשְׁתַּיֵּיר לָךְ מִדְּנַפְשָׁךְ. מֵיתִיבִי: *[ד]הָיְתָה שְׁנַת שִׁדָּפוֹן וְיֵרָקוֹן, אוֹ שְׁבִיעִית, אוֹ שֶׁהָיוּ שָׁנִים כִּשְׁנֵי אֵלִיָּהוּ — אֵינוֹ עוֹלֶה לוֹ מִן הַמִּנְיָן. קָתָנֵי שִׁדָּפוֹן וְיֵרָקוֹן דּוּמְיָא דְּשָׁנִים כִּשְׁנֵי אֵלִיָּהוּ. מַה שְּׁנֵי אֵלִיָּהוּ — דְּלָא הֲוֵי תְּבוּאָה כְּלָל, אַף הָכָא נַמִי — דְּלָא הֲוֵי תְּבוּאָה כְּלָל. אֲבָל (א) דְּאִיכָּא תְּבוּאָה — סָלְקָא לֵיהּ, וְלָא קָאָמְרִינַן מַכַּת מְדִינָה הִיא. אֲמַר רַב נַחְמָן בַּר יִצְחָק: שָׁאנֵי הָתָם, דַּאֲמַר קְרָא: °"בְּמִסְפַּר שְׁנֵי תְבוּאוֹת יִמְכָּר לָךְ" — שָׁנִים שֶׁיֵּשׁ בָּהֶן תְּבוּאָה בָּעוֹלָם. אֲמַר לֵיהּ רַב אַשִׁי לְרַב כָּהֲנָא: אֶלָּא מֵעַתָּה שְׁבִיעִית תַּעֲלֶה לוֹ מִן הַמִּנְיָן, דְּהָא אִיכָּא תְּבוּאָה בְּחוּצָה לָאָרֶץ! אֲמַר לֵיהּ: שְׁבִיעִית *אַפְקְעָתָא דְּמַלְכָּא הִיא. אֲמַר לֵיהּ מָר זוּטְרָא בְּרֵיהּ דְּרַב מָרִי לְרָבִינָא: אֶלָּא מֵעַתָּה שְׁבִיעִית לֹא תַּעֲלֶה לוֹ מִן הַגֵּירוּעַ, אַלְמָּה תְּנַן: *[ה]נוֹתֵן סֶלַע וּפוּנְדְּיוֹן לְשָׁנָה! אֲמַר לֵיהּ: שָׁאנֵי הָתָם, דַּחֲזְיָא לְמִשְׁטְחָא בָּהּ פֵּירֵי. אָמַר שְׁמוּאֵל: לֹא שָׁנוּ אֶלָּא שֶׁזְּרָעָהּ וְצָמְחָה וַאֲכָלָהּ חָגָב, [ו]אֲבָל לֹא זְרָעָהּ כְּלָל — לֹא. דְּאָמַר לֵיהּ: אִילּוּ זַרְעְתָּהּ הֲוָה מְקַיֵּים בִּי: °"לֹא יֵבֹשׁוּ בְּעֵת רָעָה וּבִימֵי רְעָבוֹן יִשְׂבָּעוּ". מְתִיב רַב שֵׁשֶׁת: *רוֹעֶה שֶׁהָיָה רוֹעֶה וְהִנִּיחַ עֶדְרוֹ וּבָא לָעִיר, וּבָא זְאֵב וְטָרַף, וּבָא אֲרִי וְדָרַס — אֵין אוֹמְרִים: אִילּוּ הָיָה שָׁם הָיָה מַצִּיל. אֶלָּא אוֹמְדִין אוֹתוֹ; אִם יָכוֹל לְהַצִּיל — חַיָּיב, וְאִם לָאו — פָּטוּר. וְאַמַּאי? נֵימָא לֵיהּ: אִי הֲוֵית הָתָם — הֲוָה מְקַיֵּים *בִּי: °"גַּם אֶת הָאֲרִי גַּם (אֶת) הַדּוֹב הִכָּה עַבְדֶּךָ"! מִשּׁוּם דְּאָמַר לֵיהּ: אִי הֲוֵית חֲזֵית לְאִיתְרְחוּשֵׁי לָךְ נִיסָּא — הֲוָה אִיתְרְחִישׁ לָךְ נִיסָּא *כר' חֲנִינָא בֶּן דּוֹסָא, דְּמַתְיָין עִיזֵּי דּוּבֵּי בְּקַרְנַיְיהוּ. וְנֵימָא לֵיהּ: נְהִי דְּלְנִיסָּא רַבָּה לָא הֲוָה חֲזֵינָא, לְנִיסָּא זוּטָא חֲזֵינָא

רש"י

מַאי. מִי אָמְרִינַן: אַרְבַּע שָׂדוֹת שֶׁסְּבִיבוֹתֶיהָ לֹא נִשְׁדְּפוּ, אוֹ דִּלְמָא אָמַר לֵיהּ: אִילּוּ הָיוּ זְרוּעוֹת תְּבוּאָה — אַף הֵן נִשְׁדְּפוּ. זֶרַע אַחֵר מַאי. אִם תִּמְצָא לוֹמַר אַסְפַּסְתָּא לָאו הַפְסָקָה הִיא, מִשּׁוּם דְּלָאו בִּכְלַל גְּזֵירַת פּוּרְעָנוּת הַתְּבוּאָה הוּא, דְּאָמַר לֵיהּ: אִילּוּ תְּבוּאָה הֲוַאי — אִיהוּ נַמִי אִישְׁתַּדּוּף, זֶרַע אַחֵר מִי הָוֵי הַפְסָקָה? וְתִגְזַר אוֹמֶר. מַה שֶּׁתְּבַקֵּשׁ מִן הַיּוֹצֵר יַעֲשֶׂה. וַאֲנִי לֹא בִּקַּשְׁתִּי מִן הַשָּׁמַיִם בִּתְחִלַּת הַשָּׁנָה שֶׁיַּצְלִיחֵנִי בִּשְׂעוֹרִים אֶלָּא בְּחִטִּין. כָּל שְׂדוֹתָיו. בְּכָל מָקוֹם שֶׁהֵן. לָתָךְ. = מַזָּלְךָ. כּוּלְּהוּ אַרְעָתֵיהּ. וַאֲפִילּוּ יֶשְׁנָן בְּבִקְעָה אַחֶרֶת. הָיְתָה שְׁנַת שִׁדָּפוֹן. גַּבֵּי מוֹכֵר, בִּזְמַן שֶׁהַיּוֹבֵל נוֹהֵג, שֶׁאֵינוֹ מוּתָּר לוֹ לִגְאוֹל פָּחוֹת מִשְּׁתֵּי שָׁנִים, תְּנַן לָהּ בַּעֲרָכִין (דף כט:). אוֹ שָׁנִים כִּשְׁנֵי אֵלִיָּהוּ. שֶׁלֹּא יָרְדוּ גְּשָׁמִים. אֵינוֹ עוֹלֶה לוֹ מִן הַמִּנְיָן. שְׁתֵּי שָׁנִים. הָא אִיכָּא תְּבוּאָה בְּדוּכְתָּא אַחֲרִיתִי. אַף עַל גַּב דְּהַהוּא בָּאגָא אִישְׁתַּדּוּף, אָמְרִינַן: לָתָא דִּידֵיהּ (מַזָּל דִּידֵיהּ) גָּרַם (ב) וְסָלְקִינַן לֵיהּ, מְגָרֵעַ מִדָּמִים מַה שֶּׁמַּגִּיעַ לְשָׁנָה אַחַת כְּאִילּוּ הָיוּ בָּהּ פֵּירוֹת. שֶׁיֵּשׁ בָּהֶן תְּבוּאָה. בְּשׁוּם מָקוֹם בָּאָרֶץ. אַפְקְעָתָא דְּמַלְכָּא. הַמֶּלֶךְ בִּיטְּלוֹ מִלְּזוֹרְעָהּ, וַהֲרֵי הִיא כְּמוֹ שֶׁאֵינָהּ, וְלֹא קְרָאָהּ הַכָּתוּב לְיִשְׂרָאֵל שְׁנַת תְּבוּאָה. אֶלָּא מֵעַתָּה. אִי כְּמַאן דְּלֵיתָהּ. לֹא תַּעֲלֶה לוֹ בְּגֵירוּעַ. מַקְדִּישׁ שָׂדֵהוּ וּבָא לִפְדּוֹתוֹ, שֶׁנָּתַן לוֹ הַכָּתוּב פִּדְיוֹן בִּתְחִלַּת הַיּוֹבֵל "חֲמִשִּׁים שֶׁקֶל כֶּסֶף" (ויקרא כז), וְאִם אַחַר הַיּוֹבֵל "וְחִשַּׁב לוֹ הַכֹּהֵן" וגו' "וְנִגְרַע מֵעֶרְכֶּךָ" (שם) — שָׁנִים שֶׁעָבְרוּ הוּא מְגָרֵעַ מִן הַחֶשְׁבּוֹן כַּמָּה שֶׁמַּגִּיעַ לָהֶם, וְנוֹתֵן כַּמָּה שֶׁמַּגִּיעַ לַשָּׁנִים הַבָּאוֹת. וְכֵיוָן דִּבִשְׁבִיעִית כְּמַאן דְּלֵיתְנְהוּ, לָמָּה הֵן נִמְנוֹת לִפְחוֹת אֶת הַפִּדָּיוֹן? דִּתְנַן: נוֹתֵן סֶלַע וּפוּנְדְּיוֹן לַשָּׁנִים הַבָּאוֹת, שֶׁזֶּהוּ הַחֶשְׁבּוֹן הַמַּגִּיעַ לְכָל שָׁנָה כְּשֶׁאַתָּה מְחַלֵּק חֲמִשִּׁים סְלָעִים לְמ"ט שָׁנִים. נִמְצְאוּ שְׁבִיעִיּוֹת מוֹעִילוֹת לְגָרֵעַ הַפִּדְיוֹן, דְּאִי מַדְלֵית שֶׁבַע שְׁמִיטּוֹת וּתְחַלֵּק חֲמִשִּׁים שְׁקָלִים לְמ"ב שָׁנָה — מַגִּיעַ לְכָל שָׁנָה קָרוֹב לְסֶלַע וְדִינָר! לְמִשְׁטַח בֵּיהּ פֵּירֵי. הִלְכָּךְ סָלְקָא לֵיהּ, דְּגַבֵּי פִּדְיוֹן שְׂדֵה אֲחוּזָּה לָא כְּתִיב שְׁנֵי תְּבוּאוֹת. לֹא שָׁנוּ. אִם מַכַּת מְדִינָה הִיא מְנַכֶּה לוֹ. אֲבָל לֹא זְרָעָהּ. וְאִשְׁתַּדּוּף רוּבָּא דְּבָאגָא — לֹא מְנַכֶּה לֵיהּ. רַבִּי חֲנִינָא בֶּן דּוֹסָא. בְּמַסֶּכֶת תַּעֲנִית. פַּעַם

תוספות

אי הוית חזית לאשתיורי לך הוי משתייר לך מדנפשך. גבי חוכר איכא למימר הכי דאפילו יפטור אותו המחכיר מליתן חכירותו — הרי לא נשתייר כלום, דנשדף כל השדה איירי. והא דקתני מנכה לו — לישנא קלילא נקט. אי נמי: נשאר קלת בשדה לאו חשיב שיור המעט הנמלא לענין שיהא קורא "כי נשארנו מעט מהרבה" כיון שפום שדה לא פלט מהפסד מרובה. אבל מחכיר, שגוף הקרקע שלו וממנו יש לו לקבל חכירותו, כדאמר לעיל מארעאי קבעינא — יכול המחכיר לומר לחוכר "כי נשארנו מעט מהרבה" והרי נשאר לי חכירותי מה שקבלתי עמך בכך וכך כורין. **אלא** מעתה שביעית תעלה כו'. תימה: מאי "אלא מעתה"? בלאו הכי תקשה אברייתא אמאי אין שביעית עולה מן המנין, כיון דלא דמי לשני אליהו? וי"ל: דשפיר קאמר אלא מעתה, דאי אמרת (ג) דמכת מדינה לא חשיב אלא דומיא דשני אליהו — אתי שפיר דהוה תלינן טעמא במה שזו השדה אינה ראויה לתבואה — לא מיקרי שני תבואות, והיינו כי ליכא תבואה בעולם כגון שני אליהו. אבל יש תבואה בעולם — חשיב שדה זו ראויה לתבואה, אף על גב דאישתדוף רובא דבאגא, אבל שביעית, ודאי אף על גב דאיכא תבואה בחו"ל — שדה זו אינה ראויה לתבואה, כיון שהיא בארץ. אבל השתא דאמר כי (ד) אישדוף רובא דבאגא הוה מכת מדינה, ולא חשיבא שדה זו ראויה לתבואה, ואפי' הכי גזירת הכתוב הוא כיון דאיכא תבואה בעולם עולה לו מן המנין — א"כ אפי' שביעית נמי. ומשני: שביעית אפקעתא דמלכא הוא, ואי אפשר להיות תבואה בארץ בהיתר כלל, ולהכי לא מקרי שנת תבואה. אבל שנת שדפון, דאע"ג דהוי מכת מדינה, אי אשתדוף רובא דבאגא חשיבא אפשר להיות בה תבואה, כיון שיש בחו"ל בשום מקום בעולם, כי באפשר להיות בה תבואה. מיקרי שנת תבואה ובשנים כבשני אליהו חשב כלא אפשר להיות בה תבואה, כיון דבשום מקום ליכא.

מתיב רב ששת רועה שהיה רועה עדרו כו'. תימה: אמאי לא פריך ממתניתין ד"הפועלים" (לעיל דף צג:) דתנן: הארי והדוב — הרי זה אונס, ואמאי? נימא אילו נלחם בהם הוה מקיים ביה "גם את הארי"! וי"ל: דהתם כיון שהיה שם ולא בא לו רוח גבורה — אין יכול לומר דהוה מקיים ביה. אבל הכא, שלא היה שם — דלמא אי הוה התם היה בו רוח (ה) וגבורה ודעת להלחם, והוה מקיים ביה "גם את הארי כו'".

לניסא זוטא מיהא חזיא קשיא. תימה: מאי קשיא? הא אמרן לעיל דכי אמר ליה זרעה חטין וזרעה שערי ואשתדוף, דמצי אמר ליה אי זרעתה חטין — הוה מקיים בי "ותגזור אומר ויקם לך" — וכ"ש כשלא זרעה כלל, דליכא הוכחה שהיה ראוי להשתדף! וי"ל: דשמואל מיירי כגון שאמר ליה זרע כל מה שתרצה, דהשתא לא מצי למימר הוה מקיים בי "ותגזור אומר ויקם לך" דבשתא לא היה מקבל הקדוש ברוך הוא תפלתו של זה שיללית כל מה שיזרע, אם לא שיעשה לו נס. ולא קאמר לעיל הוה מקויים בי ותגזר אומר, אלא לפי שמתפלל על מין אחד של חטין.

וקיימא

עין משפט נר מצוה

לו א מיי' פ"ח מהל' שכירות הלכה ה סמג עשין פט טוש"ע ח"מ סי' שכב סעיף ב:

לז ב ג מיי' שם טוש"ע שם סעיף א:

לח ד מיי' פי"א מהל' יובל הלכה י:

לט ה מיי' פ"ד מהל' ערכין הלכה ו:

מ ו מיי' פ"ח מהלכות שכירות הל' ה סמג עשין פט טוש"ע ח"מ סי' שכב סעיף ב:

הגהות הב"ח

(א) גמ' אבל היכא דאיכא תבואה סלקא: (ב) רש"י ד"ה הא איכא וכו' דידיה גרס הס"ד ואח"כ מ"ה סלקא ליה: (ג) תום' ד"ה אלא וכו' דאי אמרת בשלמא דמכת מדינה: (ד) בא"ד כי אישתדוף רובא: (ה) ד"ה מתיב וכו' רוח גבורה כצ"ל ואות ו' נמחק:

מסורת הש"ס

תורה אור: איוב כב (וְתִגְזַר אוֹמֶר); ירמיהו מב (כִּי נִשְׁאַרְנוּ); ויקרא כה (בְּמִסְפַּר שְׁנֵי תְבוּאוֹת); תהלים לז (לֹא יֵבֹשׁוּ); ש"א יז (גַּם אֶת הָאֲרִי)

ס"א אינו רש"ל (לְצַד "אִישְׁתַּדּוּף, אָמְרִינַן")

ערכין כט: [ע"ש]

[לעיל לט. לקמן קט.]

[ערכין כה.]

לעיל מא. [ע"ש] לג.

תענית כה.

מא א מיי' פ"ח מהל' שכירות הלכה ה סמג עשין פט טור ש"ע ח"מ סי' שכב סעיף ב וע"ש בה"ת:

מב ב מיי' פכ"א מהל' איסורי ביאה הלכה לא סמג לאוין קכו טוש"ע אה"ע סי' ט סעיף א:

מג ג מיי' פ"ח מהל' שכירות הל' ה סמג עשין פט טוש"ע ח"מ סי' שכב סעיף ב:

מד ד ה ו ז מיי' שם הלכה ז סמג שם טור וש"ע ח"מ סי' שכב סעיף א ב:

מה ח ט מיי' שם הל' ט סמג שם טור ש"ע ח"מ סי' שכג:

וקיימא כימה להדי רישא. פי' בקונט' דכימה זנב טלה, כדאמר בברכות (דף נח:). ולא דק, אלא אמרינן התם דעש זנב טלה, אלא שכימה סמוכה לה, ואומר הב לי בניי. ומה שפי' בקונטרס דביום ראשון של אדר בסוף שעה עשירית קיימא כימה באמצע הרקיע – קשה, דפועלים אלא אתו מדברא עד צאת הכוכבים, כדפי' בריש "הפועלים" (לעיל דף פג:). ותו: דבסוף י' שעות הן עוד היום גדול ואין נראין הכוכבים, ומשמע שבא ליתן סימן לאריסין להכיר שעה שיבאו מן השדה, וזה דוחק לומר, דה"ק: כשיחשיך לילה – אז רואין למפרע שבשעת הליכתן היתה כימה להדי רישייהו. ונראה לפרש דאתו אריסי מדברא בתחילת הלילה, וקיימא כימה להדי רישייהו – היינו בתחילת שבט, ואז כלה זמן הזרע. והא דאמר בפ' "כל הקרבנות" (מנחות דף פה. ושם ד"ה וזורע) שהיו זורעים קודם הפסח ע' יום, וזה חמשה יומי בתוך שבט – התם שקרקע חשובה היא שזורעין בה לצורך העומר, נמשך שם ימי הזרע יותר. א"נ, דבתחילת שבט של חמה הוא דקיימא כימה להדי רישייהו, ואין תחילת של שבט של חמה מתחיל ברוב שנים יותר מע' יום לפני הפסח*. **שדא** ביה **אספסתא** ועבדא. לא הוה צריך למימר דשדא ביה אספסתא, דבלאו הכי מלי למימר אילו הוה זרע אספסתא הוה עבדא, אלא מעשה הוה הכי.

האי

[עי' תוס' מנחות פה. ד"ה וזורע ביאורו יותר]

[נ"ל בה יעב"ץ]

חזינא! קשיא. [א] תני חדא: פעם ראשונה ושניה – זורעה, ושלישית אינו זורעה. ותניא אידך: שלישית – זורעה, רביעית – אינו זורעה. לא קשיא; הא – כרבי, הא כרשב"ג. הא כרבי, דאמר: *בתרי זימני הוי חזקה. הא כרשב"ג, דאמר: בתלת זימני הוי חזקה. אמר ריש לקיש: לא שנו אלא שזרעה וצמחה ואכלה חגב, אבל זרעה ולא צמחה – מצי אמר ליה בעל הקרקע: כל ימי זרע (א) זרעא לה ואזיל. ועד אימת? אמר רב פפא: עד דאתו אריסי מדברא וקיימא כימה ארישייהו. מיתיבי: רשב"ג משום ר"מ אומר, וכן היה רבי שמעון בן מנסיא אומר כדבריו: חצי תשרי, מרחשון וחצי כסליו – זרע; חצי כסליו, טבת וחצי שבט – חורף; חצי שבט, אדר וחצי ניסן – קור; חצי ניסן, אייר וחצי סיון – קציר; חצי סיון, תמוז וחצי אב – קיץ; חצי אב, אלול וחצי תשרי – חום. רבי יהודה מונה מתשרי, ר"ש מונה ממרחשון. מאן מיקל בכולהו? ר' שמעון, וכולי האי לא קאמר! לא קשיא; הא – דקבלה מיניה בחרפי, הא – דקבלה מיניה באפלי. § "רבי יהודה אומר אם קבלה ממנו במעות". § ההוא גברא דקביל ארעא למיזרעה *בהו *תומי אגודא דנהר מלכא סבא בזוזי. איסתכר נהר מלכא סבא. אתא לקמיה דרבא, אמר ליה: נהר מלכא סבא לא עביד דמיסכר, מכת מדינה היא, זיל נכי ליה. אמרו ליה רבנן לרבא, הא אנן תנן: ר' יהודה אומר: אם קבלה הימנו במעות בין כך ובין כך אינו מנכה לו מן חכורו! אמר להו: לית דחש לה לדר' יהודה. §

מתני' המקבל שדה מחבירו בעשרה כור חטים לשנה ולקתה – נותן לו מתוכה. היו חטיה יפות, לא יאמר לו הריני לוקח מן השוק, אלא נותן לו מתוכה. §

גמ' ההוא גברא דקביל ארעא לאספסתא בכורי דשערי. עבדא אספסתא, וחרשה וזרעה שערי, ולקו הני שערי. שלחה *רב חביבא מסורא דפרת לקמיה דרבינא: כי האי גוונא מאי? כי לקתה נותן לו מתוכה דמי, או לא? אמר ליה: מי דמי? התם – לא עבדא ארעא שליחותא דמרה, הכא – עבדא ארעא שליחותא דמרה. ההוא גברא דקביל פרדס מחבריה בעשר דני חמרא. תקיף ההוא חמרא. סבר רב כהנא למימר: היינו מתני' לקתה נותן לו מתוכה. אמר ליה רב אשי: מי דמי? התם – לא עבדא ארעא שליחותא, הכא – עבדא ארעא שליחותא. ומודה רב אשי בעינבי דכדום, ובשדה שלקתה בעומריה. §

מתני' המקבל שדה מחבירו לזרעה שעורים – לא יזרענה חטים. חטים – יזרענה שעורים. רשב"ג אוסר. [ב] תבואה – לא יזרענה קטנית, קטנית – יזרענה תבואה. ורשב"ג אוסר. §

גמ' א"ר חסדא: מ"ט דרשב"ג? דכתיב: "שארית ישראל (צפניה ג) לא יעשו עולה ולא ידברו כזב ולא ימצא בפיהם לשון תרמית". מיתיבי: *מגבת פורים – לפורים, ואין מדקדקין בדבר. ואין העני רשאי ליקח מהן רצועה לסנדלו, אא"כ התנה במעמד אנשי העיר, דברי רבי יעקב שאמר משום ר"מ. רשב"ג

מיקל

פעם ראשונה ושניה. זרעה ואכלה חגב או נשדפה – חוזר וזורעה שנית, ואם אינו זורעה – אינו מנכה לו, אפילו היא מכת מדינה. **פלוגתא דרבי ורשב"ג.** גבי נשואה לראשון ומת, לשני ומת, במסכת יבמות. **מצי אמר ליה בעל הקרקע כל יומי זרע זרע ואזיל.** כלומר: כל זמן הזריעה חזור וזרעה, שמא לא הגיע זמן. **ועד אימת.** הוי משך זמן הזריעה. עד זמן דכי **אתא אריסא מדברא.** ונכנס לבית, בזמן שהן רגילין ליכנס. דהיינו: לאחר תשע שעות ביום, קרוב לסוף העשירית, קיימא כימה שהוא זנב טלה להדי רישייהו בראש כל אדם. דהיינו באמצע הרקיע, שנראה לכל אדם כאילו הוא על ראשו, והן הן ימי אדר. לפי שבגלגל קבועין בו שנים עשר מזלות. וזהו סידרן: טש"ת סא"ב מע"ק גד"ד. ולעולם ששה עולין וששה שוקעין. בניסן לעולם בתחילת עלות השחר טלה מתחיל לעלות ומאזנים שוקע, וב' שעות המזל שוהה לעלות. לאחר שתי שעות העולה גמר עלייתו והשוקע גמר שיקועו. נמצא, הששה עולים בשתים עשרה שעות ביום. וששה בלילה, כל ימי ניסן ראש טלה מתחיל לעלות, ובאייר שור ובסיון תאומים, וכן הסדר. נמצא, באדר מזל דגים מתחיל לעלות. בבוקר סוף ב' שעות טלה מתחיל לעלות, ולסוף ארבע גמר עלייתו. ושור עולה לסוף שש, גמר שור עלייתו ומתחיל תאומים, לסוף שמונה גמר תאומים ומתחיל סרטן, ונמצא ראש טלה באמצע, שהרי עברו שש שעות משהתחיל. ובשש שעות ראשו מגיע לאמצע, שהרי מתחלת עליית המזל עד תחלת שיקועו שנים עשר שעות, נמצא משעה שמתחיל לעלות עד ו' שעות מגיע לאמצע הרקיע, ולסוף שמונה שעות משעלה הוי זנבו באמצע הרקיע. נמצא, באדר זנב טלה בסוף שעה עשירית באמצע הרקיע הוא, והכי אמרינן במסכת ברכות בפרק "הרואה" (דף נח:) שכימה בזנב טלה הוא. **חצי תשרי וכו'.** שש תקופות שהובטחו לנח ובניו קמפרש. **קציר.** כנגד זרע, זה בתחלת גשמים, זה בתחלת החמה. וקיץ כנגד חורף, וחורף הוא חוזקו וחורפו של סתיו וימי ליפה, לשון (איוב כט) "כאשר הייתי בימי חרפי" – חוזקי ועיקרי. קיץ הוא חוזקו של יבש, ועל שמייבשין באותו פרק תמרים ותאנים לקציעות, והן נקראין קיץ, כדכתיב (שמואל ב טז): "הלחם והקיץ לאכול הנערים וגו'". קור הוא סופו של סתיו, וכן חום סופו של שמש. וכן כל אחד שני חדשים, י"ב חדשים לששה עתים. מתחיל למנות שני חדשים בכל עת. מתחילת תשרי. **מאן קמיקל.** במשך ימי הזרע למי שבא לאחר זריעותיו. **ר"ש.** שמונה מן מרחשון, ואומר: מרחשון וכסליו זרע. **בחרפי.** חטין ושיפון הנזרעין בתחילת החורף. **באפלי.** שעורין וקטנית הנזרעין באדר. **איסתכר.** לשון (בראשית ח) "ויסכרו מעינות תהום" – נסתמה הליכתו, שעכבוהו העליונים. העליונים הסיבוהו דרך אחרת. ואין ירק מגליח אלא בקרקע נרגלת בארץ לחה. **מכת מדינה.** לא עליו לבדו עברה, ולאסוקי אדעתיה נמי לא הוה ליה, דלא הוי עביד למיסתכר. **מתני'** ולקתה. שהיו חטין שדופות וגם כחושות. וזו בחכירות הוערכה לשנותה ולא בקבלנות. דאי בקבלנות – פשיטא דכל אחד זוכה ומתחייב בחלקו. **גמ'** עבדא **אספסתא.** היא נקצרת לשלשים יום, כדאמר בריש "ח"ה" (ב"ב כח:) וחוזר וזורעה שעורים. **עבדא ארעא שליחותא.** [ג] בעליה לא חכרה אלא לאספסתא, ואילו זרע לה אספסתא והוה אזיל היה מגליח, והוא פסק עמו ליקח שעורין מן השוק. **פרדיסא.** כרם. **תקיף.** החמיץ. **עבדא ארעא שליחותא.** הענבים לא לקו אלא משנעשה יין בחביותיו בביתו לקה, ואמר בבבא בתרא (דף צו:): חמרא אכתפא דגברא שוור, זה קונהו מזה טוב, ומזלו גורם להחמיץ. **ענבי דכדום.** ענבים שהתליעו. **בעומריה.** בעודן שטוחות ליבש בימות הקיץ. דכל [זמן] זה עודן צריכין לקרקע. וכך הענבים שהתליעו בין בציר לדריכה, וכגון דלא איחרו יותר מן המנהג. **מתני'** המקבל שדה לזרעה שעורין. ובחכירות כך וכך חטין או שעורין או מעות. **לא** יזרענה חטין. שהחטין מכחישות את הקרקע יותר מן השעורין והא לא מיתוקמא אלא בחכרנות. דאי בקבלנות – הא אמרינן* תיכחוש ארעא ולא ליכחוש מרא, והרי הוא נהנה בשינוי של זה [ד]. **ורבן שמעון בן גמליאל אוסר.** וטעמא מפרש בגמרא. **תבואה לא** יזרענה קטנית. שהקטנית מכחשת הקרקע יותר מן התבואה. **גמ'**

מיקל

תורה אור

הגהות הב"ח

(א) גמ' זרעא לה ואזיל. נ"ב [ודוקא שאחר בני באגי זרעו וצמחו דאמרי' דזרע זרע שאינו ראוי לזריעה אבל אם כל בני באגי] נמי לא צמחו ליכא למימר שכל בני באגי זרעו זרע שאינו ראוי לזריעה:

הגהות הגר"א

[א] גמ' תני כו'. נ"ב רי"ף ורמב"ם השמיטוהו ולא כתבו רק להא דשמואל וכו' (ועמ"ש בהגהות על הרא"ש ובח"מ סי' שכ"ב): [ב] במשנה תבואה לא כו'. נ"ב והרי"ף והרמב"ם גרסי בהיפך: [ג] רש"י ד"ה עבדא ארעא שליחותא בעליה כו'. נ"ב ואפי' זרעה מתחלה שעורים הדין [כן] לפ"ש רבינו עבדא ארעא כו' ולא דוקא (ועמ"ש רבינו בח"מ סי' שכ"ב): [ד] שם ד"ה לא יזרענה כו' והרי הוא נהנה בשינוי של זה. נ"ב והרמב"ן כתב להיפך דבקבלנות אסור בכל ענין:

יבמות [סד:] סה: [עירובין לז. כתובות מג: סנהדרין פא: נדה י. סד.]

גירסת הערוך בערך אבא האחרון אבא אגודא פי' ר"ח אילן של ערבה

לעיל סח: הגירס' רב חנינא עי' מ"ק כ. כז.

לעיל עח: [ע"ש]

[לעיל קד:]

תורה אור

מֵיקַל. אֲמַר אַבַּיֵי: טַעְמָא דְּרַבָּן שִׁמְעוֹן כִּדְמָר, דַּאֲמַר מָר: הַאי מַאן דְּנִיחָא לֵיהּ דְּתִתְבּוּר אַרְעֵיהּ — לִיזְרְעָהּ שַׁתָּא חִטֵּי וְשַׁתָּא שְׂעָרֵי, שַׁתָּא שְׁתִי וְשַׁתָּא עֵרֶב. וְלָא אֲמָרַן אֶלָּא דְּלָא כָּרֵיב וְתָנֵי, אֲבָל כָּרֵיב וְתָנֵי — לֵית לָן בָּהּ. § "תְּבוּאָה לֹא יִזְרָעֶנָּה קִטְנִית [וכו']" § מַתְנֵי לֵיהּ רַב יְהוּדָה לְרָבִין: [א] אתְּבוּאָה יִזְרָעֶנָּה קִטְנִית. א"ל: וְהָא אֲנַן תְּנַן: תְּבוּאָה לֹא יִזְרָעֶנָּה קִטְנִית! א"ל: לָא קַשְׁיָא; *בהָא — לָן, וְהָא — לְהוּ. א"ל רַב יְהוּדָה לְרָבִין בַּר ר"נ: רָבִין אָחִי, גהָנֵי תַּחְלֵי דְּבֵי כִיתָּנָא אֵין בָּהֶן מִשּׁוּם גֵּזֶל; דעוֹמְדוֹת עַל גְּבוּלִין — יֵשׁ בָּהֶן מִשּׁוּם גֵּזֶל. הוְאִם הוּקְשׁוּ לְזֶרַע, אֲפִילּוּ דְּבֵי כִיתָּנָא נַמִי — יֵשׁ בָּהֶם מִשּׁוּם גֵּזֶל. מ"ט? מַאי דְּאַפְסִיד אַפְסִיד. א"ל רַב יְהוּדָה לְרָבִין בַּר ר"נ: רָבִין אָחִי, הָנֵי דִּילִי — דִּילָךְ, וְדִילָךְ — דִּילִי. (א) נְהוּג בְּנֵי מִצְרָא, אִילָן הַנּוֹטֶה לְכָאן — לְכָאן, וְהַנּוֹטֶה לְכָאן — לְכָאן. דְּאִיתְּמַר, אִילָן הָעוֹמֵד עַל הַמֵּיצַר. אָמַר רַב: הַנּוֹטֶה לְכָאן — לְכָאן, וְהַנּוֹטֶה לְכָאן — לְכָאן. וּשְׁמוּאֵל אָמַר: וחוֹלְקִין. מֵיתִיבִי: אִילָן הָעוֹמֵד עַל הַמֵּיצַר — יַחֲלוֹקוּ. תְּיוּבְתָּא דְּרַב! *תַּרְגְּמָא שְׁמוּאֵל אַלִּיבָּא דְּרַב: בִּמְמַלֵּא כָּל הַמֵּיצַר כּוּלּוֹ. אִי הָכִי, מַאי לְמֵימְרָא? לָא צְרִיכָא דְּתָלֵי טוּנֵיהּ לְחַד גִּיסָא. וְאַכַּתִּי, מַאי לְמֵימְרָא? מַהוּ דְּתֵימָא, *דְּא"ל: פְּלוֹג הָכִי, קמ"ל דְּאָמַר לֵיהּ: מַאי חָזֵית דְּפָלְגַתְּ הָכִי — פְּלוֹג הָכִי. א"ל רַב יְהוּדָה לְרָבִין בַּר ר"נ: רָבִין אָחִי, לָא תִּזְבֵּין אַרְעָא דִּסְמִיכָא לְמָתָא, *דְּא"ר *אַבָּהוּ אָמַר רַב הוּנָא אָמַר רַב: אָסוּר לוֹ לְאָדָם שֶׁיַּעֲמוֹד עַל שְׂדֵה חֲבֵירוֹ בְּשָׁעָה שֶׁעוֹמֶדֶת בְּקָמוֹתֶיהָ. אִינִי? וְהָא אַשְׁכַּחִינְהוּ רַבִּי אַבָּא לְתַלְמִידֵיהּ דְּרַב, אֲמַר לְהוּ: מַאי אֲמַר רַב בְּהָנֵי קְרָאֵי °"בָּרוּךְ אַתָּה בָּעִיר וּבָרוּךְ אַתָּה בַּשָּׂדֶה, בָּרוּךְ אַתָּה בְּבוֹאֶךָ וּבָרוּךְ אַתָּה בְּצֵאתֶךָ"? וַאֲמַרוּ לֵיהּ, הָכִי אָמַר רַב: "בָּרוּךְ אַתָּה בָּעִיר" — שֶׁיְּהֵא בֵּיתְךָ סָמוּךְ לְבהכ"נ. "בָּרוּךְ אַתָּה בַּשָּׂדֶה" — שֶׁיִּהְיוּ נְכָסֶיךָ קְרוֹבִים לָעִיר. "בָּרוּךְ אַתָּה בְּבוֹאֶךָ" — *שֶׁלֹּא תִמְצָא אִשְׁתְּךָ סְפֵק נִדָּה בִּשְׁעַת בִּיאָתְךָ מִן הַדֶּרֶךְ. "בָּרוּךְ אַתָּה בְּצֵאתֶךָ" — *שֶׁיִּהְיוּ צֶאֱצָאֵי מֵעֶיךָ כְּמוֹתְךָ. וַאֲמַר לְהוּ: ר' יוֹחָנָן לָא אֲמַר הָכִי, אֶלָּא: "בָּרוּךְ אַתָּה בָּעִיר" — שֶׁיְּהֵא בֵּית הַכִּסֵּא סָמוּךְ לְשׁוּלְחָנְךָ, אֲבָל בהכ"נ לֹא. (ב) וְרַבִּי יוֹחָנָן לְטַעְמֵיהּ דְּאָמַר: *שְׂכַר פְּסִיעוֹת יֵשׁ. "בָּרוּךְ אַתָּה בַּשָּׂדֶה" — שֶׁיִּהְיוּ נְכָסֶיךָ מְשׁוּלָּשִׁין: שְׁלִישׁ בִּתְבוּאָה, שְׁלִישׁ בְּזֵיתִים וּשְׁלִישׁ בִּגְפָנִים. "בָּרוּךְ אַתָּה בְּבוֹאֶךָ וּבָרוּךְ אַתָּה בְּצֵאתֶךָ" — שֶׁתְּהֵא יְצִיאָתְךָ מִן הָעוֹלָם כְּבִיאָתְךָ לָעוֹלָם; מַה בִּיאָתְךָ לָעוֹלָם בְּלֹא חֵטְא — אַף יְצִיאָתְךָ מִן הָעוֹלָם בְּלֹא חֵטְא.

לא

מֵיקַל. אע"ג דְּמְשַׁנֵּי — לָא סָבַר דְּמַקְפִּיד אִינִישׁ מִידֵּי דְּלָא חָסֵר בָּהּ. דְּאָמַר מָר. רַבָּה בַּר נַחְמָנִי רַבֵּיהּ דְּאַבַּיֵי, דְּרַבָּה גִּידְּלוֹ בְּבֵיתוֹ. דְּתִתְבּוּר. שֶׁתֵּעָשֶׂה בּוּרָה, שֶׁלֹּא יִלְמְחוּ זֵרְעוֹנֶיהָ. לִיזְרַע [שַׁתָּא] חִטִּין וכו'. ה"ג פָּסַק עִמּוֹ חִטִּין, שֶׁמָּא הוּא זְרָעָהּ חִטִּין בַּשָּׁנָה שֶׁעָבְרָה, וְאִם יִזְרָעֶנָּה זֶה שְׂעוֹרִין נִמְצָא זֶה מְקַלְקְלָהּ. דְּלָא כָּרֵיב וְתָנֵי. חֲרָשָׁהּ לְאַחַר קְצִירָה וְשִׁינָּה בִּשְׁעַת הַזֶּרַע. מַתְנֵי לָהּ רַב יְהוּדָה לְרָבִין. בְּמַתְנִי': תְּבוּאָה — יִזְרָעֶנָּה קִטְנִית. הָא לָן וְהָא לְהוּ. מַתְנִי' — בְּא"י קָאֵי, שֶׁהִיא מְקוֹם הָרִים, וְאִיכָּא לְמֵיחַשׁ לְכַחֲשָׁא דְּאַרְעָא. אֲנַן הָשְׁתָּא — בְּבָבֶל קָיְימִינַן, שֶׁהִיא מְצוּלָה וּטְבוּעָה בְּבִלְעֵי הַמַּיִם, וְלֵיכָּא לְמֵיחַשׁ לְכַחֲשָׁא דְּאַרְעָא. הִלְכָּךְ, מְשַׁנֶּה בְּכָל מָקוֹם שֶׁיִּרְצֶה מִקִּטְנִית לִתְבוּאָה, וּמִתְּבוּאָה לְקִטְנִית. וְר"ש אוֹסֵר כִּדְאֲמַרַן. תַּחְלֵי דְּבֵי כִיתָּנָא. שַׁחֲלַיִם שֶׁקּוֹרִין כרישי"ן הַגְּדֵלִים בֵּין הַפִּשְׁתָּן. אֵין בָּהֶן מִשּׁוּם גָּזֵל. לְכָל הַבָּא וְעוֹקְרָן, לְפִי שֶׁהוּא מַשְׁבִּיחַ אֶת הַבְּעָלִים, שֶׁמַּפְסִידִים פִּשְׁתָּן יוֹתֵר עַל דָּמֶיהָ. וְאִם עוֹמֶדֶת עַל גְּבוּל. הָעֲרוּגָה, שֶׁאֵין עוֹמְדִין בְּתוֹכָהּ. יֵשׁ בָּהֶם מִשּׁוּם גָּזֵל. דְּלָא מַפְסְדִי. הוּקְשׁוּ לְזֶרַע. אוֹתָן שַׁחֲלַיִם שֶׁעָמְדוּ בַּפִּשְׁתָּן יָמִים רַבִּים עַד שֶׁנִּגְמַר גִּידּוּלֵיהֶן — שׁוּב אֵין עֲקִירָתָן מוֹעֶלֶת לַפִּשְׁתָּן, וְיֵשׁ בָּהֶן מִשּׁוּם גָּזֵל. דִּילִי דִּילָךְ דִּילָךְ דִּילִי. יֵשׁ בְּאִילָנוֹתַי שֶׁהַפֵּירוֹת שֶׁלְּךָ, וּבְאִילָנוֹתֶיךָ שֶׁהַפֵּירוֹת שֶׁלִּי, שֶׁשְּׂדוֹתֵינוּ זוֹ לָזוֹ סְמוּכוֹת, וְהַמְּצָרִים גְּבוֹהִים, וְאִילָנוֹת נְטוּעִין בָּהֶם. יֵשׁ מֵהֶן נְטוּעִין בְּשֶׁלִּי שֶׁשָּׁרְשֵׁיהֶן כָּפְפוּ וְנָטוּ כּוּלָּן לְתוֹךְ שָׂדְךָ, וְיוֹנְקִין מִשֶּׁלְּךָ, וְיֵשׁ בְּשֶׁלְּךָ שֶׁנּוֹטִין לְתוֹךְ שֶׁלִּי וְיוֹנְקִים מֵאַרְצִי. וְנָהֲגוּ בְּנֵי מִצְרָא וכו' נוֹטֶה לְכָאן וּלְכָאן. נוֹטִין שָׁרָשִׁין לְשָׂדֶה זוֹ — הַפֵּירוֹת שֶׁלּוֹ. בִּמְמַלֵּא כָּל הַמֵּצַר. שֶׁנּוֹטִין שָׁרָשִׁין לְכָאן וּלְכָאן. דְּתָלֵי טוּנֵיהּ. מַשָּׂא פֵּירוֹתָיו וַעֲנָפָיו נוֹטֶה לְצַד אֶחָד. פְּלוֹג הָכִי. טוֹל אַתָּה חֶלְיוֹ שֶׁאֶצְלְךָ וַאֲנִי חֶלְיוֹ שֶׁאֶצְלִי. פְּלוֹג הָכִי. לְעֵבֶר רוֹחַב הַשָּׂדֶה חֲלוֹק הָאִילָן, אִם עוֹמֶדֶת הַשָּׂדֶה מִזְרָח וּמַעֲרָב — יַחֲלוֹק אוֹתוֹ הָאִילָן לָפוֹן וְדָרוֹם. לָא תִּזְבּוּן. לֹא תִּקְנֶה שָׂדֶה הַסְּמוּכָה לָעִיר, שֶׁעֵין בְּנֵי אָדָם שׁוֹלֶטֶת בָּהּ תָּמִיד. אָסוּר לְאָדָם כו'. שֶׁלֹּא יַפְסִידֶנָּה בְּעַיִן הָרַע. קְרוֹבִין לָעִיר. שֶׁלֹּא יְהֵא טוֹרֵחַ לְהַכְנִיס פֵּירוֹת. סָפֵק נִדָּה. וְכ"ש וַדַּאי. אָמַר לְהוּ. ר' אַבָּא: רַבִּי יוֹחָנָן לָא אָמַר הָכִי. סָמוּךְ לְשׁוּלְחָנְךָ. כְּלוֹמַר: סָמוּךְ לְבֵיתְךָ, שֶׁלֹּא תִּצְטָרֵךְ לְהַרְחִיק בַּשָּׂדוֹת. וְהַאי דְּנָקַט "שֻׁלְחָנְךָ" — שֶׁתּוּכַל לִבְדּוֹק עַצְמְךָ לִפְנֵי אֲכִילָה וּלְאַחַר אֲכִילָה, כִּדְאָמַר בְּשַׁבָּת (דף מא.) כִּדְתַנְיָא: הַנִּפְנֶה לִנְקָבָיו וְאוֹכֵל — דּוֹמֶה לְתַנּוּר שֶׁהֶסִּיקוּהוּ עַל גַּבֵּי אֶפְרוֹ. וְאַחַר אֲכִילָה — שֶׁהַמַּאֲכָל דּוֹחֵק וּמוֹצִיא אֶת הַמְּעוּכָּל. וְאִם יְהֵא צָרִיךְ לְהַרְחִיק — פְּעָמִים שֶׁהָעַמּוּד חוֹזֵר וּבָא לִידֵי הִדְרוֹקָן. אֲבָל בֵּית הַכְּנֶסֶת סָמוּךְ לְבֵיתוֹ — לְר' יוֹחָנָן לָאו מַעַלְּיוּתָא הִיא. ר' יוֹחָנָן לְטַעְמֵיהּ. דְּאָמַר בְּמַסֶּכֶת סוֹטָה (דף כב.): "שְׂכַר פְּסִיעוֹת יֵשׁ", דְּאָמַר: לָמַדְנוּ יִרְאַת חֵטְא מִבְּתוּלָה, וְקִיבּוּל שָׂכָר מֵאַלְמָנָה, שֶׁאָמְרָה לוֹ: וְלֹא שְׂכַר פְּסִיעוֹת יֵשׁ; אִם יֵשׁ בֵּית הַכְּנֶסֶת בִּשְׁכוּנָתִי, וַאֲנִי בָּאָה לְבֵית מִדְרָשְׁךָ לְהִתְפַּלֵּל?! מְשׁוּלָּשִׁין. שֶׁיֵּשׁ שָׁנָה שֶׁלּוֹקָה בִּגְפָנִים וּבְזֵיתִים וְאֵין לוֹקָה בַּתְּבוּאָה, וְיֵשׁ שָׁנָה שֶׁלּוֹקָה בָּזוֹ וְלֹא בָזוֹ, וּתְהִי לוֹ פְּלֵיטָה.

לא

האי מאן דבעי דתתבור [ארעיה]. פי' בקונט': שתקלקל שדה. וקשה: דאדרבה, כך הוא רגילות של עובדי אדמה, שזורעים שנה חטין ושנה שעורין, וכשזורעין אותה ב' שנים חטין רצופין או שעורין — מתקלקלת. וכן נמי משמע בשילהי "חזקת הבתים" (ב"ב דף מ:) גבי אחד אמר אכלה חטין ואחד אמר אכלה שעורין, כדפי' רבינו שמואל התם! לכך י"ל: האי מאן דבעי שתהא שדהו חשובה כאילו הניחה שנה אחת בורה, כי כן דרך לזורעה שנה ולהובירה שנה, כדי שתחזור לכחה ממה שהוכחשה — ליזרע שתא חטין ושתא שעורים. ולכך אסור רשב"ג, כשאמר לזרעה חטין, שלא יזרע שעורים — כי שמא אשתקד זרעה שעורים. ואי כריב ותני לית לן בה — שם לא יאסור רשב"ג.

הני תחלה דבי כיתנא אין בהם משום גזל. אע"ג שהתנה יהושע שיהא מלקטין עשבים בכל מקום, כדאמר בסוף פ' "מרובה" (ב"ק דף פא.) — התם מיירי בעשבים שאין ראוים לאדם אלא לבהמה. וכן משמע מדלא נקט ירקות, אבל תחלי שהן מאכל אדם — אסור, אא"כ הוא שדה פשתן.

אילן העומד על המיצר. פי' הקונטרס אינו מיושב, שפירש: אילן שנטוע בקרקע סמוך למיצר והשרשים נוטים בשל חבירו. אלא נראה לפרש: שהאילן עומד ממש על המיצר שהוא של שניהם, ואין השרשים מתפשטין לקרקעו של זה יותר משל זה, אך הענפים נוטין יותר לשל אחד מהם. רב אמר: הנוטה לכאן לכאן כיון שהשרשים שוים בשל זה כמו בשל זה — אזלינן בתר הענפים, מה שיש מן הענפים כנגד המיצר — חולקים, והשאר — לרשות שנוטין — הוי הכל שלו. ושמואל אמר: חולקין, אזלינן בתר השרשים שהם שוים, כמו כן יהיו שוים בענפים. אבל אי נטוע כולו ברשות אחד והענפים נוטים ברשות חבירו, בזה אמר ר' יוחנן בס"פ "לא יחפור" (ב"ב דף כז: ושם ד"ה ואחד): מביא וקורא. שעל מנת כן הנחיל יהושע את הארץ — שכל הענפים יהא לבעל השרשים. ובהא מודו נמי רב ושמואל דשמעתין, ופריך: אילן העומד על המיצר חולקים. ומשני: בממלא כל המיצר, כמו שהשרים הן כולן על המיצר — כך הם הענפים. ודתלי טעוניה לחד גיסא, דקאמר: לא שהענפים עוברים המיצר, אלא שיש פירות לצד אחד יותר מלצד חבירו, מהו דתימא: ניפלוג לאורכו של מיצר קמ"ל: דחולקין לרוחבו של מיצר. ושילהי "הבית והעלייה" (לקמן דף קיח:) דתנן: שתי גינות זו למעלה מזו וירק בינתים. השרשים לכ"ע הם של עליון, לפי שהם יונקים מגינתו. אבל הנוף, שהוא באויר התחתון — לר' יהודה הוא של תחתון, ולר"מ הוי של עליון, דאמר: שדי נופו בתר עיקרו. והתם פסיק כר"ש, דאמר: כל שיכול עליון לפשוט ידו וליטול — הרי אלו שלו, והיינו כר"מ. והשאר — מסתמא — הפקיר לתחתון. ונראה דאפי' לרב דלית ליה הכא שדי נופו בתר עיקרו סובר שפיר כר"מ, דכיון דהתם כל השרשים כולן בשל עליון — דין הוא למימר שדי נופו בתר עיקרו, כדאמר נמי רבי יוחנן בשילהי "לא יחפור". ושמואל דאמר הכא: חולקין — יכול לסבור התם כרבי יהודה, דלא אמר שדי נופו בתר עיקרו — משום דרגילות למלאות גינתו עפר ולהשוותו אל גינת חבירו. ועוד, דאין כלל מן הנוף ברשות העליון, אלא מיד שנראה חוץ לארץ — הוא ברשות התחתון, אבל בשמעתין — רוב הנוף על המיצר, רק מעט מן הענפים נוטים לכאן ולכאן חוץ לרוחב המיצר.

מו א ב מיי' פ"ח מהל' שכירות הלכה ט סמג עשין פט טוש"ע ח"מ סי' שכל:

מז ג ד ה מיי' פ"ו מהל' גזילה ואבידה הלכה ד סמג עשין עג טוש"ע ח"מ סי' רעג סעיף יז:

מח ו מיי' פ"ד מהל' שכנים הלכה ט סמג עשין פב טוש"ע ח"מ סי' קסז סעיף ב וסי' קנה סעיף כט:

הגהות הב"ח

(א) גמ' ודילך דילי ונהוג: (ב) שם ר' יוחנן לטעמיה כצ"ל ואות ו' נמחק:

הגהות הגר"א

[א] גמ' תבואה יזרענה כו'. כ"ב ורי"ף גרים תבואה לא יזרעה כו' (תנן תבואה יזרענה קטנית) א"ל ל"ק הא כו' מתני' בא"י ברייתא בבבל:

[ברכות ה: וש"נ]

[שבת נב: וש"נ]

[לעיל ז. ז:]

ב"ב ב: ע"ש

דברים כח

[ברכות נה: סנהדרין קג.]

[תענית ו.]

[סוטה כב.]

ס"א רבי אבא וכן איתא בב"ב כ:

תורה אור

לֹא קַשְׁיָא; הָא — דִּמְהַדַּר לֵיהּ שׁוּרָא וְרִתְקָא; הָא — דְּלָא מְהַדַּר לֵיהּ שׁוּרָא וְרִתְקָא. °"וְהֵסִיר ה' מִמְּךָ כָּל חוֹלִי" — אָמַר רַב: זוֹ עַיִן. רַב לְטַעְמֵיהּ, דְּרַב סָלֵיק לְבֵי קִבְרֵי, עֲבַד מַאי דַּעֲבַד. אֲמַר: תִּשְׁעִין וְתִשְׁעָה בְּעַיִן רָעָה, וְאֶחָד בְּדֶרֶךְ אֶרֶץ. וּשְׁמוּאֵל אָמַר: זֶה הָרוּחַ. שְׁמוּאֵל לְטַעְמֵיהּ, דְּאָמַר שְׁמוּאֵל: הַכֹּל בָּרוּחַ. וְלִשְׁמוּאֵל, הָא אִיכָּא הֲרוּגֵי מַלְכוּת! הָנָךְ נַמִי, אִי לָאו זִיקָא — עָבְדִי לְהוּ *סַמָּא וְחָיֵי. ר' חֲנִינָא אָמַר: *זוֹ צִינָּה, *דְּא"ר חֲנִינָא: הַכֹּל בִּידֵי שָׁמַיִם חוּץ מִצִּנִּים פַּחִים, שֶׁנֶּאֱמַר: °"צִנִּים פַּחִים בְּדֶרֶךְ עִקֵּשׁ שׁוֹמֵר נַפְשׁוֹ יִרְחַק מֵהֶם". ר' יוֹסֵי בַּר חֲנִינָא אָמַר: זוֹ צוֹאָה, דְּאָמַר מָר: צוֹאַת הַחוֹטֶם וְצוֹאַת הָאוֹזֶן — רוּבָּן קָשֶׁה וּמִיעוּטָן יָפֶה. ר' אֶלְעָזָר אָמַר: זוֹ מָרָה. תַּנְיָא נַמִי הָכִי: *מַחֲלָה — זוֹ מָרָה. וְלָמָּה נִקְרָא שְׁמָהּ מַחֲלָה? שֶׁהִיא מַחֲלָה כָּל גּוּפוֹ שֶׁל אָדָם. דָּבָר אַחֵר: מַחֲלָה שֶׁשְּׁמוֹנִים וּשְׁלֹשָׁה חֳלָאִים תְּלוּיִן בַּמָּרָה, וְכוּלָּן — פַּת שַׁחֲרִית בְּמֶלַח וְקִיתוֹן שֶׁל מַיִם מְבַטַּלְתָּן. ת"ר: י"ג דְּבָרִים נֶאֶמְרוּ בְּפַת שַׁחֲרִית: מַצֶּלֶת מִן הַחַמָּה, וּמִן הַצִּינָּה, וּמִן הַזִּיקִין, וּמִן הַמַּזִּיקִין, וּמַחְכִּימַת פֶּתִי, וְזוֹכֶה בַּדִּין, לִלְמוֹד תּוֹרָה וּלְלַמֵּד, וּדְבָרָיו נִשְׁמָעִין, וְתַלְמוּדוֹ מִתְקַיֵּים בְּיָדוֹ, וְאֵין בְּשָׂרוֹ מַעֲלֶה הֶבֶל, וְנִזְקָק לְאִשְׁתּוֹ, וְאֵינוֹ מִתְאַוֶּה לְאִשָּׁה אַחֶרֶת, וְהוֹרֶגֶת כִּינָּה שֶׁבִּבְנֵי מֵעַיִם. וי"א: אַף מוֹצִיא אֶת הַקִּנְאָה וּמַכְנִיס אֶת הָאַהֲבָה. *א"ל רַבָּה לְרָבָא בַּר מָרִי: מְנָא הָא מִילְּתָא דְּאָמְרִי אֱינָשֵׁי שִׁיתִּין רְהִיטֵי רְהוּט וְלָא מָטוּ לְגַבְרָא דְּמִצַּפְרָא כְּרַךְ — *וְאָמְרוּ רַבָּנַן: הַשְׁכֵּם וֶאֱכוֹל, בַּקַּיִץ מִפְּנֵי הַחַמָּה, וּבַחוֹרֶף מִפְּנֵי הַצִּינָּה? א"ל: דִּכְתִיב: °"לֹא יִרְעָבוּ וְלֹא יִצְמָאוּ וְלֹא יַכֵּם שָׁרָב וָשָׁמֶשׁ". "לֹא יַכֵּם שָׁרָב וָשָׁמֶשׁ" — כֵּיוָן דְּלָא יִרְעֲבוּ וְלָא יִצְמָאוּ. א"ל: אַתְּ אָמְרַתְּ לִי מֵהָתָם, וַאֲנָא אָמֵינָא לָךְ מֵהָכָא: °"וַעֲבַדְתֶּם אֵת ה' אֱלֹהֵיכֶם וּבֵרַךְ אֶת לַחְמְךָ וְאֶת מֵימֶיךָ". "וַעֲבַדְתֶּם אֵת ה' אֱלֹהֵיכֶם" — זוֹ קְרִיאַת שְׁמַע וּתְפִלָּה. "וּבֵרַךְ אֶת לַחְמְךָ וְאֶת מֵימֶיךָ" — זוֹ פַּת בְּמֶלַח וְקִיתוֹן שֶׁל מַיִם. מִכָּאן וְאֵילָךְ — "וַהֲסִירוֹתִי מַחֲלָה מִקִּרְבֶּךָ". א"ל רַב יְהוּדָה לְרַב אַדָּא מְשׁוֹחָאָה: [א]לָא תְּזַלְזֵל בְּמִשְׁחָתָא, דְּכָל פּוּרְתָּא וּפוּרְתָּא חֲזֵי לְכוּרְכְּמָא רִישְׁקָא. א"ל רַב יְהוּדָה לְרַב אַדָּא מְשׁוֹחָאָה: [ב]ד' אַמּוֹת דְּאַנִּיגְרָא — זַלְזֵל בְּהוּ, [ג]דְּאַנַּהֲרָא — לָא תְּמְשַׁחְנְהוּ כְּלָל. רַב יְהוּדָה לְטַעְמֵיהּ, דַּאֲמַר רַב יְהוּדָה: אַרְבַּע אַמּוֹת דְּאַנִּיגְרָא — לִבְנֵי אַנִּיגְרָא; דְּאַנַּהֲרָא — [ד]דְּכוּלֵּי עָלְמָא. [ה]מַכְרִיז רַבִּי אַמִי: מְלָא כַּתְפֵי נַגָּדֵי בִּתְרֵי עִבְרֵי נַהֲרָא — קוֹצוּ. רַב נָתָן בַּר הוֹשַׁעְיָא קָץ שִׁיתְסַר אַמְּתָא. אָתוּ עֲלֵיהּ בְּנֵי מַשְׁרוֹנְיָא, דַּפְנוּהוּ. הוּא סָבַר: כִּרְשׁוּת הָרַבִּים. וְלָא הִיא, הָתָם בָּעֵינַן כּוּלֵּי הַאי. הָכָא [ו]מִשּׁוּם אַמְתּוּחֵי אַשְׁלֵיהֶן הוּא — כִּמְלֹא כַּתְפֵי נַגָּדֵי סַגִּי. רַבָּה בַּר רַב הוּנָא הֲוָה לֵיהּ הַהוּא אַבָּא אַגּוּדָא דְּנַהֲרָא. אֲמַרוּ לֵיהּ: נִיקוֹץ מָר! אֲמַר לְהוּ: קוֹצוּ עִילָּאֵי וְתַתָּאֵי, וַהֲדַר נִיקוֹץ אֲנָא. הֵיכִי עָבֵיד הָכִי? וְהָכְתִיב: °"הִתְקוֹשְׁשׁוּ וָקוֹשּׁוּ" — *וְאָמַר רֵישׁ לָקִישׁ: קְשׁוֹט עַצְמְךָ וְאַחַר כָּךְ קְשׁוֹט אֲחֵרִים! הָתָם אַבָּא דְּבֵי פַּרְזַק רוּפִילָא הֲוָה, וַאֲמַר: אִי קָיְיצוּ — קָיְיצְנָא, וְאִי לָא קָיְיצוּ — אַמַּאי אֵיקוֹץ? דְּאִי מַמְתְּחֵי לְהוּ אַשְׁלַיְיהוּ — מִסְתַּגֵּי לְהוּ, וְאִי

(דברים ז) (משלי כב) (ישעיה מט) (שמות כג) (צפניה ב)

לֹא קַשְׁיָא. דְּרַב אַדְּרַב. שׁוּרָא וְרִיתְקָא. חוֹמָה וּרְתוּקַת גָּדֵר שֶׁל נְגָרִים, כְּמוֹ (איכה ב): חֵיל וְחוֹמָה. כָּל חֹלִי. דָּבָר שֶׁכָּל הַחֳלָאִים תְּלוּיִן בּוֹ, וְזוֹ הָעַיִן, עַיִן רָעָה. עֲבַד מַה דַּעֲבַד. יוֹדֵעַ הָיָה לִלְחוֹשׁ עַל הַקְּבָרוֹת וּלְהָבִין עַל כָּל קֶבֶר וְקֶבֶר בְּאֵיזוֹ מִיתָה מֵת: אִם מֵת בִּזְמַנּוֹ אִם בְּעַיִן רָעָה*. הַכֹּל בָּרוּחַ. כָּל הֶחֳלָאִים וְתוֹלָאוֹת מִיתָה עַל נְשִׁיבַת הָרוּחַ בָּאִין, הַכֹּל לְפִי הַשָּׁעָה וְהָאָדָם. יֵשׁ לְךָ אָדָם שֶׁרוּחַ פְּלוֹנִי קָשָׁה לוֹ וּבְשָׁעָה פְּלוֹנִי. וְהָאִיכָּא הֲרוּגֵי מַלְכוּת. הֲרוּגֵי חֶרֶב. אִי לָאו זִיקָא. שֶׁנִּכְנָס בְּמַכָּה. עָבְדִי סַמָּא וְחָיֵי. סַם הַמְחַבֵּר בְּשַׂר חֲתוּכָה, וּמִן הָעֲשָׂבִים הוּא, כִּדְאָמַר בְּ"הַמּוֹכֵר אֶת הַסְּפִינָה" (ב"ב דף עד:). צִינִּים פַּחִים. קוֹר הַנּוֹפֵחַ, וְלָאו הַיְינוּ רוּחַ דְּקָאָמַר שְׁמוּאֵל, דִּשְׁמוּאֵל זִיקָא בְּלָא לֵיכָּא נַמִי מַזֶּקֶת. זוֹ מָרָה. שֶׁהַמְּרִירָה שֶׁבָּהּ גְּדוֹלָה, וְנוֹבַעַת וּמִתְפַּשֶּׁטֶת בַּגִּידִין וּבָעֲצָמוֹת. וְכוּלָּן פַּת בְּמֶלַח מְבַטַּלְתָּן. כִּדְיָלֵיף לְקַמָּן מִקְּרָאֵי. וְקִיתוֹן שֶׁל מַיִם. לְמִי שֶׁאֵין לוֹ יַיִן. וְזִיקִין. הַיְינוּ רוּחַ דְּאָמַר שְׁמוּאֵל. מַחְכִּימַת פֶּתִי. שֶׁדַּעְתּוֹ מְיוּשֶּׁבֶת עָלָיו, לְפִי שֶׁאֵינוֹ מִצְטַעֵר בְּעִינּוּי. וְזוֹכֶה בַּדִּין. אִם יֵשׁ לוֹ דִּין עִם חֲבֵירוֹ — דַּעְתּוֹ מְיוּשֶּׁבֶת לְיַישֵּׁב דְּבָרָיו בְּבֵ"ד לְהַטְעִים. לִלְמוֹד וּלְלַמֵּד. מֵחֲמַת יִשּׁוּב הַדַּעַת. וּדְבָרָיו נִשְׁמָעִין. לַבְּרִיּוֹת, שֶׁיֵּשׁ לוֹ לֵב לְהַטְעִימָן. הֶבֶל. זֵיעָה וְזוֹהַם. נִזְקָק לְאִשְׁתּוֹ. אִם בַּעַל הִרְהוּרִים הוּא, וּמִתּוֹךְ שֶׁלִּבּוֹ טוֹב בַּבֹּקֶר שֶׁאָכַל קְצָת — תּוֹבֵעַ לְאִשְׁתּוֹ, וּבִצְאֵתוֹ לַשּׁוּק וְרוֹאֶה נָשִׁים — אֵינוֹ מִתְאַוֶּה לָהֶן. כִּינָּה שֶׁבִּבְנֵי מֵעַיִם. תּוֹלָעִים. מוֹצִיא אֶת הַקִּנְאָה וְאֶת הַתִּגָּר. שֶׁכְּשֶׁאֵין לִבּוֹ טוֹב עָלָיו הוּא נוֹחַ לִכְעוֹס. וְאָמְרוּ רַבָּנַן הַשְׁכֵּם וֶאֱכוֹל. בְּ"עַרְבֵי פְסָחִים" (דף קיב.) בִּדְבָרִים שֶׁצִּוָּה *רַבִּי לְבָנָיו. מְשׁוֹחָאָה. מוֹדֵד קַרְקָעוֹת הָיָה בְּשָׂכָר לַקּוֹנִים וְלַמּוֹכְרִים, וְלָאַחִין וְלַשּׁוּתָפִין הַבָּאִין לַחֲלוֹק. כּוּרְכְּמָא רִישְׁקָא. כַּרְכּוֹם שֶׁל גַּן שֶׁקּוֹרִין קרו"ג אודמינל"ט, וְהוּא מְשׁוּבָּח שֶׁבַּכּוּרְכְּמִין. אַרְבַּע אַמּוֹת דְּאַנִּיגְרָא. אַמַּת הַמַּיִם שֶׁהִמְשִׁיכוּהָ מִן הַנָּהָר הַגָּדוֹל אֶל הַשָּׂדוֹת עַל פְּנֵי הַבִּקְעָה כּוּלָּהּ, וּמַנִּיחִין בַּעֲלֵי כָּל שָׂדֶה וְשָׂדֶה מִלִּזְרוֹעַ אֶת אֲגַפֶּיהָ רוֹחַב אַרְבַּע אַמּוֹת — שֶׁלֹּא תִּתְקַלְקֵל שְׂפָתָהּ. וּמוֹדְדִין אוֹתָם כּוּלָּם בְּיַחַד, וּמְצַיְּינִים אוֹתָם שֶׁלֹּא יַחְרְשׁוּ מִן הַסִּימָן וְלַחוּץ. זַלְזֵל בָּהֶן. אַל תְּדַקְדֵּק בָּהֶן לְהַרְחִיבָן. לֹא תְּמְשַׁחְנְהוּ כְּלָל. אֶלָּא בְּאוֹמֶד הַדַּעַת תַּנִּיחֵם, כְּדֵי שֶׁיְּהוּ נִיכָּרִים לָעֵינַיִם שֶׁהֵן שְׁלֵימוֹת וּרְחָבוֹת. לִבְנֵי אַנִּיגְרָא. אֵינוֹ מַזִּיק אֶלָּא יְחִידִים, וְיֵשׁ בְּיָדָן לִמְחוֹל. לְכ"ע. וּמַאן מָחֵיל. מְלֵי כַּתְפֵי נַגָּדֵי בִּתְרֵי עִבְרֵי נַהֲרָא קוֹצוּ. הַמּוֹלֵא יַעַר אוֹ אִילָנוֹת נְטוּעִין עַל שְׂפַת הַנָּהָר יָקוֹץ בְּרוֹחַב מְלֹא כָּתֵף מוֹשְׁכֵי חֶבֶל הַסְּפִינָה. וְהֵן מַטִּין עַצְמָן בַּאֲלַכְסוֹן. וְהוֹלְכִין כְּשֶׁהֵן מְשׁוּפָּעִין לְצַד הַיַּבָּשָׁה — שֶׁלֹּא תִּמָּשֵׁךְ הַסְּפִינָה לַמַּיִם. וְכָל כַּמּוּת הַצָּרִיךְ לְהִלּוּכָם — דַּיָּים לָקוֹץ, וּבִשְׁנֵי עִבְרֵי הַנָּהָר, שֶׁפְּעָמִים שֶׁהוֹלְכִין מִכָּאן וּפְעָמִים שֶׁהוֹלְכִין מִכָּאן. קַץ שִׁיתְסַר אַמְּתָא. (א) כְּרוֹחַב דֶּרֶךְ רה"ר כִּדְתְנַן בְּבָבָא בַּתְרָא (דף צט:): דֶּרֶךְ רה"ר — שֵׁשׁ עֶשְׂרֵה אַמָּה. בְּנֵי מַשְׁרוֹנְיָא. שֵׁם הָעִיר, וְהַיַּעַר הָיָה שֶׁלָּהֶן. דַּפְנוּהוּ. הִלְקוּהוּ. אַשְׁלֵיהֶן. חֲבָלִין שֶׁלָּהֶן. אַבָּא. יַעַר. נִיקַיְיצוּ עִילָּאֵי וְתַתָּאֵי. מִי שֶׁיֵּשׁ לָהֶן יַעַר עַל הַנָּהָר אֶצְלִי, לְמַעְלָה הֵימֶנּוּ וּלְמַטָּה הֵימֶנּוּ — הִילּוּךְ דֶּרֶךְ הַמַּיִם. הָתָם דְּבֵי פַּרְזַק רוּפִילָא הֲוָה. אוֹתָן שֶׁלְּמַטָּה וְשֶׁלְּמַעְלָה לֹא שֶׁל יִשְׂרָאֵל הָיָה, שֶׁיָּכוֹל לִקְצוֹץ אוֹתוֹ יַעַר שֶׁל בֵּית פַּרְזַק — פֶּחַת פַּרְסִיִּים הָיָה, וְיָדוּעַ הוּא שֶׁלֹּא יָקוֹצוּ, וּמַה תּוֹעִיל קְצִיצָה שֶׁלִּי. אִי מַמְתְּחֵי אַשְׁלַיְיהוּ מִסְתַּגֵּי לְהוּ. אִם יוּכְלוּ לִמְתּוֹחַ חַבְלָם וְלָבֹא מִמַּסָּע לְמַסָּע אוֹ מִכְּפָר לִכְפָר לֵילֵךְ מִמַּטָּה לְמַעְלָה — יֵלְכוּ. וְאִם

תשעין וט' מתו בעין הרע ואחד בדרך ארץ. וא"ת: א"כ בני יוסף שלא שלטה בהן עין הרע *היה להן לחיות הרבה מכל השבטים?! וי"ל: שמתו בדרך ארץ יותר מאחרים, כשהקב"ה היה רוצה להמתין — היה שולח להם חלאים אחרים. צנים · קור, כדמוכח הכא. פחים — חום, כדמוכח בריש מסכ' ע"ז (דף ג: ושם ד"ה הכל). ומיירי הכא במאורעות הבאים על האדם. דאילו במדות אמר בפ' "כל היד" (נדה דף טז: ושם ד"ה הכל): הכל בידי שמים חוץ מיראת שמים. שיתין רהיטי רהוט. יש מפרשים: דנקט שיתין — לפי שימי החורף ששים, וכן ימי הקיץ, כדאמר לעיל (דף קו:), ופת שחרית מצלת מן החמה ומן הצנה. א"נ: כן דרך למינקט בכל מקום שיתין, כדאמר ב"החובל" (ב"ק דף צב:): שיתין תכלי מטייה לככא דקל חבריה שמע כו'. *ארבע גרמידי דאניגרי זלזל בהו. פירוש: ארבע אמות שאתה מודד לבני אניגרא, שדולים משם להשקות שדותיהם — זלזל. פירוש: מדוד אותם שחוקות ולא מצומצמות, כדי שיוכלו לעמוד שם בריוח, ולא כפי' הקונט'. דעל נהרא שמניחין מקום גם למושכי ספינות לא תמשח כלל, שצריכין ריוח הרבה של יפלו במים, אלא בלא מדידה יתנו — שיהא (ב) ניכרת ונראה לעינים. בתרי עברי נהרא קוצו. פי': ענפי אילנות היער קוצו, שצריכין להטות כתפיהם לצד היער, שלא יפלו במים. *וא"ת: דאמרינן בסוף פרק "המוכר פירות" (ב"ב דף צט: ושם ד"ה ואמה): אמה בית השלחין אני מוכר לך — נותן לו ב' אמות לתוכה, אמה מכאן ואמה מכאן לאגפיה?! וי"ל: דהתם מיירי באמת המים שהוא לאדם אחד, שהוא עושה חריץ תוך שדהו להשקות ממנה. ואין צריך לאגפיים, רק אמה מכאן ואמה מכאן. והכא, אניגרא — הוא יאור גדול להשקות כל אותה בקעה, לכך צריך ארבע אמות לאגפיה. תדע דהתם זורעים אותן אמות, ונוטעין שם אילנות כדאמר התם, אבל הכא אין זורעין ונוטעין כלל שכל העם הולכים שם להשקות שדותיהם. והא דקאמר דאנהרא לכ"ע — לאו משום דאניגרא ליהוו כולהו דאדם אחד, אלא אינו דכ"ע אלא לאותן המשקין שדותיהם לבד. אי נמי, ארבע אמות דהכא — היינו ב' אמות של תוכה, ואמה מכאן ואמה מכאן. ליקון

[כלאיתא ברכות דף כ.]

מט א מיי' פ"ח מהל' גניבה הלכה א סמג עשין עב טוש"ע ח"מ סי' רלא סעיף טז:
נ ב ג ד מיי' שם הל' ב טוש"ע שם סעיף יז:
נא ה ו מיי' פי"ג מהל' נזקי ממון הלכה כו סמג עשין סו טוש"ע ח"מ סי' תיז סעיף ז:

[גי' הערוך שמתר וכן גי' הרשב"ם ב"ב עד: ד"ה שמתרי]
[עי' תוס' כתובות ל. ד"ה הכל ובב"ב קמד: ד"ה חוץ ובע"ז ג: ד"ה שומר]
זה הדבור ודבור המתחיל בתרי כו' הכל ד"א. מהר"ם

הגהות הב"ח

(א) רש"י ד"ה קץ שיתסר אמתא ברוחב הס"ד ואח"כ מ"ה בני משרוניא ואח"כ ד"ה דפנוהו הלקוהו ואח"כ מ"ה כר"ה כדתנן וכו' ואח"כ ד"ה אשליהן: (ב) תום' ד"ה ארבע וכו' שיהא ניכר כנ"ל ואות ת' נמחק והד"א עם ד"ה בתרי:

קושיא זאת קאי אלעיל אד' גרמידי דאניגרא. מהר"ם

[ובערוך ערך עבד ב' פי' עבד מאי דעבד ע"י שאלת חלום וי"א נטע אילנות כו' ע"ש]
ע"ז ג: ב"ב קמד: כתובות ל. [וע"ש]
ב"ק לב: [ע"ש]
[ג"ז שם וע"ש הגי']
[שטה ר' עקיבא לבניו כנ"ל]
[פסחים קיב. ב"ק לב:]
ב"ב ס: סנהדרין יח. יט.

ואי לא — לא מיסתגי להו. רבה בר רב נחמן הוה קא אזיל בארבא. חזא ההוא אבא דקאי אגודא דנהרא. אמר להו: דמאן? אמרו ליה: דרבה בר רב הונא. אמר: °"ויד השרים והסגנים היתה במעל הזה ראשונה". אמר להו: קוצו, קוצו! אתא רבה בר רב הונא אשכחיה דקייץ. אמר: מאן קצייה — תקוץ ענפיה. אמרי: כולהו שני דרבה בר רב הונא לא אקיים ליה זרעא לרבה בר רב נחמן. *אמר רב יהודה: [א]הכל לאיגלי גפא, ואפילו מיתמי. [ב]אבל רבנן — לא. מ"ט? רבנן *לא צריכי נטירותא. [ג]לכריא דפתיא — ואפילו מרבנן. ולא אמרן אלא דלא נפקא *באוכלוזא, [ד]אבל לאוכלוזא — לא, דרבנן לאו בני מיפק באוכלוזא נינהו. אמר רב יהודה: לכריא דנהרא — תתאי מסייעי עילאי, עילאי לא מסייעי תתאי. וחילופא במיא דמיטרא. תניא נמי הכי: [ה]חמש גנות המסתפקות מים ממעין אחד, ונתקלקל המעיין — כולם מתקנות עם העליונה. נמצאת התחתונה מתקנת עם כולן, ומתקנת לעצמה. [ו]וכן חמש חצרות שהיו מקלחות מים לביב אחד ונתקלקל הביב — כולן מתקנות עם התחתונה. נמצאת העליונה מתקנת עם כולן ומתקנת לעצמה. אמר שמואל: האי מאן דאחזיק ברקתא דנהרא — חציפא הוי, סלוקי לא מסלקינן ליה. והאידנא דקא כתבי פרסאי קני לך עד מלי צוארי סוסיא מיא — סלוקי נמי מסלקינן ליה. אמר רב יהודה *אמר רב: האי מאן דאחזיק ביני אחי וביני שותפי — חציפא הוי, סלוקי — לא מסלקינן ליה. ורב נחמן אמר: [ז]נמי מסלקינן, ואי משום דינא דבר מצרא — לא מסלקינן ליה. נהרדעי אמרי: [ח]אפילו משום דינא דבר מצרא מסלקינן ליה, משום שנאמר: °"ועשית הישר והטוב בעיני ה'". אתא אימליך ביה, אמר ליה: איזיל איזבון? ואמר ליה: זיל זבון, צריך למיקנא מיניה או לא? *רבינא אמר: לא צריך למיקנא מיניה. נהרדעי אמרי: צריך למיקנא מיניה. [ט]והלכתא: צריך למיקנא מיניה. השתא דאמרת צריך למיקנא מיניה, אי לא קנו מיניה — [י]אייקור וזול ברשותיה. זבן במאה ושוי מאתן; [כ]חזינא, אי לכולי עלמא קא מוזילא ומזבין — יהיב ליה מאה ושקיל ליה; ואי לא — יהיב ליה מאתן ושקיל ליה. *זבן במאתן ושויא מאה, סבור מינה: מצי אמר ליה *לתקוני שדרתיך ולא לעוותי. אמר ליה מר קשישא בריה דרב חסדא לרב אשי: [ל]הכי אמרי נהרדעי משום דרב נחמן: *אין אונאה לקרקעות. זבין ליה גריוא דארעא במיצעא נכסיה, [מ]חזינן: אי עידית היא אי זיבורית היא — זביניה זביני, ואי

תורה אור: עזרא ט; דברים ו

רש"י

ואם לאו לא מסתגי להו. אין להם מהלך בעבר זה, והולכין על כרחן דרך שפתו השנית. שהרי על כרחן, כשהולכין כנגד היער של גוי ילכו בשפתו השנייה, ולכשיגיעו כנגד שלי, למה יטריחו לעבור את רוחב המים? והרי הן צריכין לחזור ולעבור לצד אחר כשכלתה הקלירה?! (א). חזא ההוא אבא. יער שהניח רבה בר רב הונא, לפי שאין העליונים והתחתונים קוללין. ורבה בר רב נחמן לא היה יודע שכן היה, שיהא עליון ותחתון של גוי המושל. יד השרים והסגנים. פסוק הוא בספר עזרא. תיקוץ ענפיה. ימותו בניו. לאגלי גפא. הכל מסייעין לגדור חומת העיר ולהעמיד שעריה, שלא יכנס צבא שונאים לעיר. אגלי. שערים, כמו ברכות (דף כח.) טרוקו גלי. גפא. סתימת העיר – כדתנן לעיל (דף כה:): מצא אחר הגפה גוזלות. לא צריכי נטירותא. תורתן משמרתן, כדכתיב (משלי ו): "בשכבך תשמור עליך". (ב) לכריא דפתיא. לכרות מעין או בורות למים לשתות. ואפילו מרבנן. שהרי גם הם צריכים לשתות. ועל שם כלי ששותין בו משקין – שקורין פתיא בלשון ארמי – קרי ליה כריא דפתיא. דלא נפקי באכלוזא. שאין יוצאין בעלי בתים עצמן באכלוזא ובאוכלוסא לחפור אלא גובין מעות ושוכרין פועלים. לאו בני מיפק וכו'. גנאי הוא להן. לכריא דנהרא. כשמעלת שרטון, ונופלים בה אבנים ומעכבין מרוצת המים, וכורין ומנקין אותו להעביר מכשוליו. תתאי מסייעי לעלאי. כשהעליונים מתקנין כנגדן למעלה – יש על התחתונים לסייען, שמכשולין העליונים מעכבים מים מלירד, נמצא תיקון העליונים לעזרת התחתונים. אבל העליונים אין צריכין לסייע את התחתונים. כשמתקנין למטה, שתיקון של מטה אינו לעזרת עליונים אלא לרעתם, שכל זמן שהמים רצים למטה הנהר מתמעט למעלה, והשדות שלהן מתייבשות. וחילופא במיא דמיטרא. כגון בעיר, שהמים קשים להרבות טיט ולקלקל את הדרכים. ועושין להם חריץ במורד להוריד המים חוץ לעיר. אם נתקלקל החריץ כנגד התחתונים, וכורין להם – העליונים צריכים לסייע את התחתונים לכרות כנגדן, שכל זמן שלא ירדו המים התחתונים חוץ לעיר – יעמדו העליונים במקומן, אבל תחתונים – אין להן לסייע לעליונים לכרות למעלה, שכל זמן שלא ירדו העליונים למטה – טוב להן לתחתונים. ומתקנת לעצמה. בפני עצמה. כשמגעת כנגדה – אין אחר מסייעה. המקלחות מים. מים סרוחין, מי מטר. לביב אחד. חריץ מתוקן להוריד מי גשמים בו. כולן מתקנות עם התחתונה. מסייעות אותה לתקן כנגדה, כדפרישית לעיל. האי מאן דאחזיק ברקתא דנהרא. בשני הפרסיים היה הקרקע מופקר לכל הקודם להחזיק בו ולפרוע למלך טסקא דהוא מס של קרקע. ואם בא אחד ומחזיק על שפת הנהר, מקום שהספינות עולות לגמל, וצריך מקום פנוי הרבה לפורקי משאות לספינות ולטוענין מתוכן ומוליכין, וזה החזיק לבנות שם בנין או לחרוש ולזרוע. חציפא הוי. שמקלקל מקום לרבים. אבל סלוקי. מדינא לא מסלקינן ליה. והאידנא דכתבי פרסאי. לאותן הלוקחין שדות שעל שפת הנהר: קני לך השדה עד תוך הנהר, מלא צואר הסוס. והלוקחין גודרין גדירן רחוק מן הנהר שלא לקלקל את מקום הרבים. ואם בא אחד והחזיק מן הגדר ולצד הנהר – מסלקינן ליה, לפי שהיא קנויה לבעל הגדר עד תוך המים. ביני אחי. שדה העומדת ליקח בטסקא, ושדות שני אחים סמוכין לה מכאן ומכאן. ואי משום דינא דבר מצרא. אם אינן לא אחים ולא שותפים, אלא מכח מצרנות באין על המחזיק ואומרים: אנו היינו מצפים לקחתה, שאנו צריכין לקרקע, וטוב לכל אחד לקנות בסמוך לו ולא ליקח במקום אחר. לא מסלקינן ליה. דלא איכפת לן לדינא דבר מצרא כלל. ועשית הישר והטוב. דבר שאי אתה נחסר כ"כ, שתמצא קרקעות במקום אחר, ולא תטריח על בן המצר להיות נכסיו חלוקין. אתא לאימלוכי ביה. שדה העומדת לימכר, ובא אחר ונטל רשות מבן המצרן, וא"ל: זיל זבון. נהרדעי אמרי צריך למקני. דאי לא קנה מיניה, מצי אמר ליה: משטה הייתי בך. כדי להעמידה על דמים הראויין לה. שאם באתי אני אצל הבעלים – היה מעלה לי בדמים בשביל שחביבה עלי. השתא דאמרת צריך למיקנייה מיניה. א"כ אין קניינו של זה כלום. אם אייקר או זול ארעא – ברשותא דבר מצרא אייקר או זול, ולא יוסיף ולא יגרע הלוקח מלקבל דמים שנתן בה, דכי אייקר – רווחא דבר מצרא הוא, וכי זול – פסידא דבר מצרא הוא. ואי לא יהיב ליה מאתן. דגבי דהאי הוא דאוזיל. בי מיצעי דנכסי. של מוכר שדות המוכר מקיפות לה מכל צד. חזינן אי עידית היא. דבר העשוי לימכר לעצמו שאינו דומה לשאר שדות הסמוכות לה. זביניה זביני. ואין מצרני המוכר יכולים לסלקו שהרי יש ביניהן הפסק.
ואי

תוספות

ליקוץ ענפיה. שזה היה אותו יער עצמו של פרזיק רופילא, ולא היתה ידו במעל כלל, לכך קילל. האי מאן דאחזיק ברקתא דנהרא. קיבל בטסקא מן המלך, כדפי' בקונטרס. ולהכי קאמר "דאחזיק" ולא קאמר "דזבין" כדאמרינן לקמן: זבין במאתים זבין מגוי. וכן האי מאן דאחזיק ביני אחי, דבסמוך, מפר"ת: דוקא באחזיק – שהיתה קרקע הפקר וקבלה מן המלך בטסקא – לא מסלקינן ליה. ולרב נחמן דוקא ביני אחי מסלקינן ליה, שעשה יותר מדאי שלא כהוגן להחזיק ביני אחי. אבל משום מצרנות לא מסלקינן ליה, דלא שייך כאן "ועשית הישר והטוב" כיון שיוכלו לקבל מן המלך ולא עשו. אבל במכר – מודים הם כ"ע דשייך דינא דבר מצרא, דלא הוה ליה לאסוקי אדעתיה דמצרן שהיו הבעלים רוצים למכור. ונהרדעי סברי דאפילו הכי שייך "ועשית הישר והטוב". והשתא אתי שפיר הא דאמרי נהרדעי משמיה דרב נחמן, בשמעתין: "אין אונאה לקרקעות", דאמצרנות קאמר, כדמוכח בכתובות בפ' "אלמנה" (דף לט: ע"ש ושם ד"ה ה"ג) דקאמר רבא גבי טעה השליח: והאמר מר: אין אונאה לקרקעות, גבי מצרנות שהוא כעין שליח שהמקח לא יהיה שלו. ואין צריך לדחוק כפי' הקונטרס דרב נחמן לית ליה דינא דבר מצרא. והאידנא דכתבי פרסאי. לא כפירוש הקונטרס דמפ' דמסלקינן ליה – שהראשון קנאו מן המלך, אלא דמסלקינן ליה לבא להחזיק לכתחילה משום דכיון דכתבי פרסאי כו' חיישינן שלא יבא להחזיק עד תוך הנהר כמו שכותב לו המלך, ויעכב הילוך הספינות ויאתן לגמל. וקנסינן ליה משום הכי להסתלק מכולה רקתא, אפילו ממה שחוץ לנהר.
מזבנינן

מסורת הש"ס

ב"ב ח.
[שם ז: ח.]
כמו אוכלסא פי' המון עם. ערוך
זו היא גירסת הרא"ש אבל הרי"ף ל"ג אמר רב
כרב אלפס איתא רב נחמן ומכאן ראיה לפי' ר"ת ועי' בתוספות
עי' תוספות כתובות לח. ד"ה אלמנה וכו'
קידושין מב: וש"נ
כתובות נט: ע"ש תוס'. קדושין מב:

עין משפט נר מצוה

נב א מיי' פ"ו מהלכות שכנים הלכה ו סמג עשין פב טוש"ע ח"מ סי' קסג סעיף ד:
נג ב ג מיי' שם ופ"ו מהלכות ת"ת הלכה י סמג שם סי' יב טוש"ע י"ד סי' רמג סעיף ב וטוש"ע ח"מ שם:
נד ד מיי' שם פ"ו מהל' ת"ת הלכה י וסמג שם טוש"ע ח"מ שם טור ש"ע י"ד שם סעיף א וסעיף ב:
נה ה מיי' פ"ג מהלכות שכנים הלכה ט סמג עשין פב טוש"ע ח"מ סי' קע סעיף א:
נו ו מיי' שם סמג שם טוש"ע ח"מ סי' קסא סעיף ו וטור ח"מ סי' קע:
נז ז מיי' שם פי"ב הלכה ד ועיין בהשגו' ובמ"מ סג שם טוש"ע ח"מ סי' קעה סעיף ה:
נח ח מיי' שם הלכה ה טוש"ע שם סעיף ו:
נט ט מיי' שם פי"ד הלכה א סמג שם טוש"ע שם סעיף כט:
ס י מיי' שם הלכה ד סמג שם טור וש"ע שם סעיף ו:
סא כ ל מיי' שם סמג שם טוש"ע שם סעי' ז [רב אלפס כאן ועוד במכילתין פ"ד לז:]
סב מ מיי' שם פי"ג הלכה ה סמג שם טור וש"ע ח"מ שם סעיף כח:

הגהות הב"ח

(א) רש"י ד"ה ואם לאו וכו' כשכלת' הקלירה כצ"ל והס"ד: (ב) ד"ה לכריא הד"א עם ד"ה ואפי' מרבנן וכו' ששותין בו שקורין כצ"ל ותיבת משקין נמחק:

וְאִי לָא — אִיעֲרוּמֵי קָא מַעֲרִים. ^א^מַתָּנָה לֵית בָּהּ מִשּׁוּם דִּינָא דְּבַר מִצְרָא. אֲמַר אַמֵימָר: ^ב^אִי כְּתַב לֵיהּ אַחֲרָיוּת — אִית בָּהּ מִשּׁוּם דִּינָא דְּבַר מִצְרָא. ^ג^מָכַר כָּל נְכָסָיו לְאֶחָד — לֵית בָּהּ מִשּׁוּם דִּינָא דְּבַר מִצְרָא. ^ד^לַבְּעָלִים הָרִאשׁוֹנִים — לֵית בָּהּ מִשּׁוּם דִּינָא דְּבַר מִצְרָא. *^ה^זָבַן מִגּוֹי וְזַבֵּין לְגוֹי — לֵית בָּהּ מִשּׁוּם דִּינָא דְּבַר מִצְרָא. זָבַן מִגּוֹי — דְּאָמַר לֵיהּ: אֲרִי אַבְרָחִי לָךְ מִמִּצְרָא. זַבֵּין לְגוֹי — ^ו^גּוֹי וַדַּאי לָאו בַּר "וְעָשִׂיתָ הַיָּשָׁר וְהַטּוֹב" הוּא. ^ז^שַׁמּוּתֵי וַדַּאי מְשַׁמְּתִינַן לֵיהּ, עַד דְּמַקַבֵּל עֲלֵיהּ כָּל אוֹנְסֵי דְּאָתֵי לֵיהּ מֵחֲמָתֵיהּ. ^ח^מַשְׁכַּנְתָּא לֵית בָּהּ מִשּׁוּם דִּינָא דְּבַר מִצְרָא, *דַּאֲמַר רַב אַשִׁי: אֲמַרוּ לִי סָבֵי דְּמָתָא מַחְסְיָא: מַאי מַשְׁכַּנְתָּא? דִּשְׁכוּנָה גַּבֵּיהּ. מַאי נַפְקָא מִינַּהּ? לְדִינָא דְּבַר מִצְרָא. ^ט^לִמְכּוֹר בְּרָחוֹק וְלִגְאוֹל בְּקָרוֹב, בְּרַע וְלִגְאוֹל בְּיָפֶה — לֵית בָּהּ מִשּׁוּם דִּינָא דְּבַר מִצְרָא. ^י^לְכַרְגָּא וְלִמְזוֹנֵי וְלִקְבוּרָה — לֵית בָּהּ מִשּׁוּם דִּינָא דְּבַר מִצְרָא. *^כ^דְּאָמְרִי נְהַרְדְּעֵא: לְכַרְגָּא, לִמְזוֹנֵי וְלִקְבוּרָה מְזַבְּנִינַן בְּלָא אַכְרַזְתָּא. ^ל^לְאִשָּׁה וְלִיתְמֵי ^מ^וּלְשׁוּתָּפֵי — לֵית בָּהּ מִשּׁוּם דִּינָא דְּבַר מִצְרָא. ^נ^שְׁכֵנֵי הָעִיר וּשְׁכֵנֵי שָׂדֶה — שְׁכֵנֵי הָעִיר קוֹדְמִין. *שָׁכֵן וְתַלְמִיד חָכָם — תַּלְמִיד חָכָם קוֹדֵם. קָרוֹב וְתַלְמִיד חָכָם — תַּלְמִיד חָכָם קוֹדֵם. אִיבַּעְיָא לְהוּ: שָׁכֵן וְקָרוֹב מַאי? ת"שׁ: ^ס^"טוֹב שָׁכֵן קָרוֹב מֵאָח רָחוֹק". ^ע^הָנֵי זוּזֵי טָבֵי וְהָנֵי זוּזֵי תְּקוּלֵי — לֵית בֵּיהּ מִשּׁוּם דִּינָא דְּבַר מִצְרָא. ^פ^הָנֵי צַיְירֵי וְהָנֵי שָׁרֵי — לֵית בֵּיהּ מִשּׁוּם דִּינָא דְּבַר מִצְרָא. ^צ^אָמַר: אֵיזִיל וְאֶטְרַח וְאַיְיתֵי זוּזֵי — לָא נָטְרִינַן לֵיהּ. אָמַר: אֵיזִיל אַיְיתֵי זוּזֵי, ^ק^חָזֵינַן; אִי גַּבְרָא דַּאֲמִיד הוּא, דְּאָזֵיל וּמַיְיתֵי זוּזֵי — נָטְרִינַן לֵיהּ. וְאִי לָא — לָא נָטְרִינַן לֵיהּ. אַרְעָא דְּחַד וּבָתֵּי דְּחַד — ^ר^מָרֵי אַרְעָא מְעַכֵּב אַמָּרֵי בָּתֵּי, מָרֵי בָּתֵּי לָא מְעַכֵּב אַמָּרֵי דְּאַרְעָא. אַרְעָא דְּחַד וְדִיקְלֵי דְּחַד — ^ש^מָרֵי דְּאַרְעָא מָצֵי מְעַכֵּב אַמָּרֵי דִּיקְלֵי, מָרֵי דִּיקְלֵי לָא מָצֵי מְעַכֵּב אַמָּרֵי דְּאַרְעָא. אַרְעָא לְבָתֵּי וְאַרְעָא לְזַרְעָא — ^ת^יִשּׁוּב עָדִיף, וְלֵית בָּהּ מִשּׁוּם דִּינָא דְּבַר מִצְרָא. אַפְסֵיק מְשׁוּנִיתָא אוֹ רִיכְבָּא דְּדִיקְלָא, ^א^חָזֵינָא: אִם יָכוֹל לְהַכְנִיס בָּהּ אֲפִילּוּ תֶּלֶם אֶחָד — אִית בָּהּ מִשּׁוּם דִּינָא דְּבַר מִצְרָא; וְאִי לָא — לֵית בָּהּ מִשּׁוּם דִּינָא דְּבַר מִצְרָא. ^ב^הָנֵי ד' בְּנֵי מִצְרָנֵי, דְּקָדֵים חַד מִינַּיְיהוּ וּזְבֵין — זְבִינֵיהּ זְבִינֵי. ^ג^וְאִי כּוּלְּהוּ אָתוּ בַּהֲדֵי הֲדָדֵי — פָּלְגוּ לָהּ *בְּקַרְנָזִיל.§

מתני'

וְאִי לָא אִיעֲרוּמֵי קָא מַעֲרִים. אִם בָּאתִי לִיקַּח אֶצְלָם — יְסַלְּקוּנִי. אֶקְנֶה אֲנִי בֵּית סְאָה בָּאֶמְצַע, וְאֶהְיֶה אֲנִי מִצְרָן לְכָל רוּחַ. וְאֶקְנֶה אֲנִי אַחֲרֵי כֵן לְכָל צַד, וְלֹא יוּכְלוּ לְסַלְּקֵנִי מִן הַמַּתְחָלָה *וּמִן הַנּוֹתָר לְכָל רוּחַ. הִלְכָּךְ, מֵהַשְׁתָּא מְסַלְּקִינַן לֵיהּ. וְאִי כָּתַב לֵיהּ אַחֲרָיוּת כו'. דְּוַדַּאי מֶכֶר הוּא, שֶׁאֵין כּוֹתְבִין אַחֲרָיוּת עַל הַמַּתָּנָה. מוֹכֵר כָּל נְכָסָיו לְאֶחָד. בְּכָל מָקוֹם שֶׁהֵן, זוֹ בַּמִּזְרָח וְזוֹ בַּמַּעֲרָב. וְיָצְאוּ מִצְרָנֵי אַחַת מֵהֶן וְעִרְעֲרוּ. לֵית בְּהוּ מִשּׁוּם דִּינָא דְּבַר מִצְרָא. שֶׁלֹּא תִּקְּנוּ חֲכָמִים לַלּוֹקֵחַ לְהִסְתַּלֵּק, לַעֲשׂוֹת הַיָּשָׁר וְהַטּוֹב לְבַעַל הַמֶּצֶר, שֶׁהוּא רָעָה לַמּוֹכֵר. שֶׁזֶּה לֹא יִקְנֶה הַשְּׁאָר, שֶׁיִּמְשׁוֹךְ אֶת יָדוֹ בִּשְׁבִיל זוֹ. וּבִמְקוֹם פְּסֵידָא דְּמוֹכֵר לֹא תִּקּוּן דִּינָא דְּבַר מִצְרָא. כִּדְאָמַר לְקַמָּן: הָנֵי צַיְירֵי וְהָנֵי שָׁרוּ — לֵית בָּהּ מִשּׁוּם דִּינָא דְּבַר מִצְרָא. אַרְיָא אַבְרְחִי לָךְ. וְאֵין לָךְ יָשָׁר וְטוֹב מִזֶּה. גּוֹי לָאו בַּר וְעָשִׂיתָ וכו'. וְאֵין לָנוּ לוֹמַר; עַל דִּינָא דְּבַר מִצְרָא "וְעָשִׂיתָ הַיָּשָׁר וְהַטּוֹב" אֶלָּא לַלּוֹקֵחַ, שֶׁהַמּוֹכֵר אוֹמֵר לוֹ: מֶה עָשִׂיתִי לְךָ? אִם אֶרְצֶה לֹא אֶמְכְּרֶנָּה לְךָ וּתְהֵא בְּיָדִי. אֲבָל לַלּוֹקֵחַ נֹאמַר: מְשׁוֹךְ יָדְךָ וְיִקְנֶנָּה זֶה. שַׁמּוּתֵי וַדַּאי מְשַׁמְּתִינָא לֵיהּ. לַמּוֹכֵר, לְקַבּוּלֵי עֲלֵיהּ כָּל אוֹנְסָא דְּאָתֵי לֵיהּ מֵחֲמַת הַגּוֹי. מַשְׁכַּנְתָּא. אִם מְכָרָהּ לְמִי שֶׁמְּמוּשְׁכֶּנֶת לוֹ. לֵית בְּהוּ מִשּׁוּם דִּינָא דְּבַר מִצְרָא. שֶׁזֶּה שָׁכֵן מַצְרָן מְכוּלָּן, שֶׁכּוּלּוֹ שְׁכוּנָה בְּיָדוֹ. לִמְכּוֹר בְּרָחוֹק וְלִגְאוֹל בְּקָרוֹב. אִם הַמּוֹכֵר זֶה מוֹכְרָהּ מִפְּנֵי שֶׁהִיא רְחוֹקָה מִמֶּנּוּ וְרוֹצֶה לִקְנוֹת אַחֶרֶת בְּקָרוֹב. אֵין בָּהּ מִשּׁוּם דִּינָא דְּבַר מִצְרָא. לְפִי שֶׁאֵין לָנוּ לְהַפְסִיד מוֹכֵר מִשּׁוּם טוֹב וְיָשָׁר דְּמַצְרָן, דִּכְשֵׁם שֶׁעָלֵינוּ לַעֲשׂוֹת טוֹב לָזֶה, כָּךְ עָלֵינוּ לַעֲשׂוֹת טוֹב לָזֶה — וְאִם בָּאנוּ לַעֲשׂוֹת אִיחוּר בַּדָּבָר — שֶׁמָּא בֵּין כָּךְ וּבֵין כָּךְ תִּמָּכֵר זוֹ שֶׁהָיָה רוֹצֶה זֶה לִקְנוֹת. וְכֵן לְכַרְגָּא. לִפְרוֹעַ כֶּסֶף גּוּלְגָּלְתָּא לַמֶּלֶךְ. [וְלִמְזוֹנֵי]. לָמְזוֹן אַלְמָנָה וְהַבָּנוֹת, שֶׁבֵּ"ד מוֹכְרִין בְּנִכְסֵי יְתוֹמִין. וְכֵן לִקְבּוֹר אֶת הַמֵּת. בְּלָא אַכְרַזְתָּא. וְכֵיוָן דְּמִשּׁוּם רְוָוחָא דְיָתְמֵי לֹא מַשְׁהֵינַן לְמִילְּתָא פֶּן יִכְעוֹס שׁוֹטֵר הַמֶּלֶךְ, וְכֵן חֶסְרוֹן מְזוֹנוֹת, וּלְבִזָּיוֹן הַמֵּת — כָּל שֶׁכֵּן דְּמִשּׁוּם בַּר מִצְרָא לֹא מַשְׁהֵינַן מִילְּתָא לְאוֹדוּעֵי. לְאִשָּׁה לְיָתְמֵי וּלְשׁוּתָּפֵי. מָכַר לָאִשָּׁה — לֹא מְסַלְּקִינַן (א) לֵיהּ דְּלָאו אוֹרַח אַרְעָא לְאַהְדוּרֵי וּלְבַקֵּשׁ מִי שֶׁיֵּשׁ לוֹ קַרְקָעוֹת לִמְכּוֹר. וּמַה שֶּׁבָּאָה לְיָדָהּ רִאשׁוֹן — אֵין לָנוּ לוֹמַר "וְעָשִׂיתָ הַיָּשָׁר וְהַטּוֹב", לְהַרְחִיקוֹ מֵעָלָיו, וְכֵן יָתְמֵי. וְשׁוּתָּף שֶׁמָּכַר לוֹ לַחֲבֵירוֹ חֶלְקוֹ בַּשָּׂדֶה שֶׁהֵן שׁוּתָּפִין בָּהּ — (ב) אֵין לָנוּ לְסַלְּקוֹ מִשּׁוּם דִּינָא דְּבַר מִצְרָא, וְלוֹמַר: אֵין אַתָּה בָּא בְּחֵלֶק חֲבֵירְךָ אֶלָּא כְּאֶחָד הַמִּצְרָנִין, וְיִקְחֶנָּה עִמְּךָ. אֶלָּא כֵּיוָן דְּלֹא נִתְחַלְּקוּ (ג) חֶלְקוֹ — וַהֲרֵי הוּא כְּשָׁכֵן בְּכוּלָּהּ. שְׁכֵנֵי הָעִיר וּשְׁכֵנֵי הַשָּׂדֶה שְׁכֵנֵי הָעִיר קוֹדְמִין. נִרְאֶה בְּעֵינַי, דְּלָאו בְּדִינָא דְּבַר מִצְרָא אַיְירֵי, אֶלָּא לְהַשִּׂיא עֵצָה דֶּרֶךְ יָשָׁר וְטוֹב לַמּוֹכֵר. שֶׁאִם יֵשׁ לוֹ שָׂדֶה לִמְכּוֹר וּבָאוּ עָלֶיהָ (ד) לַלּוֹקֵחַ שְׁכֵנִים הַדָּרִים אֶצְלוֹ בַּדִּירָה, וְשָׁכֵן שֶׁיֵּשׁ לוֹ בַּשָּׂדֶה, שֶׁשְּׂדוֹתֵיהֶן סְמוּכוֹת זוֹ לָזוֹ, וְזוֹ שֶׁיֵּשׁ לוֹ לִמְכּוֹר — אֵינָהּ סְמוּכָה לַמַּצְרָן — שְׁכֵנֵי הָעִיר קוֹדְמִין. וַאֲנִי לֹא דִּקְדַּקְתִּי בָּהּ מִפִּי רַבּוֹתַי כָּל צָרְכִּי. וְעַד הֵנָּה פֵּירַשְׁתִּי דְּבְמַצְרָן דִּילֵיהּ קָאָמַר, וְהַשְׁתָּא לֹא נִרְאֶה לִי. דְּאִם כֵּן, הֲוָה לֵיהּ לְמִיתְנִינְהוּ בַּהֲדֵי הָנָךְ דִּלְעֵיל, וּלְמֵימַר הָכִי: לְאִשָּׁה וּלְיָתְמֵי וּלְשׁוּתָּפֵי וְלִשְׁכֵנֵי הָעִיר וְלַת"ח — לֵית בָּהּ מִשּׁוּם דִּינָא דְּבַר מִצְרָא. מַאי שְׁנָא דְּשַׁנֵּי בְּלִישָּׁנָא דְּכוּלֵּי שְׁמַעְתָּא, לְמִינְקַט לִישָּׁנָא דְּקוֹדְמִין?! וְתוּ, דְּקָאָמַר: שָׁכֵן וְתַלְמִיד חָכָם — ת"ח קוֹדֵם, אִי הַאי שָׁכֵן מַצְרָן הוּא, אַמַּאי ת"ח קוֹדֵם? תַּלְמִיד חָכָם לָאו בַּר "וְעָשִׂיתָ הַיָּשָׁר וְהַטּוֹב" הוּא?! דְּהַאי "וְעָשִׂיתָ" — אַלּוֹקֵחַ שֶׁדִּיוּהּ רַבָּנַן, כִּדְאָמְרִינַן לְעֵיל גַּבֵּי זַבֵּין לְגוֹי: גּוֹי לָאו בַּר וְעָשִׂיתָ כו'. וְתוּ, קָרוֹב וְתַלְמִיד חָכָם — מַאי דִּינָא דְּבַר מִצְרָא אִיכָּא? וְאִי ת"ח: כְּשֶׁשְּׁנֵיהֶן מִצְרָנִין הַאוּ מִשּׁוּם דְּת"ח הוּא מְשַׁלֵּחַ גְּלִימָא דְּאִינָשֵׁי?! זוּזֵי טָבֵי זוּזֵי תְּקוּלֵי. מַצְרָן שֶׁבָּא לְעוֹרֵר עַל הַמַּקָּח מֵבִיא מָעוֹת שֶׁמִּשְׁקָלָן טוֹב יוֹתֵר עַל שֶׁל לוֹקֵחַ, אֲבָל שֶׁל לוֹקֵחַ טָבִין וַחֲרִיפִין בַּמַּטְבֵּעַ הַיּוֹצְאָה יוֹתֵר מִשֶּׁל מַצְרָן, וְאִי נַמִּי אִיפְּכָא. לֵית בָּהּ מִשּׁוּם דִּינָא דְּבַר מִצְרָא. דְּקָאָמַר לֵיהּ הַמּוֹכֵר: בְּהָא נִיחָא. הָנֵי צַיְירֵי וְהָנֵי שָׁרוּ. לוֹקֵחַ וּמַצְרָן שֶׁשָּׁלְחוּ מְעוֹתֵיהֶן — שֶׁל מַצְרָן צְרוּרִין וַחֲתוּמִין, וְזֶה יָרֵא לְהַתִּירָן שֶׁלֹּא יֹאמַר: יוֹתֵר הָיוּ, וְשֶׁל לוֹקֵחַ מוּתָּרִין. לֵית בָּהּ מִשּׁוּם דִּינָא דְּבַר מִצְרָא. דִּפְסֵידָא דְּמוֹכֵר הוּא, דְּקָאָמַר: לְזוּזֵי נְרִיכְנָא. אָמַר לֵיהּ אֵיזִיל וְאִיטְרַח וכו'. מִילְּתָא בְּאַפֵּי נַפְשֵׁיהּ הִיא, מַצְרָן שֶׁאָמַר: אֵיזִיל וְאִיטְרַח וכו'. דַּאֲמִיד הוּא. שֶׁאָנוּ אוֹמְדִין אוֹתוֹ דְּאֶפְשָׁר לוֹ לְקַיֵּים דְּבָרָיו. וּבָתֵּי דְּחַד. בִּנְיָן שֶׁעָלֶיהָ. מָרֵי אַרְעָא מְעַכֵּב אַמָּרֵי בָּתֵּי. שֶׁלֹּא לִמְכּוֹר הַבִּנְיָן לְאַחֵר, דְּהוֹאִיל וְהוּא בָּא לְמוֹכְרָם וְזֶה צָרִיךְ לָהֶם — טוֹב שֶׁיִּהְיֶה בִּנְיָנוֹ בַּקַּרְקַע שֶׁלּוֹ, וְאִיכָּא הַיָּשָׁר וְהַטּוֹב. מָרֵי בָּתֵּי לָא מְעַכֵּב אַמָּרֵי אַרְעָא. שֶׁהוּא אֵינוֹ חָשׁוּב, שֶׁכֵּן לִכְשֶׁיַּגִּיעוּ שָׁנָיו עוֹמֵד לְהִסְתַּלֵּק מִינֵּיהּ. וְדִיקְלֵי דְּחַד. שֶׁמָּכַר לוֹ דְּקָלִין בְּשָׂדֵהוּ לְהַנִּיחָן שָׁם עַד זְמַן פְּלוֹנִי, אוֹ עַד שֶׁיִּיבְשׁוּ. אַרְעָא לְזוֹרְעָהּ. הַמַּצְרָן חָפֵץ בָּהּ לִזְרִיעָה וְהַלּוֹקֵחַ צָרִיךְ בָּהּ לְבִנְיַן בַּיִת. (ה) לְבֵית דִּין וְלֹא תִּקְּנוּ כָּאן עֲשׂוֹת יָשָׁר וְטוֹב, שֶׁזּוֹ טוֹבָה מִזּוֹ. יִשּׁוּב דְּבָתֵּי עָדִיף. אַפְסֵיק מְשׁוּנִיתָא. שֵׁן סֶלַע מַפְסִיק בֵּין שָׂדֶה זוֹ לְשָׂדֶה שֶׁל מַצְרָן. אוֹ רִיכְבָּא דְּדִיקְלָא. הַדְּקָלִים הַכְּפוּפִין וּסְמוּכִין זוֹ לְצַד זוֹ וּמְסוּגָּרִין, כְּאוֹתָן שֶׁקּוֹרִין *פלשיירי בְּלַעַ"ז. אִם יָכוֹל לְהַכְנִיס הַמַּצְרָן תֶּלֶם אֶחָד. מִשָּׂדֵהוּ לְתוֹךְ שָׂדֶה זוֹ אִית בָּהּ וכו'. תֶּלֶם. שׁוּרוֹת הַמַּעֲנָה. וְאִי אַיְיתוּ בַּהֲדָדֵי. שֶׁמְּעַרְעֵר כָּל אֶחָד עַל מַצְרָנוּתוֹ. פָּלְגֵי לָהּ בְּקַרְנְזִיל. בְּאַרְבַּע אֲלַכְסוֹנוֹת, שֶׁיְּהֵא כָּל אֶחָד נוֹטֵל בָּהּ עַל פְּנֵי כּוּלָּהּ סָמוּךְ לוֹ כָּזֶה:* וּלְשׁוֹן קַרְנְזִיל — זִיל בָּהּ לְקַרְנוֹת.

מתני'

מזובנינן בלא אכרזתא. אין לפרש כל הני מילי לצורך יתומים, דא"כ הוה משמע דלשאר צורכי יתומין אין מוכרין בלא אכרזתא. כי הנהו דחשיב פי' "הנזקין" (גיטין דף נב. ושם): מוכרים שדותיהן לקנות בהן מגלה וצילית ושופר כו', וא"כ בפרק "שום היתומים" (ערכין דף כב. ושם) דפריך לרב *אשי דאמר אין נזקקין כו' מדתנן: שום היתומים שלשים יום ומכריזין בבוקר ובערב — לוקמה במילי דיתמי שצריכי הכרזה?! אלא ודאי לכל מילי דיתמי אין צריכין הכרזה, ובשמעתין מיירי בכרגא ומזוני וקבורה דאשה ובנות. ואם תאמר: לקבורה פשיטא דמזבינן בלא אכרזתא, דאטו יהיה מת מוטל באשפה כל ימי הכרזה?! וי"ל: דאם לוו לצורך קבורה קאמר דמזבנינן בלא אכרזתא *כדי לפדות. אי נמי דה"א שממשכנין מחפצי יתומים עד שמכריזין — קמ"ל.

*משמתינן ליה עד דמקבל כו'. דוקא שישראל רוצה ליקח בדמים שנתן הגוי.

שכיני העיר כו'. הא מילתא בדין הקדמה קמיירי, כששניהם מצרנים ושכן עיר — מצרן מצד העיר, שיש לו שדה אחורי ביתו הסמוכה לזו. ושכן שדה — שיש לו שדה רחוקה מן העיר, הסמוכה לזו.

ארעא דחד ובתי דחד. שהבית בנוי על גבי קרקע — מרי דארעא מעכב שלא ימכור הלה עציו ואבניו כי אם לו. אבל בבית אצל בית, או קרקע שאינו עומד לזריעה — לא שייך דינא דבר מצרא, דלא שייך התם טעמא דקאמר בסמוך: להכניס תלם אחד, ודוקא בשדה של זריעה שייך הישר והטוב שיכול לחורשה בבת אחת. וכן פר"ת בתשובה אחת המתחלת: חזרנו על כל צידי צדדים ולא מצאנו דין מצרנות בבתים. אלא

סג א ב מיי' פי"ג מהל' שכנים הלכה א סמג עשין פב טור וש"ע ח"מ סי' קעה סעיף יח וסעיף כ:

[נ"ל אסי]

סד ג מיי' שם פי"ב הלכה ו סמג שם טוש"ע שם סעיף לו:

סה ד מיי' שם טוש"ע שם סעיף לז:

סו ה מיי' שם טוש"ע שם סעיף לח:

סז ו מיי' שם טוש"ע שם סעיף לט:

סח ז מיי' שם הלכה ז טוש"ע שם סעיף מ:

סט ח מיי' שם הלכה ט טוש"ע שם סעיף נז:

כדי לפרוע כצ"ל רש"ל

ע ט מיי' שם טוש"ע שם סעיף מב:

עא י מיי' שם טוש"ע שם סעיף מג:

עב כ מיי' פי"ב מהל' אישות הלכה טז ופי"ח הלכה כ ופי"ב מהל' מלוה הלכה יא סמג עשין מח ולד טוש"ע אה"ע סי' ע סעיף ה וסי' לג סעיף כה וסי' קד סעיף ג וסי' קיב סעיף ו וטוש"ע ח"מ סי' קט סעיף ג:

עג ל מיי' פי"ב מהל' שכנים הלכה יג יד סמג עשין פב טוש"ע ח"מ סי' קעה סעיף מז:

עד מ מיי' שם הלכה ה טוש"ע שם סעי' יב מט:

עה נ ס מיי' שם פי"ד הלכה ה סמג שם טוש"ע שם סעי' נ:

עו ע פ מיי' שם הלכה א טוש"ע שם סעי' נג:

עז צ ק מיי' שם טוש"ע שם סעי' כה:

עח ר ש מיי' שם פי"ב הלכה טז סמג שם טוש"ע שם סעי' נה:

עט ת מיי' שם פי"ד הלכה א סמג שם טוש"ע שם סעי' כו:

פ א מיי' שם פי"ב הלכה יז טוש"ע שם סעי' כז:

פא ב ג מיי' שם פי"ב הלכה ה סמג שם טוש"ע שם סעי' יח:

הגהות הב"ח

(א) רש"י ד"ה לאשה וכו' לא מסלקינן לה דלאו וכו' להרחיקה: (ב) בא"ד אין לנו לסלקו נ"ב פי' בשביל המצרן עי' באשר"י: (ג) בא"ד חלקו הרי כצ"ל ואות ו' נמחק: (ד) ד"ה שכיני וכו' ובאו עליה ללקחו שכינים: (ה) ד"ה ישוב וכו' ב"ד לא כצ"ל ואות ל' ואות ו' נמחק:

תורה אור: משלי כז

מן המתחלה מן הנותר. כצ"ל רש"ל

ב"ק קיד.

שם סח.

גיטין נב: כתובות פז. ק:

כתובות פה:

[ב"ב יג.]

מתני' ^א^הַמְקַבֵּל שָׂדֶה מֵחֲבֵירוֹ לְשָׁנִים מוּעָטוֹת — לֹא יִזְרָעֶנָּה פִּשְׁתָּן, וְאֵין לוֹ בְּקוֹרוֹת שִׁקְמָה. ^ב^קִיבְּלָהּ הֵימֶנּוּ לְז' שָׁנִים — שָׁנָה רִאשׁוֹנָה יִזְרָעֶנָּה פִּשְׁתָּן, וְיֵשׁ לוֹ בְּקוֹרוֹת שִׁקְמָה.§ **גמ'** אֲמַר אַבַּיֵי: בְּקוֹרוֹת שִׁקְמָה — אֵין לוֹ, בִּשְׁבַח שִׁקְמָה — יֵשׁ לוֹ. וְרָבָא אֲמַר: ^ג^אֲפִילּוּ בִּשְׁבַח שִׁקְמָה נַמִי אֵין לוֹ. מֵיתִיבִי: ^ד^הַמְקַבֵּל שָׂדֶה מֵחֲבֵירוֹ וְהִגִּיעַ זְמַנּוֹ לָצֵאת — שָׁמִין לוֹ. מַאי לָאו — שָׁמִין לוֹ בִּשְׁבַח שִׁקְמָה? לָא, ^ה^שָׁמִין לוֹ יַרְקָא וְסִילְקָא. יַרְקָא וְסִילְקָא, נַעֲקוֹר וְנִשְׁקוֹל! ^ו^בִּדְלָא מְטָא יוֹמָא דְּשׁוּקָא. ת"ש: הַמְקַבֵּל שָׂדֶה מֵחֲבֵירוֹ וְהִגִּיעַ שְׁבִיעִית — שָׁמִין לוֹ. שְׁבִיעִית — מִי קָא מַפְקְעָא אַרְעָא! אֶלָּא אֵימָא: הַמְקַבֵּל שָׂדֶה מֵחֲבֵירוֹ וְהִגִּיעַ יוֹבֵל — שָׁמִין לוֹ. וְאַכַּתִּי, יוֹבֵל מִי מַפְקְעָא קַבְּלָנוּת? "לִצְמִיתוּת", אֲמַר רַחֲמָנָא! אֶלָּא אֵימָא: ^ז^הַלּוֹקֵחַ שָׂדֶה מֵחֲבֵירוֹ וְהִגִּיעַ יוֹבֵל — שָׁמִין לוֹ. וְכִי תֵּימָא ה"נ שָׁמִין לוֹ בְּיַרְקָא וְסִילְקָא, סִילְקָא וְיַרְקָא בְּיוֹבֵל הֶפְקֵירָא הוּא! אֶלָּא לָאו — ^ח^שְׁבַח שִׁקְמָה! *תַּרְגְּמָא אַבַּיֵי אַלִּיבָּא דְּרָבָא: שָׁאנֵי הָתָם דְּאָמַר קְרָא: (ויקרא כה) °"וְיָצָא מִמְכַּר בַּיִת", מִמְכָּר — חוֹזֵר, ^ט^שְׁבָח — אֵינוֹ חוֹזֵר. וְנִגְמַר מִינֵּיהּ! הָתָם זְבִינֵי מְעַלְּיָא הוּא, *וְיוֹבֵל אַפְקַעְתָּא דְּמַלְכָּא הִיא. רַב פַּפָּא קַבֵּיל אַרְעָא לְאַסְפַּסְתָּא. קָדְחוּ בָּהּ תָּאלֵי. כִּי קָא מִסְתַּלֵּק אֲמַר לְהוּ: הֲבוּ לִי שְׁבָחָא! א"ל רַב שִׁישָׁא בְּרֵיהּ דְּרַב אִידִי לְרַב פַּפָּא: אֶלָּא מֵעַתָּה, דִּיקְלָא וְאַלִּים — ה"נ דְּבָעֵי מָר שְׁבָחֵיהּ? א"ל: הָתָם לָאו אַדַּעְתָּא דְּהָכִי נָחֵית, אֲנָא הָכָא אַדַּעֲתָא דְּהָכִי נָחֵיתְנָא. כְּמַאן? כְּאַבַּיֵי, דַּאֲמַר: בִּשְׁבַח שִׁקְמָה יֵשׁ לוֹ? אֲפִילּוּ תֵּימָא כְּרָבָא. הָתָם — לֵית לֵיהּ פְּסֵידָא, הָכָא — אִיכָּא פְּסֵידָא. א"ל: מַאי פְּסַדְתִּיךְ? יָדָא דְּאַסְפַּסְתָּא. ^י^שְׁקוֹל יָדָא דְּאַסְפַּסְתָּא וְזִיל! אָמַר לֵיהּ: אֲנָא כּוּרְכְּמָא רִישְׁקָא רַבַּאי. א"ל: גַּלֵּית אַדַּעְתָּךְ דְּלְמִשְׁקַל וְאִסְתַּלּוּקֵי עֲבַדְתְּ. (א) שְׁקַל כּוּרְכְּמָא רִישְׁקָא וְזִיל, אֵין לְךָ אֶלָּא דְּמֵי עֵצִים בִּלְבָד. רַב בֵּיבָי בַּר אַבַּיֵי קַבֵּיל אַרְעָא וְאַהֲדַר לֵיהּ מְשׁוּנִיתָא. קָדְחוּ בֵּיהּ זַרְדְּתָא. כִּי קָא מִיסְתַּלֵּק אֲמַר לְהוּ: הֲבוּ לִי שְׁבָחַאי. *אֲמַר רַב פַּפִּי: מִשּׁוּם דְּאָתִיתוּ מִמּוּלָאֵי אָמְרִיתוּ מִילֵּי מוּלְיָיתָא? אֲפִילּוּ רַב פַּפָּא לָא אֲמַר אֶלָּא דְּאִית לֵיהּ פְּסֵידָא. ^כ^הָכָא — מַאי פְּסֵידָא אִית לָךְ?§ רַב יוֹסֵף הֲוָה לֵיהּ הַהוּא שַׁתָּלָא. שְׁכֵיב וּשְׁבַק חֲמִשָּׁה חַתְנָוָתָא. אֲמַר: עַד הָאִידָּנָא — חַד, הַשְׁתָּא — חֲמִשָּׁה. עַד הָאִידָּנָא לָא הֲווּ סָמְכוּ אַהֲדָדֵי וְלָא מַפְסְדוּ לִי. הַשְׁתָּא חֲמִשָּׁה, סָמְכוּ אַהֲדָדֵי וּמַפְסְדוּ לִי. אֲמַר לְהוּ: אִי שָׁקְלִיתוּ שְׁבָחַיְיכוּ וּמִסְתַּלְּקִיתוּ — מוּטָב; וְאִי לָא — מְסַלֵּיקְנָא לְכוּ בְּלָא שְׁבָחָא. דַּאֲמַר רַב יְהוּדָה, וְאִיתֵימָא רַב הוּנָא, וְאִיתֵימָא ר"נ: הַאי שַׁתָּלָא דְּשָׁכֵיב — יוֹרְשִׁים דִּילֵיהּ מִסְתַּלְּקִין לְהוּ בְּלָא שְׁבָחָא. ^ל^וְלָאו מִילְּתָא הִיא. הַהוּא שַׁתָּלָא דַּאֲמַר לְהוּ: אִי מַפְסַדִינָא (ב) מְסַלַּקְנָא. אַפְסִיד. אֲמַר רַב יְהוּדָה: מִסְתַּלֵּק בְּלָא שְׁבָחָא. רַב כָּהֲנָא אֲמַר: מִסְתַּלֵּק וְשָׁקֵיל שְׁבָחָא. וּמוֹדֶה רַב כָּהֲנָא דְּאִי אֲמַר אִי פָּסֵידְנָא מִסְתַּלַּקְנָא בְּלָא שְׁבָחָא — מִסְתַּלֵּק בְּלָא שְׁבָחָא. רָבָא אֲמַר: ^מ^אַסְמַכְתָּא הִיא, *וְאַסְמַכְתָּא לָא קַנְיָא. וּלְרָבָא, מַאי שְׁנָא מֵהָא *דִּתְנַן: אִם אוֹבִיר וְלָא אַעֲבִיד אֲשַׁלֵּם בְּמֵיטְבָא? הָתָם מַאי דְּאַפְסִיד מְשַׁלֵּם. הָכָא — ^נ^מַאי דְּאַפְסִיד מְנַכִּינַן לֵיהּ, וְאִידָךְ יָהֲבִינַן לֵיהּ. רוּנְיָא שַׁתָּלָא דְּרָבִינָא הֲוָה. אַפְסִיד, סַלְּקֵיהּ. אֲתָא לְקַמֵּיהּ דְּרָבָא, א"ל: חֲזֵי מָר מַאי קָא עָבֵיד לִי! א"ל: שַׁפִּיר עָבֵיד. א"ל: הָא לָא הִתְרָה בִּי! א"ל: לָא צְרִיכָא לְהַתְרוֹת. רָבָא לְטַעְמֵיהּ, *דַּאֲמַר רָבָא: ^ס^מַקְרֵי דַרְדְּקֵי, שַׁתָּלָא, טַבָּחָא, וְאוּמָּנָא, וְסַפָּר

תורה אור: ויקרא כה

רש"י

מתני' לשנים מועטות. פחות מז' שנים. **לא יזרענה פשתן.** שזרע פשתן מכחיש בארץ הרבה, ואינה חוזרת ליושנה עד ז' שנים. והא לא מיתוקמא אלא בחכירות, דאי בקבלנות — מאי דבעי ליזרע, שהרי הבעלים חולקין בו. **ואין לו בקורות שקמה.** עץ סרק הוא, וקוצצין ענפיו לקורות הבנין, והן חוזרין וגדילין, (ג) ופחות מז' שנים אין נעשות קורות. הלכך, קיבלה לפחות מז' שנים — לא יקוץ קורות שבה, דלאו אדעתא דקורות נחית, דבשנים מועטות אינם חוזרים לקורות. אבל קיבלה לז' שנים — שנה ראשונה זורעה פשתן, וקוצץ שנה ראשונה שקמה שבה. **גמ'** שבח שקמה יש לו. עשו והשביחו — שמין לו שבחם לכשיסתלק. **לצמיתות אמר רחמנא.** מי שאילולי יובל היתה נלמטת, דכתיב (ויקרא כה): "והארץ לא תמכר לצמיתות". **ונגמר מיניה.** (ד) דמקבל. **התם זביני מעליא הוא.** וכל כמה דאשבחא ארעא — ברשותיה אשבחא, וארעא דהדרא, משום דיובל אפקעתא דמלכא הוא, ומאי דלא פקע מלכא — לא מפקע. ממכר — אפקע, שבחא — לא פקע. **קדחי בה תאלי.** צמחו בה אילנות. **דיקלא ואלים.** קיבל הימנו אילן לפירותיו כך וכך שנים, ונתעבה והגבירו עיקרו ה"נ וכו'. **לאו אדעתא דהכי נחת.** אלא לאכילת פירות. הכא — אדעתא דהכי נחת לכל אשר יצמח בה. **התם לית ליה פסידא.** כל מה שהשביח שקמה, לא מנע ממנו חרישה וזריעה. **ידא דאספסתא.** מקום הדקלין היה זורע אספסתא. ידא כמו (במדבר ב) "איש על ידו". **אנא כורכמא רישקא רבאי.** אני הייתי מגדל במקומן כרכום שדמיו יקרין. **א"ל.** מדקאמרת: כורכמא רישקא רבאי, שהוא דבר הנקצר בכל שנה, ולא אמרת: אנא תאלי הייתי נוטע בה למישקל שבחייהו — גלית אדעתך, דלא נחתת להא ארעא אדעתא למיעבד בה מידי דבר קיימא, למישם ליה שבחיה ומפיק, אלא מידי דתיעקריה ותישקליה ותיזיל. כי מסתלקת — שקול כורכמך רישקך, אותו כורכמא רישקא, דהיינו תאלי שקיימו בה — עקור אותו ולך. וכשתבא לעקור, אינו אלא עצים, וזה יתן לך דמי עצים. **אהדר ליה משוניתא.** הגביהו סביב גבוליה כעין שן הר. **קדחי ביה זרדתא.** בההיא משוניתא, צמחו בה אילנות של עוזרדין, קורמיי"ר בלע"ז. **ממולאי.** *מבית עלי שהיה ממשפחה רעועה. **אמריתו מילי מולייתא.** דברים גנונים. לשון מוליא במוליא במו"ק (דף י:): גבשושית. **אפילו רב פפא.** דבעי שכר שבחא דתאלי. **דאית ליה פסידא.** שצמחו במקום הראוי לזריעה. **הכא מאי פסידא איכא.** במשוניתא אין דרך לזרוע. **שתלא.** נוטע כרם בקרקע בעל הבית, ועליו להיות אריס כל הימים. ונוטל מחצה בפירות. **אפסיד.** מאי דאשבח כבר. מיהו, אכתי הוה שבחא, ומיסתלקנא דקאמר — בלא שבחא קאמר. **ורב כהנא אמר וכו'.** ה"ק: אי מפסידנא מסתלקנא על כרחי, ושקילנא מאי דאשבחי. **לא קניא.** ואפילו *אמרת הכי — לא מסלקינן ליה בלא שבחא. **מאי דאפסיד מנכינן ליה.** שיימינן מאי דמטי לבעל הבית בהפסד, ומנכינן ליה מחלקו דשתלא בשבח. **אומנא.** *מוהל תינוקות. במותרין ועומדין דמי. לסלקינהו. **מקרי דרדקי.** פסידא דלא הדר הוא, דשבשתא כיון דעל — על.

אמר

תוספות

אלא מעתה דיקלא ואלים ה"נ. דבעי מר שבחא באלימות הדקל?! הא ודאי אפילו לאביי לית ליה. דדוקא בשבח שקמה, דליכא פרי אלא שבח דגידול ענפים — קאמר אביי דיש לו, דאדעתייהו נחת, אבל אדעתא דאלימות הדקל לא נחת. ה"נ מר לא נחת אדעתא דתאלי, אלא אדעתא דאספסתא. א"ל: התם — ודאי לאו אדעתא דהכי נחת, כדקאמרת, אבל אנא (ה) נחתינא למה שילמיח הקרקע, דהיינו אספסתא, ולא למחו במקומה.

כמאן כאביי. דאילו לרבא דאמר בשבח שקמה אין לו, אע"ג דאיכא למימר דאדעתא דהכי נחית. ומשני: דאפילו תימא כרבא, דהתם כו'. **אין** לך אלא דמי עצים בלבד. [א] ואע"ג דבסוף פרק "השואל" (לעיל דף קא. ושם) אמר דמצי למימר זיתי אני נוטל, אי לאו משום ישוב א"י — הכא לא מצי אמר ליה, [ב] דמיירי דהני תאלי לא היו ראוים לנוטעם במקום אחר, ואם היה נוטלם היו מתים, ולא היו שוים אלא לעצים. א"נ, מדלא א"ל תאלי הוה נטענא, אלא כורכמא דרישקא, שמשעוקרין אותן אין נוטעין אותן במקום אחר — גלית אדעתיך שלא היית חושש בדבר שראוי לנוטען, ולכך אין לך אלא דמי עצים, [ג] וכגון שהתאלי לא היו מכחישין אותו יותר מאספסתא וכורכמא דרישקא, שאם לא כן לא יכול לומר: תאלי הוה נטענא — שהרי לאספסתא קבלה.

וספר

עין משפט נר מצוה

פב א ב מיי' פ"ח מהלכות שכירות הלכה ג יוד טוש"ע ח"מ סי' שכה:
פג ג מיי' שם טור ח"מ שם:
פד ד ה ו מיי' שם סמג שם טוש"ע ח"מ סי' שכז סעיף א:
פה ז ח ט מיי' פי"א מהלכות שמיטה הלכה ח סמג לאוין ערה:
פו י כ מיי' פ"ח מהל' שכירות הלכה י סמג עשין פט טוש"ע ח"מ סי' שכה:
פז ל טוש"ע ח"מ סי' שכט:
פח מ נ מיי' פ"י מהל' שכירות הלכה ו סמג שם טוש"ע ח"מ סי' של סעיף ב:
פט ס מיי' פ"י מהלכות שכירות הלכה ז ועיין בהשגות ובמגיד משנה סמג עשין פח טוש"ע ח"מ סי' שו סעיף ח:

הגהות הגר"א

[א] תום' ד"ה אין לך ואע"ג וכו'. נ"ב ואף דאמר שם בהיורד לשדה כו' לחד לישנא משום כחשא דארעא וקי"ל כהאי לישנא. תוס' אזלי לשיטתייהו שכתבו למטה וכגון שהתאלי כו' אבל הטור ס"ל דבאמת שמכחישין כמ"ש למטה לכן כתב שנוטל דמי נטיעות העומדין ליטע וכמ"ש תוס' שם בד"ה ואם אמר כו': [ב] שם דמיירי כו'. נ"ב וכ"פ הטור וכ"ה אבל הרמב"ם וש"ע השמיטו וכתירוץ השני של תוס': [ג] שם וכגון כו'. נ"ב אבל הטור השמיטו דס"ל לעובדא דכאן הוא במקבל ועי' רש"י ק"ו ע"ב במתני' ד"ה לא יזרענה כו' ולהרמב"ן שם דאוסר בכל ענין במקבל א"כ לגילוי דעתו דלמשקל ואסתלוקי כו' ולכן השמיט הרמב"ם לפי שכתב הדין אצל מקבל על המתני' דכאן ולא כדעת רש"י דמתני' כאן ד"ה לא יזרענה פשתן כו' ורש"י ז"ל לשיטתו כנ"ל ועמ"ש רבינו בח"מ סי' שכה ס"ק ז).

מסורת הש"ס

[שבת נב: וש"נ]
[לעיל לט. קו.]
יבמות עה: כתובות פה. ב"ב קלז: שם קנח. [ערובין כה:]
ובערוך פירש ממולאי שם מקום ואייתי ראיה מבראשי' רבה פכ"ט וע"ש
ב"ב כא:
ולעיל נז. פי' רש"י אומנא מקיז דם. רש"ל
[לעיל סו. וש"נ]
[לעיל קד.]
[ואפי' אמר הכי כנ"ל]

הגהות הב"ח

(א) גמ' שקול כורכמא: (ב) שם מפסדינא מסתלקנא אפסיד: (ג) רש"י ד"ה ואין לו וכו' ובפחות מז' שנים: (ד) ד"ה ונגמר מיניה למקבל: (ה) תום' ד"ה אלא וכו' אבל אנא הכא נחתינא:

*וְסַפָּר מָתָא — כּוּלָּן כְּמוּתָרִין וְעוֹמְדִין דָּמֵי. כְּלָלָא דְּמִילְּתָא: כָּל פְּסֵידָא דְּלָא הָדַר — כְּמוּתָרִין וְעוֹמְדִין דָּמֵי. הַהוּא שַׁתָּלָא דַּאֲמַר לְהוּ: הֲבוּ לִי שְׁבָחַאי, דְּבָעֵינָא לְמֵיסַק לְאַרְעָא דְּיִשְׂרָאֵל. אֲתָא לְקַמֵּיהּ דְּרַב פַּפָּא בַּר שְׁמוּאֵל. אֲמַר לְהוּ: הֲבוּ לֵיהּ שְׁבָחֵיהּ. א"ל רָבָא: אִיהוּ אַשְׁבַּח, אַרְעָא לָא אַשְׁבַּח? א"ל: אֲנָא פַּלְגָּא דִּשְׁבָחָא קָאָמִינָא לָךְ. א"ל: עַד הָאִידָּנָא הֲוָה שָׁקֵיל בַּעַל הַבַּיִת פַּלְגָּא וְשַׁתָּלָא פַּלְגָּא, הַשְׁתָּא בָּעֵי לְמֵיתַב מְנָתָא לַאֲרִיסָא! א"ל: רִיבְעָא דִּשְׁבָחָא קָאָמִינָא. סָבַר רַב אַשִׁי לְמֵימַר: [א]רִיבְעָא דְּהוּא דַּנְקָא, דַּאֲמַר רַב מַנְיוּמֵי בְּרֵיהּ דְּרַב נַחוּמִי: [ב]בְּאַתְרָא דְּשָׁקֵיל שַׁתָּלָא פַּלְגָּא וַאֲרִיסָא תִּילְתָּא, הַאי שַׁתָּלָא דְּבָעֵי לְאִסְתַּלּוּקֵי יָהֲבִינַן לֵיהּ שְׁבָחָא וּמְסַלְּקִינַן לֵיהּ, כִּי הֵיכִי דְּלָא נִמְטְיֵיהּ הֶפְסֵד לְבַעַל הַבַּיִת. אִי אָמְרַתְּ בִּשְׁלָמָא רִיבְעָא דְּהוּא דַּנְקָא — שַׁפִּיר. אֶלָּא אִי אָמְרַתְּ רִיבְעָא מַמָּשׁ — קָא מָטֵי לֵיהּ פְּסֵידָא לְבַעַל הַבַּיִת פַּלְגָּא דַּנְקָא! א"ל רַב אַחָא בְּרֵיהּ דְּרַב יוֹסֵף לְרַב אַשִׁי: וְלֵימָא לֵיהּ: אַנְתְּ מְנָתָא דִּילָךְ הַב לֵיהּ לַאֲרִיסָא, וַאֲנָא — מְנָתָא דִּילִי מַאי דְּבָעֵינָא עָבֵידְנָא בֵּיהּ! אֲמַר: כִּי מָטֵית לִשְׁחִיטַת קָדָשִׁים תָּא וְאַקְשִׁי לִי. •גּוּפָא, אֲמַר רַב מַנְיוּמֵי בְּרֵיהּ דְּרַב נַחוּמִי: בְּאַתְרָא דְּשָׁקֵיל שַׁתָּלָא פַּלְגָּא וַאֲרִיסָא תִּילְתָּא, הַאי שַׁתָּלָא דְּבָעֵי (א) אִיסְתַּלּוּקֵי — יָהֲבִינַן לֵיהּ שְׁבָחֵיהּ וּמְסַלְּקִינַן לֵיהּ, כִּי הֵיכִי דְּלָא לִיפְסוּד בַּעַל הַבַּיִת. אֲמַר רַב מַנְיוּמֵי בְּרֵיהּ דְּרַב נַחוּמִי: [ג]קוּפָא סָבָא — פַּלְגָּא; [ד]שָׁטְפָה נַהֲרָא — רִיבְעָא. *הַהוּא גַּבְרָא דְּמַשְׁכִּין פַּרְדֵּיסָא לְחַבְרֵיהּ לַעֲשַׂר שְׁנִין, וְקַשׁ לְחָמֵשׁ שְׁנִין. אַבַּיֵי אֲמַר: [ה]פֵּירָא הָוֵי. רָבָא אֲמַר: קַרְנָא הָוֵי, וְיִלָּקַח בּוֹ קַרְקַע וְהוּא אוֹכֵל פֵּירוֹת. מֵיתִיבִי: *[ו]יָבֵשׁ הָאִילָן אוֹ נִקְצָץ — שְׁנֵיהֶם אֲסוּרִים בּוֹ. כֵּיצַד יַעֲשׂוּ? יִמָּכְרוּ לְעֵצִים, וְיִלָּקַח בָּהֶן קַרְקַע, וְהוּא אוֹכֵל פֵּירוֹת. מַאי לָאו יָבֵשׁ דּוּמְיָא דְּנִקְצָץ? מָה נִקְצָץ — בִּזְמַנּוֹ, אַף יָבֵשׁ — בִּזְמַנּוֹ. וְקָתָנֵי: יִלָּקַח בָּהֶן קַרְקַע וְהוּא אוֹכֵל פֵּירוֹת. אַלְמָא: קַרְנָא הָוֵי! לָא, נִקְצָץ דּוּמְיָא דְּיָבֵשׁ. מָה יָבֵשׁ בְּלֹא זְמַנּוֹ — אַף נִקְצָץ בְּלֹא זְמַנּוֹ. ת"ש: *[ז]נָפְלוּ לָהּ גְּפָנִים וְזֵיתִים זְקֵנִים יִמָּכְרוּ

א"ל אֲנָא פַּלְגָּא בִּשְׁבָחָא קָאָמִינָא. כְּדֶרֶךְ שְׁאָר שַׁתָּלִים שֶׁאֵינָן מִסְתַּלְּקִין. הַשְׁתָּא קָבָעֵי לְמֵיתַב מְנָתָא לַאֲרִיסָא. כְּלוֹמַר: כֵּיוָן דְּמִיסְתַּלֵּק לוֹ בְּלֹא זְמַנּוֹ — אַמַּאי שָׁקֵיל פַּלְגָּא בִּשְׁבָחָא? עַד הָאִידָּנָא הֲוָה שָׁקֵיל בַּעַל הַבַּיִת פַּלְגָּא בַּפֵּירוֹת. וְזֶה הָיָה עוֹשֶׂה בָּהּ כָּל עֲבוֹדָתוֹ כְּמִשְׁפַּט אֲרִיסִין. הַשְׁתָּא קָבָעֵי לְמֵיתַב מְנָתָא לַאֲרִיסָא. עַכְשָׁיו זֶה יִטּוֹל כָּל הַמַּגִּיעַ לוֹ וְיֵלֵךְ, וְעַל בַּעַל הַבַּיִת לִיטּוֹל עֲבוֹדַת הַכֶּרֶם וְיִצְטָרֵךְ לִתְּנָהּ לַאֲרִיסָא. וְדֶרֶךְ אָרִיס שֶׁיּוֹרֵד לְכֶרֶם נָטוּעַ לִיטּוֹל שְׁלִישׁ בַּפֵּירוֹת, נִמְצָא בַּעַל הַבַּיִת מַפְסִיד שְׁלִישׁ מִמַּחֲלִיתוֹ בְּכָל שָׁנָה. רִיבְעָא דִּשְׁבָחָא. לְקַמָּן מְפָרֵשׁ וְאָזֵיל. סָבַר רַב אַשִׁי לְמֵימַר רִיבְעָא. דִּתְרֵי תִּילְתֵי הַמַּגִּיעִין לְבַעַל הַבַּיִת, מִשֶּׁתּוֹצִיא הַשְּׁלִישׁ שֶׁיִּצְטָרֵךְ לִיתֵּן לַאֲרִיס שֶׁיּוֹרֵד לָהּ, דְּהוּא דַּנְקָא בְּכָל שֶׁבַח הַכֶּרֶם. כְּגוֹן: אִם הַשֶּׁבַח שִׁשָּׁה דִינָרִים — יוֹצִיא מֵהֶן שְׁלִישׁ שֶׁעָתִיד לִיתֵּן לַאֲחֵרִים — נוֹתְרוּ ד' דִּינָרִים, מֵהֶן יִטּוֹל הַשַּׁתָּל דִּינָר. וְהַיְינוּ רִיבְעָא בְּמַאי דְּמָטָא לְבַעַל הַבַּיִת, דְּהוּא דַּנְקָא דִּשְׁבָחָא כּוּלֵּיהּ. דַּנְקָא. שְׁתוּת. דְּאָמַר רַב מַנְיוּמֵי בְּאַתְרָא דְּשָׁקֵיל שַׁתָּלָא פַּלְגָּא. בַּפֵּירוֹת, וְעוֹשֶׂה עֲבוֹדָה לְעוֹלָם. וַאֲרִיסָא תִּילְתָּא. אָרִיס הַיּוֹרֵד לְתוֹךְ הַכֶּרֶם גְּמוּרָה וְעוֹבְדָהּ — נוֹטֵל שְׁלִישׁ בַּפֵּירוֹת. הַאי שַׁתָּלָא דְּבָעֵי אִיסְתַּלּוּקֵי. שָׁיְימִינַן לֵיהּ כִּי הֵיכִי דְּלָא נַפְסִיד בַּעַל הַבַּיִת. כְּלוֹמַר: מְעַיְּינִין בְּמִילְּתָא, לְמֵיתַב לֵיהּ כִּי הֵיכִי דְּלָא נִמְטְיֵיהּ פְּסֵידָא לְבַעַל הַבַּיִת בְּסִילּוּק שֶׁל זֶה. אִי אָמְרַתְּ בִּשְׁלָמָא דַּנְקָא. שָׁקֵיל שַׁתָּלָא — שַׁפִּיר. דְּכִי הָדַר שָׁקֵיל אֲרִיסֵיהּ תִּילְתָּא — הֲרֵי ג' דִּינָרִין בֵּין שְׁנֵיהֶן, פָּשׁ לֵיהּ פַּלְגָּא דְּבַעַל הַבַּיִת כְּדַהֲוָה שָׁקַל עַד הַשְׁתָּא. אֶלָּא אִי אָמְרַתְּ רִיבְעָא מַמָּשׁ. דִּינָר וָחֵצִי, וְהָאָרִיס יִטּוֹל שְׁלִישׁ שֶׁהֵן ב' דִּינָרִין. פְּסֵידָא לְבעה"ב. חֲצִי דִּינָר מִמַּחֲלִיתוֹ. וְלֵימָא לֵיהּ. שַׁתָּלָא: אַנְתְּ מְנָתָא דִּידָךְ הַב לֵיהּ לַאֲרִיסָא שֶׁיִּטְרַח בּוֹ בַּחֲצִי שֶׁלְּךָ — שֶׁהָיָה מוּטָּל עָלַי לַעֲשׂוֹת וְאַתָּה אוֹכֵל פֵּירוֹת — הַב לֵיהּ לַאֲרִיסָא וְעָלַי לְנַכּוֹת מֵחֶלְקִי כְּפִי הַמַּגִּיעַ לוֹ. וְהַיְינוּ רִיבְעָא מַמָּשׁ. דִּינָר וָחֵצִי, כֵּיצַד? טוֹל אַתָּה שְׁלֹשָׁה רִבְעֵי הַכֶּרֶם לְחֶלְקְךָ, מֵהֶן תִּתֵּן הַשְּׁלִישׁ לַאֲחֵרִים — נִמְצֵאתָ אוֹכֵל כָּל הַשָּׁנָה חֲצִי פֵּירוֹת הַכֶּרֶם בְּלֹא יְגִיעָה. מְנָתָא דִּידִי מַאי דְּבָעֵינָא עָבֵידְנָא בֵּיהּ. אֲנִי אֶמְכּוֹר לַאֲחֵרִים הָרְבִיעַ הַמַּגִּיעַ לְיָדִי. וְלֹא שַׁיָּיךְ גַּבָּאי לְמֵיתַן מְנָתָא לַאֲרִיסָא, דְּהָא מְזַבְּנִינָא וּמִסְתַּלְּקְנָא, הַקּוֹנֶה יֵרֵד וְיַעֲשֶׂה וְיֹאכַל. וְאִם בָּאתָ לְקָנוֹתוֹ הֲרֵי אֵין עָלַי לַעֲשׂוֹת לְךָ וְתֹאכַל אֶת פֵּירוֹתַי בְּחִנָּם?! אִם תִּתְּנֵהוּ לַאֲחֵרִים — לִישְׁקוֹל מִינֵּיהּ וּבֵיהּ שָׁוֶה חֲצִי דִּינָר, וְהַדִּינָר יִשָּׁאֵר לְךָ. וְהַיְינוּ תְּרֵי תִּילְתֵי, שֶׁהֲרֵי עַכְשָׁיו אַתָּה קוֹנֶה מִמֶּנִּי, וּלְעוֹלָם רִיבְעָא מַמָּשׁ קָאָמַר רַב פַּפָּא. (*וְאֵין בַּעַל הַבַּיִת מַפְסִיד כְּלוּם, שֶׁעַד עַתָּה הָיָה אוֹכֵל חֲצִי הַפֵּירוֹת, וּמֵעַתָּה אוֹכֵל ב' שְׁלִישִׁים, דְּהַיְינוּ ד' דִּינָרִים). כִּי מָטֵית לִשְׁחִיטַת קָדָשִׁים. הִכַּרְתִּי בָּךְ שֶׁאַתָּה חָדוּד וְיוֹדֵעַ לְהַעֲמִיק וּלְהַקְשׁוֹת. וְכִי מָטֵית לְמַסֶּכֶת זְבָחִים, שֶׁהִיא עֲמוּקָּה — תָּא אַקְשֵׁי לִי, וְאֶתֵּן לֵב לְתָרֵץ לְפִי שְׁאֵלָתְךָ. וְיֵשׁ אוֹמְרִים: דְּחוּיֵי מִדְּחֲיָא, וְלָא הִיא, דְּעַל כָּרְחָיךְ קַבּוּלֵי קִיבְּלָהּ. חֲדָא דְּקוּשְׁיָא מַעַלְיָא הִיא. וְעוֹד, מִדְּקָאָמַר: קָסָבַר רַב אַשִׁי לְמֵימַר — מִכְּלָל דְּמַסְקָנָא לָאו הָכִי הוּא. קוּפָא סָבָא פַּלְגָּא. גֶּפֶן שֶׁהִזְקִינָה בַּכֶּרֶם — הֲרֵי הוּא כִּשְׁאָר זְמוֹרוֹת שֶׁחוֹלְקִין בָּהֶם, וְנוֹטֵל בָּהּ שַׁתָּלָא פַּלְגָּא כִּשְׁאָר פֵּירוֹת. דְּכֵיוָן דְּאוֹרְחֵיהּ בְּהָכִי — אַדַּעְתָּא דְּהָכִי נָחַת. שָׁטְפָה נָהָר. וּבָאוּ לְחַלֵּק הָעֵצִים — הֲוָה לֵיהּ כִּי שַׁתָּלָא דְּמִיסְתַּלֵּק בְּלָא זִמְנֵיהּ, וְשָׁקֵיל רִיבְעָא. שְׁטָפָהּ נַהֲרָא — פְּעָמִים שֶׁעוֹקְרִין לְגַמְרֵי, וּפְעָמִים שֶׁשּׁוֹטֵף אֶת הַקַּרְקַע וּמַכְחִישׁוֹ, וְאֵין רָאוּי לְנְמוֹתַ בּוֹ כְּלוּם עַד זְמַן מְרוּבֶּה. הַהוּא גַּבְרָא דְּמַשְׁכִּין פַּרְדֵּיסָא לְחַבְרֵיהּ. מַשְׁכֵּן לוֹ כֶּרֶם בְּמַשְׁכַּנְתָּא דְסוּרָא, א"נ בְּנַכְיָיתָא. וְקַשׁ. הִזְקִין, וּבִזְמַנּוֹ שֶׁהָיָה רָאוּי לְכָךְ. פֵּירָא הָוֵי. עֵצִים שֶׁבּוֹ, וְיִטּוֹל הַמַּלְוֶה. יָבֵשׁ הָאִילָן. בְּמַשְׁכַּנְתָּא קָאֵי. מָה נִקְצָץ בִּזְמַנּוֹ. שֶׁאֵין אָדָם קוֹצֵץ אִילָן שֶׁעוֹשֶׂה פֵּירוֹת אֶלָּא בִּזְמַנּוֹ, שֶׁחָדַל לוֹ מֵעֲשׂוֹת פְּרִי. בְּלֹא זְמַנּוֹ. וּמוֹדֶה אַבַּיֵי בְּלֹא זְמַנּוֹ, שֶׁחָדַל לַעֲשׂוֹת פְּרִי, דְּכֵיוָן דְּלָאו אוֹרְחֵיהּ — לָאו פֵּירָא הוּא, וְלָאו אַדַּעְתָּא דְּהָכִי נָחַת. נָפְלוּ לָהּ. לְאִשָּׁה, מִשֶּׁנִּיסֵּת. מֵת אָבִיהָ וְנָפְלוּ לָהּ בִּירוּשָּׁה. יִמָּכְרוּ

וספר מתא כמותרין ועומדין. פי' בקונטרס: משום דשבשתא כיון דעל על, לכך חשיב פסידא דלא הדר. וליתא, דרבא גופיה אית ליה בפ' "לא יחפור" (ב"ב דף כא. ושם) דשבשתא ממילא נפקא. אלא להכי קרי ליה הכא פסידא דלא הדר — לפי שבאותה שעה שלימדו שיבושים נתבטל לו לימוד של אמת.

(לעיל) מסלקינן להו בלא שבחא ולאו מילתא היא. פי' ריב"ן: שלא אמר דבר זה מעולם, אלא להפחידו אמר כן. ותימה: דאם לא אמר מעולם, למה הזכיר כל כך אמוראים, רב הונא ואיתימא רב יהודה ואיתימא כו'? וי"ל: דרב יוסף לא הזכיר אלא אחד מהם, ובני בית המדרש נסתפקו בין אלו איזה מהן הזכיר. רבא אמר קרנא הוי. וא"ת: והא קופא סבא פלגא, ודוחק לומר דפליג רבא אדרב מניומי! וי"ל: דקופא סבא פלגא משום דשתלא שקיל אפילו בגוף הקרקע פלגא, וכי מסתלק בלא זמניה — הוא דשקיל ריבעא, משום דעליו לשלם אפילו מה שהבעל יצטרך ליתן לאריס שימשור חלקו שהיה מוטל על השתלא לשמור. וכן שטפה נהרא ריבעא — דאדעתא דהכי נחית, שאם יסתלק בלא זימניה, באיזה ענין שיסתלק, שלא יקח אלא ריבעא. ובקופא סבא, שאין עוד מה לשמור — שקיל פלגא. אבל הכא — המלוה אין לו בגוף כלום, אלא בפירות.

מה נקצץ בזמנו. דאין דרך לקצוץ שלא בזמנו ולהפסיד פירות. ועוד, דאמרינן בפרק "לא יחפור" (ב"ב דף כו.): האי דיקלא דטעון קבא אסור למיקציה. ואית דגרסי איפכא יבש בזמנו, ואין נראה לר"י. לא מה יבש שלא בזמנו. יבש משמע שלא בזמנו, מדלא קתני "הזקין". ואע"ג ד"הזקין" נמי משמע שלא בזמנו, כדאמרינן בסמוך: אימא והזקינו — הזקינו משמע בין בזמנו בין שלא בזמנו, אבל יבש לא משמע אלא שלא בזמנו.

אף נקצץ שלא בזמנו. וא"ת: ואמאי איצטריך למימר: אף נקצץ שלא בזמנו, והא מעיקרא לא פריך אלא מיבש דהוה דומיא דנקצץ. אבל מנקצץ בזמנו לא פריך, משום דאיכא למימר דנקצץ בזמנו — היינו לאחר שיבש שלא בזמנו. והשתא דשני ליה מיבש תו לא קשיא ליה לאביי?! וי"ל: דמעיקרא נמי קשיא ליה מנקצץ, דנקצץ משמע סתמא אחר שיבש בזמנו כמו שדרכו. והא דקאמר: מה נקצץ בזמנו אף יבש בזמנו — משום שרוצה להקשות משניהם. אי נמי, לא איצטריך — אלא לאפוקי דלא נידוק איפכא, נקצץ דומיא דיבש, כדמשני בתר הכי.

נפלו לה זיתים זקנים ימכרו וילקח בהן קרקע ובעל אוכל פירות. אבל לא יקצוץ עצים, אלמא, קרנא הוי, וקשה לאביי דאמר: עצים — פרי הוי, במקום שאין פרי אחר. ותימה דמאי פריך? דהתם ע"כ מיירי שעושין קצת פירות, מדפליג התם *רבי יהודה ואמר: לא תמכור מפני שבח בית אביה. ומוקי ליה התם — בשדה שאינה שלה, ואי ליכא פירות כלל — מה שבח בית אביה יש? הלא בעל השדה לא יניחם לעמוד שם יותר אחר שנתייבשו, והבעל יקוץ אותם לעצים?! וכן משמע נמי מעיקרא, דבעי לאוקמי פלוגתייהו בנפלו לה זיתים בשדה שלה — ופליגי, אבל בשדה שאינה שלה — דברי הכל ימכרם. ופריך: והא עבדים ושפחות זקנים, דהוי כנפלו בשדה שאינה שלה. ופליגי! והנהו עבדים ושפחות — ע"כ. כשעושין

[מקרי דרדקי כמותרין ועומדין כצ"ל]

[וע"ע תוס' ב"ב כא. ד"ה בספר מתא]

צ א ב מיי' פ"י מהל' שכירות הלכה ו טור ש"ע ח"מ סי' של סעיף ג:

צא ג ד טוש"ע שם סעיף ד:

צב ה ו מיי' פ"ז מהל' שכירות הלכה ה [רב אלפס כאן ועוד בפ"ז דף קיג.]:

צג ז מיי' פכ"ב מהל' אישות הלכה כג וחזר מפירושו שסם פסק כתנא קמא סמג עשין עת טוש"ע אה"ע סי' פה סעיף יד:

הגהות הב"ח

(א) גמ' שתלא דבעי לאיסתלוקי:

גליון הש"ס

גמ' גופא א"ר מניומי בשיטה מקובצת כ' בשם הרא"ש אע"פ שלא חידש בה דבר קאמר גופא משום דבעי מימר בה וכה"ג איתא בהגוזל קמא דף קי ע"א.

[עי' פרש"י ותוס' ב"ב כח:]

[ע' כתובות נה:]

לעיל עט.

כתובות עט:

ר"מ מ"ז ועי' רש"ל ות"ח

ס"א רשב"ג

– יִמָּכְרוּ לְעֵצִים וְיִלָּקַח בָּהֶן קַרְקַע, וְהוּא אוֹכֵל פֵּירוֹת! אֵימָא: וְהִזְקִינוּ. וְאִיבָּעֵית אֵימָא: לָאו מִי אוֹקִימְנָא לְהַהִיא אכְּגוֹן שֶׁנָּפְלוּ לָהּ בְּשָׂדֶה אַחֶרֶת, דְּקָא כַּלְיָא קַרְנָא.§ הַהוּא שְׁטָרָא דַּהֲוָה כְּתִיב בֵּיהּ שְׁנִין סְתָמָא. מַלְוֶה אָמַר: שָׁלֹשׁ, לֹוֶה אָמַר: שְׁתַּיִם. (א) קַדֵּים מַלְוֶה וְאָכְלִינְהוּ לְפֵירֵי. מִי נֶאֱמָן? רַב יְהוּדָה אָמַר: קַרְקַע בְּחֶזְקַת בְּעָלֶיהָ קַיְימָא. רַב כָּהֲנָא אָמַר: בפֵּירוֹת בְּחֶזְקַת אוֹכְלֵיהֶן קַיְימֵי. וְהִלְכְתָא כְּוָותֵיהּ דְּרַב כָּהֲנָא, דְּאָמַר: פֵּירוֹת בְּחֶזְקַת אוֹכְלֵיהֶן (*קַיְימֵי.) וְהָא קי"ל *דְּהִלְכְתָא כְּוָותֵיהּ דְּרַב נַחְמָן, *דְּאָמַר: קַרְקַע בְּחֶזְקַת בְּעָלֶיהָ עוֹמֶדֶת! הָתָם מִילְּתָא דְּלָא עֲבִידָא לְאִיגַּלּוּיֵי הִיא; הָכָא – מִילְּתָא דַּעֲבִידָא לְאִיגַּלּוּיֵי הִיא, וְאַטְרוּחֵי בֵּי דִינָא תְּרֵי זִמְנֵי לָא מַטְרְחִינַן. מַלְוֶה אוֹמֵר חָמֵשׁ, לֹוֶה אוֹמֵר שָׁלֹשׁ. א"ל: אַיְיתִי לִי שְׁטָרָךְ! א"ל: שְׁטָרָא אִירְכַס לִי. אָמַר רַב יְהוּדָה: גמַלְוֶה נֶאֱמָן, מִגּוֹ דְּאִי בָּעֵי אָמַר לְקוּחָה הִיא בְּיָדִי. א"ל רַב פָּפָּא לְרַב אָשֵׁי: רַב זְבִיד וְרַב עֲוִירָא לָא סְבִירָא לְהוּ הָא דְּרַב יְהוּדָה. מַאי טַעְמָא? הַאי שְׁטָרָא כֵּיוָן דִּלְגוּבַיְינָא קָאֵי – מִיזְהַר זָהִיר בֵּיהּ, וּמִיכְבַּשׁ הוּא דִּכְבַשֵׁיהּ לִשְׁטָרֵיהּ. סָבַר: אוֹכְלָהּ תַּרְתֵּין שְׁנִין יְתֵירָתָא. א"ל רָבִינָא לְרַב אָשֵׁי: אֶלָּא מֵעַתָּה, *הַאי מַשְׁכַּנְתָּא דְּסוּרָא דְּכָתְבִי הָכִי: בְּמִישְׁלַם שְׁנַיָּא אִלֵּין תֵּיפּוֹק אַרְעָא דָא בְּלָא כְּסַף – הֵיכָא דִּכְבַשֵׁיהּ לִשְׁטַר מַשְׁכַּנְתָּא וְאָמַר לְקוּחָה הִיא בְּיָדִי, הָכִי נַמִי דִּמְהֵימַן? וְכִי מְתַקְּנֵי רַבָּנַן מִילְּתָא דְּאָתֵי בָּהּ [לִידֵי] פְּסֵידָא? א"ל: הָתָם תַּקִּינוּ לֵיהּ רַבָּנַן דְּמָרֵי אַרְעָא יָהֵיב טַסְקָא וְכָרֵי כַּרְיָא. אַרְעָא דְּלֵית לַהּ כַּרְיָא וְלָא יָהֵיב טַסְקָא מַאי? א"ל: דאִיבָּעֵי לֵיהּ לְמִחוּיֵי. לָא אִימְחָא מַאי? אִיהוּ הוּא דְּאַפְסֵיד אַנַּפְשֵׁיהּ. אָרִיס אוֹמֵר: לְמֶחֱצָה יָרַדְתִּי, וּבַעַל הַבַּיִת אוֹמֵר: לִשְׁלִישׁ הוֹרַדְתִּיו, מִי נֶאֱמָן? רַב יְהוּדָה אָמַר: בַּעַל הַבַּיִת נֶאֱמָן. רַב נַחְמָן אָמַר: ההַכֹּל כְּמִנְהַג הַמְּדִינָה. סְבוּר מִינַּהּ: לָא פְּלִיגֵי; הָא – בְּאַתְרָא דְּשָׁקֵיל אֲרִיסָא פַּלְגָא, הָא – בְּאַתְרָא דְּשָׁקֵיל אֲרִיסָא תִּילְתָּא. אָמַר לְהוּ רַב מָרִי בְּרַהּ דְּבַת שְׁמוּאֵל: הָכִי אָמַר אַבָּיֵי: אֲפִילּוּ בְּאַתְרָא דְּשָׁקֵיל אֲרִיסָא פַּלְגָא פְּלִיגִי. רַב יְהוּדָה אָמַר: בַּעַל הַבַּיִת נֶאֱמָן, דְּאִי בָּעֵי אָמַר שְׂכִירֵי וְלַקִּיטֵי הוּא.§ *יְתוֹמִים אוֹמְרִים: אָנוּ הִשְׁבַּחְנוּ, וּבַעַל חוֹב אוֹמֵר: אֲבִיכֶם הִשְׁבִּיחַ – עַל מִי לְהָבִיא רְאָיָה? סָבַר

רש"ל ואמר

יִמָּכְרוּ וכו'. אַלְמָא קַרְנָא הָוֵי. דְּאִי פֵּירָא הֲוָה – הָא תַּקִּין רַבָּנַן פֵּירוֹת לַבַּעַל. וְהִזְקִינוּ. קְפָלָה עֲלֵיהֶן זִקְנָה בְּלֹא זְמַנָּן. לָאו מִי אוֹקִימְנָא. בִּכְתוּבּוֹת, בְּפֶרֶק "הָאִשָּׁה שֶׁנָּפְלוּ לָהּ נְכָסִים" (דף עט:). בְּשָׂדֶה אַחֶרֶת. שֶׁלֹּא הָיְתָה הַקַּרְקַע שֶׁלָּהּ, שֶׁהָיוּ דְּקָלִים בְּשָׂדֶה שֶׁל אֲחֵרִים. דְּהָא כַּלְיָא קַרְנָא דִּידָהּ לְגַמְרֵי, אִי אָמְרַתְּ (ב) לִישְׁקְלִינְהוּ בַּעַל לְכוּלְּהוּ. הַהוּא שְׁטָרָא. שְׁטַר מַשְׁכַּנְתָּא דְּסוּרָא "בְּמִישְׁלַם שְׁנַיָּא אִלֵּין", וְלֹא פֵּירֵשׁ בּוֹ מִנְיַן הַשָּׁנִים. הָכִי גָּרְסִינַן: וְקַדֵּים מַלְוֶה וְאָכְלִינְהוּ לְפֵירֵי. דְּשָׁנָה שְׁלִישִׁית, מִקַּמֵּי דְּנִתְבְּעֵיהּ לְדִינָא. קַרְקַע בְּחֶזְקַת בְּעָלֶיהָ עוֹמֶדֶת. אע"ג דְּלָא תִּבְעֵיהּ עַד לְאַחַר אֲכִילַת פֵּירוֹת – אֲנַן בָּתַר קַרְקַע אָזְלִינַן, וְכִי מְסַפְּקָא לָן שָׁנָה זוֹ שֶׁל מִי – אוֹקֵי אַרְעָא בְּחֶזְקַת מָרֵיהּ, וְשֶׁלֹּא כַּדִּין אֲכָלִינְהוּ לְפֵירֵי. בְּחֶזְקַת אוֹכְלֵיהֶן עוֹמְדוֹת. כֵּיוָן דְּקַדֵּים וְאַכְלִינְהוּ, וְאַתָּה לְאַפּוֹקֵי מִינֵּיהּ – נַיְיתֵי רְאָיָה דְּלֹא שָׁלֹשׁ הָוֵי, דְּבָתַר אֲכִילַת פֵּירוֹת אָזְלִינַן. וְהָא קי"ל הִלְכְתָא כְּרַב נַחְמָן בְּדִינֵי. וְרַב נַחְמָן – קַרְקַע בְּחֶזְקַת בְּעָלֶיהָ עוֹמֶדֶת קָאָמַר, גַּבֵּי שׂוֹכֵר מֶרְחָץ מִשְּׁנֵים עָשָׂר זְהוּבִים לְשָׁנָה, מִדִּינָר זָהָב לְחֹדֶשׁ. בְּ"הַשּׁוֹאֵל" (לעיל דף קב:). וַאֲפִילּוּ בָּא בְּסוֹף הַחֹדֶשׁ, אָמַר כּוּלּוֹ לַמַּשְׂכִּיר, כְּשֶׁנִּתְעַבְּרָה הַשָּׁנָה. הָנֵי מִילֵּי מִילְּתָא דְּלָא עֲבִידָא לְאִיגַּלּוּיֵי. כְּלוֹמַר: בָּתַר קַרְקַע דַּוְקָא אִית לָן לְמֵיזַל. וּמִיהוּ, הָנֵי מִילֵּי בְּסָפֵק שֶׁאֵין עוֹמֵד לְעוֹלָם לְהִתְבָּרֵר, כִּי הַהוּא, דְּמִסְתַּפְקָא לָן בֵּין אִם תּוֹפְסִים לָשׁוֹן רִאשׁוֹן וְאִי תּוֹפְסִים לָשׁוֹן אַחֲרוֹן. אֲבָל הָכָא מִילְּתָא עֲבִידָא לְאִיגַּלּוּיֵי. בַּסּוֹף, שֶׁיָּבֹאוּ עֵדֵי שְׁטָר וְיָעִידוּ. וְאַטְרוּחֵי בֵּי דִינָא תְּרֵי זִמְנֵי. שֶׁמָּא הַדִּין עִם הַמַּלְוֶה. וְאִם תּוֹצִיאֶנּוּ מִיָּדוֹ – עֲתִידִין אָנוּ לַחֲזוֹר וּלְגוֹבוֹתוֹ מִיַּד הַלֹּוֶה לְאַחַר זְמַן. מַלְוֶה אוֹמֵר חָמֵשׁ וכו'. מִילְּתָא אַחֲרִיתִי הִיא, מַלְוֶה וְלֹוֶה שֶׁבָּאוּ לַדִּין, מַלְוֶה אוֹמֵר: חָמֵשׁ שָׁנִים מוּשְׁכֶּנֶת לִי וְאֵין הַשְּׁטָר לְפָנֵינוּ. וְלֹוֶה אוֹמֵר: לְשָׁלֹשׁ, וּכְבָר אָכַלְתָּ שָׁלֹשׁ. מִגּוֹ דְּאִי בָּעֵי אָמַר לְקוּחָה הִיא בְּיָדִי. לְעוֹלָם, וַאֲכָלָהּ שְׁנֵי חֲזָקָה, וְאָבַד הַשְּׁטָר מִמֶּנִּי. לָא סְבִירָא לְהוּ הָא דְּאָמַר רַב יְהוּדָה. וְלָא אָמְרִינַן מִגּוֹ, שֶׁהַדְּבָרִים מוֹכִיחִין שֶׁהוּא רַמַּאי, שֶׁאָמַר אָבַד הַשְּׁטָר. וְהַאי שְׁטָרָא לָא דָּמֵי לִשְׁטַר זְבִינֵי, דְּאִילּוּ שְׁטַר זְבִינֵי – לְעֵדוּת שֶׁמְּכָרָהּ לוֹ הוּא בָּא, וְכִי עַד עוֹלָם תֹּאמַר לוֹ לְהִזָּהֵר בּוֹ? אָמוּר רַבָּנַן בֵּיהּ: עַד תְּלָת שְׁנִין – מֵהָנֵי לְאִיזְדַּהוֹרֵי אִינָשׁ בִּשְׁטָרָא, טְפֵי – לָא מִיזְדַּהַר. דְּקָסָבַר: לֹא יֵצֵא עוֹד עִרְעוּר עָלֶיהָ. אֲבָל זֶה שֶׁהוּא מוֹדֶה שֶׁשְּׁטַר מַשְׁכַּנְתָּא הוּא, לְרָאיַית מִנְיַן שָׁנִים שֶׁל אֲכִילַת פֵּירוֹת – לְגוּבַיְינָא דַּאֲכִילַת פֵּירוֹת דְּמִנְיַן הַשָּׁנִים קָאֵי, וּמִיזְדַּהֵר זָהִיר בֵּיהּ, דְּלָא לֵירְכַּס לֵיהּ עַד כְּלוֹת הַשָּׁנִים. וְהַאי דְּקָאָמַר: אִירְכַּס – לָא מְהֵימַן, דְּמִיכְבָּשׁ הוּא דִּכְבָשֵׁיהּ וכו'. אֶלָּא מֵעַתָּה. אַלִּיבָּא דְּרַב יְהוּדָה קָפָרֵיךְ, דְּקָאָמַר: אִי בָּעֵי אָמַר לְקוּחָה הִיא בְּיָדִי. הָכִי נַמִי דִּמְהֵימַן. וְכִי עָבְדִי רַבָּנַן מִילְּתָא דְּאָתֵי בָּהּ לִידֵי רַמָּאוּת, כִּי הַאי?! תַּקּוּן רַבָּנַן לְמָרֵי אַרְעָא דְּיָהֵיב טַסְקָא. לְמַלְכָּא. וְכָרֵי כַּרְיָא. מְתַקֵּן חֲפִירַת סְבִיבוֹת הַגְּבוּלִים. וְאִי אַרְעָא קַנְיָא הוּא. דְּלֵית לֵיהּ טַסְקָא, וְכַרְיָא נַמִי לֵית לֵיהּ, מַאי לֵיעֲבֵיד? לְמִחוּיֵי. הֱווּ יוֹדְעִים שֶׁלֹּא מְכַרְתִּיהָ לוֹ, אֶלָּא הִיא מַשְׁכּוֹן בְּיָדוֹ. הָכִי גָּרְסִינַן: הָא בְּאַתְרָא דְּשָׁקֵיל אֲרִיסָא פַּלְגָא הָא בְּאַתְרָא דְּשָׁקֵיל אֲרִיסָא תִּילְתָּא. וְלָא גָּרְסִינַן "שַׁפַּלְגָּא" בְּכוּלֵּי מִילְּתָא. שְׂכִירֵי. לְיָמִים, אוֹ לַחֳדָשִׁים וְלַשָּׁנוֹת. וּשְׂכַרְתִּיו בְּמָעוֹת – וְלָךְ נֶאֱמָן דְּקָאָמַר: בִּשְׁבוּעַת הֶיסֵּת הוּא. אָנוּ הִשְׁבַּחְנוּ. וְאֵין לְבַעַל חוֹב בַּמֶּה שֶׁהִשְׁבִּיחוּ יְתוֹמִים כְּלוּם. סָפֵק

כשעושין קלת מלאכה, דאי לאו הכי – מה מכירה שייך בהס. דמי יקנהו? וה"נ מיירי דאיכא בזיתים קלת פירי, ולכך הוו קרנא אפילו לאביי. ולפי שאין עושין אלא פירות מועטין, ילקח בהן קרקע ויאכל פירות, וזה טובת שניהס. אבל בשמעתין, דליכא פרי, אז העלים מיקרו פרי לאביי. וי"ל: דמ"מ מוכח שפיר דקרנא הוי, אפילו כשיבש לגמרי. ולהכי קאמר תנא קמא: ילקח בהן קרקע, אפילו מעתה שעושין קלת פירות, לטובתו של בעל. ופליג *ארשב"ג דאמר: לא תמכור משוס שבח בית אביה, ולא חיישינן לטובת הבעל, כל זמן שעושין קלת פירות. עד שתייבש לגמרי, ואז ילקח בהן קרקע. אבל לאביי דאמר פרי הוי, וכשייבש לגמרי נוטל בעל הכל – אס כן אין זה טובת הכל מה שלוקח בהן קרקע ואוכל פירות משלו, כי טוב לו יותר להמתין מעט, עד שתייבש לגמרי, ויהא הכל שלו. א"ל רבינא לרב אשי – משכנתא דסורא, אס אמר: לקוחה היא בידי – ה"נ דנאמן כו'. אלא ודאי לא מהימן. הקשה הרב רבינו אלחנן: דהא תנן (ב"ב דף כח.): חזקת הבתים כו' חזקתן ג' שנים. ואומר ר"י: דהתם בטוען שמחזיק בה בגזל – הויא חזקה, שהיה לו למחות תוך שלש כי יודע בודאי, כיון שנכנס לה בגזל – אם ישתוק לו ג' שנים ולא ימחה – שיטעון על ידי ג' שנים שיהיה שלו. ולכך היה לו למחות, שיודע לכל שתקנו חכמים למחות תוך שלש, ואס לא מיחה – הפסיד. אבל כשמשכנתא באה לידו סובר המקשה כי לא תקנו חכמים – אין לחוש שאחר ג' יטעון שקר. וא"ת: אס כן, לעולם יהיה בעל הקרקע נאמן לומר שבגזל הוא בא, מגו דאי בעי אמר במשכנתא היה אצלך או לפירות הורדתיך. וי"ל: דהוי מגו במקום עדים, דאנן סהדי: אס היה בא בגזל – לא היה שתיק, אלא היה מוחה. אי נמי, אין זה מגו – שאין טוען ברצון משכנתא היה, או לפירות הורדתיך, לפי שסבור להוליא גם הפירות שכבר אכל. אי נמי, חשיב מגו להוליא, כיון שאכלה שני חזקה. וקשה: דטעמא דבשלש שנים הויא חזקה – משום דעד שלש שנים מיזדהר איניש בשטריה, טפי לא מיזדהר, והשתא הלא ע"כ לריך לשמור לעולס, כי שמא יטעון זה משכנתא היא!? וע"כ נראה, דלא בעי למימר שלא יהא נאמן – [לומר]: לקוחה היא בידי, אלא שואל מה תקנה יעשה הממשכן, שלא יוכל להחזיק ולטעון לקוחה היא בידי? דמחאה נראה דלא מהניא, אלא כשאומר: "פלניא אכיל ארעאי בגזלנותא". ומשני רב אשי: דאיבעי ליה למחויי ולומר תוך שלשה: דעו כי משכנתא היא בידו. דמחאה שפיר מהניא בכי האי גוונא, וכי האי גוונא יש לפרש בפ' "חזקת הבתים" (שם דף לה: ושם) גבי "ואי טעין ואמר לפירות הורדתיך – נאמן". ואף על גב דהתם רב אשי פריך לרב כהנא: ואי לפירות אחתיה – מאי הוה ליה למיעבד? ורב כהנא משני: דאיבעי ליה למחויי, ומייתי ראיה ממשכנתא דסורא, ובשמעתין רב אשי משני: איבעי ליה למחויי, וכן משני רב אשי התם, בההוא פירקא (דף לה.) גבי ההוא מאן דזבין דקלא לחבריה. איכא למימר דרב אשי התם קיבל שינויא מרב כהנא, ולהכי משני ליה איהו נמי הכי. האי משכנתא דסורא כו'. אע"ג דהאי גופא דהכא, אפשר דמשכנתא דסורא הוי – שייך שפיר לאקשויי בהאי לישנא, לפי שמשכנתא דסורא הוה קים ליה שתקנו חכמים לעשות. ולהכי קאמר: אלא מעתה תקנת משכנתא דסורא וכו'.

בס"י לא גרסי' לי' ועי' בס' כ"י [כתובות יג. קידושין נט:]

לעיל סז: ב"ב לה: [לח.]

[עי' תוס' לעיל עו. ד"ה בעל חוב ותוס' כתובות נב. ד"ה ולשבח ועוד שם תוס' נו: ד"ה נכסי ותוס' כתובות נב. ד"ה והאמר]

צד א מיי' פכ"ב מהל' אישות הל' כג סמג עשין מח טוש"ע אה"ע סי' פה סעיף יד:

צה ב מיי' פ"ז מהלכות שכירות הלכה ו סמג עשין פט טור ש"ע ח"מ סי' קנ סעיף ז וסי' שח סעיף ג:

נ"א אר"י

צו ג מיי' שם סמג שם טוש"ע ח"מ סי' קנ שם וסי' שח סעיף ל:

צז ד טוש"ע שם סי' קנ סעיף ח:

צח ה מיי' פ"ח מהל' שלוחין ושותפין הל' ה סמג עשין קנג טוש"ע ח"מ סי' של סעיף ה:

לעיל קב:

הגהות הב"ח

(א) גמ' וקדים מלוה:
(ב) רש"י ד"ה בשדה וכו' דלישקלינהו:

עין משפט
נר מצוה

צט א מיי' פכ"א מהל' מלוה ולוה הלכה ז סמג עשין עג טוש"ע ח"מ סי' קטו סעיף ה:
ק ב מיי' פ"י מהלכות שכנים הלכה א ועיין שם סמג עשין פב טוש"ע ח"מ סי' קנה סעיף כב בהג"ה:
קא ג מיי' פכ"א מהל' מלוה ולוה הל' ז סמג עשין עג טוש"ע ח"מ סי' קטו סעיף ו:
קב ד מיי' פ"ג מהלכות נחלות הלכה ד סמג עשין צו טוש"ע ח"מ סי' רעח סעיף ו:
קג ה מיי' פכ"א מהל' מלוה ולוה הלכה ז ועיין שם במ"מ סמג עשין צד טוש"ע ח"מ סי' קטו סעיף ו:
קד ו מיי' שם הלכה ה טוש"ע שם סעיף א וסעיף ב:
קה ז מיי' פ"ח מהלכות שכירות הלכה ג:
קו ח ט מיי' שם פי"א הלכה ב סמג לאוין קפא טוש"ע ח"מ סי' שלט סעיף ג:
קז י מיי' שם טוש"ע שם סעיף ד:
קח כ מיי' שם טוש"ע שם סעיף ה:
קט ל מ מיי' שם הל' ה טוש"ע שם סעיף ח:
קי נ מיי' שם הלכה ד טוש"ע שם סעיף ז:

סָבַר רַבִּי חֲנִינָא לְמֵימַר: אַרְעָא בְּחֶזְקַת יַתְמֵי קַיְימָא, וְעַל בַּעַל חוֹב לְהָבִיא רְאָיָה. אֲמַר לְהוּ הַהוּא סָבָא, הָכִי א"ר יוֹחָנָן: *[א]עַל הַיְתוֹמִים לְהָבִיא רְאָיָה. מַאי טַעְמָא? אַרְעָא, כֵּיוָן דִּלְגוּבַיְינָא קַיְימָא, כְּמַאן דְּגַבְיָא דָּמְיָא, וְעַל הַיְתוֹמִין לְהָבִיא רְאָיָה. אָמַר אַבַּיֵי: אַף אֲנַן נַמִּי תְּנֵינָא: *[ב]סָפֵק זֶה קָדַם וְסָפֵק זֶה קָדַם – קוֹצֵץ וְאֵינוֹ נוֹתֵן דָּמִים. אַלְמָא: כֵּיוָן דִּלְמֵיקַץ קַיְימָא – אָמְרִינַן לֵיהּ: אַיְיתִי רְאָיָה וּשְׁקוֹל. הָכָא נַמִּי, הַאי שְׁטָרָא כֵּיוָן דִּלְגוּבַיְינָא קַיְימָא – כְּמַאן דְּגַבְיָא דָּמְיָא, וְעַל הַיְתוֹמִים לְהָבִיא רְאָיָה. אַיְיתוּ יַתְמֵי רְאָיָה דְּאִינְהוּ אַשְׁבְּחוּ. סָבַר רַבִּי חֲנִינָא לְמֵימַר: כִּי מְסַלְּקִינַן לְהוּ בְּאַרְעָא מְסַלְּקִינַן לְהוּ. [ג]וְלָא הִיא, בְּדָמֵי מְסַלְּקִינַן לְהוּ, מִדְּרַב נַחְמָן. *דְּאָמַר רַב נַחְמָן אָמַר שְׁמוּאֵל: שְׁלֹשָׁה שָׁמִין לָהֶם אֶת הַשֶּׁבַח, וּמַעֲלִין אוֹתָן בְּדָמִים, וְאֵלּוּ הֵן: [ד]בְּכוֹר לַפָּשׁוּט [ה]וּבַעַל חוֹב וּכְתוּבַּת אִשָּׁה לַיְתוֹמִים, [ו]וּבַעַל חוֹב לַלָּקוֹחוֹת. א"ל רָבִינָא לְרַב אַשִׁי: לְמֵימְרָא דְּסָבַר שְׁמוּאֵל בַּעַל חוֹב לַלָּקוֹחוֹת? (א) וּמִי אִית לֵיהּ שְׁבָחָא לַלּוֹקֵחַ? *וְהָאָמַר שְׁמוּאֵל: בַּעַל חוֹב גּוֹבֶה אֶת הַשֶּׁבַח! וְכִי תֵּימָא: לָא קַשְׁיָא, כָּאן בְּשֶׁבַח הַמַּגִּיעַ לִכְתֵפַיִם; כָּאן בְּשֶׁבַח שֶׁאֵין מַגִּיעַ לִכְתֵפַיִם – וְהָא *מַעֲשִׂים בְּכָל יוֹם, וְקָא מַגְבֵּי שְׁמוּאֵל אֲפִי' בְּשֶׁבַח הַמַּגִּיעַ לִכְתֵפַיִם! לָא קַשְׁיָא; הָא – דְּמַסֵּיק בֵּיהּ כְּשִׁיעוּר אַרְעָא וּשְׁבָחָא; הָא – דְּלָא מַסֵּיק בֵּיהּ שִׁיעוּר אַרְעָא וּשְׁבָחָא. וְכִי לָא מַסֵּיק שִׁיעוּר אַרְעָא וּשְׁבָחָא – דְּיָהֵיב לֵיהּ זוּזֵי לַלּוֹקֵחַ וּמְסַלֵּק לֵיהּ. הָנִיחָא לְמ"ד *אִי אִית [לֵיהּ] זוּזֵי לַלּוֹקֵחַ – לָא מָצֵי מְסַלֵּק לֵיהּ לְבַעַל חוֹב – שַׁפִּיר. אֶלָּא לְמ"ד אִית לֵיהּ זוּזֵי לַלּוֹקֵחַ מָצֵי מְסַלֵּק לֵיהּ לְבַעַל חוֹב, וְנֵימָא לֵיהּ: אִי הֲווּ לִי זוּזֵי – הֲוָה מְסַלֵּיקְנָא לָךְ מִכּוּלָּא אַרְעָא. הַשְׁתָּא דְּלֵית לִי זוּזֵי – הַב לִי גְּרִיוָא דְּאַרְעָא בְּאַרְעַאי שִׁיעוּר שְׁבָחַאי! הָכָא בְּמַאי עָסְקִינַן – כְּגוֹן דְּשַׁוְיָא נִיהֲלֵיהּ אַפּוֹתֵיקִי, דְּא"ל: לֹא יְהֵא לְךָ פֵּרָעוֹן אֶלָּא מִזּוֹ.§ **מתני'** [ז]הַמְקַבֵּל שָׂדֶה מֵחֲבֵירוֹ לְשָׁבוּעַ אֶחָד בְּשֶׁבַע מֵאוֹת זוּז – הַשְּׁבִיעִית מִן הַמִּנְיָן. קִבְּלָהּ הֵימֶנּוּ שֶׁבַע שָׁנִים בְּשֶׁבַע מֵאוֹת זוּז – אֵין הַשְּׁבִיעִית מִן הַמִּנְיָן. [ח]שְׂכִיר יוֹם גּוֹבֶה כָּל הַלַּיְלָה, [ט]שְׂכִיר לַיְלָה גּוֹבֶה כָּל הַיּוֹם. [י]שְׂכִיר שָׁעוֹת גּוֹבֶה כָּל הַלַּיְלָה וְכָל הַיּוֹם. [כ]שְׂכִיר שַׁבָּת, שְׂכִיר חֹדֶשׁ, שְׂכִיר שָׁנָה, שְׂכִיר שָׁבוּעַ – יָצָא בַּיּוֹם, גּוֹבֶה כָּל הַיּוֹם; יָצָא בַּלַּיְלָה – גּוֹבֶה כָּל הַלַּיְלָה וְכָל הַיּוֹם.§ **גמ'** ת"ר: מִנַּיִן לִשְׂכִיר יוֹם שֶׁגּוֹבֶה כָּל הַלַּיְלָה? ת"ל: °"לֹא תָלִין פְּעוּלַּת שָׂכִיר אִתְּךָ עַד בֹּקֶר". וּמִנַּיִן לִשְׂכִיר לַיְלָה שֶׁגּוֹבֶה כָּל הַיּוֹם? שֶׁנֶּאֱמַר: °"בְּיוֹמוֹ תִתֵּן שְׂכָרוֹ". וְאֵימָא אִיפְּכָא! *שְׂכִירוּת אֵינָהּ מִשְׁתַּלֶּמֶת אֶלָּא בַּסּוֹף. ת"ר: מִמַּשְׁמַע שֶׁנֶּאֱמַר: "לֹא תָלִין פְּעוּלַּת שָׂכִיר אִתְּךָ" אֵינִי יוֹדֵעַ שֶׁ"עַד בֹּקֶר"? מַה ת"ל "עַד בֹּקֶר"? – [ל]מְלַמֵּד שֶׁאֵינוֹ עוֹבֵר אֶלָּא עַד בֹּקֶר רִאשׁוֹן בִּלְבַד. מִכָּאן וְאֵילָךְ מַאי? אָמַר רַב: [מ]עוֹבֵר מִשּׁוּם בַּל תַּשְׁהֶא. אָמַר רַב יוֹסֵף: מַאי קְרָאָה? °"אַל תֹּאמַר לְרֵעֲךָ לֵךְ וָשׁוּב וּמָחָר אֶתֵּן וְיֵשׁ אִתָּךְ". ת"ר: [נ]הָאוֹמֵר לַחֲבֵירוֹ צֵא שְׂכוֹר לִי פּוֹעֲלִים – שְׁנֵיהֶן אֵין עוֹבְרִין מִשּׁוּם בַּל תָּלִין, זֶה – לְפִי שֶׁלֹּא שְׂכָרָן, וְזֶה

ויקרא יט
דברים כד
משלי ג

סבר ר' חנינא למימר בארעא מסלקינן להו. תימה: כיון דטעמא דעל היתומין להביא ראיה – משום שהקרקע בחזקת בעל חוב, והיינו כשעשה אפותיקי, כדמסיק, א"כ הוה ליה כיורד לתוך שדה חבירו ונטעה שלא ברשות, דפשיטא דלא שקיל מגוף הקרקע את השבח?! וי"ל: דכיון שהיה הקרקע בחזקת אביהם תחלה, ועדיין לא יצאת מרשותן – עדיפי מיורד לתוך שדה חבירו ונטעה שלא ברשות. א"נ, ביורד לתוך שדה חבירו – נמי היה סבור דמסלקינן ליה בארעא.

יצא בלילה גובה כל הלילה וכל היום. וכן ברישא בשכיר שעות דלילה, אע"פ שילא ממלאכתו ועוד לילה – גובה כל היום, ואינו עובר ב"בל תלין" בעמוד השחר, ד"לינה" – משמע כל הלילה, וזה השכירות לא לן כל הלילה. וא"ת: "לא ילין" ד"חלב חגי" (שמות כג) – הוא בעמוד השחר גרידא, שאם העלה אימורים על גבי המזבח בתחילת הלילה והורידן לפני עמוד השחר – נפסלין בלינה, כדאמרינן בזבחים (דף פו.)! וי"ל: מפני שהן ראוין להקריב בתחילת הלילה – קרינא ביה לינה אפילו בעמוד השחר, ודוחק. ועוד: דבפרק שני דזבחים (דף כ:) משמע גבי קידוש ידים ורגלים ומי כיור, דעמוד השחר פוסל בלינה, אפילו לא התחיל לינה אלא לאחר תחילת הלילה.

אמר

ספק. בְּבָבָא בַּתְרָא (דף כד:) בְּאִילָן הַנָּטוּעַ בְּתוֹךְ חֲמִשִּׁים אַמָּה סָמוּךְ לָעִיר, וְקָתָנֵי הָתָם: אִם הָעִיר קָדְמָה – קוֹצֵץ וְאֵינוֹ נוֹתֵן דָּמִים, סָפֵק זֶה קָדַם סָפֵק זֶה קָדַם – קוֹצֵץ וְאֵינוֹ נוֹתֵן דָּמִים. אַלְמָא, כֵּיוָן דְּבֵין הָכִי וּבֵין הָכִי לְמִקְצַץ קָאֵי, דְּכִי קָדַם אִילָן נַמִּי קָתָנֵי: קוֹצֵץ, כִּי מִסַּפְּקָא לָן – אָמְרִינַן: קוֹץ מִמַּה נַּפְשָׁךְ, שֶׁהֲרֵי עָלֶיךָ לַעֲשׂוֹת. נִמְצָא הַסָּפֵק מוּטָּל עַל הַדָּמִים וְלֹא עַל קְצִיצַת הָאִילָן, דְּאִילּוּ גַּבֵּי אִילָן הַסָּמוּךְ לְבוֹר שֶׁל יָחִיד, קָתָנֵי בָּהּ, גַּבֵּי וַדַּאי דִּידֵיהּ: אִם הַבּוֹר קָדְמָה – קוֹצֵץ וְנוֹתֵן דָּמִים, אִם הָאִילָן קָדַם – לֹא יָקוֹץ. תְּנַן גַּבֵּי סָפֵק זֶה קָדַם וְסָפֵק זֶה קָדַם – לֹא יָקוֹץ. אַלְמָא, גַּבֵּי סָפֵק אִילָן דְּעִיר, טַעְמָא – מִשּׁוּם דְּמִמַּה נַּפְשָׁךְ עוֹמֵד לִקְצִיצָה. וְהָכָא נַמִּי, בֵּין יְתוֹמִים הִשְׁבִּיחוּ וּבֵין אֲבִיהֶן הִשְׁבִּיחַ – דִּינוֹ לִיטּוֹל קַרְקַע עִם הַשֶּׁבַח. וְאִם הַיְתוֹמִים הִשְׁבִּיחוּ – מַעֲלֶה לָהֶן הַשֶּׁבַח בְּדָמִים, כִּדְלְקַמֵּיהּ. הִלְכָּךְ גַּבֵּי אַרְעָא עִם הַשֶּׁבַח מִמַּה נַּפְשָׁךְ, נִמְצָא הַיְתוֹמִים תּוֹבְעִין לְהוֹצִיא מִמֶּנּוּ, וַעֲלֵיהֶן הָרְאָיָה. בְּאַרְעָא מְסַלְּקִינַן לְהוּ. יָהֲבִינַן לְהוּ גְּרִיוָא דְּאַרְעָא, שִׁיעוּר שְׁבַחַיְיהוּ. וּמַעֲלִין אוֹתָן. מִן הַקַּרְקַע. בְּדָמִים. וְלָא שָׁקְלִי בְּאַרְעָא גּוּפֵיהּ. בְּכוֹר לַפָּשׁוּט. בְּכוֹר וּפָשׁוּט שֶׁהִשְׁבִּיחוּ קַרְקַע קוֹדֶם שֶׁחָלְקוּ. וְקַיְ"ל (ב"ב דף קכד.) שֶׁאֵין הַבְּכוֹר נוֹטֵל פִּי שְׁנַיִם בַּשֶּׁבַח שֶׁהִשְׁבִּיחוּ נְכָסִים לְאַחַר מִיתַת אֲבִיהֶן, דַּהֲוָה לֵיהּ "רָאוּי", וְאֵין הַבְּכוֹר נוֹטֵל הַבְּכוֹרָה בָּרָאוּי, דִּכְתִיב: "בְּכֹל אֲשֶׁר יִמָּצֵא לוֹ". וּכְשֶׁהֵן בָּאִין לַחֲלוֹק – נוֹטֵל בְּכוֹר פִּי שְׁנַיִם בַּקַּרְקַע שֶׁהִיא מְשׁוּבַּחַת, וְשָׁמִין אֶת הַשֶּׁבַח, וְנוֹתֵן לַפָּשׁוּט רְבִיעַ שֶׁהוּא מַגִּיעַ לוֹ בַּשֶּׁבַח שֶׁבְּתוֹךְ חֶלְקוֹ שֶׁל זֶה. וְכֵן בַּעַל חוֹב לִיתוֹמִין. וְכֵן בַּעַל חוֹב שֶׁקָּדַם שְׁטַר הַלְוָאָתוֹ לִשְׁטַר מִקָּח שֶׁל לָקוֹחוֹת – טוֹרְפָהּ מֵהֶן עִם מַה שֶּׁהִשְׁבִּיחוּ, וְשָׁם לָהֶן שֶׁבַח, וְנוֹתֵן דָּמִים. וְטַעְמָא דְּכוּלְּהוּ: מִשּׁוּם דְּמֵעִיקָּרָא אַרְעָא דִּידֵיהּ הוּא, וְאֵין לָנוּ לְכוֹפוֹ לִמְכּוֹר לָהֶן קַרְקַע שֶׁלּוֹ בִּשְׁבִיל הַשֶּׁבַח, אִם יֵשׁ בְּיָדוֹ מָעוֹת. וּלְקַמָּן מוֹקֵי לָהּ בְּקַרְקַע שֶׁנַּעֲשֵׂית לוֹ אַפּוֹתֵיקִי. הַמַּגִּיעַ לִכְתֵפַיִם. צְרִיכִין לַקַּרְקַע דָּבָר מוּעָט. דְּאִילּוּ אֵין צְרִיכִין לַקַּרְקַע – הָווּ לְהוּ פֵּירוֹת, וְלָא מִיקְרוּ שֶׁבַח. וּבַעַל חוֹב גּוֹבֶה הַשֶּׁבַח קָאָמַר, וְלֹא פֵּירוֹת גְּמוּרִין כִּדְאָמְרִינַן בְּפ"ק. הָנִיחָא לְמ"ד. פְּלוּגְתָּא בְּמַסֶּכֶת כְּתוּבּוֹת (*בְּ"הַכּוֹתֵב"). אִי אִית לֵיהּ זוּזֵי לַלּוֹקֵחַ. שִׁיעוּר דְּמֵי הַחוֹב. שַׁפִּיר. אִיכָּא לְמֵימַר דְּאַרְעָא מֵעִיקָּרָא דִּידֵיהּ הֲוַאי, וְהוּא דְּנָחַת לָהּ שֶׁלֹּא בִּרְשׁוּת – שָׁקֵיל שְׁבָחָא בְּזוּזֵי וְלֹא בְּאַרְעָא, הוֹאִיל וַהֲוָה מַסֵּיק בֵּיהּ שִׁיעוּר אַרְעָא כּוּלָּהּ. **מתני'** שְׂכִיר יוֹם גּוֹבֶה כָּל הַלַּיְלָה. שָׂכִיר שֶׁפְּעוּלָּתוֹ לַיּוֹם וְיוֹצֵא לָעֶרֶב – גּוֹבֶה כָּל הַלַּיְלָה. כָּל הַלַּיְלָה הוּא זְמַן גְּבִיָּיתוֹ, בֵּין לְעִנְיַן שְׁבוּעָה שֶׁתִּקְּנוּ לוֹ חֲכָמִים: שָׂכִיר בִּזְמַנּוֹ הוּא נִשְׁבָּע וְנוֹטֵל, בֵּין לְעִנְיַן שֶׁאֵינוֹ עוֹבֵר עָלָיו מִשּׁוּם "לֹא תָבֹא עָלָיו הַשֶּׁמֶשׁ" (דברים כד) אֶלָּא מִשּׁוּם "לֹא תָלִין פְּעוּלַּת שָׂכִיר אִתְּךָ עַד בֹּקֶר" (ויקרא יט). שְׂכִיר לַיְלָה. שֶׁיּוֹצֵא מִמְּלַאכְתּוֹ בַּבּוֹקֶר. גּוֹבֶה כָּל הַיּוֹם. בֵּין לְעִנְיַן שְׁבוּעָה, וּבֵין לְעִנְיַן שֶׁאֵינוֹ עוֹבֵר עָלָיו מִשּׁוּם "בַּל תָּלִין" אֶלָּא מִשּׁוּם "לֹא תָבֹא עָלָיו הַשֶּׁמֶשׁ", וּבַגְּמָרָא יָלֵיף לָהּ. שְׂכִיר שָׁעוֹת. גּוֹבֶה כָּל הַיּוֹם וְכָל הַלַּיְלָה, אֲמוֹרָאֵי מְפָרְשִׁי לָהּ בַּגְּמָ'. שְׂכִיר שָׁבוּעַ. שְׁמִיטָּה. יָצָא בַּיּוֹם. שֶׁכָּלְתָה שְׂכִירוּתוֹ לַבּוֹקֶר אוֹ בַּיּוֹם. גּוֹבֶה כָּל הַיּוֹם. וְכֵיוָן שֶׁשָּׁקְעָה חַמָּה עוֹבֵר עָלָיו. יָצָא בַּלַּיְלָה. שֶׁכָּלְתָה שְׂכִירוּתוֹ בַּלַּיְלָה. גּוֹבֶה כָּל הַלַּיְלָה וְכָל הַיּוֹם. דְּכֵיוָן דִּמְשָׁכָה פְּעוּלָּתוֹ מִשֶּׁתֶּחְשַׁךְ, הֲוָה לֵיהּ שְׂכִיר לַיְלָה, וְאֵינוֹ עוֹבֵר עָלָיו בַּבּוֹקֶר, עַד לְמָחֳרַת בִּשְׁקִיעַת הַחַמָּה. **גמ'** אֵיפוּךְ אֲנָא. ד"לֹא תָלִין" – בִּשְׂכִיר לַיְלָה, "לֹא תָבֹא" – בִּשְׂכִיר יוֹם. שְׂכִירוּת אֵינָהּ מִשְׁתַּלֶּמֶת אֶלָּא בַּסּוֹף. כִּדְאָמַר בְּ"אֵיזֶהוּ נֶשֶׁךְ" (לעיל סה.): "כִּשְׂכִיר שָׁנָה בְּשָׁנָה" – שְׂכִירוּת שָׁנָה זוֹ מִשְׁתַּלֶּמֶת בִּתְחִילַּת שָׁנָה אַחֶרֶת, אַלְמָא לָא מִשְׁתַּעְבֵּד לֵיהּ לִשְׂכִיר יוֹם עַד שֶׁתִּשְׁקַע הַחַמָּה. וְכִי כְּתִיב "לֹא תָבֹא" – עַל כָּרְחָךְ בִּשְׂכִיר לַיְלָה תּוֹקְמֵיהּ, שֶׁנִּשְׁתַּעְבֵּד לוֹ לַבּוֹקֶר מִשֶּׁכָּלְתָה שְׂכִירוּתוֹ. וְכֵן "לֹא תָלִין" נַמִּי לֹא תּוֹקְמֵיהּ בִּשְׂכִיר לַיְלָה – דְּהָא לָא מִשְׁתַּעְבֵּד לֵיהּ עַד הַבּוֹקֶר. מִמַּשְׁמַע שֶׁנֶּאֱמַר וכו'. שֶׁאֵין "לִינָה" קְרוּיָה – אֶלָּא עַד הַבּוֹקֶר, דִּכְתִיב (שמות לד): "וְלֹא יָלִין לַבֹּקֶר", וְכָל לִינָה שֶׁבַּמִּקְרָא – לִינַת לַיְלָה הוּא. מַאי קְרָאָה. הֵיכָא רְמִיזָא "בַּל תַּשְׁהֶא"? זֶה לְפִי שֶׁלֹּא שְׂכָרוֹ. וְלָא קָרֵינָא "שָׂכִיר" גַּבֵּיהּ.

וְזֶה

מסורת הש"ס
[עי' תוס' סוטה כה: ד"ה ב"ה סברי]
ב"ב כד:
ב"ק לה:
שם ולעיל יד: טו. [בכורות נב.]
[סוכה מז. וש"נ]
[לעיל טו: ב"ק נז.]
[לעיל סה. וש"נ]
נ"ל בפ' מי שהיה נשוי דף נה: [ע"ש תוס' ד"ה מאי פסידא ותוס' ב"ק נז. ותוס' ב"מ לה. ד"ה הניחא]

הגהות הב"ח
(א) גמ' דסבר שמואל בע"ח ללקוחות יהיב שבחא ומי אית:

וזה לפי שאין פעולתו אצלו. היכי דמי? אי דאמר להו שכרכם עלי – שכרו עליו הוא, דתניא: *השוכר את הפועל לעשות בשלו והראהו בשל חבירו – נותן לו שכרו משלם, וחוזר ונוטל מבעל הבית מה שההנה אותו! [א]לא צריכא, דאמר להו: שכרכם על בעל הבית. יהודה בר מרימר א"ל לשמעיה: זיל אגיר לי פועלים, ואימא להו: שכרכם על בעל הבית. מרימר ומר זוטרא אגרי להדדי. אמר רבה בר רב הונא: [ב]הני שוקאי דסורא לא עברי משום בל תלין; מידע ידעי דעל יומא דשוקא סמכי, אבל משום בל תשהא ודאי עובר.§ "שכיר שעות גובה כל הלילה וכל היום".§ אמר רב: [ג]שכיר שעות דיום – גובה כל היום; שכיר שעות דלילה – גובה כל הלילה. ושמואל אמר: שכיר שעות דיום – גובה כל היום, ושכיר שעות דלילה – גובה כל הלילה וכל היום. תנן: שכיר שעות גובה כל הלילה וכל היום. תיובתא דרב! אמר לך רב: לצדדין קתני; שכיר שעות דיום – גובה כל היום, שכיר שעות דלילה – גובה כל הלילה. תנן: היה שכיר שבת, שכיר חדש, שכיר שנה, שכיר שבוע, יוצא ביום – גובה כל היום, יוצא בלילה – גובה כל הלילה וכל היום! אמר לך רב: תנאי היא; דתניא: שכיר שעות דיום – גובה כל היום; שכיר שעות דלילה – גובה כל הלילה, דברי ר' יהודה. ר"ש אומר: שכיר שעות דיום – גובה כל היום; שכיר שעות דלילה – גובה כל הלילה וכל היום. מכאן אמרו: [ד]כל הכובש שכר שכיר עובר בה' שמות (א) הללו, ועשה: משום °בל תעשוק את ריעך, ומשום °בל תגזול, ומשום °בל תעשוק שכיר עני, ומשום °בל תלין, ומשום °ביומו תתן שכרו, ומשום °לא תבא עליו השמש. הני דאיכא ביממא – ליכא בליליא, דאיכא בליליא – ליכא ביממא? אמר רב חסדא: שם שכירות בעלמא. [ה]איזה הוא עושק ואיזהו גזל? א"ר חסדא: °לך ושוב, לך ושוב – זה הוא עושק. יש לך בידי ואיני נותן לך – זה הוא גזל. מתקיף לה רב ששת: [ו]איזהו עושק שחייבה עליו תורה קרבן? דומיא דפקדון, דקא כפר ליה ממונא! אלא אמר רב ששת: נתתיו לך – זהו עושק; יש לך בידי ואיני נותן לך – זה הוא גזל. מתקיף לה אביי: [ז]איזה הוא גזל שחייבה עליו תורה קרבן? דומיא דפקדון בעינן, דקא כפר ליה ממונא! אלא אמר אביי: לא שכרתיך מעולם – זה הוא עושק; נתתיו לך – זה הוא גזל. ולרב ששת, מאי שנא עושק דקשיא ליה, ומאי שנא גזל דלא קשיא ליה? אמר לך: גזל – דגזליה והדר כפריה. אי הכי, אפילו עושק נמי דהדר כפריה! הכי השתא? בשלמא התם כתיב: °"או בגזל" – מכלל דאודי ליה מעיקרא. אבל גבי עושק מי כתיב: "או בעושק"? °"או עשק" כתיב – שעשקו כבר. רבא אמר: זה הוא עושק זהו גזל. ולמה חלקן הכתוב? לעבור עליו בשני לאוין.§

מתני' [ח]אחד שכר אדם ואחד שכר בהמה ואחד שכר כלים – יש בו משום °ביומו תתן שכרו, ויש בו משום לא תלין פעולת שכיר אתך עד בוקר. [ט]אימתי? בזמן שתבעו. [י]לא תבעו – אינו עובר עליו. [כ]המחהו אצל חנוני או אצל שולחני – אינו עובר עליו. *[ל]שכיר בזמנו – נשבע ונוטל. *עבר זמנו – אינו נשבע ונוטל. [מ]אם יש עדים שתבעו (בזמנו) – הרי זה נשבע ונוטל. [נ]גר תושב – יש בו משום ביומו תתן שכרו ואין בו משום לא תלין פעולת שכיר אתך עד בקר.§ **גמ'** מני מתני'? לא תנא קמא דמאחיך ולא רבי יוסי ברבי יהודה! מאי היא? דתניא: מאחיך

אמר ליה לשמעיה זיל אגיר לי פועלים. לא משום שהיה דעתו לדחות, אלא היה ירא שלא יהא פנוי ליתן להם, ואפילו משום "בל תשהא" לא היה עובר, כיון שהוא עסוק במלאכה אחרת.

מתקיף לה אביי איזהו גזל כו'. תימה: וכי לא ידע אביי דרב ששת מוקי לה באודי ליה והדר כפריה? וי"ל: דסבר אביי דאית לן לאוקמי גזל דומיא דעשק, וכי היכי דלא קאי "וכחש" אעושק – לא קאי נמי אגזל. אלא תחילת גזל דקרא ותחילת עושק הוא כיחש, ולא דייק כדדייק רב ששת בסמוך, דהכא כתיב "או בגזל" והכא כתיב "או עשק" בלא בי"ת.

או עשק כתיב. לא גרסינן שעשקו כבר. **ולמה** חלקן הכתוב לעבור עליו בשני לאוין. לאו משום דכתיב גזל ועשק, ששינה בלשון, דייק, אלא משום דכתיב תרי לאוין. תימה: בשלמא הכא חילקן כדי לעבור עליו בשני לאוין, אבל גבי אשם גזילות למה נכתבו שניהם – או בגזל או עשק?

וזה לפי שאין פעולתו עליו. ולא קרינא ביה פעולתו אתך. ואימא להו וכו'. דאי לא משתלימנא – לא עברנא. אגרי להדדי. כשהיה האחד צריך לפועלים – חבירו פוסק עמהן, ואמר להן: שכרכם על בעל הבית. הני שוקאי דסורא. בעלי בתים של סורא*, שאין מגיעין למעות עד יום השוק. לא עברי. על שכר פועלין. מידע ידעי דעל יומא דשוקא סמכי. להגיע למעות. הלכך, אפילו אית ליה מעות גביה – לא עבר, דאדעתא דהכי איתגר ליה וכיון דמיומא קמא לא עברי תו לא עברי כדאמרינן לעיל שאינו עובר עליו אלא בקר ראשון. אבל משום בל תשהא עובר. מיום השוק ואילך. שכיר שעות דיום. שנשכר לו מן הבקר עד חצות. גובה כל היום. דהא כלתה שכירתו מחצות, ואיכא ב"לא תבא". שכיר שעות דלילה גובה כל הלילה. ולכשיעלה עמוד השחר עובר משום "בל תלין" – דהא נשתעבד לו קודם לכן. ושמואל אמר שכיר שעות דיום הוא גובה כל היום. כדקאמרת, ואין לילה הולך אחר יום. אבל שכיר שעות דלילה גובה כל הלילה וכל היום, שהיום הולך אחר הלילה הואיל ושכירותו בליל יום זה. ולא דמי לשכיר יום דאתמול, שאינו גובה אלא כל הלילה. תנן שכיר שעות גובה כל הלילה וכל היום. בשלמא שמואל מוקי לה בשכירות שעות דלילה אלא רב במאי מוקי לה. לצדדין. והכי קאמר: שכיר שעות יש שגובה כל הלילה, ויש שגובה כל היום, וכדאמרי אנא. יצא בלילה וכו'. אלמא: הואיל ומשכה פעולתו בלילה – הוה ליה שכיר שעות דלילה, וקתני: גובה כל הלילה וכל היום. משום לא תגזול. דהא אוקמיה ב"איזהו נשך" (דף סא.) לכובש שכר שכיר. דאי גזל ממש – מלאו דריבית ואונאה נפקא. ה' שמות. חמשה לאוין: "לא תעשוק את רעך", ו"לא תגזול", ו"לא תלין", ו"לא תעשוק שכיר עני ואביון ביומו תתן שכרו", ו"לא תבוא עליו השמש", ועשה – "ביומו תתן". שם שכירות. כולהו בחד ודאי לא משכחת לה, אלא הכי קאמר: עבירות כל השמות הללו בשם שכירות הן, יש מהן בשכירות לילה ויש מהן בשכירות יום. גזל. משמע שאנסו בידו מידו ממש, טפי מעושק, דכתיב (שמואל ב כג) "ויגזול את החנית מיד המצרי" וכן (שופטים ט) בבעלי שכם "ויגזלו את כל אשר יעבור עליהם בדרך". מתקיף לה רב ששת. על כרחיך עושק דקא כפר ליה הוא, מדמחייביה עליו בתורת כהנים קרבן שבועה, דכתיב (ויקרא ה): "וכחש בעמיתו בפקדון או בתשומת יד וגו'".

אלא אמר רב ששת וכו'. לקמן פריך: לרב ששת, מאי שנא עושק דקשיא ליה, ומ"ש גזל דלא קשיא ליה? לא שכרתיך מעולם. לא דמי לגזל, כי נתתיו לך – דהא מודי ליה דעבד בהדיה, וקא גזל ליה. מ"ש גזל דלא קשיא ליה. הא איהו נמי גבי קרבן שבועה כתיב, ואי לא כפר – שבועה היכא? דגזליה והדר כפריה. כל זמן שלא תבעו בב"ד, אלא בינו לבין עצמו היה גוזלו ואומרו "איני נותן לך", וכשתבעו בב"ד – כפר ונשבע. ולעולם גזל לא איקרי אלא א"כ אומר לו "איני נותן לך". אי הכי עושק נמי. נוקמיה כרב חסדא בלך ושוב, ודקשיא לך שבועה היכא – כגון דהדר כפריה. הכי גרסינן: הכי השתא בשלמא התם או בגזל. כתיב "וכחש" – השתא, מכלל דאודי ליה מעיקרא, כלומר: וכחש בעמיתו בגזל – במה שהיה גוזלו עד עתה בתורת גזל, כחש עכשיו וכפר. ומקודם כחש – קרוי גזל. אבל הכא מי כתיב או בעושק. דנימא וכחש בעושק דמעיקרא. או עשק כתיב. על ידי הכחשה עשקו. שעשקו כבר. משעה שהתחיל לתובעו עושקו בכחישה. ולא נקרא עשק על ידי דבר אחר קודם כחישה. **מתני'** שכר בהמה וכלים. ילפינן בגמרא. לא תבעו אינו עובר עליו. בגמרא יליף ליה דכתיב "אתך" – מדעתך, ולא מדעתו. המחהו. נתקן מאללו, והעמידו אצל חנוני. שהיה פועל צריך לקנות פירות מחנוני, ואמר לו בעל הבית לחנוני: תן לו בדינר פירות, ועלי לשלם. או אמר לשולחני: תן לו בדינר מעות. נשבע ונוטל. מפרש בגמרא. ואם יש עדים שתבעו. בזמנו. גר תושב. שקבל עליו שלא לעבוד ע"ז, ואוכל נבילות וטריפות. יש בו משום וכו'. מפרש בגמרא. **גמ'** מאחיך

תורה אור

לעיל עו. לקמן קיח.

[לעיל קג. וע' תוס' לקמן קיב: ד"ה שכיר שבועות מה:]

[לקמן קיב:]

ויקרא יט | שם | שם | דברים כד | שם שם | משלי ג | ויקרא ה | שם | דברים כד

הגהות הב"ח
(א) גמ' בה' שמות ועשה הללו:

עין משפט נר מצוה

קיא א מיי' פי"א מהל' שכירות הל' ד סמג לאוין קפא טוש"ע ח"מ סי' שלט סעיף ז:
קיב ב טוש"ע שם סעיף ט:
קיג ג מיי' שם הלכה ב טוש"ע שם סעיף ד:
קיד ד מיי' שם טוש"ע שם סעיף ב:
קטו ה מיי' פ"א מהל' גזילה ואבידה הל' ג ד סמג לאוין קנו טור וש"ע ח"מ סי' שנט סעיף ז וסעיף ח ודלא כסוגיין וע"ש:
קטז ו ז מיי' שם פ"ז הלכה א והלכה ב סמג עשין עג:
קיז ח מיי' פי"א מהל' שכירות הלכה א סמג לאוין קפא טוש"ע ח"מ סי' שלט סעיף א:
קיח ט י כ מיי' שם הל' ד טוש"ע שם סעיף י:
קיט ל מ מיי' שם הל' ו ועיין בהשגות ובמגיד משנה סמג שם טור ש"ע ח"מ סי' פט סעיף ג:
קכ נ מיי' שם הלכה א סמג שם:

מאחיך פרט לאחרים. תימה: אמאי איצטריך "מאחיך" – למעוטי גוי, מגר תושב נפקא דדוקא גר תושב ולא גוי? ועוד תימה: אמאי איצטריך למיכתב גר צדק, מגר תושב נפקא דכ"ש גר צדק? וליכא למימר דאי לאו דכתיב גר צדק הוה מוקמינן "בשעריך" לגר צדק, ד"בשעריך" לא משמע אלא גר תושב שאוכל נבילות, דומיא ד"לגר אשר בשעריך (דברים יד) תתננה ואכלה". **מגרך** זה גר צדק. תימה: אמאי איצטריך למימר גר צדק? ד"מאחיך" נפקא, דגר צדק אחיך לכ"ע לרבי יהודה ולרבנן דפליגי ב"החובל" (ב"ק דף פז. ושם) גבי אין לעבדים בושת – דיש לו אחוה, ואחיך הוא במצות! וי"ל: דשאני הכא דכתיב "מאחיך" – דמשמע ממובחר שבאחיך, כדדרשינן ב"ק (דף פח.) "מקרב אחיך". אי נמי: "מאחיך" – ולא כל אחיך, כדדרשינן קדושין (דף כד:) "מן העוף" – ולא כל העוף, והוה ממעטינן גר, אי לאו דכתיב "גרך". אבל ב"איזהו נשך" (לעיל דף עא.), גבי רבית דדריש גר – זה גר צדק, קשיא לר"י: אמאי איצטריך? פשיטא! דמה לי ישראל מה לי גר צדק! וכי בכל המצות אין גר צדק בכלל ישראל?! וכן קשה: דזימנין כתיב לאזרח ולגר, וזימנין דלא כתיב, ומ"ש?

כל שבארצך. ולא מוקמינן ליה למעוטי חוצה לארץ, דחובת הגוף היא, ואינה תלויה בארץ.

ורבי יוסי ברבי יהודה לא יליף שכיר שכיר. ובפ"ק דקדושין (דף יד: ושם) דלא משכח תנא דלא יליף שכיר שכיר – היינו דוקא גבי עבד עברי. משום דסבר דההוא דהכא לא מופנה, והאי מופנה.

ואי אשמועינן גזל משום דלא טרח. לא הוה צריך להאי צריכותא, דאי לא כתיב אלא חד – אפילו "לא תגזול" הוה מוקמינן לה בעושק, דמשתעי ביה קרא, כדאמר ב"איזהו נשך" (לעיל סא. ושם ד"ה לעבור). אבל השתא, דכתיבי תרוייהו – מוקמינן לה בגזל גוי בהא אינו ענין. אלא משום דמשכח צריכותא, אפי' מיעטיה בהדיא מגזל – לא הוה שמעינן עשק*. [ועי' תוס' לעיל סא. ד"ה לעבור]

ורבי יוסי בר' יהודה האי לא תלין אתך מאי עביד ליה. תימה: דבסמוך בברייתא דריש מיניה כמה דרשות! ומלאתי כתוב, כמדומה בתוס' רבינו אלחנן: דהכא משכיר קבעי מאי עביד ליה, דהוי ליה למיכתב "לא תלין פעולתו אתך".

לבצור אשכול אחד. היינו שכיר שעות. נראה לר"י דאיצטריך למכתב, משום דשכיר – משמע שכיר יום או חצי יום, שאין רגילות להשכיר פעולים אלא ליום או חצי יום. אבל לכל דהו – לא. אי נמי, איצטריך לאשמועינן דאפילו שכרו לבצור אשכול אחד ואכלו – אפילו הכי עובר עליו.

חוזר

תורה אור

°"מֵאַחֶיךָ" — פְּרָט לַאֲחֵרִים; "גֵּרְךָ" — זֶה גֵּר צֶדֶק; (דברים כד) "בִּשְׁעָרֶיךָ" — זֶה אוֹכֵל נְבֵילוֹת. אֵין לִי אֶלָּא שְׂכַר אָדָם. מִנַּיִן לְרַבּוֹת בְּהֵמָה וְכֵלִים? ת"ל: "בְּאַרְצְךָ", *כָּל שֶׁבְּאַרְצְךָ. וְכוּלָּן עוֹבְרִים בְּכָל הַשֵּׁמוֹת הַלָּלוּ. מִכָּאן אָמְרוּ: אֶחָד שְׂכַר אָדָם וְאֶחָד שְׂכַר בְּהֵמָה וְאֶחָד שְׂכַר כֵּלִים — יֵשׁ בּוֹ מִשּׁוּם (דברים כד) °בְּיוֹמוֹ תִתֵּן שְׂכָרוֹ וְיֵשׁ בָּהֶן מִשּׁוּם °בַּל (ויקרא יט) תָּלִין פְּעוּלַּת שָׂכִיר. רַבִּי יוֹסֵי בְּרַבִּי יְהוּדָה אוֹמֵר: גֵּר תּוֹשָׁב יֵשׁ בּוֹ מִשּׁוּם בְּיוֹמוֹ תִתֵּן שְׂכָרוֹ וְאֵין בּוֹ מִשּׁוּם לֹא תָלִין. בְּהֵמָה וְכֵלִים אֵין בָּהֶן אֶלָּא מִשּׁוּם °בַּל תַּעֲשֹׁק בִּלְבָד. (שם ודברים כד) מַנִּי? אִי תַּנָּא קַמָּא דְ"מֵאַחֶיךָ" — קַשְׁיָא גֵּר תּוֹשָׁב. אִי רַבִּי יוֹסֵי — קַשְׁיָא בְּהֵמָה וְכֵלִים! אֲמַר רָבָא: הַאי תַּנָּא — תַּנָּא דְּבֵי ר' יִשְׁמָעֵאל הוּא. דְּתָנָא דְּבֵי ר' יִשְׁמָעֵאל: אֶחָד שְׂכַר אָדָם וְאֶחָד שְׂכַר בְּהֵמָה וְאֶחָד שְׂכַר כֵּלִים — יֵשׁ בּוֹ מִשּׁוּם בְּיוֹמוֹ תִתֵּן שְׂכָרוֹ וּמִשּׁוּם לֹא תָלִין. גֵּר תּוֹשָׁב יֵשׁ בּוֹ מִשּׁוּם בְּיוֹמוֹ תִתֵּן שְׂכָרוֹ וְאֵין בּוֹ מִשּׁוּם בַּל תָּלִין. מ"ט דְּת"ק דְּ"מֵאַחֶיךָ"? גָּמַר "שָׂכִיר", "שָׂכִיר". וְרַבִּי יוֹסֵי בְּרַבִּי יְהוּדָה לָא גָּמַר "שָׂכִיר", "שָׂכִיר". נְהִי דְּלָא גָּמַר "שָׂכִיר", "שָׂכִיר", בְּהֵמָה וְכֵלִים מִשּׁוּם "בְּיוֹמוֹ תִתֵּן שְׂכָרוֹ" נַמִי נִיחַיֵּיב! תָּנֵי רַבִּי חֲנַנְיָא: אֲמַר קְרָא (דברים כד) °"וְלֹא תָבֹא עָלָיו הַשֶּׁמֶשׁ כִּי עָנִי הוּא". מִי שֶׁהֵן בָּאִין לִידֵי עֲנִיּוּת וַעֲשִׁירוּת, יָצְאוּ בְּהֵמָה וְכֵלִים שֶׁאֵינָן בָּאִין לִידֵי עֲנִיּוּת וַעֲשִׁירוּת. וְת"ק, הַאי "כִּי עָנִי הוּא" מַאי עָבֵיד לֵיהּ? הַהוּא מִיבָּעֵי לְהַקְדִּים עָנִי לְעָשִׁיר. וְרַבִּי יוֹסֵי בְּרַבִּי יְהוּדָה? הַהוּא °מִ"לֹּא תַעֲשֹׁק שָׂכִיר עָנִי וְאֶבְיוֹן" נָפְקָא. (שם) וְת"ק? חַד לְהַקְדִּים עָנִי לְעָשִׁיר, וְחַד לְהַקְדִּים עָנִי לְאֶבְיוֹן. וּצְרִיכָא, דְּאִי אַשְׁמְעִינַן אֶבְיוֹן — מִשּׁוּם דְּלָא כָּסֵיף לְמִתְבָּעֵיהּ, אֲבָל עָשִׁיר דְּכָסֵיף לְמִתְבָּעֵיהּ — אֵימָא לָא. וְאִי אַשְׁמְעִינַן עָשִׁיר — מִשּׁוּם דְּלָא צָרִיךְ לֵיהּ, אֲבָל אֶבְיוֹן דְּצָרִיךְ לֵיהּ — אֵימָא לָא. צְרִיכָא. וְתַנָּא דִּידַן: מַה נַּפְשָׁךְ, אִי יָלֵיף "שָׂכִיר" "שָׂכִיר" — אֲפִילּוּ גֵּר תּוֹשָׁב נַמִי! אִי לָא יָלֵיף "שָׂכִיר" "שָׂכִיר" — בְּהֵמָה וְכֵלִים מְנָא לֵיהּ? לְעוֹלָם לָא יָלֵיף "שָׂכִיר" "שָׂכִיר", וְשָׁאנֵי הָתָם דְּאָמַר קְרָא: "וְלֹא תָלִין פְּעוּלַּת שָׂכִיר אִתְּךָ עַד בֹּקֶר" — כָּל שֶׁפְּעוּלָּתוֹ אִתְּךָ. אִי הָכִי, אֲפִילּוּ גֵּר תּוֹשָׁב נַמִי! אֲמַר קְרָא: "רֵעֲךָ" — "רֵעֲךָ" וְלֹא גֵּר תּוֹשָׁב. אִי הָכִי, אֲפִילּוּ בְּהֵמָה וְכֵלִים נַמִי! הָא כְּתִיב "אִתְּךָ". מָה רָאִיתָ לְרַבּוֹת בְּהֵמָה וְכֵלִים וּלְהוֹצִיא גֵּר תּוֹשָׁב? מִסְתַּבְּרָא, בְּהֵמָה וְכֵלִים הֲוָה לֵיהּ לְרַבּוֹת — שֶׁכֵּן יֶשְׁנָן בִּכְלַל מָמוֹן רֵעֲךָ, גֵּר תּוֹשָׁב אֵינוֹ בִּכְלַל מָמוֹן רֵעֲךָ. וְת"ק דְּ"מֵאַחֶיךָ" *הַאי "רֵעֲךָ" מַאי עָבְדִי לֵיהּ? הַהוּא מִיבָּעֵי לֵיהּ לְכִדְתַנְיָא: "רֵעֲךָ" וְלֹא גּוֹי. גּוֹי מֵ"אַחֶיךָ" נָפְקָא! חַד לְמִשְׁרָא עוֹשְׁקוֹ, וְחַד לְמִשְׁרָא גְּזֵלוֹ. וּצְרִיכִי. דְּאִי אַשְׁמְעִינַן גְּזֵלוֹ — מִשּׁוּם דְּלָא טָרַח בֵּיהּ, אֲבָל עוֹשְׁקוֹ דְּטָרַח גַּבֵּיהּ — אֵימָא לָא. וְאִי אַשְׁמְעִינַן עוֹשְׁקוֹ — מִשּׁוּם דְּלָא אֲתָא לִידֵיהּ, אֲבָל גְּזֵלוֹ דַּאֲתָא לִידֵיהּ — אֵימָא לָא, צְרִיכָא. וְרַבִּי יוֹסֵי בְּרַבִּי יְהוּדָה, הַאי "לֹא תָלִין פְּעוּלַּת שָׂכִיר אִתְּךָ עַד בֹּקֶר" מַאי עָבֵיד לֵיהּ? מִיבָּעֵיא לֵיהּ לְכִדְרַב אַסִּי. *דְּאָמַר רַב אַסִּי: אֲפִילּוּ לֹא שְׂכָרוֹ אֶלָּא לִבְצוֹר לוֹ אֶשְׁכּוֹל אֶחָד שֶׁל עֲנָבִים — עוֹבֵר מִשּׁוּם בַּל תָּלִין. וְאִידָךְ? °מִ"וְאֵלָיו הוּא נוֹשֵׂא אֶת נַפְשׁוֹ" נָפְקָא, (שם) דָּבָר הַמּוֹסֵר נַפְשׁוֹ עָלָיו.

וְאִידָךְ

מֵאַחֶיךָ. "לֹא תַעֲשׁוֹק שָׂכִיר עָנִי וְאֶבְיוֹן מֵאַחֶיךָ". פְּרָט לַאֲחֵרִים. נָכְרִי. זֶה גֵּר אוֹכֵל נְבֵילוֹת. דִּכְתִיב בֵּיהּ "שְׁעָרֶיךָ" (דברים יד) — "לַגֵּר אֲשֶׁר בִּשְׁעָרֶיךָ תִּתְּנֶנָּה וַאֲכָלָהּ". וְכוּלָּן. עַל שְׂכַר יִשְׂרָאֵל, וְעַל שְׂכַר בְּהֵמָה וְכֵלִים, וְגֵר, וְגֵר תּוֹשָׁב. עוֹבֵר בְּכָל הַשֵּׁמוֹת הַלָּלוּ. בֵּין הַכְּתוּבִים כָּאן וּבֵין הָאֲמוּרִים בְּתוֹרַת כֹּהֲנִים, דְּיָלֵיף גְּזֵירָה שָׁוָה לְאִיתוּיֵינְהוּ הָכָא, כִּדְלְקַמָּן. וְיֵשׁ בָּהֶם מִשּׁוּם בַּל תָּלִין. הָאָמוּר בְּתוֹרַת כֹּהֲנִים, וְהוּא הַדִּין לְ"לֹא תַעֲשׁוֹק וְלֹא תִגְזוֹל" דִּכְתִיב גַּבֵּיהּ. [חגיגה יז:] וּמִיהוּ, שֶׁל שְׂכִיר יוֹם לֵיתֵיהּ בִּשְׂכִיר לַיְלָה. ר' יוֹסֵי בְּר' יְהוּדָה וכו'. לְקַמָּן מְפָרֵשׁ לָהּ. אֵין בָּהֶם אֶלָּא מִשּׁוּם לֹא תַעֲשֹׁק שָׂכִיר וְגוֹמֵר. דִּכְתִיב בֵּיהּ "בְּאַרְצְךָ" דִּמְרַבֵּי בְּהֵמָה וְכֵלִים. אֲבָל "בְּיוֹמוֹ תִּתֵּן שְׂכָרוֹ", אַע"ג דִּסְמִיךְ לֵיהּ — לָא. וּלְקַמָּן מְפָרֵשׁ טַעְמָא. קַשְׁיָא גֵּר תּוֹשָׁב. דְּמַתְנִיתִין תְּנַן: אֵין בּוֹ מִשּׁוּם "בַּל תָּלִין" הָאָמוּר בְּתוֹרַת כֹּהֲנִים, וּבְבָרַיְיתָא קָתָנֵי: כּוּלָּן עוֹבְרִים בְּכָל הַשֵּׁמוֹת הַלָּלוּ. קַשְׁיָא בְּהֵמָה וְכֵלִים. דְּקָתָנֵי מַתְנִי' יֵשׁ בָּהֶם מִשּׁוּם "בְּיוֹמוֹ תִּתֵּן שְׂכָרוֹ" וּמִשּׁוּם "לֹא תָלִין", וְר' יוֹסֵי בְּר' יְהוּדָה סָבַר אֵין בָּהֶן אֶלָּא מִשּׁוּם "לֹא תַעֲשׁוֹק" דְּמִשְׁנֵה תוֹרָה, וַאֲפִילּוּ מִשּׁוּם "בְּיוֹמוֹ וגו'" דִּסְמִיךְ לֵיהּ — לָא. גֵּר תּוֹשָׁב יֵשׁ בּוֹ מִשּׁוּם בְּיוֹמוֹ תִּתֵּן שְׂכָרוֹ. וְכָל שֶׁכֵּן מִשּׁוּם "לֹא תַעֲשֹׁק שָׂכִיר" דִּבְגַוֵּיהּ כְּתִיב "בִּשְׁעָרֶיךָ". וְאֵין בּוֹ מִשּׁוּם לֹא תָלִין. דְּתוֹרַת כֹּהֲנִים, וְכֵן מִשּׁוּם "לֹא תַעֲשֹׁק" וְ"לֹא תִגְזוֹל" דְּת"כ. וְהַאי דְּנָקַט הָנֵי — מִשּׁוּם דִּמְפָרְשִׁי בְּהוּ שְׂכִיר יוֹם וּשְׂכִיר לַיְלָה. וְה"ק: יֵשׁ בּוֹ מִשּׁוּם "בְּיוֹמוֹ תִּתֵּן שְׂכָרוֹ" דְּמִשְׁתָּעֵי גַּבֵּי שְׂכִיר לַיְלָה, וְאֵין בּוֹ מִשּׁוּם שְׂכִיר יוֹם. גָּמַר שָׂכִיר שָׂכִיר. כְּתִיב הָכָא "לֹא תַעֲשֹׁק שָׂכִיר" וּכְתִיב בִּשְׂכִיר יוֹם "לֹא תָלִין פְּעוּלַּת שָׂכִיר", מַה כָּאן גֵּר תּוֹשָׁב בְּהֵמָה וְכֵלִים אִיתְרַבַּאי — אַף בְּת"כ נַמִי, גֵּר תּוֹשָׁב בְּהֵמָה וְכֵלִים. לֹא גָּמַר. הִלְכָּךְ דְּתוֹרַת כֹּהֲנִים לֵיתְנְהוּ, לָא בִּבְהֵמָה וְכֵלִים וְלָא בְּגֵר תּוֹשָׁב. מִשּׁוּם דְּבְיוֹמוֹ תִּתֵּן שְׂכָרוֹ. לִיחַיֵּיב, דְּהָךְ סָמֵיךְ לֵיהּ, דִּבְקְרָא דִּלְעֵיל כְּתִיב "מֵאַרְצְךָ". לְהַקְדִּים עָנִי לְעָשִׁיר. נִשְׂכְּרוּ שְׁנֵי פוֹעֲלִין, אֶחָד עָנִי וְאֶחָד עָשִׁיר, וְאֵין בְּיָדוֹ לִיתֵּן אֶלָּא לְאֶחָד מֵהֶן — הֶעָנִי קוֹדֵם. אֶבְיוֹן. מְעוּנֶּה מֵעָנִי. וּלְשׁוֹן אֶבְיוֹן — הָאוֹבֶה וְאֵינוֹ מַשִּׂיג מַה שֶּׁנַּפְשׁוֹ מִתְאַוָּה לְכָל טוּב. וְאַשְׁמְעִינַן קְרָא דְּעָנִי קוֹדֵם לָאֶבְיוֹן, מִשּׁוּם דְּעָנִי כָּסֵיף לְמִיתְבְּעֵיהּ, אַף עַל גַּב דְּלָרִיךְ. אֲבָל אֶבְיוֹן. הוּרְגַּל לְבוֹשֶׁת, וְלָא כָּסֵיף לְמִיתְבְּעֵיהּ. וְאִי אַשְׁמוּעִינַן עָשִׁיר. דִּלְקַדְמֵיהּ עָנִי, מִשּׁוּם דְּלָא צָרִיךְ לֵיהּ הֶעָשִׁיר לְשָׂכָר כְּמוֹ הֶעָנִי. אֲבָל אֶבְיוֹן דְּצָרִיךְ לֵיהּ. טְפֵי מֵעָנִי, אֵימָא דְּלִיקַדְמֵיהּ לֶעָנִי – קמ"ל דְּעָנִי קוֹדֵם, דְּצָרִיךְ לֵיהּ וְכָסֵיף לְמִיתְבְּעֵיהּ. וְתַנָּא דִּידַן. וְכֵן דְּבֵי רַבִּי יִשְׁמָעֵאל דְּאָמְרוּ תַּרְוַייהוּ בְּהֵמָה וְכֵלִים אִכּוּלְּהוּ, וְגֵר תּוֹשָׁב לֵית לְהוּ *דְּת"כ אִי גָּמֵיר ג"ש — אֲפִילּוּ גֵּר תּוֹשָׁב נַמִי לִיחַיְּיבֵיהּ מִשּׁוּם שְׂכִיר יוֹם. אִתְּךָ. קְרָא יְתֵירָא הוּא. שֶׁפְּעוּלָּתוֹ אִתְּךָ. וַאֲפִילּוּ בְּהֵמָה וְכֵלִים. רֵעֲךָ. בְּהָהוּא דְּתוֹרַת כֹּהֲנִים כְּתִיב "לֹא תַעֲשֹׁק אֶת רֵעֲךָ". עֲשָׁקוֹ. שְׂכַר שָׂכִיר. גְּזָלוֹ. גְּזֵילָה מַמָּשׁ. וְר' יוֹסֵי הַאי אִתְּךָ מַאי עָבֵיד לֵיהּ. דִּמְרַבֵּי מִינֵּיהּ תַּנָּא דִּידַן בְּהֵמָה וְכֵלִים, אַף עַל גַּב דִּגְזֵרָה שָׁוָה לָא גָּמֵיר. אֶלָּא לִבְצוֹר אֶשְׁכּוֹל אֶחָד. כְּלוֹמַר: שְׂכִיר שָׁעוֹת. מִוְאֵלָיו הוּא נוֹשֵׂא אֶת נַפְשׁוֹ. כָּל שֶׁשִּׁיעְבֵּד עַצְמוֹ עָלָיו.

וְאִידָךְ

ס"א ות"ק דמאחיך ור"י ב"י האי רעך מאי עבדי כו' ועיין רש"א

[נ"א דת"ק]

[לעיל נב.]

קבא א מיי' פי"א מהל' שכירות הלכה ב סמג לאוין קפח טוש"ע ח"מ סי' שלט סעי' ב:
קבב ב עיי' כ"מ הלכה ד טוש"ע שם סעי' י:
קבג ג מיי' פ"י מהל' שכירות הלכה ד סמג עשין פט טוש"ע ח"מ סי' שו סעי' ב ועיין בטוש"ע אה"ע סי' כח סעי' טו בהג"ה:
קבד ד ה מיי' שם פי"א הלכה ג סמג לאוין קפא טוש"ע ח"מ סי' שלט סעי' ו:

תורה אור

דברים כד: וְאִידָךְ? הַהוּא מִיבָּעֵי לֵיהּ לִכְדְתַנְיָא: °"וְאֵלָיו הוּא נוֹשֵׂא אֶת נַפְשׁוֹ", מִפְּנֵי מַה עָלָה זֶה בַּכֶּבֶשׁ וְנִתְלָה בָּאִילָן וּמָסַר אֶת עַצְמוֹ לְמִיתָה? לֹא *עַל שְׂכָרוֹ? דָּבָר אַחֵר: "וְאֵלָיו הוּא נוֹשֵׂא אֶת נַפְשׁוֹ" — אכָּל הַכּוֹבֵשׁ שְׂכַר שָׂכִיר כְּאִילּוּ נוֹטֵל נַפְשׁוֹ מִמֶּנּוּ. *רַב הוּנָא וְרַב חִסְדָּא — חַד אֲמַר: נַפְשׁוֹ שֶׁל גַּזְלָן, וְחַד אֲמַר: נַפְשׁוֹ שֶׁל נִגְזָל. מַאן דַּאֲמַר נַפְשׁוֹ שֶׁל גַּזְלָן — דִּכְתִיב: °"אַל תִּגְזָל דָּל כִּי דַל הוּא וְאַל תְּדַכֵּא עָנִי בַשָּׁעַר", וּכְתִיב: °"כִּי ה' יָרִיב רִיבָם וְקָבַע אֶת קֹבְעֵיהֶם נָפֶשׁ". ומ"ד נַפְשׁוֹ שֶׁל נִגְזָל — דִּכְתִיב: °"כֵּן אָרְחוֹת כָּל בּוֹצֵעַ בָּצַע, אֶת נֶפֶשׁ בְּעָלָיו יִקָּח". וְאִידָךְ נַמִי, הָכְתִיב: "אֶת נֶפֶשׁ בְּעָלָיו יִקָּח"! בְּעָלָיו דְּהָשְׁתָּא. וְאִידָךְ נַמִי, הָכְתִיב: "וְקָבַע אֶת קֹבְעֵיהֶם נָפֶשׁ"! מַה טַּעַם קָאָמַר; מַה טַּעַם קָבַע אֶת קֹבְעֵיהֶם? מִשּׁוּם דְּנָטְלוּ נֶפֶשׁ.§ "אֵימָתַי? בִּזְמַן שֶׁתְּבָעוֹ. לֹא תְּבָעוֹ אֵינוֹ עוֹבֵר עָלָיו".§ ת"ר: "לֹא תָלִין פְּעוּלַּת שָׂכִיר". יָכוֹל אֲפִילּוּ לֹא תְּבָעוֹ — ת"ל: "אִתְּךָ", לְדַעְתְּךָ. יָכוֹל אֲפִי' אֵין לוֹ — ת"ל: "אִתְּךָ", שֶׁיֵּשׁ אִתְּךָ. יָכוֹל אֲפִי' הִמְחָהוּ אֵצֶל חֶנְוָנִי וְאֵצֶל שׁוּלְחָנִי — ת"ל: "אִתְּךָ" — וְלֹא שֶׁהִמְחָהוּ אֵצֶל חֶנְוָנִי וְאֵצֶל שׁוּלְחָנִי.§ "הִמְחָהוּ אֵצֶל חֶנְוָנִי וְאֵצֶל שׁוּלְחָנִי אֵינוֹ עוֹבֵר".§ אִיבַּעְיָא לְהוּ: חוֹזֵר אוֹ אֵינוֹ חוֹזֵר? רַב שֵׁשֶׁת אָמַר: אֵינוֹ חוֹזֵר, וְרַבָּה אָמַר: בחוֹזֵר. אֲמַר רַבָּה: מְנָא אָמֵינָא לָהּ — מִדְּקָתָנֵי: אֵינוֹ עוֹבֵר עָלָיו. מֵעֲבַר הוּא דְּלָא עָבַר, הָא מִיהְדַּר הָדַר. וְרַב שֵׁשֶׁת אָמַר: מַאי אֵינוֹ עוֹבֵר? אֵינוֹ בְּתוֹרַת לַעֲבוֹר.§ *בָּעוּ מִינֵּיהּ מֵרַב שֵׁשֶׁת: קַבְּלָנוּת עוֹבֵר עָלָיו מִשּׁוּם בַּל תָּלִין אוֹ אֵין עוֹבֵר מִשּׁוּם בַּל תָּלִין? אוּמָּן קוֹנֶה בְּשֶׁבַח כְּלִי — וְהַלְוָאָה הִיא? או גאֵין אוּמָּן קוֹנֶה בְּשֶׁבַח כְּלִי וּשְׂכִירוּת הִיא? אֲמַר לְהוּ רַב שֵׁשֶׁת: דעוֹבֵר. וְהָתַנְיָא: אֵינוֹ עוֹבֵר! הָתָם שֶׁהִמְחָהוּ אֵצֶל חֶנְוָנִי וְאֵצֶל שׁוּלְחָנִי. נֵימָא מְסַיְּיעָא לֵיהּ: *ה"הַנּוֹתֵן טַלִּיתוֹ לְאוּמָּן, גְּמָרָהּ וְהוֹדִיעוֹ — אֲפִי' מִכָּאן וְעַד עֲשָׂרָה יָמִים אֵינוֹ עוֹבֵר מִשּׁוּם בַּל תָּלִין. נְתָנָהּ לוֹ בַּחֲצִי הַיּוֹם — מִשֶּׁשָּׁקְעָה עָלָיו חַמָּה עוֹבֵר מִשּׁוּם בַּל תָּלִין. וְאִי אָמְרַתְּ אוּמָּן קוֹנֶה בְּשֶׁבַח כְּלִי, אַמַּאי עוֹבֵר? אֲמַר רַב מָרִי בְּרֵיהּ דְּרַב כָּהֲנָא: *בְּגַרְדָּא דְּסַרְבְּלָא. לְמַאי יְהָבָהּ נִיהֲלֵיהּ? לְרַכּוּכֵי, הַיְינוּ שְׁבָחֵיהּ! לָא צְרִיכָא, דְּקָא אַגְרֵיהּ מִינֵּיהּ לְבַטּוּשֵׁי, בַּטְּשָׁא וּבַטְּשָׁא בְּמָעֲתָא.§ שָׂכִיר

משלי כב
שם
שם א

וְאִידָךְ הַהוּא מִיבָּעֵי לֵיהּ לִכְדְתַנְיָא. לְהַעֲנִישׁוֹ כְּאִילּוּ הוּא נוֹטֵל אֶת נַפְשׁוֹ, כִּדְתַנְיָא וכו'. וּמַסְקָנָא: כָּל הַכּוֹבֵשׁ שְׂכַר שָׂכִיר וכו'. וְאֵלָיו הוּא נוֹשֵׂא. כָּל עַצְמוֹ הוּא מוֹסֵר נַפְשׁוֹ עָלָיו, לַעֲלוֹת בְּכֶבֶשׁ גָּבוֹהַּ וְסִיכֵּן בְּעַצְמוֹ לִיפּוֹל, וְלִתָּלוֹת בָּאִילָן כְּשֶׁעָלָה עָלָיו לִמְסוֹק זֵיתִים, וְלִגְדּוֹר תְּמָרִים וּמָסַר נַפְשׁוֹ עָלָיו לְמִיתָה, שֶׁמָּא יִפּוֹל מִן הַכֶּבֶשׁ אוֹ מִן הָאִילָן. ה"ג: ד"א וְאֵלָיו הוּא נוֹשֵׂא אֶת נַפְשׁוֹ. וּפְלִיגִי בָּהּ רַב הוּנָא וְרַב חִסְדָּא בְּמַשְׁמָעוּתָא דִּקְרָא. חַד אָמַר: נַפְשׁוֹ שֶׁל שָׂכִיר, נֶעֱנָשׁ עָלָיו כְּאִילּוּ הוֹרְגוֹ. וְחַד אָמַר: נַפְשׁוֹ שֶׁל גַּזְלָן, הִגִּיד לְךָ הַכָּתוּב שֶׁגּוֹרֵם מִיתָה לְעַצְמוֹ. וְקָבַע. וְגוֹזֵל אֶת גּוֹזְלֵיהֶם. וּמַה יִּקְבַּע מֵהֶן — אֶת נַפְשָׁם, שֶׁגּוֹרְמִים הַגַּזְלָנִים רָעָה לְעַצְמָן. אַל תִּגְזָל דָּל כִּי דַל הוּא וְאַל תְּדַכֵּא וגו'. אַף אִם דַּל הוּא וְאֵין לוֹ עֵזֶר — אַל תִּגְזְלֵהוּ. וְהוּא אֶחָד מֵאַרְבַּע לְשׁוֹנוֹת שֶׁ"כִּי" מְשַׁמֵּשׁ בָּהֶן "אִם". דְּהָשְׁתָּא. לְאַחַר גְּזֵילָה, דְּהַיְינוּ גַּזְלָן. מִשּׁוּם דְּנָטְלוּ נֶפֶשׁ. וְהָכִי מַשְׁמַע: "וְקָבַע אֶת קֹבְעֵיהֶם נָפֶשׁ" — אֶת אֲשֶׁר קָבְעוּ אֶת נַפְשָׁם מֵהֶם. לְדַעְתְּךָ. וְלֹא מִדַּעְתּוֹ. חוֹזֵר. הַשָּׂכִיר אֵצֶל בַּעַל הַבַּיִת אִם לֹא נָתַן הַחֶנְוָנִי, וְנִתְחַיֵּיב בַּעַל הַבַּיִת לְשַׁלֵּם. אֵינוֹ בְּתוֹרַת לַעֲבוֹר. כְּלוֹמַר: אֵין לוֹ עָלָיו כְּלוּם שֶׁיְּהֵא עָלָיו בְּתוֹרַת דָּמִים שׁוּם עֲבֵירוֹת שְׂכַר שָׂכִיר. קַבְּלָנוּת. אוּמָּן שֶׁקִּיבֵּל עָלָיו לַעֲשׂוֹת מְלָאכָה בְּכָךְ וְכָךְ, וְלֹא לִשְׂכִירוּת יָמִים. אוּמָּן קוֹנֶה בְּשֶׁבַח כְּלִי. וְזוֹכֶה בַּמֶּה שֶׁהִשְׁבִּיחוֹ. וּמִשּׁוּם קַבְּלָנוּתוֹ יוֹצֵא לוֹ, וּכְשֶׁמַּחֲזִירוֹ לוֹ — הֲרֵי הוּא כְּמוֹכֵר לוֹ שֶׁבַח שֶׁהָיָה לוֹ בְּתוֹכוֹ. הַלְוָאָה הִיא. וְלֹא שֵׁם שְׂכִירוּת עָלֶיהָ. בְּגַרְדָּא דְּסַרְבְּלָא. פולקיי"ר בְּלַעַ"ז. שֶׁאֵין כָּאן שֶׁבַח כְּלִי, שֶׁאִם הָיָה מַנִּיחוֹ כְּמוֹת שֶׁהִיא — הָיְתָה מִתְקַיֶּימֶת הַרְבֵּה יוֹתֵר מֵעַתָּה. לְרַכּוּכֵי. שֶׁיְּהֵא רַךְ. הַיְינוּ שְׁבָחֵיהּ. דְּאִיכָּא דְּנִיחָא לֵיהּ בְּהָכִי, מִפְּנֵי שֶׁמְּחַמֵּם יוֹתֵר וְיֵשׁ נוֹי בַּדָּבָר. דְּאַגַּר לְבִיטְשֵׁי. *אֶלָּא לְעוֹלָם לָאו בְּגַרְדָּא, אֶלָּא בַּתִּיקּוּן הָרִאשׁוֹן שֶׁקּוֹרִין פולי"ר, כְּשֶׁבָּא מִבֵּית הַגַּרְדִּי בּוֹטְשִׁין אוֹתוֹ בָּרַגְלַיִם בְּתוֹךְ כְּלִי עֵץ בַּמַּיִם וְקַרְקַע הָרְאוּיָה בְּכָךְ. מִיהוּ, לֹא בְּקַבְּלָנוּת עָסְקִינַן אֶלָּא בִּשְׂכִירוּת, בֵּין יַשְׁבִּיחַ וּבֵין לֹא יַשְׁבִּיחַ, שְׂכָרוֹ לְפִי מִנְיַן בְּטִישׁוֹתָיו, כָּךְ וְכָךְ בְּטִישׁוֹת בְּכָךְ וְכָךְ מָעוֹת. דְּאַגְרֵי' לְבִיטְשֵׁי. לְחֶשְׁבּוֹן בְּטִישׁוֹת. הֲלָכוֹת

כ"א שתתן לו שכרו רש"ל
ב"ק קיט.
שם לט.
ורש"י בפרק הגוזל פי' בע"א
ב"ק שם
נ"א בגרדא וכן הוא בערוך [פי' ערך גרד א]

חוזר עליו או אינו חוזר עליו. היכא דא"ל אני פוטרך לגמרי, אפי' לא יתן לי — פשיטא דאינו חוזר. דאם לא כן — בכל מחילה בעלמא תיבעי ליה אי בעי קנין או לא. והיכא דא"ל נמי אני פוטרך אם יפרע לי שולחני — פשיטא דחוזר, כיון דאין שולחני רוצה ליתן לו. והכא מיירי כשאמר ליה הפועל סתמא שיסמוך על שולחני, ומיבעיא ליה: מי אמרי' דאדעתא דהכי סמך אם יתן לו, או דלמא לגמרי פוטרו אפילו לא יתן לו. וא"ת: פשיטא שלא פטרו לגמרי אלא דוקא אם יתן, שהרי שולחני יכול לחזור בו אפי' במעמד שלשתן, כיון שאין לבעל הבית בידו לא פקדון ולא מלוה. וכיון דיכול לחזור — מסתמא לא פטרו לגמרי, דלאו בשופטני עסקינן! וי"ל: דלעולם איכא למימר שפטרו לגמרי, ומתחייב לו שולחני מדין ערב. דכשמסמיכו השולחני — הוי כאומר סמוך עלי ופטור בעל הבית לגמרי. וה"ה דהוה מלי למיבעי אם השולחני יכול לחזור בו אם לאו, דהא בהא תליא. והשתא מוכח דמחילה אינה צריכה קנין, דע"כ הכא בלא קנין איירי, דקנין לא שייך אלא כשפטרו לגמרי בהדיא. ואפי' לא פטרו לגמרי בפירוש, כיון שהקנה לו — דומה ודאי שלפוטרו הקנה לו, דאם לא כן מאי צריך קנין? ובפוטרו בהדיא פשיטא דאינו חוזר, כדפרישית, ובהא לא מיבעיא ליה, אלא ודאי בלא קנין איירי. ומיהו, מצינו לפרש דהכא איירי כשאמר ליה, בהדיא אני פוטרך אם יתן לי, ואם לא — אחזור עליך. ופליגי כל זמן שלא חוזר בו שולחני, אם יכול לחזור על בעה"ב, ולזה הפירוש נמי יש להוכיח קצת דמחילה אינה צריכה קנין, מדאמר רב ששת אינו חוזר — אלמא פוטרו כל זמן שירצה שולחני לפרוע לו. ובלא קנין מיירי, דבקנין אפילו רבה מודה. ועוד י"ל: דפלוגתא דהכא לא שייכא מידי למחילה, דלכ"ע פועל חוזר על בעה"ב, ולא פליגי אלא לענין "בל תלין" כשחוזר בו מיד ביום ראשון על בעה"ב, דלרב ששת אינו חוזר עליו לענין להתחייב ב"בל תלין", כיון דניתק שעה אחת ממנו כשעמד אצל שולחני — שוב אינו חוזר לאיסור "בל תלין". ורבה אמר: כיון דתוך זמנו חוזר — הוה כדמעיקרא. ודייק רבא ממתניתין, דקתני, המחהו אצל שולחני — אינו עובר עליו. משמע דוקא כל זמן שעומד אצל שולחני. הא מיהדר הדר וחוזר לאיסורו. דאי לא הדר לאיסורו — הוה ליה למיתני: אינו יכול לעבור עליו. לא דמי להא דקתני אחר זמנו אינו עובר עליו, ולא קתני אינו יכול — דהתם ליכא למיטעי. ורב ששת דחי דאינו בתורת לעבור עליו כלל, אפילו יחזור בו. ומיהו, בירושלמי דשבועות גבי חנוני על פנקסו דנשבעין ונוטלין מבעל הבית, קאמר דדוקא כשלא העמיד לפועלים אצל חנוני, אבל העמידם אצלו — אין בעל הבית חייב לפועלים כלום. ומפרש רב אלפס דירושלמי אתי אליבא דרב ששת, וסבר כמותו. אבל מ"מ, לדידן קי"ל כרבה, ומוקי ההיא דלא פליגי לענין "בל תלין", אלא לענין אם צריך בעל הבית לשלם לפועלים אם לאו. וכן משמע בפ"ק דקדושין (דף טו. ושם) דמחילה אינה צריכה קנין גבי עבד עברי, דקאמר: למה לי שטרא? לימא ליה באפי תרי: זיל. אמר רבא: זאת אומרת עבד עברי גופו קנוי, והרב שמחל על גרעונו — אין גרעונו מחול. משמע דאי לאו דגופו קנוי לו — היה יכול למחול. ובלא קנין איירי, דבקנין לא היה צריך שטר, דאפילו עבד כנעני קונה עצמו בחליפין, כדמוכח ב"השולח" (גיטין דף לט: ושם). דקאמר: שקל כומתא ושדא ביה, ואמר קני הא וקני נפשך. וקאמר דלא עשה ולא כלום — משום דהוה ליה בכליו של מקנה, אבל אי הוה בכליו של קונה — הוה קניא נפשה בחליפין. וכן בפרק "הנושא" (כתובות דף קד.). אמרינן דלאחר כ"ה שנה אבדה כתובתה משום דמסתמא מחלה, ואע"ג דלא עשתה שום קנין. דקנין לאלתר נמי אבדה כתובתה. ומדאמר לעיל ב"איזהו נשך" (דף עא:) תן על גבי קרקע והפטר, ובפרק "הזורק" בגיטין (דף עח: ושם) זרוק לי והפטר — אין ראיה, דאיכא למימר דאיירי בקנין. ואין להקשות מה"ג שפירש בפ"ק דסנהדרין (דף ו. ד"ה צריכה) גבי פשרה צריכה קנין דשניהם צריכין קנין, המוחל צריך להקנות — שמחל לו, והמשלם צריך להקנות — שישלם לו החצי, דשאני פשרה, משום דדמי למחילה בטעות. שאילו היה יודע שהיה זוכה בדין — לא היה מוחל, ולהכי צריכה קנין, דאלים טפי. ומהאי טעמא נמי איכא מאן דבעי ג' ולא סגי בב', משום דדמי למחילה בטעות. כל שכן אם לא נפרש כמו שמפרש בהלכות גדולות. אלא הקנין עושין קודם שישמעו שיקיימו דברי הפשרנים, דלבא קני יוכלו לחזור בהן כשישמעו הפשרה, דאז לא קשה כלום.

אומן קונה בשבח כלי כו' אמר להו עובר. פי': יש ענין שעובר, כגון היכא דליכא שבח כלי, כמו בשליחא דאגרתא או דאגריה לבטשי. אבל רב ששת סבר שפיר דאומן קונה בשבח כלי, כדמוכח ב"הגוזל קמא" (ב"ק דף לט. ע"ש ושם ד"ה דאגריה) דקאמר התם: לימא רב ששת פליגא אדרב *אמי, דאמר אומן קונה בשבח כלי. אמר רב אשי בר חמא: דרב ששת בשליחא דאגרתא. והנך דבעו מרב ששת לא הזכירו בבעייתן אומן קונה בשבח כלי, אלא סתם שאלו קבלן עובר ב"בל תלין" או לאו? והגמרא הוא שאומר אומן קונה כו'. שלפי הפשט בו תליא הבעיא. ולהכי קאמר נמי לימא מסייע ליה, שהיה סבור הגמרא דהא בהא תליא. ורב ששת שהשיב עובר — סבר דאין אומן קונה.

[נ"ל אסי]

שכיר

קכה א מיי' פי"א מהל' שכירות הלכה ו ועיין בהשגות ובמגיד משנה ופ"ט מהל' טוען הלכה ב סמג לאוין קפא טוש"ע ח"מ סי' פט סעי' א:

קכו ב מיי' שם הל' ח טוש"ע שם סעי' ה:

"שָׂכִיר בִּזְמַנּוֹ נִשְׁבָּע וְנוֹטֵל" וכו'. § *שָׂכִיר אַמַּאי תַּקִּינוּ לֵיהּ רַבָּנַן לְמִשְׁתַּבַּע וְשָׁקֵיל? אָמַר רַב יְהוּדָה אָמַר שְׁמוּאֵל: הֲלָכוֹת גְּדוֹלוֹת שָׁנוּ כָּאן. הָנֵי הִלְכְתָא נִינְהוּ? הָנֵי תַּקָּנוֹת נִינְהוּ! אֶלָּא, אָמַר רַב יְהוּדָה אָמַר שְׁמוּאֵל: תַּקָּנוֹת גְּדוֹלוֹת שָׁנוּ כָּאן. גְּדוֹלוֹת מִכְּלָל דְּאִיכָּא קְטַנּוֹת? אֶלָּא אָמַר רַב נַחְמָן אָמַר שְׁמוּאֵל: תַּקָּנוֹת קְבוּעוֹת שָׁנוּ כָּאן. שְׁבוּעָה דְּבַעַל הַבַּיִת הִיא וַעֲקָרוּהָ רַבָּנַן לִשְׁבוּעָה דְּבַעַל הַבַּיִת וְשַׁדְיוּהָ אַשָּׂכִיר, מִשּׁוּם כְּדֵי חַיָּיו דְּשָׂכִיר. וּמִשּׁוּם כְּדֵי חַיָּיו דְּשָׂכִיר מַפְסַדְנָא לֵיהּ לְבַעַל הַבַּיִת? בַּעַל הַבַּיִת גּוּפֵיהּ נִיחָא לֵיהּ דְּמִשְׁתַּבַּע שָׂכִיר וְשָׁקֵיל, כִּי הֵיכִי דְּלִיתַּגְּרוּ לֵיהּ פּוֹעֲלִים. שָׂכִיר גּוּפֵיהּ נִיחָא לֵיהּ דְּמִשְׁתַּבַּע בַּעַל הַבַּיִת וְיִפָּקַע, כִּי הֵיכִי דְּלִיגְרוּהוּ! בַּעַל הַבַּיִת עַל כָּרְחֵיהּ אָגַר. שָׂכִיר נַמִּי בְּעַל כָּרְחֵיהּ אִיתַּגַּר! אֶלָּא, [א]בַּעַל הַבַּיִת טָרוּד בְּפוֹעֲלִים הוּא. אִי הָכִי נֵיתַב לֵיהּ בְּלָא שְׁבוּעָה! כְּדֵי לְהָפִיס דַּעְתּוֹ שֶׁל בַּעַל הַבַּיִת. וְנֵיתַב לֵיהּ בְּעֵדִים! טִרְחָא לְהוּ מִילְּתָא. וְנֵיתַב לֵיהּ מֵעִיקָּרָא! שְׁנֵיהֶם רוֹצִים בְּהַקָּפָה. אִי הָכִי, אֲפִי' קָצַץ נַמִּי. אַלְמָה תַּנְיָא: *[ב]אוּמָּן אוֹמֵר שְׁתַּיִם קָצַצְתָּ לִי, וְהַלָּה אוֹמֵר לֹא קָצַצְתִּי לְךָ אֶלָּא אַחַת – הַמּוֹצִיא מֵחֲבֵירוֹ עָלָיו הָרְאָיָה! קְצִיצָה וַדַּאי מִידְכַּר דְּכִירֵי לָהּ אֱינָשֵׁי. אִי הָכִי, אֲפִי' עָבַר זְמַנּוֹ נַמִּי. אַלְמָה תְּנַן: *עָבַר זְמַנּוֹ אֵינוֹ נִשְׁבָּע וְנוֹטֵל! חֲזָקָה אֵין בַּעַל הַבַּיִת עוֹבֵר מִשּׁוּם בַּל תָּלִין. וְהָא אָמְרַתְּ בַּעַל הַבַּיִת טָרוּד בְּפוֹעֲלָיו הוּא! הָנֵי מִילֵּי מִקַּמֵּיהּ דְּלִימְטְיֵיהּ זְמַן חִיּוּבֵיהּ,
אֲבָל

הֲלָכוֹת גְּדוֹלוֹת שָׁנוּ כָּאן. כְּלוֹמַר שֶׁמָּנוּ חֲכָמִים בְּנִשְׁבָּעִין וְנוֹטְלִין בְּמַסֶּ' שְׁבוּעוֹת (דף מד:): דְּשָׂכִיר וְנִגְזָל וְנֶחְבָּל וְחֶנְוָנִי עַל פִּנְקָסוֹ. הָנֵי הֲלָכָה נִינְהוּ. בִּתְמִיָּה: וְכִי הֲלָכוֹת לְמֹשֶׁה מִסִּינַי הֵם? וַהֲלֹא אֵינָם אֶלָּא תַּקָּנוֹת חֲכָמִים, כִּדְמְפָרֵשׁ הָתָם. תַּקָּנוֹת קְבוּעוֹת. רָאוּי לַעֲשׂוֹתָן קֶבַע לַעֲקוֹר עֲלֵיהֶם דָּבָר מִן הַתּוֹרָה. דְּמִדְּאוֹרַיְיתָא מִי שֶׁיֵּשׁ עָלָיו לְשַׁלֵּם הוּא נִשְׁבָּע, דִּכְתִיב (שמות כב): "וְלָקַח בְּעָלָיו וְלֹא יְשַׁלֵּם", וְהָכָא שַׁקְלוּהָ לִשְׁבוּעָה מִבַּעַל הַבַּיִת וְשַׁדְיוּהָ אַשָּׂכִיר. וְיִפָּקַע. יַפְסִיד שְׂכָרוֹ. כִּי הֵיכִי דְּלִיגְרוּהוּ. שֶׁלֹּא יִמָּנְעוּ מִלְּשׂוֹכְרוֹ, שֶׁיִּדְאֲגוּ לוֹמַר חָשׁוּד הוּא זֶה לִתְבּוֹעַ שְׂכָרוֹ מִשֶּׁקִּבְּלוֹ. עַל כָּרְחֵיהּ אָגַר. כְּשֶׁהוּא צָרִיךְ לְפוֹעֲלִין – עַל כָּרְחוֹ שׂוֹכְרָם. עַל כָּרְחֵיהּ מִיתַּגַּר. נִשְׂכָּר, שֶׁצָּרִיךְ לִמְזוֹנוֹת. טָרוּד בְּפוֹעֲלָיו. וְסָבַר שֶׁנָּתַן לוֹ וְלֹא נָתַן. לֵיתִיב לֵיהּ בְּעֵדִים. וְיִתֵּן לוֹ בְּלֹא שְׁבוּעָה, לְתַקְּנוּ לָהֶן לְכָל שׂוֹכְרֵי פוֹעֲלִין שֶׁיִּתְּנוּ שְׂכָרָם בְּעֵדִים, וְאִם יֹאמַר "פְּרַעְתִּיו שֶׁלֹּא בְּעֵדִים" – יִתֵּן בְּלֹא שְׁבוּעָה. טִרְחָא לְהוּ מִילְּתָא. לַחֲזוֹר בָּתַר עֵדִים כָּל הַיּוֹם. וְנֵיתִיב לֵיהּ מֵעִיקָּרָא. לְתַקּוּן לְבַעַל הַבַּיִת, דְּיָהֵיב אַגְרֵיהּ בְּצַפְרָא מִקַּמֵּי עֲבִידְתַּיְיהוּ. דְּאִי קָאֵי שָׂכִיר – לָא מְהֵימַן. שְׁנֵיהֶם רוֹצִים בְּהַקָּפָה. בַּעַל הַבַּיִת פְּעָמִים שֶׁאֵין לוֹ, וּפוֹעֵל שֶׁמָּא יִפְּלוּ מִמֶּנּוּ. אִי הָכִי. דְּבַעַל הַבַּיִת טָרוּד וְשָׁכַח. אֲפִי' עָבַר זְמַנּוֹ נַמִּי. וּתְבָעוֹ לְמָחָר, לְהֵימְנוּהוּ לְפוֹעֵל!
גַּבֵּי

שכיר בזמנו נשבע ונוטל. בפ' "כל הנשבעין" (שבועות דף מה: ושם ד"ה מתוך) מפרש: לא שנו אלא ששכרו בעדים, אבל שכרו שלא בעדים, מתוך שיכול לומר לא שכרתיך מעולם – יכול לומר שכרתיך ונתתי לך שכרך. תימה: דהיכי נאמן במגו? דהא מפרש בגמ' דטעמא דשכיר נשבע – משום דבעה"ב טרוד בפועליו ואנן חושבין אותו כאילו אומר איני יודע. מדפריך בגמ': אי הכי ניתיב ליה בלא שבועה. וא"כ, מה מועיל מגו? דאילו אומר איני יודע – לא הוה מהני שום מגו והוה חייב, דהוה ליה כאומר "הלויתני ואיני יודע אם פרעתיך" דחייב, כדתנן ב"הגוזל בתרא" (ב"ק דף קיח.). וביבמות בפרק "האשה שהלכה" (דף קיד:) משמע נמי דלא מהני מגו בכי האי גוונא, דאמר: אינה נאמנת לומר מת בעלי במלחמה, משום דאמרה בדדמי לה, ואינה יודעת בברור שמת. ולא מהני לה מגו, דאי בעיא אמרה מת על מטתו.

מכלל דאיכא קטנות. אע"ג דבפרק "השולח" (גיטין דף לו.) אמרינן: תקנה גדולה התקינו שיהיו מפרשין שמותיהן בגיטין, וכן ב"הגוזל קמא" (ב"ק דף קג:): תקנה גדולה התקינו שאם *יגלה יתירה על הקרן כו'. [הוצאה יתירה כצ"ל] לא פריך אלא הכא, דקאמר "שנו כאן" דמשמע ולא במקום אחר.

תקנות קבועות. הא דנקט לשון רבים – משום דקאי אכל הנהו דנשבעין ונוטלין בפרק "כל הנשבעין" (שבועות דף מד:) דשכיר ונגזל ונחבל ושכנגדו חשוד על השבועה וחנוני על פנקסו. וקרי להו קבועות – משום דעקרו לשבועה ממקומה, וקבעוה לשכנגדו, שיהא נשבע ונוטל. והגמרא לא הוצרכה לפרש טעם כולם, אלא טעמא דשכיר.

שקלוה רבנן לשבועה מבעה"ב ושדיוה אשכיר. וא"ת: והלא אף בכופר הכל איירי ת"ק, מדפליג עליה ר' יהודה* ואמר דשכיר אינו נשבע אלא במודה מקצת, ובכופר הכל מי מחייב בעל הבית שבועה דאורייתא? ומאי קאמר דשקלוה רבנן מבעל הבית! וי"ל: דאמודה במקצת קאמר דשקלוה מבעל הבית, ואפי' היכא דכופר הכל – טפי הוה לן לחיוביה בעל הבית שעליו לשלם, שהרי אם מודה מקצת הוא נשבע, ולפי שהיתה ראויה להיות על בעל הבית קאמר דשקלוה. טרוד בפועליו הוא. וחשוב כמו איני יודע, דחייב אפי' כופר הכל, כדתנן ב"הגוזל בתרא" (ב"ק דף קיח.) הלויתני ואיני יודע אם פרעתי לך – חייב, ולא פליג בין אם יש לו פועלים הרבה בין אין לו.

אי הכי ניתיב ליה בלא שבועה. וא"ת: מאי פריך; וכי לעולם ישכח? פעמים שאומר בעל הבית אמת, ולכך לא רצו לתקן שיטול בלא שבועה. תדע, דאי חשוב בודאי שכח – אמאי פטר ר' יהודה כופר הכל אלא ודאי חששא בעלמא, דחיישינן שמא שכח, ולהכי פטר ר' יהודה בכופר הכל דליכא שבועה דאורייתא אבעל הבית, דלא חשבינן ליה לבעה"ב כאומר איני יודע, כי רגילות הוא שיודע יפה. אבל כשמודה מקצת – חששו לשמא שכח, כי פעמים שהוא שוכח מחמת שהוא טרוד בפועליו וישבע לשקר, לפי שסבר שפרע. וה"נ לרבנן, דלא מחזקינן ליה בודאי שכח! וי"ל: דנראה לגמ' דלת"ק מחזקינן ליה בודאי שכח, ואומר איני יודע, מדמחייב כופר הכל. שאם לא היתה אלא חששא בעלמא – אמאי שקיל שכיר אפי' בשבועה? כיון דאיכא למימר דבעה"ב יודע יפה שפרע. אלא ודאי דחשיב ליה כאומר איני יודע. ומשני: להפיס דעתו של בע"ה, לפי שסבר בדעתו בברור שפרע. אבל בהלויתני ואיני יודע אם פרעתיך – אין צריך שבועה, דלא שייך *הספק כיון שהוא מודה שאינו יודע אם פרע.

וניתיב ליה בעדים. פי': נתקן שלא יתן לו אלא בעדים, ואם יפרע בלא עדים – איהו דאפסיד אנפשיה, ולא נצטרך להפיס דעתו. דכל כמה שנוכל לתקן שלא ישבע על חנם – יש לתקן. וכן ניתיב ליה מעיקרא פריך דנתקן אם לא יקח שכרו מתחלה – שיפסיד, קודם שנתקן שבועה על חנם. אי הכי אפילו קציץ נמי. וא"ת: והא קציצה הוי כאומר איני יודע אם הלויתני, דפטור לר"נ ור' יוחנן דאמרי (לעיל דף לז:): מנה לי בידך והלה אומר איני יודע – פטור! וי"ל: דהכא שמודה מקצת יש לחייבו, דהוה כחמשין ידענא וחמשין לא ידענא (שם לח.). וא"ת: לוקי כגון שאותה אחת שמודה כבר פרע, דהשתא הוי כופר הכל! וי"ל: דניחא ליה לשנויי קציצה מידכר דכירי, שהוא מתורץ גם לרב הונא ורב יהודה. ועוד: אפי' לר"נ ור' יוחנן ניח אליה לשנויי הכי, כדי לאוקמי בכל ענין, אפי' לא פרע אותה אחת שמודה. ועוד: דהפשט משמע שלא פרע, דומיא דמילתיה דר' יהודה. שתים קצצת לי כו'. המוציא מחבירו עליו הראיה, ואם לא הביא ראיה – ישבע בעה"ב ויפסיד אומן. דבלא שבועה אינו יכול להפטר כיון שמודה במקצת. והכי מפרש לה בהדיא בריש "כל הנשבעין" (שבועות דף מו.). וא"ת: דהכא קתני המוציא מחבירו עליו הראיה, וב"חזקת הבתים" (ב"ב מה: ושם ד"ה נתנה) תניא דבקבלנה נמי נשבע ונוטל! וי"ל: דבריש "כל הנשבעין" פריך כי האי גוונא, ומשני דהך ברייתא ד"חזקת הבתים" – ר' יהודה היא. קציצה מידכר דכירי אינשי. לא מצי לשנויי דהכא משום הכי אין שכיר נשבע ונוטל – משום דאיירי כששכרו שלא בעדים, דאי איכא עדים – נחזי עדים מאי קאמרי, כמה קצץ. דהכי פריך בפ' "חזקת הבתים" (שם דף מה:) בהלכה דאומן. דהא ע"כ איירי כשיש עדים, דומיא דרישא דקתני שכיר בזמנו נשבע ונוטל, דמוקי לה רב ושמואל ששכרו בעדים, כדאמרי' התם בשבועות (דף מה:) בהדיא. וה"נ סיפא איירי בשכרו בעדים ולא שמעו הקציצה, או שמעו ושכחו. וב"חזקת הבתים" דפריך רבא לאביי, דאמר: אי לא ראה, אע"ג דאיכא עדים – יש לאומן חזקה. ואי ראה, אע"ג דליכא עדים – אין לו חזקה. מהנותן טליתו לאומן ואומר שתים קצצת לי ובעל הבית אומר לא קצצתי לך אלא אחת – כל זמן שהטלית ביד אומן – על בעה"ב להביא ראיה. ואי דאיכא עדים – ניחזי מאי קאמרי! אלא לאו – דליכא עדים, ואע"ג דראה אומן – נאמן, התם לא הוה מצי למימר דאיכא עדים וכגון ששכחו או לא שמעו הקציצה – דא"כ אף לדידיה תקשי, דכיון דמשמע ליה דאיירי בכל ענין, אפילו בראה. אי מיירי נמי דאיכא עדים – אמאי נאמן אומן? דבאיכא עדים וראה לכולי עלמא אין לו חזקה, כדתנן במתני'. ורבא דקאמר אלא לאו דליכא עדים (ולא ראה) – אינו אומר כן אלא כדי שלא יקשה לו למה סרלה להעמידו אף בראה. ואביי דמשני ליה: לא, דליכא עדים ולא ראה – הוי מצי לאוקמה דאיכא עדים ולא ראה, וכגון שלא שמעו הקציצה. אלא, משום דרבא אוקמה בדליכא עדים – אוקמה איהו הכי. ועוד נראה: דאי משום מגו בעל הבית נאמן – אמאי נקט שחולקין בקציצה, ושבק לומר שחולקין בפריעה, זה אומר נתתי וזה אומר לא נתת, כדתנן בפ' "כל הנשבעין" (שבועות דף מד:). ועוד יש לתרץ: דאפילו איירי בששכרו שלא בעדים אין נאמן במגו, כיון שהוא מודה במקצת, שאל היה יכול להעיז ולכפור ולומר לא שכרתיך מעולם כדין כל מודה מקצת דאין נאמן במגו, דאי בעי כפר הכל. ועוד אומר ר"י: דודאי כי איכא עדים – רגילות שיודעים וזוכרין הקציצה, כדאמרינן ב"חזקת הבתים", וברייתא כולה בדליכא עדים איירי. ורישא דקתני נשבע
ונוטל

שבועות מה.

ג"ז שם מו. ב"ב מה:

[לעיל קיא.]

[שבועות מד:]

בס"י הפסקה

גַּבֵּי בַּעַל הַבַּיִת. כְּלוֹמַר: בִּזְכוּתָא דְּבַעַל הַבַּיִת – אִיכָּא תְּרֵי חֲזָקֵי לִזְכוּתוֹ. וְהָא תָּבַע לֵיהּ קַמָּן. וּמָה עֵדִים שֶׁתְּבָעוֹ אוֹתוֹ מַצְרִיכִין? וְדִלְמָא לְבָתַר הָכִי. דְּאָזְלֵי עֵדִים מֵהָתָם – פְּרָעֵיהּ בּוֹ בַּיּוֹם, דְּלֹא עָבַר בְּ"בַל תָּלִין". כָּל זְמַנּוֹ. עַד שֶׁעָבַר עָלָיו. וּלְעוֹלָם. בִּתְמִיהָה. וּבִשְׁבִיל שֶׁתְּבָעוֹ כָּל הַיּוֹם וְלֹא נָתַן יְהֵא שָׂכִיר זֶה נֶאֱמָן לְעוֹלָם לוֹמַר לֹא הִתְקַבַּלְתִּי, וְאִם רוֹצֶה בעה"ב לִישָּׁבַע לֹא נֶאֱמָן, וְכִי כָּל כָּךְ הַשְׁהָה שָׂכִיר שְׂכָרוֹ? א"ר חָמָא בַּר עוּקְבָא כְּנֶגֶד כָּל הַיּוֹם שֶׁל תְּבִיעָה. יוֹם אֶחָד לְאַחַר זְמַנּוֹ נָתְנוּ לוֹ חֲכָמִים לִישָּׁבַע וְיִטּוֹל. מתני' הַמַּלְוֶה אֶת חֲבֵירוֹ. וְהִגִּיעַ זְמַן וְלֹא פָּרַע לוֹ. לֹא יְמַשְׁכְּנֶנּוּ. אֲפִי' בַּשּׁוּק, אֶלָּא בְּב"ד. וְלֹא יִכָּנֵס לְבֵיתוֹ. בַּגְּמָ' מְפָרֵשׁ בְּמַאן קָאֵי. הָיוּ לוֹ שְׁנֵי כֵלִים. וְחוֹבוֹ כְּנֶגֶד שְׁנֵיהֶם, וּמִשְׁכְּנוֹ בִּשְׁנֵיהֶם. נוֹטֵל אֶחָד וּמַחֲזִיר אֶחָד. בְּשָׁעָה שֶׁהוּא צָרִיךְ לָזֶה יַחֲזִירֶנּוּ לוֹ מִשּׁוּם הַחְזָרַת הָעֲבוֹט, וִיעַכֵּב אֶת הַשֵּׁנִי. וּכְשֶׁיִּצְטָרֵךְ זֶה לַשֵּׁנִי – יִטּוֹל זֶה אֶת הָרִאשׁוֹן וְיַחֲזִיר אֶת הַשֵּׁנִי, כִּדְמְפָרֵשׁ וְאָזֵיל: מַחֲזִיר אֶת הַכַּר בַּלַּיְלָה וְאֶת הַמַּחֲרֵישָׁה בַּיּוֹם. מֵת. הַלֹּוֶה אֵין מֵשִׁיב הָעֲבוֹט לַיּוֹרְשִׁין, שֶׁאֵין כָּאן מִצְוַת הָעֲבוֹט, אֶלָּא יִמְכְּרֶנּוּ וְיִגְבֶּה חוֹבוֹ. דְּ"הָשֵׁב תָּשִׁיב לוֹ" כְּתִיב, וְלֹא לַיּוֹרְשִׁין. שְׁלֹשִׁים יוֹם. זְמַן ב"ד. גמ' וּשְׁלִיחַ ב"ד מְנַתֵּחַ נַתּוּחֵי. אַף הוּא אֵינוֹ רַשַּׁאי לִיכָּנֵס לְבֵיתוֹ וּלְמַשְׁכְּנוֹ, אֶלָּא רוֹאֵהוּ בַּשּׁוּק וּמְנַתֵּק דָּבָר שֶׁאוֹחֵז בְּיָדוֹ מִמֶּנּוּ. מְמַשְׁכְּנִין. מַשְׁמַע: בְּתוֹךְ הַבַּיִת. חֲבִילָה. מִתּוֹךְ הַבַּיִת מַשְׁמַע, דְּהָא רֵיחַיִם וָרֶכֶב בְּגוֹ בֵּיתָא שְׁכִיחֵי. לְעוֹלָם בְּבַעַל חוֹב. קָאָמַר, וְלָא תֵּידוֹק מִינָּהּ הָא כֵּלִים אֲחֵרִים חָבוּל, דִּבְכֵלִים אֲחֵרִים – עוֹבֵר מִשּׁוּם "לֹא תָבֹא אֶל בֵּיתוֹ" וּלְהָכִי אִיצְטְרִיךְ לְהוֹסִיף לָאו שֵׁנִי מִשּׁוּם רֵיחַיִם וָרֶכֶב, וְחַד מִשּׁוּם "לֹא תָבֹא אֶל בֵּיתוֹ". מִמַּשְׁמַע שֶׁנֶּאֱמַר בַּחוּץ תַּעֲמוֹד. וְיוֹצִיא אֵלֶיךָ אֶת הָעֲבוֹט, וְכִי אֵינִי יוֹדֵעַ שֶׁהָאִישׁ יוֹצִיאֶנּוּ? אֶלָּא מִי יוֹצִיאֶנּוּ אִם לֹא בעה"ב? מַאי לָאו לְרַבּוֹת שְׁלִיחַ ב"ד כו'. שֶׁיִּכָּנֵס לְתוֹךְ הַבַּיִת. וְה"ק: וְהָאִישׁ – דְּהוּא שְׁלִיחַ ב"ד, וַאֲשֶׁר אַתָּה נוֹשֶׁה בּוֹ – יוֹצִיא אֵלֶיךָ. לֹא

אֲבָל מְטָא זְמַן חִיּוּבֵיהּ – רָמֵי אַנַּפְשֵׁיהּ וּמִידְכַּר. וְכִי שָׂכִיר עוֹבֵר מִשּׁוּם בַּל תִּגְזוֹל? הָתָם תְּרֵי חֲזָקֵי, הָכָא חֲדָא חֲזָקָה. גַּבֵּי בַּעַל הַבַּיִת אִיכָּא תְּרֵי חֲזָקֵי: חֲדָא דְּאֵין בַּעַל הַבַּיִת עוֹבֵר מִשּׁוּם °בַּל תָּלִין, וַחֲדָא דְּאֵין שָׂכִיר מַשְׁהֶא שְׂכָרוֹ. וְהָכָא – חֲדָא חֲזָקָה.§ "אִם יֵשׁ עֵדִים שֶׁתְּבָעוֹ הֲרֵי זֶה נִשְׁבָּע וְנוֹטֵל".§ וְהָא (א) קָתָבְעוֹ לְקַמָּן! א"ר אַסִּי: [א]שֶׁתְּבָעוֹ בִּזְמַנּוֹ. וְדִלְמָא לְבָתַר הָכִי פָּרַע! אָמַר אַבַּיֵי: שֶׁתְּבָעוֹ כָּל זְמַנּוֹ. וּלְעוֹלָם (*לָא פָּרַע לֵיהּ?) א"ר חָמָא בַּר עוּקְבָא: [ב]כְּנֶגֶד אוֹתוֹ הַיּוֹם שֶׁל תְּבִיעָה.§ מתני' [ג]הַמַּלְוֶה אֶת חֲבֵירוֹ – לֹא יְמַשְׁכְּנֶנּוּ אֶלָּא בְּב"ד. [ד]וְלֹא יִכָּנֵס לְבֵיתוֹ לִיטּוֹל מַשְׁכּוֹנוֹ, שֶׁנֶּאֱמַר: °"בַּחוּץ תַּעֲמוֹד". [ה]הָיוּ לוֹ שְׁנֵי כֵּלִים – נוֹטֵל אֶחָד וּמַנִּיחַ אֶחָד. *[ו]וּמַחֲזִיר אֶת הַכַּר בַּלַּיְלָה וְאֶת הַמַּחֲרֵישָׁה בַּיּוֹם. וְאִם מֵת – אֵינוֹ מַחֲזִיר לְיוֹרְשָׁיו. רשב"ג אוֹמֵר: אַף [ז]לְעַצְמוֹ אֵינוֹ מַחֲזִיר אֶלָּא עַד שְׁלֹשִׁים יוֹם, וּמִשְּׁלֹשִׁים יוֹם וּלְהַלָּן מוֹכְרָן בְּב"ד.§ גמ' אָמַר שְׁמוּאֵל: *[ח]שְׁלִיחַ ב"ד, מְנַתֵּחַ נַתּוּחֵי – אִין, אֲבָל מַשְׁכּוֹנֵי – לָא. וְהָתְנַן: הַמַּלְוֶה אֶת חֲבֵירוֹ לֹא יְמַשְׁכְּנֶנּוּ אֶלָּא בְּב"ד – מִכְּלָל דִּבְב"ד מְמַשְׁכְּנִין! *א"ל שְׁמוּאֵל: אֵימָא לֹא יְנַתְּחֶנּוּ אֶלָּא בְּב"ד. הָכִי נַמִי מִסְתַּבְּרָא, דְּקָתָנֵי סֵיפָא: לֹא יִכָּנֵס לְבֵיתוֹ לִיטּוֹל מַשְׁכּוֹנוֹ. מַנִּי? אִילֵימָא בַּעַל חוֹב – מֵרֵישָׁא שְׁמַע מִינָּהּ; אֶלָּא לָאו שְׁלִיחַ ב"ד. אִי מִשּׁוּם הָא לָא אִירְיָא. (ב) ה"ק: הַמַּלְוֶה אֶת חֲבֵירוֹ לֹא יְמַשְׁכְּנֶנּוּ אֶלָּא בְּב"ד. מִכְּלָל דִּבְב"ד – מְמַשְׁכְּנִים. וּבַעַל חוֹב אֲפִי' נַתּוּחֵי נַמִי לָא, (ג) שֶׁלֹּא יִכָּנֵס לְבֵיתוֹ לִיטּוֹל מַשְׁכּוֹנוֹ. מְתִיב רַב יוֹסֵף: °[ט]"לֹא יַחֲבֹל רֵחַיִם וָרָכֶב", הָא דְּבָרִים אֲחֵרִים – חָבַל. °"לֹא תַחֲבֹל בֶּגֶד אַלְמָנָה", הָא שֶׁל אֲחֵרִים – תַּחְבֹּל. מַאן? אִי נֵימָא בַּעַל חוֹב – הָא כְּתִיב: °"לֹא תָבֹא אֶל בֵּיתוֹ לַעֲבוֹט עֲבוֹטוֹ". אֶלָּא לָאו שְׁלִיחַ ב"ד! תַּרְגְּמָהּ רַב פַּפָּא בְּרֵיהּ דְּרַב נַחְמָן קַמֵּיהּ דְּרַב יוֹסֵף, וְאָמְרִי לָהּ רַב פַּפָּא בְּרֵיהּ דְּרַב יוֹסֵף קַמֵּיהּ דְּרַב יוֹסֵף: לְעוֹלָם בְּבַעַל חוֹב, וְלַעֲבוֹר עָלָיו בִּשְׁנֵי לָאוִין. ת"ש: מִמַּשְׁמַע שֶׁנֶּאֱמַר °"בַּחוּץ תַּעֲמוֹד" אֵינִי יוֹדֵעַ שֶׁ"הָאִישׁ אֲשֶׁר אַתָּה נוֹשֶׁה בּוֹ יוֹצִיא"? אֶלָּא מַה תַּלְמוּד לוֹמַר °"וְהָאִישׁ"? לְרַבּוֹת שְׁלִיחַ בֵּית דִּין. מַאי לָאו – שְׁלִיחַ בֵּית דִּין כְּלָוֶה? לָא

ונוטל הכי פירושו: יביא ראיה ששכרו, ואז יהיה נשבע ונוטל. *והיכא דקתני המע"ה – היינו יביא עדים שקצץ לו שתים. שהעדים יודעים הקצילה אם יודעין ששכרו, (ד) כדפריך. וכן משמע בפרק "כל הנשבעין" דקאמר עלה: ראיה דלשלם קתני, ראיה דלשבע לא קתני. משמע, דנשבע ונוטל – היינו שיביא ראיה ששכרו, ויהיה נשבע ונוטל.

השתא דמטא זמן חיוביה רמי אנפשיה ומדכר. וא"ת: א"כ, בזמנו אמאי נשבע שכיר ונוטל? לימא בעה"ב: איני זוכר עתה, אבל הניחו לי עד שיעלה עמוד השחר, שאזכור אם נתתי אם לאו. כיון שאחר זמנו אנו פוטרים אותו מטעם זה?! ועוד קשה: במודה במקצת, אמאי אין בעל הבית נשבע, דרמי אנפשיה ומדיכר שלא ישבע לשקר?! וי"ל: דחזקה שאין בעה"ב עובר ב"בל תלין" לא מהני אלא היכא דאיכא חזקה דאין שכיר משהה שכרו בהדיה, כמו שאפרש בסמוך. ואם היה יכול בעה"ב לטעון הניחו לי עד שיעלה עמוד השחר – לא היתה כאן חזקה דאין שכיר משהה שכרו, שהרי לא השהה (ה) אתו אלא תבעו ממנו בב"ד, ולא רצו ליתן לו ושהו אותו לעמוד השחר. **וכי** שכיר עובר בבל תגזול. וא"ת: בעל נמי אית ליה הך חזקה, שאינו עובר ב"בל תגזול". וי"ל: דחמיר ליה לא אחר כמו שניס. א"נ: בלאו הכי משני ליה שפיר. וא"ת: ומ"מ, היכא חזקה דאין בעה"ב עובר ב"בל תלין" כנגדו, והוה ברי וברי, והמע"ה! וי"ל: דחזקה של בעל הבית אינה חזקה טובה כשל שכיר, דזימנין לא רמי אנפשיה למידכר. והוה לן למימר דנשבע ונוטל. וחזקה דאין שכיר משהה שכרו לבדו (ו) לא חשיבא כחזקת שכיר, אלא כששתיהן ביחד הוו כנגד חזקת שכיר, והוי ברי וברי והמע"ה.

והא תבע ליה קמן. ס"ד השתא אם יש עדים שתבעו – היינו אפי' אחר זמנו, ולכך פריך דמה אנו צריכין לעדים? הלא תובעו השתא בפנינו? ולמאי דס"ד הוה מצי למיפרך: אמאי נשבע ונוטל? אלא פריך שפיר.

ולעולם. פי' בקונטרס: וכי שכיר משהה שכרו כ"כ? ואינו מיושב, דאין בזה ראיה שנפרע. דחזקה דאין שכיר משהה שכרו אינה מועלת אלא היכא דאיכא חזקה דאין בעה"ב עובר ב"בל תלין" בהדה, ו"בל תלין" אינו עובר אלא בוקר ראשון. אלא הכי פירושו: ולעולם שכיר נשבע ונוטל? אין זו תקנה טובה שיהא נאמן לומר "לא פרע לי". **מחזיר** את הכר בלילה. בריש תמורה (דף ו. ושם ד"ה מחזיר) פריך לרבא, דאמר: כל דאמר רחמנא לא תעביד, אי עביד – לא מהני. והרי השבת העבוט, דאמר רחמנא "לא תעבוט עבוטו" ותנן: מחזיר את הכר בלילה, אלמא דמהני! וקשה, דמלניה דמתני' איירי במשכנו באיסור? וא"ל דסמיך אברייתא ד"אלו מציאות" (לעיל דף לא:) דקתני משכנו שלא ברשות מנין כו' – דא"כ מאי קשה לן? דהא בברייתא גופה יליף מ"השב תשיב" כדמשני התם, ואי אדשמואל סמיך – א"כ מה צריך לתרץ מ"השב תשיב"? הלא עיקר קרא לשמואל איירי במשכנו באיסור, דאם חבל וגו' משמע דמשכנו בביתו! וי"ל: דסמיך אמעשים בכל יום דמחזיר אפי' משכנו שלא ברשות. א"נ: סמיך אברייתא דלקמן (דף קיד:) דמתרץ לה רב ששת המלוה [את] חבירו אינו רשאי למשכנו. משכנו – חייב להחזיר לו. אע"ג דהאי דפריך לרבא בתמורה לא אתי אליבא דשמואל, דלשמואל אין שייך להקשות, דעיקר קרא במשכנו באיסור כתיב – מ"מ אין להוכיח משם שלא יהא הלכה כשמואל, כי כן דרך גמרא להקשות ולתרץ אפילו דלא כהלכתא. כדאשכחן בפ"ב דכתובות (דף כו.*) וברייתא ד"אלו מציאות" (לעיל דף לא:) דקאמר: אין לי אלא במשכנו ברשות, אין צריך לומר דשמואל יהפוך וישנה אין לי אלא משכנו שלא ברשות, אלא יעמידנה כתנא דפליג אתנא דקאי כוותיה, ויהפוך הדרשה.

ואת המחרישה ביום. קשה לר"ת: דתניא בסוף פירקין (דף קטז.): חבל זוג של ספרים וצמד של פרות – חייב משום ב' כלים. ופירש בקונטרס: פרות החורשות וחייב עליהן החובלן, לפי שעושין אוכל נפש. א"כ היאך נטל את המחרישה דקתני ומחזיר? *הא עבר "כי נפש הוא חובל" (דברים כד)! ועוד: דאין נראה לחייב אלא דוקא דומיא דריחיים ורכב שמתקנים האוכל עצמו בכלי. [א] לכן מפרש ר"ת: צמד פרות – היינו פרות המרכסות בתבואה. וגרים ר"ת נמי: זוג של מספרים, ולא גרסינן זוג של ספרים, וכן גרים ר"ת. והם תספורת של ירק, או לגזוז בית השחיטה, כדאמרינן בבכורות (דף כה.) שדרכן היה לגזוז. אבל פרות החורשות – לא מיקרי כלי שעושין אוכל נפש. ועוד נראה לר"ת: דמחרישה דהכא לאו היינו מחרישה שחורשין בה את הקרקע, דנראה דלא מחייב בהשבת העבוט, אלא בכלי העשוי לגוף האדם ולהנאתו. ועוד: דמוקי בגמ' במחרישה דכספא, ואין דרך לחרוש קרקע במחרישה של כסף. אלא נראה לר"ת דהיינו מגרדתא שמגרדין בו בני אדם בבית המרחץ, כדאמר בפרק "חבית" (שבת דף קמז:): עבדא ליה אימיה מגרדתא דכספא, וכן בפרק "מציאת האשה" (כתובות דף סח.) במחרישה דכספא פר"ח דהיינו מגרדתא. **אימא** לא ינתחנו אלא בבית דין. וא"ת: מנין דניתוח אסור לבעל חוב? ואומר ר"י: דמדרבנן הוא, כדאמר בסמוך בעל חוב ניתוח נמי לא, גזירה שמא יכנס בביתו. **וחסורי** מיחסרא והכי קתני. תימה: דקאמר חסורי מיחסרא כדי לדחות! וי"ל: דאין לחוש, כיון שאינו מגיה כ"כ. ורוב ספרים גרסי "הכי קאמר".
מטה

ר"ל מוחק ג' תיבות אלו

תמורה ו.

[ע' תוס' לקמן קטו. ד"ה אלמנה]

אמר לך

[ועס כתו' ד"ה והאמר רבי יוחנן]

עי' מ"מ פ"ג ממלוה מה שתירץ בשם הרשב"א

עין משפט נר מצוה

נ"ל וסיפא

קכז א ב מיי' פי"א מהל' שכירות הל' ו ועיין שם סמג לאוין קפא טור ש"ע ח"מ סי' פט סעי' ג:

קכח ג ד מיי' פ"ג מהל' מלוה ולוה הל' ד סמג שם טוש"ע ח"מ סי' לז סעי' ו:

קכט ה מיי' שם הל' ו ועיין בהשגות ובמ"מ טוש"ע שם סעיף יח:

קל ו מיי' שם הל' ה טוש"ע שם סעי' טז:

קלא ז מיי' שם הלכה ו טוש"ע שם סעי' יח:

קלב ח ט מיי' שם הל' ד ועיין שם טוש"ע שם סעי' ו:

הגהות הב"ח

(א) גמ' והא קתבע ליה קמן: (ב) שם משום הא לא אירא (הכי קאמר) תא"מ ונ"ב ס"א חסורי מיחסרא והכי קתני: (ג) שם נתוחי נמי לא גזירה שמא יכנס לביתו: (ד) תד"ה קלילה וכו' אם יודעין ששכרו כדפרישית וכן משמע בפ': (ה) ד"ה השתא שהרי לא השהה אותו אלא: (ו) ד"ה וכי שכיר וכו' לבדו נמי לא חשיבא:

הגהות הגר"א

[א] תוס' ד"ה ואת. לכן מפר"ת כו' ועוד נראה לר"ת כו'. נ"ב וכן פי' הרא"ש וטור אבל הרמב"ם ורמב"ן ורשב"א וש"פ מפרשים כפירש"י החורשות וכן מחרישה דמתני' מחרישה ממש וקושית תוס' תירץ בסה"ת דמתני' מיירי בעבר ומשכנו ובזה מתורץ קושית תוס' ד"ה מחזיר כו' ומש"ש זיל אהדריה ר"ל בשעת מלאכה דא"צ להחזיר כלי א"נ אלא בשעת מלאכה ודוקא הצריך לגוף אדם או כלי א"נ אבל ש"ד כמו גלוחית כו' א"ל. והרמב"ן והרשב"א תירצו דאף לכתחלה מותר למשכן שלא בשעת מלאכה כלי א"נ וכ"ה בירושלמי אבל דעת הרמב"ם בזה כדעת תוס' דכלי א"נ אסור לעולם למשכן ואם משכנו חייב להחזיר מיד והרז"ה תירץ דמתני' מיירי בנתנו מדעתו ואפ"ה חייב להחזיר וכ"כ הרמב"ם אחד כו' ואחד שנתנו לו מדעתו וכמ"ש בש"ע שם (בח"מ סי' לז) סעי' טז וע"ש בסעי' יב דפסק דכלי א"נ מחזיר מיד וע"ש בהג"ה אבל בסוף סעי' ו' כתב ומחזיר אותם בשעת מלאכה והעיקר כדעת רמב"ם דמחזיר מיד:

לא, שליח ב"ד כמלוה. ת"ש: °"אם חבל תחבל שלמת רעך" — בשליח בית דין הכתוב מדבר. אתה אומר בשליח בית דין הכתוב מדבר, או אינו אלא בבעל חוב? כשהוא אומר: °"לא תבא אל ביתו לעבוט עבוטו" — הרי בע"ח אמור. הא מה אני מקיים "אם חבל תחבל שלמת רעך"? בשליח ב"ד הכתוב מדבר! תנאי היא; דתניא: [א]שליח ב"ד שבא למשכנו — לא יכנס לביתו למשכנו, אלא עומד מבחוץ והלה מוציא לו משכון, שנאמר: °"בחוץ תעמוד והאיש". ותניא אידך: בע"ח שבא למשכנו — לא יכנס לביתו למשכנו, אלא עומד בחוץ, והלה נכנס ומוציא לו משכונו, שנאמר: "בחוץ תעמוד". ושליח ב"ד שבא למשכנו — הרי זה נכנס לביתו וממשכנו. [ב]ולא ימשכננו דברים שעושין בהן אוכל נפש. [א] [ג]ונותן מטה, ומטה ומצע — לעשיר. מטה, ומטה ומפץ — לעני. לו, [ד]אבל לא לאשתו, ולא לבניו ולבנותיו. כדרך שמסדרין לבע"ח כך מסדרין בערכין. כלפי לייא? עיקר סידור בערכין כתיב! אלא אימא: כדרך [ה]שמסדרין בערכין — כך [ו]מסדרין בבע"ח. אמר מר: נותן מטה ומטה ומצע לעשיר, מטה ומטה ומפץ לעני. למאן? אילימא לאשתו ולבניו ולבנותיו — הא אמרת: לו, אבל לא לאשתו ולבניו ולבנותיו! אלא, אידי ואידי לדידיה. תרתי למה לי? חדא דאכיל עלה, וחדא דזגי עלה. כדשמואל, דאמר שמואל: כל מילי ידענא אסותייהו, לבר מהני תלת: מאן דאכיל אהינא מרירא אליבא ריקנא; ומאן דאסר מיתנא דכיתנא רטיבא אחרציה; *ומאן דאכיל נהמא ולא מסגי ארבעה *גרמידי. תני תנא קמיה דרב נחמן: כדרך שמסדרין בערכין — כך מסדרין בבע"ח. א"ל: השתא זבוני מזבנינן ליה, סדורי מסדרינן ליה? ומי מזבנינן ליה? והתנן: מחזיר את הכר בלילה ואת המחרישה ביום! תנא כרשב"ג תנא קמיה, והכי קאמר ליה: השתא לרשב"ג זבוני מזבנינן ליה, סדורי מסדרינן ליה? דתנן, רשב"ג אומר: אף לעצמו אינו מחזיר אלא עד שלשים יום, מכאן ואילך מוכרן בב"ד. וממאי דהכי קאמר רשב"ג זבוני לגמרי קאמר? דלמא הכי קאמר: עד שלשים יום — הדר ליה בעיניה; מכאן ואילך — מיהדר ליה למאי דחזי ליה, ומזבנינן מאי דלא חזי ליה. אי סלקא דעתך אית ליה לרשב"ג האי סברא — ליכא מידי דלא חזי ליה. דאמר אביי: *רשב"ג ורבי שמעון ורבי ישמעאל ורבי עקיבא, כולהו סבירא להו: כל ישראל בני מלכים הן. רשב"ג *דתנן: [ז]לא את הלוף ולא את החרדל. רשב"ג מתיר בלוף, מפני שהוא מאכל לעורבין. רבי שמעון — *דתנן: [ח]בני מלכים סכין שמן וורד על גבי מכותיהן בשבת, שכן דרכן לסוך בחול. ר' שמעון אומר: כל ישראל בני מלכים הן. רבי ישמעאל ורבי עקיבא, דתניא: [ט]הרי שהיו נושין בו אלף זוז ולבוש איצטלא בת מאה מנה — מפשיטין אותה ממנו, ומלבישים אותו איצטלא הראויה לו. ותנא משום רבי ישמעאל, ותנא משום רבי עקיבא: כל ישראל ראוין לאותה איצטלא. ולמאי דסליק אדעתין מעיקרא, דיהיב ליה מאי דחזי ליה, ומזבנינן מאי דלא חזי ליה — בשלמא כר וכסת חזי ליה דביני ביני. אלא מחרישה למאי חזיא? *אמר רבא בר רבה: *מחרישה דכספא. מתקיף לה רב חגא: ולימא ליה לאו עלי קרמית! אמר ליה אביי:

איברא

תורה אור: שמות כב; דברים כד; שם

[עי' תוס' כתובות סה. ד"ה ונותן תירצו באופן אחר]

[עי' שבת מח.]

כתובות סח.

רש"י

לא שליח ב"ד כמלוה. והכי קאמר: "בחוץ תעמוד" אתה והאיש שהוא שליח ב"ד, ואשר אתה נושה בו יוציא אליך. הרי בעל חוב אמור. שאינו רשאי. הכתוב מדבר. שהוא רשאי ליכנס לחובלו. והכי קאמר קרא: אם חבול תחבול על ידי שליח ב"ד — עד בוא השמש תשיבנו לו. שנאמר בחוץ תעמוד והאיש. שהוא שליח בית דין — גם הוא יעמוד בחוץ. לא ימשכננו כלים שעושין בהן אוכל נפש. דאיתרבו מ"כי נפש הוא חובל". מטה ומטה. לקמן הוא מפרש: אחת לאכול ואחת לישן. מצע. של לבד שקורין פולטר"א, במקום שאין כסתות. לעשיר. שהורגל במצעות. ומפץ לעני. לפי מה שהורגל. דגבי ערכין כתיב "ואם מך הוא מערכך", ודרשינן (ערכין דף כד.) החייהו מערכך. גזבר הבא למשכנו כשאין ידו משגת והוא נידון בהשגת יד, דכתיב (ויקרא כז) "והעמידו לפני הכהן והעריך אותו הכהן" — משייר לו כדי חייו, ונוטל השאר, ויצא ידי הקדש. ואפי' העשיר לאחר שאמדוהו ונטל מה שבידו. ומינה נמי גמרינן לבעל חוב שמשיירין לו כדי חייו, כדאמר לקמן (דף קיד.) דגמר מיכה מיכה. לו. הוא צריך ליתן מטה, אבל לא לאשתו ולבניו. דהחייהו כתיב, ולא הוטל על המלוה להחיות את בני ביתו. שמסדרין. שמין להניח לו צרכי חייו, לשון "והעריך אותו". לישנא אחרינא: שמשרדין לשון 'שריד'. ושתיהן שמעתי. אדרבה עיקר סידור בערכין כתיב. כדפי' לעיל. למאן. המטה השנית. מיתנא רטיבא דכיתנא אחרציה. חבל לח של פשתן על מתניו. אהינא. תמרה. אליבא ריקנא. קודם אכילה. ולא מסגי ארבעה גרמידי. קודם שיישן. הלכך יהבינן ליה מטה שניה, ומושיבה ברחוק ארבע אמות ממקום אכילתו, ועל כרחו ירגיל לעמוד וללכת במשכב ולא יישן על מטה שאכל. זבוני מזבנינן ליה. לאחר שלשים יום אף כלים הצריכין לו, כדתנן: משלשים ולהלן מוכרן. תנא כרבן שמעון תני תנא קמיה. דרב נחמן להך מתני' רשב"ג אומר כדרך שמסדרין וכו'. זבוני לגמרי. שלא ישאיר לו לפי צרכו כלום. בעיניה. כמות שהיא חשובה, אם חבל כסות של מעיל — יחזיר לו הוא בעצמה. מהדר ליה מאי דחזי ליה. ימכור לו של שיראין, ויתן לו אחת של צמר ואחת של קנבוס. אי אית ליה לרבן גמליאל האי סברא. לסדר לבעל חוב. ליכא מידי דלא חזי ליה. מאחר שהורגל בו. דהא שמעינא ליה דאמר כל ישראל בני מלכים הם, דאמר אביי וכו'. לא את הלוף ולא את החרדל. מטלטלין בשבת, שאינם ראויים היום לא זה לבשל ולא זה לטחון. לוף — מין קטנית, ואינן ראוין למאכל כשהוא חי, ואפילו לעופות. לעורבים. וישראל בני מלכים, ויש להם לגדל עורבים לנוי ולשחוק. שכן דרכן לסוך בחול. בלא שום מכה. הלכך, כי איכא מכה — נמי לא מוכחא מילתא דלרפואה עביד, *(דכי גזרו) רבנן משום שחיקת סממנין. מפשיטין אותה ממנו. לפרוע לבעל חוב את חובו. בשלמא כר וכסת. דתנן במתניתין, איכא למימר מוכרן דקאמר רשב"ג — לביני ביני קאמר, לקנות גרועה הימנו. וביני ביני יטול בחובו. אלא מחרישה. דקתני במתניתין, ועלה קאמר רשב"ג מוכרן, מאי ביני ביני איכא? ונימא ליה. מלוה. לאו עלי דידי רמית. לפרנסך.

איברא

[פי' אמות וכן פי' רש"י לעיל סד. ד"ה בני גרמידא]

[שבת קכח.]

שבת קכו:

שבת קיא.

[פי' כמין מסרק הוא ומחכך בה בשרו במרחץ ערוך ערך מחרש ועי"ל עמוד א' בתוס' סד"ה ולא המחרישה]

[דליגזרו כצ"ל]

תוספות

מטה ומטה. בפ' "שום היתומים" (ערכין דף כג:) לא תני אלא מטה המולעת, משום דמולעת לא שבקינן ליה אלא אחת, כדאמר נמי הכא מטה ומטה ומצע. ובפ' "אע"פ" (כתובות דף סד:) גבי משרה אשתו על ידי שליש בעני שבישראל דלא יהיב לה אלא מטה ומפץ — משום דהתם קודם שנשאת לו לא היה לה אלא חדא מטה*. **השתא** זבוני מזבנינן הכסת והכר שיש לו בעין סדורי מסדרינן? — בתמיה. פירוש: ואנן נסדר לו להניח מן המעות כדי לקנות כסות לצורך שנים עשר חדש כמו שעושין בערכין? **נימא** ליה לא עלי דידי רמית. לאו אמתני' פריך אמאי מחזיר לו הכא — דא"כ למה המתין עד כאן? ועוד: דמה צריך טעם על מלות המקום? ועוד: וכי לא ידע דכתיב (דברים כד) "ולך תהיה צדקה"? אלא על כרחך ידע, ואפילו הכי מקשה ליה, וא"כ, מה מתרץ לו? אלא נראה דארבי עקיבא ורבי ישמעאל פריך, דאמרי כל ישראל בני מלכים הם וכולן ראוין לאותה איצטלא, ואמאי? כיון דאינו לובשה אלא לכבוד ולנוט בעלמא למה יש לנו לומר שכל זה הטיל הכתוב על המלוה? כיון שלא פירש הכתוב בהדיא, ולא היה שייך עליו יותר מעל אחר, כיון דסגיא ליה בלאו הכי? ומשני: גם באיצטלא שייך לומר "לך תהיה צדקה" והטיל עליו הכתוב שלא למנוע ממנו הנוי והכבוד והתענוג שהורגל בו עד עתה.

הקדש

עין משפט נר מצוה

קלג א מיי' פ"ג מהל' מלוה הל' ד סמג לאוין קע"ה טוש"ע ח"מ סי' צז סעיף ו:

קלד ב מיי' שם הל' ב טוש"ע שם ובסעי' יז:

קלה ג מיי' שם הל' ו ועיין בהשגות ובמ"מ טוש"ע שם סעי' יז וסעי' כג:

קלו ד מיי' פ"א שם הל' ז טוש"ע שם סעי' כג:

קלז ה מיי' פ"ג מהל' ערכין הל' יד סמג עשין קלא:

קלח ו מיי' פ"א מהל' מלוה הל' ז סמג לאוין קפא טוש"ע ח"מ סי' צז סעי' כג:

קלט ז מיי' פכ"ו מהל' שבת הל' טז סמג לאוין סה טוש"ע א"ח סימן שח סעי' כט:

קמ ח מיי' שם פכ"א הלכה כג סמג שם טוש"ע א"ח סי' שכז סעי' א:

קמא ט מיי' פ"א מהל' מלוה הלכה ז סמג לאוין קפא טוש"ע ח"מ סי' צז סעי' כג:

הגהות הגר"א

[א] גמ' ונותן מטה כו'. נ"ב דעת הרמב"ם שאינו נותן אלא אלו בלבד אבל לא שאר שמסדרין בשעת גביה והרמב"ן ורשב"א כתבו דכל הסדור מסדרין לו ג"כ כאן וז"ש כדרך כו' ודעת הרא"ש דאין נותן לו כלום ומ"ש ונותן כו' קאי אשעת גביה וה"ה כל הסידור וז"ש (במתני') ומחזיר כו' ודעת הרמב"ן שמניחין לו כל הסידור כנ"ל רק מה שא"צ לו תמיד כגון כר ומחרישה אינו מניח לו כי אם בעת שצריך וז"ש במתני' ומחזיר כו' ולהרמב"ם י"ל דכר לאו בכלל מצע וכן משמע בדבריו (ועמ"ש רבינו בח"מ סי' צז ס"ק נה):

תורה אור

אִיבְרָא, עֲלֵיהּ קָרָמֵי, מִשּׁוּם שֶׁנֶּאֱמַר: (דברים כד) "וּלְךָ תִּהְיֶה צְדָקָה". אִיבַּעְיָא לְהוּ: מַהוּ שֶׁיְּסַדְּרוּ בְּבַעַל חוֹב? מִי גָּמַר "מִיכָה", "מִיכָה" מֵעֲרָכִין אוֹ לֹא? ת"ש, דְּשָׁלַח רָבִין בְּאִגַּרְתֵּיהּ: דָּבָר זֶה שָׁאַלְתִּי לְכָל רַבּוֹתַי וְלֹא אָמְרוּ לִי דָּבָר. בְּרַם כָּךְ הָיְתָה שְׁאֵלָה: הָאוֹמֵר הֲרֵי עָלַי מָנֶה לְבֶדֶק הַבַּיִת מַהוּ שֶׁיְּסַדְּרוּ? ר' יַעֲקֹב מִשְּׁמֵיהּ *דְּבַר פַּדָּא, וְר' יִרְמְיָה מִשְּׁמֵיהּ דְּאִילְפָא אָמְרִי: ק"ו מִבַּעַל חוֹב. וּמַה ב"ח שֶׁמַּחֲזִירִין – *אֵין מְסַדְּרִין, הֶקְדֵּשׁ שֶׁאֵין מַחֲזִירִין – אֵינוֹ דִּין שֶׁאֵין מְסַדְּרִין? וְר' יוֹחָנָן אָמַר: "נֶדֶר בְּעֶרְכְּךָ" כְּתִיב, מָה עֲרָכִין מְסַדְּרִין – [א]אַף הֶקְדֵּשׁ מְסַדְּרִין. וְאִידָךְ? הַהוּא לְנִידּוֹן בִּכְבוֹדוֹ הוּא דַּאֲתָא. מָה עֲרָכִין *[ב]נִידּוֹן בִּכְבוֹדוֹ – [ג]אַף הֶקְדֵּשׁ נִידּוֹן בִּכְבוֹדוֹ. וִיסַדְּרוּ בְּבַ"ח ק"ו מֵעֲרָכִין: וּמָה עֲרָכִין [ד]שֶׁאֵין מַחֲזִירִין – מְסַדְּרִין; בַּעַל חוֹב שֶׁמַּחֲזִירִין – אֵינוֹ דִּין שֶׁמְּסַדְּרִין? אֲמַר קְרָא: (ויקרא כז) "וְאִם מָךְ הוּא מֵעֶרְכֶּךָ" – "הוּא" וְלֹא ב"ח. וְאִידָךְ? *[ה]הַאי – עַד שֶׁיְּהֵא בְּמָכוּתוֹ מִתְּחִילָּתוֹ וְעַד סוֹפוֹ. וְיַחֲזִירוּ בְּהֶקְדֵּשׁ קַל וָחוֹמֶר מִבַּ"ח: וּמַה בַּעַל חוֹב שֶׁאֵין מְסַדְּרִין – מַחֲזִירִין, הֶקְדֵּשׁ שֶׁמְּסַדְּרִין אֵינוֹ דִּין שֶׁמַּחֲזִירִין? אֲמַר קְרָא: (דברים כד) "וְשָׁכַב בְּשַׂלְמָתוֹ וּבֵרְכֶךָּ" – יָצָא הֶקְדֵּשׁ שֶׁאֵין צָרִיךְ בְּרָכָה. וְלָא? וְהָכְתִי': (שם ח) "וְאָכַלְתָּ וְשָׂבָעְתָּ וּבֵרַכְתָּ" וגו'! אֶלָּא אֲמַר קְרָא: "וּלְךָ תִּהְיֶה צְדָקָה" – מִי שֶׁצָּרִיךְ צְדָקָה, יָצָא הֶקְדֵּשׁ שֶׁאֵין צָרִיךְ צְדָקָה. אַשְׁכְּחֵיהּ רַבָּה בַּר אֲבוּהּ לְאֵלִיָּהוּ דְּקָאֵי בְּבֵית הַקְּבָרוֹת שֶׁל גּוֹיִם. א"ל: מַהוּ שֶׁיְּסַדְּרוּ בְּבַ"ח? א"ל: גָּמַר "מִיכָה", "מִיכָה" מֵעֲרָכִין; גַּבֵּי עֲרָכִין כְּתִיב: "וְאִם מָךְ הוּא מֵעֶרְכֶּךָ", גַּבֵּי ב"ח כְּתִיב: (ויקרא כה) "וְכִי יָמוּךְ אָחִיךָ". מִנַּיִן

רש"י

איברא. באמת. **עליה רמי.** שיהא לו צדקה, שהכתוב הטיל עליו לעשות לו צדקה להלך לפניו. **מיכה מיכה.** גבי לוה ומלוה כתיב: "וכי ימוך אחיך ומטה ידו עמך", וגבי ערכין כתיב: "ואם מך הוא מערכך". **דבר זה [שאלתי].** אם למדנו גזירה שוה ד'מיכה' 'מיכה', ולא אמרו לי דבר. **ברם כך היתה שאילה.** אבל כן נשאלה שאילה אחת בבית המדרש, מינה יש ללמוד שאין מסדרין. **הרי עלי מנה לבדק הבית.** והשגת יד לא כתיב אלא בערכין, אבל שאר הקדשות אין נידונין בהשג יד, ומה שיש לו גובין הימנו – והמותר יגבו לאחר זמן אם יעשיר. **מהו שיסדרו לו.** כשבאין למשכנו. **שמחזירין.** שמלוה מלווה להשיב לו את העבוט. **אין מסדרין.** להשאיר לו כלום משבא למכור לאחר שלשים. **נדר בערכך.** "כי יפליא נדר בערכך נפשות" (ויקרא כז) הקיש נדרים לערכין. **ההוא לנידון בכבודו.** היקש נדר לערכין להכי אתא, שאם אמר דמי לבי או ראשי או כבידי עלי – נותן דמי כולו. אבל אם אמר על אבר שאין הנשמה תלויה בו דמיו עלי – שמין אותו כעבד הנמכר בשוק, כמה הוא שוה ביד וכמה הוא שוה בלא יד. להא מילתא איצטריך למיגמר נדר מערכין. גבי ערכין כתיב (שם) "ערכך נפשות" אם אמר ערך אבר שהנשמה תלויה בו עלי – נותן דמי כולו, ואם אמר ערך ידי עלי – לא אמר כלום, שאין ערך כתוב אלא לנפש. **נידון בכבודו.** האבר נידון לפי כבודו, שאם הנשמה תלויה בו – נותן דמי כולו. **ויסדרו לב"ח.** גמרא קא פריך לה. **שמחזירין.** מיום אל יום את כלי הצריך לו. **אינו דין שמסדרין.** כשבא למכור לאחר שלשים יום ישאיר לו כדי חייו, כגון מטה ומפץ והנך דאמר בערכין (דף כג:). **ואידך.** תנא קמא דמתני' דאמר מסדרין לבעל חוב, דקתני: אם מת אינו מחזיר ליורשיו, הא לו – מחזיר לעולם. **האי.** "הוא" דכתיב בערכין דריש ליה עד שיהא במכותו מתחילתו ועד סופו, שאם העריך עצמו עני והעשיר קודם שהעריכו כהן – אינו נידון בהשגת יד, אלא נותן ערך עשיר. **ויחזירו בהקדש.** העבוט עד שלשים יום.

ערות

תוספות

הקדש שאין מחזירין אינו דין שאין מסדרין. וא"ת: ערכין יוכיח שאין מחזירין ומסדרין! ויש לומר: דמה לערכין – שהם קלים, ואינן נוהגים אלא באדם, ובבן ברית, ולא בטומטום ואנדרוגינוס, ופחות מבן חדש. אבל הקדש – חל על כל דבר. **ואידך** ההוא לנדון בכבודו הוא דאתא. וא"ת: מ"מ, נילף נמי בהיקישא דמסדרין, *דאין היקש למחצה! ואין לומר דהיקישא משמע דלא אתא אלא לנדון בכבודו, דכתיב "נדר בערכך נפשות" דמשמע (א) דבר שהנפש תלוי בו, אבל לדבר אחר לא הוקשו. דהא בפרק "שום היתומים" (ערכין ד' כד.) אמרינן: מנין שלא ישהא מרגלית לקליס. פירוש: אם אמר ערכי עלי, ויש לי מרגלית שוה מנה, ובמקום שעומדין אינה שוה אלא חמשים לפי שאין שם עשירים שיקנו אותה, מנין שאין להעריכה אלא בנ' זוזים – שנאמר (ב) "והיה ערכך ביום ההוא" – כמו ששוה ביום ההוא. ובפ' "השיג יד" (שם דף יח.) אמרינן: אתא הקשת הקדש לערכין לנידון בכבודו, ולמרגלית לקליס, והכא (ג) חד מינייהו. אלמא: לכל מילי מקשינן! ◉וצריך לומר דסברא דק"ו מבטל הקישא, כיון שנוכל להעמיד ההיקישא לדבר אחר. *כן משמע בפרק קמא דזבחים (דף י:) דקאמר, תנן התם: ר"ע אומר כל הדמים שנכנסו להיכל לכפר פסולים, וחכ"א: חטאת בלבד. ר' אליעזר אומר: אף האשם, שנאמר "כחטאת כאשם" ופריך: בשלמא רבי אליעזר – כדאמר טעמא, אלא רבנן מאי טעמייהו? אמר רבא: אשם שנכנס דמו לפנים פסול לא מלית אמרת מק"ו כו'. אלמא: ק"ו מבטל הקישא ד"כחטאת כאשם", כיון דאיכא לאוקמא הקישא לדבר אחר. והיא דס"פ "כל הבשר" (חולין דף קטו:) דגמרי בשר בחלב אסור באכילה בג"ש דקדש קדש מ"אנשי קודש תהיון לי וגו'". ואיסור הנאה יליף מק"ו מערלה. ואית דדריש בג"ש *לגמרי לאיסור אכילה ולהיתר הנאה – לא דמי להכא, אפילו יהא הקישא וק"ו כמו ג"ש וק"ו, דאפילו מאן דיליף התם ק"ו – מצי סבר הכא דאין הקישא למחצה. דהתם ע"י ק"ו אין סותר ג"ש כלל, משום דקרא ד"בשר בשדה טרפה" דאיירי בבשר שיצא חוץ למחיצתו איירי גם באיסורי הנאה, כגון בשר קדשים שיצא חוץ ממחיצתו, שהוא בשריפה. ומאן דלא יליף איסור הנאה בק"ו משום ג"ש – היינו משום דאכילה והנאה חדא היא. אבל הכא מודה דעבדינן ק"ו למסדרין, כיון דמתוקם ההיקש למילתא אחריתי. וצ"ע, דהרבה מקומות בת"כ ובגמרא שרוצה לעשות ק"ו וסותר אותו ע"י היקש או ג"ש, אם יש בכל מקום שלא נוכל להעמיד ההיקש או הג"ש לד"א. וא"ת: דאמרינן בערכין בפרק קמא (דף ד:) ראש חמור זה הקדש, ראש עבד זה הקדש – הוא והקדש שותפין בו, ולא אמר דנידון בכבודו! בערכין פריך לה, ומשני: כאן בקדשי מזבח, כאן בקדשי בדק הבית, דהכא מיירי בקדשי מזבח. ר"י.

מה ערכין נידון בכבודו. פי' בקונט': דדרשינן מ"נפשות". וא"ת: מה צריך קרא? דמאי שנא מנזקין, דאם קיטע ידו אומדין כמה הוא יפה בידו וכמה הוא יפה בלא יד, וה"נ יש לנו לשום כמה הוא שוה באבר שהנשמה תלויה בו, וכמה הוא שוה בלא ממנו, דהיינו ערך כולה דאינו שוה כלום אם היה נוטל אותו אבר! וי"ל: דאמר בפרק "האומר משקלי" (ערכין דף יט.) דאין שמין בערכין אומד של נזקין, אלא שמין אותו כאילו היתה ידו מוכתבת לרבו ראשון, ולא כמו שנטלה לגמרי – דאז מתגנה העבד ושוה הרבה פחות. וה"נ אין שמין באבר שהנשמה תלויה בו אי לאו דכתיב "נפשות". **מה** ערכין שאין מחזירין מסדרין. וא"ת: כיון שמסדרין ומניחין לו שיעור המפורש במשנה א"כ מה חזרה שייך, דהרי מניחין לו לגמרי כדי צרכו ומה יחזיר לו עוד? ואור"ת: דכשנוטל ממנו בתורת פרעון אז מסדרין, אבל כשנוטל בתורת משכון דחייבי ערכין ממשכנין אותן – אז אין מסדרין ושייך חזרה.

ואידך עד שיהא במכותו כו'. פירש בקונטרס: דהיינו רבנן דמתני'. ולפי' ר"ת דלקמן, רבנן דמתניתין מצי סברי דאין מסדרין – צ"ל ואידך היינו הני דאיבעיא להו מהו שיסדרו בבעל חוב. אי נמי: ברייתא דתנא לעיל דמסדרין. **במכותו** מתחילתו ועד סופו. למעוטי עני והעשיר וחזר והעני דנותן ערך עשיר, כרבי יהודה דבפרק "השיג יד" (שם דף יז:).

מהו שיסדרו בבעל חוב. *פסק ר"ת בספר הישר דאין מסדרין בבעל חוב, דהא רשב"ג דמתני' מסיק לעיל דסבר דאין מסדרין בב"ח, וקי"ל (ב"ק דף סט.): הלכה כרשב"ג במשנתנו היכא דלא פסק גמרא כמאן דפליג עליה. ולא מצינו בכל אמוראים דשמעתא שום אמורא שסבר בהדיא שמסדרין. ורבה בר אבוה דאמר ליה לאליהו מהו שיסדרו לבעל חוב, וא"ל גמר "מיכה מיכה" מערכין – נראה לר"ת דגרסינן: מנין שמסדרין לבעל חוב, כלומר: מגליה למאן דאית ליה מסדרין, וכן גריס בה"ג, וכן נראה. דאי כגי' הספרים דקבעי מה שיסדרו לבעל חוב – הוה ליה למימר 'מסדרין', שהרי הטעם לא היה שואל, אלא ודאי מנין גרס, ולעולם אין מסדרין ס"ל. ובפ' "השיג יד" (ערכין שם) דפליגי רבי יהודה ורבנן בעני והעשיר וחזר והעני, דר' יהודה סבר נותן ערך עשיר, ומפרש בגמרא דטעמא דרבי יהודה משום דכתיב "ואם מך הוא" – עד שיהיה במכותו מתחילתו ועד סופו, מכלל דרבנן דפליגי עליה דרשי הוא – ולא בבעל חוב, דדוקא בערכין מסדרין ולא בבעל חוב, כדדריש לעיל, ויחיד ורבים הלכה כרבים. ויש לדחות: דדרשינן: הוא ולא אשתו, כדדרשינן לעיל. ועוד הביא ראיה, דאמרי' בפ"ק דב"ק (דף יא: ושם ד"ה אפילו): מיניה – ואפילו מן גלימא דעל כתפיה. וכי תימה דהיינו שמפשיטין אותו גלימא דאלפא זוזא ויהבינן ליה גלימא אחרינא דחזיא ליה – הא ליכא מידי דלא חזי ליה כרשב"ג דלעיל. ועוד: דפסיק רב אלפס בפרק "שמנה שרצים" (שבת דף קיא.) כר"ש דאמר כל ישראל בני מלכים, ומיהו, אמרינן התם דפסיק כר"ש ולא מטעמיה. ורבנן דמתני' נמי מצי סברי דאין מסדרין, ומיירי

מסורת הש"ס

[ע' תוס' תמורה י. ד"ה איתמר]

נדרים סה:

[ערכין ד: יח.]

[ערכין יז:] גי' רש"ל האי הוא וכו'

עיין רש"א

עין משפט נר מצוה

קמב א מיי' פ"ג מהל' ערכין הל' טו סמג עשין קלא:

קמג ב מיי' שם פ"ב הל' א:

קמד ג מיי' שם הל' ז:

[נדרים ז.]

קמה ד מיי' שם פ"ג הל' יד סמג שם:

קמו ה מיי' שם הל' ה:

[וכן משמע כל"ל]

[שם קטז.]

גליון הש"ס

תוס' ד"ה ואידך ההוא כו' וצ"ל דסברא דק"ו. עיין בכורות דף לג ע"א תוס' ד"ה וכ"ה:

הגהות הב"ח

(א) תוס' ד"ה ואידך ההוא וכו' דמשמע לדבר: (ב) בא"ד בנ' זוזים שנאמר ונתן את הערכך ביום: (ג) בא"ד חדא מינייהו נקט אלמא:

עין משפט נר מצוה

קמז א מיי' פ"ד מהל' תרומות הל' ז:
קמח ב מיי' פ"א מהל' טומאת מת הל' יג:
קמט ג ד ה מיי' פ"ג מהל' מלוה ולוה הלכה ה סמג לאוין קפא טוש"ע ח"מ סי' נז סעי' טז:
קנ ו מיי' שם הל' ו ועיין שם טוש"ע שם סעיף יט:

תורה אור

א מנין לערום שלא יתרום? דכתיב: °"ולא יראה בך ערות דבר" (דברים כג). אמר ליה: לאו כהן הוא מר? מאי טעמא קאי מר בבית הקברות? א"ל: לא מתני מר טהרות? דתניא, *ר"ש בן יוחי אומר: ב קבריהן של גוים אין מטמאין, שנאמר: *°"ואתן צאני צאן מרעיתי אדם אתם" (יחזקאל לד) — אתם קרויין אדם, ואין גוים קרויין אדם. אמר ליה: בארבעה לא מצינא, בשיתא מצינא? א"ל: ואמאי? אמר ליה: דחיקא לי מילתא. דבריה ועייליה לגן עדן. אמר ליה: פשוט גלימך, ספי שקול מהני טרפי. ספא שקל. כי הוה נפיק שמע דקאמר: מאן קא אכיל לעלמיה כרבה בר אבוה! נפץ שדנהו. אפילו הכי, אתייה לגלימיה, סחט גלימא ריחא, זבניה בתריסר אלפי דינרי, פלגינהו לחתנוותיה. ת"ר: °"ואם איש עני הוא לא תשכב בעבוטו" (דברים כד), *הא עשיר — שכיב. מאי קאמר? אמר רב ששת: הכי קאמר: ג ואם איש עני הוא לא תשכב ועבוטו אצלך, הא עשיר — שכיב ועבוטו אצלך. ת"ר: המלוה את חבירו אינו רשאי למשכנו, ואינו חייב להחזיר לו, ועובר בכל השמות הללו. מאי קאמר? אמר רב ששת, הכי קאמר: המלוה את חבירו אינו רשאי למשכנו, ואם משכנו — חייב להחזיר לו; ועובר בכל השמות הללו — אסיפא. רבא אמר: הכי קאמר: המלוה את חבירו אינו רשאי למשכנו, ואם משכנו — חייב להחזיר לו. ד במה דברים אמורים — שמשכנו שלא בשעת הלואתו, ה אבל משכנו בשעת הלואתו — אינו חייב להחזיר לו. ועובר בכל השמות הללו — ארישא. תני רב שיזבי קמיה דרבא: °"עד בא השמש תשיבנו לו" (שמות כב) — זו כסות לילה; °"השב תשיב לו את העבוט כבוא השמש" (דברים כד) — זו כסות יום. אמר ליה: דימגא בליליא למה לי, ודליליא בימגא למה לי? אמר ליה: איסמייה? אמר ליה: לא, הכי קאמר: "עד בא השמש תשיבנו לו" — זו כסות יום שניתנה לחבול בלילה; "השב תשיב לו את העבוט כבוא השמש" — זו כסות לילה שניתנה לחבול ביום. אמר ר' יוחנן: *ו משכנו ומת — שומטו מעל גבי בניו. מיתיבי, אמר ר' מאיר: וכי מאחר שממשכנין למה מחזירין? למה מחזירין? רחמנא אמר אהדר! אלא: מאחר שמחזירין, למה

רש"י

ערות דבר. בשעה שאתה מדבר בו לא יראה בך ערות דבר. ש"מ: אין אדם מברך כשהוא ערום, ותורם בעי ברכה. והאי דבעי מיניה לענין תורם — דהתם תנן (תרומות פ"א מ"ו): אין מגביהין תרומה ערום. לאו כהן מר. דאיכא למ"ד דאליהו הוא פינחס, דכתיב ביה "קנא קנאתי" וכן בפינחס "בקנאו את קנאתי". אין מטמאין. דגבי אהל כתיב "אדם" (במדבר יט): "אדם כי ימות באהל". בארבעה לא מצינא. בגירסא דארבעה סדרין, כגון מועד ישועות נשים שהן נוהגות בזמן הזה כבזמן הבית, וקדשים נמי כדכתיב: "ובכל מקום מוקטר מוגש לשמי" ואמרי' (מנחות דף קי.): אלו תלמידי חכמים העוסקין בהלכות עבודה בכל מקום — מעלה עליהן הכתוב כאילו מקריבין אותן בבית המקדש. בשיתא מצינא. בתמיה. זרעים אינו נוהג בחוצה לארץ, וכן טהרות. ספי. לקוט. טרפי. עלין. נפץ. אשקוש"ט בלע"ז. סחט גלימא. נסחט ריח מתוך העלין לתוך טלית, וקלטה טליתו את הריח. וזבני'. לגלימ' בי"ב אלפי דינרי. לא תשכב בעבוטו. הא עשיר — שכיב בעבוטו. מאי קאמר. וכי בשביל שהוא עשיר התירו לשכב על טליתו? והרי הוא רבית אללו, שישתמש במשכונו חנם. הכי קאמר לא תשכב ועבוטו בידך. אלא השיבנו לו כבוא השמש, כדכתיב: "השב תשיב לו את העבוט כבוא השמש". ה"ג: המלוה את חבירו אינו רשאי למשכנו ואינו חייב להחזיר לו. ועובר בכל השמות הללו. "השב תשיב", ו"לא תשכב בעבוטו", ו"עד בא השמש תשיבנו לו". מאי קאמר. דקתני אינו חייב להחזיר לו, ועוד הדר תני עובר בכל השמות הללו (עובר בכל השמות הללו) "השב תשיב", "לא תשכב בעבוטו", ו"עד בא השמש תשיבנו". אסיפא. אם לא החזיר. ורבא אמר הכי קאמר וכו'. לא טעי תנא במאי דאתנייה חייב להחזיר לאוסופי ולמימר אינו חייב להחזיר. אלא ודאי אינו חייב להחזיר נמי אתנייה, והכי קאמר וכו' ושכח וחיסר ודילג מחייב להחזיר באינו חייב להחזיר. שמשכנו שלא בשעת הלואתו. בבית דין. אבל משכנו בשעת הלואתו. שהביא לו משכונו. אינו חייב להחזיר. דקרא בחובלו לאחר הלואה כתיב, דהיכא דאתייה ניהליה — לאו חובלו הוא. ארישא. אמשכנו שלא בשעת הלואתו ולא החזיר לו — עובר בכל השמות הללו. עד בא השמש תשיבנו לו. משמע בבוקר תשיבנו לו. ויהא בידו עד בא השמש, ויקח לו ממנו. זה כסות לילה. לקמן פריך: דלילה לאהדורי ליה בימאא למה לי? כבא השמש. בלילה החזירו לו. איסמייה. אסיר ברייתא זו מסדר משנתי. אמר ליה לא. תסמייה, דהא כסות לילה וכסות יום דקאמר — לאו תשמיש יום ותשמיש לילה קאמר, אלא: כסות העשויה למשכב בלילה, וכסות העשויה למשכב ביום קאמר. והכי קאמר: "עד בא השמש תשיבנו לו" וכבא השמש תטלנו — זה כסות יום, ולימדך הכתוב שניתנה לו רשות לחובלה בלילה, ולענין חבלה קרי ליה כסות לילה. משכנו ומת. לוה לאחר שהשיב לו את העבוט. שומטו. מלוה מעל גבי בניו ואין נעשה אללו כשאר מטלטלים שלהן דלא משתעבדי לב"ח, דכיון דמשכניה — קנייה.

למה

תוספות

ומיירי בבא ליטול בתורת משכון. דרבנן סברי שמחזירין לו כל ימי חייו, ורשב"ג סבר: דאמר שלשים יום מוכרו. אבל היכא דנטל בתורת גבייה — יכול למוכרו מיד, ולא יסדרו כלל. וא"ת: אמאי לא מייתי מרשב"ג דאין מסדרין? ויש לומר: דסבר גמרא דשקלינן מידי דלא חזי ליה, ויהבינן ליה מידי דחזי ליה. כמו שלמעלה לא היה יודע הגמרא. ואע"ג ששנינו דרשב"ג מתיר בלוף — לא ידע דהוי טעמא (א) דליכא מידי דחזי ליה. ומר' עקיבא ור' ישמעאל דאמרי (לעיל דף קיג:) כל ישראל ראויין לאותה איצטלא — אין להוכיח דסבירא להו מסדרין, דמיירי דגבה בתורת משכון, דת"ק סבר דמפשיטין אותה איצטלא בת מאה מנה ונותנין לו הראויה לו, וממנה עושין הֲסָבַת העבוט בכל יום ויום, והמותר יהיה לו למלוה בתורת משכון ולא יחזיר אותו כלל. ורבי עקיבא ור' ישמעאל סברי דמן הטובה עושה השבת העבוט — אבל בתורת גבייה לא הדר כלל. ומדמהדר ליה אליהו מיכה מיכה — לא בעי למיפשט, אפילו גרס מהו שיסדרו — משום דאליהו דחוי הוה מדחי ליה, (ב) והיה לו להשיב "אין מסדרין". תדע, שהרי השיב לו קברי גוים אינם מטמאים באהל כר"ש בן יוחי, אע"ג דלא קי"ל כוותיה, אלא כרשב"ג דמתני' דאהלות דאסר מדורות גוים משום אהל. וטעמיה דאליהו משום דרוב ארונות יש בהן פותח טפח, ויש מקום שלא גזרו, כגון *לצאת לקראת מלכים וכיוצא בו. • וכן מצינו כשהיה קובר את רע"ע היה דוחה, שאמר ליה: וכי אינך כהן? אמר ליה: צדיקים אין מטמאין. ודחה אותו כן משום כבודו דר"ע, ועיקר טעמו היה לפי שהיה מת מלוה, לפי שהיו יראים לקברו שהיה מהרוגי מלכות. וכן נמצא בתשובת גאון, שכתב: שיש בסדר אליהו רבה שנחלקו עליו, יש אומרים שהיה מבני בני בניה של לאה, ואמר להם: איני אלא מזרעה של רחל, וא"כ לא היה כהן, וכאן אומר שכהן היה. ומסיים התם, אמרו לו: תן סימן לדבריך, אמר להן: כך כתוב ביחוסו של בנימין "ויערשיה ואליה וזכרי בני ירוחם". אמרו לו: לא כך אמרת לאותה אלמנה *"עשי לי משם עוגה קטנה *ולך ולבנך תעשה באחרונה" ולא כהן אתה? פי': לפי שכהן הוא היה רוצה ליטול חלה תחילה. אמר להם: אותו תינוק משיח בן יוסף היה, ורמז רמזתי לעולם שאני בא תחילה. ובאותה תשובה מביא נמי הא דגמרי' מיכה מיכה, וגרס: מנין שמסדרין לבעל חוב כמו שגורס ר"ת. וכן בב"ר, גבי "ותאמר לאה בגד" נחלקו, רבי נהוראי אמר דאליהו מגד, ור"א אמר משל בנימין, ועמד לפניהם ואמר להם: רבותי, למה אתם נחלקים עלי אני מבני בניה של רחל.

מנין לערום שלא יתרום. הוה ליה למימר מנין שלא יברך, דבשעה שתורם ממנו אינו אסור אלא בשעת ברכה, ושאר ברכות אסור לברך כשהוא ערום. אלא נקט הכי משום דמשנה היא: ערום לא יתרום. **אמר** ליה לאו כהן (*אתה). תימה לר"י היאך החיה בנה של האלמנה, כיון שכהן היה, דכתיב (מלכים א יז) "ויתמודד על הילד וגו'"! ויש לומר: שהיה ברור לו שיחייהו, לכך היה מותר משום פיקוח נפש.

ה"ג **דתניא** ר' שמעון [בן יוחי] אומר. דאינה משנה בשום מקום, ועוד: דמשניות אף של זרעים וטהרות היו שגורות להם, כדמשמע בכמה *דוכתין. והא דקאמר בארבע לא מצינא, בשיתא מצינא – היינו בתוספתא.

למה

הגהות הב"ח

(א) ד"ה מהו שיסדרו וכו' לא ידע דהוי טעמא משום דבני מלכים אלא דליכא דלא חזי ליה: (ב) בא"ד דחויי הוה מדחי ליה (והוה לו להשיב אין מסדרין). תא"מ ונ"ב ס"א והיה לו להשיב מסדרין אלא סבר אין מסדרין כו':

גליון הש"ס

גמ' הא עשיר שכיב מאי קאמר. עיין כתובות דף קה ע"ב תוס' ד"ה אפי': **רש"י** ד"ה מאי קאמר וכו' והרי הוא רבית. עיין לעיל דף סד ע"ב תוס' ד"ה ולא: **תום'** ד"ה מהו וכו' וכן מצינו כשהיה קובר את ר"ע. במדרש ילקוט משלי בפסוק חכמות נשים בנתה ביתה.

מסורת הש"ס

יבמות סא.
[כריתות ו:]
[ע' תוס' כתובות קה: ד"ה אפילו]
[לעיל קד. ע"ש]
[וע' תוס' חולין קו: ד"ה דתקן]
[ברכות יט:]
[מלכים א יז]
[בראשית]
לאו כהן מר

לָמָּה חוֹזְרִין וּמְמַשְׁכְּנִין? אשֶׁלֹּא תְהֵא שְׁבִיעִית מְשַׁמַּטְתּוֹ, וְלֹא יַעֲשֶׂה מִטַּלְטְלִין אֵצֶל בָּנָיו. טַעְמָא — דַּהֲדַר וּמַשְׁכְּנֵיהּ, הָא לָא הֲדַר וּמַשְׁכְּנֵיהּ — לָא! אָמַר רַב אַדָּא בַּר מַתְנָא: וְלָאו תֵּרוּצֵי קָא מְתָרְצַתְּ לָהּ? תְּרֵיץ הָכִי: וְכִי מֵאַחַר שֶׁמַּחֲזִירִין בלָמָּה מְמַשְׁכְּנִין מֵעִיקָּרָא? שֶׁלֹּא תְהֵא שְׁבִיעִית מְשַׁמַּטְתּוֹ, וְלֹא יַעֲשֶׂה מִטַּלְטְלִין אֵצֶל בָּנָיו. דברים כד *ת"ר: °"לֹא תָבֹא אֶל בֵּיתוֹ לַעֲבוֹט עֲבוֹטוֹ". לְבֵיתוֹ אִי אַתָּה נִכְנָס, אֲבָל גאַתָּה נִכְנָס לְבֵיתוֹ שֶׁל עָרֵב. וְכֵן הוּא אוֹמֵר: °"לְקַח בִּגְדוֹ כִּי עָרַב זָר" משלי כ וגו'. וְאוֹמֵר: °"בְּנִי אִם עָרַבְתָּ לְרֵעֶךָ תָּקַעְתָּ לַזָּר כַּפֶּיךָ, נוֹקַשְׁתָּ בְאִמְרֵי פִיךָ נִלְכַּדְתָּ בְּאִמְרֵי פִיךָ, שם ו עֲשֵׂה זֹאת אֵפוֹא בְּנִי וְהִנָּצֵל כִּי בָאתָ בְכַף רֵעֶךָ לֵךְ הִתְרַפֵּס *וּרְהַב רֵעֶיךָ". אִם מָמוֹן יֵשׁ לוֹ בְּיָדְךָ — הַתֵּר לוֹ פִּיסַּת יָד; וְאִם לָאו — הַרְבֵּה עָלָיו רֵעִים. לְצַד שֵׁנִי: לְבֵיתוֹ אִי אַתָּה נִכְנָס, דאֲבָל אַתָּה נִכְנָס לִשְׂכַר כָּתֵף, לִשְׂכַר חַמָּר, לִשְׂכַר פּוּנְדָּק, לִשְׂכַר דְּיוֹקְנָאוֹת. יָכוֹל אֲפִילּוּ זְקָפָן עָלָיו בְּמִלְוָה — הת"ל: "מַשַּׁאת מְאוּמָה".§ **מתני'** ואַלְמָנָה, בֵּין שֶׁהִיא עֲנִיָּה בֵּין שֶׁהִיא עֲשִׁירָה — אֵין מְמַשְׁכְּנִין אוֹתָהּ, שֶׁנֶּאֱמַר: °"לֹא תַחֲבוֹל דברים כד בֶּגֶד אַלְמָנָה".§ **גמ'** ת"ר: *אַלְמָנָה, בֵּין שֶׁהִיא עֲנִיָּה בֵּין שֶׁהִיא עֲשִׁירָה — אֵין מְמַשְׁכְּנִין אוֹתָהּ, דִּבְרֵי ר' יְהוּדָה. ר"ש אוֹמֵר: עֲשִׁירָה — מְמַשְׁכְּנִין אוֹתָהּ, עֲנִיָּה — אֵין מְמַשְׁכְּנִין אוֹתָהּ, *שֶׁאַתָּה חַיָּיב לְהַחֲזִיר לָהּ וְאַתָּה מַשִּׂיאָהּ שֵׁם רַע בִּשְׁכֵנוֹתֶיהָ. לְמֵימְרָא דְּר' יְהוּדָה לָא דָּרֵישׁ טַעְמָא דִּקְרָא, וְר"ש *דָּרֵישׁ טַעְמָא דִּקְרָא? וְהָא אִיפְּכָא שָׁמְעִינַן לְהוּ, *דְּתַנְיָא: °"וְלֹא יַרְבֶּה לּוֹ נָשִׁים" — ר' יְהוּדָה אוֹמֵר: מַרְבֶּה הוּא, דברים יז וּבִלְבַד שֶׁלֹּא יְהוּ מְסִירוֹת אֶת לִבּוֹ. ר"ש אוֹמֵר: אֲפִילּוּ אַחַת וְהִיא מְסִירָה אֶת לִבּוֹ ה"ז לֹא יִשָּׂאֶנָּה. א"כ מַה ת"ל "וְלֹא יַרְבֶּה לּוֹ נָשִׁים" — אֲפִילּוּ כַּאֲבִיגַיִל! לְעוֹלָם ר' יְהוּדָה לָא דָּרֵישׁ טַעְמָא דִּקְרָא, וְשָׁאנֵי הָכָא דִּמְפָרֵשׁ קְרָא: "וְלֹא יַרְבֶּה לּוֹ נָשִׁים וְלֹא יָסוּר". מַאי טַעְמָא לֹא יַרְבֶּה לּוֹ נָשִׁים? מִשּׁוּם דְּ"לֹא יָסוּר". וְר"ש: מִכְּדֵי בְּעָלְמָא דָּרְשִׁינַן טַעְמָא דִּקְרָא — לִכְתּוֹב רַחֲמָנָא "לֹא יַרְבֶּה" וְלָא בָּעֵינַן "לֹא יָסוּר", וַאֲנָא יָדַעְנָא: מַאי טַעְמָא "לֹא יַרְבֶּה"? מִשּׁוּם דְּ"לֹא יָסוּר". "לֹא יָסוּר" דִּכְתַב רַחֲמָנָא לָמָּה לִי? אֲפִילּוּ אַחַת וּמְסִירָה אֶת לִבּוֹ — הֲרֵי זֶה לֹא יִשָּׂאֶנָּה.§ **מתני'** זהַחוֹבֵל אֶת הָרֵיחַיִם עוֹבֵר מִשּׁוּם לֹא תַעֲשֶׂה, וְחַיָּיב מִשּׁוּם שְׁנֵי כֵלִים, שֶׁנֶּאֱמַר: °"לֹא יַחֲבוֹל רֵיחַיִם וָרָכֶב". חוְלֹא דברים כד רֵיחַיִם וָרֶכֶב בִּלְבַד אָמְרוּ, אֶלָּא כָּל דָּבָר שֶׁעוֹשִׂין בּוֹ אוֹכֶל נֶפֶשׁ, שֶׁנֶּאֱמַר: "כִּי נֶפֶשׁ הוּא חוֹבֵל".§ **גמ'** אָמַר רַב הוּנָא: חָבַל רֵיחַיִם — לוֹקֶה שְׁתַּיִם, מִשּׁוּם "רֵיחַיִם" וּמִשּׁוּם "כִּי נֶפֶשׁ הוּא חוֹבֵל". רֵיחַיִם וָרֶכֶב — לוֹקֶה שָׁלֹשׁ, מִשּׁוּם "רֵיחַיִם וָרֶכֶב", וּמִשּׁוּם "כִּי נֶפֶשׁ הוּא חוֹבֵל". טוְרַב יְהוּדָה אָמַר: חָבַל רֵיחַיִם — לוֹקֶה אַחַת; "וָרֶכֶב" — לוֹקֶה אַחַת; "רֵיחַיִם וָרֶכֶב" — לוֹקֶה שְׁתַּיִם. "כִּי נֶפֶשׁ הוּא חוֹבֵל" — לִשְׁאָר

לָמָּה חוֹזְרִין וּמְמַשְׁכְּנִין. הֲרֵי עָלָיו לְהַחֲזִיר לוֹ לְמָחָר. שֶׁלֹּא תְהֵא שְׁבִיעִית מְשַׁמַּטְתּוֹ. דְּלֶהֱוֵי מַשְׁכּוֹנוֹ בְּיָדוֹ, וְהַמַּלְוֶה עַל הַמַּשְׁכּוֹן אֵינוֹ מְשַׁמֵּט. וְלֹא יַעֲשֶׂה מִטַּלְטְלִין אֵצֶל בָּנָיו. שֶׁלֹּא יָמוּת בְּעוֹד הַמַּשְׁכּוֹן מוּחְזָר לוֹ, וִיהֵא מִטַּלְטְלִין אֵצֶל בָּנָיו. טַעְמָא דַּהֲדַר מִשְׁכְּנֵיהּ. שֶׁהָיָה בְּיָדוֹ כְּשֶׁמֵּת לֹוֶה. לָמָּה מְמַשְׁכְּנִין מֵעִיקָּרָא. דָּבָר שֶׁעָלָיו לְהַחֲזִיר, מַה מּוֹעִיל לוֹ?. שֶׁלֹּא תְהֵא שְׁבִיעִית מְשַׁמַּטְתּוֹ וְכוּ'. דְּמִדְּמִשְׁכְּנֵיהּ קָנְיֵיהּ, וְכִי מְהַדַּר לֵיהּ — הָוֵה פִּקָּדוֹן גַּבֵּיהּ. בְּנִי אִם עָרַבְתָּ לְרֵעֶךָ אוֹ אִם נוֹקַשְׁתָּ בְּאִמְרֵי פִיךָ. שֶׁהוֹנִיתוֹ בִּדְבָרִים. עֲשֵׂה זֹאת וְהִנָּצֵל. הִתְרַפֵּס יָד אִם עֲרַבְתּוֹ. וְאִם לֹא עֲרַבְתּוֹ אֶלָּא נוֹקַשְׁתָּ בְּאוֹנָאַת דְּבָרִים — רְהַב רֵעֶיךָ, הַרְבֵּה עָלָיו רֵעִים לְבַקֵּשׁ מְחִילָה. אִם מָמוֹן יֵשׁ לוֹ בְּיָדְךָ. אִם נַעֲשָׂה לוֹ עָרֵב, וְאִם נוֹקַשְׁתָּ בִּדְבָרִים — רְהַב רֵעֶיךָ. לְצַד שֵׁנִי. כְּמוֹ דָּבָר אַחֵר. לְבֵיתוֹ. שֶׁל לֹוֶה בְּמִלְוֶה אִי אַתָּה נִכְנָס, אֲבָל אַתָּה נִכְנָס לְמַשְׁכְּנוֹ חוֹב אַחֵר שֶׁאֵינָהּ מִלְוֶה. שְׂכַר פּוּנְדָּק. הִשְׂכִּיר לוֹ פּוּנְדָּק. דְּיוֹקְנָאוֹת. צָר לוֹ צוּרוֹת בְּבֵיתוֹ בְּשָׂכָר. מַשִּׂיאָהּ שֵׁם רַע. שֶׁאַתָּה יוֹצֵא וְנִכְנָס אֶצְלָהּ שַׁחֲרִית וְעַרְבִית. מִכְּדֵי בְּעָלְמָא דָּרֵישׁ טַעְמָא דִּקְרָא. אַע"ג דְּלָא מְפָרֵשׁ טַעְמָא כִּדְאוֹקִימְנָא גַּבֵּי חוֹבֵל. **מתני'** מִשּׁוּם שְׁנֵי כֵלִים. הָעֶלְיוֹנָה רֶכֶב, וְהַתַּחְתּוֹנָה רֵיחַיִם. **גמ'** לִשְׁאָר

למה ממשכנין מעיקרא ומשכנין? הקשה ה"ר אלחנן: ולמה חוזרים וממשכנין? וי"ל: כדי שלא יוכל הלוה לכפור, וגם ימהר לפרוע חובו ולבקש מעות, כי מתבייש שבכל יום ויום יחזירו משכונו, ומ"מ לא רצה הגמרא לתרץ כן, כשאומר למה ממשכנו מעיקרא, דעדיפא מיניה משני ליה.

אלמנה בין שהיא ענייה בין שהיא עשירה אין ממשכנין אותה. וא"ת: אמאי לא פריך מהכא לשמואל, *דמשמע הא אחרים ממשכנין? וליכא למימר דהאי אין ממשכנין (א) דהיינו אין מנתחין, הא אחרים מנתחין. דהא "לא תחבול" כתיב, דמשמע בבית, ומנלן לאסור ניתוח? דמדרבנן ליכא למיגזר בשליח ב"ד גזירה שמא יכנס בביתו, דבשליח ב"ד ליכא למיגזר, מדשרי בעלמא לנתח ולא גזרינן. ואין סברא לגזור באלמנה יותר משום דאית בה תרי לאוין. וי"ל: דלכך לא פירך ממתניתין דהכא — משום דאיכא למידחי אין ממשכנין אותה משום לאו ד"לא תחבול", הא אחרים — לית בהו האי לאו. לכך עדיפא ליה למיפרך מברייתא. ור"ש דקאמר בגמ' עשירה ממשכנין אותה — איכא למימר נמי דסבר כשמואל, ומשכנין — היינו מנתחין. דלדידיה ענייה דקאמר אין ממשכנין אותה — היינו אין מנתחין. דטעמא דאתה משיאה שם רע בשכנותיה שייך אפילו בניתוח. והא דכתב רחמנא "לא תחבול" ולא כתיב לא תנתח — היינו כדי לחייב על משכון שני לאוין. אבל קשה: דאי סבר ר"ש, כשמואל ולא שרי בעשירה אלא ניתוח, ות"ק שרי ניתוח בין בעשירה בין בענייה — א"כ מחמיר ר"ש יותר מת"ק, ולשון הברייתא משמע שבא להקל ולהתיר בעשירה מה שאסר ת"ק! לכך נראה: דר"ש לית ליה דשמואל, ומתיר למשכן עשירה ושאר בני אדם. וה"מ למפרך שפיר לשמואל מר"ש, אלא דלא איירי ר"ש במתני' אלא בברייתא, ושפיר פריך מברייתא אחריתי. ועוד, נראה לפרש: דלכ"ע "לא יחבול ריחים" ו"לא תחבול בגד אלמנה" אתא קרא לאסור בה ניתוח דשרי בעלמא, והא דאפקיה בלשון חבלה ולא בלשון ניתוח — כדי לעבור במשכון בשני לאוין. ולהכי, לעיל כי אקשינן מינייהו לשמואל — איצטריך לשנויי לעבור בשני לאוין, ולא קאמר לאסור ניתוח — משום דהוה קשה ליה אמאי אפקיה בלשון חבלה. ואע"ג דאיצטריך לשני לאוין לשמואל — מ"מ מיסתבר דעיקר קרא אתא לאסור ניתוח דשרי בעלמא, ולא ללאו יתירא לחוד. והשתא לא קשה לשמואל מידי מפלגותא דרבי יהודה ור"ש, דהשתא אין ממשכנין אותה — היינו אין מנתחין אותה, ולהכי לא פריך מיניה דפשיטא דכי היכי דמשנין לא ימשכננו אלא בב"ד לא ינתחנו — דה"נ איכא לשנויי הכא. ופי' זה נראה עיקר, דאסור גם לשמואל *ניתוח אפי' בכלים שעושין בהן אוכל נפש. דלפי' קמא דלא אתא לשמואל אלא ללאו יתירא, ולא לאסור ניתוח — לא אתי שפיר. דלמאן דפליג עליה נראה דבריחים ורכב אסור אפי' ניתוח, דכיון דשליח ב"ד בדברים אחרים מותר אפילו למשכן, ובריחים ורכב אסור — ה"ה אפילו ניתוח דשרי בעלמא אפילו למלוה, דאסור בריחים ורכב. דמיסתבר לאסור כל משכונה שמישכן בשוה. אבל לשמואל שאינו מתיר למשכן לשליח ב"ד בדברים אחרים אלא ניתוח — יש לנו לומר דבריחים ורכב נמי דוקא משכן הוא דאסור כמו שכתוב, ולא ניתוח. ונמצא ששמואל דמשמע דבא להחמיר מיקל יותר לענין ריחים ורכב, שמתיר לנתח. ומאן דפליג עליה אסר כדפרישית. **וחייב** משום ב' כלים. פי': אפילו בהתראה אחת, אם חבל בפעם אחת ריחים ורכב והתרו בו משום "לא יחבול ריחים ורכב" לוקה שתים. דאי בשתי התראות — אפי' ריחים וריחים חייב כדאמר גבי נזיר (מכות דף כא.), אמרו לו "אל תשתה אל תשתה" — חייב על כל אחד ואחד. ואין לומר לעולם איירי בשתי התראות, וקא משמע לן דריחים ורכב אינם כלי אחד שלא להתחייב אלא עד שיחבול שניהם — דא"כ ה"ל למיתני: החובל ריחים או רכב בלא תעשה כו', ותו לא. אלא ודאי אתא לאשמועינן דבהתראה אחת חייב שתים. וכן משמע בהדיא בגמ' דחייב שתים בריחים ורכב בהתראה אחת. דאמר רב הונא: חבל ריחים ורכב — לוקה ג'. והיינו בהתראה אחת, דאי בשתי התראות — לוקה שתים על הריחים ושתים על הרכב. וכיון דבהתראה אחת איירי — א"כ חייב שתים דקתני — היינו שתי מלקיות. ותימה: דהיכי לקי? והא חשיב לה בגמרא (דף קטז.) לאו הניתק לעשה, מדאמר ליה אביי: זיל אהדר, וכי תימא דמש"ה א"ל לאהדורי דכל מילתא דאמר רחמנא לא תעביד אי עביד לא מהני — הא אביי גופיה קאמר בפ"ק דתמורה (דף ד:) דאי עביד מהני! ואין לומר דהאי דלקי — היינו כגון ששבר הריחים ואת הרכב, דשוב אינו ניתק לעשה, שאינו יכול להחזיר הריחים, ולהכי לקי. כדאמרינן בפרק "שילוח הקן" (חולין דף קמא.) דאם הרג את האם — שוב לא חשיב ניתק לעשה, ולקי. הא ליכא למימר, דשאני הכא כיון דמפקיד

ב"כ קעג: (ליד "רהב רעיך")
[יומא פז.] (ליד "פונדק")
סנהדרין כא.
[עי' בסנהדרין כא. וצריך קצת יישוב]
נ"ל דתנן יעב"ץ
[לעיל קיג.]
[נסמן בקדושין סח:]
רש"א נ"ל אפילו ניתוח בכלים וכו'

קנא א ב מיי' פ"ג מהל' מלוה ולוה הל' ה סמג לאוין קפח טוש"ע ח"מ סי' צז סעי' טז:
קנב ג ד ה מיי' שם הלכה ז טוש"ע שם סעיף יד:
קנג ו ז מיי' שם הלכה א ב ועיין בהשגות ובמ"מ טוש"ע שם סעי' יד:
קנד ח מיי' שם הלכה ב טוש"ע שם סעי' ו:
קנה ט מיי' שם הל' ג ועיין בהשגות ובמ"מ:

הגהות הב"ח
(א) תוס' ד"ה אלמנה וכו' אין ממשכנין היינו כצ"ל ואות ד' נמחק:

עין משפט
נר מצוה

קנו א מיי' פ"ח מהל' קרבן פסח הל' ד ופי"ח מהל' סנהדרין הלכה ג:

מסורת הש"ס

לִשְׁאָר דְּבָרִים הוּא דַּאֲתָא. לֵימָא אַבַּיֵי וְרָבָא בִּפְלוּגְתָּא דְּרַב הוּנָא וְרַב יְהוּדָה קָמִיפַּלְגִי; *דַּאֲמַר רָבָא: אָכַל נָא — לוֹקֶה שְׁתַּיִם, מִשּׁוּם "נָא", וּמִשּׁוּם °"כִּי אִם צְלִי אֵשׁ" (שמות יב). "מְבוּשָּׁל" — לוֹקֶה שְׁתַּיִם, מִשּׁוּם "מְבוּשָּׁל" וּמִשּׁוּם "כִּי אִם צְלִי אֵשׁ". "נָא וּמְבוּשָּׁל" — לוֹקֶה שָׁלֹשׁ: מִשּׁוּם "נָא", וּמִשּׁוּם "מְבוּשָּׁל", וּמִשּׁוּם "לֹא תֹאכְלֶנּוּ כִּי אִם צְלִי אֵשׁ". אַבַּיֵי אֲמַר: *אאֵין לוֹקִין עַל לָאו שֶׁבִּכְלָלוֹת. לֵימָא אַבַּיֵי דַּאֲמַר כְּרַב יְהוּדָה, וְרָבָא דַּאֲמַר כְּרַב הוּנָא! אָמַר לָךְ רָבָא: אֲנָא דַּאֲמַרִי — אֲפִילּוּ כְּרַב יְהוּדָה. עַד כָּאן לָא קָאָמַר רַב יְהוּדָה הָתָם אֶלָּא דְּ"כִי נֶפֶשׁ הוּא חוֹבֵל" לָא מַשְׁמַע רֵיחַיִם וָרֶכֶב. הִלְכָּךְ לִשְׁאָר דְּבָרִים הוּא דַּאֲתָא. אֲבָל הָכָא "כִּי אִם צְלִי אֵשׁ" לְמַאי אֲתָא? ש"מ — לְלָאו. וְאַבַּיֵי אָמַר לָךְ: אֲנָא דַּאֲמַרִי אֲפִילּוּ לְרַב הוּנָא. ע"כ לָא קָאָמַר רַב הוּנָא הָתָם אֶלָּא דְּ"כִי נֶפֶשׁ הוּא חוֹבֵל" יְתֵירָא

יְתֵירָא

לִשְׁאָר דְּבָרִים. וְלָאו לְאוֹסוּפֵי לָאו אֲרֵיחַיִם וָרֶכֶב, דְּהָא רֵיחַיִם וָרֶכֶב כְּתִיב בְּרֵישָׁא, וְאִיצְטְרִיךְ "כִּי נֶפֶשׁ" לְרַבּוֹת שְׁאָר כֵּלִים שֶׁל אוֹכֶל נֶפֶשׁ. עַל לָאו שֶׁבִּכְלָלוֹת. מִשּׁוּם "לֹא תֹאכְלֶנּוּ כִּי אִם צְלִי אֵשׁ" דְּכָיֵיל נָא וּמְבוּשָּׁל, וְאֵין לוֹקִין אֶלָּא עַל נָא וּמְבוּשָּׁל שֶׁהֵן מְפוֹרָשִׁין. אַבַּיֵי כְּרַב יְהוּדָה. דְּהֵיכָא דְּעָבַר עַל הַכְּלָל וְעַל הַפְּרָט, וְהֵן שְׁנֵיהֶן בְּלָאו אֶחָד — לָא לָקֵי אַכְּלָלָא. ע"כ לֹא קָאָמַר רַב יְהוּדָה הָתָם. דְּלָא מְהַנֵּי "כִּי נֶפֶשׁ" לְאוֹסוּפֵי לָאוֵי יְתֵירֵי אֲרֵיחַיִם וָרֶכֶב. אֶלָּא מִשּׁוּם דְּכִי נֶפֶשׁ. דִּמְרַבֵּי שְׁאָר דְּבָרִים, אִי לָאו דִּכְתִיב (א) בֵּיהּ לָא מִישְׁתַּמְּעֵי לֵיהּ מֵרֵיחַיִם וָרֶכֶב, דְּה"א הָנָךְ דַּוְקָא. הִלְכָּךְ לִשְׁאָר דְּבָרִים אֲתָא, וְלָא תִּישַׁדְיֵיהּ נַמִי אַהָנֵי דִּמְפָרֵשׁ לָאו דִּידְהוּ לְאַטְפוּיֵי לָאוֵי. אֲבָל הָכָא. אִי לָאו לְטַפּוּיֵי לָאוֵי אַנָּא וּמְבוּשָּׁל אֲתָא. כִּי אִם צְלִי אֵשׁ לְמַאי אֲתָא. אֵין לְךָ דָּבָר שֶׁאֵינוֹ בִּכְלַל נָא וּמְבוּשָּׁל חוּץ מִצָּלִי דְּנֵיתֵי לְאַזְהוּרֵי לָאו עֲלַיְיהוּ, וְאִי אַשְׁמְעִינַן מִצְוַת צָלִי — קְרָא אַחֲרִינָא כְּתִיב "צְלִי אֵשׁ וּמַצּוֹת וְגו'". יְתֵירָא

פסחים מא. [ועמ"ש על הגליון שם]
[מנחות נח. וש"נ]

דמפסיד בחובו כנגד הריחים – הרי כאילו החזיר הריחים עלמו, והוי לעולם ניתק לעשה. כדאמר בפרק בתרא דמכות (דף טז.) אַהֲשָׁבַת העבוט דהוי ניתק לעשה, אפילו נאבד לו העבוט, משום דכיון דאיתיה בתשלומין – לא לקי. ועוד: דלא משכחינן במכות ביטלו ולא ביטלו בשום לאו הניתק לעשה, כמו בשילוח הקן, ובפאה שלא הפריש ואכל הכל. ואם הלאו דחבלת ריחים חשיב ניתק לעשה, ואם שיבר לוקה – ה"ל למיחשבי' נמי התם! וע"ק: דהיכי חשיב ליה אביי ניתק לעשה? הא לא אשכחן דנתקו הכתוב, כדאשכחן גבי השבת העבוט. ד"לא תבא אל ביתו לעבוט עבוטו" דהתם – ודאי נתקו הכתוב, דכתיב "השב תשיב" מ"מ, אפי' משכנו באיסור, ולהכי חשיב בפרק בתרא דמכות (שם) לאו הניתק לעשה! וי"ל: דטעמא דאביי דא"ל לאהדורי – משום דאי עביד לא מהני, כיון שהיה שוגג, שאם היה יודע שהוא אסור לא היה חובלו, והוה ליה זכייה בטעות וחוזרת*.

[וע"ע תוס' תמורה ו. ד"ה שאני התם]

שנאמר לא יחבול ריחים ורכב. וא"ת: לר' יאשיה מנלן דחייב על כל אחת בפני עלמו, כיון דמלריך "או" לחלק? ולר' *יונתן נמי, דלא מלריך לחלק, מנלן דחייב שתים משום ב' כלים? כיון דבלאו אחד נאמרו. דהכי אמרינן בסוף "גיד הנשה" (חולין דף קב: ושם ד"ה לר"י) לר' (יונתן*), דלא לקי אלא חדא אם אכל בשר מן החי ובשר מן הטריפה, משום דתרוייהו בלאו אחד נאמרו. ומיהו, לר' יאשיה י"ל: כיון דכתיב "ורכב" ולא כתיב "רכב" – הוי כאילו כתיב "או רכב". וכן בנא ומבושל כתיב "ממנו" דמשמע אפילו באחד מהן. וכן גבי שאור ודבש, דאמרינן בפרק "כל המנחות" (מנחות דף נח: ושם ד"ה אין) דלוקה על כל אחד בפני עלמו, דכתיב "לא תקטירו ממנו", וגבי חרלן וזג כתיב "ועד" דמשמע שפיר לחלק. ועוד: דגבי ריחים ורכב אי לא מיחייב אלא על שניהם יחד – לשתוק קרא מרכב, ולא לכתוב אלא ריחים, דמשמע שניהם ביחד. אבל קשה: לר' יאשיה מנלן דחייב שתים כיון דבלאו אחד נאמרו, אבל לר' יונתן, דאילטריך חילוק בכולהו חייב על כל אחד! ושמא יש לומר דגם לר' יאשיה, כיון דאיכא קראי בכולם לחלק – חייב על כל אחד, דלא דמי ל"בשר בשדה טריפה" דליכא שום חילוק. א"נ, יש לומר: כיון שהאיסורין מפורשין – קאי לאו אַכָּל אחד ואחד, כדפי' בקונטרס בפרק בתרא דמכות (דף יח.) גבי "לא תוכל לאכול בשעריך מעשר דגנך וגו'" דלא חשיב לאו שבכללות אפילו הוה כתיב "לא תוכל לאכלם", ואם אכל מכולם – היה חייב על כל אחד ואחד, דלא דמי ל"בשר בשדה טריפה" ו"לא תאכל הנפש עם הבשר" דמשמע דליכא אלא חדא מילתא, אע"ג דדרשינן מניה תרי מילי, כיון דכתיב בלשון איסור אחד – אין חייב אלא אחת. והא דמלרכי' קרא לחלק בין אלמנה שהיא גרושה לכ"ג בפרק "עשרה יוחסין" (קדושין עז:) – היינו משום דבגוף אחד אין לחייב שתים בלא פסוק, ולכן לריך יתור לחייב שתים באשה אחת. וא"ת: דבפ"ק דכריתות (דף ד.) אמרינן דבחלב שור וכשב ועז לא לקי אלא חדא, וכן לחם קלי וכרמל וכן מעשר דגן תירוש וילהר לא הוי לקי אלא חדא אי לאו דאיכא קראי יתירי, בפ"ק דכריתות! וי"ל: דזג וחרלן שני שמות נינהו, וכן ריחים ורכב, וכן כולם. אבל חלב שור וכבש ועז – שם חלב אחד הוא, וכן שם לחם, וכן שם מעשר אחד הוא.

נ"ל ולר' יוחנן
[נ"ל יוחנן]

לימא אביי ורבא בפלוגתא דרב הונא ורב יהודה קמיפלגי. וא"ת: טעמא דרב יהודה הוי משום ד"כי נפש הוא חובל" לשאר דברים הוא דאתא, ולא משום לאו שבכללות, כדקאמר אביי! וי"ל: שכן דרך הגמ', דאע"ג שכבר פירש הטעם אומר "לימא", דכשנאמר ה"לימא" בבית המדרש עדיין לא נודע להם טעם המפורש, אלא היה סבור דטעמא דרב יהודה משום דאין לוקין על לאו שבכללות, ולרב הונא לוקין. וכה"ג איכא נמי בפרק "החולץ" (יבמות דף לח.) גבי ספק ובני יבם שבאו לחלק בנכסי יבם. דאחר שכבר פירש דטעמא של אדמון ורבנן כמו שמפרש לבסוף, כשדוחה הלימא שלא נחלקו בקם דינא והדר דינא, אמר אחרי כן: לימא דמ"ד קם דינא – כרבנן, ומ"ד הדר דינא – כאדמון.

אמר לך רבא אנא דאמרי אפי' לרב יהודה כו'. תימה: והא גבי זג וחרלן נמי נחלקו בפ' "ג' מינין" (נזיר דף לח:) ובפרק "כל שעה" (פסחים דף מא:) דרבא אמר: אבל זג וחרלן – לוקה ג' משום זג וחרלן ומשום (ב) "כל אשר יעשה", אע"ג דמ"כל אשר יעשה" אתא לשאר דברים דמרבה בפרק "ג' מינים"! וי"ל: ד"מכל אשר יעשה" משמע שהוא בלשון לאו יותר מכולם, ולהכי מוקמינן ליה ללאו אזג וחרלן, אע"ג דלריך נמי לשאר דברים. א"כ "כי נפש הוא חובל" – משמע דלא אתא אלא לשאר דברים. ולא לאטפויי לאוי על ריחים ורכב. דודאי, אי הוה כתיב כל נפש הוא חובל, כדכתיב (במדבר ו) מ"כל אשר יעשה" – הוה קאי נמי אריחים ורכב. וא"ת: אביי מ"מ לא יוכל לדחות אזג וחרלן כמו שדוחה הכא אפלוגתא דנא ומבושל, ע"כ לא קאמר רב הונא אלא משום ד"כי נפש הוא חובל" קרא יתירא הוא. ובפי' הקונטרס: וכי היכי דאתא לשאר דברים – אתא נמי לריחים ורכב. וא"כ, בזג וחרלן נמי נימא לילקי ג', דכי היכי דאתא לשאר – אתא נמי לזג וחרלן! וי"ל: דלא נפרש כפירש הקונט', אלא הכי פי': נפש הוא חובל קרא יתירא הוא, ולא לריך לשאר דברים, דשמעינן להו מריחים ורכב דלא הוו ב' כתובים הבאים כאחד, דהא אילטריכו לחייב עליהם משום ב' כלים. ולא אילטריך "כי נפש הוא חובל" לשאר דברים טפי מלריחים ורכב, ולהכי שדייה נמי אריחים ורכב. אבל (ג) "כל אשר יעשה מגפן היין" – לשאר דברים דוקא הוא דאתא, דלא שמעינן להו מזג וחרלן. ומיהו, גם על פי' הקונט' לא קשה, דלהכי לא הביא ההוא דזג וחרלן – לפי שאינו יכול לדחות, או אינו מביא אלא דבר שיכול לדחות. וכן דרך הגמ', שאינו מתחיל אלא כדי להוכיח ולהראות דמהכא ליכא למשמע מינה. וכי דחי נמי דרב הונא כאביי – היינו במאי דקאמר אביי אכל נא ומבושל לוקה שתים, ואינו לוקה משום "כי אם צלי אש" "כי אם צלי אש" אתא לכדתניא. אבל במאי דמפרש טעמא דאביי משום דאין לוקין על לאו שבכללות – לא מצי סבר כרב הונא, דהא "כי נפש הוא חובל" הוי נמי לאו שבכללות, ולקי עליה לרב הונא. וא"ת: ואמאי אילטריך אביי הכא טעמא דאין לוקין משום "כי אם צלי אש" משום דהוי לאו שבכללות, תיפוק ליה דאילטריך לכדתניא! וי"ל: דגמ' הוא דקמפרש, ומפרש ההוא טעמא אליביה משום דידע גמרא דאביי אית ליה הכי בעלמא גבי זג וחרלן ושאור ודבש. א"נ: אביי לדבריו דרבא דקאמר וה"ק: לדידי לא אתי "כי אם צלי אש" ללאו אלא להקישא נכתב. אלא אפי' לדידך דללאו אתא – אין לוקין על לאו שבכללות. ומטעמא דאמר אביי אין לוקין אלאו שבכללות קאמר בסוף פרק "כל שעה" תרתי הוא דלא לקי – חדא מיהא לקי. אבל לטעמא דמפרש כאן אביי אליבא דרב הונא ד"כי אם צלי אש" לכדתניא – אפי' חדא לא לקי.

אבל [הכא] כי אם צלי אש למאי אתא. וא"ת: והא אילטריך לכדתנא, כדקאמר אביי! וי"ל: דרבא עביד הקישא מצלי אש דכתיב בקרא דלקמיה "צלי אש ומצות על מרורים יאכלוהו" (שמות יב) וסמיך ליה "אל תאכלו ממנו נא וגו'". אע"ג דבברייתא פ' "כל שעה" (פסחים דף מא:) נקיט קרא ד"כי אם צלי אש" – לאו משום דמיניה דריש, אלא ניחא ליה למנקט קרא גופיה דנא ומבושל. ואביי סבר: דדוקא נקט ליה ברייתא "כי אם צלי אש", אבל קרא אחריתי – לא סמיכה הוא. וא"ת: והא אכתי אילטריך "כי אם צלי" לחי ומבושל בחמי טבריא, דרבא גופיה קאמר בסוף פ' "כל שעה" (שם.) מאי חייב דקאמר – משום "כי אם צלי אש" גבי מבושל בחמי טבריא! וי"ל: דאינו לוקה בחי ומבושל בחמי טבריא, כדתניא התם: יכול יהא לוקה – ת"ל "נא ומבושל", נא ומבושל אמרתי לך ולא חי. בשמעתין ה"ק רבא: כי אם צלי אש למאי אתא, פי': לאיזה לאו ללקות אם לא לטפויי לאוי על נא ומבושל. וא"ת: הא "כי נפש הוא" (ד) לרב יהודה קאמר רבא, דאתא לדברים אחרים ללקות עליהם, ולא אמרי' ריחים ורכב אמרתי לך ולא שאר דברים! וי"ל: ד,כי נפש הוא חובל" מזכיר האיסור שעושה שחובל, לכך אתי לשאר דברים ללקות עליהם. אבל "כי אם צלי אש" – אינו מזכיר שם איסור, ולכך לא אתי ללקות על דברים אחרים כי אם אנא ומבושל שכתב בהן לאו בהדיא. השתא משמע הכא דאפילו לרבא

לרבא

הגהות הב"ח

(א) רש"י ד"ה אלא וכו' אי לאו דכתב ליה לא: (ב) תוס' ד"ה אמר וכו' ומשום מכל אשר: (ג) בא"ד אבל מכל אשר: (ד) ד"ה אבל וכו' נפש הוא חובל לרב יהודה:

תורה אור

יתירא הוא, כיון דיתירא הוא – שדייה אריחים ורכב. אבל הכא "כי אם צלי אש" לאו יתירא הוא. דמבעי ליה לכדתניא: *[א]בשעה שישנו בקום אכול צלי – ישנו °ב"בל תאכל נא"; בשעה שאינו בקום אכול צלי – אינו ב"בל תאכל נא". שמות יב
תניא כוותיה דרב יהודה: [ב]חבל זוג של ספרים *וצמד של פרות – חייב שתים. זה בעצמו וזה בעצמו – אינו חייב אלא אחת. ותניא אידך: חבל זוג של ספרים וצמד של פרות, יכול לא יהא חייב אלא אחת – ת"ל: °"לא יחבול ריחים ורכב". דברים כד
מה ריחים ורכב שהן מיוחדין, שני כלים ועושין מלאכה אחת וחייב על זה בפני עצמו ועל זה בפני עצמו – אף כל דברים שהן שני כלים מיוחדים, ועושין מלאכה אחת – חייב על זה בפני עצמו ועל זה בפני עצמו. ההוא גברא דחבל סכינא דאשכבתא מחבריה. אתא לקמיה דאביי, [ג]א"ל: זיל אהדריה, דהוי ליה כלי שעושים בו אוכל נפש, ותא קום בדינא עלה. רבא אמר: [ד]לא צריך למיקם בדינא עלה, ויכול לטעון עד כדי דמיהן. ואביי לית ליה ההיא סברא? מאי שנא *מהנהו עיזי דאכלי חושלא בנהרדעא, ואתא מרא דחושלא ותפס להו וקא טעין טובא. ואמר אבוה דשמואל: יכול לטעון עד כדי דמיהן. [ה]התם לאו מידי דעבדא לאושולי ולאוגורי הוא; הכא – מידי דעביד לאושולי ולאוגורי הוא. דשלח רב הונא בר אבין: [ו]דברים העשויין להשאיל ולהשכיר, ואמר לקוחין הן בידי – אינו נאמן. ורבא לית ליה האי סברא? *והא רבא [ז]אפיק זוגא דסרבלא וספרא דאגדתא מיתמי בדברים העשויין להשאיל ולהשכיר! אמר לך רבא: [ח]האי נמי, כיון דמי פגמא – קפדי אינשי ולא מושלי.§

הדרן עלך המקבל

פסחים מא:
[ע' תוס' לעיל קיג. ד"ה ואם המתריסה]
ב"ב לו.
שבועות מו: ב"ב נב.

יתירא הוא. לגאו משום שאר דברים. וכיון דיתירא הוא לגאו וכתביה סתמא – שדייה נמי אריחים ורכב, שאין לך להוציאם ממשמע' כי נפש הוא חובל על כרחך. אבל הכא "כי אם צלי אש" – לאו לאזהרה אתא, לאוסופי לאו יתירא, אלא כדתניא. ומ"מ נא ומבושל משמע ביה, שאינו עובר בנא ומבושל ביום אלא בלילה. ה"ג תניא כוותיה דרב יהודה חבל זוג וכו' ותניא אידך וכו' ולא גרסינן תניא אידך. דמתרוייהו מתני' מתרץ סייעתא ולא מחדא מינייהו, דאי משום דקתני חייב ב' ולא ג' – הא אפילו רב הונא מודה דמהיכא תיתי? הא הני לא כתיבי ומ"כי נפש הוא חובל" הוא דנפקי, דאכל חד קאי כי נפש, אלא מתרוייהו מתני' מיתוקמא סייעתא לרב יהודה. חבל זוג של ספרים. = מספרים של ספרים. והן של פרקים, וכל חד כלי באפי נפשיה, ועושין המלאכה בין שניהם כריחים ורכב. חייב שתים. משום "כי נפש" על כל אחד; אע"פ ששניהן צריכין למלאכה אחת. וכן צמד של פרות – חבל ב' פרות חורשות עם למדן, דהיינו נמי כלי אוכל נפש. ונראה בעיני שהעול שלהן – של פרקים הוה. ותניא אידך. דיליף להו מריחים ורכב, דאיתקוש שאר דברים לריחים ורכב בחד קרא מה ריחים ורכב וכו'. וחייב על זה בעצמו ועל זה בעצמו. שהרי פירשן הכתוב, לברר אזהרה לכל אחד לעצמו. אף כל וכו'. ומדיליף להו מריחים ורכב – ש"מ בריחים ורכב חייב נמי שתים קאמר, ולא שלש, והיינו כרב יהודה. וא"ת: מתני' קמייתא למאי אייתיה? ה"נ שמעי' לה מבתרייתא?! אי מבתרייתא חייב על זה בעצמו ועל זה בעצמו קאמר, דלא אזלינן בתר מלאכה אלא בתר כלים, ולעולם שלש מלקיות: אחת משום רכב ואחת משום ריחים, ואחת משום "כי נפש" דקאי אתרוייהו. ולהכי אשמעינן קמייתא, דקתני בה בהדיא: חייב (א) שנים. סכינא דאשכבתא. של בית המטבחים שמקצבים בו בשר. ותא קום בדינא. תבעהו לדין על חובך. אם מודה לך או אם יש עדים – ישלם, ואם לאו – ישבע שבועת היסת. רבא אמר. כיון דמשכניה. ואין עדים שמשכנו, היה יכול לטעון: לקוחה היא בידי – לא צריך למיקם בדינא עילויה, דקנה ליה משכון לישבע וליטול עד כדי דמיו. חושלא. = שעורין קלופים. לאו מידי הוא דעביד לאושולי וכו'. שאין אדם משכיר ומשאיל עזים שלו, הלכך יכול לטעון: לקוחין הן בידי, היכא דאין עדים שאספם מרשותם של בעליהן. זוגא דסרבלא. = מספרים שגוזזין בהן צמר. אפילו מיתמי. שהביאו הבעלים עדים שהיו שלהן, והן טוענין השאלנום לאביהם של אלו, ואפקינהו רבא מינייהו. משום דדברים העשויין להשאיל ולהשכיר, ואם איתא דיכול לטעון "לקוח הוא בידי" יתמי כי לא טענו נמי – אנן טענינן להו.

הדרן עלך המקבל

לרבא אין לוקין אחי ומבושל בחמי טבריא, מדקאמר: אלא "כי אם צלי אש" למאי אתא? וכ"ש לאביי דאמר: אין לוקין על לאו שבכללות, ומוקי כי אם צלי אש לכדתניא. ומכאן קשה על פירוש הקונט' דפי' בפרק "כל שעה" (פסחים דף מא.) דההיא ברייתא דקתני: נא ובשל אמרתי לך ולא חי – אתא כמ"ד: אין לוקין על לאו שבכללות! ועוד, דתיקשי מיניה לרבא דאמר לוקין! ועוד פירש בקונט' אהא דקאמר התם תרתי הוא דלא לקי, לאביי דאמר אין לוקין על לאו שבכללות, חדא מיהא לקי. ופירש: על 'נא' אינו לוקה שתים, משום נא ומשום "כי אם צלי אש". אבל במילתא אחריתי דלא שייך אלא "כי אם צלי אש", כגון חי ומבושל בחמי טבריא – לוקה. והשתא נראין דבריו כסותרין זה את זה, דהשתא ברייתא לא אתיא אפילו כאביי לכך נראה, דברייתא אתיא לכ"ע, ולא לקי בשום ענין אחי ומבושל בחמי טבריא, כדפרישית לעיל. והא דקאמר "חדא מיהא לקי" – מפרש ר"ת: תרתי לא לקי, דאם התרו בו משום 'נא' ומשום 'כי אם צלי אש' – אינו עובר אלא משום 'נא', וכן ב'מבושל'. אבל היכא דלא התרו בו אלא משום 'כי אם צלי אש' – כשאוכל נא ומבושל לוקה. **וצמד** של פרות. פי' בקונטרס: ב' פרות חורשות עם למדס. ואין נראה לר"י, דבפרות לא איירי. **ותניא** אידך. לפי מה שפירש בקונטרס דמקמייתא ליכא לאוכוחי, קשה לר"י: דא"כ מבתרייתא נמי ליכא להוכיח, דאיכא למימר שלא בא ללמד אלא שחייב על זה בעצמו ועל זה בעצמו, אבל לא (ב) לחייב שלש. ועוד, דמקמייתא איכא לאוכוחי שפיר כדרב יהודה. דלרב הונא אי חייב שתים ע"כ חייב שלש, דכיון דיליף מריחים ורכב ליתן בהן לאו של ריחים ורכב, וכן חייב שתים: אחת משום ריחים ואחת משום רכב, א"כ חייב נמי מלקות שלישי משום "כי נפש הוא חובל". ואי לא יליף ליתן בהן לאו של ריחים, אלא לאו של "כי נפש הוא חובל" לחודיה, א"כ לא יחייב אלא אחת, דמ"כי נפש הוא חובל" – לא מיחייב אפילו בריחים ורכב אלא אחת. ע"כ נראה לר"י דגרס: תניא אידך בלא וי"ו, וכן גרס ר"ת.
כלים שעושין בהם אוכל נפש. נראה לר"י: דוקא כלים, אבל אוכלים עצמן מותר לחבול.
והא רבא אפיק זוגא דסרבלא וספרא דאגדתא כו'. ותימה: דהכא משמע (ג) מטעם דעשויין להשאיל ולהשכיר לחוד אינו נאמן לומר: לקוחין הן בידי. ובפרק "כל נשבעים" (שבועות דף מו:) גבי ראוהו שהטמין כלים תחת כנפיו ואמר לקוחין הן – אינו נאמן, קאמר: ולא אמרן אלא בבעל הבית שאינו עשוי למכור כליו, וכלים שאין דרכן להטמין, ובאיניש דלא צניע, אבל ליכא כל הני – נאמן, ולא אמרן אלא בדברים העשויין להשאיל ולהשכיר. משמע, אפילו בדברים העשויין להשאיל ולהשכיר בעי כל הני. ונראה לר"ת כגרסת הספרים ישנים, וכן ר"ח: ובכולהו לא אמרן אלא בדברים שאין עשויין להשאיל ולהשכיר, אבל עשויין אין ,נאמן אפילו ליכא חדא מכל הני. וא"ת: דהכא משמע דספרים עשויין להשאיל ולהשכיר אפילו ספרא דאגדתא, כל שכן שאר ספרים כדאמר בכתובות (דף ג.): "וצדקתו עומדת לעד" – זה הכותב ספרים ומשאילן לאחרים. וקשה, דתנן ב"הגוזל בתרא" (ב"ק דף קיד: ושם): המכיר כליו וספריו ביד אחר, אם יצא לו שם גניבה בעיר – ישבע כמה נתן ויטול, ואם לאו – לאו כל הימנו, שאני אומר: מכרם לאחר ולקחם זה הימנו. ואמאי? יהיה נאמן זה לומר: נגנבו לי, במגו דאי בעי אמר: השאלתיו לך?! ואף על גב דקאמר בפרק "כל הנשבעין" דאחזוקי אינשי בגנבי לא מחזקינן, ואין נאמן לומר: גנובים במגו דאי בעי אמר שאולים – היינו היכא דאמר "גנבת לי", אבל היכא דאמר "גנב אחר גנבם לי ומכרם לך" – לאו היינו אחזוקי אינשי בגנבי, דהא כמה גנבי איכא בשוקא. ונראה לרבינו תם: דהתם איירי במכירים שאין בעל הספרים רגיל להשאיל (ד) אותן שהם בידו. ולמורי ה"ר דודי נראה לתרץ: דמגו להוציא לא אמרינן. ומיהו, למ"ד ב"חזקת הבתים" (ב"ב דף מד) דאמר מגו להוציא – צ"ל כפירש ר"ת. וא"כ אפילו לא יצא לו שם גניבה בעיר, נאמן לומר גנובים – היכא דמצי למימר "השאלתים לך".

הדרן עלך המקבל

קנז א מיי' פ"ה מהל' קרבן פסח הל' ד:
קנח ב מיי' פ"ג מהל' מלוה ולוה הל' ג ועיין בהשגות ובמגיד משנה סמג לאוין קפא טוש"ע ח"מ סי' צז סעיף י:
קנט ג מיי' שם טוש"ע שם סעי' ח:
קס ד מיי' פי"ג מהל' מלוה ולוה הל' ג ועיין בהשגות ובמ"מ ובכ"מ ופ"ח מהל' טוען ונטען הלכה ב סמג עשין צה טוש"ע ח"מ סי' עב סעי' יז:
קסא ה מיי' פ"ח מהל' טוען ונטען הלכה ג סמג שם טוש"ע ח"מ שם ובסעי' יח וסעי' יט:
קסב ו מיי' שם סמג שם טוש"ע ח"מ סי' ל סעי' יא יב יג וסי' קלג סעי' ה:
קסג ז מיי' שם הל' י:
קסד ח מיי' שם ועיין במ"מ סמג שם טוש"ע ח"מ סי' עב סעי' יט וע"ש:

הגהות הב"ח
(א) רש"י ד"ה אף כל וכו' חייב שתים: (ב) תום' ד"ה ותניא וכו' אבל לא שלא לחייב: (ג) ד"ה והא וכו' דמטעם: (ד) בא"ד רגיל להשאיל לאותו שהם בידו:

גליון הש"ס
תד"ה והא רבא. ומיהו למ"ד בח"ה ע"ל דף ב ע"א תד"ה וזה:

הַבַּיִת ^[א]וְהָעֲלִיָּיה שֶׁל שְׁנַיִם שֶׁנָּפְלוּ, שְׁנֵיהֶם חוֹלְקִין בָּעֵצִים וּבָאֲבָנִים וּבֶעָפָר, וְרוֹאִין אֵלּוּ אֲבָנִים הָעֲשׂוּיוֹת לְהִשְׁתַּבֵּר. אִם הָיָה אֶחָד מֵהֶן מַכִּיר מִקְצָת אֲבָנָיו — נוֹטְלָן, וְעוֹלוֹת לוֹ מִן הַחֶשְׁבּוֹן.§ **גמ'** מִדְּקָתָנֵי רוֹאִין — מִכְּלָל ^[ב]דְּאִיכָּא לְמֵיקַם עֲלַיְיהוּ אִי בַּחֲבָסָא נָפֵיל אִי בַּחֲבָטָא נָפֵיל. אִי הָכִי, רֵישָׁא אַמַּאי חוֹלְקִין? נֶחֱזֵי: אִי בַּחֲבָטָא נָפֵיל — עִלָּיְיתָא אִיתְּבוּר; אִי בַּחֲבָסָא נָפֵיל — תַּתָּיְיתָא אִיתְּבוּר! ^[ג]לָא צְרִיכָא, דְּנָפֵיל בְּלֵילְיָא. וְלֶיחֱזִינְהוּ בְּצַפְרָא! דְּפַנִּינְהוּ. וְלֶיחֱזֵי מַאן פַּנִּינְהוּ וְלִישַׁיְּילֵיהּ? דְּפַנִּינְהוּ בְּנֵי רְשׁוּת הָרַבִּים וְאָזְלוּ לְעָלְמָא. וְלֶיחֱזֵי בִּרְשׁוּת דְּמַאן יָתְבָן, וְלֶיהֱוֵי אִידָּךְ הַמּוֹצִיא מֵחֲבֵירוֹ עָלָיו הָרְאָיָה! לָא צְרִיכָא, דְּיָתְבָן בְּחָצֵר דְּתַרְוַיְיהוּ. אִי נַמִּי: בִּרְשׁוּת הָרַבִּים. וְאִיבָּעֵית אֵימָא: שׁוּתָּפִין בְּכִי הַאי גַּוְונָא לָא קָפְדֵי אַהֲדָדֵי.§ "אִם הָיָה אֶחָד מֵהֶן מַכִּיר" כו'.§ וְהַלָּה מַה טוֹעֵן? אִי דְּקָאָמַר אִין — פְּשִׁיטָא! וְאִי לָא אָמַר אִין — לָמָּה נוֹטֵל? אֶלָּא, דְּא"ל: אֵינִי יוֹדֵעַ. לֵימָא תֶּהֱוֵי תְּיוּבְתָּא דְּר"נ? דְּאִיתְּמַר: *מָנֶה לִי בְּיָדְךָ וְהַלָּה אוֹמֵר אֵינִי יוֹדֵעַ, רַב הוּנָא וְרַב יְהוּדָה אָמְרִי: חַיָּיב. ר"נ וְר' יוֹחָנָן אָמְרִי: פָּטוּר. כִּדְאָמַר ר"נ: כְּגוֹן שֶׁיֵּשׁ עֵסֶק שְׁבוּעָה בֵּינֵיהֶן — הָכָא נַמִּי כְּגוֹן שֶׁיֵּשׁ עֵסֶק שְׁבוּעָה בֵּינֵיהֶן. הֵיכִי דָּמֵי עֵסֶק שְׁבוּעָה? כִּדְרָבָא. *דְּאָמַר רָבָא: מָנֶה לִי בְּיָדְךָ וְהַלָּה אוֹמֵר אֵין לְךָ בְּיָדִי אֶלָּא חֲמִשִּׁים וְהַשְּׁאָר אֵינִי יוֹדֵעַ, מִתּוֹךְ שֶׁאֵינוֹ יָכוֹל לִישָּׁבַע — יְשַׁלֵּם.§ ^[ד]"וְעוֹלוֹת לוֹ מִן הַחֶשְׁבּוֹן".§ סָבַר רָבָא לְמֵימַר: לְפִי חֶשְׁבּוֹן שְׁבוּרוֹת. אַלְמָא, כֵּיוָן דְּאָמַר אֵינִי יוֹדֵעַ — רֵיעַ טְפֵי. א"ל אַבַּיֵי: אַדְּרַבָּה, הָא רֵיעַ טְפֵי. מִדְּהָנֵי יָדַע, טְפֵי לָא יָדַע — תּוּ לֵית לֵיהּ, וְאִידָּךְ כּוּלְּהוּ — דְּהֵיאַךְ נִינְהוּ. אֶלָּא אָמַר אַבַּיֵי: ^[ה]לְפִי חֶשְׁבּוֹן שְׁלֵימוֹת. אִי הָכִי מַאי קָמְהַנֵּי לֵיהּ? לְמַלְבְּנָא רַוְוחָא, אִי נַמִּי טִינָא דִּמְעַבְּדָא.§ **מתני'** ^[ו]הַבַּיִת וְהָעֲלִיָּיה, נִפְחֲתָה הָעֲלִיָּיה וְאֵין בַּעַל הַבַּיִת רוֹצֶה לְתַקֵּן — הֲרֵי בַּעַל הָעֲלִיָּיה יוֹרֵד וְדָר לְמַטָּה, עַד שֶׁיְּתַקֵּן לוֹ אֶת הָעֲלִיָּיה. ר' יוֹסֵי אוֹמֵר: הַתַּחְתּוֹן נוֹתֵן אֶת הַתִּקְרָה, וְהָעֶלְיוֹן אֶת הַמַּעֲזִיבָה.§ **גמ'** *נִפְחֲתָה, בְּכַמָּה? רַב אָמַר: בְּרוּבָּהּ, וּשְׁמוּאֵל אָמַר: ^[ז]בְּאַרְבָּעָה. רַב אָמַר: בְּרוּבָּהּ, אֲבָל בְּאַרְבָּעָה — לָא, אָדָם דָּר חֶצְיוֹ לְמַטָּה וְחֶצְיוֹ לְמַעְלָה. וּשְׁמוּאֵל אָמַר: בְּאַרְבָּעָה, אֵין אָדָם דָּר חֶצְיוֹ לְמַטָּה וְחֶצְיוֹ לְמַעְלָה. ה"ד? אִי דְּאָמַר עֲלִיָּיה זוֹ — אָזְדָא. אֶלָּא דְּאָמַר לֵיהּ עֲלִיָּיה סְתָם — לוֹגַר לֵיהּ אַחֲרִיתִי! אָמַר רָבָא: לָא צְרִיכָא, דְּא"ל עֲלִיָּיה זוֹ שֶׁאֲנִי מַשְׂכִּיר לָךְ, כִּי סָלְקָא — סָלֵיק בַּהֲדָהּ, וְכִי נָחֵית — חוּת בַּהֲדָהּ. אִי הָכִי, מַאי לְמֵימְרָא? אֶלָּא אָמַר רַב אַשִׁי: ^[ח]דְּא"ל עֲלִיָּיה זוֹ שֶׁעַל גַּבֵּי בַּיִת זֶה אֲנִי מַשְׂכִּיר לָךְ, דְּהָא שַׁעְבֵּיד בַּיִת לָעֲלִיָּיה. וְכִי הָא דְּאָמַר רָבִין בַּר רַב אַדָּא אָמַר ר' יִצְחָק: ^[ט]מַעֲשֶׂה בְּאֶחָד שֶׁאָמַר לַחֲבֵירוֹ דָּלִית שֶׁעַל גַּבֵּי פַּרְסֵק זֶה אֲנִי מוֹכֵר לָךְ, וְנֶעֱקַר הַפַּרְסֵק, וּבָא מַעֲשֶׂה לִפְנֵי רַבִּי חִיָּיא וְאָמַר: ^[י]חַיָּיב אַתָּה לְהַעֲמִיד לוֹ פַּרְסֵק, כָּל זְמַן שֶׁהַדָּלִית קַיְּימָא. בָּעֵי ר' אַבָּא בַּר מָמֵל
כְּשֶׁהוּא

רש"י

הַבַּיִת וְהָעֲלִיָּיה שֶׁל שְׁנַיִם. כְּגוֹן שְׁנֵי אַחִים שֶׁחָלְקוּ, אֶחָד נָטַל בַּיִת וְאֶחָד נָטַל עֲלִיָּיה שֶׁעַל גַּבָּיו. וְהָאֲבָנִים שֶׁל חוֹמַת הַבַּיִת — מִן תִּקְרַת הַבַּיִת הַתַּחְתּוֹנָה שֶׁהִיא קַרְקָעִיתָהּ שֶׁל עֲלִיָּיה, וּלְמַעְלָה — שֶׁל עֶלְיוֹן, וְהֵימֶנָּה וּלְמַטָּה — שֶׁל תַּחְתּוֹן. שְׁנֵיהֶם חוֹלְקִים. הַכֹּל לְפִי (א) הַגָּבוֹהַּ, *שֶׁהָאֶחָד הוּא גָּבוֹהַּ מֵחֲבֵירוֹ, וַאֲבָנָיו וַעֲפָרוֹ מְרוּבֶּה מִשֶּׁל חֲבֵירוֹ — חוֹלְקִים. לְפִי שֶׁאֵין נִיכָּר אֵיזוֹ אֲבָנִים שֶׁל עֶלְיוֹן, וְאֵיזוֹ אֲבָנִים שֶׁל תַּחְתּוֹן. רוֹאִים אֵלּוּ אֲבָנִים רְאוּיוֹת לְהִשְׁתַּבֵּר. אִם יֵשׁ אֲבָנִים שְׁבוּרוֹת שֶׁל לְבֵנִים, זֶה אוֹמֵר: שְׁלֵימוֹת שֶׁלִּי, וְזֶה אוֹמֵר: שְׁלֵימוֹת שֶׁלִּי. רוֹאִין אֵלּוּ אֲבָנִים רְאוּיוֹת לְהִשְׁתַּבֵּר, אִם שֶׁל עֶלְיוֹן אִם שֶׁל תַּחְתּוֹן. וְהַכֹּל לְפִי הַמַּפּוֹלֶת; שֶׁאִם נֶחְבַּט הַבַּיִת מִיסוֹדוֹ, וְנָפַל תַּחְתָּיו הַחוֹמָה בִּמְקוֹמָהּ — יֵשׁ לָדַעַת שֶׁהַתַּחְתּוֹנוֹת נִשְׁבְּרוּ, וּלְכָךְ נָפְלָה *הַבַּיִת, וְאִם נֶחְבַּט הַכּוֹתֶל לְהַלָּן, כְּמַקֵּל שֶׁהָיָה עוֹמֵד זָקוּף וְנָפַל, שֶׁהָעֶלְיוֹנוֹת שֶׁל כּוֹתֶל נָפְלוּ לְהַלָּן מִמֶּנּוּ הַרְבֵּה — אָז הָעֶלְיוֹנוֹת נִשְׁבְּרוּ, שֶׁנָּפְלוּ מִגּוֹבַהּ רַב וְהַתַּחְתּוֹנוֹת שְׁלֵימוֹת, שֶׁנָּפְלוּ מִמָּקוֹם נָמוּךְ. מִקְצָת אֲבָנָיו. וְהֵן שְׁלֵימוֹת. וְעוֹלוֹת לוֹ מִן הַחֶשְׁבּוֹן. שֶׁחֲבֵירוֹ יִקַּח אֲחֵרוֹת כְּנֶגְדָּן. וּבַגְּמָרָא מְפָרֵשׁ מַאי יִטּוֹל כְּנֶגְדָּן, שְׁלֵימוֹת אוֹ שְׁבוּרוֹת. **גמ'** מִכְּלָל דְּאִיכָּא לְמֵיקַם עֲלֵיהּ. דְּמַפּוֹלֶת זוֹ הֵיאַךְ נָפְלָה. אִי **בַּחֲבָסָא** נָפְלָה. וְתַתָּאָה אִיתַּבּוּר, כִּדְפָרֵישִׁית. **אִי בַּחֲבָטָא** נְפוּל. כַּחֲבָטַת מַקֵּל, וְעִלָּיָיתָא אִיתַּבּוּר. **אִי** הָכִי. דְּאִיכָּא לְמֵיקַם עֲלַיְיהוּ. רֵישָׁא **אַמַּאי** תָּנָא חוֹלְקִין. יִטּוֹל הָעֶלְיוֹן הָרְחוֹקוֹת — אִם בַּחֲבָטָה נְפוּל, וְאִם בַּחֲבָסָה נְפוּל — יִטּוֹל הָעֶלְיוֹנוֹת, הֵן שְׁלֵימוֹת וְהֵן שְׁבוּרוֹת. **לָא** קָפְדִי **אַהֲדָדֵי**. לְמִיקְנֵי רְשׁוּתָא דִּידֵיהּ. דְּאַפְקוּרֵי מַפְקַר לֵיהּ כָּל חַד רְשׁוּתֵיהּ לְגַבֵּי חַבְרֵיהּ, לְהָנִיחַ שָׁם חֲפָצָיו. הִלְכָּךְ, כִּי נַמִּי יָתְבָן בִּרְשׁוּת דְּחַד מִינַּיְיהוּ — לָא הָוֵי אִידָּךְ מוֹצִיא. דְּבִרְשׁוּתָא דְּהַאי נַמִּי יָתְבִי, דְּהָא לָא קָפֵיד עֲלֵיהּ מִלְּאַשְׁלֵיהּ דּוּכְתָּא. **דְּאָמַר** אֵינִי יוֹדֵעַ. בָּרִי וְשֶׁמָּא — בָּרִי עָדִיף. **חַיָּיב** לְשַׁלֵּם. דְּבָרִי עָדִיף. **פָּטוּר** מִלְּשַׁלֵּם. אוֹקֵי מָמוֹנָא בְּחֶזְקַת מָרֵיהּ, וְצָרִיךְ לִישָּׁבַע שֶׁאֵינוֹ יוֹדֵעַ. **עֵסֶק** שְׁבוּעָה וְכוּ'. וְה"נ כֵּיוָן דְּמוֹדֶה בְּמִקְצָת. וְקָאָמַר "אֵינִי יוֹדֵעַ בְּמִקְצָת" — דְּחַיָּיב שְׁבוּעָה דְּאוֹרַיְיתָא, מִשּׁוּם הוֹדָאָה בְּמִקְצָת. **לְחֶשְׁבּוֹן** שְׁבוּרוֹת. *(שֶׁכְּנֶגְדָּן) נוֹטֵל שְׁבוּרוֹת כְּנֶגְדָּן, וְזֶה יִטּוֹל אֶת אֵלּוּ לְפִי הַחֶשְׁבּוֹן. **לְחֶשְׁבּוֹן** שְׁלֵימוֹת. (שֶׁכְּנֶגְדָּן), אַף הוּא יִטּוֹל שְׁלֵימוֹת כְּנֶגְדָּן. **לְמַלְבְּנָא** רַוְוחָא. יֵשׁ לְבֵנִים הָעֲשׂוּיוֹת כְּמַלְבֵּן, שֶׁהוּא רָחָב מֵחֲבֵירוֹ. **א"נ** לְטִינָא **דִּמְעַבְּדָא**. יֵשׁ טִיט שֶׁעוֹשִׂין מִמֶּנּוּ לְבֵנִים, שֶׁמְּעוּבָּד וּמְגוּבָּל יָפֶה מֵחֲבֵירוֹ. **מתני'** הַבַּיִת וְהָעֲלִיָּיה. "וְנִפְחֲתָה הָעֲלִיָּיה" גָּרַס וְלֹא גָּרַס הָכָא "שֶׁל שְׁנַיִם" — דְּהָא בְּשׂוֹכֵר קָאֵי, כִּדְאָמַר בַּגְּמָרָא. **וְאֵין** בַּעַל הַבַּיִת. מַשְׂכִּיר. **מַעֲזִיבָה**. טִיחַ שֶׁל טִיט שֶׁנּוֹתְנִין עַל הַתִּקְרָה שֶׁקּוֹרִין אשטרי"ך. וְדוֹמֶה לוֹ בַּמִּקְרָא "וַיַּעַזְבוּ (אֶת) יְרוּשָׁלַיִם" בְּסֵפֶר עֶזְרָא (נחמיה ג). וּבַגְּמָרָא מְפָרֵשׁ פְּלוּגְתַּיְיהוּ. **גמ'** אֲבָל **בְּאַרְבָּעָה** לָא. שֶׁאֵינוֹ מְחוּסָּר אֶלָּא מָקוֹם *הַנָּחַת כְּלִי אֶחָד, וּכְנֶגְדּוֹ יִתֵּן כְּלִי אַחֵר, כְּגוֹן תֵּיבָה אוֹ עֲרֵיבָה לְמַטָּה וּכְשֶׁיִּרְצֶה לְהִשְׁתַּמֵּשׁ בּוֹ — יִשְׁתַּמֵּשׁ. **חֶצְיוֹ** לְמַטָּה. כְּלוֹמַר: מִקְצָת תַּשְׁמִישׁוֹ לְמַטָּה, וּמִקְצָת תַּשְׁמִישׁוֹ לְמַעְלָה. **בְּאַרְבָּעָה**. כֵּיוָן שֶׁנִּפְחֲתָה בְּאַרְבָּעָה — יוֹרֵד וְדָר בַּבַּיִת לְגַמְרֵי, וְלָא כָּפֵינַן לֵיהּ, לָדוּר חֶצְיוֹ לְמַעְלָה וְחֶצְיוֹ לְמַטָּה. **אָזְדָא**. מַזָּלוֹ גָּרַם לוֹ. **לוֹגַר** לוֹ אַחֶרֶת. אִם יֵשׁ לוֹ, וְלָמָּה אָנוּ כּוֹפִין אֶת הַמַּשְׂכִּיר לְקוֹלְטוֹ עִמּוֹ בַּבַּיִת? **כִּי** סָלְקָא. בְּעוֹדָהּ קַיֶּימֶת. **וְכִי** נָחְתָא. אִם תִּפָּחֵת — נָחֵית בַּהֲדָהּ, גּוּר בַּבַּיִת. **דְּשַׁעְבֵּיד** הַבַּיִת לְגַבֵּי עֲלִיָּיה. דְּאִי לָא שַׁעְבְּדוֹ, לָמָּה לֵיהּ לְמֵימַר "שֶׁעַל גַּבֵּי בַּיִת זֶה", וְהָא קָא חָזֵי לֵיהּ, דַּ"עֲלִיָּיה זוֹ" קָאָמַר לֵיהּ. **דָּלִית**. גֶּפֶן מוּדְלֶית, שֶׁקּוֹרִין פליד"א. **פַּרְסְקָא**. אִילָן שֶׁפֵּירוֹתָיו אֲפַרְסְקִין. לְבַדּוֹ

תוספות

הבית והעלייה: **וליחזי** ברשות דמאן קיימי כו'. וא"ת: דהכא פשיטא ליה דאיירי בנפל לרשות דחד מינייהו, שכן רגילות הוא שאינו נופל בנאמנוס בשוה. ובריש בבא בתרא (דף ז.) פריך: פשיטא, דאם נפל הכותל, דהוי של שניהם?! ומשני: לא נריכא, דנפל לרשות דחד. וי"ל: משום דאוקי לה הכא, דמונחים בשל זה כמו בשל זה — פריך התם: "פשיטא", דהוה משמע ליה לאוקמיה דומיא דהכא, שנשנית לפניה בסמוך. ועוד, דהתם (ב) פריך מתוך הסוגיא דשפיר פריך פשיטא.

לימא תיהוי תיובתא דר"נ. דאמר פטור, ואע"ג דטעמא דר"נ, משום דאוקי ממונא בחזקת מריה. והכא אוקימנא דקיימי ברה"ר, או בחצר א] שאינה של שניהם, שאין האחד מוחזק יותר מחבירו — מ"מ, בהכי חשיב מוחזק, שאנו יודעין שהאי שלו. לכך פריך שפיר. ועוד, דבפ' "השואל" (לעיל דף לה: ושם) פירש, דכל ממון המוטל בספק — חשיב כאילו שניהם מוחזקים בו.

סבר רבא למימר לפי חשבון שבורות. נראה לר"י שר"ל לפי חשבון שבורות ושלימות, כמו שהן מעורבות שם במקום שנפלו. דמה סברא הוא לומר שיברור, ולא יקח כי אם שבורות דוקא כנגדו.

הבית והעלייה של שנים. בקונט' לא גרס "של שנים". ולר"ת נראה דאע"ג דמוקי לה בגמ' בשוכר ומשכיר — מ"מ שייך למיתני "של שנים", כיון דקתני בה "בעל הבית" ו"בעל עלייה". ובגמרא, דמוקי לה בשוכר ומשכיר —[א] משום דבאין שחלקו, אין על התחתון לבנות תקרה. אבל קשה: אי אין עליו לבנות, מאי קאמר בגמר' תחתון שבא לסכך בארזים שומעין לו. למה בא לסכך, כיון דאין מוטל עליו, דבאין שחלקו מיירי.

אי דא"ל עלייה זו ונפל אזדא ליה. ויתן לו שכרו שכבר דר, שאם דר חצי — יתן חצי. כדאמר ב"האומנין" (לעיל דף עט.) גבי שוכר את החמור ומת לו בחצי הדרך — נותן לו שכרו של חצי הדרך. ושם [ד"ה ואם] פירשתי אמאי לא אמר הכא ובסוף "השואל" (לעיף דף קג.) גבי המשכיר בית לחבירו ונפל, אם יש בדמים ליקח — יקח, ולשכור — ישכור, כדאמר גבי חמור.
איפסית

עין משפט נר מצוה

א א ב ג מיי' פ"ד מהל' שכנים הל' ב סמג עשין פב טוש"ע ח"מ סי' קסל סעיף ג:
ב ד ה מיי' שם טוש"ע שם סעיף ד:
ג ו ז ח מיי' פ"ה מהל' שכירות הלכה ח סמג עשין פט טוש"ע ח"מ סי' שיב סעי' יח:
ד ט י מיי' שם טוש"ע שם סעי' כ:

הגהות הב"ח

(א) רש"י ד"ה שניהם חולקין הכל לפי הגובה לפי מה שהאחד היה גבוה מחבירו: (ב) תום' ד"ה וליחזי וכו' דהתם מפורש מתוך הסוגיא:

הגהות הגר"א

[א] תום' ד"ה הבית. משום כו'. נ"ב וכ"כ הרא"ש. ורי"ף ורמב"ם כ' דבחלקו מודי רבנן לר' יוסי ועי' רי"ף וע"ל קי"ז ב' ד"ה וכן כו'. (ועמ"ש רבינו בח"מ סי' קס"ד ס"ק ד' ולא כמש"ש בליקוט):

הגהות מהר"ב רנשבורג

א] תום' ד"ה לימא תהוי כו' או בחצר שאינה של שניהם. מלת שאינה נמחק:

מסורת הש"ס

רש"ל לפי
ס"א החומה
ב"ק קיח. לעיל לז: כתובות יב: [ב"ב קלה. ע"ש]
לעיל לח.
[לקמן קיח.]
[נ"ל שכנגדו וכן בסמוך יעב"ץ]
ס"א ל"ג
ס"א הנחת כלי כגון תיבה או מגדל וכנגדו ליטול מקום הנחת כלי למטה וכשירצה כו' וכן הוא ברש"י של אלפסי

כְּשֶׁהוּא דָּר, לְבַדּוֹ הוּא דָּר כִּדְמֵעִיקָּרָא? אוֹ דִּלְמָא שְׁנֵיהֶם דָּרִין, דְּא"ל: אַדַּעְתָּא לְאַפְּקִינַן — לָא אָגְרִי לָךְ? אִם תִּמְצָא לוֹמַר [א]שְׁנֵיהֶם דָּרִין בּוֹ, כְּשֶׁהוּא מִשְׁתַּמֵּשׁ — דֶּרֶךְ פְּתָחִים מִשְׁתַּמֵּשׁ אוֹ דֶּרֶךְ גַּגִּין מִשְׁתַּמֵּשׁ? מִי אָמַר: כִּדְמֵעִיקָּרָא, מַה מֵּעִיקָּרָא — דֶּרֶךְ גַּגִּין, הָשְׁתָּא נַמִי — דֶּרֶךְ גַּגִּין. אוֹ דִּלְמָא מָצֵי אָמַר לֵיהּ: עֲלִיָּיה — קַבִּילִי עִלָּאִי, עֲלִיָּיה וִירִידָה — לָא קַבִּילִי עִלָּאִי. אִם תִּמְצָא לוֹמַר, [ב]מָצֵי אָמַר לֵיהּ: עֲלִיָּיה וִירִידָה לָא קַבִּילִי עִלָּאִי, שְׁתֵּי עֲלִיּוֹת זוֹ עַל גַּב זוֹ מַהוּ? אִיפְּחִית עֶלְיוֹנָה — נָחֵית וְדָר בַּתַּחְתּוֹנָה. אִיפְּחִית תַּחְתּוֹנָה מַהוּ לְמִיסְלַק לְגַמְרֵי בָּעֶלְיוֹנָה? מִי אָמְרִינַן, דְּא"ל: שֵׁם עֲלִיָּיה קַבֵּילִית עֲלָךְ? אוֹ דִּלְמָא: חַד עֲלִיָּיה — קַבֵּיל עֲלֵיהּ, שְׁתֵּי עֲלִיּוֹת — לָא קַבֵּיל עֲלֵיהּ? [ג]תֵּיקוּ. § "רַבִּי יוֹסֵי אוֹמֵר הַתַּחְתּוֹן נוֹתֵן אֶת הַתִּקְרָה" כו'. § מַאי תִּקְרָה? רַבִּי יוֹסֵי בַּר חֲנִינָא אָמַר: קִינִּים *וּסְנָאִין. וּסְטִינֵי אָמַר רַבִּי שִׁמְעוֹן בֶּן לָקִישׁ: לְוָוחִים. וְלָא פְּלִיגִי, *מָר כִּי אַתְרֵיהּ וּמָר כִּי אַתְרֵיהּ. הָנְהוּ בֵּי תְּרֵי דַּהֲווּ דָּיְירִי, חַד עִילָּאִי וְחַד תַּתָּאֵי. אִיפְּחִית מַעֲזִיבָה. כִּי מָשֵׁי מַיָּא עִילָּאִי — אָזְלִי וּמַזְּקִי לְתַתָּאֵי. (מִי מְתַקֵּן?) ר' חִיָּיא בַּר אַבָּא אָמַר: הָעֶלְיוֹן מְתַקֵּן, וְר' אֶלְעַי מִשּׁוּם ר' חִיָּיא בְּר' יוֹסֵי אָמַר: [ד]הַתַּחְתּוֹן מְתַקֵּן. וְסִימָן °"וְיוֹסֵף הוּרַד מִצְרָיְמָה". לֵימָא ר' חִיָּיא בַּר אַבָּא וְרַבִּי אֶלְעַי בִּפְלוּגְתָּא דְּרַבִּי יוֹסֵי וְרַבָּנַן קָמִיפַּלְגִי? לְמַאן דְּאָמַר הָעֶלְיוֹן מְתַקֵּן — קָסָבַר: עַל הַמַּזִּיק לְהַרְחִיק אֶת עַצְמוֹ מִן הַנִּיזָּק, וּמַאן דְּאָמַר תַּחְתּוֹן מְתַקֵּן — קָסָבַר: [ה]עַל הַנִּיזָּק לְהַרְחִיק אֶת עַצְמוֹ מִן הַמַּזִּיק. וְתִיסְבְּרָא רַבִּי יוֹסֵי וְרַבָּנַן לְעִנְיַן נְזָקִין פְּלִיגִי? וְהָא אִיפְּכָא שָׁמְעִינַן לְהוּ, דִּתְנַן: *מַרְחִיקִין אֶת הָאִילָן מִן הַבּוֹר עֶשְׂרִים וְחָמֵשׁ אַמָּה. וּבֶחָרוּב וּבְשִׁקְמָה — חֲמִשִּׁים אַמָּה, בֵּין מִלְמַעְלָה בֵּין מִן הַצַּד. אִם הַבּוֹר קָדַם — קוֹצֵץ וְנוֹתֵן דָּמִים; אִם הָאִילָן קָדַם — לֹא יָקוֹץ. סָפֵק זֶה קָדַם סָפֵק זֶה קָדַם — לֹא יָקוֹץ. רַבִּי יוֹסֵי אוֹמֵר: [ו]אע"פ שֶׁהַבּוֹר קוֹדֶמֶת לָאִילָן — לֹא יָקוֹץ, שֶׁזֶּה חוֹפֵר בְּתוֹךְ שֶׁלּוֹ, וְזֶה נוֹטֵעַ בְּתוֹךְ שֶׁלּוֹ. אַלְמָא, ר' יוֹסֵי סָבַר: עַל הַנִּיזָּק לְהַרְחִיק אֶת עַצְמוֹ, וְרַבָּנַן סָבְרִי: עַל הַמַּזִּיק לְהַרְחִיק אֶת עַצְמוֹ. אֶלָּא, אִי אִיכָּא לְמֵימַר (א) פְּלִיגִי — בִּפְלוּגְתָּא דְּר' יוֹסֵי וְרַבָּנַן דְּהָתָם קָמִיפַּלְגִי. וְרַבִּי יוֹסֵי וְרַבָּנַן דְּהָכָא בְּמַאי פְּלִיגִי? בְּחוֹזֶק תִּקְרָה קָמִפַּלְגִי. רַבָּנַן סָבְרִי: [ז]מַעֲזִיבָה אַחְזוּקֵי תִּקְרָה הוּא, וְאַחֲזוּקֵי תִּקְרָה עַל הַתַּחְתּוֹן בָּעֵי לְאַחֲזוּקֵי. וְרַבִּי יוֹסֵי סָבַר: מַעֲזִיבָה אַשְׁוּוּיֵי גּוּמּוֹת הוּא, וְאַשְׁוּוּיֵי גּוּמּוֹת עַל הָעֶלְיוֹן לְאַשְׁוּוּיֵי. אִינִי? *וְהָאָמַר רַב אַשִׁי: כִּי הֲוֵינָא בֵּי רַב כָּהֲנָא הֲוָה אָמְרִינַן: [ח]מוֹדֶה רַבִּי יוֹסֵי בְּגִירֵי דִּילֵיהּ! [ט]דְּפָסְקֵי מַיָּא וְהָדַר נָפְלֵי. § מתני' *[י]הַבַּיִת וְהָעֲלִיָּיה שֶׁל שְׁנַיִם שֶׁנָּפְלוּ, אָמַר בַּעַל הָעֲלִיָּיה לְבַעַל הַבַּיִת לִבְנוֹת וְהוּא אֵינוֹ רוֹצֶה לִבְנוֹת — הֲרֵי בַּעַל הָעֲלִיָּיה בּוֹנֶה אֶת הַבַּיִת וְדָר בְּתוֹכָהּ, עַד שֶׁיִּתֵּן לוֹ אֶת יְצִיאוֹתָיו. ר' יְהוּדָה אוֹמֵר: אַף זֶה דָּר בְּתוֹךְ שֶׁל חֲבֵירוֹ, צָרִיךְ לְהַעֲלוֹת לוֹ שָׂכָר. אֶלָּא, בַּעַל הָעֲלִיָּיה בּוֹנֶה אֶת הַבַּיִת וְאֶת הָעֲלִיָּיה, (ב) מְקָרֶה אֶת הָעֶלְיוֹנָה וְיוֹשֵׁב בַּבַּיִת עַד שֶׁיִּתֵּן לוֹ אֶת יְצִיאוֹתָיו. §

גמ'

רש"י

לְבַדּוֹ הוּא דָּר. וּבַעַל הַבַּיִת יוֹצֵא מִבֵּיתוֹ בְּעַל כָּרְחוֹ. דֶּרֶךְ גַּגִּין. לַעֲלוֹת מִבַּחוּץ דֶּרֶךְ סוּלָּם הַקָּבוּעַ לִכְנִיסַת פֶּתַח הָעֲלִיָּיה, וְיִכָּנֵס לָעֲלִיָּיה הַנִּפְחֶתֶת, וּמִשָּׁם יֵרֵד לַבַּיִת בְּסוּלָּם. עֲלִיָּיה קַבִּילַת עִילָּוַאי. לַעֲלוֹת דֶּרֶךְ סוּלָּם, וְלִיכָּנֵס לַפֶּתַח, וְלָדוּר לְמַעְלָה. אֲבָל טוֹרַח שֶׁל עֲלִיָּיה וִירִידָה לֹא קַבֵּילִית עָלַי. שְׁתֵּי עֲלִיּוֹת זוֹ עַל גַּב זוֹ מַהוּ. וְהַגְּמָרָא מְפָרֵשׁ לְבַעְיָא וְאָזֵיל. אִיפְּחִית (ג) עֲלִיָּיה עֶלְיוֹנָה. וְהוּא שָׂכַר הָעֶלְיוֹנָה — פָּשׁוּט לִי דְּדָר בַּתַּחְתּוֹנָה, דְּכ"ש דְּהָא עֲדִיפָא לֵיהּ. אֶלָּא אִיפְּחִית תַּחְתּוֹנָה. וְהוּא שָׂכַר אֶת הַתַּחְתּוֹנָה, מַהוּ דְּנִידְחֵיהּ מַשְׂכִּיר אֵצֶל הָעֶלְיוֹנָה, אוֹ נָכוֹף אֶת הַמַּשְׂכִּיר וְיָדוּר עִמּוֹ בַּבַּיִת. חֲדָא עֲלִיָּיה. מַעְלָה. קִינִּים וּסְנָאִים. מַעֲשֵׂה תִּקְרָה כְּעֵין מַחְצָלוֹת, שֶׁקּוֹרִין קלידי"ש. וּסְטִינֵי אָמַר רֵישׁ לָקִישׁ. שֵׁם חָכָם, תַּלְמִידוֹ שֶׁל רֵישׁ לָקִישׁ. לְוָוחִין. פלנק"ש בְּלַעַ"ז, מִנְּסָרִים שֶׁל אֶרֶז. אִיפְּחִית מַעֲזִיבָה. וְהַתִּקְרָה קַיֶּימֶת, אֶלָּא שֶׁהַמַּיִם שׁוֹתְתִין וְיוֹרְדִין דֶּרֶךְ הַפְּתָחִים הֲווּ. וְלָאו שׂוֹכֵר וּמַשְׂכִּיר הֲווּ, אֶלָּא בַּיִת שֶׁל זֶה וְהָעֲלִיָּיה שֶׁל זֶה. וְיוֹסֵף הוּרַד. תַּרְגּוּמוֹ אִיתָּחַת. ר' חִיָּיא בּ"ר יוֹסֵי אָמַר תַּחְתּוֹן וכו'. בִּפְלוּגְתָּא דְּר' יוֹסֵי וְרַבָּנַן. דְּמַתְנִיתִין, דְּס"ד דְּהָא דְּקָאָמַר ר' יוֹסֵי "הָעֶלְיוֹן נוֹתֵן אֶת הַמַּעֲזִיבָה" — כְּדֵי שֶׁלֹּא יַזִּיקוּ מֵימָיו אֶת הַתַּחְתּוֹן הוּא, דְּקָסָבַר עַל הַמַּזִּיק לְהַרְחִיק אֶת עַצְמוֹ. וְהַתַּחְתּוֹן נוֹתֵן תִּקְרָה — שֶׁהֲרֵי הִשְׂכִּיר לוֹ מָקוֹם לָגוּר. וְת"ק סָבַר: עַל הַנִּיזָּק לְהַרְחִיק אֶת עַצְמוֹ. הִלְכָּךְ מַעֲזִיבָה נַמִי, עַל הַתַּחְתּוֹן לְעַכֵּב הַמַּיִם שֶׁלֹּא יֵרְדוּ עָלָיו. וְתִיסְבְּרָא דְּרַבִּי יוֹסֵי וְרַבָּנַן. דְּהָכָא, בְּהֶיזֵּיקָא דְּתַחְתּוֹן פְּלִיגִי, וּמַעֲזִיבָה זוֹ — לְעַכֵּב הַמַּיִם, וּבִשְׁבִיל נִזְקֵי הַתַּחְתּוֹן. אִיפְּכָא שָׁמְעִינַן לְהוּ. דְּר' יוֹסֵי סָבַר: עַל הַנִּיזָּק לְהַרְחִיק אֶת עַצְמוֹ. מִן הַבּוֹר. שֶׁהַשָּׁרָשִׁין מִתְפַּשְּׁטִין וְנוֹקְבִין בְּכוֹתְלֵי הַבּוֹר, וּמַחֲלִידִין אֶת הַקַּרְקַע, וְהַכְּתָלִים נוֹפְלִים. חָרוּב וְשִׁקְמָה. יֵשׁ לָהֶן שָׁרָשִׁין יְתֵירִין וַאֲרוּכִּין מִשְּׁאָר אִילָנוֹת. בֵּין מִלְמַעְלָה. בֵּין שֶׁהָאִילָן נָמוּךְ מִן הַבּוֹר, שֶׁקַּרְקָעִית הַבּוֹר לְמַעְלָה מִשָּׁרָשֵׁי הָאִילָן. שֶׁהָאִילָן נָטוּעַ בְּבִקְעָה, וְהַבּוֹר בָּהָר. וְהָתָם מְפָרֵשׁ: מִפְּנֵי שֶׁמַּחֲלִידִין אֶת הַקַּרְקַע, וּמַעֲלִין עָפָר, וּמְקַלְקְלִין קַרְקָעִיתוֹ שֶׁל בּוֹר. מִן הַצַּד. שֶׁשְּׁנֵיהֶם בְּקַרְקַע הַשָּׁוֶה. וְנוֹתֵן דָּמִים. בַּעַל הַבּוֹר לְבַעַל הָאִילָן. אֶלָּא אִי אִיכָּא לְמֵימַר דִּפְלִיגִי. אִם יֵשׁ לִתְלוֹת פְּלוּגְתָּא דְּהָנָךְ אֲמוֹרָאֵי דִּלְעֵיל, בִּפְלוּגְתָּא דְּתַנָּאֵי. בִּפְלוּגְתָּא דְּרַבִּי יוֹסֵי וְרַבָּנַן דְּהָתָם הוּא דִּפְלִיגִי. מ"ד עַל הָעֶלְיוֹן לְתַקֵּן — כְּרַבָּנַן, וּמ"ד עַל הַתַּחְתּוֹן — כְּרַבִּי יוֹסֵי. בַּחֲזוּקֵי תִּקְרָה. וּכְשֶׁאֵין הַתַּחְתּוֹן נוֹעֵק, שֶׁאֵינוֹ חָשׁ לְמֵימָיו. אֶלָּא הָעֶלְיוֹן נוֹעֵק, וְאוֹמֵר: כְּשֶׁאֲנִי דּוֹרֵךְ עַל הַנְּסָרִים הֵם מִתְנַעְנְעִים, וַאֲנִי דּוֹאֵג שֶׁמָּא תֵּהָפֵךְ אֶחָד מֵהֶן תַּחְתַּי, אוֹ תִּשָּׁמֵט מִן הַקּוֹרָה וְאֶפּוֹל. חִזּוּקֵי תִּקְרָה הוּא. מֵאַחַר שֶׁהוּא טָח בְּטִיט אֵין הַנְּסָרִים נָדִין מִמְּקוֹמָן. אַשְׁוּוּיֵי גּוּמּוֹת הוּא. דְּחִזּוּקֵי תִּקְרָה סַגִּי לֵיהּ בִּיתֵידוֹת, שֶׁקּוֹרִין קבליי"ש בְּלַעַ"ז. אִינִי וְהָאָמַר רַב אַשִׁי וכו'. אַדְּרַבִּי חִיָּיא בַּר יוֹסֵי פָּרֵיךְ. דְּקָאָמַר: "עַל הַתַּחְתּוֹן לְתַקֵּן", וְאוֹקִימְנָא כְּרַבִּי יוֹסֵי. וְהָא מוֹדֶה רַבִּי יוֹסֵי בְּגִירֵי דִּילֵיהּ: אע"ג דְּאָמַר עַל הַנִּיזָּק לְהַרְחִיק אֶת עַצְמוֹ — ה"מ הֵיכִי דְּלָאו אָדָם עַצְמוֹ מַזִּיקוֹ, כְּגוֹן אִילָן וּבוֹר שֶׁבִּשְׁעַת נְטִיעָתוֹ אֵינוֹ מַזִּיקוֹ אֶלָּא הַשָּׁרָשִׁים גְּדֵלִין וּמִתְפַּשְּׁטִין מֵאֲלֵיהֶן לְאַחַר זְמַן, אֲבָל הֵיכָא דְּאָדָם עַצְמוֹ מַזִּיקוֹ וְזוֹרֵק בּוֹ חִצָּיו, כִּי הָכָא שֶׁשּׁוֹפֵךְ הַמַּיִם עַל רֹאשׁוֹ — מוֹדֶה הוּא דְּלָא גְּרָמָא דִּנְזָקִין הוּא דְּתִיפָּטֵר, אֶלָּא מַזִּיק מַמָּשׁ הוּא, וְאָדָם מוּעָד לְעוֹלָם, עֵר וְיָשֵׁן, שׁוֹגֵג וּמֵזִיד. דְּפָסְקֵי וְהָדַר נָפְלֵי. לֹא הָיְתָה מְקוֹם רְחִיצַת יָדַיִם שֶׁל עֶלְיוֹן עַל מְקוֹם נִזְקֵי תַּחְתּוֹן, אֶלָּא בְּמָקוֹם אַחֵר. מִשָּׁם הֵן נִמְשָׁכִין, עַד שֶׁנּוֹפְלִים בַּמָּקוֹם שֶׁמַּזִּיקִין. **מתני'** שֶׁל שְׁנַיִם. בַּיִת שֶׁל זֶה וְהָעֲלִיָּיה שֶׁל זֶה, שֶׁחָלְקוּ כָּךְ בְּנַחֲלַת אֲבִיהֶן. אָמַר בַּעַל הָעֲלִיָּיה לְבַעַל הַבַּיִת לִבְנוֹת. הַחוֹמָה וְהַתִּקְרָה הַתַּחְתּוֹנָה הַמּוּטָּלִין עָלָיו לִבְנוֹת, וְהוּא יִבְנֶה הַחוֹמָה מִן הַתִּקְרָה וּלְמַעְלָה, וְתִקְרָה הָעֶלְיוֹנָה שֶׁל גַּג. בּוֹנֶה בַּיִת. לְבַדּוֹ, עַד תִּקְרָה הַתַּחְתּוֹנָה. עַד שֶׁיִּתֵּן לוֹ יְצִיאוֹתָיו. וְאַח"כ יֵצֵא מִמֶּנּוּ, וְיִבְנֶה עֲלִיָּיתוֹ. אָמַר ר' יְהוּדָה אַף זֶה דָּר בְּתוֹךְ שֶׁל חֲבֵירוֹ. אִם כֵּן הוּא, אַף *בַּעַל הָעֲלִיָּיה זוֹ כְּשֶׁהוּא חוֹזֵר (ד) מָעוֹתָיו לָזֶה שֶׁהוּא דָּר בְּתוֹךְ שֶׁלּוֹ, וְאִי נַמִי זֶה לֹא חָסֵר, דְּהָא בְּלָאו הָכִי לָא הֲוֵי בָּנֵי לַהּ אִיהוּ — צָרִיךְ לְהַעֲלוֹת לוֹ שָׂכָר, דְּזֶה מִיהָא נֶהֱנֶה, שֶׁאִלּוּלֵי בַּיִת זֶה אֵין לוֹ מָקוֹם לָדוּר שָׁם. וְקָסָבַר: זֶה נֶהֱנֶה וְזֶה לֹא חָסֵר — חַיָּיב, וְצָרִיךְ לְהַעֲלוֹת לוֹ שָׂכָר. וְאִי לָא — מִיחְזֵי כְּרִבִּית. אֶלָּא בּוֹנֶה וְגוֹמֵר אֶת הַכֹּל. וּמְקָרֶה אֶת הָעֲלִיָּיה לְמַעְלָה וְכָל הַצָּרִיךְ לָהּ. וְיוֹשֵׁב בַּבַּיִת. הַתַּחְתּוֹן, דַּהֲוָה לֵיהּ "זֶה לֹא נֶהֱנֶה וְזֶה לֹא חָסֵר". הוּא לֹא נֶהֱנֶה — שֶׁהֲרֵי עֲלִיָּיתוֹ מוּכֶנֶת לוֹ לָדוּר בָּהּ, וְזֶה לֹא חָסֵר — דִּבְלָאו הָכִי לָא חָזְיָא לֵיהּ, דְּהָא לָא הֲוָה בָּנֵי לָהּ.

גמ'

תוספות

איפחית תחתונה מהו למידר בעליונה. וא"ת: אי דאמר ליה "עלייה שתחת עלייה זו אני משכיר לך" – פשיטא שידור בעליונה שנשתעבד לו! ואי אמר: "שעל גבי בית זה אני משכיר לך" – פשיטא שלא יכול לסלקו לילך לעליונה! וי"ל: דלעולם דא"ל "שעל גבי בית זה אני משכיר לך". ומספקא ליה, דלמא עלייה עליונה נמי היא בכלל בית, והא דא"ל "שעל גבי בית זה" – משום דעיקר הבית היא למטה. ואף על גב דמוכר את הבית לא מכר את העלייה – לענין שיעבוד זה מיהא הוי בכלל בית.

רבי יהודה אומר אף הדר בתוך של חבירו צריך להעלות לו שכר. מה שפירש בקונטרס דאם אין נותן לו שכר מיחזי כרבית – אין נראה לר"י. דמה רבית שייך הכא, דלא הלווהו כלום? שהרי אם הבית נשרף – לא היה נותן לו יציאותיו. וגם אין אנו צריכין לטעם דרבית – שהרי טעמו הוא משום ד"זה נהנה וזה חסר", כדמפרש בגמרא.

ויושב בבית עד שיתן לו יציאותיו. פי' בקונטרס דטעמא משום דהשתא לא נהנה, דהרי עלייתו מוכנת לו. וקשה: דהא נהנה הוא שאין צריך לעלות?! ונראה, דגרס: ומקרה את העלייה ויושב בתוכה, פי' בעלייה. ולא יניח לבעה"ב ליכנס בתוכו עד שיתן לו יציאותיו.

בשלשה

עין משפט נר מצוה

ה א ב מיי' פ"ה מהל' שכירות הל' ח סמג עשין פט טוש"ע ח"מ סי' שיב סעי' יח:

ו ג מיי' שם טוש"ע שם סעי' יט:

ז ד מיי' פ"י מהל' שכנים הל' ו סמג עשין פב טוש"ע ח"מ סי' קנה סעי' ז:

ח ה מיי' שם הל' ה טוש"ע שם סעי' לא לב:

ט ו מיי' שם הל' ז סמג שם טוש"ע שם סעי' לב:

י ז מיי' פ"ו מהל' שכירות הל' ד סמג עשין פט טוש"ע ח"מ סי' שיד סעי' א ועיין מ"ש בזה המ"מ בפ"ד מהל' שכנים הל' א:

יא ח מיי' פ"י מהל' שכנים הל' ה סמג עשין פב טוש"ע ח"מ סי' קנה סעי' לא:

יב ט מיי' שם הל' ו טוש"ע שם סעי' ד:

[גי' הערוך וסנאין וטינא רשב"ל אמר לוחאי ע"ש ערך מעזב וע' עוד בערך קר י' ומ"ש שם הרב המוסף]

יג י מיי' שם פ"ד הל' ג סמג שם טוש"ע ח"מ סי' קסד סעי' ה:

מסורת הש"ס

[פסחים ג. וש"נ]

רש"ל מ"ז

בראשית לט

[לעיל נה.] [ב"ב כה:]

[ב"ב כב: כה:]

[ב"ק כ:]

הגהות הב"ח

(א) גמ' דפליגי בפלוגתא:

(ב) במשנה ומקרה את העלייה ויושב בבית:

(ג) רש"י ד"ה איפחית עליונה והוא שכר כצ"ל ותיבת עלייה נמחק:

(ד) ד"ה אמר ר' יהודה וכו' בעל העלייה זו כשהוא חוזר ומקבל מעותיו מזה הוה ליה שהוא דר בתוך שלו ואי נמי זה לא חסר דהא בלאו הכי לא הוי בני לה איהו זה מיהא נהנה שאלולי בית זה כצ"ל:

[דברים הללו צריכין מובן ול' רש"י שבאלפסי בזה"ל אף זה אף שבעל הבית אינו חסר כלום צריך להעלות לו הדר שכר כיון שנהנה דקסבר זה נהנה וכו' וע"ע בפי' הרב ברטנורה ד"ה ר"י אומר וכו' ע"ש]

עין משפט
נר מצוה

מסורת הש"ס

גמ' אָמַר רַבִּי יוֹחָנָן: בִּשְׁלֹשָׁה מְקוֹמוֹת שָׁנָה לָנוּ רַבִּי יְהוּדָה אָסוּר לְאָדָם שֶׁיֵּהָנֶה מִמָּמוֹן חֲבֵירוֹ. חֲדָא – הָא דִּתְנַן. אִידָךְ מַה הִיא? דִּתְנַן: *הַנּוֹתֵן צֶמֶר לְצַבָּע לִצְבּוֹעַ לוֹ אָדוֹם וּצְבָעוֹ שָׁחוֹר, שָׁחוֹר וּצְבָעוֹ אָדוֹם, ר' מֵאִיר אוֹמֵר: נוֹתֵן לוֹ דְּמֵי צַמְרוֹ. רַבִּי יְהוּדָה אוֹמֵר: אִם הַשֶּׁבַח יוֹתֵר עַל הַהוֹצָאָה – נוֹתֵן לוֹ הַיְּצִיאָה וְאִם הַהוֹצָאָה יְתֵירָה עַל הַשֶּׁבַח – נוֹתֵן לוֹ אֶת הַשֶּׁבַח. וְאִידָךְ מַאי הִיא? דִּתְנַן: *מִי שֶׁפָּרַע מִקְצָת חוֹבוֹ וְהִשְׁלִישׁ אֶת שְׁטָרוֹ, וְאָמַר לוֹ: אִם אֵין אֲנִי נוֹתֵן לְךָ מִכָּאן וְעַד זְמַן פְּלוֹנִי – תֵּן לוֹ שְׁטָרוֹ. הִגִּיעַ זְמַן וְלֹא נָתַן, רַבִּי יוֹסֵי אוֹמֵר: יִתֵּן. רַבִּי יְהוּדָה אוֹמֵר: [א]לֹא יִתֵּן. (א) אַמַּאי? דִּלְמָא עַד כָּאן לָא קָאָמַר רַבִּי יְהוּדָה הָכָא – אֶלָּא מִשּׁוּם (ב) דְּאִיכָּא שַׁחְרוּרִיתָא. אִי נַמִּי לִצְבּוֹעַ לוֹ אָדוֹם וּצְבָעוֹ שָׁחוֹר – מִשּׁוּם דְּקָא מְשַׁנֶּה, (ג) וְהָתְנַן: *כָּל הַמְשַׁנֶּה יָדוֹ עַל הַתַּחְתּוֹנָה. וּמִי שֶׁפָּרַע מִקְצָת חוֹבוֹ נַמִּי, הָוֵי אַסְמַכְתָּא, וְשָׁמְעִינַן לֵיהּ לְר' יְהוּדָה דַּאֲמַר *[ב]לָא קָנֵי. אָמַר רַב אַחָא בַּר אַדָּא מִשְּׁמֵיהּ דְּעוּלָּא: [ג]תַּחְתּוֹן הַבָּא לְשַׁנּוֹת בְּגְוִיל – שׁוֹמְעִין לוֹ; בְּגָזִית – אֵין שׁוֹמְעִין לוֹ; בִּכְפִיסִין – שׁוֹמְעִין לוֹ; בִּלְבֵנִים – אֵין שׁוֹמְעִין לוֹ. לְסַכֵּךְ בַּאֲרָזִים – שׁוֹמְעִין לוֹ; בְּשִׁקְמִים – אֵין שׁוֹמְעִין לוֹ. לְמַעֵט בַּחַלּוֹנוֹת – שׁוֹמְעִין לוֹ; לְהַרְבּוֹת בַּחַלּוֹנוֹת – אֵין שׁוֹמְעִין לוֹ; לְהַגְבִּיהַּ – אֵין שׁוֹמְעִין לוֹ; לְמַעֵט – שׁוֹמְעִין לוֹ. [ד]עֶלְיוֹן שֶׁבָּא לְשַׁנּוֹת בְּגָזִית – שׁוֹמְעִין לוֹ; בִּגְוִיל – אֵין שׁוֹמְעִין לוֹ; בִּכְפִיסִין – אֵין שׁוֹמְעִין לוֹ; בִּלְבֵנִים – שׁוֹמְעִין לוֹ; בַּאֲרָזִים – אֵין שׁוֹמְעִין לוֹ; בְּשִׁקְמָה – שׁוֹמְעִין לוֹ. לְרַבּוֹת בַּחַלּוֹנוֹת – שׁוֹמְעִין לוֹ; לְמַעֵט בַּחַלּוֹנוֹת – אֵין שׁוֹמְעִין לוֹ; לְהַגְבִּיהַּ – אֵין שׁוֹמְעִין לוֹ; לְמַעֵט – שׁוֹמְעִין לוֹ. אֵין לוֹ לָזֶה וְלֹא לָזֶה, מַאי? (*תַּנְיָא: "אֵין לוֹ לֹא לָזֶה וְלֹא לָזֶה" – אֵין לוֹ לְבַעַל עֲלִיָּיה בַּקַּרְקַע כְּלוּם.) תַּנְיָא – רַבִּי נָתָן אוֹמֵר: [ה]תַּחְתּוֹן נוֹטֵל שְׁנֵי חֲלָקִים, וְהָעֶלְיוֹן שְׁלִישׁ. וַאֲחֵרִים אוֹמְרִים: תַּחְתּוֹן נוֹטֵל שְׁלֹשָׁה חֲלָקִים, וְהָעֶלְיוֹן נוֹטֵל רְבִיעַ. אָמַר רַבָּה: נְקוֹט דְּרַבִּי נָתָן בִּידָךְ, *דְּדַיָּינָא הוּא וְנָחֵית לְעוּמְקָא דְּדִינָא. קָא סָבַר: כַּמָּה מַפְסִיד עֲלִיָּיה בַּבַּיִת? תִּילְתָּא; הִלְכָּךְ אִית לֵיהּ תִּילְתָּא.§

מתני' [ו]וְכֵן בֵּית הַבַּד שֶׁהוּא בָּנוּי בְּסֶלַע, וְגִינָּה אַחַת עַל גַּבָּיו וְנִפְחַת – הֲרֵי בַּעַל הַגִּינָּה יוֹרֵד וְזוֹרֵעַ לְמַטָּה, עַד שֶׁיַּעֲשֶׂה לְבֵית בַּדּוֹ כִּיפִּין. *[ז]הַכּוֹתֶל וְהָאִילָן שֶׁנָּפְלוּ לִרְשׁוּת הָרַבִּים וְהִזִּיקוּ – פָּטוּר מִלְּשַׁלֵּם. נָתְנוּ לוֹ זְמַן לָקוֹץ אֶת הָאִילָן וְלִסְתּוֹר אֶת הַכּוֹתֶל וְנָפְלוּ, בְּתוֹךְ הַזְּמַן – פָּטוּר; לְאַחַר הַזְּמַן – חַיָּיב. [ח]מִי שֶׁהָיָה כּוֹתְלוֹ סָמוּךְ לְגִינַּת חֲבֵירוֹ וְנָפַל, וְאָמַר לוֹ: פַּנֵּה אֲבָנֶיךָ, וְאָמַר לוֹ:

הִגִּיעוּךְ

גמ' שֶׁיֵּהָנֶה מִמָּמוֹן חֲבֵירוֹ. שֶׁלֹּא בְּמַתָּנָה, עַד שֶׁתְּהֵא מִדַּעְתּוֹ וְנוֹחָה לוֹ. נוֹתֵן לוֹ דְּמֵי צַמְרוֹ. לָמֶר לָבָן כְּמוֹ שֶׁמָּסַר לוֹ דְּקַנְיֵיהּ בְּשִׁינּוּי וְנִתְחַיֵּיב מָעוֹת. ר' יְהוּדָה אוֹמֵר. אִם כֵּן תְּחַיְּיבוֹ – נִמְצָא זֶה נֶהֱנֶה, שֶׁזֶּה הֱבִיאוֹ לוֹ מִן הַשּׁוּק. אֶלָּא מַחֲזִיר לוֹ אֶת הַצֶּמֶר כְּמוֹת שֶׁהוּא צָבוּעַ, וְיָדוֹ עַל הַתַּחְתּוֹנָה. אִם הַשֶּׁבַח. שֶׁהִשְׁבִּיחַ הַצֶּמֶר יָתֵר עַל הַיְּצִיאָה שֶׁהוֹצִיא לְצֶבַע זֶה בְּסַמְמָנִין וְעֵצִים, וּשְׂכַר טָרְחוֹ כִּשְׂאָר שְׂכִיר יוֹם. נוֹתֵן לוֹ אֶת הַיְּצִיאָה. וְלֹא מַה שֶּׁרָאוּי בְּקַבְּלָנוּת דְּהָוֵי טְפֵי, וְאִם הַהוֹצָאָה וכו'. וְהִשְׁלִישׁ אֶת שְׁטָרוֹ. הִפְקִידוֹ בְּיַד נֶאֱמָן, לְפִי שֶׁדָּאַג הַלֹּוֶה שֶׁיַּחֲזוֹר וְיִתְבָּעֶנּוּ כָּל הַחוֹב. וְאָמַר לוֹ. לֹוֶה לַשָּׁלִישׁ. אִם אֵין אֲנִי נוֹתֵן לוֹ. אֶת הַמּוֹתָר מִכָּאן עַד יוֹם פְּלוֹנִי. תֵּן לוֹ שְׁטָרוֹ. וְיַחֲזוֹר וְיִתְבַּע הַכֹּל. וְדִלְמָא. לֹא הִיא, זֶה נֶהֱנֶה וְזֶה לֹא חָסֵר – לָא קָאָסַר רַבִּי יְהוּדָה, אֶלָּא זֶה נֶהֱנֶה וְזֶה חָסֵר הוּא דְּאָסַר. וּמַתְנִיתִין זֶה נֶהֱנֶה וְזֶה חָסֵר הוּא, דְּאָמַר לֵיהּ בַּעַל הַבַּיִת: קָא מַשְׁחַרְתְּ לְכוֹתְלַאי. שֶׁאַתָּה בּוֹנֶה חֲדָשִׁים וְיָפִים, וְכָל הַדָּמִים עָלַי, וְאַתָּה מַשְׁחִירָן בְּעָשָׁן לִפְנֵי יְלִיאָתְךָ. דַּהֲוָה לֵיהּ מְשַׁנֶּה. וְקָנְסָא קָנֵים לֵיהּ. אֲבָל זֶה נֶהֱנֶה וְזֶה לֹא חָסֵר, כְּגוֹן לְעֵיל (דף סד:): הַדָּר בַּחֲצַר חֲבֵירוֹ בְּחָצֵר דְּלָא קָיְימָא לְאַגְרָא, וְהַדָּר זֶה אֲפִילּוּ עֲבִיד לְמֵיגַר דְּה"ל נֶהֱנֶה וְזֶה אֵינוֹ חָסֵר – אֵינוֹ צָרִיךְ לְהַעֲלוֹת לוֹ שָׂכָר. וְשָׁמְעִינַן לֵיהּ וכו'. הָכָא אַשְׁמְעִינַן הָכִי. תַּחְתּוֹן שֶׁבָּא לְשַׁנּוֹת. בַּבִּנְיָן חוֹמָה שֶׁעָלָיו, מִן הַיְסוֹד עַד הַתִּקְרָה. בִּגְוִיל שׁוֹמְעִין לוֹ. אִם הָיָה מַתְחִילָּה מֵאַבְנֵי גָזִית, וּבָא לְשַׁנּוֹתוֹ כְּשֶׁנָּפְלָה וְלִבְנוֹת בְּאַבְנֵי גְוִיל – שׁוֹמְעִין לוֹ, מִפְּנֵי שֶׁהוּא מַחֲזִיק אֶת הַבִּנְיָן, שֶׁחוֹמַת גְּוִיל רְחָבָה מִשֶּׁל גָּזִית וְטֶפַח, כִּדְאָמַר בְּפ"ק דְּבָבָא בַּתְרָא (דף ג.): בִּגְוִיל – זֶה נוֹתֵן ג' טְפָחִים וְזֶה נוֹתֵן ג' טְפָחִים, וּבְגָזִית – זֶה נוֹתֵן טְפָחַיִים וּמֶחֱצָה וְזֶה נוֹתֵן טְפָחַיִים וּמֶחֱצָה. וְהָתָם מְפָרֵשׁ: גְּוִיל – אֲבָנִים דְּלָא מְשַׁפְּיָין, דְּמוּרְשֵׁי דִּידְהוּ מַטְפֵּי בָּהּ טֶפַח. כְּפִיסִים. אָרְחֵי, חֲצָאֵי לְבֵינִים, וְרָחְבָּן טֶפַח וּמֶחֱצָה. וְנוֹתֵן אָרִיחַ מִכָּאן וְאָרִיחַ מִכָּאן וְטֶפַח אֲבָנִים דַּקּוֹת וְסִיד בֵּינֵיהֶם, וְהָוֵי עוֹבִי הַחוֹמָה ד' טְפָחִים. בִּלְבֵינִים. שְׁלֵימוֹת. וְאֵין עוֹבְיוֹ שֶׁל כּוֹתֶל אֶלָּא כְּמִדַּת רוֹחְבָּן, וְהֵן ג' טְפָחִים. כְּלַל הַדָּבָר: הַתַּחְתּוֹן שֶׁמַּרְחִיב עוֹבִי הַבִּנְיָן וּמַחֲזִיקוֹ – שׁוֹמְעִין לוֹ, אִם מְמַעֵט חִיזּוּקוֹ – אֵין שׁוֹמְעִין לוֹ, שֶׁהָעֶלְיוֹן טוֹעֲנוֹ: לְמָחָר יִפּוֹל. וְעֶלְיוֹן שֶׁבָּא לְהַכְבִּיד אֶת הַמַּשָּׂא – תַּחְתּוֹן מְעַכֵּב עָלָיו, וְכָל זְמַן שֶׁמְּמַעֵט כּוֹבְדוֹ – שׁוֹמְעִין לוֹ. אֲרָזִים. בְּקוֹרוֹת שֶׁל תִּקְרָה תַּחְתּוֹנָה קָמַיְירֵי, וַאֲרָזִים *מִתְקַיְּימִין מִן הַשִּׁקְמִין, וּמַשָּׂאָן כָּבֵד. בָּא לְשַׁנּוֹת תַּחְתּוֹן. מִשִּׁקְמִים לַאֲרָזִים – שׁוֹמְעִין לוֹ. שֶׁמְּהַנֵּהוּ לָעֶלְיוֹן – שֶׁמִּתְקַיֵּים וְחָזֵק מְקוֹם מִדְרַךְ רַגְלָיו. מֵאֲרָזִים לְשִׁקְמִים – אֵין שׁוֹמְעִין לוֹ, מִפְּנֵי שֶׁהֵן נוֹחִין לְהִשָּׁבֵר. לְהַרְבּוֹת בַּחַלּוֹנוֹת. מְמַעֵט חוֹזֶק הַבִּנְיָן, וְהָעֶלְיוֹן מְעַכֵּב עָלָיו. לְהַגְבִּיהַּ. חֲלַל הַבַּיִת – אֵין שׁוֹמְעִין לוֹ, שֶׁמַּטְרִיחַ אֶת הָעֶלְיוֹן לַעֲלוֹת. וְעוֹד, שֶׁהַנָּמוּךְ חָזָק מִן הַגָּבוֹהַּ. עֶלְיוֹן שֶׁבָּא לְשַׁנּוֹת וכו'. טַעְמָא דְּכוּלְּהוּ שׁוֹמְעִין לוֹ מִפְּנֵי שֶׁמְּמַעֵט כּוֹבֶד הַמַּשָּׂא, וְהֵיכָא דְּמוֹסִיף עַל כּוֹבְדוֹ – תַּחְתּוֹן מְעַכֵּב עָלָיו, שֶׁהַתַּחְתּוֹן אֵינוֹ חוֹשֵׁשׁ אִם תִּפּוֹל הַחוֹמָה שֶׁמִּן הַתִּקְרָה וּלְמַעְלָה. אֵין לוֹ לֹא לָזֶה וְלֹא לָזֶה. לִבְנוֹת, שֶׁעֲנִיִּים הֵם וּבַעַל הַקַּרְקַע רוֹצֶה לִמְכּוֹר הַקַּרְקַע. מַאי. אִית לֵיהּ לְבַעַל הָעֲלִיָּיה בַּקַּרְקַע, אוֹ לָא? דְּדַיָּינָא הוּא. אַב"ד הָיָה, כִּדְאָמְרִינַן בְּהוֹרָיוֹת בְּפֶ' בַּתְרָא (דף יג:). כַּמָּה מַפְסִיד שְׁלִישׁ. יְמֵי קִיּוּמָהּ, הִיא מְמַהֶרֶת לִיפּוֹל מֵחֲמַת מַשָּׂא הָעֲלִיָּיה. **מתני'** בֵּית הַבַּד. בַּיִת לַעֲצוֹר זֵיתִים, וְגִינָּה אַחַת עַל גַּבּוֹ שֶׁחָקַק אָדָם בַּסֶּלַע תַּחְתֶּיהָ כְּגוֹן כִּיפָּה, וְהָיָה גִּינָּתוֹ לְמַעְלָה וּבֵית בַּדּוֹ מִלְּמַטָּה. וּכְשֶׁמֵּת – נָטְלוּ בָּנָיו זֶה בֵּית הַבַּד וְזֶה גִּינָּה. וְנִפְחַת גַּגּוֹ שֶׁל בֵּית הַבַּד שֶׁהוּא מְקוֹם זְרִיעָתוֹ שֶׁל הָעֶלְיוֹן. כִּיפִּין. אַרְקוּולט"ו. הָעֶלְיוֹן יִתֵּן עָלָיו עָפָר וְיִזְרַע. פָּטוּר. מִלְּשַׁלֵּם, דְּמַאי הֲוָה לֵיהּ לְמֶיעְבַּד? אָנוּס הוּא! נָתְנוּ לוֹ זְמַן. שֶׁרָאוּהוּ ב"ד שֶׁהָיָה נוֹטֶה, וְאָמְרוּ לוֹ: סְתוֹר. וְנָפַל. לְתוֹךְ גִּינָּתוֹ שֶׁל חֲבֵירוֹ.

הִגִּיעוּךְ

בשלשה מקומות שנה לנו ר' יהודה **אסור** לאדם שיהנה ממחון חבירו שלא מדעתו. אע"פ שמן הדין היה נראה לומר שיהנה. חדא, דאע"ג דזה נהנה *וזה לא חסר, אפי' הכי תיקנו חכמים שיהא חייב, דאין לו ליהנות מממון חבירו שלא מדעתו. ואידך, דאמר רבי יהודה: אם השבח כו' דאע"ג דגזלן קונה בשינוי – הכא תקינו דלא ליקני – כיון שאין מתכוין לגזול ולקנות, משום דאין לו ליהנות מממון חבירו. שחבירו הביאו מן השוק וטרח בו כדפירש בקונט'. וא"ת: לפי מאי דס"ד השתא דטעמא משום דאסור שיהנה מממון חבירו, ולא משום דכל המשנה ידו על התחתונה, נהי דלא קני בשינוי, משום שהבעלים טרחו להביאו מן השוק, מ"מ לא הוה ליה למימר ידו על התחתונה?! ואור"י: דהמ"ל "וליטעמיך". א"נ: מן הדין לא קנאו בשינוי כיון שאינו מתכוין לקנות, ומיהו, מ"מ היה לו ליתן שכר כפי מה שהשביחו בצביעת שחור. ורבנן תקנו שלא יהנה מממון חבירו שלא מדעתו, דהיינו בצביעת השחור שמעשה שלא מדעתו. הלכך ידו על התחתונה. וגם משליש שטרו נמי, אע"ג דאסמכתא קניא – הכא, כיון שאין זו מתנה גמורה, שאין נותנה בלב שלם, תקנו חכמים שלא יהנה מלוה הימנו.

אם השבח יתר על היציאה. *פי' בירושלמי בפרק "הגוזל" קמא (ב"ק דף ק: ד"ה אם).

לא לזה ולא לזה מאי. אין נראה לר"י פירוש הקונט' שפי' שבעה"ב רוצה למכור את הקרקע. דהא לא קמבעיא ליה דפשיטא דאין יכול למוכרו, שהרי משועבד לזה לבנות עלייה שם כשירצה. ואי רוצה למכור הקרקע לעשות הבית, ואין מוכר אלא כח שיש לו בתוכה – הא נמי פשיטא שבענין זה יכול למוכרה, דלמה לא ימכור כח שיש לו בה? אלא נראה לר"י, דמיירי שרוצה בעה"ב לזורעה, ובעל עלייה אמר: גם אני אזרע, שגם לי הקרקע משועבד לעלייה. או דלמא מני א"ל היאך: אין לך כלום בקרקע אלא לענין העלייה בלבד.

וכן בית הבד כו'. פי' בקונטרס דאיירי באחין שחלקו כמו פלוגתא דר' יהודה ורבנן, ולא בשוכר ומשכיר. וקלת קשה: דמשמע – דמדפליגי הכא רב ושמואל בגמרא – דמיירי בשוכר ומשכיר, דומיא דההיא דפליגי לעיל. ועוד, אי באחין שחלקו – מוטל על התחתון לבנות התקרה, אמאי אצטריך לאוקמי ההיא דלעיל בנפחת העלייה בשוכר ומשכיר? לוקמה באחין שחלקו. ואי האי "וכן" – אנפחת העלייה דלעיל קאי, אמאי הפסיק ביניהם ולא הסמיכם?

זמן

[זה לא חסר כצ"ל]

יד א מיי' פי"א מהל' מכירה הל' ה סמג עשין פב טוש"ע ח"מ סי' נה סעי' א וסי' רז סעי' יב:
טו ב מיי' שם סמג שם טוש"ע ח"מ שם:
טז ג מיי' פ"ד מהל' שכנים הל' ה סמג שם טוש"ע ח"מ סי' קסד סעי' ו:
יז ד מיי' שם טוש"ע שם סעי' ז:
יח ה מיי' שם הל' ד טוש"ע שם סעי' ה:
יט ו מיי' שם הל' ח סמג שם טוש"ע ח"מ סי' קסה:
כ ז מיי' פי"ג מהל' נזקי ממון הלכה יט סמג עשין סח טוש"ע ח"מ סי' תיו סעי' א:
כא ח מיי' פ"ג מהל' שכנים הל' ח סמג עשין סב טוש"ע ח"מ סי' קסו:

[פירשתי בשם ירושלמי כצ"ל]

ב"ק לה. ק: קב. לעיל עח: ע"ז ו:

ב"ב קסח. נדרים כז:

[לעיל עו. וש"נ]

[לעיל סו. וש"נ]

רש"ל מ"ז בשם הרא"ש אבל הרי"ף גרס לה

[ב"ק לט. נג.]

שם ו:

ס"א חזקים

הגהות הב"ח

(א) גמ' ר' יהודה אומר לא יתן (אמאי). תז"מ ונ"ב כ"ל ממאי: (ב) שם דאיכא שחרוריתא. נ"ב אע"פ שזה חסר דאיכא שחרוריתא דאשייתא אפ"ה אם העלייה הוה מקורה פטור הואיל ולא נהנה דא"ל להעלות לו שכר היכא דזה לא נהנה וזה חסר כמ"ש התוס' בב"ק דף כ' ע"א: (ג) שם דקא משנה דתנן כצ"ל:

הַגִּיעוּד – אֵין שׁוֹמְעִין לוֹ. [א]מִשֶּׁקִּבֵּל עָלָיו, אָמַר לוֹ: הֵילָךְ אֶת יְצִיאוֹתֶיךָ, וַאֲנִי אֶטּוֹל אֶת שֶׁלִּי – אֵין שׁוֹמְעִין לוֹ. [ב]הַשּׂוֹכֵר אֶת הַפּוֹעֵל לַעֲשׂוֹת עִמּוֹ בְּתֶבֶן וּבְקַשׁ, וְאָמַר לוֹ: תֵּן לִי שְׂכָרִי, וְאָמַר לוֹ: טוֹל מַה שֶּׁעָשִׂיתָ בִּשְׂכָרְךָ – *אֵין שׁוֹמְעִין לוֹ. [ג]מִשֶּׁקִּבֵּל עָלָיו, וְאָמַר לוֹ: הֵילָךְ שְׂכָרְךָ וַאֲנִי אֶטּוֹל אֶת שֶׁלִּי – אֵין שׁוֹמְעִין לוֹ.§ **גמ'** *נִפְחֲתָה – רַב אָמַר: בְּרוּבָּהּ, וּשְׁמוּאֵל אָמַר: [ד]בְּאַרְבַּע. רַב אָמַר: בְּרוּבָּהּ, אֲבָל בְּאַרְבַּע – אָדָם זוֹרֵעַ חֶצְיוֹ לְמַטָּה וְחֶצְיוֹ לְמַעְלָה. וּשְׁמוּאֵל אָמַר: בְּאַרְבַּע. אֵין אָדָם זוֹרֵעַ חֶצְיוֹ לְמַטָּה וְחֶצְיוֹ לְמַעְלָה. וּצְרִיכָא. דְּאִי אַשְׁמוּעִינַן דִּירָה – בְּהָא קָאָמַר שְׁמוּאֵל, מִשּׁוּם דְּלָא עָבְדִי אֱינָשֵׁי דְּדָיְירֵי פּוּרְתָּא הָכָא וּפוּרְתָּא הָכָא, אֲבָל לְעִנְיַן זְרִיעָה – עָבְדִי אֱינָשֵׁי דְּזָרְעֵי הָכָא פּוּרְתָּא וְהָכָא פּוּרְתָּא, אֵימָא מוֹדֶה לֵיהּ לְרַב. וְאִי אִיתְּמַר בְּהַךְ – בְּהַךְ קָאָמַר רַב, אֲבָל בְּהָא – אֵימָא מוֹדֶה לֵיהּ לִשְׁמוּאֵל. צְרִיכָא.§ "נָתְנוּ לוֹ זְמַן".§ וְכַמָּה זְמַן ב"ד? א"ר יוֹחָנָן: [ה]שְׁלֹשִׁים יוֹם.§ "מִי שֶׁהָיָה כּוֹתְלוֹ" כו'.§ הָא מִדְּקָתָנֵי סֵיפָא הֵילָךְ יְצִיאוֹתֶיךָ – מִכְּלָל דְּפַנְּיִנְהוּ עָסְקִינַן. טַעְמָא [א] – דְּפַנְּיִנְהוּ, הָא לָא פַּנְּיִנְהוּ – לָא. אַמַּאי? וְתִקְנֶה לֵיהּ שָׂדֵהוּ, *דְּאָמַר ר' יוֹסֵי בְּר' חֲנִינָא: חֲצֵירוֹ שֶׁל אָדָם קוֹנָה לוֹ שֶׁלֹּא מִדַּעְתּוֹ! ה"מ – הֵיכָא דְּקָא מִיכַּוֵּין לְאַקְנוּיֵי לֵיהּ, אֲבָל הָכָא – אִישְׁתַּמּוֹטֵי הוּא דְּקָא מִשְׁתַּמֵּיט לֵיהּ.§ "הַשּׂוֹכֵר לַעֲשׂוֹת עִמּוֹ בְּתֶבֶן" כו'.§ וּצְרִיכָא. דְּאִי אַשְׁמוּעִינַן לְהַךְ קַמַּיְיתָא, דְּכִי קָאָמַר לֵיהּ הַגִּיעוּךְ אֵין שׁוֹמְעִין לוֹ – מִשּׁוּם דְּלֵית אַגְרָא גַּבֵּיהּ, אֲבָל הָכָא דְּאִית לֵיהּ אַגְרָא גַּבֵּיהּ – אֵימָא שׁוֹמְעִין לוֹ. *דְּאָמְרִי אֱינָשֵׁי: מִמָּרֵי רַשְׁוָתֵיךְ – פָּארֵי אִפָּרַע. וְאִי אַשְׁמוּעִינַן הָכָא – הָכָא שֶׁמִּשֶּׁקִּבֵּל עָלָיו אֵין שׁוֹמְעִין לוֹ – מִשּׁוּם דְּאִית לֵיהּ אַגְרָא גַּבֵּיהּ, אֲבָל הָכָא דְּלֵית לֵיהּ אַגְרָא גַּבֵּיהּ – אֵימָא שׁוֹמְעִין לוֹ, צְרִיכָא.§ "אֵין שׁוֹמְעִין לוֹ".§ וְהָתַנְיָא: שׁוֹמְעִין לוֹ! אָמַר רַב נַחְמָן: לָא קַשְׁיָא. כָּאן – בְּשֶׁלּוֹ, כָּאן – בְּשֶׁל חֲבֵירוֹ. א"ל (א) רָבָה לְרַב נַחְמָן: בְּשֶׁלּוֹ מ"ט? דא"ל: אַגְרָא עֲלָךְ; בְּשֶׁל חֲבֵירוֹ נַמִי שְׂכָרוֹ עָלָיו! דְּתַנְיָא: *הַשּׂוֹכֵר אֶת הַפּוֹעֵל לַעֲשׂוֹת בְּשֶׁלּוֹ וְהֶרְאָהוּ בְּשֶׁל חֲבֵירוֹ – נוֹתֵן לוֹ שְׂכָרוֹ מְשַׁלֵּם, וְחוֹזֵר וְנוֹטֵל מִבַּעַל הַבַּיִת מַה שֶּׁהֶהֱנָה אוֹתוֹ. אֶלָּא אָמַר רַב נַחְמָן: לָא קַשְׁיָא. כָּאן – בְּשֶׁלּוֹ, כָּאן – בְּשֶׁל הֶפְקֵר. אֵיתִיבֵיהּ רָבָא לְרַב נַחְמָן: *מְצִיאַת פּוֹעֵל – לְעַצְמוֹ. אֵימָתַי – בִּזְמַן שֶׁאָמַר לוֹ בַּעַל הַבַּיִת נַכֵּשׁ עִמִּי הַיּוֹם, אוֹ עֲדוֹר עִמִּי הַיּוֹם. אֲבָל אִם אָמַר לוֹ עֲשֵׂה עִמִּי מְלָאכָה הַיּוֹם – מְצִיאָתוֹ לְבַעַל הַבַּיִת. אֶלָּא אָמַר רַב נַחְמָן: [ו]לָא קַשְׁיָא. כָּאן – בְּהַגְבָּהָה, כָּאן – בְּהַבָּטָה. אָמַר רַבָּה: הַבָּטָה בְּהֶפְקֵר תַּנָּאֵי הִיא. דִּתְנַן: *[ז]שׁוֹמְרֵי סְפִיחֵי שְׁבִיעִית נוֹטְלִין שְׂכָרָן מִתְּרוּמַת הַלִּשְׁכָּה. ר' יוֹסֵי אוֹמֵר: הָרוֹצֶה מִתְנַדֵּב הוּא, וְשׁוֹמֵר חִנָּם. אָמְרוּ לוֹ: אַתָּה אוֹמֵר כֵּן – [ח]אֵין בָּאִין מִשֶּׁל צִבּוּר! מַאי לָאו בְּהָא קָמִיפַּלְגִי: דְּת"ק סָבַר: הַבָּטָה בְּהֶפְקֵר קָנֵי, וְאִי יָהֲבֵי לֵיהּ אַגְרָא – אִין, וְאִי לָא – לָא. וְרַבִּי יוֹסֵי סָבַר: [ט]הַבָּטָה בְּהֶפְקֵר לָא קָנֵי, וְכִי אָזְלֵי צִבּוּר וּמַיְיתִי – הָשְׁתָּא הוּא דְּקָא זָכֵי בֵּיהּ. וּמָה אַתָּה אוֹמֵר – הָכִי קָאָמְרִי לֵיהּ: מִדְּבָרֶיךָ לִדְבָרֵינוּ אֵין עוֹמֶר וּשְׁתֵּי לֶחֶם בָּאִין מִשֶּׁל צִבּוּר. אָמַר רָבָא: לָא. דְּכ"ע הַבָּטָה בְּהֶפְקֵר קָנֵי, וְהָכָא – חָיְישִׁינַן *שֶׁמָּא לֹא יִמְסְרֵם יָפֶה יָפֶה קָמִיפַּלְגִי; דְּרַבָּנַן סָבְרֵי: יָהֲבִינַן לֵיהּ אַגְרָא, וְאִי לָא חָיְישִׁינַן שֶׁמָּא לֹא יִמְסְרֵם יָפֶה יָפֶה. רַבִּי יוֹסֵי סָבַר: לָא חָיְישִׁינַן שֶׁמָּא לֹא יִמְסְרֵם יָפֶה יָפֶה. וּמָה אַתָּה אוֹמֵר – הָכִי קָאָמְרִי לֵיהּ: מִדְּבָרֶיךָ לִדְבָרֵינוּ, דְּחָיְישִׁינַן שֶׁמָּא לֹא יִמְסְרֵם יָפֶה יָפֶה – אֵין עוֹמֶר וּשְׁתֵּי לֶחֶם בָּאִין מִשֶּׁל צִבּוּר. אִיכָּא דְּאָמְרִי, רָבָא אָמַר: דְּכ"ע הַבָּטָה בְּהֶפְקֵר לָא קָנֵי, וְהָכָא בְּחָיְישִׁינַן לְבַעֲלֵי זְרוֹעוֹת קָמִיפַּלְגִי. דְּת"ק סָבַר: דְּתַקִּינוּ רַבָּנַן לְמֵיתַב לֵיהּ אַרְבַּע זוּזֵי, כִּי הֵיכִי דְּלִישְׁמְעִי בַּעֲלֵי זְרוֹעוֹת וְלִיפְרְשׁוּ מִינַּיְיהוּ. וְר' יוֹסֵי סָבַר: לָא תַּקִּינוּ

וּמָה

רש"י

הַגִּיעוּךְ. הֵם שֶׁלְּךָ, וּפַנֵּה אוֹתָן לְעַצְמְךָ. אֵין זֶה רוֹצֶה אֵין קוֹנֶה לוֹ דְּבַר הֶפְקֵר אוֹ מַתָּנָה. בְּתֶבֶן וּבְקַשׁ. לְלַקֵּט לוֹ מִשֶּׁלּוֹ אוֹ מִן הָהֶפְקֵר. טוֹל מַה שֶּׁעָשִׂיתָ. כָּל מַה שֶּׁלִּקַּטְתָּ – יְהֵא שֶׁלְּךָ. אֵין שׁוֹמְעִין לוֹ. אע"ג דִּבְכָל דּוּכְתֵּי אִית לֵיהּ שָׁוֶה כֶּסֶף כְּכֶסֶף, הָכָא גַּבֵּי פּוֹעֵל "בַּל תָּלִין שְׂכָרוֹ" כְּתִיב (ויקרא יט) – מַאי דְּאַתְנֵי בַּהֲדֵיהּ מַשְׁמַע. **גמ'** דְּלֵית לֵיהּ אַגְרָא גַּבֵּיהּ. וְזֶה אֵינוֹ חָפֵץ בְּמַתְּנָתוֹ, וְהוּא מַזִּיקוֹ, שֶׁמְּנָעוֹ מִזְּרִיעָתוֹ. אֲבָל סֵיפָא דְּאִית לֵיהּ אַגְרָא גַּבֵּיהּ. וְזֶה בָּא לְכוֹפוֹ עַל שְׂכָרוֹ, וְהוּא אוֹמֵר לוֹ טוֹל זֶה בְּפֵרָעוֹן אֵימָא כו'. מִמָּרֵי רַשְׁוָתֵיךְ. מִבַּעַל חוֹבְךָ. פָּארֵי אִפָּרַע. אֲפִי' נוֹתֵן לְךָ סוּבִּין – קַבְּלֵם. מִשּׁוּם דְּאִית לֵיהּ אַגְרָא גַּבֵּיהּ. מִשֶּׁקִּבֵּל עֲלֵיהּ קַנְיֵיהּ בְּאַגְרֵיהּ. צְרִיכָא. דְּאֵין שׁוֹמְעִין לוֹ דְּקַנְיֵיהּ לֵיהּ חֲלָרוֹ. וְהָתַנְיָא שׁוֹמְעִין לוֹ. לָאוֹמֵר לַפּוֹעֵל: טוֹל מַה שֶּׁעָשִׂיתָ בִּשְׂכָרְךָ. בְּשֶׁל חֲבֵירוֹ. שֶׁהָיְתָה מְלֶאכֶת חֲבֵירוֹ – שׁוֹמְעִין לוֹ. בְּשֶׁל הֶפְקֵר. שׁוֹמְעִין לוֹ, דְּא"ל קָנֵי בֵּיהּ אַתְּ, דִּלְדִידֵיהּ לָא קָנֵי לֵיהּ. ר"נ לְטַעְמֵיהּ, דְּאָמַר לְעֵיל (דף י.): הַמַּגְבִּיהַּ מְצִיאָה לַחֲבֵירוֹ לֹא קָנָה חֲבֵירוֹ. נִמְצָא שֶׁאֵין פְּעוּלָּתוֹ עָלָיו, וְאֵין כָּאן "בַּל תָּלִין". וְלָא דָּמֵי לְשֶׁל חֲבֵירוֹ, דְּהָתָם לֵיכָּא לְמֵימַר זְכֵי בֵּיהּ אַתְּ, וְכִי לָא א"ל שְׂכָרְךָ עַל בַּעַל הַבַּיִת – עַל כָּרְחוֹ שְׂכָרוֹ עָלָיו, אֲבָל הָכָא – לָא. אֵיתִיבֵיהּ רָבָא לְרַב נַחְמָן. לְמֵימַר דְּפוֹעֵל לָאו בִּכְלַל הַמַּגְבִּיהַּ מְצִיאָה לַחֲבֵירוֹ הוּא, אֶלָּא כְּיַד בעה"ב הוּא, וְקַנְיֵיהּ בעה"ב בְּהַגְבָּהָה דְּפוֹעֵל, אֲפִילּוּ אָמַר לוֹ עֲשֵׂה עִמִּי מְלָאכָה סְתָם – וְכָל שֶׁכֵּן הָכָא, דִּשְׂכָרוֹ לְלַקֵּט מְצִיאוֹת מַמָּשׁ. כָּאן בְּהַגְבָּהָה כָּאן בְּהַבָּטָה. וְאִידִי וְאִידִי בְּשֶׁל הֶפְקֵר, מַתְנִי' כְּשֶׁשְּׂכָרוֹ לְלַקֵּט תֶּבֶן וְקַשׁ בְּהַגְבָּהָה דְּפוֹעֵל – וְע"כ שְׂכָרוֹ עָלָיו, וּבָרַיְיתָא כְּשֶׁשְּׂכָרוֹ לִמְלֶאכֶת הַבָּטָה כְּגוֹן לִשְׁמוֹר אוֹ לְהַשְׁלִיךְ מֵעֲלִיָּיה לָאָרֶץ, דְּלֵיכָּא הַגְבָּהָה. דְּא"ל: אַכַּתִּי לָא זַכַּאי בֵּיהּ אֲנָא, זִיל אַתְּ זְכֵי בֵּיהּ. תַּנָּאֵי הִיא. אִי קָנְיָא אִי לָא. שׁוֹמְרֵי סְפִיחִים. שֶׁל שְׂעוֹרִין לְצוֹרֶךְ מִנְחַת הָעוֹמֶר, אוֹ שֶׁל חִטִּין לְצוֹרֶךְ שְׁתֵּי הַלֶּחֶם. אַתָּה אוֹמֵר אֵינָן בָּאִין מִשֶּׁל צִבּוּר. אִם נִשְׁמַע לְךָ לֹא יָבִיאוּ עוֹמֶר וּשְׁתֵּי הַלֶּחֶם מִשֶּׁל צִבּוּר אֶלָּא מִשֶּׁל יָחִיד, זֶה שֶׁקָּנָה מִן הַהֶפְקֵר בִּשְׁמִירָתוֹ. דִּסְבִירָא לְהוּ הַבָּטָה קָנְיָא בְּהֶפְקֵר, הוֹאִיל וּדְבַר טוֹרַח הוּא, וְדַעְתּוֹ לְכָךְ עַל יָדוֹ נִשְׁמָר. וּמָה אַתָּה אוֹמֵר אֵין בָּאִין וכו'. הָא אִיהוּ סָבַר דְּלָא קָנְיָא. מִדְּבָרֶיךָ. שֶׁאַתָּה אוֹמֵר לְשָׁמְרוֹ בְּחִנָּם. לִדְבָרֵינוּ. שֶׁאָנוּ אוֹמְרִים הַבָּטָה בְּהֶפְקֵר קָנֵי אֵין וכו'. אָמַר רָבָא. גָּרְסִינַן הָכָא. וּלְעֵיל: אָמַר רַבָּה. דְּכ"ע הַבָּטָה בְּהֶפְקֵר קָנֵי. וְטַעֲמָא דְּר' יוֹסֵי דְּקָסָבַר מְסָרָהּ זֶה לַצִּבּוּר, וְנִמְצְאוּ בָּאִין מִשֶּׁל צִבּוּר. וְרַבָּנַן. חָיְישִׁי שֶׁמָּא לֹא יְהֵא בְּלִבּוֹ לִמְסוֹר יָפֶה יָפֶה בְּלֵב שָׁלֵם, דְּנוֹחַ לוֹ שֶׁיַּקְרִיבוּהוּ מִשֶּׁלּוֹ. מִדְּבָרֶיךָ. שֶׁאַתָּה אוֹמֵר יִשְׁמְרֵם חִנָּם. לִדְבָרֵינוּ. שֶׁאָנוּ חוֹשְׁשִׁין שֶׁמָּא לֹא יִמְסְרֵם יָפֶה יָפֶה, אֵין עוֹמֶר וּשְׁתֵּי הַלֶּחֶם וכו'. בְּחוֹשְׁשִׁין לְבַעֲלֵי זְרוֹעוֹת. שֶׁאִם לֹא נוֹצִיא עֲלֵיהֶן קוֹל שֶׁהֵן שֶׁל הֶקְדֵּשׁ – יֵשׁ בַּעֲלֵי זְרוֹעוֹת שֶׁלּוֹקְחִין אוֹתָם בְּחָזְקָה, וּלְעַצְמָן.

תוספות

זמן ב"ד ל' יום. ומכאן אנו למדים זמן ב"ד לפרוע חובו, ולכמה דברים, דהוי ל' יום. ורשב"ג נמי אמר לעיל (דף קיג.) אף לעצמו אין מחזיר אלא שלשים יום. ומיהו, לכל נזיקין לא אמר שיהא זמן ב"ד ל' יום כמו הכא, דהא לעיל (דף פב:) גבי נשברה כדו ולא סילקו נפלה גמלו ולא העמידה, ר"מ מחייב בהזיקן, אין זמן ב"ד שלשים יום שם, כדמשמע ב"המניח את הכד" (ב"ק דף כט.), והיינו טעמא שבשעה קלה יכול להסירם משם.

*__אמר__ ליה הגיעוך אין שומעין לו. אע"ג דמפקיר נזקיו לאחר נפילת אונס אמרי' בפרק "המניח" (שם דף כט.) דפטור – הכא דאישתמוטי קא מישתמיט. ואינו מפקירו, כדאמר בגמרא.

ליקני ליה חצרו כו'. אבל אי לאו דר"י ברבי חנינא – אתי שפיר, דאין קונה לו, אלא היכא דעומד בצד שדהו, לכך כי לא פנינהו לא, דכשאמר ליה הגיעוך – לא היה אכתי עומד שם.

כאן בשל חבירו. תימה: למאי דס"ד השתא, אמאי צריך לומר לו טול מה שעשית בשכרך? יאמר לא אתן לך כלום, שלא עשית לי כלום.

לעשות בשלו והראהו בשל חבירו. [ב] משמע דוקא לעשות בשלו אז נותן לו שכרו משלם, אבל סתמא – לא. תימה: א"כ אמאי איצטריך לשנויי כאן בשלו כאן בשל הפקר? לישני: כאן ששכרו לעשות שלו, כאן ששכרו סתמא בשל חבירו! ואור"י: דמשום הכי לא משני הכי, דהא פשיטא דאם שכרו לעשות בשל חבירו – דשומעים לו. אבל הא דמשני לעיל הא בשל חבירו חידוש הוא דשומעין לו דהא לא קאי הכי. וכן כאן בשל הפקר – חידוש הוא, וכן מה שמתרץ לסוף דבהבטה שומעין לו – חידוש הוא, דקא משמע לן דהבטה בהפקר לא קני.

שומרי ספיחים. פירשתי בסוף פ' "הזהב" (ג) (לעיל דף נח.).

מסוורתא

עין משפט נר מצוה

כב א מיי' פ"ג מהל' שכנים הל' ח סמג עשין סב טוש"ע ח"מ סי' קסו:

כג ב ג מיי' פ"ט מהל' שכירות הל' י סמג עשין פט טוש"ע ח"מ סי' שלו סעיף ב:

שייך לעיל

כד ד מיי' פ"ד מהל' שכנים הלכה ח סמג עשין כב טוש"ע ח"מ סי' קסה:

כה ה מיי' פ"ג מהל' נזקי ממון הלכה יט סמג עשין סח טוש"ע ח"מ סי' תטז:

כו ו טוש"ע ח"מ סימן שלו סעיף ב וסעי' ג:

כז ז מיי' פ"ד מהל' שקלים הלכה ה:

כח ח מיי' שם הל' ו:

כט ט מיי' פ"ב מהל' נדרים הל' יט טוש"ע ח"מ סי' רעג סעיף יא:

ל י מיי' פ"ד מהל' שקלים הלכה ו:

הגהות הב"ח

(א) גמ' א"ל רבה לר' נחמן בשלו: (ב) תוס' ד"ה שומרי וכו' פ' הזהב. נ"ב דף נח ד"ה לשמור:

הגהות הגר"א

[א] גמ' טעמא דפנינהו כו'. נ"ב אבל בסיפא בפועל אפי' בלא"ה. רשב"א וטוש"ע אבל ר"נ ונ"י חולקין וטעמו של רשב"א כיון דחייב לו מקני ליה ועי' סי' שלו ס"ב וסי' ע"ב סכ"ו (וע"ש בדברי רבינו ס"ק קכ"ט ול"ע): [ב] תוס' ד"ה לעשות. משמע דוקא כו'. נ"ב ודוקא דלא א"ל שכרכם עלי וע"ל ע"ו א' (ועמ"ש רבינו בח"מ סי' של"ו ס"ק ב'):

מסורת הש"ס

[עי' תוס' ב"ק ע. ד"ה רב הונא]

[לעיל קטז: ושם איתא נפחתה בכמה רב אמר וכו' וכן יתכן להיות כאן נפחתה בכמה]

ב"ק מט: לעיל יא. ודף קב. חולין קמא:

ב"ק מו: ב"ב לג:

לעיל טו. קיח.

לעיל י. יב:

שקלים ו. מנחות פד.

[ר"ה ז. יומא לה: ועי' בתוס' שם]

"וּמָה אַתָּה אוֹמֵר" — הָכִי קָאָמְרִי לֵיהּ: מִדְּבָרֶיךָ לִדְבָרֵינוּ אֵין בָּאִין מִשֶּׁל צִבּוּר. וְכֵן כִּי אֲתָא רָבִין אָמַר רַבִּי יוֹחָנָן: חוֹשְׁשִׁין לְבַעֲלֵי זְרוֹעוֹת אִיכָּא בֵּינַיְיהוּ.§ **מתני'** אהַמּוֹצִיא זֶבֶל לִרְשׁוּת הָרַבִּים, הַמּוֹצִיא — מוֹצִיא, וְהַמְזַבֵּל — מְזַבֵּל. באֵין שׁוֹרִין טִיט בִּרְשׁוּת הָרַבִּים, וְאֵין לוֹבְנִים לְבֵנִים. גאֲבָל גּוֹבְלִין טִיט בִּרְשׁוּת הָרַבִּים, אֲבָל לֹא לְבֵנִים. דהַבּוֹנֶה בִּרְשׁוּת הָרַבִּים — הַמֵּבִיא אֲבָנִים מֵבִיא, וְהַבּוֹנֶה בּוֹנֶה. הוְאִם הִזִּיק — מְשַׁלֵּם מַה שֶּׁהִזִּיק. רַבָּן שִׁמְעוֹן בֶּן גַּמְלִיאֵל אוֹמֵר: אַף מְתַקֵּן הוּא אֶת מְלַאכְתּוֹ לִפְנֵי שְׁלֹשִׁים יוֹם.§ **גמ'** לֵימָא מַתְנִי' דְּלָא כְּרַבִּי יְהוּדָה, דְּתַנְיָא: *רַבִּי יְהוּדָה אוֹמֵר: ובִּשְׁעַת הוֹצָאַת זְבָלִים אָדָם מוֹצִיא זִבְלוֹ לרה"ר, וְצוֹבְרוֹ כָּל שְׁלֹשִׁים יוֹם, כְּדֵי שֶׁיְּהֵא נִישּׁוֹף בְּרַגְלֵי אָדָם וּבְרַגְלֵי בְהֵמָה, שֶׁעַל מְנָת כֵּן הִנְחִיל יְהוֹשֻׁעַ לְיִשְׂרָאֵל אֶת הָאָרֶץ. אֲפִילּוּ תֵּימָא רַבִּי יְהוּדָה. זמוֹדֶה ר' יְהוּדָה שֶׁאִם הִזִּיק — חַיָּיב לְשַׁלֵּם. וְהָתְנַן: (א) *מוֹדֶה רַבִּי יְהוּדָה בְּנֵר חֲנוּכָּה שֶׁהוּא פָּטוּר, מִפְּנֵי שֶׁהוּא עוֹשֶׂה בִּרְשׁוּת. מַאי לָאו — רְשׁוּת דְּבֵית דִּין? לָא, רְשׁוּת דְּמִצְוָה. וְהָתַנְיָא: כָּל אֵלּוּ שֶׁאָמְרוּ מוּתָּרִין לְקַלְקֵל בְּרה"ר, אִם הִזִּיק — חַיָּיב לְשַׁלֵּם, וְרַבִּי יְהוּדָה פּוֹטֵר! אֶלָּא מְחַוַּורְתָּא, מַתְנִי' דְּלָא כְּרַבִּי יְהוּדָה. אָמַר אַבָּיֵי: רַבִּי יְהוּדָה וְרַבָּן שִׁמְעוֹן בֶּן גַּמְלִיאֵל וְר' שִׁמְעוֹן כּוּלְּהוּ סְבִירָא לְהוּ: כָּל מָקוֹם שֶׁנָּתְנוּ לוֹ חֲכָמִים רְשׁוּת וְהִזִּיק — פָּטוּר. רַבִּי יְהוּדָה — הָא דַּאֲמָרַן. רשב"ג — דִּתְנַן: רשב"ג אוֹמֵר: אַף מְתַקֵּן הוּא אֶת מְלַאכְתּוֹ לִפְנֵי שְׁלֹשִׁים יוֹם. רַבִּי שִׁמְעוֹן — דִּתְנַן: *חהָיָה מַעֲמִידוֹ בַּעֲלִיָּיה — צָרִיךְ שֶׁיְּהֵא תַּחְתָּיו מַעֲזִיבָה שְׁלֹשָׁה טְפָחִים, וּבְכִירָה — טֶפַח. טוְאִם הִזִּיק — מְשַׁלֵּם מַה שֶּׁהִזִּיק. רַבִּי שִׁמְעוֹן אוֹמֵר: לֹא אָמְרוּ כָּל הַשִּׁיעוּרִים הַלָּלוּ אֶלָּא שֶׁאִם הִזִּיק פָּטוּר מִלְּשַׁלֵּם. ת"ר: יהַחַצָּב שֶׁמָּסַר לַסַּתָּת — הַסַּתָּת חַיָּיב. הַסַּתָּת שֶׁמָּסַר לַחַמָּר — הַחַמָּר חַיָּיב. הַחַמָּר שֶׁמָּסַר לַכַּתָּף — הַכַּתָּף חַיָּיב. הַכַּתָּף שֶׁמָּסַר לַבַּנַּאי — הַבַּנַּאי חַיָּיב. הַבַּנַּאי שֶׁמָּסַר לָאַדְרִיכָל — אַדְרִיכָל חַיָּיב. וְאִם הִנִּיחַ אֶבֶן עַל הַדִּימוֹס וְהִזִּיקָה — כּוּלָּן חַיָּיבִין לְשַׁלֵּם. וְהָתַנְיָא: כאַחֲרוֹן חַיָּיב וְכוּלָּן פְּטוּרִים! לָא קַשְׁיָא: לכָּאן — בִּשְׂכִירוּת, כָּאן — בְּקַבְּלָנוּת.§ **מתני'** *שְׁתֵּי גִנּוֹת זוֹ עַל גַּב זוֹ וְהַיָּרָק בֵּינְתַיִם, ר"מ אוֹמֵר: שֶׁל עֶלְיוֹן. ר' יְהוּדָה אוֹמֵר: שֶׁל תַּחְתּוֹן. אָמַר ר"מ: אִם יִרְצֶה הָעֶלְיוֹן לִיקַּח אֶת עֲפָרוֹ — אֵין כָּאן יָרָק! אָמַר ר' יְהוּדָה: אִם יִרְצֶה הַתַּחְתּוֹן לְמַלְאוֹת אֶת גִּנָּתוֹ — אֵין כָּאן יָרָק! אָמַר ר"מ: מֵאַחַר שֶׁשְּׁנֵיהֶן יְכוֹלִין לִמְחוֹת זֶה עַל זֶה — רוֹאִין מֵהֵיכָן יָרָק זֶה חַי. אָמַר ר"ש: מכָּל שֶׁהָעֶלְיוֹן יָכוֹל לִפְשׁוֹט אֶת יָדוֹ וְלִיטּוֹל — הֲרֵי הוּא שֶׁלּוֹ, [א] וְהַשְּׁאָר שֶׁל תַּחְתּוֹן.§ **גמ'** אֲמַר רָבָא: בְּעִיקָּרוֹ — כּוּלֵּי עָלְמָא לָא פְּלִיגִי דְּעֶלְיוֹן הָוֵי. כִּי פְּלִיגִי — בְּנוֹפוֹ. ר"מ סָבַר: *שָׁדֵי נוֹפוֹ בָּתַר עִיקָּרוֹ, וְר' יְהוּדָה סָבַר: לָא אָמְרִינַן שָׁדֵי נוֹפוֹ בָּתַר עִיקָּרוֹ. *(וְאָזְדָא לְטַעְמַיְיהוּ,) דְּתַנְיָא: (ב) הַיּוֹצֵא מִן הַגֶּזַע וּמִן הַשָּׁרָשִׁין — הֲרֵי אֵלּוּ שֶׁל בַּעַל הַקַּרְקַע, דִּבְרֵי ר' מֵאִיר. ר' יְהוּדָה אוֹמֵר: *נמִן הַגֶּזַע — שֶׁל בַּעַל הָאִילָן, וּמִן הַשָּׁרָשִׁין — שֶׁל בַּעַל הַקַּרְקַע.

וּתְנַן

מחוורתא מתני' דלא כר' יהודה. וא"ת: ואמאי לא מסני: מתני' שלא בשעת הוצאת זבלים, ודברי הכל, כדמשני ב"המניח" (ב"ק דף ל. ושם) אמתני' דהתם?! וי"ל: דהכא פשיטא ליה דאיירי שלא בשעת הוצאת זבלים, ולהכי לא הוה קשיא ליה הא דמתני' מצרכת לזבל לאלתר, ור' יהודה מתיר להניח ל' יום! אלא להכי לא מצי אתא כר' יהודה — משום דמחייב לשלם מה שהזיק, אפילו הזיק בההיא שעה קטנה שיש לו רשות להניח. ולרבי יהודה, אותה שעה כיון שיש לו רשות — פטור. ועי"ל: דמתניתין משמע דאיירי בשעת הוצאת זבלים, מדקתני המזבל מזבל — משמע בשעה שרגילין לזבל. והא דלא הוה קשה ליה דרבי יהודה שרי שלשים יום, ומתני' לאלתר — משום דאיכא למימר דמתניתין עלה טובה קמ"ל — שימהר, שלא יצטרך לשלם מה שהזיק.

ותניא

וּמָה אַתָּה אוֹמֵר. אֵינָן בָּאִין מִשֶּׁל צִבּוּר — הָא אֲמַרַן דְּלָא קָנֵי. הָכִי קָאָמְרִי לֵיהּ מִדְּבָרֶיךָ. דְּקָאָמְרַתְּ יִשְׁמְרֵם חִנָּם. לִדְבָרֵינוּ. דִּסְבִירָא לָן דְּתַקִּינוּ רַבָּנַן אַרְבָּעָה זוּזֵי מִן הַתְּרוּמָה לְשׁוֹמְרֵי סְפִיחִים, וְזֶה מוֹחֵל עֲלֵיהֶן, וְנִמְצְאוּ לוֹ בַּתְּרוּמָה אַרְבָּעָה זוּזִים שֶׁאֵין לַצִּבּוּר חֵלֶק בָּהֶם. וְאִם קוֹנִין מֵהֶן תְּמִידִין וּמוּסָפִין וּשְׁאָר קָרְבְּנוֹת צִבּוּר — אֵין תְּמִידִין בָּאִין מִשֶּׁל צִבּוּר. **מתני'** הַמּוֹצִיא מוֹצִיא וְהַמְזַבֵּל מְזַבֵּל. כְּלוֹמַר: אֵינוֹ רַשַּׁאי לְהַשְׁהוֹתוֹ שָׁם, אֶלָּא זֶה מוֹצִיאוֹ מִן הָרֶפֶת לרה"ר, וְהַנּוֹשְׂאוֹ יְהֵא מְזוּמָּן לִישָּׂאֶנּוּ לַשָּׂדֶה וְלַגִּנָּה לְזַבֵּל. אֵין שׁוֹרִין טִיט. מְקוֹמוֹת יֵשׁ שֶׁשּׁוֹרִין אוֹתוֹ יָמִים רַבִּים צָבוּר בְּמָקוֹם אֶחָד. וְאֵין לוֹבְנִים לְבֵנִים. לְפִי שֶׁמַּשְׁהֶה אוֹתָן לְיַיבְּשָׁן, שֶׁשּׁוֹטֵחַ הַטִּיט בְּקַרְקַע חֲלָקָה כְּעוֹבִי הַלְּבֵנִים, וְחוֹרֵץ בּוֹ חֲרִיצוֹת שְׁתִי וָעֵרֶב כְּמִדַּת הַלְּבֵנִים, וּמַנִּיחָן שָׁם עַד שֶׁיִּיבְשׁוּ. וְגוֹבְלִין טִיט. לָתֵת מִיָּד בַּבִּנְיָן. וְהַבּוֹנֶה בּוֹנֶה. מְקַבֵּל מִיַּד הַמֵּבִיא וּבוֹנֶה. מְתַקֵּן. מְזַמֵּן בִּרְשׁוּת הָרַבִּים, וְאֵינוֹ חַיָּיב בִּנְזָקִין. **גמ'** וְצוֹבְרוֹ כָּל שְׁלֹשִׁים יוֹם. מִשְּׁלֹשִׁים לִשְׁלֹשִׁים חוֹזֵר וְצוֹבְרוֹ, כְּדֵי שֶׁיְּהֵא נִישָּׁף יָפֶה. מוֹדֶה רַבִּי יְהוּדָה וכו'. וּמַתְנִי' נַמִּי עֵצָה טוֹבָה קָאָמַר, שֶׁלֹּא יִתְחַיֵּיב בְּנִזְקוֹ. בְּנֵר חֲנוּכָּה פָּטוּר. גַּבֵּי הַנִּיחַ חֶנְוָנִי נֵרוֹ מִבַּחוּץ וְעָבַר גָּמָל טָעוּן פִּשְׁתָּן וְדָלְקָה בַּנֵּר וְהִדְלִיק אֶת הַבִּירָה, בְּב"ק (דף סב:). מַאי לָאו בִּרְשׁוּת ב"ד. אַלְמָא: כָּל מִידֵּי דְּיָהֲבוּ לֵיהּ רַבָּנַן רְשׁוּתָא, אִם הִזִּיק — פָּטוּר. כָּל אֵלּוּ שֶׁאָמְרוּ וכו'. כָּל אוֹתָן נְזָקִין שֶׁנָּתְנוּ חֲכָמִים עֲלֵיהֶם רְשׁוּת, וְאָמְרוּ מוּתָּרִין לְקַלְקֵל בְּרה"ר וּלְהַשְׁלִיכָן לְשָׁם, כְּגוֹן הוֹצָאַת זְבָלִים לְר' יְהוּדָה, וּכְגוֹן פּוֹתְקִין בִּיבוֹתֵיהֶם וְגוֹרְפִין מְעָרוֹתֵיהֶן בִּימוֹת הַגְּשָׁמִים, דִּבְרְשׁוּת קָא עָבְדִי, בְּב"ק (דף ו.). אַף מְתַקֵּן הוּא. וְקָאֵי אַתַּנָּא קַמָּא, דְּאָמַר: אִם הִזִּיק מְשַׁלֵּם, וְקָאָמַר לֵיהּ אִיהוּ: אַף בִּשְׁלֹשִׁים יוֹם קוֹדֶם לָכֵן מְתַקֵּן וּפָטוּר. הָיָה מַעֲמִידוֹ בַּעֲלִיָּיה. מִשְׁנָה הִיא בְּב"ב בְּ"לֹא יַחְפּוֹר": לֹא יַעֲמִיד אָדָם תַּנּוּר בְּתוֹךְ הַבַּיִת אא"כ יֵשׁ עַל גַּבָּיו חָלָל גּוֹבַהּ ד' אַמּוֹת מִפִּי הַתַּנּוּר לָעֲלִיָּיה. הָיָה מַעֲמִידוֹ בַּעֲלִיָּיה. עַד שֶׁיְּהֵא תַּחְתָּיו עוֹבִי מַעֲזִיבָה שְׁלֹשָׁה טְפָחִים. וּבְכִירָה. שֶׁאֵין הֶיסֵּק שֶׁלָּהּ גָּדוֹל. וְטֶפַח. מַעֲזִיבָה יְהֵא תַּחְתֶּיהָ. וְאִם הִזִּיק. שֶׁדָּלַק הַבַּיִת וְהִדְלִיק אֶת סְדִינָיו. חַצָּב. הַחוֹצֵב אֶבֶן מִן הָהָר לַעֲקָרָהּ מֵחִיבּוּרָהּ. סַתָּת. הוּא הַמְרַבְּעָהּ וּמַחֲלִיקָהּ. חַמָּר. נוֹשְׂאָהּ מִן הָהָר, שֶׁסִּיתְּתָהּ הַסַּתָּת שָׁם, וּמוֹסְרָהּ לַכַּתָּף, הַמּוֹשִׁיטָהּ לַבַּנַּאי הָעוֹמֵד עַל מַעֲמַד הַחוֹמָה הֶעָשׂוּי לְהִילּוּךְ הָאוּמָּנִין. אַדְרִיכָל. *הוּא אֲבִי הָאוּמָּנִין, שֶׁהוּא מְדַקְדֵּק בְּהַנָּחַת הָאֶבֶן לְגַדְּדָהּ עַל מוֹשָׁבָהּ בְּשָׁוֶה שֶׁלֹּא תָּמִישׁ וְלֹא תַּטֶּה, וְלֹא תְּהֵא בּוֹלֶטֶת חוּץ לַדִּימוֹס. חַיָּיב. זֶה שֶׁהִיא בְּיָדוֹ חַיָּיב בְּנִזְקָהּ, אִם תִּפּוֹל מִיָּדוֹ וְתַזִּיק אֶת אֲחֵרִים אוֹ תִּשָּׁבֵר הִיא — הוּא חַיָּיב לְשַׁלֵּם. וְאע"ג דְּמוֹקְמִינַן לְהָא לְקַמָּן בְּקַבְּלָנוּת, וְכוּלָּן שׁוּתָּפִין בַּמְּלָאכָה — אֵין חַיָּיב אֶלָּא מִי שֶׁהָיְתָה מְסוּרָה לוֹ, דְּכֵיוָן דְּכֹחוֹ הוּא — הֶיזֵּק מוּטָּל עָלָיו כָּל הֵיכָא דְּמִיתְרְמֵי. דִּתְנַן: אָדָם מוּעָד לְעוֹלָם שׁוֹגֵג וּמֵזִיד אוֹנֶס וְרָצוֹן, דְּנָפְקָא לָן בְּב"ק (דף כו:) "פֶּצַע תַּחַת פָּצַע" — לְחַיֵּיב עַל הַשּׁוֹגֵג כְּמֵזִיד, וְאוֹנֶס כְּרָצוֹן. כּוּלָּן. אֵלּוּ שֶׁהָיוּ שׁוּתָּפִין בִּמְלָאכָה אַחַת, וּמִשֶּׁהִנִּיחוּ אֶבֶן עַל הַדִּימוֹס, הִיא שׁוּרַת הַבִּנְיָן, נָפְלָה וְהִזִּיקָה, הוֹאִיל וְלָאו כֹּחוֹ דְּאַדְרִיכָל הוּא, שֶׁלְּאַחַר שֶׁהִנִּיחָהּ נָפְלָה וְלֵיכָּא לְחַיּוּבֵיהּ מִשּׁוּם גִּירֵי דִּילֵיהּ — כּוּלָּן חַיָּיבִין יַחַד, שֶׁכּוּלָּן שׁוּתָּפִין בַּדָּבָר וַעֲלֵיהֶן הַמְּלָאכָה לַעֲשׂוֹת, וְקִיבְּלוּ אַחֲרָיוּת הַנֶּזֶק יַחַד. וְהָתַנְיָא הָאַחֲרוֹן חַיָּיב. אַדְרִיכָל שֶׁהִנִּיחָהּ. בִּשְׂכִירוּת. הָאַחֲרוֹן חַיָּיב. בְּקַבְּלָנוּת. כּוּלָּן חַיָּיבִין הֵיכָא דְּלֹא נָפְלָה מִיַּד אֶחָד מֵהֶן, דְּעַל כּוּלָּן לִשְׁמוֹר שֶׁתְּהֵא מְיוּשֶּׁבֶת יָפֶה. **מתני'** שְׁתֵּי גִנּוֹת זוֹ עַל גַּב זוֹ. סְמוּכוֹת זוֹ לָזוֹ, הָאַחַת קַרְקָעִיתָהּ גָּבוֹהַּ וְשֶׁאֶצְלָהּ קַרְקָעִיתָהּ נָמוּךְ. וְהַיָּרָק בֵּינְתַיִם. בִּזְקִיפַת הַגּוֹבַהּ, שֶׁזּוֹ גְּבוֹהָה מִזּוֹ, יֵשׁ שׁוּמִים אוֹ בְּצָלִים. שֶׁל עֶלְיוֹן. שֶׁהֲרֵי עֲפָרוֹ הוּא וּמִשֶּׁלּוֹ הוּא יוֹנֵק. שֶׁל תַּחְתּוֹן. שֶׁבַּעַל אֲוִירוֹ הוּא מוּנָּח. **אָמַר ר"מ מֵאַחַר שֶׁשְּׁנֵיהֶן הֵן יְכוֹלִין לִמְחוֹת** זֶה עַל זֶה. שֶׁלֹּא יְהֵא יָרָק זֶה כָּאן עֶלְיוֹן לִיטּוֹל עֲפָרוֹ וְהַתַּחְתּוֹן לְמַלְאוֹת גִּנָּתוֹ. רוֹאִין מֵהֵיכָן יָרָק זֶה חַי. מִמָּקוֹם שֶׁהוּא יוֹנֵק וְגָדֵל לוֹ יִנָּתֵן. כָּל שֶׁעֶלְיוֹן יָכוֹל לִפְשׁוֹט יָדוֹ וְלִיטּוֹל הֲרֵי אֵלּוּ שֶׁלּוֹ. כִּדְקָאָמַר ר"מ, הוֹאִיל וּמֵעֲפָרוֹ הִיא חָיָה. וְהַשְּׁאָר שֶׁל תַּחְתּוֹן. וְעֶלְיוֹן הוּא גּוּפֵיהּ אַפְקוּרֵי מַפְקַר לְהוּ לְגַבֵּיהּ, שֶׁגְּנַאי הוּא לוֹ לִיטּוֹל רְשׁוּת לִיכָּנֵס לְתוֹךְ שֶׁל חֲבֵירוֹ וְלִלְקוֹט. **גמ'** בְּעִיקָּרוֹ. שָׁרְשֵׁי הַיָּרָק. בְּנוֹפוֹ. לְפִי שֶׁהֵן תְּלוּיִין בַּאֲוִירוֹ שֶׁל תַּחְתּוֹן, פְּלִיגִי בְּהוּ.

אִילָן

לא א מיי' פי"ג מהל' נזקי ממון הלכה טו סמג עשין סז סח טוש"ע חו"מ סי' תיד סעיף ב:
לב ב ג מיי' שם הלכה טז וסמג שם טוש"ע ח"מ סי' תיז סעיף ה:
לג ד מיי' שם הל' יז טוש"ע שם סעיף ו:
לד ה מיי' שם טוש"ע שם סעיף ז:
לה ו ז מיי' שם הלכה טו סמג שם טוש"ע ח"מ סי' תיד סעיף ב:
לו ח ט מיי' פ"ט מהל' שכנים הלכה יא סמג עשין פב טוש"ע ח"מ סי' קנה סעיף א:
לז י כ ל מיי' פי"ג מהל' נזקי ממון הל' יח סמג עשין סז סח טוש"ע ח"מ סי' שפד סעיף ד:
לח מ מיי' פ"ד מהל' שכנים הלכה ט סמג עשין פב טוש"ע ח"מ סי' קסז סעיף א:
לט נ מיי' פכ"ד מהל' מכירה הלכה ז ועי' במ"מ סמג עשין סב טוש"ע ח"מ סי' רטז סעיף י:

הגהות הב"ח

(א) גמ' והתנן רבי יהודה אומר בנר חנוכה פטור כצ"ל ותיבת מודה ותיבת שהוא נמחק. וכ"כ סוף הכונס בב"ק: (ב) שם דתניא אילן היוצא מן הגזע:

הגהות הגר"א

[א] במשנה הרי הוא שלו והשאר כו'. נ"ב משמע דבעיקר דינא ס"ל כר"י ונ"מ למכירה וערלה ולכן כתב הרמב"ם בבעיא דלקמן דלכתחלה לא יטול העליון כו' (ועמ"ש רבינו בח"מ סי' קס"ז ס"ק ג'):

[ב"ב פא.]

עי' רש"י עירובין כו. ד"ה אדרכלין

ב"ק ל. פח: [תוספתא פי"א]

[ועי' ב"ק ל.]

ב"ק סח: ב"ב כ:

גיטין כב.

[שבת ד: ח.]

רש"ל מ"ז והכי גורס ותני' נמי גבי מקח וממכ' כי האי גוונא דתניא היוצא וכו' [ועי' תוס' גיטין כב. ד"ה ובלאשרוש וכו']

אִילָן הַיּוֹצֵא מִן הַגֶּזַע וכו׳. בְּלוֹקֵחַ אִילָן אֶחָד בְּתוֹךְ שֶׁל חֲבֵירוֹ דְּקִי״ל בְּבָבָא בַּתְרָא (דף פא.) דְּדִבְרֵי הַכֹּל לֹא קָנָה קַרְקַע. וְאִילָן קָטָן הַיּוֹצֵא (מִן הַגֶּזַע אוֹ) מִן הַשָּׁרָשִׁין – לֵית דִּינָא וְלֵית דַּיָּינָא דְּקַרְקַע גְּמוּרָה הִיא. וּמִן הַגֶּזַע נַמִי, ר״מ סָבַר: שְׁדִי נוֹפוֹ בָּתַר עִיקָּרוֹ. וְהָתָם מְפָרֵשׁ מַאי גֶּזַע וּמַאי שָׁרָשִׁין: גֶּזַע – כֹּל שֶׁרוֹאֶה פְּנֵי חַמָּה, שָׁרָשִׁין – שֶׁאֵין רוֹאִין פְּנֵי חַמָּה. וְאַע״ג דְּשֶׁבַח נוֹף הָעֶלְיוֹן לְבַעַל הָאִילָן, כִּדְקָתָנֵי הָתָם: הִגְדִּילוּ לֹא יְשַׁפֶּה – הָתָם הוּא דְּאַדַּעְתָּא דְּהָכִי נָחַת, שֶׁכָּל זְמַן שֶׁיְּהֵא רָאוּי לַעֲשׂוֹת פְּרִי יְהֵא בַּקַּרְקַע, וְיִשָּׂא עָנָף וּפֵירֵי. אֲבָל אִילָן אַחֵר הָעוֹלֶה מִן הַגֶּזַע – אִילָנָא אַחֲרִינָא הוּא. חַיָּיב בְּעָרְלָה. גָּרְסִי׳ לְר״מ, דְּאִילָן הוּא לְעַצְמוֹ. דְּגֶזַע הַסָּמוּךְ לַקַּרְקַע [ב] בְּתוֹךְ שְׁלֹשָׁה כַּקַּרְקַע הוּא, וְאַע״ג דְּלָא מֵאַרְעָא מַמָּשׁ יָנִיק – שְׁדִי נוֹפוֹ בָּתַר עִיקָּרוֹ. מַגִּיעַ לְעִיקָּרוֹ וְאֵינוֹ מַגִּיעַ לְנוֹפוֹ. כְּגוֹן שֶׁנּוֹטֶה נוֹפוֹ לְמַטָּה. קַמֵּיהּ דְּשָׁבוּר מַלְכָּא. לִי נִרְאֶה: שָׁבוּר (א) מַלְכָּא מַמָּשׁ, וּמֶלֶךְ פָּרַס הָיָה, וּבָקִי בְּדִינִים. וַאֲמָרוּהָ לְהָא דְּר״ש דְּמַתְנִי׳ קַמֵּיהּ, וְקִלְּסֵיהּ, וְאָמַר: אַפִּרְיוֹן נִמְטְיֵיהּ לְר״ש – יְקַבֵּל חֵן מֵאִתָּנוּ עַל דָּבָר זֶה. וְאִית דְּאָמְרִי שָׁבוּר מַלְכָּא – שְׁמוּאֵל, דְּבְכַמָּה דּוּכְתֵּי קָרֵי לֵיהּ הָכִי. וְאֵין מְיוּשָּׁב בָּהּ, דְּמַאי אֲמָרוּהָ, אִי לְהָא דְּר״ש דְּמַתְנִי׳ – אַטּוּ שְׁמוּאֵל לָא הֲוָה יָדַע לָהּ לְמַתְנִי׳? וְאִי לְהָא דְּאֶפְרַיִם סָפְרָא – אַטּוּ אִי לָא אֲמַר רֵישׁ לָקִישׁ הֲלָכָה כְּר״ש שְׁמוּאֵל מִי לָא קִים בְּדִינֵי לְמִיקַלְּסֵיהּ לְר״ש עַד דְּשָׁמַע מִשְּׁמֵיהּ דְּרֵישׁ לָקִישׁ דְּהִלְכְתָא כְּוָותֵיהּ? אַפִּרְיוֹן. ״חֵן שֶׁלָּנוּ.

*וְתָנַן נַמִי גַּבֵּי עָרְלָה כִּי הַאי גַּוְונָא: אִילָן הַיּוֹצֵא מִן הַגֶּזַע וּמִן הַשָּׁרָשִׁין – חַיָּיב בְּעָרְלָה, דִּבְרֵי רַבִּי מֵאִיר. רַבִּי יְהוּדָה אוֹמֵר [א]מִן הַגֶּזַע – פָּטוּר, מִן הַשָּׁרָשִׁין – חַיָּיב. וּצְרִיכִי, דְּאִי אַשְׁמוּעִינַן קַמַּיְיתָא – בְּהָא קָאָמַר רַבִּי יְהוּדָה, מִשּׁוּם דְּמָמוֹנָא. אֲבָל גַּבֵּי עָרְלָה דְּאִיסּוּרָא – אֵימָא מוֹדֵי לֵיהּ לְר׳ מֵאִיר. וְאִי אִיתְּמַר בְּהָא – בְּהָא קָאָמַר ר׳ מֵאִיר, אֲבָל בְּהַהִיא אֵימָא מוֹדֵי לֵיהּ לְר׳ יְהוּדָה, צְרִיכִי.§ [״אָמַר] ר״ש: (אוֹמֵר) כָּל שֶׁהָעֶלְיוֹן יָכוֹל לִפְשׁוֹט״ [וכו׳]§ אָמְרִי דְּבֵי רַבִּי יַנַּאי: [ב]וּבִלְבַד שֶׁלֹּא יֵאָנֵס. *) בָּעֵי רַב עָנָן וְאִיתֵּימָא רַבִּי יִרְמְיָה: מַגִּיעַ לְנוֹפוֹ וְאֵין מַגִּיעַ לְעִיקָּרוֹ, [א] מַגִּיעַ לְעִיקָּרוֹ וְאֵין מַגִּיעַ לְנוֹפוֹ, מַאי? [ג]תֵּיקוּ.§ אָמַר אֶפְרַיִם סָפְרָא תַּלְמִידוֹ שֶׁל רֵישׁ לָקִישׁ מִשּׁוּם רֵישׁ לָקִישׁ: הֲלָכָה כְּר״ש. אֲמָרוּהָ קַמֵּיהּ דְּשָׁבוּר מַלְכָּא. אֲמַר לְהוּ: *אַפִּרְיוֹן נִמְטְיֵיהּ לְרַבִּי שִׁמְעוֹן.§

*) עי׳ בהרא״ש ובספר ת״ח ובספר כה״י

*ותניא נמי גבי מקח וממכר כה״ג. תניא גרסינן, דאינה משנה בשום מקום. ולא הוי כה״ג ממש, דאפילו אמר ר״י היוצא מן הגזע של בעל הקרקע – לא יקשה כלום, שהרי עומד באוירו של בעל הקרקע וגם יונק מן הקרקע. ועוד: שלא היה בדעת המוכר למכור אלא זה האילן, שהיה כעין שמכר, אבל לא אילן חדש שעתיד לצאת מן הגזע דלא חשיב כאילן עצמו הענפים המתחדשים, אלא נחשב כאילן אחר. וכן ר׳ מאיר, אם היה אומר כאן של בעל האילן – לא היה קשה על משנתנו, שכמו שהענפים המתחדשים בכל שנה הם של בעל האילן – ה״נ היוצא מן הגזע יהיו שלו. והא דקאמר כה״ג – היינו שמיפה ר״מ כאן כחו של בעל הקרקע טפי מרבי יהודה כמו במתני׳. ולהכי לא עביד צריכותא בסמוך אלא אערלה ואמקח וממכר, ולא אמתניתין.

שבור מלכא. נראה לפרש כפי׳ הקונטרס, דשבור מלכא היה בקי בהלכות, כדאמרינן בסוף מסכת ע״ז (דף עו:) שנעץ הסכין עשר פעמים בקרקע קשה כשחתך האתרוג בסכין לרב יהודה.

הדרן עלך הבית והעלייה וסליקא לה מסכת בבא מציעא

[נ״ל ותניא והיא תוספתא דערלה ע״ש]

גליון הש״ם

רש״י בד״ה אפריון חן שלנו. וכ״כ רש״י בחומש פ׳ ויחי בפסוק בן פורת יוסף. אבל הרמב״ן שם כ׳ דהגו״ן פרסית והוא לשון שבח ורווחא כמו פורנא ליתמי (כתובות ד׳ נד) ועי׳ ברא״ש שם:

גי׳ הערוך הבו ליה אפרייא לריש לקיש פי׳ חוזק בלשון פרסי יישר כחו יישר חילו ס״א אפרייא לריש לקיש ברכה ומלשון בן פורת כלומר יפרו וירבו חכמים ונבונים כמותו.

סייד לעיל קיח: וכגי׳ רש״ל

מ א מיי׳ פ״י מהלכות מעשר שני ונטע רבעי הלכה יט סמג עשין קלו טור י״ד סי׳ רלד [חפשתי בטור ובסמג שם ולא מצאתי]:

מא ב ג מיי׳ פ״ד מהל׳ שכנים הל׳ ט סמג עשין פב טוש״ע ח״מ סי׳ קסז סעיף א:

הגהות הב״ח

(א) רש״י ד״ה קמיה דשבור וכו׳ מלכא ממש. נ״ב ובב״ב סוף דף י מבואר דהוה עכו״ם ע״ש ובב״ב דף קטו ע״ב איתא דשמואל נקרא כך וכן בפסחים דף נד:

הגהות הגר״א

[א] גמ׳ (מגיע לעיקרו ואין מגיע לנופו) תא״מ ונ״ב הרמב״ם והרא״ש ל״ג לה וכ׳ דכה״ג ודאי נקרא מגיע: [ב] רש״י ד״ה חייב. הסמוך לקרקע בתוך כו׳. נ״ב ומכאן כתב הרא״ש לג׳ טפחים סמוך לתחתון הרי הוא של תחתון אף לר״מ ור״ש:

הדרן עלך הבית והעלייה וסליקא לה מסכת בבא מציעא

The following paragraph is recited three times:

הַדְרָן עֲלָךְ מַסֶּכֶת בָּבָא מְצִיעָא וְהַדְרָךְ עֲלָן, דַּעְתָּן
עֲלָךְ מַסֶּכֶת בָּבָא מְצִיעָא וְדַעְתָּךְ עֲלָן, לָא נִתְנְשֵׁי מִנָּךְ
מַסֶּכֶת בָּבָא מְצִיעָא וְלָא תִתְנְשֵׁי מִנָּן, לָא בְּעָלְמָא
הָדֵין וְלָא בְּעָלְמָא דְאָתֵי.

יְהִי רָצוֹן מִלְּפָנֶיךָ יהוה אֱלֹהֵינוּ וֵאלֹהֵי אֲבוֹתֵינוּ,
שֶׁתְּהֵא תּוֹרָתְךָ אֻמָּנוּתֵנוּ בָּעוֹלָם הַזֶּה, וּתְהֵא עִמָּנוּ
לָעוֹלָם הַבָּא. חֲנִינָא בַּר פַּפָּא, רָמֵי בַּר פַּפָּא, נַחְמָן
בַּר פַּפָּא, אֲחַאי בַּר פַּפָּא, אַבָּא מָרִי בַּר פַּפָּא, רַפְרָם
בַּר פַּפָּא, רָכִישׁ בַּר פַּפָּא, סוּרְחַב בַּר פַּפָּא, אַדָּא בַּר
פַּפָּא, דָּרוּ בַּר פַּפָּא.

הַעֲרֶב נָא יהוה אֱלֹהֵינוּ אֶת דִּבְרֵי תוֹרָתְךָ בְּפִינוּ וּבְפִי
עַמְּךָ בֵּית יִשְׂרָאֵל, וְנִהְיֶה אֲנַחְנוּ וְצֶאֱצָאֵינוּ (וְצֶאֱצָאֵי
צֶאֱצָאֵינוּ) וְצֶאֱצָאֵי עַמְּךָ בֵּית יִשְׂרָאֵל, כֻּלָּנוּ יוֹדְעֵי
תהלים קיט שְׁמֶךָ וְלוֹמְדֵי תוֹרָתְךָ לִשְׁמָהּ. מֵאֹיְבַי תְּחַכְּמֵנִי מִצְוֹתֶךָ
כִּי לְעוֹלָם הִיא־לִי: יְהִי־לִבִּי תָמִים בְּחֻקֶּיךָ לְמַעַן לֹא
אֵבוֹשׁ: לְעוֹלָם לֹא־אֶשְׁכַּח פִּקּוּדֶיךָ כִּי־בָם חִיִּיתָנִי:
בָּרוּךְ אַתָּה יהוה לַמְּדֵנִי חֻקֶּיךָ: אָמֵן אָמֵן אָמֵן סֶלָה
וָעֶד.

מוֹדִים אֲנַחְנוּ לְפָנֶיךָ יהוה אֱלֹהֵינוּ וֵאלֹהֵי אֲבוֹתֵינוּ
שֶׁשַּׂמְתָּ חֶלְקֵנוּ מִיּוֹשְׁבֵי בֵּית הַמִּדְרָשׁ, וְלֹא שַׂמְתָּ חֶלְקֵנוּ
מִיּוֹשְׁבֵי קְרָנוֹת. שֶׁאָנוּ מַשְׁכִּימִים וְהֵם מַשְׁכִּימִים,
אָנוּ מַשְׁכִּימִים לְדִבְרֵי תוֹרָה, וְהֵם מַשְׁכִּימִים לִדְבָרִים
בְּטֵלִים. אָנוּ עֲמֵלִים וְהֵם עֲמֵלִים, אָנוּ עֲמֵלִים וּמְקַבְּלִים
שָׂכָר, וְהֵם עֲמֵלִים וְאֵינָם מְקַבְּלִים שָׂכָר. אָנוּ רָצִים וְהֵם
רָצִים, אָנוּ רָצִים לְחַיֵּי הָעוֹלָם הַבָּא, וְהֵם רָצִים לִבְאֵר
תהלים נה שַׁחַת, שֶׁנֶּאֱמַר: וְאַתָּה אֱלֹהִים תּוֹרִדֵם לִבְאֵר שַׁחַת
אַנְשֵׁי דָמִים וּמִרְמָה לֹא־יֶחֱצוּ יְמֵיהֶם וַאֲנִי אֶבְטַח־בָּךְ:

יְהִי רָצוֹן מִלְּפָנֶיךָ יהוה אֱלֹהַי, כְּשֵׁם שֶׁעֲזַרְתַּנִי לְסַיֵּם
מַסֶּכֶת בָּבָא מְצִיעָא כֵּן תַּעַזְרֵנִי לְהַתְחִיל מַסֶּכְתּוֹת
וּסְפָרִים אֲחֵרִים וּלְסַיְּמָם, לִלְמֹד וּלְלַמֵּד לִשְׁמֹר וְלַעֲשׂוֹת
וּלְקַיֵּם אֶת כָּל דִּבְרֵי תַלְמוּד תּוֹרָתְךָ בְּאַהֲבָה, וּזְכוּת
כָּל הַתַּנָּאִים וְאָמוֹרָאִים וְתַלְמִידֵי חֲכָמִים יַעֲמֹד לִי
וּלְזַרְעִי שֶׁלֹּא תָמוּשׁ הַתּוֹרָה מִפִּי וּמִפִּי זַרְעִי וְזֶרַע זַרְעִי
משלי ו עַד עוֹלָם, וְיִתְקַיֵּם בִּי: בְּהִתְהַלֶּכְךָ תַּנְחֶה אֹתָךְ בְּשָׁכְבְּךָ
משלי ט תִּשְׁמֹר עָלֶיךָ וַהֲקִיצוֹתָ הִיא תְשִׂיחֶךָ: כִּי־בִי יִרְבּוּ יָמֶיךָ
משלי ג וְיוֹסִיפוּ לְּךָ שְׁנוֹת חַיִּים: אֹרֶךְ יָמִים בִּימִינָהּ בִּשְׂמֹאולָהּ
תהלים כט עֹשֶׁר וְכָבוֹד: יהוה עֹז לְעַמּוֹ יִתֵּן יהוה יְבָרֵךְ אֶת־עַמּוֹ
בַשָּׁלוֹם:

The following paragraph is recited three times:

הַדְרָן We shall return to you, tractate *Bava Metzia,* and your glory is upon us. Our thoughts are upon you, tractate *Bava Metzia,* and your thoughts are upon us. We will not be forgotten from you, tractate *Bava Metzia,* and you will not be forgotten from us; neither in this world nor in the World-to-Come.

יְהִי רָצוֹן May it be Your will, Lord our God and God of our ancestors, that Your Torah will be our avocation in this world and will accompany us to the World-to-Come. Ḥanina bar Pappa, Ramei bar Pappa, Naḥman bar Pappa, Aḥai bar Pappa, Abba Mari bar Pappa, Rafram bar Pappa, Rakhish bar Pappa, Surḥav bar Pappa, Adda bar Pappa, Daru bar Pappa.

הַעֲרֶב נָא Please, Lord our God, make the words of Your
Torah sweet in our mouths and in the mouths of Your
people, the house of Israel, so that we, our descendants
(and their descendants), and the descendants of Your
people, the house of Israel, may all know Your name and
study Your Torah for its own sake. Your commandments Psalms 119
make me wiser than my enemies, for they are ever with
me. Let my heart be undivided in Your statutes, in order
that I may not be put to shame. I will never forget Your
precepts, for with them You have quickened me. Blessed
are You, O Lord; teach me Your statutes. Amen, Amen,
Amen, Selah, Forever.

מוֹדִים We give thanks before You, Lord Our God and
God of our ancestors, that You have placed our lot
among those who sit in the study hall and that you have
not given us our portion among those who sit idly on
street corners. We rise early and they rise early. We rise
early to pursue matters of Torah and they rise early to
pursue frivolous matters. We toil and they toil. We toil
and receive a reward and they toil and do not receive a
reward. We run and they run. We run to the life of the
World-to-Come and they run to the pit of destruction,
as it is stated: But You, God, will bring them down into Psalms 55
the pit of destruction; men of blood and deceit shall not
live out half their days; but as for me, I will trust in You.

יְהִי רָצוֹן May it be Your will, Lord my God, just as you
have assisted me in completing tractate *Bava Metzia*
so assist me to begin other tractates and books and
conclude them to learn and to teach, to observe and to
perform, and to fulfill all the teachings of Your Torah with
love. And may the merit of all the *tanna'im* and *amora'im*
and Torah scholars stand for me and my descendants so
that the Torah will not move from my mouth and from
the mouths of my descendants and the descendants of
my descendants forever. And may the verse: When you Proverbs 6
walk, it shall lead you, when you lie down, it shall watch
over you; and when you awaken, it shall talk with you
be fulfilled in me. For in the Torah your days shall be Proverbs 9
multiplied, and the years of your life shall be increased.
Length of days is in her right hand; in her left hand are Proverbs 3
riches and honor. May the Lord give strength to His Psalms 29
people; the Lord will bless His people with peace.

The following קדיש *requires the presence of a* מנין.

יִתְגַּדַּל וְיִתְקַדַּשׁ שְׁמֵהּ רַבָּא
בְּעָלְמָא דְּהוּא עָתִיד לְאִתְחַדָּתָא
וּלְאַחֲיָאָה מֵתַיָּא, וּלְאַסָּקָא יָתְהוֹן לְחַיֵּי עָלְמָא
וּלְמִבְנֵא קַרְתָּא דִירוּשְׁלֵם, וּלְשַׁכְלָלָא הֵיכְלֵהּ בְּגַוַּהּ
וּלְמֶעְקַר פֻּלְחָנָא נֻכְרָאָה מֵאַרְעָא
וְלַאֲתָבָא פֻּלְחָנָא דִשְׁמַיָּא לְאַתְרֵהּ
וְיַמְלִיךְ קֻדְשָׁא בְּרִיךְ הוּא בְּמַלְכוּתֵהּ וִיקָרֵהּ
(נוסח ספרד: וְיַצְמַח פּוּרְקָנֵהּ וִיקָרֵב מְשִׁיחֵהּ)
בְּחַיֵּיכוֹן וּבְיוֹמֵיכוֹן וּבְחַיֵּי דְכָל בֵּית יִשְׂרָאֵל
בַּעֲגָלָא וּבִזְמַן קָרִיב, וְאִמְרוּ אָמֵן.

יְהֵא שְׁמֵהּ רַבָּא מְבָרַךְ לְעָלַם וּלְעָלְמֵי עָלְמַיָּא.

יִתְבָּרַךְ וְיִשְׁתַּבַּח וְיִתְפָּאַר וְיִתְרוֹמַם וְיִתְנַשֵּׂא
וְיִתְהַדָּר וְיִתְעַלֶּה וְיִתְהַלָּל
שְׁמֵהּ דְּקֻדְשָׁא בְּרִיךְ הוּא
לְעֵלָּא מִן כָּל בִּרְכָתָא
/בעשרת ימי תשובה: לְעֵלָּא לְעֵלָּא מִכָּל בִּרְכָתָא/
וְשִׁירָתָא, תֻּשְׁבְּחָתָא וְנֶחֱמָתָא, דַּאֲמִירָן בְּעָלְמָא
וְאִמְרוּ אָמֵן. (קהל: אָמֵן)

עַל יִשְׂרָאֵל וְעַל רַבָּנָן
וְעַל תַּלְמִידֵיהוֹן וְעַל כָּל תַּלְמִידֵי תַלְמִידֵיהוֹן
וְעַל כָּל מָאן דְּעָסְקִין בְּאוֹרַיְתָא
דִּי בְּאַתְרָא (בארץ ישראל: קַדִּישָׁא) הָדֵין, וְדִי בְּכָל אֲתַר וַאֲתַר
יְהֵא לְהוֹן וּלְכוֹן שְׁלָמָא רַבָּא
חִנָּא וְחִסְדָּא, וְרַחֲמֵי, וְחַיֵּי אֲרִיכֵי, וּמְזוֹנֵי רְוִיחֵי
וּפֻרְקָנָא מִן קֳדָם אֲבוּהוֹן דִּי בִשְׁמַיָּא
וְאִמְרוּ אָמֵן.

יְהֵא שְׁלָמָא רַבָּא מִן שְׁמַיָּא
וְחַיִּים (טוֹבִים) עָלֵינוּ וְעַל כָּל יִשְׂרָאֵל
וְאִמְרוּ אָמֵן.

Bow, take three steps back, as if taking leave of the Divine Presence, then bow, first left, then right, then center, while saying:

עֹשֶׂה שָׁלוֹם/ בעשרת ימי תשובה: הַשָּׁלוֹם/ בִּמְרוֹמָיו
הוּא יַעֲשֶׂה בְרַחֲמָיו שָׁלוֹם, עָלֵינוּ וְעַל כָּל יִשְׂרָאֵל
וְאִמְרוּ אָמֵן.

The following Kaddish requires the presence of a minyan.

Magnified and sanctified may His great name be,
in the world that will in future be renewed,
reviving the dead and raising them up to eternal life.
He will rebuild the city of Jerusalem
and in it re-establish His Temple.
He will remove alien worship from the earth
and restore to its place the worship of Heaven.
Then the Holy One, blessed be He,
will reign in His sovereignty and splendor.
May it be in your lifetime and in your days,
(*Nusaḥ Sepharad:* make His salvation flourish,
and hasten His messiah,)
and in the lifetime of all the House of Israel,
swiftly and soon – and say: Amen.

May His great name be blessed for ever and all time.

Blessed and praised,
glorified and exalted,
raised and honored,
uplifted and lauded
be the name of the Holy One,
blessed be He,
beyond any blessing,
song, praise and consolation uttered in the world –
and say: Amen.

To Israel, to the teachers,
their disciples and their disciples' disciples,
and to all who engage in the study of Torah,
in this (*in Israel add:* holy) place or elsewhere,
may there come to them and you great peace,
grace, kindness and compassion,
long life, ample sustenance and deliverance,
from their Father in Heaven –
and say: Amen.

May there be great peace from heaven,
and (good) life for us and all Israel –
and say: Amen.

Bow, take three steps back, as if taking leave of the Divine Presence, then bow, first left, then right, then center, while saying:

May He who makes peace in His high places,
in His compassion make peace for us and all Israel –
and say: Amen.